FORCED NATIVE LABOR IN
SIXTEENTH-CENTURY CENTRAL AMERICA

"En verdad, si los indios no son hombres, sino monas, *non sunt capaces injuriae*. Pero si son hombres y prójimos, *et quod ipse prae se ferunt*, vasallos del emperador, *non video quomodo* excusar a estos conquistadores de última impiedad y tiranía, ni sé que tan grand servicio hagan a su magestad de echarle a perder sus vasallos."

Francisco de Vitoria, 1534, in *Relectio de Indis o Libertad de los Indios*, pp. 138–39.

FORCED NATIVE LABOR IN SIXTEENTH-CENTURY CENTRAL AMERICA

William L. Sherman

UNIVERSITY OF NEBRASKA PRESS
Lincoln and London

Library of Congress Cataloging in Publication Data
Sherman, William L
   Forced native labor in sixteenth-century Central
America.

   Bibliography: p. 459
   Includes index.
   1. Indians, Treatment of—Central America—History.
2. Forced labor—Central America—History.   3. Labor
and laboring classes—Central America—History.
4. Slavery in Central America—History.   I. Title.
F1434.S54   1978   301.44'93'09728   78–13521
ISBN 0–8032–4100–3

For my family

Contents

Preface

SOCIETY IN THE SPANISH INDIES during the sixteenth century remains little studied, yet it was during those formative decades that Latin American class structure evolved. The Spanish conquest of the Indians produced social dislocations of the most serious order. The subsequent ethnic fusion notwithstanding, there persisted two communities—the Spanish and the Indian. Forming on the fringe, culturally adrift, was the group of the mixed-bloods.

In the new order of things following the conquest, many Spaniards of low station found themselves members of a new, rustic aristocracy, while proud native lords were often reduced to the meanest circumstances. The social and economic implications of the resulting system of Indian servitude were of such dimension that they transcend the drama of the conquest itself. For native labor was the base upon which Spanish colonial society rested, and without it the empire would have been but a pale imitation of the vast and rich complex it became. The degrees to which the conqueror depended upon the vanquished at once reflect the weak edifice of colonial Spanish society and define the relationship between the two races. The first bishop of Guatemala was moved to remark that "Spaniards in these parts are worthless without native friends."

Europeans who shipped to the New World during the sixteenth century sought opportunity, but not at the end of a hoe. Cortés spoke for them all when he stated that he had not left Spain to plow the land. Spanish artisans of course came to ply their trades, merchants negotiated, lawyers, physicians, and other professionals established practices, and a burgeoning bureaucracy spread to all corners. Indeed, Spaniards representing practically every type in Spain migrated to perform all kinds of work—except common labor. A peasant in Spain saw little to gain by becoming a peasant on the frontiers of the Indies, despite efforts to convince him otherwise. The labor crisis was met by the available force of conquered Indians who

ix

were, however, reluctant to labor for the benefit of their new masters. Nevertheless, work they did. Through outright slavery and other contrived systems of free labor, the most remarkable of which was that of the *encomienda*, natives formed the laboring base of the colonial economy.

The most dramatic aspect of native labor was that of chattel slavery, and it was to that subject that I began to direct my research in Spanish manuscripts in the early 1960s. The general outlines of Indian slavery were known. Many early accounts were fragmentary, but the nineteenth-century Cuban historian José Antonio Saco left an impressive study based on wide documentation, much of which was taken from the Muñoz collection of transcripts in Madrid. It was, however, very broad in scope, which necessarily rendered it superficial with respect to specific regions and times. In more recent years the studies of Silvio Zavala probed in greater depth than others, and his large study of Indian slavery in New Spain was the culmination of decades of research. The area I had chosen to study was Central America, which, while it was properly within the jurisdiction of greater New Spain, was for all intents and purposes largely autonomous. Zavala had dealt with those provinces, but not in great detail, and his emphases were different from mine. Ultimately it became clear to me that slavery was, in the totality, quite a restricted view of the scope of native labor. Other forms, although less well studied, emerged as the more important, and not less interesting, part of the picture.

The subject of nonslave labor had not been ignored by historians: again Zavala had done important work, especially on the encomienda; José Miranda had published his study of tribute; the various archival findings of France V. Scholes and Eleanor B. Adams furnished important information on both; and in a series of scintillating studies Lesley Byrd Simpson offered the most comprehensive picture of Indian labor written in English. Then the publication of Charles Gibson's superb study of the Aztecs under Spanish rule explored the subject in great depth. Other aspects of the problem had been examined; José María Ots Capdequi occupied himself with the legal ramifications, and both Lewis U. Hanke and Benjamin Keen discussed the philosophical considerations. Many other modern works have touched on the subject, but the list is too long to cite here.

Still, there was no detailed study devoted to the social aspects of labor in Central America during the sixteenth century. The closest thing to it was the *Relación* written by the royal judge Alonso de Zorita, but, although it was a valuable contemporary account, it was devoted in large part to Mexico. Anyway, it was one man's version, contradicted by others. Many writings from the colonial period presented a variety of views, most of them still unpublished. The most influential of the sixteenth-century writers on the subject was the formidable Bartolomé de Las Casas, whose views have tended to prevail above all others, at least in non-Spanish circles. Persuasive as the general thrust of the Dominican's writings is, it is generally accepted that he exaggerated in his use of figures. Did he distort in other respects, and if so to what degree? Seldom has a historian writing in English been inclined to take sharp issue with the Lascasian view. Today few would be sympathetic to the *encomendero* position, but it required a fuller discussion, if for no other reason than to try to understand the problem from all facets. By no means were most contemporary writers hostile to the encomenderos; but they had no pen comparable to that of Las Casas, nor for that matter of Zorita. However, since most of those pro-encomendero views remained unpublished, or at least had not found their way into English print, a thorough examination of the documents was necessary. If their arguments are unacceptable to most people today, it is still incumbent upon the historian to give them an airing, for only in that way can we gain some insight into the society and its controversies.

It is generally conceded that while Crown Indian legislation was enlightened for the time, the laws were not implemented for various reasons, principal among which was expediency. Other reasons are imputed as well, but often the impression is left of the basest hypocrisy, however simplistic that proves to be. The whole question of forced native labor is far more complex. I have not dealt with the legal considerations to any degree, although their presence is unavoidable. One problem, in fact, is that too many histories have been based to great extent on the laws, in particular the *Recopilación de Leyes de los Reynos de las Indias*. Those laws record the putative royal intent, but studies based on them do not sufficiently take into account what truly happened in the colonies, which has been my primary concern.

In order to present a reasonably accurate and detailed picture of native labor, I decided to concentrate my research on the sixteenth century, which would cover three generations, and to restrict the study to Central America. My plan was to make a thorough examination of the original manuscripts, which alone occupied me for the better part of a decade. Beyond that, there were many important published works, but I have used them sparingly and only where I thought they would add some dimension to the study. Consequently, except for some background materials for which there are few archival sources, most of what follows is based on letters, reports, and lawsuits of the time. There are drawbacks to this methodology, particularly in that the documents tend to dictate, and therefore inhibit, a flow of style. On the positive side, I began with no prefigured model and, to a considerable degree, the work went where the manuscripts took it. The most vexing problem was that of organization, a dilemma not mitigated by the wish to base as much as possible on sixteenth-century documents.

It is to be hoped that the result is an examination of the subject that is not patently of either the *indigenista* or the *hispanista* school. In point of fact, while there is much to admire in both the native and Spanish cultures, neither comes off well in the present work. This derives from no melancholy predisposition on my part, but rather from the nature of the sources, which reflect what seems to be the common propensity of man —to dwell on the darker side of events. But if in that misanthrope's delight there were acts of terror and violence perpetrated by the Spaniards on the native peoples, the point should not be missed that many other Spaniards were sufficiently appalled to leave us abundant documentation of such atrocities. While it is regrettably true that few Indian accounts are available, there are plenty of Spanish records that defend the Indian cause with vehemence.

Although what follows is social history, it also borders on ethnohistory. In both types of research the evidence is much more elusive than for other historical studies. Often one finds very significant information in an off-hand comment made in an unpromising document. Evidence that is vital for the social historian was frequently of no interest whatsoever to those writing in the sixteenth century, so that our image of their society is imperfect to say the least. More than that, there is considerable disagreement among those correspondents about almost any issue, so that reaching reasonably accurate conclusions is made difficult. Each writer betrays his particular biases, and few were moderate in their attitudes. *Cabildo* correspondence generally echoes the encomendero view, although it is not unusual for the *regidores* to express concern for the plight of the Indians. There is quite a diversity of opinion shown by the judges of the *audiencia;* for while they were all officers of the Crown, there was no official viewpoint to which they adhered with consistency. Moreover, their own personal, and unofficial, interests frequently conditioned their policies. There was sharp disagreement among clergymen, and even the bishops held no unanimity of opinion. Various other officials and private individuals reflected an even greater range of views. Aside from providing a variety of thinking, however, the papers also give a substantial amount of detailed information, and none more so than the books of the notaries, with particular reference to contract labor. These are standard sources for investigators, although few have examined them with the care they warrant. Despite the conflicting data contained within such documents, certain truths ultimately emerge with some clarity.

Among the most neglected sources have been those of the *Justicia* section of the Archivo General de Indias in Seville. Combing those lawsuits is a tedious business, but they are often rewarding, as are the same types of documents in the Archivo General de Centro América in Guatemala. Of special interest are the *juicios de residencia*, the judicial reviews to which officials submitted at termination of their offices. Those trials are often quite long, sometimes running to thousands of pages; others are relatively short. They can be of great importance, especially for social history, because the community at large, including Indians, was encouraged to post charges against the official. In the resulting testimony, items of interest ordinarily not dealt with in other sources, including a certain amount of gossip, are revealed. In the process of this research more than thirty of the residencias, some of which yielded substantial profit, were studied.

In the end, perhaps only about half of the notes accumulated could be utilized for this study. Chapters on the special roles of the audiencia, the various minor judges and petty officials, encomenderos, the Church, and a section devoted to tribute are not included. All of those subjects figure into these chapters to some extent, but a fuller discussion of them as they related to Indian labor would have made an unwieldy volume.

Within the limits thus imposed, I have tried to present a detailed record, exposing all viewpoints. It seemed advisable to cite numerous examples with a view toward forestalling charges of generalizing, which in fact has been the weakness of some works attempting synthesis. Regrettably, our ignorance of race relations in sixteenth-century Central America is such that another quarter century or so of what is fashionably disparaged as "traditional" research is necessary before a synthesis worthy of the ink can be written. Nonetheless, history is inquiry, and where evidence warrants, I have not hesitated to offer analysis and interpretation.

Central America as the focus of this work was an outgrowth of my original, and continuing, interest in the career of Pedro de Alvarado. The attraction to the scenes of his adventures was reinforced by the growing awareness that the region had been relatively neglected by modern historians. There are important chronicles of the colonial period, almost all written by men of the Church whose peculiar biases are evident. Moreover, they reflect the idiosyncrasies of times past, occupying themselves with boresome minutiae while slighting those concerns of the modern reader. Other early chroniclers, such as Gonzalo Fernández Oviedo y Valdés (who was not an ecclesiastic), included Central America in their discussions. Antonio de Remesal, the Dominican historian, was the first, and in most respects the best, of the chroniclers devoting their work specifically to Central America, and both he and Oviedo were copied shamelessly by those who followed. The chroniclers are very important sources, with all their limitations, because they made use of some documents that no longer exist.

The fascinating account of Thomas Gage, the Englishman who spent several years in seventeenth-century Central America, awakened some interest in the area for readers of English, but it was not until the nineteenth century with the publication of John L. Stephens and Ephraim Squier that a broader readership resulted. Nonetheless, they were not, strictly speaking, historical studies. The significant contribution along those lines lay in the publication of the monumental treatise by Hubert H. Bancroft. His three-volume *History of Central America*, although a popular target for critics in recent years, was a signal achievement for the time. And despite some errors, his pontificating, and various prejudices common to his age, Bancroft remains a formidable source.

Owing to the overwhelming intrigue of the brilliant Maya civilization, it was anthropologists who continued research into the Central American past, from the late nineteenth century and into the twentieth. Recently some of them tend more to ethnohistory, but most of their investigations have been concerned with prehispanic cultures, or in later years with socioeconomic aspects of modern Indian communities.

Until quite recently, the research of Robert S. Chamberlain remained one of the few scholarly works done on sixteenth-century Central America in English. A tireless scholar, Chamberlain assiduously searched the documents of Spain and Central America to produce works of uniformly impressive scholarship. The present study owes much to the groundwork laid by him.

About the same time the present work was undertaken, Murdo Mac-Leod had started his important research on a very significant topic. Working at opposite ends of the axis (he beginning in Central America, I in Spain), we were unaware of each other's investigations until both were well advanced. The publication of MacLeod's broad, imaginative *Spanish Central America: A Socio-Economic History, 1520–1720,* opens up the area to the consideration of themes hitherto only lightly touched by others. Future historians, particularly those interested in the early economic history of Central America, will owe a great debt to him for his admirable pioneering work. Professor MacLeod very kindly made available for my study his manuscript, which unfortunately I had for only a very brief time. The fruition of his research was reached at the time the present study was in its final stages, which accounts for the limited use I could make of it; otherwise more of his findings would have been incorporated here. Although he and I cross paths on certain topics (and sometimes disagree), the two studies complement each other, as our emphases are different.

Other significant studies by diligent young scholars are being put together. Christopher Lutz has completed an excellent doctoral dissertation on a history of the city of Antigua (Santiago) under the late Professor John L. Phelan. Henry Ibargüen has recently investigated the subject of land tenure in sixteenth-century Guatemala, under the guidance of Professor Charles Gibson. Salvador Rodríguez of the University of Seville has published his work on encomiendas for the same period, and Pilar Sanchíz's study of hidalgos in Guatemala is now available. These works, too recently completed to be utilized here, are significant contributions to an important area of colonial history that has, until recently, been slighted by modern historians.

Without some institutional support it would have been impossible to carry out the necessary research for this project. A grant for a year's investigation, primarily in Seville, was partially financed through the generosity of the Del Amo Foundation. A return to Spain for more investigation was funded by the Faculty Improvement Committee of Colorado State University, which institution also made available funds for the purchase of microfilm and other materials. The University of Nebraska Research Council helped finance a trip to Central America for research in the Archivo General de Centro América, in addition to aiding in the purchase of microfilm and photocopies of documents, and a typing grant. A Woods Foundation grant enabled me to take leave to write, and assistance from the Nebraska Foundation made possible my return to Central America for more research. To all I am most grateful.

Over the years one accumulates many debts to individuals who have lent encouragement and support of various kinds. Their help has been of varying degrees, but all of those mentioned here (and doubtless others who slip my mind) were helpful. I am grateful to the late William Lytle Schurz who first interested me in Latin American history. As a student, and later colleague, at Mexico City College, I first gained some insight to native cultures from Wigberto Jiménez Moreno, Fernando Horcasitas, and the late Pablo Martínez del Rio. In particular I wish to express thanks to Richard E. Greenleaf and Paul V. Murray for their support. At the University of New Mexico Edwin Lieuwen, Troy S. Floyd, France V. Scholes, and Donald C. Cutter were of much help.

In Seville, two directors of the Archivo General de Indias, José de la Peña and Rosario Parra, were of considerable assistance, as was the staff of the AGI. Carlos Molina Argüello shared his wide familiarity with Central American documents, and I share the debt owed by many visiting scholars to Miguel Maticorena. The late José Joaquín Real Díaz, Antonia M. Heredia, and Luis Navarro García were always generous with their time and knowledge. When I was unable to be in Seville, Angeles Flores sent microfilm my way with great efficiency.

In Guatemala I was treated with great kindness by Ricardo and Juanita Barrios, Manuel Rubio Sánchez, and David Vela, and various fellow *socios* of the Sociedad de Geografía e Historia de Guatemala. The interim director of the Archivo General de Centro América, Rigoberto Bran Azmitia, and the present director, Arturo Valdés Oliva, along with the staff of the archive, were always gracious and accommodating. I owe a special debt of gratitude to the late secretary of the archive, Carmen Peláez Olivares, for her assistance and consideration.

My colleagues at the University of Nebraska–Lincoln, Ralph H. Vigil and Michael C. Meyer (now at the University of Arizona), were patient listeners and contributors of ideas over the years. Christopher Lutz has contributed to this work through his generosity in sharing information, and it certainly benefits from the criticism of Benjamin Keen, Murdo MacLeod, and Dave Warren. Finally, and most importantly, I am grateful for the forbearance over many years of my wife, Carolina, and my children, Bill, Cristina, and Rowena.

Forced Native Labor in
Sixteenth-Century Central America

Introduction

SPANIARDS UNDERTOOK THE CONQUEST of Central America in 1523–24. They found a land teeming with people of diverse cultures, long in decline from the magnificence of the Maya past, the great stone temples overgrown with vegetation. Yet it was a vigorous race that resisted the foreign intrusion with great defiance before finally submitting.

For the first quarter century following the conquest Central America was a colony of considerable worth in the Spanish empire of the Indies. It gave promise of mineral wealth and was the center for a thriving trade in Indian slaves. It became a vital middle ground between the European settlements of the north (Mexico and the Antilles) and the expeditions moving into Peru and Tierra Firme. Within two decades the supply of native slaves dwindled, and the modest production of the mines was dwarfed by the rich silver strikes in Peru and Mexico during the 1540s. But while those developments relegated Central America to secondary rank, its provinces continued to be of consquence throughout the sixteenth century. There were still rich cacao-producing regions, and later silver discoveries renewed optimism in its potential. Santiago de Guatemala, the capital, grew into an attractive and prosperous center, the most important between the city of Mexico and Lima.

The regions under consideration here were those comprehended within the political jurisdiction of the Audiencia de los Confines. That district comprised the area of present-day Central America north of Panama: Costa Rica, Nicaragua, Honduras, Guatemala, and El Salvador (then called San Salvador and belonging to the province of Guatemala). In addition, the *audiencia* included the modern Mexican regions of Chiapas (which was spelled Chiapa in the sixteenth century) and Soconusco. For a few short years Yucatán, Tabasco, and Cozumel also formed part of the district, but they are scarcely touched on in this study. Taken altogether, it was a colony of good size, measuring some six hundred leagues in length

3

(including Yucatán) and eighty to ninety across at the widest point.[1] The
land was varied in nature, containing within its boundaries highlands
punctuated by dramatic volcanic peaks where the air was chill in the cold
months and temperate in the summer. There were natural ports on both
coasts, muggy tropical regions, breeding grounds for fevers and other
tropical illnesses. While most of the landscape was rough and mountainous, some provinces, such as Nicaragua, had much flat land. There were
rivers, swollen over their banks in the rainy season, and many lakes,
among them the beautiful Atitlán and the sizable *lago de Nicaragua*. In the
extremes of nature lay the wealth: silver in the mountains so difficult of
access, and cacao in the wilting humidity of the lowlands.

How many natives lived in Central America before the advent of the
white man is a question that has long perplexed scholars. The disagreement is such that one cannot confidently offer a reasonable estimate. A
conservative figure of two and a quarter million has been advanced; but
others go up to six million and far beyond.[2] The reports of early *conquistadores* that there were as many Indians as in Mexico or Peru are no help at
all. Initial impressions should not be taken too seriously. There was a
tendency at the time to use figures with abandon, and it was all to a
captain's advantage to give the impression that he had discovered and
conquered a great civilization. Later writers seized on the high population
figures in order to dramatize the shocking decline in the native population. Until a couple of decades had passed there were few reliable figures,
and even then the disparities confuse the issue.

Leaving aside the unsubstantiated estimates of some private individuals, we must pay more attention to reports of clergymen and royal officials,
some of whom had reason to keep records. But they often resorted to
round figures, and sometimes they used old counts. Moreover, the figures
seldom, if ever, included all of the Indian villages under administrative
control and certainly not those beyond the Spanish pale. Tribute assessments would be reliable, except that counts for some pueblos are usually
missing and the figures occasionally included Indians long dead.

Further complicating the picture is the uncertain application of ter-
minology. Tribute assessments took into account only those Indians who
actually paid tribute. But other reports do not always make clear whether
their counts refer to *tributarios*, as they are sometimes clearly designated;
frequently reference is merely to "indios," which could include all natives.
It is probable that in most cases the term *indios* means tributaries,
although in Appendix A I have made the distinction in most instances. The
remaining task is to ascertain the ratio of tributaries to those who were

exempt from payment. Just who constituted these *reservados* varied from time to time, but they were usually children, the aged and infirm, sometimes women, Indians who worked in various capacities for the Church, and certain native officials, including the nobility. For periods of time Indians (usually from Mexico) who aided the Spaniards in the conquest were exempt.[3]

It is difficult to arrive at a reasonably accurate ratio of tributaries to the reservados. It could be altered over the years by war or pestilence, as opposed to periods of peace and relative prosperity. Among other results, the birthrate could vary according to conditions. A notable statistic in some tribute assessments is the few children in Indian families, with a good number of couples showing no children at all, others with only one, and relatively few with more than two.[4] However, the other members of families who were exempted have to be taken into account. With some reservations, it appears to me that one tributario represented a count of close to four people.

Rarely did anyone assess the population for the entire audiencia district, since most are local estimates. But the royal cosmographer-chronicler, Juan López de Velasco, undertook the task in the early 1570s. There are reasons for questioning the degree of accuracy in his figures, but they are the best we have. His assertion that there were 120,000 tributaries is not greatly different from composite estimates made by others around the same time, few as such comparisons are. The Indians, most of whom were assigned in *encomienda*, lived in about one thousand *pueblos*. Something like a third of them lived in Guatemala. The *cosmógrafo* admitted that he had no count for some towns.[5] Using a ratio of 1:4, we arrive at a figure of 480,000 Indians in Central America by the early 1570s. Allowing for those he missed, the district had perhaps about half a million natives following half a century of Spanish occupation. Some authorities favor a ratio of 1:5, which would raise the total to over 600,000.[6]

If we accept the fairly conservative figure of two and a quarter million Indians in pre-conquest times, the decline to half a million after five decades is disastrous; but it may be remarked that some, using a higher initial count and a lower survival figure, see the proportion of loss in even more catastrophic terms. Although the rate of declining population was clearly drastic, a great deal of specialized research will have to be undertaken before we have an acceptable approximation. It is not likely that truly accurate numbers will ever be known. While some authorities, citing hyperbolic estimates, write of decimation (such as occurred in the Antilles), there are good indications that the reduction should be tallied in slightly less calamitous terms. Reference was made by the president of

the audiencia in 1582 to a decline of some two-thirds from the original
population, a tragedy proportionately exceeding that of the Black Death in
Europe, but still less than figures often quoted. Clergymen witnesses in
the president's report attributed most of the loss to three or four pestilences, which they said came from Mexico.[7] Whether or not the allusion
is only to the province of Guatemala is unclear. How much of the loss
of life can be ascribed to plagues is debatable, but I am inclined to
think the percentage is very high. MacLeod is of the opinion that at
least a third of the population of the Guatemalan highland died very early
from pestilence.[8]

For the Spanish population of Central America during the sixteenth
century we have a much more reliable settlement pattern and a fairly
accurate count of *vecinos* (householders). What strikes one initially about
the figures, especially in the early years, is the very small number of
Spaniards given, with some towns appearing to be tiny hamlets, hardly
worthy of recognition. One reads of settlements with ten to twelve
Spaniards, or even fewer. Those figures are, however, deceptive; for
while many of the towns were indeed small, a visitor to them would have
seen many more people than the counts indicate. The designation of
vecinos represented only heads of households, citizens inscribed on the
town rolls. That is to say, the vecino was a permanent resident of the
community, a property owner, usually the head of a family, and an
active participant in local affairs. In the earliest years he was more often
than not an *encomendero* and a conqueror. How many others were represented by a vecino in a census count could vary considerably. During
the conquest period a vecino would represent no more than himself;
even though his household would likely consist of an Indian mistress,
mestizo children, and various Indian or perhaps black retainers, he
probably would be the only Spaniard. Before long, however, the conqueror was joined by various relatives and friends from Spain who
would reside in his house. Almost all eventually took Spanish wives and
had children.

Prosperous encomenderos usually had large households, and the same
was often true for royal bureaucrats, lawyers, merchants, members of the
higher clergy, and other successful settlers. To take one example, in a
probanza of 1551, Francisco Sánchez observed that he had thirteen
children (one of whom was "natural"), plus seven grandchildren and
sons-in-law.[9] Thus his household represented more than twenty
Spaniards, without taking into account the probability of his having
Spanish *criados* in residence or nearby. Including non-Spanish servants,

Sánchez must have fed at least thirty people within his household alone, and perhaps more.

Doubtless the Sánchez household was larger than most, but there are few easily accessible records from which to deduce the size of an average family. If we use a ratio of one vecino to five Spaniards there is little chance of inflating the figures, in my view. It must be borne in mind that the ratio would be smaller in the first few years and then would increase considerably with the proliferation of families. The extended-family concept was well developed in the second half of the century, with the result that some households must have been quite large indeed. Spaniards imported from Spain unmarried sisters and nieces, as well as brothers, nephews, parents, cousins, and friends. Within the communities there were many other Spaniards unattached to an established household. Some had the impermanent status of *estantes*, while others were merely spending a few days visiting or passing through. And, despite efforts to keep them out, there were always vagabonds lounging about.

Population figures for port cities remained small in most cases, owing to the unhealthful climates. When ships pulled in for trade, merchants arrived to transform the towns into bustling centers for a short time. Sailors, a fair number of whom were foreigners, moved among the crowds and sometimes jumped ship.

Taking into account the above factors, a town with a hundred Spanish vecinos by 1575 most likely had a total of at least five hundred Spaniards, and probably that many more from among the other racial groups. Perhaps some will disagree, believing that a postulation of ten inhabitants (of all races) for one listed Spanish vecino is distorted one way or the other. But it is helpful to have some idea of the total numbers of people in Central American settlements beyond the misleading figures for vecinos. While my estimate is based on no hard information, I believe that it is within reason.

Some of the Spanish settlements lost population, while others simply disappeared. What, for instance, happened to the Villa de Santa María de Esperança? That mining settlement, which had some seventy encomenderos in 1531, appears to have vanished.[10] In a few instances names were changed, adding to the confusion. While location changes were sometimes tied to lack of economic opportunity, other reasons, such as bad climate or better port facilities, caused removal. Indian threats were responsible for the relocation of the first Santiago; a mudslide destroyed the second; and the third had to be abandoned in the eighteenth century because of a terrible earthquake. A volcanic eruption, beginning in the late sixteenth century, finally caused the withdrawal from the city of León

in the early part of the seventeenth century. The location of the new city of
León a few leagues distant is often shown on maps as the site of the
original. It was, in fact, only a few years ago that the ruins of León *viejo*
were discovered in a field near the lake, ominously close to the peak of
Momotombo.[11]

The figures of López de Velasco (see Appendix B) show nineteen
Spanish towns for Central America in the early 1570s, with a population of
between twenty-two and twenty-three hundred vecinos; the Pineda account of 1594 shows only sixteen settlements, with a population of more
than 1,760; Vázquez de Espinosa, writing about 1620, lists only fifteen
towns and more than 2,840 Spanish vecinos. For several town counts both
Pineda and Vázquez de Espinosa add "more than" to the figures given,
and both overlooked some settlements. The most arresting statistic shows
that from a total population for Central America in 1570 of more than two
thousand vecinos, there was a decline to only 1,760 about a quarter of a
century later. The loss is even more remarkable comparing the latter
figure with the count of López de Velasco of ca. 1572–73, showing
twenty-two hundred to twenty-three hundred, a reduction of some five
hundred vecinos. That was a very serious development considering
that altogether about twenty-five hundred Spaniards left the sparsely
settled colony.

There are at least a couple of reasons to explain the exodus. Between
1576 and 1581, a pandemic of *cocoliztli-matlazáhuatl* (or *gucumatz*,
probably pulmonary plague) swept Central America, taking a dreadful toll
of Indians lives, which by extension reduced the labor force upon which
Spaniards depended.[12] Moreover, the economic problems of which Mac-
Leod writes were having an effect. The economy was showing some signs
of recovery by the second decade of the seventeenth century, although
there were fewer towns. During the population decline, Santiago, the
largest city, had five hundred vecinos, according to Pineda. By 1620,
Vázquez de Espinosa shows that the population had doubled to more than
one thousand. Santiago was by then an important city, with a probable
total population of some ten thousand inhabitants.

Finally, the shifting demographic pattern of the early decades should be
emphasized, as at least one explanation for the apparent discrepancies of
the population figures given. To take one example, Oviedo's count of León,
Nicaragua, showed that city to have more than two hundred Spaniards
from about 1527 to 1530, after which the number dropped off. The
obvious reason is that many Spaniards from that region followed the
expeditions for the conquest and settlement of Peru. Other population
drops doubtless occurred when many men joined the Alvarado expedition

to Peru (Quito) in 1534–35, and his armada to explore the Pacific, 1539–41. A shift of the population in Nicaragua certainly followed the Contreras revolt of 1550.

The conquest of Central America followed the inevitable expansion of Spanish positions on both geographical extremes, and the land became a battleground among contending forces for years. Eager to extend his jurisdiction, Fernando Cortés dispatched Pedro de Alvarado to the south in late 1523. From Panama, the men of Pedrarias Dávila (Pedro Arias de Avila) moved up into Nicaragua and beyond in 1523–24. Shortly thereafter Cortés personally led a calamitous march to Honduras, an area that was disputed by many factions in following years. In all cases, the rewards to the conquerors were Indians, taken either as slaves or assigned to individual Spaniards to whom they owed labor and tribute. Subsequent to the initial conquest there followed a period of twenty-five years which may be termed a conquest society, years when the conquistador-encomendero had little opposition, living off the labor of the conquered people.

The abusive exploitation of the Indians existed almost unchecked because men of power wanted it that way. Perhaps even more importantly, unlike Mexico (where similar conditions existed under slightly different political circumstances), it would be two decades before Central America had a centralized bureaucratic structure. Instead, there was rule by provincial strongmen.

While Cortés retained political power in Mexico for a relatively short time before being displaced by royal appointees, his erstwhile lieutenant, Pedro de Alvarado, was able to maintain his control over much of Central America for seventeen years. His dominance was never seriously challenged. Alvarado was the quintessential *caudillo*, whose charisma derived from his imposing physical presence, exploits on the field of battle, grace, charm, self-assurance, a mercurial character, and an inclination to violence combined with a generous spirit—all of which impressed the Indians quite as much as his Spanish companions. To the natives he was known as "Tonatiuh"—the sun. The flattering sobriquet (supposedly given for his fair complexion and cheerful disposition) implied awe more than affection; indeed, the Indians feared him, and it was said that his very presence had the effect of calming—or better put, intimidating—the local populace.[13] Magnanimous to his friends and ruthless to his enemies, Alvarado was master of Guatemala from 1524 to 1541. Through careful marriages, guile, and force, he found himself with the titles of *adelantado*, governor, and captain general.[14] As such, he allowed unrestricted use of the Indians, to the immense satisfaction of his followers.

No less remarkable in his way was the caudillo of the southern region, Pedrarias Dávila. Much older than Alvarado, he too had an impressive record as a warrior and athlete, dating back long before his arrival in the Indies. Were it not for the cruelties he committed in Panama and Nicaragua, he doubtless would have gone down in history as a man of heroic proportions. His savage treatment of the natives and his predilection for beheading good and popular Spaniards precluded that. With powerful friends at court, Pedrarias was, nevertheless, able to retain power until his death at an advanced age in 1531.[15] Like Alvarado, he governed with tenacity for seventeen years. Following a period of about three years during which time the government was held by *licenciado* Francisco de Castañeda, who didn't help matters much, the son-in-law of Pedrarias, Rodrigo de Contreras, succeeded to the governorship.[16] For a decade (1534–44) he and his family had the run of Nicaragua. It was a period of violence and unrestrained oppression of the native population.

Still another powerful individual exerted authority in Central America during the early years. He was Francisco de Montejo, the frustrated adelantado who spent years trying to conquer Yucatán. Having finally been named governor of Honduras, he was later forced out by Alvarado.[17] There were other governors during the early, chaotic years, but for the most part they were ineffectual and maintained only tenuous control.

The fact that Central America had little in the way of an experienced and dedicated bureaucracy—aside from the ever-present treasury officials —does not satisfactorily explain the failure to protect the Indians. After all, Mexico had a royal high court (audiencia) with high-minded judges and an enlightened viceroy many years before substantial reforms were effected there. The truth is that Mexico ultimately lagged behind Central America in implementing significant Indian labor legislation.

Nor was there lacking a body of laws to be applied. Some twelve years prior to the initial conquest of Central America the humane legislation known as the Laws of Burgos was issued, in 1512. Indians were to be well treated and converted to the Christian faith. Although they would be required to work nine months a year for Spaniards, during the remaining three months they could either work their own fields or hire out as wage-earners. Aside from general provisions, the legislation dealt in specifics: Indians were to be provided with hammocks so they would not have to sleep on the ground; encomenderos were to give each of their Indians a gold peso every year in order for them to clothe themselves adequately; and no Spaniard was to dare hit an Indian or call him "dog" or anything else except his true name. No Indian was to be used as a burden-bearer, and official visitors were to inspect towns to make sure the laws were being obeyed.[18]

Royal edicts proclaiming that Indians were free men and not subject to servitude were given on at least six occasions between 1526 and 1542—that is, from the early years of colonization in Central America up to the issuance of the celebrated New Laws.[19] There were, furthermore, numerous less formal admonitions to royal officials on the same subject, to little avail.

Eventually the situation changed somewhat, as the period of independent strong governors, who favored the encomenderos, gave way to royal bureaucracy in Central America. It came about for both political and humanitarian reasons.

The distance of the Indies from the royal court gave justifiable concern to the Crown, particularly with regard to the loyalty of the encomenderos and the ability of administrators to control them. The rebellions against authority that subsequently broke out in various New World colonies during the sixteenth century confirmed the very real danger. At least to some extent, such apprehension was probably a factor in the removal of Columbus from power in the Antilles many years before. And later Charles V, with his distrust of the aristocracy reinforced by a power struggle with Spanish nobility precisely during the conquest of Mexico, moved before long to ease Cortés from perpetuating his political influence. The prestige of New World conquerors portended the formation of a colonial aristocracy that could again challenge royal authority in the Indies.

But while royal appointees took charge of affairs in Mexico, provincial governors in Central America remained to create a crisis in administration; they either governed arbitrarily or they were unable to cope with local problems. Accordingly, the Crown determined to abolish the system and to replace the independent governors with an audiencia that would give strong, centralizing administration, reflecting the Crown's interests, not those of individuals. The corporate structure of judges was to bring about justice and order through the implementation of existing legislation, averting the dangers inherent in the system of provincial one-man rule. In that way control would pass from the unruly conquistadores to bureaucrats, sober men of integrity and learning. All things considered, it made good sense.

The timing of all this was fortunate because the most powerful leaders were not present to put up effective resistance. Alvarado had been killed in 1541, a decade after the passing of Pedrarias. Coincident with the political change was the issuance of a comprehensive set of humane laws—the New Laws of the Indies for the Good Treatment and Preservation of the Indians, proclaimed in 1542–43. At the same time, the order was given for the establishment of the new court—the Audiencia de los

Confines. Thus a new phase emerged, in which the judges were specifically charged to implement the reforms.

But what appeared to be so auspicious a change for the native peoples in reality relieved them very little. From 1544 to 1548, the judges (*oidores*) were able to bring about better administration and some measure of justice. However, the plight of the Indians remained much as before, except that there was gradually less violence, owing more to the eventual process of pacification and acculturation than to any resolute action by the first audiencia. The natural process of settlement acted as some restraint. And despite the concern of the colonists about the threatened application of Indian labor legislation, a concern bordering on panic, the judges allowed affairs to continue with little change.

It came as a shock, therefore, when, in 1548, a new audiencia was formed under the presidency of licenciado Alonso López de Cerrato. A dour, dedicated judge who brooked no nonsense, Cerrato set in motion a policy that was seen by the colonists as their complete ruination—that is to say, he was completely intent on enforcing the laws. His substantial achievement of that goal, in the face of incredible odds, was a landmark in the history of Indian labor in the New World. By 1550 the situation of the Indians was significantly altered because of Cerrato's actions, and their condition was never again quite so deplorable as in the past. This is not to say that the high ideals of Spanish legislation were fully realized; indeed, life for the Indians remained that of servitude to their white masters throughout the sixteenth century and beyond. Officials who followed Cerrato were not his equal in zeal and courage, and the social patterns of the conquest society took further root.

What follows is an account of a conquered people and the tragic fate to which they were subjected by their masters. More than that, it attempts to describe in detail the ways in which it came about, and seeks to explain in part why it happened at all.

PART I

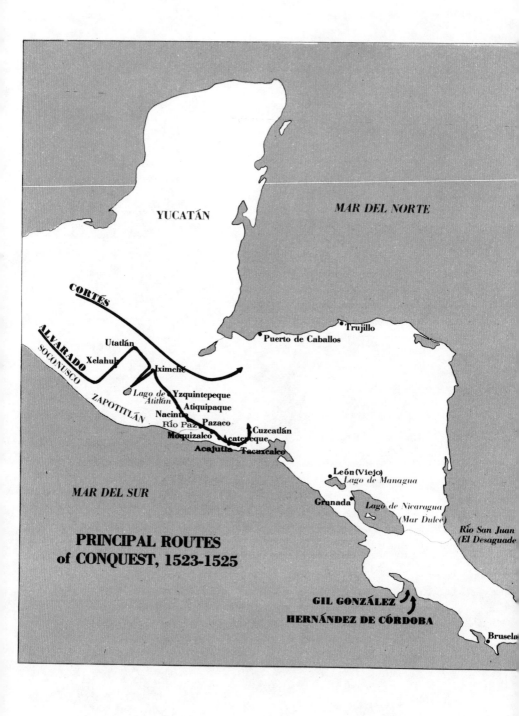

YUCATÁN

MAR DEL NORTE

CORTÉS

ALVARADO

SOCONUSCO

Utatlán

Xelahuh

Iximché

Trujillo

Puerto de Caballos

Lago de Atitlán

Yzquintepeque

Atiquipaque

ZAPOTITLÁN

Nacintla

Río Paz

Pazaco

Moquizalco

Acatepeque

Cuzcatlán

Acajutla

Tacuxcalco

León (Viejo)

Lago de Managua

MAR DEL SUR

Granada

Lago de Nicaragua

(Mar Dulce)

Río San Juan

(El Desaguade

PRINCIPAL ROUTES

of CONQUEST, 1523-1525

GIL GONZÁLEZ

HERNÁNDEZ DE CÓRDOBA

Brusela

1
Prehispanic Slavery

SLAVERY WAS WELL ESTABLISHED among the indigenous peoples of Central America long before the coming of the Spaniards, and it appears to have been widespread as far back as records obtain.[1] Slaves formed a distinct class in the social order, which was typically formed as follows: (a) nobles *(pipiltin);* (b) merchants *(pochteca)* and artisans *(amanteca);* (c) plebeians *(macehualtin);* and (d) slaves *(tlatlacotin).*[2]

As in most ancient stratified societies, class differences were manifest not only in occupation, but in manner of dress, living conditions, and privileges, or the lack of them. In Nicaragua slaves were given permanent brands. A black powder called *tile* made from charred and ground pine trees was rubbed into a cut made on the slave's face or arm, and when the wound healed the black mark remained.[3] In Yucatán the heads of slaves were shorn.[4]

Slaves were usually either prisoners of war or criminals enslaved by their own society, but their children were sometimes born free. *Caciques* in preconquest Santiago de Atitlán, Guatemala, had vassals and received both male and female slaves in tribute from their subjects.[5] In early El Salvador those who broke laws were expelled and sold into slavery, although their condition was not inherited.[6] In other areas slavery was passed on to offspring; however, in Yucatán, "children had the right to redeem themselves by settling on unoccupied lands and becoming tribute-payers."[7]

Edward Calnek notes that there was a class of slaves in preconquest Chiapas and that a distinction was made in local languages for a slave purchased *(munat* or *manbil munat)* and one captured in war *(tzoc).* He adds that "definition of *Oghouh* and *Aghauetic* as 'señor de siervos' in the Tzotzil dictionary suggests that such slaves were purchased or owned by members of the ruling class. The term defined as 'siervo nacido en casa' suggests that some forms of slavery could be inherited."[8]

In nearby Acalán, where less is known of social organization, slaves were clearly identified. In a Chontal text published by authorities, "they are called 'meya uinicob' or 'working people' in Chontal, and 'esclavos' in Spanish." The Yucatecan Maya manuscripts, the authors note, "with the exception of the Crónica de Calkini, avoid mention of slavery; but the Chol words for male and female slaves, *pentac* and *mun*, are almost identical with the Maya, which are *ppentac* and *ah munil*, so it is to be suspected that the Chontal expression mentioned above was a euphemism."[9]

Slave raids were common, and war was often fomented with the precise objective of taking slaves for sacrifice or labor. In Honduras some tribes went through the formality of sending ambassadors out to demand the delivery of slaves, failing which they were taken by force. To distinguish the captured slaves, their noses were cut off—that is, provided they were tractable; otherwise they were thrown off a cliff so they would cause no more trouble.[10] Among native societies the need for slaves was justification in itself for making war, as a result of which the Indians did not trouble themselves to frame a rationale for their actions. Apparently they had little concept of what Spaniards called "just war"; but if they failed to make legal and philosophical distinctions, neither was there hypocrisy in their direct, if merciless, behavior. Unrestrained by such considerations, Indians had as their greatest source of slaves captives taken in war.[11] Thus the Spanish designation "esclavo de guerra" was easily comprehensible to the New World natives.

The coastal people of Honduras were sometimes in the habit of killing their prisoners, but more generally captives were held in thrall to serve their masters. In Nicaragua captured chiefs were occasionally killed and eaten, while the commoners were simply enslaved. In some areas prisoners of high rank were frequently sacrificed. Perhaps only as a captive was the plebeian in a position preferential to that of a noble; although, if his captors lacked an aristocratic victim, the commoner might find himself offered to the gods.[12] In Verapaz slaves were sometimes purchased for sacrifice, but towns able to muster a sizable force of warriors sent out expeditions to seize them instead. Fifteen days prior to a religious rite they invaded their enemies' territories and took as many slaves as they needed. If they captured more than the sacrificial ceremony required some were given to the ruler and the remainder were divided among the warriors. All enemies taken in war, male and female, young and old, were enslaved.[13]

In addition to slaves taken in war, others were enslaved among their own people. Reasons were based on a different set of principles from those which induced the condition in Europe, and they provided a wider range of possibilities for forced labor than those which the Spanish invaders would introduce.

In Guatemala, under the stern code of justice prevailing, many crimes called for the death penalty, and it was common among some groups for the executed criminal's wife and children to be enslaved. The penalty for rape was death if the act was consummated; if not, the assailant would be enslaved. If one stole something sacred and valuable from a temple he was pushed over a precipice; but if the theft was something of less importance the offender was reduced to slavery.

In Nicaragua when a thief was apprehended he was forced to serve as the slave of the owner of the stolen property until it was paid for. As a slave, he could be sold to someone else, though with the approval of the cacique he could be redeemed. When a cassal fled from his lord he was killed, if captured, and his wife and children were made slaves. The same fate awaited the family of a traitor. If an Indian from an enemy tribe was caught poaching in tribal hunting or fishing territories he could either be executed or enslaved.[14]

It was common among the Indians of Verapaz to sell one another. One would exercise great care and cunning to locate a buyer, presumably outside the tribe, for one of his own people. Once the sinister agreement was reached, the victim was kidnaped and sold. Because of the gravity of this crime there was a harsh law against it—anyone found guilty of it was summarily put to the garrote. Moreover, his family was sold into slavery, and from the proceeds of the sale food and drink were bought for the villagers who assembled for the execution and celebration that followed.[15]

Bartolomé de Las Casas notes that kidnaping was not uncommon in Guatemala, despite the punishment, which was that the offender was clubbed to death, and his wife and children enslaved. He adds, furthermore, that in Nicaragua a father sometimes sold himself and his children into slavery owing to poverty, although redemption was possible.[16] Later the Spaniards found many Indians who had been sold into slavery for the same reason.

The severe laws extended even to the king himself, the concept of regicide for tyrants pertaining. The custom in Guatemala was that if a king was a cruel, unjust, tyrant the heads of families who felt aggrieved communicated their sentiments in secret to leading citizens of the kingdom. If their argument was compelling, a conspiracy formed and the ruler was put to death, after which all his wives and concubines were taken, along with his children, as slaves. The deceased king's property was then divided among the people. If the plaintiffs lacked sufficient support in the city or kingdom, the plotters then presented their plan to the most powerful of the surrounding lords, offering to him the king's family as slaves, as well as his holdings.[17]

A slave was considered a piece of property pure and simple, and one could therefore physically abuse or even kill his own slave with impunity, without any accounting whatsoever. Nor was it a serious crime to kill another's slave, although restitution had to be made to the owner for the loss of his property. On the other hand, the penalty for killing a free Indian was invariably death by hanging or the garrote.[18] All of this is clear indication of the low esteem in which slaves were held. Apparently they were easily obtained, for we are told that in pre-conquest Nicaragua one could be purchased for only 100 cacao beans.[19]

Among the Guatemalans if one had sexual relations with a female slave he was punished with a fine, which sometimes equaled her value. On occasion the fornicator was required to purchase another slave of the same value for the owner. If the offense was committed with a slave belonging to a lord who had himself had carnal access to her, the fine was doubled.

In some regions sex with a slave or a widow resulted in a fine of 60 precious quetzal feathers, and sometimes 100, depending on the circumstances. Payment could also be in other goods such as cacao or cloth. But if anyone became intimate with a woman slave within the house of her lord, the couple was taken outside of the village and stoned to death. On some occasions the woman was strangled or killed by a stake driven through her throat, while the man was taken for sacrifice.[20] If a slave, or anyone else, was caught in adultery with the woman of a noble, the penalty was death by the garrote, although he was sometimes reserved for sacrifice during a fiesta.[21]

In some Indian groups fornication with a slave resulted in the Indian's own enslavement, though he could be pardoned by a high priest for distinction in battle. In Verapaz the hapless male slave was for all practical purposes denied sex: "If slaves committed fornication with women of their own condition, both parties were slain by having their heads broken between two stones, or by a stick driven down the throat, or by the garrote; the man, however, was sometimes sold for sacrifice." Anyone caught in a lie was severely whipped, with the exception that if the lie concerned a matter of war the liar was made a slave for treason.[22]

Free women sometimes married slaves, but in Verapaz at least, the children inherited the condition of the father. When sons of native lords married very young girls, the bride's family provided the bridegroom with a slave woman with whom to disport himself until the child-wife was old enough to receive him. Sons of the union with the slave woman could not inherit noble status, even if the father had no sons by his legitimate wife.[23]

An incorrigible adultress could be enslaved by her husband, who was permitted to sell her as such if he chose. When an important cacique became gravely ill his children by his slave women were sometimes sacrificed to the gods as an offering; if he had no illegitimate children others by his legal wives could be offered. After that ceremony the cacique confessed his sins, which usually involved simple fornication and adultery. Adultery with a free woman was a grievous sin since there was an injured party; if the object of the man's attentions had been his slave, however, it was not considered a grave offense because she was for his use as he saw fit.[24] Squier comments that in some tribes the adulterer was enslaved by the injured husband.[25]

Many slaves were taken for the purpose of selling them to others, and the trade was often brisk in order to meet the demands of both domestic needs and the export trade. Slaves in fact made up one of the most important items of trade from the Yucatán peninsula to Honduras, and Cortés mentioned that at Acalán there was considerable commerce in the slave trade. Slaves were transported from Yucatán to Guatemala as well.[26]

Mexican codices show us that slaves were burdened with wooden yokes and marched off to alien lands, separated from their families. The description by the historian Fray Diego Durán involving a slaving expedition of the Totonacs in the valley of Mexico in 1454 would no doubt be apt for a similar scene in early Central America:

> They placed yokes around the neck of young and old. The slaves, lined up one behind the other, were led out of the cities in a pitiful manner, the husband leaving his wife, the father his son, the grandmother her grandson. They went along weeping and their wails reached the heavens. In this way they bought a great number of slaves from all these nations.[27]

In Indian society slaves performed menial tasks similar to those which they would do for the Spaniards. The men hauled water and firewood, paddled canoes, hunted, fished, farmed their masters' fields, and carried his goods. Occasionally they were sacrificed. The women worked in households, spun and wove cloth, cooked, ground maize, and sometimes shared their masters' beds. With the coming of the Spaniards the role of the slave remained essentially the same, but an important difference was the inclusion in the new slave society of Indians enslaved on different pretexts. And, very significantly, the pre-existence of slavery as a native institution served to reinforce the justification for its continuance under Spanish rule.[28]

2
Slavery and the Spanish Conquest

WHEN SPANIARDS FIRST ARRIVED in the Antilles they began to enslave the natives, and even though Queen Isabella was distressed about this treatment of her vassals and tried to check it, communication was so poor and administration so ineffective in the islands that it continued. She was succeeded by Ferdinand, who was less concerned about the welfare of the Indians.[1] By the time Fernando Cortés mounted his conquest of Mexico in 1519, Charles V ruled Spain, and during his long reign slavery flourished, despite many equivocal decrees aimed at preventing it. Before his abdication, however, Indian slavery as a legal institution was abolished. In Central America lawful enslavement of the natives by Spaniards lasted just about a quarter of a century.[2]

Among the conquerors of Central America were many who had accompanied Cortés. They were accustomed to taking Indians as part of the spoils of conquest, and it was with that same understanding that they invaded lands south of the Aztec domain. Other adventurers sent north from Panama by Pedrarias Dávila expected nothing less. The Spaniards had hopes of finding ready treasure; if not, the land, rumored to be very populous, would at least yield Indians to be taken and sold at good profits as slaves.

Slavery had a long history in the Old World, so that Spanish behavior in the Indies was reinforced by customs of antiquity. Even though many considered it natural that enemies taken in just war could be enslaved, there were those who questioned the legality of Spanish conquests in the New World.[3] Other considerations were insinuated, however, to justify enslavement, among which was the issue of immorality. As early as 1504, Carib Indians had been enslaved in the New World "for the sins of sodomy, idolatory, and because they ate human flesh."[4] It is not the intention here to become involved in the interminable philosophical treatises that occupied the attention of humanists and others during the

20

sixteenth century, but suffice it to say that all shades of opinion were expressed, usually in lengthy and often contrived disquisitions.[5]

Owing to the overwhelming complexities of the arguments advanced, Charles V and his advisors reluctantly allowed the enslavement of Indians,[6] but only under certain circumstances. Those who stubbornly refused to recognize the authority of the Spanish Crown and Church, and who would not submit peacefully to the conquerors, surrendered their rights as free men. Those who readily agreed to become vassals of the Spanish sovereign were not to be enslaved; but those who remained obstinate and resisted by force of arms could be taken in just war and made to serve as slaves.

So that the natives would be apprised of the terms, they were to hear the reading of the *requerimiento*—the "requirement," that most curious of documents—explaining the authority of the Spanish kings and the succession of the popes. It was to be presented, through translators, to the assembled Indians. No doubt the device seemed perfectly reasonable to jurists sitting in the councils of Castile. Probably it appealed to their sense of legality and justice, and very likely helped to salve the royal conscience. But in actual fact it made little sense on the alien frontiers of the Indies. If the natives were hostile they did not wait for the proclamation. Often there was not a competent translator available, and even when there was, the document perforce lost something in translation. If the contents were less than edifying to the bewildered Indians, the ultimatum was usually clear enough: they were to submit peacefully or the women and children would be seized and sold as slaves. The blame for such a turn of events, the requirement asserted, would not be that of the Spaniards, but of the intransigent Indians themselves.[7]

To make matters worse, the document allegedly was read out of earshot on occasion. During the conquest of Central America some chiefs did submit peacefully, whether or not they understood the nebulous terms of the requerimiento, but hostilities were frequent enough to insure a good supply of slaves. The concept of just war extended to rebellions as well, so that, even later, Indians once pacified could place themselves in jeopardy. Evidence suggests that revolts were sometimes provoked by Spaniards to furnish a pretext for enslaving the rebels.

Certain *caciques* (chiefs) in Central America, learning of the fall of Mexico-Tenochtitlán, sent ambassadors to the Spaniards offering submission. As Pedro de Alvarado pushed southward through Soconusco towards Guatemala he received more overtures of peace. He sent messengers to the Cakchiquel capital at Iximché (Patinamit), and King Belehe Qat agreed to an alliance with the invaders. More promising yet, on their return the messengers were accompanied by five thousand slaves bearing riches of the land worth 20,000 pesos.[8] Encouraged by this show of goodwill and opulence, Alvarado returned to Mexico to make preparations for the conquest of Guatemala. In the meantime, other emissaries sent by Cortés returned from the Quiché stronghold of Utatlán (Gumarcaah) with gifts and assurances of peace, lending even greater optimism to the enterprise. But, diverted by problems in Mexico, Alvarado did not set out for Guatemala until December 1523.

In the interim, however, some of the Guatemalans made an alliance with those of Soconusco to resist the Spaniards, with the result that Soconusco had to be retaken by combat. Many of those captured in the fighting were made *esclavos de guerra*—slaves of war. Alvarado then marched to the south, his army cutting its way through the dense jungles into Zapotitlán (Suchitepéquez) to secure that coastal region.[9]

As in most of the native states of the New World, those of Central America could not settle squabbles among themselves long enough to present a united resistance to the Spaniards. The most powerful kingdoms were those of the Maya-Quiché, with their capital at Utatlán, and the Cakchiquels. But the Cakchiquels quarreled among themselves and divided: one group, retaining the name, had its capital at Iximché, while the other, known as the Zutugils (Zutuhils) had its center at Atitlán. Consequently, the Quiché were the dominant power, the Cakchiquel forces having been further weakened by devastating plagues in 1520 and 1521. A proposed alliance of the three powers failed to materialize owing to their differences, and each was therefore destined to face the Spanish host alone.[10]

Still, the Quiché force itself, said, with probable exaggeration, to number two hundred thousand warriors, was formidable. Alvarado led about 420 Spaniards, of whom 120 were cavalry, along with something like twenty thousand Indian allies. The armies met at the large, fortified city of Xelahuh, and after furious fighting the Quichés were subdued and demoralized in the spring of 1524. The survivors retired to the imposing capital of Utatlán, which was by its situation deemed impregnable. To that stronghold Alvarado was invited with offers of peace and friendship. It appears, however, that the real intent of the ruler, Oxib Quieh, was to entrap the Spaniards in the city. But Alvarado, the veteran of Cholula, saw through the deceit, and in the ensuing battle Spanish arms were ultimately victorious. The king and certain nobles were either burned or hanged, including those in line of succession. Others were enslaved, one-fifth part of whom were given to the Spanish treasurer to sell for the *quinto* owed as the Crown's share.

Writing to Cortés from Utatlán in April 1524, Alvarado noted that he had forwarded terms of the requerimiento to the Quichés, inviting their fealty. He informed them that they would be favored if they came in peace; "and if not, I threatened to make war on them as on traitors rising in rebellion against the service of our Lord the Emperor and that as such they would be treated, and that in addition to this, I would make slaves of all those who should be taken alive in the war."[11]

Following the impressive evidence of Spanish force, Sinacam, the Cakchiquel ruler at Iximché, sent assurances of friendship to Alvarado. The Spaniards now had dependable allies and a base from which to operate. Meanwhile, Tepepul, the Zutugil king at Atitlán, remained defiant. On two occasions messengers sent by Alvarado were put to death. The Spaniards marched on the Zutugils, and after spirited fighting on the lake shore Alvarado invested the city and accepted the submission of Tepepul.

The Spanish captain then returned to Iximché where relations with the Cakchiquel lord deteriorated owing to Alvarado's desire for an aristocratic native woman—the beautiful Suchil, wife of Sinacam himself. On the pretext of disloyalty, Alvarado made Sinacam his prisoner and took his woman. The ruler was released only after he paid a ransom of both male and female slaves, along with some jewels. According to a witness, the female slaves were turned over to the soldiers. Alvarado accepted the treasure and slaves, keeping Suchil as well, giving her up only later.[12]

On learning that the people of Yzquintepeque (Escuintla) mocked the Christians, Alvarado attacked the capital of Panatacat at night during a rainstorm without going through the formality of the requerimiento (although it was proffered once the city was subdued). The Indians' ready acquiescence deprived the conquerors of taking large numbers of slaves on that occasion. Marching southward, the Spaniards arrived at Atiquipaque, where after an initially friendly welcome the natives fled to the hills. Their defection exasperated the Spanish commander whose army had arrived exhausted, seeking food and shelter. Later accused of unjustly enslaving the people there, he denied that he had done so; if, he added, some of his men or the native auxiliaries did so it was without his knowledge.[13]

Again Alvarado wrote Cortés, on July 28, 1524, telling of an attack by the people of Nacendelan (Nacintla). He had sent Indians of the area in with the requerimiento, but the people refused to come in peace. Apparently he omitted describing all of what happened subsequently, since other accounts state that hostile forces fell on his rear, killing Indian allies and making off with many valuable supplies of war, which could not be recovered because of widespread resistance. After failing to induce the inhabitants to come in peace, Alvarado fired the city and burned some captive nobles.

While Alvarado was still at that location, some of his native servants informed him that the people of Pazaco were coming to make war. As the Spaniards advanced to meet them, however, the Indians fled, taking their provisions with them. This reaction of the natives occurred frequently, and it seems to have particularly angered the captain, because his large army on the march depended on the native settlements providing food.

Discussing the incident later, Alvarado said that on entering the town of Pazaco the Spaniards saw many arrows stuck in the ground and came across a sacrificed dog, which was the sign of war. He did not dare send a messenger for fear the Indians would kill him, as had happened before. Suddenly the natives attacked, and everything happened so fast that he had no time to proclaim the requerimiento. During the battle Alvarado was wounded several times, from which he was on the point of death, according to his version. Moreover, the Indians killed the sorrel he was riding.[14] To pay for the horse, he demanded that slaves be given. He also required some Spanish soldiers to give up some of their slaves to compensate those Spaniards whose valuable horses had been killed. Although the price of a slave fluctuated, it might well take two hundred or more slaves to offset the cost of a horse at the time. Those present agreed that the Indians had ridiculed the Spaniards and tried their patience. They refused to bring food for the strangers and sometimes deceived them by first coming in peace and then attacking. This scorn of their arms was an insult the Spaniards felt had to be avenged for the good of the land.[15]

As the Spaniards crossed the Río Paz to present-day El Salvador, the territory and regional capital then both known as Cuzcatlán, the natives once more fell away before the Spanish advance. Frustrated by these repeated "desertions," Alvarado sent men to round up as many Indians as possible to be branded as slaves. One apparent reason for these actions was to warn the other Indians that the same would happen to them if they did not cooperate, but it often happened that the fear of enslavement only made them keep their distance.

At his judicial review (juicio de residencia) five years later, Alvarado was accused of mistreating inhabitants of the pueblo of Moquizalco (Mosuis-calco) near Sonsonate, as well as those in Acatepeque. When the people came out to greet him, it was charged, he ordered them to bring food; but being frightened of the Spanish cruelties, they did not return. Then, on the orders of Alvarado, the soldiers seized and branded as many of the natives as they could put their hands on. Alvarado admitted that they had enslaved Indians at those towns, but he said that his men were fatigued and suffering, cut off from assistance and mocked by the Indians. Under the circumstances, he felt that his response was justified.[16]

Near Acajutla a large, menacing force confronted the Spaniards. Although they were out-maneuvered and decisively defeated, the Indians seriously wounded Alvarado. He took an arrow in the thigh, shot with such force that it penetrated his saddle as well. Thereafter the elegant captain limped on one leg shorter than the other by four fingers. A few days later the Spaniards subdued an even larger force at Tacuxcalco while their lame leader watched.

Alvarado now moved on the regional capital of Cuzcatlán, encountering more deserted villages on the way. A short while later he described what happened in a letter to Cortés. Finding the city of Cuzcatlán empty, he sent assurances to the hills that the Indians would be treated kindly if they would submit to the service of God and His Majesty. "They sent word," he wrote, "that they did not know either of them, and they did not wish to come, and that if I wanted anything from them, they were there waiting with their arms." When the Indians persisted in this, he went on, "I sentenced them, as traitors, to death, both the chiefs of these provinces and all the others that had been taken during the war, and might be taken henceforth, until such time that they would give obedience to His Majesty, should be slaves and branded."[17]

However, charges posted against Alvarado years later give a different version, according to which the nobles of Cuzcatlán met him on the road, where many mounds of fruit and other food had been placed. Then, with the Spaniards comfortably lodged in the town, the accusers stated, Alvarado ordered his men to take as many Indians as possible, including the lords, and they were branded as slaves. In rebuttal, Alvarado testified that the villagers "revolted" the next day and disappeared into the woods, and that despite many appeals they would not return. Because of the multitude of Indians and the small number of Christians, the land could not be won for the king in any other way, in his opinion. Passive resistance was, in Alvarado's view, justification for enslavement.[18]

Fray Bartolomé de Las Casas gives an account that is perhaps fanciful to some degree, but interesting as a contemporary version:

> This captain [Alvarado] asked the lords to bring much gold, because it was principally to that end that they came. The Indians replied that they were happy to give all the gold they had, and they collected a very great quantity of the hachets they use which are made of gilded copper and look like gold, though there is little in them. The captain ordered that they should be tested and because he saw they were of copper, he said to the Spaniards: "to the devil with such a country: let us

leave it because there is no gold, and let each one put the Indians who serve him, in chains, and I will order that they be branded as his slaves." This was done, and they marked as slaves with the King's brand, all they could bind. And they saw the son of the prince of that town thus branded.[19]

There is some evidence that the king of the Cuzcatecs, Atlacatl, did indeed welcome the Spaniards before the inhabitants fled the city. When threats and cajolery failed to induce the Indians back, the conquerors resorted to force, without success. It was a costly encounter in which the Spaniards lost eleven valuable horses, and in the end all they held was a city deserted by its inhabitants.

Alvarado returned to the Cakchiquel capital of Iximché and formally established the Spanish settlement of Santiago in July 1524. In June 1525, he wrote the lieutenants governing Mexico during the absence of Cortés in Honduras. He made note of the founding of Santiago as well as San Salvador, down to the jurisdiction of Pedrarias.[20] Subsequently, as a result of increased demands from the conquerors, the Cakchiquels rebelled; the Spaniards withdrew from their settlement and finally defeated the rebels after a long campaign. Later the Spaniards would settle two more towns named Santiago: the first at the present-day site of Ciudad Vieja, which lasted until the disastrous deluge of 1541; and the second founded nearby at today's Antigua a short time later.

Alvarado was accused of enslaving other Indians unjustly during the conquest, but he answered that it was usually because the natives refused to submit to Spanish authority. On other occasions he justified his actions because of the guile and duplicity of the caciques. He recounted that in one instance various nobles had dined at his table, only to rebel later. They made war, "bien cruda," digging pits with sharp stakes in the bottom and covered with grass, into which many Spaniards and horses fell to their deaths. His brother Gonzalo confirmed this, noting that his own horse was maimed in that way.[21]

After several months of bitter fighting Alvarado had brought Soconusco, Guatemala, and El Salvador to the service of the Spanish sovereign. The first phase of the conquest was over and the most important indigenous groups were subdued. But the process of pacification would continue for many years, and Alvarado would later invade Honduras to fight other tribes. The policy of enslavement there was similar to those already recounted, and again he was charged with illegalities. In his defense, Alvarado admitted that he had branded some Chontal Indians because they "issued forth in war and had consistently resisted service to the Crown." His men had to be rewarded, and it was suitable that they be given the slaves because the Chontales were "perverse, bad and bellicose." His reason for making slaves near the Spanish villa of San Miguel was more candid: there was very little else with which the settlers of that new settlement could sustain themselves, except for slaves.[22]

Commenting on Alvarado's sanguinary career, Las Casas said that his soldiers would each take 50 or 100 Indians as slaves, and, the Dominican continued,

> Having thus killed all the lords and the men who could make war, they put all the others into the aforesaid infernal slavery; they demanded slaves as tribute, so the Indians gave their sons and daughters as they have no other slaves, all of whom they loaded into ships and sent them to be sold in Peru. By other massacres and murders besides the above, they have destroyed and devastated a kingdom more than a hundred leagues square, one of the happiest in the way of fertility and population in the world. This same tyrant wrote that it was more populous than the kingdom of Mexico; and he told the truth.
>
> He and his brothers, together with the others, have killed more than four or five million people in fifteen or sixteen years, from the year 1525 until 1540, and they continued to kill and destroy those who are still left; and so they will kill the remainder.[23]

This is of course gross distortion on the part of the master polemicist. Other writers have been only slightly less hyperbolic: Bancroft blames Pedrarias for the deaths of "hundreds of thousands of slaughtered savages," and he quotes Oviedo as saying that from the arrival of Pedrarias in 1514 until his death in 1530, he was responsible for the deaths of two million Indians.[24] Almost certainly the first Spaniards exaggerated the number of natives in Central America to begin with, and very likely the most telling factor in the population decline was that of the tragic plagues that swept the land with frequency.[25] There is no way of even approximating the number of Indians killed in combat, but it strains one's imagination to believe that the total was even remotely close to those stated above.

Probably more slaves were taken by the various expeditions of conquest and pacification commanded by Alvarado than any others, but it should be borne in mind that other captains conquered parts of Central America and that they too put Indians to the branding iron. In point of time, the first thrust into Central America came from the south. In January 1522, Gil González Dávila left Panama with a royal commission to explore northward. His experience was quite different from that of most such expeditions. Gil González marched to the land of the cacique Nicoya, after whom the territory took its name, where peaceful relations were established with the Indians.

Proceeding to the land of the more powerful chief Nicarao (hence

Nicaragua), the Spaniards sent messengers ahead with a requerimiento. After a long philosophical discussion with the curious ruler, Gil González peacefully converted him and his people to Christianity. Soon surrounding natives came in peace, asking for baptism, bringing, among other gifts, slaves for the Spaniards, without their having been requested. To that point, the expedition of Gil González was singular for the ease with which the Indians submitted, a happy circumstance owing no less to the peaceful attitudes of the natives than to the intelligent and humane policy of the Spanish captain. Then the powerful chieftain Diriangen approached with a splendid retinue, professing interest in what the Spaniards offered, but later attacking them. On the return journey to Panama the Nicaraguans made a halfhearted assault on the Spanish column; otherwise, the expedition made a peaceful return to Panama, arriving in June 1523, after a successful and profitable venture.

Subsequently a colonizing expedition was organized by Pedrarias. That hoary governor, now long in the tooth, was being replaced, and he was anxious to reestablish his favor with the Crown. To that end, in 1524 he dispatched a lieutenant, Francisco Hernández de Córdoba, to the north. Hernández de Córdoba founded the Spanish town of Bruselas on the Gulf of Nicoya, though it would last but three years. Some ninety miles beyond he settled Granada on the shore of Lake Nicaragua, and further on, the city of León.

From then forward, the early history of Central America, particularly in the unhappy province of Honduras, becomes very complicated owing to the disputing factions: Gil González returned to the Caribbean coast only to be challenged by Hernando de Soto, sent by Francisco Hernández de Córdoba; Cortés sent his lieutenant Cristóbal de Olid to settle Honduras as well; and the royal officials of Santo Domingo, desiring to assert their authority over the same province, sent their agent, Pedro Moreno.[26] The Spaniards there gave Moreno assurances of their loyalty, insincere as they were, and the agent prepared to leave. Before doing so, however, he raided an Indian village and seized forty slaves. Later Cortés filed formal charges against Moreno, resulting in an order from Charles V for the release of the Indians and an investigation into the affair. Cortés had marched overland from Mexico to Honduras, arriving in 1525. Moreno's kidnapping of the natives created hostile feelings, and Cortés insisted that Moreno be put in chains. Moreover, Cortés suspected that the slaves had been made with the consent of the judges of the audiencia at Santo Domingo.[27]

In the turbulent years following, slaves were taken on various forays into the backcountry and to nearby islands. A slaving expedition in 1525 seized Indians on Guanaja Island off the coast of Honduras to be taken to the mines of Cuba and Jamaica. The slavers had official license to do so, but Cortés procured the slaves' release. Although Cortés opposed the illegal enslavement of Indians, he recognized that those who had been slaves in native society could legally remain in that condition under the Spaniards. An expedition of Gabriel de Rojas from Nicaragua invaded Olancho, Honduras, and made slaves, and in late 1526 Nicaraguan Indians were branded and shipped to Panama. Hoping to straighten out the political mess in Honduras, the Crown appointed Diego López de Salcedo governor in 1525. He pursued a harsh policy with Indians, hanging some suspected of complicity in a rebellion and condemning others to slavery.[28]

Salcedo informed the Crown that while some of the natives submitted peacefully, others had to be conquered. He felt particularly justified in enslaving those who had been friendly at first, only to rebel later.[29] A royal order of 1527, noting that rebellious Indians had fortified themselves, killing both Spaniards and their native allies, ordered that the rebels be allowed to surrender with amnesty; but that if they refused the offer, they were to be taken and condemned to perpetual slavery.[30] Then, in 1530, the Crown forbade the making of any more slaves.[31]

Andrés de Cerezeda, the acting governor of Honduras in 1533, insisted that he was observing the decree that no slaves of any kind be made, even though he believed that the ruling encouraged the Indians to revolt. More to the point, he added that without slaves the Spaniards had nothing with which to trade in order to sustain themselves.[32] Cerezeda complained that when his enemy, Vasco de Herrera, had governed before, the Spaniards made war on the Indians and enslaved them. Because of the harsh treatment, the natives rebelled—which in turn gave further excuse for the Spaniards to enslave more of them as esclavos de guerra.[33]

Cerezeda also pointed out that despite the rich mines in Honduras, there were few Spaniards in the province because the land could not be pacified without rewarding the young soldiers with slaves. If they could have license to enslave the rebels, he was sure between a thousand and two thousand could be taken, a number sufficient to sustain the land.[34] Although the Crown had made a strong case against enslavement of Indians in 1530 and outlawed the practice, it revoked its previous firm and considered resolution in the face of opposition from the conquerors. The argument that without the threat of enslavement the Indians were encouraged to resist, thus resulting in more deaths, convinced the Crown that slaves taken in war was justifiable. Since those slaves already held by Indians remained in idolatry, it would be better from them to become slaves of *rescate*, in the hands of Christians.[35]

Slaves were taken the following year, 1534, when a Spanish captain took fifty men to punish an uprising in Naco. The punitive expedition failed in its main objective because of rough terrain, but the soldiers captured about sixty Indians, who were enslaved and shipped out of the province with others. Appealing to Crown interests, the treasurer, Diego García de Celis, added that good deposits of gold had been discovered in streams, but that the Indians shot arrows at the miners and frustrated the search.[36] Although enslavement of the sixty Indians was freely admitted, it was apparently still illegal, because only a month later the *veedor* (royal inspector) sought royal permission to brand rebels as slaves.[37]

A royal *cédula* issued in early 1534 did again allow Indians taken in just war to be enslaved, though it was not proclaimed in Central America until February 1535.[38] A year and a half later, however, the cabildo of Puerto de Caballos wrote that because it was illegal to make any slaves whatsoever, the vecinos suffered, not having any income, while the Indians were emboldened to resist. They were perverse and inclined to kill Spaniards without the threat of their enslavement.[39] Yet, about the same time, in the summer of 1536, Pedro de Alvarado was entering the area to take command, and he lost no time in making slaves of those rebellious Indians who killed Spaniards and their native allies. That policy had the effect of pacifying the land, according to an official. He also said that the Crown had allowed only the enslavement of males over the age of fifteen, and that it would be better to enslave the women, who were needed for labor, instead of having them die in the fighting.[40] The foregoing correspondence about Indian slavery in Honduras during the 1530s indicates the muddled conception of the law on the local level, or perhaps only confusion feigned as a pretext for the continuation of past policies favoring enslavement.[41]

When Pedrarias was restored to power in Nicaragua he sent Martín Estete to eastern Nicaragua where many slaves were taken. Despite royal injunctions to protect the natives, Pedrarias gave Estete a branding iron, which was supposed to be used only for rebels and criminals. Estete illegally branded large numbers without restraint, sending the Indians in chains to Pedrarias at León.[42]

When don Cristóbal de la Cueva took some seventy Spaniards to settle the villa of San Miguel he was subsequently charged with violating royal provisions by his cruel treatment and enslavement of the inhabitants of the region. The charge stated that when the natives came in peace, he sent one of his lieutenants to make war on them, as a consequence of which about two hundred Indians were killed; and others, some of whom were only four and five years old, were taken as slaves. Witnesses verified this version, one stating that all the captives were branded, even small children at their mothers' breasts. It may be noted, however, that small ones, "a las tetas de las indias," did not necessarily mean tiny babies—children commonly suckled to the age of four or five. Other witnesses questioned said that while the natives were peaceful at first, word came of a conspiracy to revolt. To punish the rebels, the Spaniards fought them and enslaved some, as was the custom in war. Don Cristóbal himself rebutted the charge, saying that the Indian carriers *(tamemes)* he had taken with him as allies had mutinied and fled, leaving him stranded in a hostile territory. When he sent couriers to ask the Indians to come in peace the messengers were sacrificed. In sum, the Spaniards maintained that, being warned that the Indians were determined to kill them, they attacked in fear for their lives, enslaving the survivors as punishment, because they were deceitful.[43]

These practices of enslaving Indians during the conquest of the Central American provinces were repeated from Chiapas to Costa Rica with only slight variations, and it serves little purpose here to recite more of the dismal circumstances. But while it seems apparent that many of the conquerors sought any pretext for taking slaves, it has also been seen that some, like Cortés and Gil González, curtailed indiscriminate enslavement. If one accepts the long and tiresome accounts of the querulous Francisco de Montejo (most of which are written in a diminutive hand), one would be inclined to place the adelantado in the same company. However, the evidence is strong that Montejo enslaved large numbers of Indians in Yucatán before going to Honduras, as noted further on. It seems that he had requested permission to reward his men, and that it had been carried out within the confines of the law, claims other conquerors could make as well. It does indicate that he could ignore scruples if expediency demanded it.

To his credit, Montejo did hold down slaving in Honduras, and his desire to be recognized for his policies was no doubt to some extent because of his jurisdictional dispute with Alvarado over the territory of Honduras. To that end, he was anxious to demonstrate to the Crown that his methods were humane in contrast to those of his rival, and apparently they were. He wrote the king that after he had settled the land there was an uprising during which some Christians were killed. In pacifying the land once again, the Spaniards had suffered and sustained many deaths over a period of two years; yet, he said, they had taken no slaves, whereas Alvarado came in and made "very crude" war, taking many slaves. Later he commented that he had taken the land "without killing fifty Indians nor having taken as many as a hundred slaves." Yet, despite his apparent antipathy to human servitude, he seems to have left some slaves in his own estate.[44] And even he capitulated to the realities of the situation. Chamberlain writes that "notwithstanding his general principle, Montejo believed that some Indian slaves were needed for labor and therefore permitted the taking of natives in war in accordance with royal law."[45]

Because it was traditional to enslave prisoners of war, and since Indians who refused submission to the Spain sovereign were judged to be traitors, the conquerors seized many Indians, usually with impunity. After the initial pacification of most of Central America, fighting continued fitfully for many years as a result of isolated resistance and frequent revolts of those previously subdued. Intransigence was often interpreted as treason, as a consequence of which many more could be enslaved. Such unsettled conditions would lead to a profitable trade in slaves.

3

Slaves of Rescate

ASIDE FROM THE ESCLAVOS DE GUERRA taken during the conquest and pacification, the Crown also sanctioned the taking of *esclavos de rescate* —that is, those Indians who had already been slaves among their own people. At the point of contact, there were large numbers of natives in that category, a situation of which the Spaniards were well aware.[1] A basic premise of Spanish legislation for the Indies was that natives should benefit as vassals of Charles V, and that in no way should their circumstances be more prejudicial than those existing under their native rulers. While slaves could be taken in war or rebellion—because it was a nearly universal custom in the New World as in the Old—it was reasoned that slaves of rescate suffered that condition through no fault of the Spaniards. Since they were found in that place in native society, they could remain so, as long as they were no worse off than before.

Official Spanish logic held that such slaves would benefit from serving the Spaniards because they would be taken into the Holy Faith, enjoying the benefits of Christianity. They would escape the sins of paganism, their souls would be saved, and at least some of them would be snatched from the sacrificial altars. Moreover, being in close contact with their masters, they would be exposed to the superior civilization of the Europeans, and would thus be assimilated more easily into Spanish culture. This last point, however, was stoutly, but vainly, denied by members of the clergy, who maintained that the Indians learned bad habits from association with Spaniards. So it was that the conquerors were allowed to barter for these slaves, or, in some instances, to receive them as tribute. Even though all officials were cautioned to establish that the Indians involved were truly slaves of rescate, needless to say the amenities were not always observed.

Among the few captains endeavoring to observe the royal will in the manner stipulated was Cortés. In 1525 he wrote his lieutenant in Trujillo, Honduras, with respect to the acquisition of esclavos de rescate. The

33

substance of his letter was that the king had granted all the vecinos of New Spain the privilege of receiving such slaves from the native lords of the land. Accordingly, Cortés gave permission to grant license to those Spaniards who held Indian towns in encomienda, allowing them to acquire slaves from the caciques. The lieutenant, Hernando de Saavedra, was to determine the numbers each Spaniard was to have, according to the merit of each, and in accordance with the number of Indians living in the pueblo where the slaves were to be obtained.

Furthermore, all natives secured through rescate, or trading, were to be taken before Saavedra and his notary, in the presence of the Indian lord, or whomever was trading the slave. The owner was then to be questioned about the way in which, in olden times, slaves were made among the Indians themselves. Thus, it could be determined which ones were legitimately slaves in conformance with native custom, and those so judged could then be awarded to the person holding a license. It was also to be ascertained that the native master was content to release the slave and that he was satisfied with the terms of the trade. And in verifying this, the lieutenant was to take the Indian señor outside so that he could speak freely, without fear of intimidation from the Spanish buyer.[2]

In early Spanish Honduras many of the Indians who were slaves among their own people freely confessed their status to the conquerors. When a cacique took a slave for barter, the Spaniard was required to prove that the Indian was truly a slave, to inquire as to his place of origin and the status of his parents, as well as their whereabouts, and to ask if the parents were slaves. Furthermore, the buyer was to find out if the Indian had ever been sold, and if so, how many times and for what price. Once it was substantiated that he was in fact a thrall, and therefore a legitimate esclavo de rescate, the native was branded on the face to be traded to merchants from the islands. Because supplies were very meager in Honduras during the 1520s, and since there was a demand for labor in the Antilles, there was brisk trading. In 1526 a brigantine from Fernandina (Cuba) and another vessel from Española put into a Honduran port for the purpose of trading food for slaves. An *arroba* (twenty-five pounds) of wine or vinegar was worth four pesos, and although precise information on the price of slaves at that time and place is scarce, it is likely that one of the small casks could be traded for one human, or perhaps two. Some of the merchants' agents were less scrupulous about determining the legal status of the Indians, many of whom were simply seized and put aboard ships.[3]

In 1527 Governor Diego López de Salcedo issued instructions to his lieutenant in Trujillo, Diego Méndez, cautioning him to make no slave of rescate without prior examination by himself or the *alcalde* of the villa of

Trujillo. The person who brought the Indian was to give sworn testimony, and there was to be no intimidation of the Indian to make him falsely confess being a slave. Indians were to be asked the questions mentioned above, and if it was determined that they were legitimate slaves they could be branded with the royal iron. This was to apply to those Indians offered by caciques, whereas slaves of war could be held only through a *proceso*.

Because there had been so much disorder in Trujillo, arising from the sale of unbranded slaves, the branding irons were to be put in the hands of a person of good habits and reputation, someone who was zealous in the service of the king, so that there would be no fraud perpetrated. A slave given by a cacique who confessed that he and his mother were slaves was to be branded on the face. He could then be sold or traded as a piece of property. However, the one who did not confess that his mother was a slave, but who had been sold into slavery by his parents out of need, was to be branded on the thigh, thereafter to serve perpetually as a servant (*naboría*) as remuneration for the sacrifices made by his master during the conquest of the land. Those servants could be exchanged within the area, but they were not to be taken out of the province under pain of 100 lashes and a fine of 100 pesos.[4]

In 1530, the Crown ruled that no Indian was to be enslaved. Violators were to lose their property and were to pay for the cost of returning the Indian to his village. Officials lax in enforcing the law would lose their offices and be fined 100,000 *maravedís*.[5] Little attention seems to have been paid to the decree, for in 1532 the Crown pointedly forbade Alvarado to acquire esclavos de rescate, a ruling appealed by a *procurador*. The Crown relented in 1532 before the argument that slaves remaining under the power of native caciques were in danger of being sacrificed; henceforth, slaves could be acquired from caciques, but they were not to be alienated from their lands. Before long that law was also revoked.[6] However, by 1534 it was observed that some Indians continued to resist, as a result of which the land was still not pacified, some ten years after the conquest began. The natives, seeing that they were not being enslaved for rebellion, as before, were emboldened to oppose Spanish authority with increasing audacity. Moreover, while the Spaniards "suffered" without slaves, Indian noblemen held slaves from their own kind; and, the royal opinion stated, experience had shown that slaves held by the Indians remained in a state of idolatry, "keeping the vices and abominable customs" of old, all of which would cease if they became slaves of the Christians instead.

Thus a new cédula was given: henceforth, when just war was made in accordance with the prescribed qualifications, captured Indians could be enslaved and sold, but they could not be taken to the islands—unless religious and secular officials approved. This kind of exception, so common in royal legislation, offered discretionary powers that were frequently abused by unscrupulous officials, thereby inviting the trafficking in slaves. Under the new regulations, women and children under the age of fourteen were not to be enslaved, but were to be put in their captors' houses as naborías, which usually meant household service. But they were free, not slaves. In all the pacified villages a *matrícula* was to be drawn up before a notary, listing all the slaves held by caciques and other Indians, recording not only each slave's name, but the names of his parents, as well as that of his master. If he admitted being a slave of rescate he would be branded as such. These slaves could then be purchased or traded, but the caciques were not to be forced or pressured into the transactions.

Nor could a Spaniard trade or buy a slave from among his encomienda Indians, either personally or through another person; neither could he negotiate such an arrangement with another encomendero by way of exchange of encomienda villagers. The penalty for a transaction of that sort was loss of the slave and a fine. Caciques had in former times unjustly enslaved other Indians for slight causes, but in 1534 they were to be informed that they could no longer hold slaves.[7]

It was common practice for Spaniards to ask, or demand, that the native señores bring slaves from the Indian pueblos for purchase or trade. When the town of Santiago de Atitlán in Guatemala was subjected to Spanish rule the caciques delivered as tribute four to five hundred slaves of both sexes for the mines.[8] As items of exchange, the Spaniards often used merchandise paid to them as tribute by the *maceguales* (commoners) of native villages. The goods could consist of almost anything, but the caciques preferred cacao, which Indians used as money. Once it was established that the Indian was a slave, he was branded and purchased. Both caciques and the slaves were made to understand that the slaves then belonged to the Spanish master, who could sell them to whomever he pleased.

Such explanations notwithstanding, there were complaints from the Spaniards that the caciques without shame sometimes stole back the slaves they had bartered. This occurred, the Spaniards said, even though the Indians could be identified through brands. Moreover, it sometimes happened that when rescates fled to their pueblos, the caciques would not cooperate in turning them back to their Spanish owners. Caciques were often reluctant to trade their own slaves, or even to act as agents in securing others for the Spaniards, in spite of the fact that it had been the custom among prehispanic Indians publicly to sell, like merchandise, "the slaves that go around like the cattle in Spain." The practice persisted into the post-conquest period; a witness, in 1531, told of buying slaves in the *tianguez,* or native marketplace.[9] Because the Crown had authorized the branding of rescates in Guatemala, the Audiencia of Mexico professed shock and incredulity, fearing that great damage would result. On various occasions in the early 1530s, the oidores wrote with such conviction that the royal policy was modified, probably at least in part owing to their sentiments.[10]

Anyway, the acquisition of slaves from caciques was canceled—by law if not in fact—by royal provisions forbidding Indians to make slaves among themselves.[11] Restrictions on these trades were given in 1534, and in 1536 the Crown ruled that no slaves could be made through trade (rescate). The edicts were apparently ineffective, for cédulas of 1538 and 1539 stated that, owing to continuing and excessive trading of Indians and their maltreatment, no Spaniard was to acquire any Indian slave from a cacique or principal, either directly or indirectly.[12] The emphatic decree notwithstanding, the *regidores* of *cabildos* in four important settlements responded with a common complaint: that without means of sustenance, many Spaniards were leaving Central America, having no slaves for mining. They asked that they be allowed to trade with the caciques for slaves of rescate.[13]

Caciques generally were allowed to retain some semblance of authority with their own people because it was through their agency that Spaniards obtained services from the pueblos, and because the chiefs were helpful in the administration of the native masses. In order to preserve those privileges, many of the Indian lords were overly anxious to ingratiate themselves with their European masters, to the extent that they were not above turning over free Indians when no slaves were available. Francisco Marroquín, the first bishop of Guatemala, wrote that licenciado Alonso Maldonado, president of the audiencia (1543–48), was curious about the procedure for making slaves, because if the royal provisions had been followed to the letter, all of the Indians could have been branded without examination. The reason, he said, was that the selection of the slaves was left to the native señores, and "since they wish to please their masters, their own sons confess to being slaves." Moreover, according to the royal provision recently made, there was no need for any examination to determine which ones were truly slaves. "So," continued the bishop,

I adopted another method, which was to inform myself by talking to the lords. And when that was done, I sent them from the room from where the slaves were and talked to the slaves in general, saying that we already knew for certain how the lords had cheated them and made them slaves at their pleasure, and that they should not be afraid, and that if they were not slaves they should not say they were;

and if they were, they were asked why, or in what principal manner they had been enslaved, paying particular attention to their ages to see if they were of a young age. And even if they said they were slaves, if they were young, I did not have the authority to brand them. . . . Once the examination was made by me, the governor—or in his absence the lieutenant governor—watched while the branding was done. Do not believe, Your Highness, that such examinations were very rigorous—it is just enough to prevent the Spaniards from doing what they want to do.[14]

Consequently, under the circumstances there was little deterrent to the procedure of enslavement. And there was the additional conflict as to whether or not converted Indians could be made slaves.

Despite the efforts of Marroquín and others to protect those who were legally free men, their good intentions were frustrated by the intimidation of Indians. In some instances when caciques were threatened by Spaniards to produce slaves, the native rulers simply rounded up free Indians and stated that they *were* slaves. In anticipation of the interrogation by officials, the caciques briefed the hapless pawns on what answers were to be given. Some of them refused to cooperate, telling the examiners that they were free. Accordingly, they were not branded as slaves, but later the caciques whipped them soundly and told them to return with different answers, and to explain that they had lied in the first place because they had feared the glowing iron nearby, ready to be applied to their faces. In the end, the fear of more beatings, or perhaps death, was stronger than their dread of the branding iron.[15]

Don Pedro de Alvarado was the master of much of Central America until his death in 1541, and the practice of acquiring esclavos de rescate was one to which he readily subscribed. Royal officials reported to the king that the conqueror himself had taken three thousand of them in one year; hence, he was in no good position to question the procedure, even if he had been so disposed.[16] Some Spaniards, to appear reasonable, were asking the Crown that only those Indians already slaves of the caciques be acquired by Spaniards. But, according to a letter of Las Casas written in Nicaragua in 1535, the intent was "diabolical" because under that pretext caciques were enslaving half to two-thirds of their vassals, who were then traded to the Spaniards.[17] All the evidence indicates that many of the abuses of making slaves of rescate were checked, but the trading continued for a number of years.

4
The Slave Trade

THE DEMAND FOR SLAVE LABOR stimulated a lively traffic in the acquisition and sale of Indians. Some of the less sedentary Spaniards were more interested in the quick profits to be had from that commerce than from other more mundane occupations. Early prospects for easy wealth were disappointing, since the conquerors found relatively little in the way of gold, silver, and precious jewels. There was, however, a good market for slaves outside of Central America, and some unscrupulous traders found ready buyers. Their activities were restricted by general laws governing slavery, but their nomadic habits, and the poor communication and administrative control, combined to encourage violations. It is probable that some of them were not even familiar with the latest changes in the laws, in view of the fact that the Crown often reversed itself or qualified earlier legislation. Moreover, in some regions the highest Spanish officials were themselves often involved to some extent in the slave trade, particularly during the first decade. And, under the pretext of awaiting clarification of a new ruling, officials frequently allowed established practices to continue, pending new information, which was often a matter of a year or more in resolving.

Slaving expeditions date from the early years of Spanish occupation in the Antilles, and by the early sixteenth century raids were being made to the other islands and eventually to the mainland areas. The first two expeditions sent to Yucatán, preceding Cortés, had as important objectives the taking of slaves to work in the settled islands. As the rapid decline of the natives caused increasing labor shortages in the Antilles, more and more slave raids were made to neighboring territories.

In Central America slaves were claimed by disappointed conquistadores as rewards for their sacrifices. Furthermore, the availability of free labor was one way in which the Crown hoped the restless and ambitious Spaniards would be induced to settle the land. But though the concession

39

was made to assist individual Spaniards in establishing themselves, the Crown did not countenance the trading of slaves for profit.

It was repeatedly stated that Indians were not to be taken out of their native territories, because of the social dislocation that followed, and because of the threat to their health. The constitutions of the Indians could not resist the rigors of a sharp change in climate. Moving them from the cool highlands, where freezing temperatures were not uncommon, to the steamy tropical lowlands caused the illness and death of many natives, particularly those forced to perform heavy labor. The same tragedies occurred when lowlands Indians were taken to the mountains. A further reason for not transporting them out of their traditional lands was the probability of creating a labor shortage in the place of origin. If effectively enforced, this constraint would have stopped the trade in slaves, for all practical purposes. Unfortunately for the credibility of the Crown's resolve, a royal cédula sent in 1535 allowed rebellious Indians in Honduras to be branded and sent to the islands, or anywhere else, to be sold. Although this was a temporary lapse, it was another typical example of equivocation that encouraged Spaniards to press their cause.[1]

At the same time, the order against the transferring of Indians from their lands, which was generally in effect, inhibited the travel of Spaniards with their servants, who quite often were slaves. Furthermore, while the Crown had recognized the Spaniards' requests for servants, the concession was abused when some vecinos traveled abroad taking large numbers of "servants" who were then sold as slaves at good profits. Hoping to block that aspect of the slave trade, the king ruled in 1531 that no Indian slaves could be taken out of the province of Guatemala. When the vecinos complained about the order, the Crown gave in and allowed seven Indians to be taken by each Spaniard for his service, provided it could be demonstrated that they were legally one's slaves and that a bond was posted for their return. A month later, in June 1532, the number of slaves allowable for travel was raised to ten, again with a deposit to guarantee their return.[2] Three years later Spaniards leaving Central America were allowed to take only four slaves with them to Spain, provided they registered the slaves by name at the Mexican port of Veracruz. A year later, in March 1536, a cédula declared that no slaves could be taken to Castile.

At the beginning of 1538, it was declared that, because so many Indians were being taken out of Honduras, it was forbidden to take more than one or two of them as servants. Five years later no Spaniard could legally transfer an Indian to another province, neither a slave nor a free Indian, even if he agreed to go. Violators would suffer a fine of 100,000 maravedís and would be banished in perpetuity from the Indies. If the guilty person could not pay the fine, he would receive 100 hundred lashes in public. The return of the native would also be at the expense of the guilty Spaniard.[3] Such dizzying changes as these within the space of a few years illustrate the difficulties of making valid generalizations about Spanish Indian policy.

Even though the greatest concentration of Indian population in Central America was in the highlands of Guatemala, as it is today, the centers of the most active slave trading were Honduras and Nicaragua, the former because of the proximity of its ports to the Antilles, and the latter because it was the nexus between New Spain and the recently discovered Peru. Both provinces had the busiest ports, and it was to them that Indians slaves were taken for shipment. Consequently, it follows that Honduras and Nicaragua were the scenes of the most notorious abuses.

Brief mention was made earlier of the kidnaping of Honduran Indians by the *fiscal, bachiller* Pedro Moreno, sent by the Audiencia of Santo Domingo. Cortés filed a formal charge, accusing Moreno of taking more than fifty men and women and illegally branding them as slaves, despite the admonitions of the vecinos of Trujillo. A witness testified that the bachiller had taken "ciertas pieças de indios e indias" against the order of the alcalde. Juan de Medina, the *alcalde ordinario*, said that he had confronted Moreno and warned him that he was not to take the natives, but they were branded nonetheless. One of them was a noble, and two others were peaceful porters who happened to carry a Spaniard's clothes, with the promise that they could leave. The natives were carried away in Moreno's ships to Española. It appears that later the fiscal was ordered punished by the king.[4] If Cortés was correct, Moreno had the approval of the Audiencia of Santo Domingo, and the fiscal was no doubt little concerned about the injunction of the local officials in Honduras.

Not long after the above incident, Governor Diego López de Salcedo attacked the inhabitants of Valle de Olancho as punishment for their having killed some Spaniards. He hanged some of those captured and called in representatives from other pueblos and told them the terms of the requerimiento. Nevertheless, Indians near Trujillo rebelled and fled to the mountains in fear of being enslaved. Slaves were indeed taken, and López de Salcedo took some of them away from Spaniards who held them, redistributing them among his friends and criados, but keeping the best ones for himself.

His actions produced discontent not only among the Spaniards, but also among the natives who, in their anger, ceased gathering gold and cultivating the land. This intransigence on their part decreased the modest incomes of the Spanish vecinos, and at the same time created a food shortage for themselves. They became so desperate, according to the chronicler Herrera, that they assaulted other Indians and ate them. Cannibalism was an extreme the Spaniards did not want encouraged, and, added to the natives' general attitude, it made a good case for enslavement, in the eyes of the Europeans. License was granted to brand them and send them to Panama.[5] In this way slave trading continued with official permission.

A royal provision had already been issued in late 1526, ordering the justices to determine who held Indian slaves alienated from their native habitats. Such Indians were to be returned to their lands if they wished, provided it could be accomplished without inconvenience. In the event that it could not be done easily, however, they were to be set free and treated as free men. The Indians were to be given assistance, but were to be directed into labor that was not excessive. If they were Christians, the Indians were not to return to their former lands because of the dangers of their reversion to paganism.[6]

There were early attempts to alleviate the labor problem in Central America through the introduction of slaves, and these operations were planned on the highest level. In 1527, Pedro de Alvarado made a contract with Francisco de los Cobos, the secretary to Charles V, and with Dr. Diego Beltrán, a member of the Council of the Indies, to ship 600 slaves to work the mines of Guatemala. But they were to be black slaves, which was quite a different matter; the indigenous peoples of the new kingdoms were considered vassals of the king and under the special tutelage and protection of Crown and Church, a consideration not enjoyed by the Africans. Because of market conditions, however, this project was never carried out.[7] Blacks would be introduced gradually, but their numbers were never great, and native labor continued to be the base on which the economy depended.

The early years in Honduras saw a dreadful spectacle of slaving operations, the blame for which can be attributed in large measure to the insensibilities of the royal officials. Bernal Díaz described conditions in this way:

I will go on to tell of the governors of the province of Honduras sent by the Geronimite Friars who were Governors of the Island of Santo Domingo—and pray God they will never send such men [again]—for they were very bad and never did any justice at all; for besides illtreating the Indians of that province, they branded many of them as slaves, and sent them to be sold to Hispaniola and Cuba, and to the Island of San Juan de Baruquén.

And, the chronicler continues,

These evil governors were named:—the first Fulano de Arbitez, and the second Cereceda, a native of Seville, and the third Diego Días de Herrera who was also from Seville, and these three commenced the ruin of that province, and what I state here I know, for when I came with Cortés on the expedition to Honduras I was present in Trujillo, and I was at Naco and the Río de Pichín, and that of Balama, and that of Ulúa, and in nearly all the pueblos of that neighbourhood, and it was thickly peopled and at peace [and the people were living] in their houses with their children; but as soon as those bad governors came they destroyed them to such an extent, that in the year fifteen hundred and fifty-one, when I passed through there on my return from Castile, two Caciques who had known me in the old days told me with tears in their eyes of all their misfortunes and the treatment [they had received], and I was shocked to see the country in such a condition.[8]

The assessment by Díaz of the damage done to the province seems to have been by no means exaggerated, but it should be observed that, under the circumstances, the governors were hard put to control the intractable conquistadores. The continued bickering and disorder among the Spaniards contributed to the discontent of the natives, and as Herrera writes:

From this discord of the Castilians there ensued encouragement to the Indians, who were peaceful, to rebel, and it taught them to fight, because they were also unhappy about the order that Don Hernando Cortés had left [to the effect] that if they rebelled they would be had as slaves; and the use they made of the Indians from the islands that they called Guanaxos [Guanaja] gave them little satisfaction, because being peaceful and obedient to the King, the ships from Cuba stole them and took them as slaves, under the pretext of going to las Ybueras [Higueras] to buy them, where, because of the Castilians not having any profits, and because the land was very expensive as a result of the little commerce that came from Castile, and [since] from the islands there were no clothes or food; and the Indians gave them little sustenance because they were not working, thinking that with the lack of it [a labor supply] the Christians would go.[9]

Robert Chamberlain adds these comments about slavery in early Honduras:

The practice of unrestrainedly enslaving Indians in large numbers had been carried on, or permitted, in Honduras-Higueras by the governors who preceded Montejo. Not only had natives taken in war been enslaved under law, but illegal slave raids were made against peaceful towns. Many Indians, first from Trujillo, and after 1534 from Higueras, were carried to the West Indies to be sold. Some were branded according to royal ordinances governing enslavement, but the majority seem to have been taken with but little pretense to legality. Before Montejo came a large proportion of the colonists appear to have been engaged in slaving operations in one form or another. They had kept comparatively few Indian slaves, despite the numbers taken under earlier governors, including Cerezeda and Alvarado, since it seems to have been much more lucrative to sell them outside the province. As their situation became more permanent, and as mining developed and needs for labor in general increased, the Spaniards became convinced that large numbers of Indian slaves were necessary for the economic development of the province.[10]

Reacting to inhumane treatment, Indians frequently rose up in rebellion, which in turn provided a convenient excuse for taking them as "esclavos de guerra." The ambitious regidor, Vasco de Herrera, seized more than three hundred Indians as slaves.[11] Other more responsible regidores in the cabildo of Trujillo acknowledged that the natives had sufficient cause to revolt. Many, among both the Spaniards and the Indians, were pleased enough with the overthrow of Saavedra, the lieutenant left by Cortés; but the entrance of Diego López de Salcedo led to a situation even more harrowing for the natives. He took Indians as carriers to transport his goods to the city of León in Nicaragua, including not only his personal effects, but also iron bars and tools, some of which were for trading. More than three hundred loads were carried by Indians, among whom were found those of the nobility, forced by chains and iron rings around their necks. According to the cabildo report, López de Salcedo left orders that any Indians who returned were to be hanged, a command that was subsequently carried out. But, as it happened, most of the carriers perished from fatigue or ill-treatment.[12]

At the same time, other reports reached the emperor that rebellious Spaniards were stealing slaves from Honduras and that others had raided the island of Guanaja, kidnaping peaceful natives. One group of slavers had seized more than 150 Indians and branded them.[13]

Perhaps the most graphic and damaging commentary on the early years of slaving in Honduras was set down by licenciado Cristóbal de Pedraza, the Protector of the Indians and later bishop of Honduras. In his "Informacion contra los gobernadores," Pedraza presents his own views, as well as those of witnesses. He is especially critical of the cruelty of López de Salcedo, in referring to the expedition to León mentioned above. After the party left Honduras, he said, the land was almost ruined, because those who remained, seeing so many of their men and women taken away, fled from the pueblos. Many of them died in the mountains and the others never reappeared.

A witness to the cruelties perpetrated at this time stated that among those killed were small children. He added that a captain under López de Salcedo named Alonso de Solis burned alive fourteen Indians in the pueblo of Canola, "which seemed to this witness the greatest cruelty in the world, and it made his [the witness'] flesh creep." Many villages were almost destroyed, and Tepusteca, which belonged to Diego Nieto, was made "a wilderness," and left without a single inhabitant. When some of the Indians forced on the journey realized that they were being taken far from home they tried to escape. According to the bishop, Spaniards pursued them and ran them through with lances.[14]

Violence in some instances was so gratuitous as to appear sadistic. Pedraza charged that when the Indians were taken on the road in chains by López de Salcedo and his men some of the carriers faltered under the strain and could not continue. In order to avoid the delay caused by opening the rings to release stragglers, their heads were cut off and the victims were left on the road, "the head on one side and the body on the other; and they went on their way." The alcalde ordinario testified that he had witnessed such barbaric behavior: when an Indian leader named Migesti crumpled under his load the lock did not open immediately, and his neck was severed. The accusers hastened to add that the one committing such atrocities was not really a Spaniard, but rather a *levantisco* named Agostín de Candía. Furthermore, a witness saw Candía take another Indian in chains, and

one of them, tired and weak, fell to the ground, and he [Candía] wanted to cut off his head, as he had done to others. And the witness and other Christians begged him not to do it; and he opened the chain and released the Indian. And, then, seeing that he could not do what he wished (which was to decapitate him), he jumped on top of him (the Indian still being prostrate on the ground) and straddled him, and took his sword with both hands and began to plunge it into his body, and he plunged it two or three times from one part of his body to another, so that the Indian died there; and this witness and others regretted it. And afterwards God permitted the said Agostín to die in the hands of the Indians, who cut him into pieces, severing his head and feet.[15]

The testimony relating these acts of barbarism reveals not only the depravity of the Levantine, but also the shocked sensibilities of the Spanish witnesses. Such an observer was the regidor Diego de Caçorla, who wrote that the same Candía committed further vicious acts in the pueblo of Telicachima. There he killed an Indian and some children who lay ill under a blanket; and Caçorla continued, when he saw the cruelty he wanted to kill Candía, and he called him "a dog, a bad Christian, and a white Moor." Although the Levantine was a particularly sadistic type, it was also reported that a perverted *peón* by the name of Mexía had also beheaded an ill-disposed Indian to avoid having to open the chain.[16]

Bishop Pedraza noted that some of the Indians managed to escape from the López de Salcedo expedition, but on the way back to their lands they died from starvation or at the hands of hostile natives. He characterized López de Salcedo as a man in debt who traded in slaves to become solvent. According to the testimony of Francisco Vásquez, he took "herds" of Indians from his own encomienda pueblos, as well as from others, in order to pay his debts. Vásquez saw them branded and sold, and he noticed various ships loaded with slaves. Caçorla, after observing what had taken place, estimated that the share of Diego López de Salcedo was more than five hundred slaves taken from the Indian towns. His majordomos went to the peaceful communities and asked the leaders for slaves to help pay for the expenses of López de Salcedo, and when they were delivered, the slaves were branded. This occurred in several villages, until finally the entire region rose in rebellion.[17]

Rodrigo del Castillo, another high official of Honduras, gave further details of the same expedition, lending credibility to the Pedraza account. On their way from Honduras to Nicaragua, the Spaniards burned towns and caused great destruction. Recently-delivered babies were taken from their mothers' breasts and tossed aside. Caciques and *principales* were put in collars and chains in groups of ten. More than four hundred Indians were taken from the valley of Guamira loaded down with the merchandise of the governor and his companions. If an Indian fell his head was cut off.

In Aguatega 200 Indians were punished: one-third of them were put in a large hut and burned to death; another one-third were torn to pieces by dogs; eyes were plucked out, arms were cut off, and other cruelties were practiced on the remaining one-third of the Indians. The writer importuned the Crown to see that guilty Indians were punished according to Castilian law, not by being roasted alive, disemboweled by dogs, or in other savage ways.[18] Perhaps neither the king nor the Council of the Indies saw the foregoing report. In any event, several months later, noting that slaves were being taken in the "pacification," the Crown seemed most intent on cautioning the Spaniards that one-fifth of the slaves were to be sold for the royal share.[19]

With the death of Diego López de Salcedo, Andrés de Cerezeda, the *contador*, began to govern. At that time, the previous depredations notwithstanding, Cerezeda was of the opinion that rebellious Indians should be enslaved and sold. Taking two thousand of them, he told the king, would not harm the land.[20] There were still pueblos with two hundred to five hundred heads of families, and some with as many as eight hundred. But the destruction continued under Cerezeda, as the villages were pillaged and the inhabitants carried off to be traded to shipmasters for wine, oil, and other merchandise.

Elaborating on slaving operations at that time, the regidor Paz stated that he saw a captain of Cerezeda named Alonso Ortiz taking Indians from his encomienda of Juticalpa, including a principal (so he heard) in chains. The village contained five hundred men when Cerezeda's rule began, and it was one of the better pueblos in the valley. Ortiz completely depopulated it. Cerezeda himself did the same thing with one of his own encomiendas, the large town of La Haga. Another encomendero, Sancho Esturiano, cleaned out his encomienda of Sonaguera, taking all its people indiscriminately, bound in chains. Some of the Indians were carried off in ships, others by land. A populous town called Ylniga (?) was depopulated by Diego Bravo, its encomendero; the people of Taguala, belonging to Diego Maldonado, were all taken away; and the Indians of Papayeca were enslaved by Alonso de Pareja.

In this way, with no pretense to legality, Cerezeda and his followers took their toll of the population. Making slaves of free encomienda Indians was clearly against the law, and the very fact that they enslaved their own tributaries demonstrates their aversion to settling down to live on the tribute and labor of their Indians. More than that, Cerezeda sent some of his Spaniards, along with the mulatto Antonio Herrera, to waylay and carry off naborías belonging to the vecinos who remained in the city of Trujillo.[21]

Pedro Morillo, who was lieutenant governor at the time of Pedraza's inquiry, said there had been an infinity of people in Honduras and that, the harm done by Diego López de Salcedo notwithstanding, there were still many natives left to be taken by Cerezeda and his men. Per Afán de Ribera, the king's alcalde, confirmed this and gave some indication that Indian settlements were not always simple villages. In many pueblos he had seen thirteen or fourteen chambers where the caciques and principales had lodged, "and they seemed like royal chambers of kings and lords." In one of them fifty to seventy men had slept, and each had spread out his mat, without any one of them touching another. "And all this was destroyed," he asserted, ". . . because the governors who ruled in that time did not seem to be going to conquer and pacify, but to destroy and rob, and thus they consented to their men doing such things."[22]

Antón de la Torre testified that very few Indians were able to escape the slavers, and the ones remaining in the pueblos, belonging to Spanish vecinos, rebelled at the cruelties and the sight of their fathers and sons being taken away in chains. He recalled that a cacique's son from Guayava Island arrived in Trujillo to see his master, and,

the said Andrés de Cerezeda called this Indian, and with his own hands put a chain around his throat, put him in the collar, and took him off with the others. And

seeing this, another principal of the said pueblo, being an old man, seeing the
Indian put in the chain, came weeping to the house of this witness; and at the same
time Cerezeda came to say goodbye to this witness, and as the said Indian saw him,
he fled in such haste that he broke the wall of the house, thinking that the said
Cerezeda would do the same to him that he did to the other.[23]

Witnesses testified that when the land was almost ruined, with hardly
an Indian left, Andrés de Cerezeda and his advisors, including padre Juan
de Avela, decided to leave the land. They then rounded up whatever stray
Indians they could find and packed them off to the ports. After some of the
slaves were exchanged for shirts, wine, oil, and other staples, the remainder were shipped out from Puerto de Caballos and Puerto de Sal.[24]

So many witnesses agreed on the details of what happened that the
report of Pedraza is no doubt substantially accurate. Yet there were
obvious distortions: one is led to believe that the land was almost depopulated under Diego López de Salcedo, but others testified that when
Cerezeda arrived there were still pueblos containing a few hundred up to a
thousand men. Cerezeda's encomienda of La Haga had a population of a
thousand male adults, and it was stated that when he left it was deserted.
In all probability, it is an exaggeration when witnesses referred to various
villages being completely enslaved. No doubt some towns were deserted
when the inhabitants fled to the mountains to escape the Spaniards. When
Cerezeda and his companions left, according to Gonzalo Herrera, a
regidor, they carried off more than 1,900 Indians by actual count.
Not 50 of them ever returned.[25]

While ships carried off the slaves, Cerezeda continued overland with
other captives, many of whom died because of the change of climate and
the difficult terrain. Also contributing to the deceased ranks was fatigue,
since some of the Indians' loads consisted of heavy iron tools and grinding
stones. Compounding the hardships was the lack of food, which required
the Indians to forage for the Spaniards. Mistreatment and illness added to
the number of deaths that occurred along the way.

Cerezeda stopped over at Valle de Naco, where the Spaniards took food
belonging to the natives, who were then enslaved. In this same way they
went from village to village. Cerezeda left to settle a Spanish villa in
nearby Valle de Zura, which at the time had more than twenty-five
good-sized pueblos with many people. The towns were destroyed and the
crops were ruined by the cattle of Cerezeda and padre Avela. If an Indian
complained, he was tied and whipped or thrown to the dogs.[26]

In summing up his charges, Pedraza stated that Andrés de Cerezeda,
having been ordered by the king not to make any slaves, sought a subter-
fuge by which those who were at peace as free men could be enslaved. He

conspired to have them accused of crimes for which they could be exiled from théir lands in perpetuity. Vessels were standing by to take them away, and at the ships they were traded for gold pesos, as well as hatchets, machetes, oil, wine, and other merchandise. Thus enslaved, the Indians were taken to Cuba, Santo Domingo, and Jamaica. If Pedraza did not exaggerate, this one operation must have been profitable indeed, for he contended that when Cerezeda entered the pueblo of Naco there were eight to ten thousand men, aside from women and children, and at the time of Pedraza's report, in 1539, there were not 250 Indian males left. In the time since Cerezeda had departed there were no doubt many Indians who had died from the pestilence or who were killed or enslaved, but a large quantity of them were taken by Cerezeda. One of his soldiers took 100 Indians to the island for his own use. [27]

The common complaint of Spaniards who went to Honduras was that the land had little wealth to offer a colonist. There were signs of gold and silver, but it would be years before mining became a stable and consistently profitable enterprise. Even if one had an encomienda, the tribute offerings were so poor as to make them unattractive, and there was little productive outlet for free Indian labor. The only incentive was the slave trade, which was hardly conducive to a settled society.

A witness said in 1531 that four colonizing expeditions had been made, but that the captains, seeing the shortage of dried, salted meat, decided not to establish towns. Doubtless there were other more compelling reasons; in any event, the expeditions, ostensibly formed as colonizing ventures, became merely slaving forays. [28] The invasion of Higueras-Honduras by don Cristóbal de la Cueva and his sixty men, at the orders of acting governor Jorge de Alvarado, seems to have been such an expedition. Although the party was supposedly seeking a good port, which would then be connected by a road to Santiago, the Spaniards and their five hundred native allies began raiding villages and taking many slaves. [29]

Cristóbal de Pedraza wrote other reports which were so graphic as to rank him with Las Casas as a critic of Spanish treatment of Indians; but, less prone to hyperbole than the bishop of Chiapas, Pedraza is the more credible. Among those he attacked during the years of pacification was the foremost figure of his time in Central America, the adelantado Pedro de Alvarado. When Alvarado went in to pacify Honduras he took with him *cuadrillas*, or slave gangs, to seek out and work mines. But he took other Indians as "amigos," allies who were deadly effective.

One reason for Alvarado's success in subduing native forces was his strategy of inspiring fear among his enemies, and nowhere was this better demonstrated than in the Honduras campaign. Accompanying his Spanish forces were native auxiliaries from Guatemala called Achies (Achis), described by Pedraza as "the cruelest people in the Indies and the greatest butchers and cannibals." He added that it broke his heart on being informed of their gruesome practices. Their very presence terrified the relatively peaceful Indians of Honduras, because "as the natives of this land do not eat human flesh, nor did they ever hear of such a thing, they were left very frightened and chastized." The Achies seized many Hondurans, accounting for more than six thousand persons, young and old of both sexes, three thousand of whom were enslaved. Pueblos that had four hundred or five hundred houses when Alvarado entered had only about thirty left when Montejo arrived a short time later. The principales of the village of Taloa told Pedraza that between those carried off as slaves and those consumed by the Achies, some two hundred Indians were lost in his pueblo alone.[30]

The Christians who marched with Alvarado were vecinos of Guatemala and San Salvador, whose intent was less to settle the territory than to take slaves. Consequently, they seized all the Indians they could with little consideration of the damage done to the land, since they entertained no thoughts of remaining there. They were, as they acknowledged, plundering. The Achie amigos formed their own bands as they looted the towns, although perhaps without Alvarado's full knowledge of their methods. One vecino of Guatemala had sent his criado on the mission to gather slaves for him, and the servant branded 120 of them as his employer's share, in addition to branding other free Indians that he purchased for himself from the native auxiliaries. Again, these slaves, including women who were pregnant or with babies at their breasts, were taken by force and put in chains. Children from the ages of three to five were enslaved. Witnesses said that from one thousand to fifteen hundred Indians died around Trujillo from maltreatment and the deleterious effects of dislocation. They added that for certain more than three thousand free Indians had been taken against their will, in addition to those who were legally slaves. Many of the Indians went to Pedraza in tears for help, but there was little he could do at the time.[31]

Honduras was so devastated, Pedraza wrote, that whereas at the time López de Salcedo and Cerezeda governed a pueblo might have had a thousand Indians—or a thousand houses, as some said—it did not have a single one left by 1539. The diminution of the native inhabitants was so extensive, he claimed, that one *repartimiento* in Mexico, or the holdings of one conquistador or settler there, had more Indians than all the government of Honduras from cape to cape. He assured the king that this was no fable, and that he did not believe there were fifteen thousand Indians in the whole *governación;* whereas, to hear those who went in with Gil González de Avila and the *marqués,* Fernando Cortés, the area had almost as many people as Mexico. There had been much order and reason among the natives, who were a people well-disposed and well-dressed, with about the same skill as the natives of New Spain. He wrote of the peaceful lives of the Hondurans before the Spaniards arrived, and he lamented the departure of Cortés and his lieutenant Saavedra. The slave trade continued unchecked until the arrival of Francisco de Montejo as governor. Then, Pedraza wrote, "according to what I have been informed, he [Montejo] had not consented that anyone take a person out of the land." And, he went on, it was necessary for the province that this practice be continued, for two reasons:

> One, so that these natives might see that Your Majesty, as their king and lord and true father, will return to them their sons and women and brothers and husbands like the just judge he is; and the other, that this land be settled again because [of] the bad things of the past, and the destruction that they have made in the said pueblos, and to the natives in them . . . by the governors, or [rather] the un-governors, of the past since the time that Diego Lopez de Saucedo [Salcedo] and Cereçeda governed here.[32]

Outspoken though Pedraza was in his writings, one gets the impression that he was rather more circumspect at the scene, for he asked that his *relación* be kept secret. His explanation was that he liked the "caballeros" involved, and he did not want his written views to cause his relationship to them to be like that of "a dog in the street." It is to his credit, however, that he was not one to criticize without offering solutions, including suggestions that involved certain sacrifices on his part. He felt that Indians who had been alienated from their lands should be returned, and for that purpose he requested permission from the Crown to go to Guatemala to look for Honduran natives with the idea of removing them from the Spaniards who held them. Other Indians had been taken illegally to other places, such as Cuba, and he would seek their return as well.

The justices "and other good men" could help him, and the prelates in regions where the slaves and free men had been taken could be ordered to give letters of excommunication to those who obstructed this justice. No appeal should be granted to those who held Indians unjustly; rather, as soon as the origins of the Indians could be verified, they should be ordered set free. Arrangements for their return should not be left to the natives themselves because the Christians would intimidate them so that the Indians would say that they did not want to leave, but would prefer to remain. And that, Pedraza observed, "is against true nature, because each one wants and wishes to live and die in his own native land, as Your

Majesty well knows." So much did the injustices weigh on his conscience that the bishop volunteered to go to all the places necessary to repatriate his charges, at his own expense, as his own mission.[33]

It seems clear, as Pedraza understood, that the policy of Montejo with regard to slavery was more stringent than any previous government in Honduras. But Montejo's role in the larger question of slavery is more controversial. He was accused of taking a great many slaves in Yucatán, and it appears that some of them were pledged to raise money for his expedition to Honduras. If other testimony is reliable, one cannot say that the adelantado opposed slavery on principle, unless he had a change of heart.[34] His alleged enslavement of fifty thousand Indians in Yucatán far surpasses any similar operation with which I am familiar in Central America.

Writing from Yucatán in 1534, Montejo said that the Spaniards suffered hardships without slaves, and that he had sent some slaves to Mexico to bring some ironwork, but that they had been set free by others. He appealed to the Audiencia of Mexico to let him make slaves of rescate and war, because the land had nothing else to offer, as a result of which two hundred of his men had already left for Peru.[35] Nonetheless, he seems to have moderated his course considerably in Honduras, in spite of complaints about Spaniards from Guatemala entering with their cuadrillas of slaves to exploit the mining strikes. Three or four miners from Honduras, each of whom had fifteen to twenty slaves, had found gold, but the outsiders came in with their large slave gangs and drove them out. At the same time, Montejo felt pressures from the vecinos, and despite his attempts to check abuses, he admitted that there was considerable commerce in slaves, owing to the poverty of the land.[36]

Chamberlain adds that,

Montejo's policy displeased the colonists, accustomed to laxity in the enforcement of royal regulations designed to protect the natives and used to following their own inclinations with regard to the taking of slaves. About the time the great general revolt broke out [1537], the colonists demanded of Montejo that for a period of six months he permit enslavement of Indians above the age of fifteen under conditions until then permitted by law. They told Montejo that this measure was necessary to prevent the abandonment of the province since they could not maintain themselves without a sufficient number of slaves. Under this pressure, Montejo yielded somewhat and, against his will, sanctioned their petition, prescribing, however, that royal laws should be observed with the utmost care. He was aware that it would be difficult to enforce the pertinent laws, but, under the circumstances, felt it necessary to meet the colonists' needs temporarily. He wrote to the Crown, requesting approval of the measure, and meanwhile placed it in effect. However, not many slaves seem to have been taken during the six months period involved.[37]

The Crown, however, gave way to opposing arguments and directly forbade Montejo to allow the export of slaves. "This cedula, which arrived after the general uprising had been suppressed," Chamberlain writes, "strengthened Montejo's hand in breaking indiscriminate enslavement and preventing extensive commerce in slaves."[38] Official restraints seem to have combined with the reduced native population to check fairly effectively what had been a flourishing slave trade in Honduras.

But in 1539, Montejo, maintaining that no vecino had any slaves from Honduras, complained that the lack of slaves was a hardship because the Spaniards could not mine gold without them. Therefore, he was in favor of allowing a few slaves, apparently from other provinces, to work the mines, along with some naborías who volunteered. At the petition of his men, who threatened to leave, Montejo gave them license to brand women over fifteen years of age for a period of six months, although he later insisted that it was done according to royal rules and that not more than twenty women had been branded. At that time, in 1545, he said there were only three or four vecinos taking out gold with fifteen to twenty slaves each.[39] As late as 1540, the cabildo of Trujillo complained that, contrary to law, twenty free Indians, along with some legitimate slaves, had been forcibly put on ships and carried off.

In 1543 a criminal accusation was brought against Miguel Díaz, a vecino of the city of Gracias a Dios. It was charged that in 1541, and shortly before, he went to the pueblo of Alcatoa in Honduras and asked the caciques for slaves to be used in the mines. When they failed to deliver as many as he wanted, Díaz sent his blacks to kill the caciques and some other Indians. After the native leaders were hanged, their houses and corn granaries were burned. Later Díaz, with his black and Indian friends, returned to the town and killed three more caciques, hanged more men and women, burned more granaries, and kidnaped many Indian boys as slaves. And while his encomienda people were still at peace, Díaz, for no apparent cause, tied many Indians to stakes and put some in stocks. Others less fortunate were put into huts which were then fired. And, it was alleged, in order to terrify others, he put them in jail so they would do as he commanded. Many Indians were then loaded with excessive cargoes and marched to the mines of Cuyapeque, more than sixty leagues distant, as a result of which many more died.[40] Other illegal slaving activities consisted of the sale of encomienda Indians as late as 1546.[41]

No less critical was the threat to free Indians in Nicaragua, where slavers acted with little restraint. After his visit to that troubled province in 1544, licenciado Diego de Herrera reported that there had been many excesses committed from profiteering in slavery.[42] Although it eventually

came under the jurisdiction of Guatemala, Nicaragua was first pillaged by
men from Panama, beginning with Pedrarias Dávila, who in the version of
Las Casas, entered like a "hungry wolf" to prey on the "lambs." Licenciado Francisco Castañeda,[43] the *alcalde mayor*, objected in 1529 to the
branding of free Indians, and when he required the alcalde ordinario of
Granada to provide information identifying those who were taking the
natives outside the province, Governor Pedrarias Dávila became very
angry with him. The governor himself had been giving licenses to make
slaves, for which reason Indians were disappearing. Castañeda was informed that licenses had been given for more than three thousand slaves.

Later, probably because of the growing shortage of mine labor, Pedrarias ordered that no slaves were to be exported. Two ship captains in
port ignored the order, however, loading their vessels with Indians, both
slave and free. They refused to allow indignant officials aboard. This affair
caused a great scandal and uproar, since the ships were bound for Panama;
but Pedrarias made no move to prevent the crime, because the ships'
masters were his good friends.

Like Honduras, Nicaragua was an impoverished land that yielded only
corn and some cacao. Although both would eventually produce silver and
some gold, in the early years the only profitable enterprise was that of
trading in slaves. Those who sought to redress the injustices were frustrated because in order to present a case one had to make the long journey
to Santo Domingo. An official was named as Protector of the Indians, but,
according to Castañeda, he did nothing and the office was a joke. Consequently, Pedrarias had his way.[44]

This is not to say, however, that abuses always went unnoticed. A
lawsuit was brought against Rodrigo Núñez, a vecino of León, and probably no particular friend of Pedrarias. Núñez was charged with having gone
among his encomienda Indians at night and seizing some of them to be
branded on their faces as slaves. It was also alleged that he forced the
Indian caciques and other principales to find more "slaves," and when
they failed to deliver, had them whipped.[45]

During the long years of Pedrarias's rule a great many slaves were
made, and the centers of León and Granada became headquarters for the
trade. The traffic between Nicaragua and Panama and points south was
brisk. The governor was involved in the trade himself, and among other
prominent Spaniards profiting was Hernando de Soto. In Panama the
Indians were auctioned off at the slave market, some of them destined for
labor in Peru.[46]

Following the death of Pedrarias in 1531, Castañeda became governor,
1531–35. The tenor of his correspondence with the Crown reflects a

sincere regard for the condition of the natives. He said that he had tried to stop the exporting of Indians to Panama, but Pedrarias, considering him an enemy, had provoked indignities against him, telling the vecinos that it was Castañeda who prevented their prosperity in the slave trade. As governor, Castañeda claimed that he had not allowed a single Indian to leave, even though Spaniards begged him for license, promising to return the Indians. Many of the natives had been taken as "servants" to Panama or Peru, with the understanding that they would come back with their masters; but all too often they were sold and never saw their families again.

There was a serious decline in the population, he said, but that was because of "our sins." He had reference to a pestilence which had struck León and the surrounding area, from which many natives died with stomach aches and fever. About two-thirds of the Indians had tumors. The plague had affected all categories of Indians, he added, and the deaths could not be attributed to their maltreatment. If the illness did not lift, in Castañeda's opinion, soon there would be no one left to support the Spaniards living in the province. He asked the king to rule that Indians enslaved for rebellion not be taken out of the land so that the villages could be maintained.[47]

The regidores of León were equally concerned about the labor short-age. Alluding to an earlier cédula (Burgos: 29 November 1527) authoriz-ing the vecinos to enslave Indians, they requested, in 1531, a law against the slave trade because of the excesses. At the same time, they petitioned exemption from the payment of the quinto and other taxes on slaves.[48] Meantime, the vecinos of Panama wrote of the shortage of natives there as a result of a disastrous plague. They wanted to import slaves and naborías from Nicaragua, as well as Peru, but only those condemned to death.[49] Whatever the Crown response, the trade continued: licenciado de la Garra, in three letters during 1533, wrote of the continuing injustice perpetrated by the *factor,* Miguel Juan de Ribas, who took slaves from Nicaragua to Panama.[50]

As in the case of so many others, Castañeda found it easy enough to criticize the Indian policy of someone else, but quite another matter effectively to deal with the same problems once in power. He, too, would feel compelled to placate the soured colonists. Writing in 1533, he told the king that a plague of smallpox had taken the lives of six thousand Indians, which had serious repercussions for mine labor. Moreover, In-dian uprisings had resulted in the deaths of Christians in some new mines. The Chontal Indians were especially bellicose, and their repeated attacks had upset the operation of the mines. Consequently, he sought permis-sion to enslave them so they could be taken from the land, because with their absence black slaves could productively work the mines. The contentment of the vecinos was crucial for the settlement of Nicaragua, especially in light of the successes in Peru, which were attracting many Spaniards. At the same time, it was the location of Nicaragua as an embarkation point for Peru that made it an entrepôt for the slave trade. Not only were Indians needed for servants and other personal service, but many were shipped off to Panama and Peru for profits. Women served the same purpose, and some of them were simply rented out to sailors who wanted companionship on their voyages.[51]

Castañeda, who earlier had written of his concern for the unfortunate natives and of his efforts to help them, now found himself the target of criticism. The regidores of Granada wrote in 1535 that in the more than four years Castañeda had governed, the injustices committed were frightful. With Crown sanction, the branding of slaves was continuing, even though stipulated conditions were ignored, and the result was ruinous.[52]

The royal edict of early 1534, calculated to stop the exporting of Indians, allowed the enslavement of those taken in just war, but forbade their sale or removal from their native provinces.[53] By the time it was announced in Santiago, in February of 1535, Alvarado had been gone for a year on his expedition to Peru. His army, according to Francisco de Barrionuevo, took four thousand Indians, leaving both Guatemala and Nicaragua very depopulated. To make matters worse, he said, many would never return, because they would die from the shortage of food in the new lands or from the severe climate changes.[54]

One of the first settlers in Nicaragua wrote in 1535 that affairs had deteriorated because there had been a thousand abuses and not a single residencia, or judicial review,[55] and despite the bounty of the land conditions were bad. The change of governors and the bickering among the Spaniards added to the disturbance of Indian communities. The concern of the natives was such, according to a chronicler, that "for two years they did not sleep with their women, so that no slaves would be born for the Castilians."[56]

One reason that the law was flouted with such ease was that violators were seldom brought to justice, or if so they were given only light fines. Castañeda condemned to death, by "definitive sentence," in absentia, a Juan Fernández, the master of a galleon, for having transported many free Indians to Peru and other places. When, however, Fernández returned to Nicaragua, he was pardoned, allegedly because Diego de Almagro sent from Peru a gold crown worth 1,000 to 2,000 pesos to Castañeda in exchange for the life of the captain. Another witness said that gold vases were given to the alcalde and the notary to gain their favor in the case. In his defense, Castañeda stated that the sentence of death for the absent Fernández was merely a convenient device by which he hoped to warn ship captains who were taking out so many Indians without licenses. He asserted that he never had any intention of actually executing Fernández, and he denied having received the gift in question.[57]

The illegal trade persisted also for the reason that officials were often parties to the transactions. Again, Castañeda was accused of letting Alvarado put in at the port of Realejo with illegal slaves from Guatemala. Moreover, it was charged, he let Alvarado take more slaves out of Nicaragua, all for a consideration of more than a thousand pesos. He purportedly allowed another Spaniard to carry free Indians to Peru, in exchange for a gift of the Spaniard's encomienda. His nephew and another captain, who was a special friend, were also allowed to export Indians, some of whom were from encomiendas.[58] The alcalde ordinario, and sometime lieutenant of Castañeda, Fernando de Alcántara, was also accused of allowing many free Indians to be shipped out.[59]

Furthermore, another of Castañeda's lieutenants, Luis de Guevara, was involved as well. The register books showed that he allowed 206 Indians to pass to Panama and Peru.[60] The treasurer, Pedro de los Rios, had also been a lieutenant of the governor, and he, too, was charged with the same crime. It was claimed that he issued licenses for 80 Indians to be shipped out, as the register books showed, and that he personally took another 100 that were never registered. He was also accused of letting Spaniards seize and bind free Indian men and women to be taken on the conquest of Nueva Segovia. In rebuttal, the treasurer said that he took only 8 to 10 Indians to Panama. They were registered, he insisted, and if some died it was from fevers. Those Indians taken to Nueva Segovia, he claimed, were rebels who had been killing Spaniards.[61]

Although the Crown ordered Nicaraguan Indians freed and returned to their provinces, it seems not to have been an order that was implemented with great effectiveness, despite the assurance of the oidores of Santo Domingo that they were taking measures to free those unjustly enslaved in Nicaragua and Honduras, and to punish those culpable.[62] Years later the Crown remonstrated that Spaniards were still illegally buying free Indians at low prices in Nicaragua and selling them abroad. Again the natives were ordered freed, and they were to be returned at the cost of those who took them out.[63]

Slavers had been plying their trade with relative impunity because by late 1535 the governor of Nicaragua was Rodrigo de Contreras, the son-in-law of Pedrarias Dávila. Contreras, whose own economic interests were varied, not only allowed slaves to leave Realejo, but he personally invaded Costa Rica and seized more slaves for himself from other Spaniards who were pacifying the region.[64] By 1545, he was charged with having allowed five hundred Indians to be taken out of Nicaragua without seeing to their return.[65] Aside from those Indians shipped out to Panama and Peru during his administration, many others, estimated at between three hundred and five hundred, were taken by Contreras during the conquest of the region of the *desaguadero*, the San Juan River, which drains Lake Nicaragua. He allowed Spaniards to go out "rancheando," that is, raiding and collecting Indians, some of whom were stolen from encomiendas. Of those taken to the desaguadero many had perished.

Confronted with these charges, Contreras said that it could not be proved that he took Indians against their will. It was true that he had taken some who were runaways, but even they went willingly, he said, and they were not taken in chains, as his detractors stated. Without the services of Indians, the soldiers would have refused to go on the expedition. If some of the natives died, it was from illnesses that also killed Spaniards, not, he insisted, from excessive labor or maltreatment. Furthermore, he claimed that he had freed slaves illegally brought from San Miguel by a Juan Díez Guerrero. When they arrived at the Puerto de la Posesión (Realejo), headed for Panama, he had them taken off the ship and returned to their province in canoes. Some Indians, he admitted, were taken out of Nicaragua during his absence, and he allowed others to leave that were not native to Nicaragua. Spaniards leaving the province were authorized to take five or six Indians for their personal service, provided they returned them.

As to the enslavement of encomienda Indians, Contreras noted that at least one encomendero who branded natives from his pueblo was deprived of the encomienda and put in jail.[66] The impression one gets is that Contreras did enforce the law on occasion, but that he was less scrupulous when those close to him were involved. He seems simply to have followed the established policy of selective enforcement. And although the slave trade in Nicaragua gradually diminished, as late as 1548 naborías and other free Indians were being branded and shipped south.[67]

As an inland city, Santiago de Guatemala was less of a center for the slave trade than those settlements whose port locations made for convenience in slipping Indians on board slave ships. The province of Guatemala as a whole, however, because of its dense native population, was fruitful ground for slave raiders. Its proximity to Mexico also made it attractive to dealers sending Indians to the north, and the number of Guatemalans in Mexico was apparently considerable. There were frequent pretexts for making esclavos de guerra because of isolated pockets of resisters, or rebellions on the part of those already pacified. The most flagrant cases were those in which slavers, making no pretense of legality, boldly raided ecomiendas and kidnaped free Indians. Royal officials complained that before Alvarado returned as governor, Captain Martin Estete, sent by Pedrarias, had entered San Salvador and raided six encomiendas, carrying off fifteen hundred peaceful natives as slaves. A counter force of vecinos pushed out the intruders, who relinquished a thousand of the captives. The other five hundred had already been sent in bondage to León.[68] Fray Pedro Angulo wrote that seven hundred Indians had been enslaved in the town of Tecucitlán alone.[69]

Among those most active in slaving was Pedro de Alvarado. It was said that he had fifteen hundred branded slaves working his mines, and that by the summer of 1531 he had smelted an amount equaling 12,000 pesos.[70] Later when Alvarado brought suit to recover property appropriated when he left Honduras, he claimed that he had 17,000 *castellanos* coming, primarily from slaves and their mining activities. But Montejo, who was a principal in the suit, responded by stating that in the fifteen months Alvarado was in Honduras his slaves did not even mine 3,000 castellanos worth, and that Alvarado's profits cost the lives of half the slaves in his cuadrillas, or gangs.[71]

In his 1535 residencia, Alvarado was called to account for having taken Indians out of their native habitats, even though some of them were slaves. The diversity of the adelantado's interests required considerable manpower, and he moved Indians about at will. When he entered Honduras he took slaves from Guatemala for his mining cuadrillas, and some of the slaves he took out of San Salvador were sent to Mexico. In addition, he was charged with sending a ship with two hundred slaves to Panama, and while this clearly appeared to be illegal, he declared that he had a special license from Spain to authorize the transaction. In any event, the venture was frustrated when the ship was forced to return. Unfortunately, the mishap resulted in the death of some of the Indians by drowning.[72]

In preparing his ambitious expedition to Peru, Alvarado made liberal use of available Indians, both free and slave. Many of them were used to carry equipment down to León, and on their way back a number were killed by warlike natives. According to a witness, the ships in the armada sailed "full of slaves and *maceguales.*" The official charge was that he took 1,184 Indians. All of the adelantado's companions were allowed to take slaves; depending on his status, a soldier could take from 2 to 8 Indians to serve him. Most of the slaves who survived that ill-fated expedition were sold in Peru.[73]

Accused of allowing his brother Diego to sell his encomienda villagers as slaves, Alvarado answered that Diego had performed great services for the king, but had found himself in debt nevertheless. The concession was to enable him to put his affairs in order so that he could give further service to the Crown in Peru.[74] Others contributed to the decline in population, and by 1543 it was asserted that "in those provinces" more than fourteen thousand Indians were missing.[75]

The Chiapas frontier, situated between Guatemala and Mexico, was also the scene of considerable slaving activity. A cabildo report of 1537 gave a detailed account of one expedition, carried out not by renegades, but by Spaniards under the command of Captain Francisco Gil, who was clothed with official authority. In late 1535 Gil was sent by Governor Alvarado to plant a settlement in the valley of Tequepán-Pochutla so that the Indians in that region would not have to travel all the way to San Cristóbal to have contact with Spaniards. Gil left with about forty Spaniards and some native allies taken from the encomiendas of San Cristóbal. He was instructed to name the new town San Pedro. At Tequepán-Pochutla they paused for several days, during which time they caused disturbances among the inhabitants; and then, instead of settling there, Gil pushed on to the Tanochil River in the province of the same name, where he established the Spanish town. Having thus disregarded orders, the captain proceeded to hand over the staffs of office to Francisco de Montejo, under whom he placed his command. Montejo, then governor of Yucatán, made Gil lieutenant governor.[76]

Since the founding of San Cristóbal some nine years before, the Indians of Tequepán-Pochutla had given tribute and services to the vecinos of San Cristóbal. With the founding of the villa of San Pedro, the pueblos were to continue serving their encomenderos, but Gil and his companions interfered and imposed their wishes on encomienda Indians belonging to other Spaniards. They intimidated the peoples of Tuni (Xitultepeque), Tesco, Nogango, Ocingo (Ocosingo?), Suteapa (Suchiapa?), and others. Gil made it known that he intended to take two hundred slaves to the city of Mexico, and to profit as well by arranging for merchants to secure other slaves.

To further those ambitions, Gil moved on peaceful villages. He struck first at Tila, held in encomienda by Francisco Ortes, making two or three *entradas de guerra* (military campaigns), but failing to take any slaves. He then resorted to more subtle means by making his camp in a little village outside Tila and calling the people to come to him in peace. The exact details of what happened next are somewhat obscured by differing witnesses, though all are uniformly damaging to Gil.

The cabildo statement related that Gil had made unjust war on the pueblos for no more reason than to take advantage of the opportunity to make slaves. He required fourteen señores and principales to appear before him and then demanded burden bearers, or tamemes. When they were delivered, the tamemes were branded as slaves of war. After the captain took his pick of the captives, the others were divided up among his companions, whereupon the fourteen lords of Tila were burned to death. The nose and a hand of another lord were cut off and hung around his neck, after which he was sent out to his people as a warning.

Cristóbal de Aguilar testified that when Gil called the people of Tila to come in peace about seventy of them came, and Gil asked their help in making war. That night many of them fled, but the twenty-six who remained were bound and taken to Tila, where half were enslaved and the others burned. When Gil again summoned Indians to come in peace only two señores came forth. One of them was sent to bring in more of his people, but when neither he nor any others showed up, the nose and hand were cut from the remaining lord, who was then released.

Lucas de Beneçiano said that after the Indians of Tila were called, some who were said to be principales appeared with some tamemes. The lords were burned and the others marked with brands of war on their faces and divided up.

According to Antón Portugués, two principales and six or seven other natives answered the summons. Two Indians were sent back to coax more of their people to come, while the others were bound. The people of Tila were given a limit of three days within which to comply or see their leaders burned. Since no one, including the messengers, came, one of the principales was burned, and the nose and hand of the other were strung around his neck. The disfigured lord was then sent to his people to give them Gil's message, which was that they should arm themselves and make entrenchments because he would return to make war on them in a month. The remaining five or six Indians were branded. About fifteen or twenty days later, the witness recalled, they took an Indian from Tila who said that sixty Indians had been on their way to the Spanish camp when they came upon the mutilated principal on the road, and then they turned back.

Captain Gil then marched toward the peaceful pueblo of Petalçingo, subject to Tila and giving service to Francisco Ortes as well. After settling his camp two leagues from the village, Gil sent word to the señores of Petalçingo. One of them came with about forty of his people, bearing gifts of honey. The Indians were sent to clean the road that day, but the following day they were put to the use for which Gil had requested them, that is, carrying his supplies. Twenty or twenty-five were taken as tamemes and marched a day's journey when they were tied and branded as slaves. A day later Gil sent his *maestre de campo*, Lorenzo de Godoy, and five men (one account says eight) back to Petalçingo with orders to burn the village and to take all the slaves they could. The plan was frustrated when the band of raiders found the village already burned and the people gone.

With that turn of events, Gil and his party set out for the pueblo of Yzcatepeque, held in encomienda by Bernaldino de Coria. Before reaching the village, the Spaniards suddenly fell on two or three Indians who appeared and branded them. When others came to give supplies to the Spaniards they, too, were seized without provocation and put to the brand. A merchant who had passed through there before said the people were friendly and gave him food. The cabildo claimed that two hundred men, women, and children were taken from the village, although a witness who had remained at the camp said that the others returned with about sixty slaves.

Suteapa, belonging to a vecino of San Cristóbal, was approached by Lorenzo de Godoy. Many of the women and children fled in fear of the Christians, but some of the señores gave supplies and services to them. Godoy, "wishing to have a pretext to say that the pueblo was in rebellion," ordered the Indians to come back to settle the town, giving them three days within which to comply. Those already in the village told the Spaniards that they should leave, and then the other Indians would return and serve. Seven Indians, said to be señores and principales, "and who, by their aspect, appeared to be," refused to cooperate. Godoy's response was to have them chained and put in a straw house, which was set afire, consuming all of them. With that act as an admonition, Godoy ordered twenty-five youths bound and taken to San Pedro as slaves. They would doubtless have remained so had not Francisco de Montejo interceded angrily. He reprimanded the Spaniards for having unjustly taken the Indians, freed the youths, and ordered them returned to the village, which had, however, been burned at Godoy's departure. Montejo, "because of his anger . . . did not wish to stay longer . . . and he went to Tabasco."

The pueblo of Tuni belonged to Joan de Alcántara, a vecino of San Cristóbal, who complained that his Indians had been chased into the forest or enslaved. It is clear from the testimony of various witnesses that Gil had ordered the village destroyed and its people taken as slaves. The essence of what happened is as follows: Francisco Gil had made camp at the town of Canopochil, where he ordered Godoy on the mission to Tuni. All element of surprise was lost when two natives of Zinacantlán went ahead to warn the people of Tuni, who then fired the village and retired to the forests. When Godoy arrived to find the village destroyed, he sent word for the people to come in peace. When two natives came forward, Godoy gave them a hat as a gift, telling them to call the others to bring food. When seven or eight natives appeared with chickens and other food, they were subsequently bound and, according to one witness, burned. One Spaniard testified that twenty-nine Indians came, and that the eldest was sent out to call more. When the witness left for San Cristóbal, the Indians were tied up, but he did not discuss their ultimate fate.

In summary, the cabildo of San Cristóbal accused Gil and Godoy of ruining Spanish vecinos by raiding their encomiendas, of making crude and unjust war, causing the deaths of many Indian auxiliaries, and of illegally enslaving free and peaceful encomienda Indians. Gil, the regidores asserted, had operated in collusion with retail merchants whom he allowed to trade in slaves and to take Indians out of their lands. And all of this was done by them "as men who have used royal offices in alien jurisdiction, where they had no power." For these crimes, the cabildo implored the viceroy and Audiencia of Mexico to see the offenders punished.[77]

The slaving operations touched on here, although they are among the more notorious examples, are only a few of the countless instances in which Indians were enslaved in the years following the initial conquest. Many individuals took an Indian here and there under various pretexts, and it appears that most Spaniards had at least a couple of slaves to serve them, while others had many more. Some were actively involved in the slave trade, and a few became wealthy in the process. Perhaps the most pernicious aspect of the trade was that the highest officials were in large measure responsible. With few exceptions, they allowed friends and relatives to participate in the illicit traffic, and all too often they were themselves in collusion. More often than not offenders went unpunished.[78]

5
The Branding of Slaves

GIVEN THE LAWLESS CHARACTER of the early Central American frontier, some means had to be devised by the Crown to indicate which Indians were legitimate slaves. Those who had been justly enslaved, according to law, were to be branded under regulated circumstances, but there were numerous and flagrant violations, which led to the branding of those who were in fact free men and women.

In 1526 a royal cédula noted that many free Indians were being unjustly branded. Henceforth, branding was to be done in the presence of the governor and other officials, but only after sufficient care had been taken to verify their status. Spaniards who illegally used the branding iron were to suffer the extreme penalty of death and the loss of property.[1]

According to fray Bartolomé de Las Casas, some Spaniards took a light view of the Crown's concern, despite the stern punishment. He recounts that a vecino named Orduña had a slave woman with the brand "free" on her arm, which mark was customarily applied when a slave was liberated. When Las Casas arrived, Orduña, fearing the woman would be taken away, added after the brand more letters that read "'so long as she serves her master,' or something like that." Las Casas asked that the vecino be punished as a kidnaper and as one who held a free person as his slave. He insisted that the woman be set free to do as she wished, and that all Spaniards guilty of such infractions be punished in order to arrest the "horrible crimes."[2]

Indians were, naturally enough, terrified of the searing irons. Ironically, once stigmatized, they could be set free again only with yet another brand so indicating their liberated status. When a ship put in at a Nicaraguan port loaded with illegally enslaved encomienda Indians, the governor freed them and sent them home. But first the natives, some of whom were women and suckling children, had their face brands canceled. Fresh letters spelling "libre" were burned into their scarred faces. That same year, 1532, the Crown ruled that no one was to dare brand an Indian on the face.[3]

One way in which indiscriminate branding of Indians was controlled was through limiting the possession of branding irons. To that end, it was repeatedly decreed that they be deposited with the justice and other officials, and that all branding was to be done in the presence of persons of authority. When not in use, the irons were to remain locked in the official chest having three keys, each of three officials retaining one of the keys. These regulations were effective to some degree, but the repetition of the order indicates that infractions were not infrequent. An official at Trujillo informed the king that there had been in that area three royal branding irons, but that they had been in the hands of private persons. Seeing the possibility of fraud, he requested the governor, Diego López, to collect them and to bring them to him. Only two of them could be found. It was said that the third had been broken, but it could not be verified.[4]

Another way in which the law was circumvented was by counterfeit irons. As one example, during the chaotic early years in Honduras, Vasco de Herrera branded fifty Indians, not with the official royal iron, but with one made by himself. Some even had the audacity to use a different mark altogether. A witness told how Alonso Cáceres, a lieutenant of Montejo, had taken Indians at Cerquín and branded them on their chins with the mark of a cross to identify them, saying that they would serve as naborías. This was clearly against the law, because the royal brand formed the letters "ROC," although the brand for rescates was sometimes "R,"[5] which also was used occasionally for naborías. Nevertheless, about thirty natives were impressed with the cross of Cáceres.[6]

It was not uncommon for some conquistadores to brand their slaves with the Spanish master's name. In response to information that Honduran Indians were being kidnaped and enslaved by deceit, after which their owners' names were seared into their faces, the queen ordered such practices to cease. Moreover, all those so enslaved under the administrations of Cerezeda, Alvarado, and Montejo were to be returned to their homes.[7] Some slaves in Guatemala from Mexico, enslaved for rebellion in Jalisco, had distinctive "columns" branded on their faces.[8] During the early conquest years other marks were sometimes used: Bernal Díaz del Castillo notes that in the conquest of Mexico it was common to brand Indians taken in war with the letter "G" for guerra;[9] and a contemporary said that when Cortés was in Honduras during 1525 he ordered some rebellious Indians enslaved and branded on their faces with the letter "C," presumably to identify them as property of Cortés himself.[10]

—G for guerra   —R for rescate

The irregularities did not go unnoticed in Spain. A general cédula, dated in 1528, made reference to the slaves that had been unjustly enslaved and branded on the face, adding that those free Indians had been disaffected. Therefore, anyone having just claims to slaves was to appear before the president and judges of the audiencia to produce titles and justification for holding them as slaves. The slaves were to be registered, and if the owner wanted to brand them it could be done only with the license and order of the justice, and only then with a recognized brand. The iron was to be in the possession of the justice and no one else. If irons were found in the possession of another, or if a slave was branded with other than an official iron, or without the license of the justice, the guilty person would be fined half his property and lose the slave.[11]

There was an additional reason for the branding and enslavement being performed in the presence of royal officials, for in that manner the collection of the king's quinto was assured, that is, one-fifth of the value of the slave. The officials, for their part, were all too eager to comply, because a law of 1534 allowed them to charge a tax of up to a silver *real* and a half for use of the official iron, and the notary collected his fee as well.[12]

The obviously brutalizing aspects of branding humans like cattle aside, the argument was made that there were more practical considerations in support of the practice. Some felt that permanent identification was preferable in order to protect free men, who might otherwise be suspected of being slaves, and to isolate those who were truly chattels. When the New Laws for the protection of the Indians were issued in 1542–43, forbidding slavery, it was decreed that servants who were not slaves could not be branded. But they frequently ran away, and since they were not identified with any mark, Spaniards in other parts did not know the status of such Indians, which sometimes led to their outright enslavement.

The other practical consideration was that some servants had been condemned to servitude for serious crimes. Occasionally they fled their masters, and not being identified with marks, they were seldom returned. Because of that situation, criminals went unpunished, with the result that authorization was given to brand those who had been sentenced to temporal service because of their crimes.[13]

The Crown wanted branding supervised by the bishop and the governor, or his lieutenant, but the circumstances under which some slaves were taken obstructed that procedure. When Alvarado was accused of branding slaves without the bishop's presence, he responded that the slaves he took were at San Miguel and Puerto de Fonseca, almost one hundred miles from the seat of the bishopric at Santiago. If, he said, he had to march them all the way to the capital, some would die of exhaustion on the long journey and others would escape along the way without brands identifying them as slaves. Witnesses in Alvarado's support noted that while slaves had been branded along the coast without the bishop, Alvarado, the governor, was present, in addition to a priest. In their view, the distance from Santiago was not quite so far as Alvarado had stated, but even so, the way crossed many dangerous rivers and marshes.[14]

A similar complaint about branding procedures came from Nicaragua. In 1529, there was criticism of the way in which the restrictions were affecting the economy, since, it was stated, there was no other income except that from slaves. The cabildo of Granada had requested that the regidores be given permission to brand Indians in their city, since León was the only authorized site. Finally, the governor, the Protector of the Indians, and other officials agreed that a branding iron would be entrusted to the care of Captain Martín Estete, who would take the iron to Granada, branding slaves along the way. This, an official asserted, was a mockery of the Crown's rule, even though some felt that it served the interest of the settlers.[15]

But six years later the regidores of the city of Granada, referring to royal authority given to the governor and other officials in León to brand slaves under certain conditions, said that the regulations were not being observed and that the land was being ruined. Perhaps this querulous reaction, while no doubt reflective of the true situation, stemmed at least in part from the rivalry of the two settlements.[16]

The Crown did not sanction indiscriminate branding of Indians, even those taken in war. It was eventually decreed that no female could be branded as a slave, nor could boys under the age of fourteen be enslaved. There were, however, many violations of that law. A Diego Monroy, whom Alvarado identified as his enemy, stated that at Naco, Honduras, the adelantado had branded both women and youths under fourteen, even though the royal provision prohibiting it was well known.[17] And when the Crown forbade branding at one point, Alvarado allegedly suppressed the royal order until he and his followers had finished marking a large number of slaves of rescate they had acquired.[18] A cédula of 1552 prohibited the branding of Indians as property, but by then legal slavery of Indians, except in rare cases, was a thing of the past.[19]

6
Prices and Numbers of Slaves

AS A COMMODITY ON THE MARKET, the slave brought a price relative to the supply, the demand being constant. During the first years of conquest and pacification Spaniards came by slaves of war in large numbers, along with acquiring slaves of rescate. Consequently, for some time captives were worth very little from the standpoint of trading. But as more natives were consumed by pestilence, exhaustion, and maltreatment, and since many were shipped out to other colonies, the supply diminished sharply. Other factors causing the price of slaves to rise were the increasing numbers of Spaniards entering Central America and the concomitant pressures of the Crown to limit slavery. Where native labor was in short supply, as in the Antilles, slaves brought higher prices, a market condition that gave impulse to the exporting of Indians. The value of a slave was also tied to the inflationary trends of the period.[1]

Certainly an Indian was held to be worth much less than a horse during the conquest, the animal being valued at between 500 and 800 pesos.[2] During the initial stages of Spanish domination, in 1524, the cost of a slave was probably near 2 pesos. That same year, during the pacification of Soconusco, swine sold for 20 *pesos de oro* each, and a load of cacao brought 10 pesos de oro.[3] Slaves were often traded for food and supplies, both of which were in short supply in the early years of conquest. In 1526, during the pacification of Honduras, Salcedo said that the traffic in slaves was the only thing that allowed Spaniards to exist, since the land offered nothing else for barter. Slaves were traded for food from the islands, which was very expensive. Twenty-five pounds—an arroba—of salted meat was valued at 4 pesos, a bushel and a half (a *fanega*) of maize cost 4 pesos, as did an arroba of wine or vinegar. An arroba of oil or the same quantity of cassava went for 6 pesos, and other items were proportionately high.[4] With slaves worth a couple of pesos each, it can be calculated what one was

68

worth in terms of trade for food. In 1531, slaves could be purchased for 2 to 5 pesos.[5] Oddly enough, even a black slave was worth only 9 pesos in 1530, according to Pedro de Alvarado.[6]

In the summer of 1533, some Franciscans in Mexico showed concern about the branding of slaves in Guatemala, noting that they sold for only two pesos each.[7] In a comment on their report, the president of the Audiencia of Mexico stated that in 1532 slaves in New Spain had been worth forty pesos, as compared to two pesos in Guatemala in 1533.[8] One authority on slavery concludes from this correspondence that it is proof of the great abundance of slaves in Guatemala.[9] There may well be some truth in the assumption, for in 1533 or 1534, a vecino of Santiago de Guatemala, referring to the many slaves in Guatemala, asserted that there was a shortage of them in the city of Mexico. Because there were so many gold mines in Mexico, the vecino requested license to take 200 Indians to them, but the Crown gave him permission to take only 20.[10] The availability of slaves very likely accounts for the fact that, according to witnesses, an Indian slave sold for anywhere between three and six and a half pesos during the decades of the 1530s.[11] These prices no doubt refer to unskilled labor.

As the natives gradually acquired European skills, some were obviously more sought after than others. An Indian with experience in building construction or blacksmithing was worth much more than one used only to guard cattle or to carry hod or a pack. By 1530, reference was made to "un esclavo yndio muy bueno" who was worth fifty pesos de oro in Trujillo, and the owner confessed that the slave was his "hands and feet."[12]

Francisco de Barrientos, the veedor in Honduras, wrote in 1534 that slaves, "the best in the land," could be purchased for about 33 pesos apiece.[13] By mid-century another Spaniard, whose slaves were taken from him, claimed that his mining cuadrilla of thirty slaves, plus a half dozen in his household and fields, were worth more than four thousand pesos, or roughly 112 pesos each. The man who sold the cuadrilla to him a few days before the slaves were freed said that the sale price had been 3,000 pesos, or 100 pesos a slave. The injured owner insisted that his losses were even greater because he could not run his mining operation, for which he had also bought tools and equipment, as well as cattle and food for the slaves.[14]

The conquistador Diego Holguín in San Salvador, protesting the loss of his fifty slaves in 1548, stated that they had cost him 3,000 pesos; but that was very likely an exaggeration, inasmuch as he was emphasizing his loss.[15] Another Spaniard of Chiapas had bought slaves at auction, the proceeds of which were for the royal quinto. His son testified that 200

slaves were taken from the family in 1548, at which time they were worth
70 to 80 pesos apiece. Witnesses said they had observed a couple of those
slaves purchased four years before at 50 pesos each.[16]

Another factor that sometimes drove up the prices of slaves was the
control exercised by local officials. In Nicaragua during the 1530s, there
was great fluctuation because Governor Francisco de Castañeda was
buying slaves cheap and selling them dear, a situation he could control
because he was master of the province. Among his powers was that of
issuing the licenses necessary to take Indians out to Panama and Peru. A
notary in the city of Granada bewailed the fact Castañeda had forced him
to sell to him twelve very good slaves worth more than ten to fifteen pesos
each for only seven pesos each. The notary said that he was intimidated
and had no choice.

Castañeda made his highest profits from the sale of female slaves. In
depositions it was revealed that the governor sold several of these esclavas
for 200 pesos, when in fact they were worth only somewhere between 25
and 40 pesos. In order to obtain a license to take a slave out of the province
it was necessary to buy the slave from Castañeda, at his price. According to
some of the testimony, good male slaves could be purchased for as little as
6 or 7 pesos, whereas the women brought higher prices because of their
special attractions. A female Indian would occasionally bring as much as
100 pesos in a fair transaction. Castañeda, however, maintained that the
esclavas were generally selling for 200 to 300 pesos and that the ones he
sold for 200 were very good laundresses and seamstresses. Whether or not
such skills were uppermost in the minds of the adventurers who bought
them we are not told; but his case is unconvincing, notwithstanding his
witnesses' statements to the contrary. Although the governor was heavily
fined later on, whether or not he finally paid is open to question. In any
event, he was surely far ahead on his profits: others testified that in one
period six ships left Nicaragua for Peru loaded with Indians, many of
whom were free men.[17]

It is clear from the foregoing that establishing what might be considered
standard prices for slaves over the years is difficult. During the first stages
of the conquest they sold for one to three pesos. Prices remained low
during the decade of the 1530s, and then rose in the following decade to
fifty or sixty pesos a slave. The cost varied considerably, according to the
slave's skills and sex, while the labor shortage and inflationary trends are
variables to be taken into consideration.

Estimating the total number of slaves made in Central America is a task
that bears little fruit. Record books were to have been kept to account

for the Crown's share, but few such registers survive. Many other slaves taken illegally were never inscribed at all. Consequently, there is very little in the nature of hard information on which to base a reasonable approximation. Still, it is a question that merits some examination.

We do have fragmentary documentation on the holdings of several individual Spaniards who had slaves working for them, which offers some indication of how many a few of the more prominent vecinos held. It has been noted that, according to some officials, Alvarado took three thousand slaves of rescate in one year; but even if that figure is accurate, there is no certainty that he kept all of them for himself. The same sources allege that in 1531 the adelantado had fifteen hundred branded slaves working in his mines.[18] One writer asserts that Alvarado had five hundred Indian slaves working streams for gold before he left in 1534 for Peru (Quito), but he does not document the statement.[19] There is little doubt that Alvarado's slave holdings far exceeded the numbers held by other Spaniards in Central America, with the possible exceptions of Pedrarias Dávila and Rodrigo de Contreras.

Alvarado's brother Jorge at one time held half the town of Atitlán in encomienda, from which he was given slaves in the amount of 200 to 270, depending on which witness one follows. He probably had others as well. The other half of Atitlán belonged for a time to Sancho Barahona, who had a cuadrilla of about 100, or perhaps 120, mining for gold.[20]

Juan de Espinar stated in 1537 that his encomienda of Huehuetenango gave him 250 slaves and that he had another 100 made up of Mixtecas from Mexico and various others.[21] Baltasar Guerra, the encomendero of Chiapas, had more than 200 illegal slaves working in his sugar mill, according to the chronicler Remesal; and Diego Holguín, an encomendero of San Salvador had 50.[22] Cristóbal Lobo of Chiapas reported his holdings as 42 slaves in 1549.[23] Juan Pérez Dardón, a prominent conqueror and one-time lieutenant governor, appeared on February 11, 1549, and declared 107 slaves, both men and women, who were subsequently taken from him.[24] The treasurer, Francisco de Castellanos, certainly a powerful figure, was allegedly "very rich, and he has eighty to a hundred slaves, as he confesses."[25] A Francisco de León complained that judge licenciado Pedro Ramírez liberated his cuadrilla of more than 100 slaves without a hearing.[26]

These figures show how many slaves a few prosperous Spaniards held at one time, but over the years they undoubtedly had others. Apparently the majority of settled Spaniards prior to mid-century had some slaves, but lesser functionaries and many vecinos often did not have the money to buy and maintain very many of them. In 1544, the Crown ordered justices in the towns to compile secret information about the number of slaves and their treatment.[27] If the reports are extant I've not seen them.

It is reasonable to suppose that a conqueror in Guatemala during the governorship of Alvarado would have held more slaves than one under Montejo in Honduras. Thus, local strictures, along with the availability of slaves, had a bearing on the numbers of slaves made. Also contributing to the unclear picture is the fact that some encomienda Indians and naborías were used as slaves. In order to increase gold production, Alvarado told Spaniards to put their Indians to work mining, in language that implies they were not legal slaves. This order increased the work force from ten cuadrillas to ninety, according to testimony in 1531.[28] At that time there were probably fewer than a hundred vecinos living in Santiago, and though it might appear from the foregoing that almost all vecinos had a cuadrilla, it must be borne in mind that some had more than one slave gang. There were of course many Spaniards present who were not vecinos.[29] Cuadrillas frequently consisted of 100 to 120 Indians, and sometimes as many as 150. It appears that the most common size was about 100, which suggests that the ninety cuadrillas represented about 9,000 Indians. But probably many of those were not legally slaves; and in any case, a cuadrilla could consist of as few as 10 or 12 people.

A royal official of Honduras stated in 1537 that there were about thirty cuadrillas from Guatemala working the mines in Honduras. Those Indians, numbering perhaps three thousand, had taken out 28,000 to 30,000 pesos worth of precious metal in a period of four or five months.[30] In 1539, writing shortly after his arrival, licenciado Cristóbal de Pedraza claimed that three thousand Indians had been enslaved in Honduras.[31] As Protector of the Indians and a zealous guardian of his charges, Pedraza should not have been inclined to minimize the extent of slavery in Honduras, but that low figure is misleading. The vecinos of San Pedro, complaining of the pressures to curtail slavery, had twenty cuadrillas of 100 or more slaves in each. Each gang could mine 5,000 to 6,000 pesos worth yearly, and aside from the minimum 100,000 peso annual income to the community, it was pointed out that the Crown could lose its share of 20,000 pesos or more.[32]

The numbers advanced for Guatemala, particularly in the environs of Santiago, the only settlement of any size in Guatemala proper, refer to those used primarily for mining. Evidence for the numbers of slaves in non-mining occupations, and figures for Nicaragua, Chiapas, San Salvador, and minor settlements are elusive.

Scattered accounts by treasury officials shed some light on the quantity of slaves taken in certain years, and they offer more information on prices as well. According to law, one-fifth of all Indians enslaved were to be set aside for the royal quinto. Those slaves were later sold at public auction, the proceeds of which were put into the royal account. In 1530, the Crown's share in Guatemala amounted to only 345 pesos, six *tomines*, indicating that the full value of the slaves taken in war at that time amounted to about 1,725 pesos, not a large sum. Moreover, it appears that part of the 345 pesos represented some fines levied. If slaves were selling for about 2 pesos at the time, it follows that somewhere around eight hundred slaves of war were taken legally during that time. But that is probably the maximum figure, and it could be considerably smaller. Since they are specified "esclavos de guerra," the amount evidently does not take into account those who were taken as esclavos de rescate.[33]

Of course there is no way of knowing how many slaves were taken illegally with no payment of the quinto. If the above is an accurate reflection, it is indeed surprising that only about eight hundred slaves were taken as slaves of war in Guatemala during the turbulent months of 1530.

When Pedro de Alvarado invaded the province of Puynmatlan in early January 1531, the Crown's share of the slaves he seized was declared to be a mere 33 pesos, the total value thereby amounting to 165 pesos. This means that probably between 50 and 80 Indians were enslaved.[34] By 1536, the price of slaves had risen when officials stated that 221 had been taken for the king from a total of 1,136 seized. Those Indians were Chontales captured by Alvarado during the conquest of the Honduran province of Naco and Zula. Sold at public auction, their average price was slightly under 7.5 pesos each.[35] Additional detailed evidence of this sort would give us a much more complete knowledge of the numbers of Indian slaves and their value.

When the liberation of slaves on a wide scale began in 1548, the incoming president of the audiencia wrote that he freed some in Honduras, after which he took away five hundred slaves held by forty vecinos in San Salvador.[36] Unfortunately, he does not give figures for the other provinces. At least none were found in the present research. Perhaps the most solid information is the statement of licenciado Pedro Ramírez, a judge of integrity, who wrote that five thousand Indians were liberated.[37] He referred to the numbers freed in his time of service (1544–59), but no doubt almost all of those slaves were liberated between 1548 and 1551. We may take his total as a fairly reliable figure for the number of slaves held by vecinos in Central America around mid-century; as one of those responsible for abolition, he would not likely underestimate. However, by that time Spaniards had been enslaving Indians for a quarter century, and

over the years large numbers of them had either been shipped out or had
succumbed. Still others died resisting enslavement. Unfortunately, even
the recorded figures we have are imprecise; Pedraza wrote that, according
to witnesses, "between 1,000 and 1,500" Indians died when Alvarado was
making forays into Honduras.[38]

How shall we try to arrive at a reasonable sum for those Indians shipped
out in the slave trade? We do have some figures, but the disparities are so
great as to render any conclusions very tenuous. Let us begin with low
figures. Pedraza, as noted above, wrote in 1539 that three thousand slaves
had been made in Honduras. Since that number seems low, especially in
view of his general picture of desolation, perhaps he meant that three
thousand had been enslaved in a limited period prior to his arrival, not
since the beginnings of conquest.

Although the first Spaniards in Honduras began to export Indians to the
Antilles, by 1539 the trade had dwindled to a negligible volume in all
probability. It was a mining region, and many of the slaves were put into
that work, while others were taken to Nicaragua. If Pedraza's figure was
meant to include all slaves made dating from the conquest, I am inclined to
believe that he was misinformed, because there were almost certainly
more than that. Slavery continued for a few years after he wrote that letter,
but I have not seen additional figures for the numbers of Indian slaves
made subsequently. Perhaps it would not be too far off the mark to
suggest, with reservation, that altogether something like four thousand
were shipped out of Honduras in the slave trade. Others were
undoubtedly sent to the islands from areas bordering on Honduras.

President Alonso López de Cerrato, who was not prone to distortion,
said in 1548 that more than six thousand slaves had been taken out of
Nicaragua.[39] Cerrato was a harsh critic of the slavers, and it is safe to
assume that he was not minimizing. Including those exported from Honduras, a tentative total of ten thousand shipped out of the two areas for sale
as slaves is a very small sum compared to many accounts, and it probably
represents the minimum figure; but it is based on figures given by two of
the highest authorities in Central America, both of whom were incensed
by the traffic in humans. It may be added that perhaps as many as a
thousand slaves were taken up to Mexico, but that is pure conjecture on
my part.

Other authorities present a vastly different picture. Bartolomé de Las
Casas is cited as stating that in 1536 no less than 52,000 slaves had been
shipped southward from Nicaragua—25,000 to Panama and 27,000 to
Peru; yet later he gave a total for the slave trade as 500,000 Indians.[40]

Although the first total is probably inflated, it is certainly conceivable. However, an additional 448,000 slaves in the next decade or so is not credible. In his recent, excellent study, Murdo MacLeod takes a somewhat more moderate stance: "Ten thousand slaves per year for the decade between 1532 and 1542 would certainly seem to be a low figure and a total of two hundred thousand Indians for the whole Nicaraguan slaving period appears to be conservative."[41] Professor MacLeod may well be correct, but I have seen no documents substantiating such numbers, and I remain skeptical that the trade reached that volume.

To illustrate the wide divergence of views expressed, we may cite the curious letter of Martín de Esquivel, the factor and veedor (and therefore concerned with such matters) who criticized Contreras and his loose policies affecting the slave trade. Regarding the approximate period to which MacLeod refers, Esquivel informed the king that in the eight years Contreras had governed (in fact it was almost nine years, 1535–44), the treasurer, Pedro de los Ríos, had taken out, or allowed others to take out, more than five hundred Indians without their being returned.[42] Perhaps he referred only to those taken out who were not legally slaves, although we are led to believe that that would include the majority; maybe it is simply a slip of the scribe's pen; but in any event, his low figure must be questioned along with the high count of Las Casas.

Assuming that large numbers of Indians were available for shipment to Panama and Peru, did the facilities exist to transport them? Vessels at the time were those built on the Pacific (or South Sea) coast, mostly in Nicaragua, because although Magellan had sailed through the straits a few years before, it would be many more years before ships would pass through again. Satisfactory information on the numbers and sizes of ships is lacking, even though we do have some figures. There were a few fairly large ships plying the South Sea in that period, but many others were small. We know that ships rigged for the Atlantic crossing were modest in size; in fact, most of those on the Indies route were around 150 tons (*toneles*, one tonel equaling 5/6 of a ton), and the largest was no more than 400.[43]

If we read of a ship off the coast of Central America packing aboard as many as four hundred slaves, other reports mention only ten or twelve. How many Indians could be loaded onto a ship of a given size depends on various factors. Without pursuing the subject of ratios of slaves to tonnage with any diligence, it may be of interest to observe that in the seventeenth century the Dutch put as many as six hundred black slaves on a 400-ton slave ship. Those conditions were so cramped (causing a death-rate of 20–30 percent) that improvements were made. However, in the eighteenth century English and French slave ships had a ratio of two slaves per ton.[44] I have seen no comparable figures for Spanish slave ships, but such comparisons would obviously have severe limitations in any case, arguing both sides of the question of the volume of the traffic.

On the one hand it could be said that the vessels off Central America in the sixteenth century were probably not constructed in the same way as later slave ships, with special decks for the express purpose of crowding in every possible body. Most likely they were designed for the transportation of regular passengers and merchandise, with a few exceptions. At the same time, for the relatively short trip from Nicaragua to Panama at least, it would be possible to pack Indians aboard like sardines. Moreover, as MacLeod has suggested to me, it is very likely that many Indians were taken to Panama on badly overcrowded rafts. If, however, we are to consider his estimate of the numbers of slaves shipped out of Nicaragua, and if for purposes of discussion we take 100 slaves as the average cargo, it would require 100 such voyages a year to reach a figure of 10,000, or roughly a total of two hundred thousand slaves for the two decades of the trade.

Now, all this is not beyond the realm of feasibility. It seems possible that the available ships could have conveyed the numbers MacLeod suggests under certain circumstances. But infrequency of voyages casts some doubt on the practicability of it. If ships could navigate between Nicaragua and Panama with relative ease, the voyage to Peru was another matter. In this regard, the findings of James Lockhart are pertinent:

West coast navigation was strongly influenced by the prevailing south wind, which made it nearly impossible to reach Peru from Panama except during the months of January and February. The great basic voyage from Panama (or Nicaragua or Mexico) to Lima and back was therefore undertaken only once a year, though under optimum conditions there would have been time for several voyages. When the winds were right, a ship could reach Piura from Panama in nine or ten days. Ordinarily the trip took longer, and if the ship left too late it could spend three or four months tacking in the wind before getting as far as Manta, Peru's northernmost port, near Puertoviejo. . . . The return voyage from Peru to Panama presented little problem, and could be undertaken at most times of the year, the trip between Lima and Panama, even with frequent stops, lasting usually less than a month.[45]

It would seem probable that the years of heaviest traffic in slaves preceded Contreras, during the Pedrarias and Castañeda periods when violations of the law were widespread. For those years, and indeed up until 1536, Las Casas, who has never been accused of minimizing, gave a total of 52,000 slaves shipped southward, as noted above. But even he referred to only five or six vessels engaged in the slave trade out of Nicaragua for six or seven years between 1523 and 1533. When Pedrarias Dávila moved from Panama to Nicaragua in 1528, the trade quickened. Still, during his years (he died in 1531) there were few ships; in March 1529, only five were trading between Panama and Nicaragua, "making the round trip usually in from fifteen to twenty days in all but the worst weather," according to Professor Woodrow Borah.[46]

Surely those few ships were carrying other important, bulky cargoes besides Indian slaves. After 1530, shipbuilding activity increased substantially, largely as a result of the penetration of Peru. Not only did the men of Pizarro's expedition have to be transported, but by 1532 both Almagro and Alvarado were putting together fleets. Borah adds that "by late 1533 or early 1534 between fifteen and twenty caravels were reported as being engaged exclusively in the slave trade with Panama," but he quite correctly questions the assertion of his source (the chronicler Antonio de Herrera y Tordesillas) that all were caravels, which usually ranged in size from four to fifty tons. Of more than thirty ships sailing the Pacific side by October 1533, Borah states that more than half were involved in the slave trade.[47] Twelve of them, however, belonged to Alvarado and formed part of his armada for Peru, and Almagro was also preparing to go with his own ships.[48] Francisco de Barrionuevo wrote the king three months later that while there were only twenty ships in the South Sea at that time, within a year or eighteen months there would be forty.[49] It is difficult to ascertain if the writer was justified in his optimism, although one reads that in August 1533, there were as many as twenty ships engaged only in the slave trade between Nicaragua and Peru.[50]

Writing a few weeks later from Granada, Las Casas stated that in the previous two years more than twelve thousand Indians had been sent to Peru, and "all are dead," not one surviving. Evidence for this, he stated, was recorded in the royal books, but apparently those registers have not survived. Other Indians had been transported from Nicaragua to Panama in the number of twenty-five thousand, and again, "all are dead." Not a ship left Nicaraguan ports, he maintained, that did not carry more than three hundred Indians, and all perished of thirst and hunger before reaching Peru.[51] Responding to his letter, the Crown ordered that no Spaniard was to take more than one or two legal slaves for service. The governors of Castilla del Oro (Panama) and Peru were advised not to allow Indians from Nicaragua to be landed at their ports.[52]

Yet Lockhart has pointed out that there were more Indians from Nicaragua in early Peru than from any other foreign source: "In a sampling of documents dated from 1531 to 1543, over two-thirds of the Indians were from Nicaragua, with the rest divided quite evenly between Mexico and Guatemala."[53] Given the proximity of Panama to Nicaragua, and the demand for Indians, one would expect to find large numbers of them on the isthmus. But despite the depopulation of the area because of the exodus to Peru, an official wrote in 1534 that there were so few Indians to go around that not only was no gold being taken out, but that there were barely enough of them to raise corn.[54]

According to an early settler, the original population of Nicaragua had been diminished by up to four-fifths as a result of mistreatment. More than a third of the Indians, though free men, had been enslaved, branded, and sent out of Nicaragua, which was, he said, the same as a death sentence. He was of the opinion that not one-twentieth of those taken to Panama and Peru survived. One ship left with 400 Indians, and before the voyage ended not 50 remained alive.[55] Indian slaves could be purchased in Nicaragua for very little, it is true; but one marvels that if almost all the slaves died before reaching markets the avaricious slave merchants would continue to suffer such intolerable losses year after year.

There are reports of a catastrophic population decline that would tend to support the probability of a very high volume of slave traffic southward. Licenciado Diego de Herrera noted that of the six hundred thousand inhabitants of Nicaragua at Spanish contact only thirty thousand remained.[56] Herrera had that high original count by hearsay, since he was not present at the time of the conquest. Moreover, after he took the residencia of Governor Contreras there was enmity between the two, and perhaps he exaggerated the loss of life to the discredit of the Contreras administration. Las Casas, who also stressed the drastic decline in population, had trouble with the governor that ended with his being forcibly removed from the pulpit in Nicaragua by the criados of Contreras.[57]

Those two accounts notwithstanding, it is curious that we have seen such low numbers given by officials on the spot in Nicaragua who were so critical of the slave traffic. The highest figure referred to here previously was the 3,000 licenses allegedly given out by Pedrarias, but others cited speak in terms of hundreds or less. And how is it that Alonso López de Cerrato, the great enemy of Indian slavery, and the one who finally abolished it in Central America, reported in 1548 only that "more than 6,000" Indians had been shipped out, a figure which was enough to shock him?

Barrionuevo's estimate that there would be forty ships available by 1535 may well have been accurate in light of the assertion of Francisco Sánchez that there were twenty ships involved exclusively in the slave trade by that year. I have seen no evidence that directly refutes that claim, although there are reasons to question it. The early 1530s were busy years for shipping, not only because of the Pizarro force, including groups that joined him from Nicaragua, but also because of vessels of Almagro (three in 1533) and the twelve of the Alvarado fleet, which altogether tied up many ships for nonslave traffic, or at least quite limited the numbers of Indians they could carry.[58] Alvarado was accused of taking large numbers (four thousand), although the actual count was probably about one thousand—and that was for his twelve ships.

One wonders if most of those ships could use much of the valuable space for Indian slaves, because aside from the Spaniards and all of their supplies, armor, weapons, and other equipment, they also took many horses and black slaves. Alvarado once claimed that he had 260 cavalrymen (although he apparently took fewer), and their animals, together with their fodder and water, would have taken up a good amount of space.[59] Furthermore, merchants were eager to transport horses to Peru because of the great profits to be made: at that time a horse in Peru was worth 1,000 to 1,300 pesos, and a "good" black slave brought 100 to 130 pesos.[60] What an Indian slave from Central America sold for in Peru at that time I cannot say; but when an unskilled Indian could be purchased for as little as 5 or 6 pesos in Central America, it is not likely that he brought a very high price in the south, and it must be asked if the profit margin really made him the most sought after cargo for merchants.[61]

Other goods such as the necessary casks of wine, oil, wax, paper, clothing, preserves, livestock, and countless other items of trade surely took up considerable space on the ships. Soon Spaniards' families, along with bureaucrats and men of the church, sailed for the new provinces. Could all those have been accommodated and still allow room for great numbers of Indian slaves?

No doubt many more ships were built in the years following 1535,[62] although there was apparently a lessening demand for space for merchandise inasmuch as one official reported in October, 1536, that Peru was full of goods, prices were low, and trade had slackened.[63] That would indicate more ships available for the slave trade. Thus, it would appear that the following conclusions should be considered: (1) Between 1526 and 1532 the Indian slave trade to the south was limited by the small number of ships, and (2) from 1532 to 1536 heavy demands for space resulting from the conquest and settlement of Peru must have limited the slave trade.

MacLeod is of the opinion that the slave trade was at its height between 1536 and 1540,[64] which is logical enough if more shipping was freed from other supply pressures. Nevertheless, although Governor Contreras and his friends were certainly involved in the slave trade, there seems to be no evidence that it was heavier than before. Enemies of Contreras and his lieutenants had ample opportunity to charge them with illegal slaving activity, but large numbers are not referred to in the residencias.

If we have a paucity of information on the number of ships in the South Sea in the decade after 1535, we are equally uninformed on the sizes of the vessels. Probably there were rafts and other very small craft negotiating between Nicaragua and Panama, and even some caravels were as small as 4 tons. Probably the largest ship along the coast in the 1530s was 300 tons, and there were several others half that size. We hear of one launched in Nicaragua in 1544 that carried ninety horses.[65] On the face of it, that report appears to be more sixteenth-century hyperbole. Fernand Braudel informs us that "the transport of horses required a tonnage of at least 20 tons per horse."[66] Thus our Spanish informant asks us to believe that there sailed along the coast of Central America in 1544 the spectacle of an 1,800-ton vessel.

However, it appears likely that the ratio to which Braudel refers did not apply to the Indies, according to information at hand. As early as 1532 it is stated that Almagro had a ship, "the largest that has been built in this sea," that could carry forty horses, and the same writer noted over a year later that Almagro's *capitana* was only 150 tons.[67] At the same time, he reported that Alvarado's capitana was 300 tons; and another official asserted a few months later that one of Alvarado's ships (presumably the same flagship) could transport fifty horses.[68] He added that, in January, 1534, of the twenty ships then in the South Sea there were six or seven capable of carrying fifty horses. Since the largest ship was apparently 300 tons, we have a ratio of one horse for every six tons at the most. Therefore the ship of 1544 could have been 540 tons, which was still very large for the time; and in all probability it was smaller, more like 400 tons. If Almagro's 150-ton ship could take forty horses, and if we assume that some of the six or seven ships mentioned as being able to carry fifty horses in 1534 were no larger than 300 tons, then it is difficult to establish a customary ratio.

We do have more specific information regarding some of the ships of the time. In 1532 Alvarado had eight vessels: one of 300 tons, another of 160, two of 150, a caravel of 60 tons, a *patache* of 50, and two smaller caravels.[69] The following year he had ten ships, but two were lost along the Guatemalan coast, only to be replaced by two he seized in Realejo. By January 1534, he was ready to leave for Peru with twelve ships, eight of which were over 100 tons, the smallest 40.[70] About the same time, Almagro had, in addition to his 150-ton ship, two small vessels of 40 and 50 tons each.[71] In 1538, Alvarado owned five ships: two *navíos*, a small brigantine, and two galleons then in a shipyard.[72] In November of the following year he added to his holdings; he had completed the formation of his armada for the Spice Islands and the conquest of "China," and he was ready to sail with fourteen vessels: twelve large galleons and *naos*, a galiot ("de veinte bancos"), and a brigantine of thirteen *bancos*.[73]

A report of 1545 showed that the treasurer in Nicaragua, Pedro de los Ríos, who had been involved in the slave trade, owned three large ships.[74] Specialized research on the subject would turn up more information, but even from the sketchy details presented here it is clear that a large percentage of the naval tonnage of the 1530s was tied up by Alvarado, for whom the slave trade was a minor operation.

Finally, even if the ships were available to carry the great numbers of Indian slaves that some have suggested, were large groups of slaves readily available for loading most of the time? Were there large slave raids unknown to us? I am inclined to think that the records of the more notorious expeditions have come down to us through one account or another. Certainly there were "rancherías" that were little more than minor slaving parties, and no doubt there were many unrecorded instances in which a few Indians were seized. But all leaders had enemies who were eager enough to accuse them in writing if the opportunity arose, as it almost always did. And, Las Casas aside, where is there attributed to any conqueror in Central America enslavement on the scale comparable to the alleged fifty thousand Indians taken out of Yucatán by Montejo and his followers? It is possible of course that additional accounts have been destroyed or lie buried in some obscure *legajo*.

Despite the great numbers supposedly taken to Panama, when the slaves were freed there in 1550, only 821 were brought forward. Of those, 158 were from Nicaragua, 18 from Guatemala, 5 from Honduras, 2 from Veragua, and 2 from Realejo.[75] It is true that the life of a slave in Panama was short, but it is odd nevertheless that of the very large total suggested (apparently in excess of 150,000 for Panama alone), only 185 Central American Indians survived to be liberated at mid-century.

In our age of technology we often lose sight of the fact that sixteenth-century Spaniards were very loose with figures, and our mistake so often has been to take them literally. Las Casas is frequently singled out for greatly inflating numbers, but that is because he is the best known of the writers on the subject of Indian treatment. However, he was by no means alone, and many Spaniards of the time, in various capacities, resorted to hyperbole for their own reasons.[76] At the same time, understatement was uncommon, which makes lower counts appear more reliable.

A great many slaves were taken for export, while others were used in

Central America, enough so that some shipmasters and traders became men of substance. Scholars will occupy themselves with the dimensions of Indian slavery in years to come, and perhaps they will offer more complete answers. It is perhaps incumbent upon one who spends years studying the subject to go beyond merely taking issue with the conclusions of others and to risk an estimate of his own. On the basis of documentation now brought to light, I would be surprised if the total number of chattel slaves made in all of Central America between 1524 and 1549 surpassed a hundred and fifty thousand, no more than a third of whom were shipped out to other lands. As in Mexico, the percentage of Indians who were truly slaves was relatively small.[77] The number forced into labor under circumstances often little better than slavery is, however, another matter.

PART II

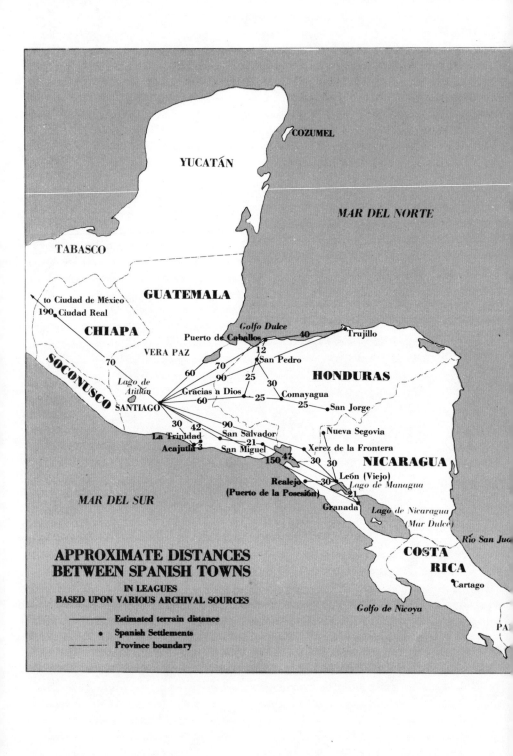

COZUMEL

YUCATÁN

MAR DEL NORTE

TABASCO

to Ciudad de México
190 Ciudad Real

GUATEMALA

CHIAPA

VERA PAZ

Golfo Dulce

Puerto de Caballos   40   Trujillo

12

70

70   San Pedro

60   90   25   30

SOCONUSCO

Lago de
Atitlán

Gracias a Dios   60   25

HONDURAS

Comayagua

25

San Jorge

SANTIAGO

30   42   90

La Trinidad   San Salvador   Nueva Segovia

21

Acajutla 3   San Miguel   Xerez de la Frontera

150 47   30   30

NICARAGUA

Realejo   30   León (Viejo)

(Puerto de la Posesión)   Lago de Managua

21

Granada   Lago de Nicaragua

(Mar Dulce)

MAR DEL SUR

Río San Juan

COSTA
RICA

Cartago

Golfo de Nicoya

PA

APPROXIMATE DISTANCES
BETWEEN SPANISH TOWNS
IN LEAGUES
BASED UPON VARIOUS ARCHIVAL SOURCES

——— Estimated terrain distance
• Spanish Settlements
----- Province boundary

7
Personal Service:
Forced Tributary Labor, 1524–49

FROM THE CONQUEST UP TO MID-CENTURY, most native labor fell either
under the category of legal slavery or what was called personal service.
Despite the large numbers of slaves made, the majority of the Indians
were considered free vassals of the Spanish crown. It is true enough that
their conditions were often little better than those of chattel slaves, but it
is careless inference on the part of some writers that the Indians were
actually enslaved *en masse*. The distinction is that while the chattel slave
was in the legal sense a piece of property which could be bought and
sold—and could be used much as the owner wished—a free vassal belonged to no man, even though, if he was part of an encomienda grant, he
came under the jurisdiction of an encomendero.

Generally speaking, the forms of labor to which the conquered peoples
were subjected were adaptations of Indian forms that already existed.
Alonso de Zorita, a judge who spent many years in Mexico and Central
America, commented on prehispanic practices as follows:

> Personal service (provision of water, fuel, and domestic service) was assigned or
> apportioned for each day among the ruler's towns and their barrios in such a way
> that each individual had to go only twice a year at most, and, . . . those who went
> twice were those who lived nearby. Such individuals also paid a somewhat lighter
> tribute than others. Sometimes a whole town would bring the portion of fuel that
> was its share at one time, especially if the people lived a fair distance away from the
> ruler's residence. However, most household work was done by slaves, of whom
> the lords had a great number.[1]

Indians under the Spanish encomienda system, which is to say most of
those within the pale of Spanish administration—either under the control
of an individual Spaniard or in a royal encomienda (crown town)—were
obligated to contribute labor without compensation, along with the payment of tributes. Accordingly, Indians entrusted to encomenderos were
exploited for all kinds of labor, sometimes under the direction of the

encomendero himself, but more often answering to the overseer—the *calpixque* (or *calpisque*), as he was commonly called. Calpixques existed in preconquest Indian societies as tribute collectors, and the designation continued under the Spaniards for the same function, having in addition the responsibility of managing other financial concerns of the encomendero. The difference was that Spaniards seldom used Indians as calpixques in Central America; sometimes they were Spaniards, but later many were mestizos, blacks, or mulattoes. In the case of a crown town, it was the royal agent, eventually a *corregidor,* who saw to the king's tribute and labor interests.

Personal service began very early in the New World, as Simpson explains:

> Its first adumbration was a position of Columbus to the Crown begging that the colonists be permitted to use the labor of the natives for a year or two until the colony should be able to support itself. He had, indeed, already invoked the same principle, after the rebellion of 1494, when in some cases he commuted into personal service the tribute laid upon the native towns. . . . In the allotment of the lands of Española to the Spaniards Columbus permitted them to compel the cacique and the people of each plot to work it for the owners' benefit.[2]

Although one generally associates tribute with the encomienda system more than labor, the latter was often the more important contribution of Indians, despite some attempts to limit the labor aspect. By 1523, Cortés had instituted the use of personal service in New Spain, with specific regulations:

> The Indians were to work for twenty days; their working hours were from sunrise until one hour before sunset with an hour at noon for rest, and while employed they were to be fed. After working twenty days they were not to be called upon again for another thirty days. In return for a year's work the Indians were paid one-half peso.[3]

On December 4, 1518, the Crown issued instructions to restrict the personal service of Indians: encomienda Indians were not to be used to carry loads, for work in the mines, or for the construction of houses. Furthermore, they were not to be taken from their fields during planting and cultivating seasons.[4] While the use of Indian labor by individual encomenderos may have been limited by those laws, other Indians were pressed into service. Gibson notes:

> In the corregimientos of the 1530's and after, labor provisions were specified in tribute regulations. The early church, by persuading and influencing the caciques, employed Indian workers in the construction of ecclesiastical buildings and in other *servicios personales.* In Tenochtitlan and Tlatelolco the first Spanish tribute

exactions consisted almost wholly of demands for labor, with service to the viceroy, the construction of canals, and other tasks contributing to the maintenance of the colonial capital.[5]

In the strict sense, if we accept Fr. Miguel Agia's distinction below, labor contributed for the good of the community at large was not truly personal service. Not that it made much difference to the Indians involved, but such work did not benefit any particular individual personally, but rather all the vecinos collectively.

There is good indication that by the 1530s the Crown was still pursuing a wavering position on the matter of personal service. Walter Scholes points out that the

instructions of Antonio de Mendoza given on April 25, 1535, showed a shift away from the idea of the free Indian toward one favoring personal service. Mendoza was ordered to take a census of the land and to discover how much tribute the Indians were paying and if they could pay more. They were not allowed to pay tribute in kind. The instructions continued that if the Indians could not pay tribute in money they should then be allowed to work out, voluntarily, the amount of assessment. Since most of the Indians had no money, this put the tribute system on the basis of personal service.[6]

In some provinces the land yielded little in the way of valuable tribute, and in such instances the income to the encomendero consisted almost entirely of labor, which came to be substituted for tribute. In other regions—cacao-producing lands for example—the fruits of the land were valued so highly that Indians were likely to be assessed a high tribute in that product, and they spent most of their time growing cacao, which was more profitable for the encomendero than almost any other kind of occupation.

Fundamental to Crown Indian policy was the conviction that the conquered peoples should be kept busy. Idleness, it was believed, would lead them into lives of sloth and vice; but, more importantly, their labor was needed for sustenance of the empire. Moreover, the Crown view of the natives as moral delinquents in need of close supervision inevitably led to a policy of paternalism characterized by regimentation. It was a system to which the Church subscribed, for only under such an arrangement, in their view, could the natives be properly indoctrinated. On the whole, the plan, as conceived, was not unreasonable, although in operation it opened the way for a multitude of abuses, despite royal and local legislation intended to thwart the unjust exploitation of the natives.

The concept of personal service has been little understood, and even those authorities of the encomienda and labor systems do not always clarify the term.[7] While references to it abound, it is rare that anyone

88   FORCED NATIVE LABOR

explains exactly what constituted personal service. It does not denote, as
the term infers, a personal servant, at least not in the sense of a valet, even
though an Indian contributing personal service could serve in that capacity. Those who gave personal service were involved in almost every kind of
work imaginable for the time and place. Generally, their tasks fell under
one of the following categories:

a) Service for agriculture, stock-raising, mining, and industry;
b) Service in construction, consisting of the building and repair of residences for the encomendero and others who worked for him; the
   construction of stables and corrals; or any other kind of similar work,
   such as the building of a dam or a road. In addition to their labor, the
   Indians were frequently required to supply part of the materials,
   such as lumber or lime;
c) The transporting of merchandise and personal effects, as well as anything else that had to be carried from one place to another. These
   porters were called tamemes, a special class of workers who are given
   separate treatment in this chapter.
d) Domestic service in Spanish households for the encomendero as well as
   the calpixque. Appropriately, much of this service consisted of Indian women for cooking and care of the houses.[8]

Although those categories cover most of the labor given under personal
service, Indians were required to perform whatever task assigned to them
by the encomendero or his administrator.

It is not surprising that the term is nebulous today, considering that
clear distinctions were not always made at the time. Fr. Miguel Agia, who
spent several years in Guatemala in the late sixteenth century, notes the
confusion between personal service and repartimiento labor, a misunderstanding that will be dealt with later in these pages. For the moment,
suffice it to say that such forced service was called *personal* because it was
for the personal benefit of the encomendero, as opposed to the good of the
community at large. It had been, according to Agia, a custom since early
years in the Antilles. The source became a system of virtual enslavement,
notwithstanding orders against it from Queen Isabella after she received
notice of the abuses from the first governors, including Columbus (referred to by Agia as "cierto almirante"). She ruled that in no case was personal service to be allowed, an order repeated by Charles V in June
1523 to Cortés.[9]

In a 1529 cédula for New Spain, the emperor stated that Indians should
be, by law and reason, completely free and not obligated to give personal
service, but only to pay tribute.[10] Over the years similar orders were

given, with little apparent effect, and in Central America encomenderos took personal service for granted.

Compulsory labor without pay was seen as necessary because there was always a short supply of workers. Lesley B. Simpson writes:

> In reality the encomienda, at least in the first fifty years of its existence, was looked upon by its beneficiaries as a subterfuge for slavery, and it was only after half a century of furious agitation on the part of las Casas and the reformers, and the active interest of the Crown in suppressing it, that it was shorn of its most profitable and harmful feature, the privilege of using the services of the Indians, and was reduced to some semblance of a social system. Indeed, the metamorphosis of the encomienda, which achieved lasting notoriety for its shocking waste of labor, into a kind of benevolent paternalism is one of the most curious phenomenon of colonial history.[11]

Apparently coming to regard this obligatory labor as a necessary evil, the Crown sought nevertheless to ameliorate the system and to regulate it. Although Indians had no choice but to work, royal policy tried, without success, to see that they were paid.[12] For a while, during the 1530s, some officials in Honduras and Guatemala sought to implement royal wishes on this matter but were only sporadically effective.[13]

Particularly in those areas where there was little valuable tribute to be given, encomenderos increasingly came to regard forced labor of their Indians as a substitute for tribute. Indians in Honduras often had meager offerings, but since that province had many mines, encomenderos were inclined to prefer the labor of the natives in the mines to the tributes. Mining was such fatiguing labor, however, that the bishop of Honduras implored the Crown to order that no other assessment be made with regard to labor than the requirement that the Indians serve one month on the farms of the encomendero, to be followed by a free month, during which time they could work their own plots. This rotation, which the natives called "lunas," would give the workers some relief so that they could bear the arrangement.

The problem, as Bishop Pedraza saw it, was in the nature of the tribute assessments. These obligations, in many of the provinces, were so high that Indians often could not meet them, as a result of which they had to contribute their labor to make up the difference. As Protector of the Indians in Honduras, Pedraza took it upon himself to reassess the tributes personally, so that the president of the audiencia and his judges "would not have to strain themselves, and so that they could stay home in the shade and play cards and ball games all day." The judges had previously delegated the responsibility of the tribute assessment to parish priests; but since the priests owed their positions to the town councils, the regidores ordered them around "like Negroes," and the priests did what they were told, under penalty of being thrown out of the towns forthwith. If the king would agree to the bishop's making reassessments of tribute, he could do it satisfactorily with two priests or friars, without the judges of the audiencia having a thing to do with it. He asked the Crown to order that this be the only assessment, and that the labor provision be the system of lunas. Pedraza was of the opinion that personal service should be against the law, since that was the opinion of all the theologians. If it had to exist, he said, at least the abuses could be curtailed.[14]

At the same time, the bishop realistically was aware of the labor shortage, noting that there was not even an Indian to carry a cask of water nor a container of mortar. If both menial and skilled labor had to be performed by Spanish workers, all the gold in the mines would not suffice to pay the costs, he said, because a maestro made no less than two pesos daily, and apprentices earned one peso a day. Even hod carriers made a gold ducat for a day's work. His solution was to make the modest request for half a dozen black slaves to relieve the labor shortage, adding that after their work for the vecinos was done, they could revert to the Crown for sale. The royal treasury would profit from these "bozales," (unacculturated blacks) because the good workers would learn trades, such as masonry and carpentry, so that their sale price would be double what the Crown would pay for them originally.

Furthermore, since there were no men available to hire for public works, as bricklayers or any other work, he asked the king to allow the use of Indians in pueblos near Trujillo to make mortar and to carry it, along with other necessary tasks, as they had done formerly. This could be done, he suggested, on a voluntary basis, so that those Indians who wished could work on free days when they were not occupied by their encomenderos. On such days the encomenderos should not detain them or keep them busy with other matters, and if they did, they should be punished. In that way, many Indians would be helped with the wages they earned, and they would learn something of the trades of construction. It would not only be advantageous for the city, and profitable for the workers, but it would also be edifying for their souls. Working one month for the encomendero and the next month for themselves should make everyone involved satisfied. Finally, he wrote that encomenderos should not interfere with Indians working on the church, since they were free men.[15]

While it was never seriously suggested that the Spanish conquerors and other early colonists work with their hands, the idea of using laborers from Spain was not completely overlooked. At least as early as 1531, a friar conducted thirty married farmers to Honduras, with the understanding that they were to be given land and were to be well treated.[16] There were other such experiments, none of which was very successful. In 1540, Pedraza tried to relieve the Indians from their burdens by contracting for 165 blacks, who were apportioned to three Spanish settlements in Honduras. Although there were perhaps between fifteen hundred and two thousand blacks in Honduras-Higueras by 1545, their numbers in Central America were never sufficient to meet the demand.[17]

The first Indians to serve Spaniards in Central America arrived with the conquistadores from other regions. Both slave and free, they acted as personal servants, carrying their masters' food, clothing, and equipment. They tended to all the needs of the Spaniards, suffering the same hardships, and occasionally dying from one thing or another. Some of them were accidentally killed in battle. Others were active combatants known as "amigos," and they were sometimes given preferential treatment once hostilities ended.[18] Those who survived tended to remain with their *amos* (masters) in one capacity or another. Shortly following the conquest, the native villages of Central America were divided among the Spaniards in encomienda, and a large labor force was created from among the vanquished.

Since Indians performed almost all the labor in the provinces, the scope of their activities was broad. The majority of the Indian commoners (maceguales) were unskilled, but almost immediately Spanish artisans began to train native apprentices in the various trades necessary to create communities as nearly Spanish as feasible. An indication of the training can be seen in tribute lists showing Indians' occupations. One such register reveals that while most of the tributaries had no specialization, others were identified as carpenters, potters, salt-makers, mat-makers, sawyers, brick- and tile-makers, lime-makers, blacksmiths, cooks, fishermen, sacristans, swineherds, merchants and traders, apprentice teachers in the Church (*teupantlacas*), as well as various kinds of officials.[19] This is by no means a complete list of the various trades learned by Indians, but it is evidence of the development of skilled native labor over the years.

In addition to paying tribute and laboring for their encomenderos, Indians also had to support themselves and their families. Tribute assessments show that most Indians had their own private plots, or *milpas*, for the planting of maize, chile, beans, and other staple food crops. Many of them maintained beehives for their production of honey. A number of them raised chickens, which were highly valued by the natives.[20] In order to assure their own welfare, Indians were required by Spanish law to maintain their huts and milpas for their food under penalty of 100 lashes.

On many occasions, however, maceguales were kept from their villages, working for the Spaniards so much that they did not have time to tend properly their own plantings, their crops failing as a consequence. A further burden was the requirement to contribute labor for the community fields, as well as to furnish a certain amount of one commodity or another for the common storehouse, both for purposes of village tribute and for security against crop failure.

Such procedures were close enough to Indian custom to constitute no great problem in themselves. It was the additional responsibility of cultivating Spanish fields, or performing other work for the conquerors, that made their schedules onerous. Food had to be supplied for the Spanish towns, and some agricultural crops would eventually be grown for export. Although the greatest profits were taken from the mines, agriculture often paid good returns. While the encomendero of Huehuetenango made 8,700 pesos in a year from the slaves working mines, the town also gave him two hundred to three hundred other "indios de servicio" who hauled ore and wood for the mines, as well as women who prepared food. Those who tilled his fields and tended his swine produced an extra 3,000 pesos for the encomendero.[21]

A president of the audiencia noted that there were three basic types of work for the Indians in Guatemala: 1) cultivating Spaniards' fields, 2) public works projects, i.e., primarily construction, and 3) *servicio ordinario*—the many routine, often daily, tasks such as household work, cooking meals, making bread, hauling water, supplying firewood, carrying fodder for beasts, and grooming horses, to mention only a few.[22]

As more Spaniards entered Central America there was increasing demand for a more European diet, which meant the growing of wheat for bread to supplement the Indian corn tortilla and cassava cakes. Toward that end, Spaniards were allowed to use Indians in wheat fields, plowing with oxen. That concession to the Spaniards was abused when laborers were made to clear the land and gather the wheat in addition to the plowing, all of which took so much of their time during the year that they had to neglect their own milpas.[23]

There were certain tasks that Indians could perform for the Spaniards in their own homes, principally the weaving of cloth by women. Most labor, however, required the Indians to leave their homes, often for extended periods. A royal order of 1531 prohibiting Spaniards to obligate the natives to leave their villages for work notwithstanding, the law was neither practical nor enforceable.[24] Some of the Indians were required to travel a hundred miles or more to work, carrying their own food, as well as loads of tribute for their masters. Apart from those who dropped from exhaustion, many starved because their food was consumed before they arrived at their destination.[25]

Although the second half of the sixteenth century would see a wider variety of crops grown for export, the first quarter century of settlement, 1524–49, found Spaniards more preoccupied with endeavors that had possibilities of quicker wealth—that is, primarily, the Indian slave trade and mining ventures. But, aside from subsistence crops for local consumption, there was some attempt to capitalize on European demands for sugar.

While sugar plantations never were as important in Central America as in other parts of the Indies, there were a few in operation, and of course the labor was supplied by Indians, supplemented by a few blacks. In Chiapas the encomendero Baltasar Guerra held a fertile site called La Vega, where he had built a large sugar plantation, with more than two hundred Indian laborers. Those workers, according to Remesal, were very unjustly enslaved, although among the deceits Guerra first related to the padres was that all the Indians had been liberated. Work on the plantation was so strenuous that many maceguales died, and it was feared by some that all of them would succumb to fatigue. For their labors, the chronicler added, the Indians were paid about one-hundredth of what they deserved.[26]

Alonso López de Cerrato observed that in Chiapas there was a "tyranny" of the sugar planters, to whom encomenderos rented their pueblo Indians. That labor, he claimed, was much worse than even that of the mines, indeed so bad that one sugar plantation was enough to kill two thousand Indians a year.[27] Perhaps unaware of the dangers presented to the native laborers, the humanitarian bishop of Honduras tried to promote the planting of sugar in 1547. He told the Crown of a large, fertile valley six leagues from Trujillo where there were rivers and where many types of plants grew. Because of the favorable conditions, he said that it would be wise to plant cane, especially since some that had been cultivated grew to a very large size.[28]

And even Cerrato was not resolutely opposed to sugar plantations; he wrote the Crown that after an order was given for loans from the royal treasury to a vecino of San Pedro for the purpose of constructing a sugar mill, some other vecinos of Santiago had approached him to inquire if the Crown would lend them money for the same purpose. He answered that he had no commission for granting such loans himself, but that he would look into the matter. Then Cerrato, who a few months before had written of the disastrous effects of the sugar plantations in Chiapas, encouraged its production in Guatemala by telling the Crown that there was good disposition for such an enterprise, particularly since he had ordered the opening of a road to the Caribbean port. He assured the king that he would recommend a reliable person—but he added nothing about his concern for the welfare of the Indian laborers who would have to work plantations.[29] Perhaps both Cerrato and the bishop of Honduras were of the opinion that the work was harmful only if the maceguales were worked to the point of exhaustion, and that a moderate policy would not be excessively harmful.

The growing of sugar was a profitable operation under the right circumstances, and a successful planter could become rich. But it required considerable capital outlay. The chronicler Oviedo, writing of plantations in Española, mentions the various buildings necessary, along with a minimum of 80 to 120 black laborers. He omits mentioning that with Indian labor more workers would be required. In addition, Oviedo added, there were the expenses involved in maintaining the 1,000 to 2,000 head of cattle, which were used to haul the logs for the almost constantly burning fires, to pull carts, and sometimes to power the mills. Carts were expensive, and the processing of the sugar was a long, arduous operation. All of this, he said, could cost up to 15,000 gold ducats just to get started.[30]

When slaves were taken away from a Spaniard in Chiapas, he complained that he was not able to complete the sugar operation he had started, and he requested a loan from the Crown of 3,000 pesos for a period of four years. The loan was authorized, with the provision that it be a water-powered mill, not a "trapiche," that is, a mill powered by animals or men. The other stipulation was that the Spaniard was to be prepared to invest a total of at least 6,000 ducats.[31]

Because of the capital necessary to start a sugar operation, the labor problems, uncertain transportation for the exporting of the yield, and competition from other parts of the Indies, sugar did not become an important industry.

Much of the native labor prior to mid-century was devoted to building construction. One of the first concerns of the new masters of the land was to erect suitable living quarters, since they had little desire to stay long in native huts. The first crude residences for shelter were later replaced to show neighbors the standing and dignity of the owners by raising impressive *casas solariegas*. Those prominent conquistadores and high officials who could afford them wanted large, fortress-like homes worthy of *magníficos* of the Indies, within whose walls the large numbers of *paniaguados*, relatives, friends, and sycophants could reside at the pleasure of the lord of the house, all of which was a sign of his munificence. Even more than in our own society, such a stately pile was a status symbol richly to be desired.

Following the pacification of a region, the town corporation was formed with elected officials whose responsibilities included that of seeing the community settled. Thus, after some apparent laxity on the part of un-committed vecinos, on March 23, 1528, the cabildo of Santiago ordered all who held Indians in encomienda to have their workers begin construc-tion of houses on the Spaniards' lots. Within three days of notice they were to commence building the required walls around the houses and having the streets in front of them cleaned. Those who did not comply were to lose their lots as well as their Indians, and they would be fined fifty castellanos in addition.[32] Still, it appears that most needed little prod-ding, for Remesal writes that the Spaniards were in such a hurry to have their houses that they did not even allow the natives to rest on days of fiesta. The cabildo ultimately ruled, in 1534, that since some encom-enderos made their Indians work on Sundays, against the rule of the Church, offending Spaniards would be fined three pesos de oro for each Sunday that Indians were used to work on any building. The same ap-plied to illegal use of Indians during general fiestas.[33]

No less important in the eyes of officials was the need for public edifices in which to house the cabildo and other offices, while men of the Church wanted houses of worship and monasteries for contemplation. In order to muster all possible workmen, the regidores of Santiago proposed using Tlaxcalan and Cholulan allies, who had only recently fought under Al-varado during the conquest, for public-works projects. For the moment at least, the Crown honored its concession to the "amigos" from Mexico and rejected the proposal.[34] By 1538 the Crown had ordered monasteries built in Indian pueblos, or in the vicinities, and Indians not belonging to an encomienda were obligated later to contribute one-third of the cost of the building of a cathedral in Guatemala.[35] Over the years, large numbers of Indians would contribute labor for the building of striking churches and monasteries, often against their will, and usually without pay.

Subsequent to the calamitous deluge of 1541 that destroyed the Spanish capital at Santiago (now Ciudad Vieja), the colonists moved nearby to settle another capital, also to be called Santiago (now Antigua). The new site would itself be greatly damaged during a great earthquake in the eighteenth century, causing removal to present-day Guatemala City, but the magnificent ruins that still stand in the romantic city of Antigua attest to the great labor and consummate skill that went into its building.[36]

Moving to that site, the third Santiago in Guatemala, called for considerable regimentation of native labor for the construction of the new capital. Once again town lots were apportioned to the deserving, while plans were drawn for government and religious structures, and the commons laid out. According to one authority, "every month the Cakchiquels of the dependence of the Ahpozotzil [King] were compelled to furnish 1000 laborers of both sexes to aid the prisoners of war in the building of the city," and the audiencia and viceroy of New Spain sent word that Indians from the estate of the late adelantado Pedro de Alvarado were to take part in the construction.[37]

Fearing the threat of rootless adventurers, and feeling the need to give more stability to the colonies, the Crown decreed that good, permanent buildings be erected. At the same time, its restrictive policy regarding Indian labor inhibited the achievement of that aim. Royal cédulas prohibited the assessment of encomienda tribute in tamemes, or burden bearers, forbade Indians to cut lumber, and disallowed the hiring of those from encomienda villages.

As one example, the regidores of San Salvador complained that with such provisions it was impossible to proceed with plans for their new town. Inasmuch as the old location of San Salvador was poor, they were starting to rebuild at a more satisfactory site. Their plans were frustrated, however, because there were no Spanish maestros, artisans skilled in construction, nor were there available the necessary materials to which they were accustomed in Spain. Furthermore, they were eighty leagues from the port where they might expect to find the building materials, and without pack trains there was no recourse but to use Indian carriers. And how were they to build if the Indians could not even be used to cut lumber? Nor could Indians be hired for other kinds of labor, and there were no slaves, either Indians or blacks—or in case some could be found, they were occupied in the gold and silver mines, so that to divert them from their mining would mean the diminution of Crown revenues. Many of the Spaniards, according to the regidores of San Salvador, were pleased with the new site and had already begun to build their houses, using native laborers who were compensated, all under the supervision of officials who could prevent abuses.

One problem was that the encomiendas consisted of few Indians, and even the encomenderos had insufficient labor. If the building stopped, even the married vecinos might have to leave, and the town would be abandoned. The cabildo members, who wanted to be free to hire Indians, who could in turn use the wages to pay their tributes, implored the Council of the Indies to revoke the cédulas so that solid houses could be constructed.[38] The demands of construction labor were in almost constant conflict with the Crown attempting to ameliorate the conditions of the Indians, and the case cited above is only one of many similar controversies.

During the invasion and pacification of Central America optimism ran high over the prospect of discovering deposits of precious metals. Prior to that time the quantities of gold and silver found in the Indies had been disappointingly small, as a result of which sanguine reports of wealth to the south of Mexico added stimulus to the expanded conquest. Earth deposits and auriferous streams were fruitful enough to sustain interest in the search for many years, and for the first two decades it appeared that Central America was Spain's best hope for mineral wealth. Consequently, for a score of years the new provinces acquired considerable status in the estimation of the Crown, owing not only to the mining potential, but also to early estimates that equated the population with that of Mexico, which appeared to insure the labor with which to exploit the mines.

Then, within a short, dramatic period, the great silver strikes in Peru and Mexico during the 1540s relegated the district of the Audiencia de los Confines to a position of relative neglect. Even before then, during the 1530s, a number of Central American conquistadores, disappointed with their slight rewards and despairing of the promise, packed up and joined the company of Pizarro. After the strike at Potosí in 1545, they swarmed southward. At least for some Spaniards, however, Central America had mineral wealth sufficient to offer entrepreneurs modest fortunes, and mining continued to be profitable throughout the sixteenth century. The familiar lament that ran over the decades was that mines could not be worked properly because of the shortage of labor.

So eager were the Spaniards to keep the natives mining that grave problems resulted.[39] It was brought to the attention of the Crown prior to 1530 by Francisco Marroquín, the first bishop of Guatemala, that Indians of the highlands working the mines found it very difficult, as well as perilous, during the rainy season. In his opinion, they should labor in the mines during the dry months only—that is, November through March —because, quite aside from the dangers, when the rains began in April it was also time for the Indians to plant their crops, at which season they should be in their villages. The Crown agreed and so ordered.[40]

Overworked Indians in Honduras (Gilotepeque and three other towns) took matters into their own hands in the spring of 1531 by rebelling against the harsh labor in the mines, mounting one revolt which resulted in the deaths of five Spaniards.[41] Yet, the Spaniards could usually contain the natives, and though the threat of rebellion continued, the profits seemed to justify the risk. Francisco de Montejo informed Spain in 1537 that 50,000 pesos de oro had been mined in Honduras, a sum no doubt sufficient to affect royal Indian labor policies.[42] Chamberlain points out that Montejo opposed forced labor in mining, believing that only legally enslaved Indians should be used, or those who voluntarily worked for pay. The arrival of Cristóbal de Pedraza as Protector of the Indians in 1538 added a strong voice for the Indian cause, but neither he nor Montejo was greatly successful in checking excesses.[43]

Although silver and gold in Honduras offered the best mining prospects, gold was being found in limited quantities in other areas. At least by 1531, ore was being taken out in Nicaragua, and officials wrote with enthusiasm that they were discovering promising new mines with frequency.[44] Hoping to spur settlers on to more strikes, the queen authorized officials in Guatemala to offer a reward of a hundred pesos to anyone discovering a new mine.[45]

Intolerable conditions for Indian miners in Nicaragua caused them to rise up. After some Spaniards had been killed, the rebels, led by some of their caciques, were subdued and returned to the mines, where they remained for the rest of the season (demora). While the demora apparently became standardized at a period of eight months eventually, in the sixteenth century it was more often nine or ten months. The period referred to here ended in August, hence Bishop Marroquín's plea for cessation of mining during the wet season evidently had not been effectively followed. The author of this report was licenciado Francisco Castañeda, the alcalde mayor of Nicaragua, who evinced some sympathy for the plight of the maceguales. Aside from those workers who had died in the mines, a plague of measles had recently left about six thousand Indians dead. Pestilences had altogether carried away approximately one-third of the native population, he said.

Castañeda and other officials agreed that Indians should have a break after the mining season in order to plant their crops before returning to the mines. Not only were the new mines dangerous for the Indians, but their isolation posed a threat from the local natives. Since so many Spaniards had left for Peru, there were fewer to protect the country, and the new mines were in wild, rough country where the hostile Chontales lived.[46]

Castañeda was most concerned about the declining native population, perhaps from humanitarian sentiments, but, given his subsequent behavior, more likely from a concern over the resulting labor shortage. He said there would be no Indians left within four years if something were not done to conserve them, not only because of the widespread pestilence and other illnesses that were present every year, but also because the exhausting work of the mines alone was enough to finish them off. The workers had to travel forty leagues from León and Granada up into the mountains, and once there they labored in the cold and rain, which combined with fatigue to weaken Indians from the hot lands. Their accustomed diet in the tropics included a wide variety of fruits and fish, without which nourishment their physical condition deteriorated.[47] They were, in any event, a people of weak constitutions and lacking in energy. Those who did not die in the mining regions fell on the roads leading to them, the paths strewn with the bones of Indians. Castañeda said he knew for certain of an encomendero who had lost two hundred of his pueblo natives during just one mining season, and others who originally had good repartimientos of Indians no longer had any of their charges left. Because of the widespread loss of life, the alcalde mayor said he did not believe the mines would be able to operate two years hence.[48] Three years later, the governor of Nicaragua said the mines could not be maintained because of the remote location in rough terrain and because they had no Indian women to prepare food for the miners.[49]

The promise of quick wealth was sufficient to dampen humanitarian impulses among most Spanish encomenderos. One of the prominent conquistadores, Sancho de Barahona, will serve to illustrate the temptation. He held half of the Indians of the large settlement of Atitlán, from which he took a team (cuadrilla) of 100 Indian miners (village witnesses testified that the team was made up of 120 men and women) who could produce 2,000 pesos de oro for Barahona in a ten-month demora. Spanish witnesses said that the cuadrilla mined 6 to 7 pesos daily. Two thousand pesos annually was not in itself sufficient to enrich Barahona, but mining was only a part of the income he enjoyed from the prosperous town of Atitlán.[50]

A royal treasurer, Diego García de Celis, described the potential of mining in Honduras by noting that four rivers near the coast had been sampled for gold and that all yielded good promise of wealth. A youth and three Indians working only half-heartedly took out seven reales worth of gold in a few hours.[51] A few months later the governor of Honduras informed the king that only two or three leagues from the settlement of Buena Esperanza mines were discovered in which eight or ten Indians mined more than two hundred pesos in a short time. Even without the large cuadrillas of Guatemala and New Spain (which, he mentioned, sometimes consisted of 120 or 150 Indians), Honduras could field sizable teams, and over a demora of nine months they could take out good sums of gold.[52] Within a few years the sums of precious metals in Central America would seem paltry, but in the 1530s the Crown was most interested.

In the mountains of Honduras, situated midway between the two seas in a prosperous region of many Indian towns, a Spanish city called Gracias a Dios was being settled. Municipal officials were appointed and repartimientos de indios were awarded to eighty encomenderos. Significantly, the site was located fairly near mines—eight leagues from those of Alax and fourteen leagues from others being exploited at the time. According to the governor, the new mines were rich, and he saw a cuadrilla of twenty men and forty women from Guatemala produce 150 pesos de oro in twenty-seven days. Usually, he said, an Indian could mine from three tomines to half a peso daily, although sometimes a peso or more. [53]

All this did not go forward without opposition from those concerned about the welfare of the natives. Pedraza was a vigorous opponent of the indiscriminate use of Indian labor. Chamberlain notes that "Pedraza renewed the prohibition against employment of free and household Indians in the mines, a measure instituted by Montejo between 1537 and 1539, but ignored after Alvarado's return." The same author sums up the conflict between Pedraza and the vecinos:

Pedraza's efforts to protect the Indians and enforce royal ordinances which favored them aroused the same kind of opposition that similar measures by Montejo had evoked. The cabildo of Gracias a Dios even instructed Pedraza, as procurador of Honduras-Higueras at Court, to petition royal measures permitting employment of Indians in the mines, contrary to his own regulations. Then, after he had left Castile, the royal treasury officials strongly denounced their letter of protest against his policies, that he had represented conditions among the natives as much worse than they actually were, and that, through his protective measures, he had hindered the development of mining. They went so far as to request the Crown to ignore Pedraza as a procurador until the despatches and documents drawn up by Montejo against Pedraza as a result of his removal of office in Honduras-Higueras in 1539, and other protests from the cabildos, had been carefully examined at Court. The royal treasury officials repeated the old arguments that the Indians gave little tribute in Honduras-Higueras as compared with other provinces and that the mines were the only real source of Crown revenues and individual wealth for the colonists. They consequently emphasized, by implication, the close relationship between mining and the permanence of the colony as they saw it, and advocated freer use of the Indians in exploitation of precious metals. The Crown, however, firmly supported Pedraza's measures. [54]

Writing of his arrival in Honduras, Montejo said that he found Spaniards taking out gold with men and women from villages because they had no slaves, and that the resulting disorder had destroyed the native pueblos. He requested a thousand blacks to alleviate the labor situation. [55]

Testifying at Seville in 1543, a Spaniard who had spent six or seven years in Honduras said that the encomienda Indians there gave only personal service for their tribute, according to the whims of their Spanish masters. For the most part they were used to carry supplies to the mines and elsewhere, and their encomenderos sometimes rented out the Indians to others for portage to the mines. In addition, some of them were required to work the Spanish maize plantings. They did not, however, have to work in the mines, which labor was performed by native slaves, blacks, and naborías.[56]

The New Laws of 1542 had as their prime objective the palliation of the abuses to which the Indians had been subjected. Among the provisions was one that prohibited the use of Indians in taking out gold. Although the natives continued to be employed in the mining operations, the Spaniards contended that since the workers were not actually washing the ore for gold, they were not really taking out gold and that consequently what they were doing was not illegal.[57] It was precisely that kind of caviling which led to the interminable evasions of the law.

Mining was interrupted into the 1540s by continuing attacks of hostile Indians. In 1544, a large force of them from the villas of Comayagua, Ulancho, and Nueva Segovia, along with others on the outskirts of San Pedro, rose up and killed many Spaniards and some blacks in the mining cuadrillas, as a result of which some rich mines had to be abandoned.[58]

A few months later a royal cédula stressed that no Indians were to work in mines, nor in any kind of labor that fatigued them or endangered their health. The Crown observed that, according to its information, in the tribute assessments encomienda pueblos were required to offer personal service, to include both burden bearers and mine laborers. The latter were required to take out ore, as well as to carry wood and to serve the mines in other ways. Referring to the nice distinction made earlier—that since the workers did not actually wash the ore, they were not really mining—the Crown ruled that no work in any way involved in the mining process was allowable, under pain of the loss of one half the violator's goods. A second offense was to result in the loss of all his goods, as well as exile from the province.[59] The decree was sent to the audiencia, whose members were much involved in mining themselves, as a consequence of which little substantive change was made. As will be seen, it was not until the coming of the second audiencia that things would take a dramatic turn.

Of all the various categories of labor under personal service, those of naborías and tamemes are important enough to merit extended discussion. Not only were they essential to the general labor force, but they are forms of labor that have persisted into modern times in only slightly modified guise.

Naborías

An exact definition of the term "naboría" is elusive because it apparently meant different things, according to time and place. It was a designation used in prehispanic times and retained by the Spaniards with only minor variations. But even among contemporary Spaniards the distinctions were somewhat blurred. Note what the knowledgeable Bartolomé de Las Casas wrote in his *Historia de las Indias:*

> There were in these Islands among the Spaniards two kinds of perpetual slaves: one, those who could be sold publicly, like those taken in war; and the other, those who could not be sold openly, and these were called naborías, for they were acquired and sold secretly, and they had a thousand cunning ways to do so. In their language the Indians commonly called retainers and ordinary house servants *naborías.* [60]

Perhaps this was the early interpretation, but it is misleading if applied to Central America. Naborías were not precisely slaves; legally they were free people who could not be bought and sold. Sometimes they were designated "naborías perpétuos," but their condition of servitude was not always perpetual by any means. It appears to me that their status more resembled that of the debt peón, who is probably a lineal descendant of the sixteenth-century naboría.

Those Indians taken from the "useless" islands, the lesser Antilles, were made naborías without due consideration of their consent. Simpson observes that "Indians given in encomienda were not slaves, but *naborías,* because Ferdinand felt that it would be a burden on his conscience to make them slaves."[61] By 1512, in Puerto Rico a royal order permitted vecinos to acquire Indians as naborías with the consent of the Indians and their caciques, "because they would thus be well treated." At least in the beginning, the similarity of their circumstances to that of encomienda Indians is clear; but while both contributed labor, naborías were not required to pay tribute. The legal position of naborías was clarified by 1531, when it was ruled that only those Indians who agreed to the condition could be made naborías. No longer were they to serve perpetually, but only for the time they wished, a point to be made clear through interpreters. Nor were they to be given in encomienda, or in any other way against their wills; they were to choose the Spaniard for whom they would work.[62]

Naborías were Indians who worked for Spaniards primarily as domestic servants, although their duties were not necessarily confined to the household.[63] They contributed personal service, but they were in a category of their own, distinct from encomienda Indians who performed much the same tasks. In early years at least, it appears that naborías were those who were, by the fortunes of war, rootless. That is, they were usually from another territory, sometimes from one of the Caribbean islands, and they found themselves in alien lands, without identifying with the local natives. Having no secure place in a village, with no family or established friendships, such Indians were footloose, a condition not to be tolerated by Spanish officialdom.[64] Because they belonged to no village, they did not fall under an encomienda grant.

Eventually, however, some of them came to form part of the repartimientos in which displaced persons were assigned to Spaniards in order to keep them occupied and under supervision. Being legally free persons, despite the fact that they were in most cases forcibly removed from their lands, they should have been affected by the laws stating that free natives who had been taken from their homes were supposed to be free to return to them. Designating those natives as "free" is a fine bit of casuistry to our eyes; the distinction was made, nonetheless, that they could not be bought and sold, and hence they were not slaves. Thus, *ipso facto*, they were "free."

Despite their legal right to return to their lands, the barriers were usually overwhelming: it often meant a long and difficult journey, not to mention the expense. Thus most of them remained in the new lands. Some had been forced into service during stages of the conquest and pacification, after having been seized on earlier raids. In the years of pacification, Indians, especially women and children, were not enslaved, but were made "perpetual" naborías. They could not be sold, but they were hardly free vassals. The naborías came to be considered "natural servants" of the Spaniards.[65]

The invading Spaniards had naborías with them when they conquered Central America, and those with Alvarado, identifying their own security with his in hostile territory, once warned the adelantado of an impending attack by his enemies.[66] In the early years many naborías who accompanied soldiers during the pacification were from Mexico, and some of them saw themselves in the role of adjunct conquerors and not simply as humble servants. It was brought to light during a meeting of the cabildo of Santiago in 1529 that some of the encomenderos were sending their naborías to the pueblos not only to obtain household necessities, but also to collect tributes. In the encomienda towns the naborías maltreated the señores and the maceguales, tying them up and beating them. The principales complained of the treatment, and an uprising was feared if it did not cease. The cabildo ruled that any Spaniard who sent a naboría to molest other Indians would lose the naboría and would be subject to a fine

of twenty-five pesos de oro. Henceforth, naborías could be sent to the
villages, but they were not to molest anyone or they would be punished.
If, however, they convinced the judge that their actions were taken on the
orders of the Spanish master, the encomendero would be punished as
well.[67] Such aggressive acts on the part of naborías were unusual and
apparently limited to those from outside Central America during the early
years.

As in the case of any servant, it is not easy to generalize about naborías in
terms of their duties and status. While one chronicler equates naborías
with criados, that is misleading. The term criado, today ordinarily used in
the same sense as servant, often referred to a trusted Spanish aide to a
prominent man, and the criado was frequently a person of some responsibility, although with little social standing. While naborías were usually
humble and exploited Indians, there is an interesting example of a naboría
having been given a charge of some power. During a bloody expedition in
1541, Miguel Díaz, without having the power to do so, gave the staff of
justice to Perico, his naboría. This was no doubt a farce, enabling Díaz to
have his way.[68]

While Indians who had been enslaved in their own societies were
ordinarily made esclavos de rescate, it was not always so. A conqueror in
Honduras, in 1527, was informed that those who had been sold into
slavery by their parents out of necessity, or others taken in battle who had
not been slaves, were to be branded on the thigh and made naborías, to
serve their captors in perpetuity, as rewards for the soldiers who had
conquered the land. It was explicitly stated that these naborías were not to
be taken from their own territories, under pain of 100 lashes, a fine of 100
pesos de oro, and loss of the Indians involved.[69]

In flagrant violation of such laws was the practice of raiding other areas
for the express purpose of taking Indians, either as naborías or slaves, and
this was particularly true in the Antilles where the Spaniards had not
settled the smaller islands. In the 1540s Spaniards were still taking
Indians from Curaçao and the Islas de los Gigantes to be used as naborías.
The king ordered them released, stressing that the New Laws decreed for
the good treatment of the natives applied to all areas of the New World.[70]

Another law stipulated that women and children under fourteen taken
in just war were not to be enslaved, but they could be kept as household
servants, or in other work, in the category of naborías. They were to be
treated as free persons and were to be given food and shelter as well as
other necessities, and they were to be treated well, as the law regarding
naborías provided.[71]

Subsequently, naborías were not to be branded;[72] however, it was charged in 1544 that Alonso de Cáceres, a lieutenant of Montejo, had seized Indians near the site of the great seige of Cerquín and branded them on the chins with the sign of a cross, saying they would serve as naborías. The controversy at the time was not that he was branding naborías, but that he had used an illegal brand.[73]

Whatever their previous circumstances in Spain, most Spaniards took Indian servants for granted, as their just due. The treasurer of Honduras observed that because of the primitive conditions there, Spaniards relied on, and became accustomed to, the service of naborías, who were at hand for every small task.[74] Because there was no Castilian bread nor other things to which they were accustomed, Spaniards had from the beginning contended that servants were necessary. It was difficult to retain them, because being free to go where they wished, by law, and not to be subjected to pressure, some of them left their Spanish masters.[75]

In the early years naborías had been available for all, but a scarcity of these servants developed quite early. The treasurer, who had arrived about October 1533, complained that he did not have sufficient service, despite his high station. While it was true, he said, that the province had comparatively few natives, there were nevertheless some Spaniards who had as many as sixty to eighty naborías, although most had only eight to ten. The governor had seen fit to give him only a boy for a servant. He had ten others, but those he had purchased, and if he had twenty they would not suffice for all the many chores. He was of the opinion that because of the many journeys he had to make throughout the province, the governor could have given him a dozen naborías. If one did not have enough of the peaceful Indians ("yndios mansos") he would be lost, because the "bravos" would run off. And, like other officials, he traveled about with a staff, and they, too, needed servants. Two naborías were needed to care for each horse, because among other duties, they would often have to forage some distance in order to find good grass. Others were needed for the daily grinding of corn on the *metates* for the preparation of tortillas, and some had to catch the fish they usually ate, going either to the sea or rivers, along with other miscellaneous tasks.[76]

This shortage of naborías, even for high officials, was confirmed a few weeks later by the veedor, who said that he was one of those with the fewest servants in the province. To make matters worse, just after the division of the available naborías, most of his ran off to the hills and he was left with only five or six of them to care for his needs.[77]

The first conquerors naturally took the greatest share of all spoils, and this extended to personal service. A large staff lent prestige to the master of the household and made his life one of relative ease—and, at least in the early years, the conquerors had this service free, aside from whatever meager supplies of food they had to provide. Jorge de Alvarado, who held half the town of Atitlán for awhile, kept no fewer than forty Indians in his household service, according to a witness. In addition to their labor, they also gave him fowls and other food. If, in the ten months he resided there, he had actually paid for the service and the food, it would have amounted to more than 500 pesos de oro, or so the witness stated.[78]

A later president of the audiencia wrote that even the most humble of the Spaniards had these servants, because he had seen no vecino who did not have at least five or six Indians serving in his house. Upon investigation, he found that in the repartimiento and assessment made by the first audiencia, Spaniards were given Indians for personal service, and although they were free persons, they were treated like slaves, despite their being called naborías. One inevitable result that he noted was the tragic separation of families.[79]

Despite the president's justifiable concern, Indians who worked as household servants were comparatively well off, unless they happened to be under the thumb of a particularly harsh master. On the whole, domestic service was less strenuous, and there was food and shelter from the elements. Usually they could stay with their families. As in the case of slaves, household workers were subjected to much less harassment than field workers or those who worked in mines. One indication that it was less exacting labor is the fact that, according to testimony from a former resident of Honduras, about the only Indians being Christianized were the naborías. It is true that they were more accessible for indoctrination, but it is also evident that they, in contrast to other workers, were at least given time off for instruction.[80] As one might expect, those in the household were often treated with some care and affection.

It sometimes happened that the Spaniard for whom a naboría worked went on an entrada de guerra, in which case the Indian might have to accompany him, a situation that usually meant not only extra labor and hardship, but also danger. To cite one example, on an expedition in Honduras, a Spanish party was attacked by hostile Indians, and some of the naborías, having no protection, were wounded. To make matters worse, the party ran out of food, and it was the naborías who were left without, as a result of which most of them died.[81]

Other naborías were used in the first years in mining enterprises, however illegally. Francisco de Montejo, who reminded the king on more than one occasion that he had not allowed Indian slaves to be made in Honduras, nevertheless allowed Spaniards to use the free naborías in mining. It was, he explained, precisely because there were no slaves that other Indians had to be used if the ore was to be mined. But, he added, only those naborías who volunteered for the work were allowed to mine, because there were few natives and they were delicate. In such hard work they had to be well cared for. [82] I cannot avoid the suspicion that those who volunteered were given more than a little encouragement to do so. It appears that by the early 1540s the common practice of using naborías as miners ceased, at least in Honduras. [83]

Because many of the naborías were females, some of them were inevitably called upon to perform services of a more personal nature, so that a more attractive woman might find herself in special demand. The oidor, licenciado Herrera, borrowed a naboría from one of the vecinos of Santiago. The vecino went to the judge's house several times for the return of the woman, since his wife had need of her, but Herrera would not give her up. It was said that the judge was sleeping with her and that, in bed, he called her "doña Ysabelica," which gossip the witness had on the authority of one Villalobos, who had himself made love to the naboría. [84]

Legislation was given designed to protect the rights of the naborías, but it was to a great extent ineffective. While a 1536 law prevented the taking of naborías to Castile as servants, the repetition of the ruling fifty years later indicates that no firm adherence had been practiced. [85] If an Indian was taken to Spain the authorities would certainly be aware of it, but moving a naboría about from one province to another was an entirely different matter. After the conquest, naborías had been assigned to Spaniards, much in the same way that encomienda Indians had been, though the former were supposedly independent.

Governor Contreras of Nicaragua was brought to account for reassigning naborías whose masters had died, and for handing them out to whomever he chose, without their having any voice in the matter. Some of them he gave to a friar and to his mother, and others were passed on by "cédulas de encomienda" to serve as naborías for his nephew, among others. In answering the charges, Contreras said that when he arrived in Nicaragua it was the custom to distribute naborías in encomienda if their former owners had died, and that the Crown had instructed him to do the same. A witness confirmed it, adding that he had four or five of the cédulas de encomiendas de naborías from Pedrárias Davila and licenciado Castañeda. [86]

A good number of the naborías were taken illegally to Peru on ships, where many of them remained. When the armada of Alvarado left for Peru he took many naborías as servants, without whom the soldiers felt they could not manage. [87] Some naborías were sold and traded for other Indians, as well as for jewels, clothing, cattle, and food. As a result, many of

them fled, while others hanged themselves or starved themselves rather
than be returned to the Christians. The queen decreed that the selling and
trading of naborías would cease, under pain of a fine of 100,000 marvedís
for first offenses, and loss of half of one's goods and exile from the Indies for
second offenses.[88]

The myth of the independent naboría is also exposed by the fact that
arbitrary officials were taking naborías away from vecinos without a hearing and investigation, which was seen as a violation of the rights of the
vecinos, not the Indians.[89] When licenciado Castañeda, the erstwhile
alcalde mayor and governor in Nicaragua, surreptitiously left for Peru, he
took about thirty-five naborías and encomienda Indians on board his ship
in chains.[90] His successor, Rodrigo de Contreras, allowed naborías of both
sexes to be carried off to Peru. He imposed the qualification of posting a
bond for their safe return, but many were never seen again.[91] No doubt
there was much more of this activity than comes to light in judicial reviews
of important officials.

This is not to say, however, that no naborías ever enjoyed some independence. Local officials complained in 1539 that when they came on the
conquest they had with them many Indians from other areas. Because
they were well treated and because they too had profited from the wars,
they were happy to be in the company of Spaniards. But once the land was
settled they saw themselves in an elevated position, and with the favor of
some rich Spaniards, they refused to recognize their obligations of servitude to the Crown or to anyone else. Rather, they lived by stealing and
gambling, much to the scandal of the local Indians and to the prejudice of
the Spaniards, because, since they were idle, they committed many sins
and caused trouble. Such Indians were called "naborías" in Guatemala,
and the officials implored the king to see that they served their former
masters. And they asked that those who arrived without amos be put
under the care of Spaniards so that they would behave and learn their
doctrine.[92]

Generally, however, naborías were denied the freedom of movement
given them by law, and their supposed option in the choice of an employer
was ignored as well. It was noted that some Spaniards treated them little
differently than their slaves, that they were transferring the Indians and
selling them, both as individual "pieças" and as part and parcel of estates.
When this practice was again brought to the attention of the Crown, it was
decreed that those who sold, transferred, or alienated any naboría from his
ancestral territory would be punished. Any Spaniard who sold a naboría,
or any who knowingly purchased one, was to lose half his property and
would be exiled from the province in perpetuity. Furthermore, since

naborías were to be free persons, they could live with whomever they preferred as master and they could leave anyone's service, as they saw fit. Those who violated their rights in this regard would be fined 100 pesos de oro, half of which would go to the accuser.[93]

Even though one of the New Laws provided that no one could use the service of a naboría or *tapia* against his will, and despite the fact that the king cited that law as a reminder, the legislation was almost impossible to implement, and the abuse continued.[94] The Protector of the Indians in Honduras wrote in 1547 that naborías were still being held involuntarily in Spanish residences, and that they were being killed by whips, clubs, and kicks. They were tied to poles like slaves, he said, with no one to help them nor even to give them so much as a shirt, and in desperation many of those men and women hanged themselves. He requested permission to have the naborías appear before him to question them to see if they were held by force, and to free them if they were. He also wanted the right to determine if they had been whipped or burned by dripping bacon grease, as many were, and to punish the offending Spaniards.[95]

Spaniards had from the beginning tried to justify the use of Indians as naborías. In 1531 the alcalde mayor of Nicaragua said that the "mansos" served in Christian homes, where they were well clothed and cared for, and if it was charged that many of them were dying it was owing principally to the pestilence, which struck down Spaniards as well.[96] Those in Honduras were most concerned about the restricted role of naborías in accordance with the law. Legally, naborías were not to be used for mining, but Spaniards complained that without mining there was no income. Because there were few Indians there and almost no slaves, the vecinos had used some naborías in the mines, but when licenciado Pedraza arrived as Protector of the Indians in late 1538 things changed. Pedraza affixed to the doors of the church orders that no naboría or encomienda Indian was to be used for such labor, which caused great confusion and scandal among the settlers and others because they were in debt to the Crown and others. Despite the wealth in the mines they would not be able to get at it. Consequently, the cabildo reported, many Spaniards were thinking of leaving the land, bitter about having made so many sacrifices and ending up poor.[97]

Later the cabildo of Gracias a Dios asked the Crown to concede to them the use of naborías and other Indians taken in rebellion to work the mines. Otherwise they could not sustain themselves, for they had no slaves and no means to purchase any. They requested 500 blacks, with the understanding that the vecinos would reimburse the Crown for them in instalments.[98] The restriction on the use of naborías in mining was a blow, particularly since black slaves were expensive and naborías were practically free, usually getting no wages and receiving little food. Nevertheless, despite the laments, mining went forward; the labor shortage notwithstanding, it was reported to the king in 1542 that 45,000 pesos of gold had been smelted.[99]

One of the difficulties of dealing with the position of the naborías was the vagueness of their classification. They could be differentiated from Indian slaves until the late 1540s because of the facial brands of slaves. On the other hand, there was little apparent distinction between them and encomienda Indians. In fact, there was little difference between the two categories insofar as labor was concerned, despite legislation to the contrary.

The judges of the first audiencia maintained the fiction that the New Laws had been observed and that no naborías were being used, whereas the testimony of Spaniards indicated that almost all vecinos had naborías serving in their homes. The truth was, a witness contended, that the judges of the audiencia themselves not only used naborías, but also enticed those employed by others to enter their own service, under the pretext of allowing the Indians full freedom of choice, and later refusing to return them to their original masters. It had been specifically ruled that no women were to be used as naborías, or in any other way, but the oidores made them work without pay and allowed the vecinos to do likewise.

In response, the officials argued that they had used no Indians as naborías or tapias, but rather utilized the services of free Indians who worked of their own volition, receiving food, clothing, and other necessities, as was the custom. The workers, they insisted, were free to come and go as they pleased. When assessments were made for encomenderos, the judges explained, the encomenderos were not assigned naborías; however, they were allowed to use maceguales from their pueblos for service. And, although such practice was not provided for by specific legislation of the Crown, it was permitted, they said, by the New Laws, in which provision was made for service that Indians were obligated to give.[100]

Nebulous as the classification of the naborías was, in practice they formed the large class of household servants for the Spaniards, usually serving without pay. Their status, like that of other native laborers, would undergo some adjustment with the reforms at mid-century. But the persistence of the naboría type, whatever else he may have been called later, is of some consequence for labor history. Identified with, and attached to, certain families and their lands, the sixteenth-century naborías may well be the origin of the debt-peonage system in modern

Latin America. Sons of the naboría worked for the sons of the same
Spanish amo, and no doubt debts were incurred somewhere along
the way.

Tamemes

If the conditions of many naborías were comparatively reasonable, the
same cannot be said for the Indians who served as burden bearers. A high
official of Nicaragua wrote that if a Spaniard wanted to go from León or
Granada to the mines, there was no need to take a guide or to ask
directions if he did not know the way; he had only to follow the trail
made by the bones of fallen Indians leading there.[101] Perhaps this
was an exaggeration, but it is clear that the use of humans as beasts of
burden took a terrible toll among the indigenous population. The use
of these tamemes was not originated by the Spaniards, for they had
long served native society in precolumbian times.[102] Since the Indians
had developed no practical use of the wheel and were without draft
animals, goods could only be transported by humans. Hence, there had
always been those whose primary function in the economy was to sling
packs, often supported by tumplines, on their backs. In Indian society, as
in that of the Spanish, such unskilled laborers were low on the social and
economic scale.

The arrival of the more materialistic Spaniards only increased the
demand for tamemes. The simple movement of goods from one place to
another constituted no mean logistical problem; the need to transport
merchandise imported from Spain complicated the labor picture even
more. The supplies that arrived on Spanish ships, both staples and luxuries, meant that every kind of cargo had to be carried from the tropical
coasts up to the cold highlands, a journey fraught with many physical
barriers and the onslaughts of the elements. Not content with the exotic
products of the Indies, the conquerors and those who followed demanded
wine, oil, vinegar, preserves, paper, books, weapons, tools, plants, and
just about every item associated with their lives in Spain, as they tried to
re-create a corner of Castile on the frontiers.

But a long time would elapse before a system of transportation would
evolve in Central America that would in any way approach the distribution
of goods in Europe. Indian America had had no use for anything more than
crude trails, and despite the urgency with which the Crown ordered the
construction of roads to accommodate teams and carts, such roads were
woefully inadequate throughout the sixteenth century.[103] Although
horses, mules, and oxen would eventually proliferate in Central America,

it would take many decades for the supply to meet the demand. Even when draft animals became available, the nature of the terrain in so many places was such that they were of limited use, especially in view of the lack of roads. Thus the Spaniards relied, as they did in so many instances, on the traditional native ways. The demand for tamemes became so great under the conquerors that Indians from all social classes were pressed into the fatiguing service.

Certainly in the beginning there was a legitimate need for porters.[104] Crown policy on the matter seems to have been that the use of tamemes was authorized when absolutely necessary, but a royal cédula sent to officials in New Spain in 1528 forbade Indians to carry to mines or any other places for the purpose of profit.[105] If the system had been supervised with justice and moderation, one could excuse its existence, at least for the first years. The same could be said for many other colonial labor practices—but, again, a fundamentally reasonable system was abused. Although prehispanic tamemes carried over long distances—as, for example, transporting cacao from Soconusco to Tenochtitlán—there is little information on the details of their work in Central America. Was there a limit on the weights they were required to carry, and if so, what was it? Was provision made for rest stops, particularly in the mountains and during heavy rains? Was adequate food provided for them? What was their compensation? Did they work in relays? Answers to these questions and others must be known before one can make comparisons of the tameme's lot before 1524 and afterwards.

It is clear enough that tamemes suffered great hardships after the conquest. On occasion they were made to haul cargoes from the Mexican port of Veracruz to Santiago, a distance of some nine hundred miles over rugged terrain. Journeys between 200 and 400 miles were not uncommon. Even for shorter hauls, the work could be extremely exhausting owing to the tortuous trails that ran up and down, twisting around the steep inclines and valleys that dominate the face of Central America.

If passage was fatiguing under the best of circumstances, it was unmitigated torture during the rainy season. Picture the carriers traversing those slopes in driving rain, bent under packs of 75 to 100 pounds, slogging through mud, slipping and sliding, goaded on by a driver with a schedule to meet. If a tameme did not drop from exhaustion, he might well become ill from exposure, drown in a river swollen by flash floods, or have some accident that would lay him up, perhaps crippled for life. The latter possibility would be seen by some as a blessing that would take them out of the carrying trade. The eroding effects of the wet season were such that bridges washed out and trails became impossible messes, so that it was virtually impossible to travel in certain areas during the wettest months.

An Indian from the cool highlands frequently became ill when he had to descend with his pack into the sweltering hotlands along the coasts, and many deaths resulted from the severe change of climate. In a steamy province like Soconusco the heat and humidity became almost unbearable for one used to the mountains, especially when strenuous labor was involved. And the coastal Indians fared no better when they were exposed to the chilling rains of the highlands. The extreme fatigue suffered by tamemes was all the more dangerous to their health because of the miserable diet on which they had to subsist. Usually they had to carry their own food, which often consisted of one *tamal* daily and nothing else. They were so undernourished that they easily became ill from consumption, fevers, pestilence, and a variety of other disorders.

Many of the foregoing were conditions of nature over which Spaniards had little control. Other sufferings could have been, and sometimes were, alleviated. Excessive loads, long journeys, recruitment by force and intimidation, work without pay, malnutrition, and mistreatment were all abuses that the Crown and some concerned individuals sought to avert —albeit halfheartedly at times—throughout the sixteenth century. Improvements in transportation were never sufficient to abolish the use of tamemes, although some discernible easing of the excesses eventually came about.

Tamemes played a crucial role during the conquests, and many of the Spanish veterans of the Mexican campaign were accustomed to having Indians carry their personal effects and supplies. More often than not, caciques offered carriers to the arriving Spaniards, but if not, the request, or demand, was made and the chiefs usually delivered.[106] Those given were often tamemes in their own societies, although in many instances others were handed over. Even though tamemes were legally free people, they sometimes lost that status once in the hands of the conquerors. Alvarado allegedly received Indians as bearers and later enslaved them during the early years of pacification.[107] When he sailed with his armada to Peru in 1534, it was said that he took many maceguales for use as tamemes and that many of them died.[108]

Nevertheless one does not hear of atrocities attributed to Alvarado's use of tamemes comparable to the expedition of López de Salcedo when he loaded down Indians and marched them from Honduras to Nicaragua, a tragedy that was particularly harmful for sparsely populated Honduras.[109] In one of the most catastrophic examples, one expedition saw 4,000 tamemes loaded for a journey from which no more than 6 survived to return to their homes.[110] Regidores in Chiapas wrote in 1537 that Francisco Gil has summoned señores and principales and demanded tamemes, who were then tied up and branded on their faces as slaves and distributed among his men.[111]

As the Spanish bureaucracy moved in, Indians were assigned to encomenderos, put in crown towns, and commended to the care of clergymen or let out as naborías, as a result of which the availability of carriers almost ceased precisely at the time that the demand was increasing. Consequently, it became customary for encomenderos to utilize Indians from their pueblos as tamemes, either for their own needs or to profit from their services by renting them out to merchants and others. This was brought to the attention of the emperor, who wrote in 1541 that the practice was to cease. A few months later a cédula was directed to Nicaragua, where encomenderos and their *estancieros* were renting villagers to others and making the Indians haul wood and other materials in excessive weights, which had resulted in many deaths.[112] Encomenderos were letting out their Indians to merchants who made them carry 100 and sometimes 200 leagues, bringing profits to the encomenderos but usually no wages for the tamemes.

Even the creation of the audiencia did not check this abuse of the encomienda system.[113] On the contrary, encomenderos came to rely more and more on the rental of their villagers as important sources of their income. Even though encomenderos could not legally take tameme service as part of their tribute, they continued to do so. The New Laws of 1542 prohibited the use of all tamemes, except in special cases, but the provision was never effectively applied.[114] In some regions the rental of carriers became the mainstay of the encomenderos, whose representatives remonstrated that without use of the tamemes some of the Spaniards would not be able to remain in the land. Their only source of income was from "pueblos de tamemes," a designation that indicates the blatant violation.[115]

The oidor licenciado Herrera observed that in Nicaragua the principal tribute offered to encomenderos was the income from the rental of their Indians as burden bearers, and he suggested to the Crown that tamemes be disallowed as part of tribute assessments. Carriers should be taken from the ranks of slaves, in his opinion, not from Indians whose work was reserved for personal service.[116] Several months later the Crown reprimanded the audiencia for assessing the encomienda pueblos for tamemes as part of their obligatory tribute and reminded the judges that it was illegal to do so.[117]

In reaction to the ruling limiting the practice, the cabildo of Gracias a Dios complained that the vecinos of Honduras suffered because no crops were grown in the mountainous province and that the natives had nothing to give their encomenderos other than their labor. There was no cacao, cloth, salt, or anything else of value. The only source of income, and very modest at that, was the service of the tamemes, who were, the regidores insisted, well treated so that the population was not declining.[118] They might have added that there were mines but that they were not allowed to use Indian labor to extract the ore. Judges of the audiencia informed the Crown about the same time that the rule against assessing pueblos for tamemes was being observed, even though it was creating great hardships for the Spaniards.[119]

Shortly thereafter, however, licenciado Alonso López de Cerrato arrived as president of the audiencia, and in reviewing the oidores for their performances in office, he found that in fact they had not enforced the decree effectively. While they may have stopped the practice of actually assessing villages for tamemes, they allowed encomenderos to use the villagers to carry, assessment or no. To cite one charge, an encomendero named Pedro Cava rented forty Indians to carry from San Pedro to the port, and others were sent to carry to San Miguel and Comayagua. Instead of depriving the encomendero of the pueblos, as the judges should have done for a violation that caused deaths, they merely fined him, and no punishment was given to the Spaniard who had illegally rented the Indians.

The judges said they had complied with the order not to require villages to furnish porters as part of their tribute; however, they had allowed encomenderos to use their Indians for that purpose because the land was so sterile that that form of personal service was the only profit they could realize. In any event, they added, the Indians were accustomed to carrying and they were supposed to be paid in cacao for their labor. Encomenderos continued renting out their pueblo Indians to merchants who made the tamemes carry excessive loads over long distances. It became a way of life for some Indians. Being so occupied, they contributed nothing else to their encomenderos and derived no benefits for themselves.[120]

The encomenderos, for their part, were satisfied with the arrangement in those situations where their villages did not produce worthwhile tribute. The president of the first audiencia, Alonso Maldonado, gave the village of Macholoa in encomienda to his first cousin, who profited 2,000 pesos a year just from the rental of the Indians of that village. It was not uncommon for villages by the late 1540s to be contributing tamemes as their primary tribute.[121] President Maldonado favored his criado, a youth

who was neither a conqueror nor even a married man, with the pueblo of
Çolomba, which offered no other tribute than tamemes. Nevertheless,
the boy realized the goodly sum of 800 to 1,000 pesos a year from
their labor.[122]

The Crown, informed by Spaniards of conscience, was well aware of the
evils of the tameme system, and as early as 1529 the emperor ruled that
no Christian could load an Indian, even for a short distance, under heavy
penalty.[123] The law proved to be impractical, but while the system
seemed to be a necessary burden on the natives, there was an attempt to
meliorate the conditions. In 1533 it was decreed that no Indian would be
allowed to carry a weight exceeding fifty pounds (two arrobas).[124] With so
much of the carrying in remote places, it was very difficult to regulate
weights, although it appears that even in and around the capital of Santiago itself the law was not rigidly observed. In 1542, the cabildo of that
city issued a regulation in which it was stated that, since the Indians were
kept so busy conveying many foodstuffs and materials, they should not be
obligated to pack more than two arrobas at a time.[125]

As more reports of overloading reached Spain, the Crown issued a
vague, equivocal order that Indians were not to bear heavy loads; and
finally, at the request of the cabildo of Santiago, instructed the audiencia
to enforce the law limiting the weights to fifty pounds.[126] The decrees
notwithstanding, witnesses continued to tell of overburdened tamemes,
who were sometimes forced to carry as much as 100 pounds.[127] One
account notes that a Spaniard was not even able to lift off the ground a pack
already carried a considerable distance by a tameme.[128]

Attempts were made as well to limit the distances that tamemes would
be required to take their loads. In response to the queen's order to revise
ordinances regarding the use of carriers, the Audiencia of Mexico, after
consultation with clergymen, ruled by 1531 that tamemes were to travel
no more than a day's journey from their villages, and that a new group of
them would have to be found for the next day's haul.[129] Such legislation
was ineffective in Central America, where Indians continued to carry over
long distances. Las Casas was upset when a procurador sought permission
for Indians to transport tribute on their backs thirty to forty leagues to
Spanish settlements. On those trips, he wrote, the natives perished,
because in addition to their cargoes they had to take along their meager
food for the journey, thirty leagues each way. Since they could not
manage sufficient provisions, they died.[130] Indians from encomiendas,
rented by their masters to merchants, were forced to carry merchandise as
far as 200 leagues, as a result of which a royal order decreed the loss of the
encomienda to anyone guilty of renting out Indians for that purpose.[131]

The longest journeys were those between the city of Mexico and Santiago, a distance of some 700 miles. Sometimes the additional 200 miles to or from Veracruz were involved. Merchants not infrequently rented tamemes who carried for distances up to 600 miles.[132] The first audiencia, illegally allowing the rental of tamemes, sought to restrict the distances, but their ungenerous ruling provided that Indians could carry up to four or five days from their villages. And, curiously enough, witnesses hostile to the audiencia judges considered that a limitation of four days' journey was reasonable.[133] Without specifying destinations, it was stated that Spanish vecinos required tamemes to haul maize to mines almost 600 miles away.[134] Throughout the sixteenth century reports issuing from Central America informed the Crown of the failure to limit effectively the distance an Indian was required to carry.

One of the stipulations regarding the use of tamemes was that only those who volunteered to serve in that capacity were to be used. That was not entirely a naive or vain ruling, for there had always been those Indians whose occupation was the transportation of goods on their backs. It was a trade like any other. However, given the excesses of the system as it subsequently operated under the Spaniards, few Indians were disposed to offer their services for journeys from which they might well never return. Consequently, no provision of the Crown regarding the conveyance of goods was more chimerical than the myth of the volunteer tameme, and it is clear enough that the Indian who carried of his own volition was the exception, Spanish protests to the contrary notwithstanding.

The rationale behind Spanish legislation was that a free Indian, carrying a moderate load over a short distance, would be willing enough to earn wages. Native attitudes were such, however, that it would be quite some time before Indians were Hispanicized to the point of acquiring a consuming interest in accumulating more than immediate needs required, as a result of which they seldom volunteered for any kind of labor. Still, if an equitable arrangement had evolved, there was some merit in the royal proposal. The existence of tamemes, or *cargadores,* into modern times is evidence that under reasonable circumstances Indians would willingly take the place of pack animals as burden bearers.

While Indians were not for the most part materialistic, they had at least some interest in receiving wages for their work if only to help meet their tribute requirements. Given a choice, it appears that they preferred not to work for the Spaniards; if they had no choice they expected pay.[135] Without at least the promise of pay, they had to be coerced into carrying, and the New Laws of 1542, which allowed the use of tamemes under special circumstances, stated that in no case were they to labor without wages.[136] In provisions made by the Audiencia of Mexico, by 1531 tamemes who wished to carry were to be paid 100 cacao beans daily.[137] In Guatemala, too, Pedro de Alvarado had been paying his tamemes in cacao, which was as acceptable to the natives as gold or silver.[138]

By the 1540s encomenderos could rent their pueblo Indians for one peso, two tomines apiece for a day's work to merchants, as exemplified in the instance of the encomendero of Canpa, who on one occasion let out forty tamemes at that price.[139] But the Indians themselves frequently received nothing in such arrangements, and even when they worked for their encomenderos they often had no reward. Neither the Crown nor local officials made strong representations for the establishment of minimum-wage standards; on the other hand, an official requested a maximum level of wages like the one imposed in Mexico.[140]

While it was in the interest of most Spaniards to perpetuate the tameme system, the Crown, along with some humanitarians, would much rather have abolished it. Ultimately conceding the temporary necessity of tamemes, the Crown instructed royal officials to construct roads over which carts and pack animals could be driven eventually. The royal preoccupation with roads persisted throughout the sixteenth century, however fruitlessly, with a few exceptions. The most forceful and consistent argument of the vecinos against the prohibition of tamemes was the absence of thoroughfares over which beasts could travel loaded with cargoes. Thus the remedy was to construct suitable roads that would take away the need for tamemes, and hence the abuse of the Indians in that regard.

Concurrent with orders for road building was the insistence that animals be used to carry whenever possible. Initially there was a shortage of them and they were very costly. As a consequence, even over trails where horses or mules could be used as pack animals, it was cheaper to use humans, who cost little or nothing. The cabildo of León, in the interest of increasing herds of livestock, asked the king to forbid anyone from taking from the province of Nicaragua any mares for a period of five years. During that time pack trains could be formed and tamemes would become anachronistic.[141] The demand for horses in Nicaragua was particularly critical because that province was the jumping-off point for the conquest and settlement of Peru, and horse traders were in a position to make enormous profits. Shortly, however, livestock began to reproduce rapidly, and Las Casas, urging the Council of the Indies to press for the opening of roads, pointed out that there were plenty of draft animals.[142]

The Crown had ordered that no Indians be allowed to carry between Puerto de Caballos and Santiago, the largest settlement in Central

America. Therefore, goods were being taken from the Rio de Guaçacualco by water and then overland on the backs of Indians to Chiapas, and from there to Santiago, the last leg of the trip being sixty to seventy leagues over bad trails. The royal factor (treasury official) in Honduras, in describing the unsatisfactory nature of this route, stressed the urgent need for opening the important road between the port and Santiago.[143] The road from Chiapas to Santiago would in any case remain in frequent use because of the intercourse with Mexico, but it was a perilous route. It was especially dangerous for the tamemes who had to cross swollen rivers on rafts that often capsized, drowning Indians and losing the loads. Moreover, lions in the mountains killed other tamemes, and still others succumbed to the chilling mountain rains. Since there were only three or four Indian towns along the way, the food supply was uncertain, so that some of the tamemes dropped from lack of nourishment. One Spaniard testified that of his Indians making the trip, some of whom were carrying gold to be smelted, sixteen were lost on the way to Santiago.[144]

Not only was communication and transportation wretched among the provinces, but even within the provinces themselves it was difficult. The bishop of Honduras complained that roads were almost nonexistent in his region and that travel was extremely arduous. It was thirty leagues from Puerto de Caballos to Trujillo and there was no road; consequently, travel was often by sea, which was dangerous. He mentioned a recent shipwreck between the two sites which resulted in the deaths of all aboard, including the tamemes who were transporting a gold shipment. The Indians, he said, were either drowned or killed by savage natives on the shore or dead from starvation in the wilderness. Going by sea had been no blessing for those tamemes—and, he hastened to add, the gold was lost.[145]

The prospect was brighter in Nicaragua, where much of the land was flat. Although in the early years there was a shortage of pack animals, which meant that Indians had to carry corn from the *estancias* and transport all other goods, the tamemes' circumstances were to some extent eased. Witnesses for Rodrigo de Contreras, who became governor of Nicaragua in 1535, stated that when he arrived at the settlement of Granada there were at most one or two carts. Contreras ordered that no Indians were to carry loads. Henceforth, carts were to be used for the conveyance of goods, and, according to the testimony, many vecinos complied. Carts pulled by oxen began replacing tamemes, and a new enterprise began. One witness claimed that he had built four carts himself. Contreras also prohibited the carrying of lumber by Indians to the port of Realejo for the shipyards, which resulted in the use of carts even outside the cities of Granada and León. If these reports were true, the picture improved considerably in Nicaragua, although tamemes were still in use.[146]

Informed by 1545 of an abundance of horses, oxen, and carts to sustain trade, the king again ordered roads opened in Guatemala and Honduras along with maintenance reviews twice a year. Repair of the roads was to be financed from public works funds, and it was not to result in any imposition on, or harm to, Indians. In the Crown view, with this accomplished there would no longer be an excuse for the existence of tamemes.[147] More than two years later, however, treasury officials reported that no roads were opened, and that because of the rough terrain and flooded rivers the traveling was exceedingly difficult. The writers were of the opinion that if roads were not built commerce would be ruined. A number of blacks were needed to construct the highways, and another dozen should be kept constantly checking to keep them in good repair, especially since in the wet season parts of the roads would be washed out.[148]

With the formation of the second audiencia in 1548, more vigorous enforcement resulted. The Crown responded to the new president's appeal that tamemes could not be abolished without the existence of roads by authorizing the use of 1,000 pesos de oro from the royal treasury funds, both for the construction of thoroughfares and bridges.[149] One of President Cerrato's appointments was Alvaro de Paz as veedor to Honduras, where apparently considerable progress was made. Writing in 1549, Paz informed the king that in Honduras most of the trade was sustained through animal pack trains, and he requested that roads be opened up all over the audiencia district so that mules could carry everywhere, as they did in his province.[150]

From January 1541 to May 1576, there were at least eight royal directives ordering the construction and maintenance of roads, not counting the many references to those orders in other correspondence.[151] Gradually crude road systems evolved along with increasingly larger herds of livestock and carts. But no system of transportation was so inexpensive and so convenient for the Spaniard as the Indian's back. And especially since the roads connected only the few relatively important settlements, tamemes remained vital to the economy of Central America.

The royal stance on the matter of tamemes was as vacillating as it was concerning other Indian legislation. Even in the comparatively explicit New Laws, number 24 of the regulations stated that audiencias were to take special care that Indians did not carry loads, but—so characteristic of the irresolute (or flexible) attitude of the Crown and its advisors—it adds, "or in case that in some places this can not be excused," certain considerations were to be observed. That exception—the allowing of carriers where it was necessary—invited interpretation of need. The conditions were that when Indians had to carry they were to pack moderate loads, that they were not to be placed in danger of their lives or health, and they were to work voluntarily for pay. Anyone who disregarded these injunctions was to be very severely punished.[152]

Licenciado Diego de Herrera, one of the audiencia oidores responsible for enforcing the New Laws, and often in disagreement with his fellow judges, related to the Crown two years later that article 24 was not being observed.[153] Yet, the law was enforced to some extent, as can be seen from the complaints of vecinos. They were being hurt because of the lack of service and food supply, and those who depended on the rental of tamemes for their incomes were in depressed circumstances.[154] Much of the conflicting testimony over the extent to which laws were implemented is due to the selective enforcement. Officials in the provinces often tended to enforce royal provisions where the general populace was concerned, while they personally broke the laws with impunity and allowed their relatives, friends, and servants to do the same.

Spanish legislation did aim to exempt from the fatiguing service of carrying those who were not qualified. In 1530, the queen wrote to the bishop in Guatemala, agreeing that natives below the age of fourteen should not be obligated to bear burdens. Her concern was not for the obvious reason that they were not sufficiently developed physically, but rather because it interfered with their religious instruction.[155] From the first, women had been regularly used as tamemes. Often they had an added burden, feeling the need to carry their small children along with their loads of corn or other produce.[156] According to Governor Contreras of Nicaragua, the forcing of Indian women to act as tamemes ceased during his administration.[157] But for some time little distinction was made, at least in certain areas, between men and women when it came to hard labor: Francisco de Montejo noted that in Honduras women were being used along with men to carry maize to mines almost 150 miles distant, over an unpopulated route.[158]

The deleterious effects on the health of tamemes resulting from a change of climate from the cold *sierra* to the hot tropics was recognized early. This was especially true when the tamemes were exhausted by heavy labor. According to one account, half the carriers who went from one of the zones to the other did not survive. In 1530, the queen ruled that Indians were not to carry from the coast to the highlands, or vice versa.[159] Colonists paid scant attention to the stricture, however, and five years later a royal official lamented the continuance of the practice, observing that nothing else harmed the Indians quite so much, and that if the land was to progress the practice should cease. It was unnecessary that so many of them fell ill and succumbed, he said, because there were mules to be used.[160] Cédulas of 1538 and 1540 again forbade the carrying by tamemes from one climatic zone to another, and although these checked the custom to some degree, it was not completely stopped by any means.[161]

Other laws were issued by which the Crown sought to alleviate the conditions under which tamemes suffered. In 1536, a regulation prohibited the transporting of any Spaniard, of whatever rank, in a hammock or palanquin.[162] An early ruling by the Audiencia of Mexico restricted the number of tamemes a Spaniard could use for his personal needs: a married man traveling without his wife could have only four, but eight tamemes were authorized if his wife accompanied him. A bachelor was allowed only two tamemes, for short distances.[163] The Crown further stipulated that Indians were not to haul during harvest time, and that none was to perform more personal service than that provided by the encomienda assessment.[164]

A widespread problem by the late 1540s was that some Indians were spending so much time as tamemes that they could not raise crops for themselves and the Spaniards. The consequent food shortages resulted in the starvation of Indians and their families. This had not happened formerly, according to the regidores of Gracias a Dios, because if a Spaniard had twenty Indians available for work he would allow only ten of them to carry, and the other Indians would take along good food for the tamemes, a practice no longer followed because the tamemes cost the Spaniards so little that they did not place a high value on them, and because the Indians were so "simple."[165]

It is a simplistic conclusion, reached by some, that regulations controlling Indian labor were ineffective owing to the complacency of the Crown and the inefficiency, lack of resolve, and collusion of the royal officials. Those were indeed contributing factors, but the situation was much more complex than that. With regard to tamemes, there was a genuine need to get goods about, and at least in some instances it was fair to argue that using Indians was the only way to get the job done under the primitive conditions.

As far as I know, no one in Central America suggested seriously that Spaniards carry their own loads, although Las Casas was of that general attitude.[166] The problem was a very real one, and it is misleading to assume that all Spaniards were insensitive to the consequences, or to believe that no thought was given to alternatives. As early as 1527, with much of the land still hostile, when the conquerors were planning a new site for their permanent city of Santiago, one of the subjects discussed was the availability of firewood and other necessities requiring the use of tamemes.[167] No doubt their considerations were more practical than humanitarian—and perhaps they anticipated a royal provision against the use of Indian carriers—but it indicates their concern with the problem of transportation.

Spaniards sometimes justified their illegal use of tamemes for projects of extraordinary importance, such as Alvarado's argument in support of his voyage to South America. The adelantado took tamemes from Chiapas to his shipyards on the west coast of Central America to haul anchors, munitions, and other provisions for the armada because, he maintained, the rugged terrain precluded his use of pack animals. The expedition was of such importance for the Crown, in his opinion, that there was no choice but to use tamemes if he was to explore the South Sea. Beyond that, Alvarado added that Spaniards who arrived in Guatemala from Veracruz in Mexico had their wine and other necessities transported from Chiapas to the port because the mountains did not allow the passage of beasts.[168] In a different justification, the governor of Honduras informed the Crown in 1536 that he had no choice but to be carried by Indians in a hammock when he was ill because the land was too rough for horses.[169]

If uneven landscapes were the persistent excuse for the use of human carriers, Nicaragua presented an interesting contradiction. Claiming that he had stopped the use of tamemes, Governor Contreras said they were uncalled for because Nicaragua was flat. Carts could be built with the plentiful supply of lumber, and there was stock from which to increase herds of cattle. As already noted, many carts were built after he prohibited the use of tamemes to carry lumber to the coast, and he was of the opinion that within three years the number of carts would be sufficient to make native porters unnecessary. His qualification was that Indians could still carry light loads, such as oil or wine, within Spanish settlements.[170] Unfortunately, the governor's optimism was unjustified: despite the flat land and the carts, the use of tamemes did not disappear from Nicaragua, even though Contreras had ruined the pretext for their continuance in that province.

The royal officials, representatives of the king and responsible for implementation of legislation, often failed to enforce laws relating to tamemes for various reasons. There was, to begin with, no immediately viable alternative to their use in the early decades, so that there was for a time reasonable argument for delaying application of restrictive decrees. Moreover, there were instances where the officials themselves were profiting from the illicit use of tamemes. Even an official dedicated to the abolishment of the carriers found it an unpopular, and sometimes dangerous, task full of frustrations. Consequently, expediency more often than not dictated the official stance in the colonies.

The members of the first audiencia in Central America were in no way remarkable in their zeal in applying any legislation designed for the good of the Indians, since it was ultimately detrimental to the interests of the Spaniards; because they were personally involved in mining enterprises, the laws against Indians carrying maize to feed miners touched their own purses. Official advices to the Crown of course made no mention of their own interests, but rather were directed toward what they said was the inevitable decline in royal revenues, because without the service of tamemes the mines could not operate. On a more dutiful note, they acknowledged that when one of the judges had to make a tour of inspection four tamemes were used to carry his personal effects.[171]

While the judges claimed that they had enforced laws against the rental of tamemes and taking them down to the coast, or unnecessarily using them in any way, witnesses implicated the audiencia members themselves in these malpractices. One of the oidores, licenciado Juan Rogel, allegedly sent one of his criados to the crown pueblo of Quimistan, outside of San Pedro, where the criado loaded a group of Indians with wine at a merchant's house and marched them off to Gracias a Dios. Juan de Lerma, the factor, observed to a witness: "Look, there goes a flock of Indians carrying for licenciado Rogel, who breaks the laws he should be abiding by even more than ourselves." When the witness was in San Pedro he saw about a hundred Indians from the pueblo of Yamala, an encomienda town of President Alonso de Maldonado, being taken by a black named Marquillos to the sea to pick up a shipment of wine and other merchandise. The witness asked the black how it happened that Indians were being used when it was prohibited, and Marquillos answered that the adelantado Montejo and his wife ordered him to do so because they were going to transport things for the marriage of Maldonado to Montejo's daughter.[172]

To the credit of the judges, they did not consistently protect each other, a tendency apparently stemming from personal differences more than rectitude. One of those who occasionally wrote independently to the Crown or council was licenciado Diego de Herrera, no paragon of virtue himself. In 1546, he informed the Crown of the collusion of President Maldonado with his father-in-law, Montejo, in illegal conquests, and added that Montejo had left Gracias a Dios the day before with his household. Maldonado went along on the expedition, saying he would return in fifteen days. The president took 200 tamemes loaded for the trip to Chiapas, 120 leagues distant, and from there he was to continue to

Yucatán. The tamemes, according to Herrera, were forced to go, and were not to be given either wages or food.[173]

The president of the audiencia was not alone in violating the laws regarding tamemes. A cacique of Tencoa named don Francisco grumbled that even though the oidores ordered the Indians not to carry for Spaniards, the judges themselves made free use of them, taking them whenever they wished. Licenciado Rogel purchased 100 fanegas (160 bushels) of maize, sold from the Crown's tribute, which he then sent on the backs of natives to the mines of Zula, a distance of some fifteen leagues. Another witness, who had acted as the executor of an estate, said that licenciado Herrera illegally took twenty-seven Indians from the estate to carry wine from Puerto de Caballos up to Gracias a Dios, paying them in cacao. It was further alleged that President Maldonado and his wife used tamemes from their encomiendas of Ocotepete, Ytalna, Yamala, and Yxalapa, which towns they held for about a year by authority of a royal cédula.

When Rogel was on his way to visit Chiapas he compelled thirty encomienda villagers to carry for his party for a day and a half for no pay. On his return trip he again used Indians from the same pueblo to carry toward Guatemala, again without compensation. Moreover, the judges sent tamemes to the villas of San Salvador and San Miguel for supplies of salt, cacao, and other provisions. Both Rogel and Herrera had sent carriers down to the coast, even though it was prohibited, and despite the fact that there were pack animals available to make the trip from the shore to the mountains. The loads sometimes included iron tools and other heavy items. Herrera was accused of loading twenty-five or thirty Indians with such weighty packs that they could hardly move. Aside from the numbers of tamemes sent to the sea by the officials, more and more merchants were renting Indians for the same purpose, in such numbers that the towns were being destroyed.

Among those testifying against the oidores were Indians, who complained that the corregidor in Tencoa made them carry wine to the mines of Guayape, some sixty to seventy leagues away. The wine belonged to the corregidor and his friend licenciado Rogel. The natives also stated that Rogel had purchased maize from the royal tribute offered by Tencoa and made tamemes transport about 200 fanegas of it to his mines at Zula, where Rogel kept his black slaves.

Once again, one can see the selective implementation of the law, because while tamemes were not to carry beyond San Pedro to the coast, there were exceptions. Some persons of "calidad" were able to send six

or seven Indians. Supposedly even this exception was only for the purpose of carrying wine, oil, and vinegar, and nothing else; but a witness
said he had seen Herrera send eight or ten tamemes to the port to
pick up some cloth. Although the oidores insisted that the vecinos pay
tamemes, they did not ordinarily do so themselves.

In response to all the testimony against them, the oidores maintained
that they allowed the use of tamemes only when necessary and because of
the mountainous configuration of the land. Moreover, they said the Indians volunteered, received pay, and carried light loads, as a consequence
of which no laws were broken.[174]

Licenciado Herrera, accused of illegally using tamemes himself, was
nonetheless outspoken on the matter of abuses. The practice of assessing
tribute in tamemes was, in his opinion, wrong. Personal service, he said,
was really the work of slaves, who were regularly rented out to work
in mines and sugar mills. On this issue his fellow judges gave little discernible support.[175]

That perceptive and articulate critic of Spanish labor practices in early
Central America, licenciado Cristóbal de Pedraza, bishop of Honduras
and Protector of the Indians, left for the historian detailed accounts of the
system in practice. Although he was clearly biased in favor of the natives,
Pedraza's comments vary in no significant way from the flood of testimony
that issued from the colonies. In despair of the lamentable situation in
which the Indians found themselves, the bishop related the tragedy in
accents that must have had a decided influence on the reform legislation
that followed.

In reassessing what the Indians owed in a report of 1547, Pedraza felt
that under no circumstances should tamemes be permitted, except to
carry tribute from their pueblos to the encomendero, provided the carrier
lived nearby in either a city or villa. Moreover, in his opinion, personal
service in general should be abolished. If it had to exist, excesses such as
renting tamemes to merchants for stipulated sums, or taking them from
their native highlands to the coast and vice versa, could be curbed. On
such journeys they died on the roads, where, he wrote, "I have seen them
dead many times, huddled under trees and in the middle of fields." Others
were physically broken by the excessively heavy loads thrown on them as
they were rented to traders to carry clothing and wine in earthen jars, the
merchant paying the Indian's master a peso or two, depending on where
the tameme was to go.

Thus the Spaniard turned his Indians over to those who, to get their
money's worth, took it from the sweat of the natives, loading at the
merchants' pleasure any merchandise they wanted on the backs of the

tamemes, "fall as they may and die as they may." The Indian carried 75 to 100 pounds for fifty and sixty leagues, over hills and mountains, along with whatever food he had for the journey, with the overseer after him. The merchant, or whoever rented them, turned the tamemes over to a trail boss, either black or white, "the cruelest one he can find," to keep the column moving. And the driver never said, "Come on, brother," but rather, "Come on, dog." The bosses sometimes forced the Indians to their knees with their clubs. The encomendero provided no food for them, and what little they took was often consumed before the destination was reached, and there was no road taken on which ten or twelve—or even twenty—of the tamemes did not die.

"The principal renter of Indians is the president of Your Majesty's royal audiencia," the bishop related. And the oidores, to please President Maldonado and to cultivate their own interests, agreed to let the Indians be rented out; for if the oidor had to bring his wine and other necessities for his household, he would have to pay the muleteer eight to ten pesos for every mule loaded. Consequently, their friends, relatives, and partisans allowed the judges to use their Indians to carry for them, as a result of which those close to the oidores were permitted to impose any hardship and torment on the Indians. Because of this, the audiencia did not want the bishop to go to the towns where he would learn of such practices. The truth was, Pedraza stated, that Francisco de Montejo had made a profit in excess of 10,000 pesos renting out Indians, and his son-in-law, President Maldonado, had taken in more than 6,000 with the same tamemes. Most deplorable was the fact that more than five hundred of the carriers—men and women—had died from exhaustion, a figure that was no exaggeration according to the bishop's informants.

Pedraza beseeched the king not to be deceived by Spaniards who said that the Indians wanted to carry and that they were happy to do so, because the natives were forced to say such things by threats and beatings. If Spaniards said Indians carried only necessities to their households —there being no alternative without animals—and that Indians carried only the cargoes they wanted to, and that they were allowed to walk leisurely, stopping to eat at each brook, river, and ravine, resting or sleeping whenever they chose—all that was deception. The truth was, the bishop said, that the tormentors who goaded them on did not let them eat or drink or rest, nor even permit them to scratch their heads. On the contrary, the driver beat them and told them to keep moving. If by chance one of them became ill he was beaten even more and knocked to the ground for feigning illness. "Who would believe those *verdugos* who say the Indians *want* to hire out? And that they want to go through mud and over mountains, collapsing and dying in the manner I have described, instead of being home with their wives and children, having their meals prepared, eating on time (as it is their custom to eat a hundred times a day), and planting their crops?" But, Pedraza wrote, the Indians had no time for all that, being occupied in carrying the finery, silks, and games of the Spaniards.

Beasts of burden there were, the bishop wrote, and plenty of them. They traveled most of the roads with ease, and even if the roads were rough in places, they could easily be repaired, even for the passage of carts, at little expense. If the roads were put in good shape, and if at the same time tamemes were prohibited, the problem would be solved. Moreover, there would be better trade and communication between Christian settlements and other places as well. It would also be helpful to construct boats like those in Castile for use on the rivers. Different ways would be found to carry wine and other necessities without tamemes, "for there are men who, even if an arroba of wine cost eight or ten pesos, would rather go without a cape than be without wine in their homes; and even if the mountain is higher than the sky they will level it like the palm of your hand so that pack animals can pass over." Finally, the bishop suggested that the king could order each town to be responsible for that part of the road nearby. Each Spaniard who had blacks could lend one to assist Indians in clearing the road and keeping it in good repair, for the advantage of everyone. Thus, in the end merchandise would be less expensive, and the royal revenues would be augmented, especially if the roads from Trujillo and San Pedro were opened.[176]

8
The Cerrato Reforms

AMONG THE PROVISIONS of the New Laws of the Indies for the Good
Treatment and Preservation of the Indians (or the Ordinances of Barcelona) decreed in 1542–43, was one creating the Audiencia de los
Confines, so called because it was to be situated on the confines of the
borders of Guatemala, Honduras, and Nicaragua. It specified a court of
four judges, one of whom was to be president. Named to preside was the
veteran judge (oidor) of the Audiencia de Mexico, Alonso Maldonado.[1] To
serve under Maldonado, the Crown appointed three other judges still in
Spain: licenciados Diego de Herrera, Pedro Ramírez de Quiñones, and
Juan Rogel. They were ordered to leave for the Indies forthwith.[2] The site
chosen as the seat of the audiencia was the Honduran town of La Villa de la
Concepción del Valle de Comayagua, referred to locally as La Nueva Villa
de Valladolid for short. All the oidores were there in early 1544, but since
the town had been settled only two years before, they found its facilities
inadequate, and the court was removed to the more convenient location
of Gracias a Dios. Finally, in May 1544, the Audiencia de los Confines
convened formally.[3]

Because of his wide experience in affairs of the Indies, the brunt of
responsibility lay with Alonso Maldonado, scion of a distinguished family
from Salamanca. His father was called "el bueno," a nickname later
bestowed on Alonso by Bernal Díaz and passed on by other historians. (It
turned out to be something of a misnomer; but Maldonado was good to
encomenderos and Bernal was an encomendero.) Maldonado took a licenciate in law, no doubt from the great university in his native city. After
serving as *colegial mayor* of Cuenca, he was given an appointment in the
New World as oidor in the second Audiencia of Mexico.[4] He and his
distinguished colleagues were received in Mexico in 1530, and that
extraordinary body began to bring some order to the chaotic situation in
Mexico. Maldonado served as oidor in Mexico for more than twelve years,
which is some evidence of his competence.[5]

Maldonado was no stranger to Central America, having been three times in Guatemala, once as "juez de agravios" and twice to take charge of the government, during which time he presided over the residencia of Pedro de Alvarado.[6] In 1535 the Crown ordered him to Guatemala, and he seems to have left Mexico sometime in March 1536, assuming the government in Santiago on May 10 of that year.[7] Meanwhile, Alvarado left for Spain to defend his interests, and Maldonado acted as governor until the adelantado's return in September of 1539, at which time the oidor returned to his duties in Mexico. When Alvarado was killed during the Mixtón War in Jalisco the governorship became vacant. Fray Pedro de Angulo, a Dominican and a close associate of Bartolomé de Las Casas, wrote the king in February 1542, to note that the governors to that point had been self-serving, but that either Alonso Maldonado or Bishop Francisco Marroquín of Guatemala would be good as governor, because neither had self-interest at heart, but rather only service to the king.[8]

The viceroy of New Spain, Antonio de Mendoza, dispatched Maldonado to Guatemala to take charge of the government, and on May 17, 1542, he took possession at Santiago. As early as November of that year he was selected to be president of the audiencia which would be formally established by royal decree ten months later. Concerned colonists elected him, in October 1543, to travel to Spain to protest the recently issued New Laws.[9] In the meantime, however, the Crown had appointed the other oidores for the audiencia, and he apparently did not make the voyage.

Later he wrote the king that during his fourteen years of service in the Indies he had tried on various occasions to get permission to return to Spain to marry and to take care of some business affairs. Despite having received permission to make the journey, pressing official matters in New Spain had kept him in the Indies. Now, he wrote, he had married the daughter of the adelantado Montejo, and the death of his parents and some of his brothers meant that certain suits in Spain no longer required his attention. Moreover, he felt that he could not leave his duties at the audiencia because the judges in his court had little experience in, and knowledge of, matters of the Indies.[10]

On May 15, 1544, the royal seal was received in Gracias a Dios, thereby formalizing the establishment of the audiencia. Two days later the oidores began to work.[11] One of the first considerations was the implementation of the New Laws, a charge emphasized at the audiencia's creation. This legislation embodied a comprehensive set of regulations for the treatment of Indians, particularly regarding the use of labor. No more slaves were to be made for any reason, and those who already held slaves would have to prove just title to them or set them free. Spaniards were not to be served by naborías, and tamemes were not to be used, except in case of dire need, in which instance they would be paid, and care was to be taken that their loads were light and that no harm to them would result. No Indians could be taken from their lands under pain of death. Tributes were to be revised. A Spaniard who wounded or killed an Indian, or even put his hands on one to harm him, was to be punished severely. The same extended to one who took an Indian's wife or daughter, or caused any harm to a native. [12]

Vecinos of the towns of Santiago, San Salvador, and San Miguel lost no time in protesting the provision calling for proof of ownership of a slave. They claimed that the existence of a brand should be sufficient to prove ownership; yet in some cases it would be difficult, if not impossible, to verify it, because some slaves had passed from one Spaniard to another. Nevertheless, the owners had paid a tax (quinto) for each slave, and it did not seem fair to them that the Crown had taken the fifth, while the Spaniards were to lose the slaves after having purchased them and having paid the tax on them to the king. Many of the slaves had been bought at public auction, after which they were branded with the royal iron. This procedure had occurred daily. Now if a Spaniard were to lose his slaves because of not being able to prove legal ownership it would be a great injustice, they insisted, because some of them had all their money invested in slaves. In order to avoid confusion or misunderstandings, licenciado Rogel had ordered Spaniards to register their slaves with the local notary public. However, the town representatives asked that the order calling for proof of legal ownership of slaves be rescinded. [13]

The provisions as a whole were enough to cause an outcry, but the most explosive parts were those threatening to erode the whole encomienda system, the implementation of which would eventually have ruined the positions of the conquerors and first settlers, as well as their descendants. The storm of reaction was so intense that the Crown revoked some of the provisions affecting encomiendas with laws issued at Mechlin on October 20, 1545. On other articles affecting Indian labor, however, the Crown held fast and insisted on their application.

It is well known that the consequences of the New Laws provoked rebellion in the Viceroyalty of Peru and that the viceroy of New Spain demurred in their implementation, fearing the same. Even if violence was averted, it was thought, the settlers would, in any event, desert the Indies, having no further reasons to remain. Probably the members of the Audiencia de los Confines saw matters in much the same light, as a result of which we need not judge them too harshly. In other respects, however, they were culpable.

The oidores were the highest officials in Central America, judges who were paid salaries to carry out royal orders. They were not to engage in extraofficial business activities, nor could they hold encomiendas. As it developed, however, their own interests became closely identified with the colonists whose excesses they were to have restrained. Consequently, they did not enforce the law with any vigor. President Maldonado wrote the Crown in late 1544 that the New Laws seemed very harsh and that the audiencia had held back on applying them, awaiting advice from Spain in view of what was happening in Peru and Mexico.[14]

The end result was that the New Laws were not applied in Central America or anywhere else—except for a reforming judge in Santo Domingo who was making the attempt. The encomenderos and other Spanish settlers were pleased to see that little had changed with the coming of royal bureaucracy. There were scattered protests: the bishop and Protector of the Indians in Honduras, licenciado Cristóbal de Pedraza, wrote bitter accounts to Spain; and the indefatigable Las Casas withheld absolution to illegal slaveholders in Chiapas for three years.[15] In some respects, it is fair to say, the audiencia gradually brought about better order, and one can find accounts of their having checked some abuses; but on the whole it cannot be said that the oidores sought to ameliorate the plight of the natives with any vigor. And so matters stood until 1548.

While Alonso Maldonado and his fellow judges were commissioned to apply the New Laws in Central America, the Crown named Alonso López de Cerrato for the same purpose in Santo Domingo.[16] The honor was, in retrospect, a dubious one, but it was no doubt considered a reward for long and dedicated service in Spain, the nature of which is vague. The historian Oviedo who was in Santo Domingo during Cerrato's administration there (1543–48), notes that Cerrato was a native of the town of Mengabril in the province of Medellín.[17] Bernal Díaz, who knew him in Guatemala, writes that Cerrato came from Estremadura.[18] Although there is a relative dearth of documentation on his earlier life and career, it is safe to conclude that, being a licenciado, he was a man of good education. Because he was president of two audiencias, it is clear that he was a man of tested ability and loyalty. In the Indies he proved to be a man of dedication and zeal in the service of the Crown. Certainly he was imbued with the singleness of purpose (some said fanaticism) that drives all successful reformers. In the matter of implementation of the humanitarian New Laws he appears to have been eminently the most effective of those officials charged with primary responsibility.

Cerrato was sent to Santo Domingo in 1543 as juez de residencia to take the judicial review of the outgoing president of that audiencia, Bishop Alonso de Fuenmayor, and his fellow judges.[19] Following that, he set about freeing the few remaining Indians from the most onerous burdens, and he soon had the reputation for indifference to public opinion in pursuit of the Crown's justice.

Cerrato and his fellow judge, Alonso López de Grajeda, wrote the king that they had found the Indian slaves on the island being traded like merchandise. They made an examination to determine if the titles to the slaves were just, according to the law. The members of the cabildo said that the slaves were legal because they had been branded on their faces with the royal iron. That alone sufficed, they insisted, because it had been recognized by custom since the first settlement. Some slaves were taken in war, others by rescate, but all, they said, were better off as slaves of the Spaniards because their souls were being saved.

Continuing the investigation outside the city of Santo Domingo, the judges found some 5,000 Indians held as slaves, of whom 100—male and female—were illegally held. Those were liberated without protest from the owners. A defender of the Indians was appointed with a salary. It was also ordered that no Indians could leave the island. With so few Indians left, slavers were importing them from other areas: two caravels arrived with more than 50 slaves from Margarita and Cubagua, the owners of the "miserable looking" Indians claiming that they were taken before the New Laws were announced. The judges impounded those slaves and others in the number of 250.[20]

When Bartolomé de Las Casas arrived at the city of Santo Domingo on September 9, 1544, he was on his way to Chiapas with forty-six Dominicans. Fray Tomás de la Torre, who was in the party, wrote that President Cerrato went to visit them because he was a great friend of Bishop Las Casas. The writer noted that Cerrato was favorably disposed toward the friars and made arrangements for their next voyage. Fray Tomás said that while there had been great numbers of Indian slaves there, Cerrato was bringing about a solution, despite the headstrong Spaniards.[21]

Las Casas wrote that Cerrato "is most righteous and a great judge. It would please God if Your Majesty had at least four here like him to entrust with the reformation of these Indies." No sooner had Cerrato arrived on the island, Las Casas stated, than he began freeing slaves.[22]

The vecinos of Santo Domingo, feeling the results of Cerrato's actions, began writing to Spain to complain. If he was going to be judged by what people said about him, Cerrato informed the king, "it would be better to have had my legs broken than to have come to the Indies." He had not exceeded his authority by a hair, despite their exaggerations. The excuse was made that slavery saved the Indians from drunkenness and the women from loose behavior, but, he said, the natives continued in those ways even when they were slaves because they did not consider them sinful or wrong. Moreover, he added, if all the drunk Spaniards and loose Spanish women were to be made slaves there would be a surplus of them and they would go cheap.[23]

Despite the general discontent aroused by his policies, the Crown gave its approval.[24] But Cerrato wearied of the struggle by March 1547, observing that he had already spent longer in the Indies than he had planned, and requesting license to return to Spain.[25] Despite his reforming vigor, he was disappointed by the lack of support and the fact that he had not completely done away with illegal slavery.[26] No longer young, he wanted to spend his last years peacefully in Spain.

When Cerrato opened his correspondence from Spain later that year he found no permission to return; instead, a royal order dated May 21, 1547, directed him to assume the presidency of the Audiencia de los Confines and to conduct the residencia of the oidores there within ninety days after arrival.[27] One can only imagine what misgivings he felt, but he wrote the king to express his gratitude for the new opportunity.[28]

When knowledge of his imminent transfer became public, there were demands on the part of some for his judicial review. The cabildo, which usually reflected the interests of the vecinos, nevertheless noted that there had previously been no call from the city for his residencia, and the regidores, feeling that it would only stir up passions, advised against it.[29] One of those present was the chronicler, Gonzalo Fernández de Oviedo, serving at the time as *alcaide* (commander of a fort). He was no friend of Cerrato, who had written the Crown protesting Oviedo's blasphemous criticism of him and charging the chronicler with malfeasance.[30]

In view of their differences, Oviedo's history is remarkably objective in its assessment of the judge, despite a few oblique thrusts. Regarding the many laments in consequence of Cerrato's administration, Oviedo wrote that he did not know if the dissatisfaction of the vecinos was justified, but that Cerrato had made a bad impression and that his reliability was questioned. At the same time, Oviedo qualified his own position by observing that he had himself been appointed a procurador to represent the city of Santo Domingo at the Spanish court, which meant in effect that he was bound to oppose legislation harmful to the interests of the vecinos. Still, the historian commented that he did not have the low opinion of Cerrato that many did, and that Cerrato was a lawyer versed in the affairs of justice. In Oviedo's opinion Cerrato's vote would be admitted among his peers. But, he continued,

it is another thing to be governor, and to have no one restrain his hand. I know at least that he is resolute and that he does not control his tongue with those who litigate in opposition to him, or with those who seek justice; because I think he wanted most to frighten them or correct them with an angry aspect, or rough words, with the whip or the knife . . . those threats and words of his made him detestable; because, in the end, men should not be treated badly by a judge's tongue, nor vituperated under the pretext of the office and authority of the justice and superior office.[31]

Oviedo wrote, somewhat to his relief and to those residing in Santo Domingo, that he had been assured by one of the gentlemen of the royal council that Cerrato would be removed and that his residencia would be taken. (In fact, it would not be taken until four more years, without Cerrato's presence.) Despite Oviedo's guarded criticism, and his opinion that there had been a lack of good government in Santo Domingo, the Crown saw fit to entrust to Cerrato the vexing problem of reforming the Central American frontiers. And, Oviedo concludes, "there was much rejoicing in the island of Espanola at his departure."[32]

In sum, the experience of Santo Domingo was a training ground for what Cerrato would face in Central America. He had at least attempted to enforce the New Laws, and he succeeded to some degree. He had the support of Las Casas, and his trial by invective prepared him for the ordeal of establishing royal authority in the loosely administered Audiencia de los Confines.

Not until April 28, 1548, in a letter sent from Santo Domingo, did Cerrato inform the cabildo of Santiago de Guatemala that he would soon leave to take possession of the audiencia at Gracias a Dios.[33] The following month, on May 26, the new president assumed the government, making it just about a year since the cédula appointing him had been issued. The next day he wrote the cabildo of Santiago of his investiture as juez de residencia.[34]

Cerrato no doubt sympathized with the reluctance of the oidores in applying the laws, knowing full well the weight of censure that would follow. But the dour judge brooked no nonsense, and he was incensed at the drift of affairs in the colony. He told the king that he found none of the royal provisions being followed. And, he wrote,

in all this the blame is thrown at the President because the oidores say that since he was President and experienced in the land, and so old, that they had followed his example. And since he had encomienda Indians—as did his father-in-law [Montejo], his brothers-in-law, and his brothers—nothing was observed that would be favor of the Indians; all of which caused no little damage for the reformation that I have wished to make.[35]

The tribute assessments were excessive and in need of revision downward. "Every encomendero," he added, "did as he wished, and although they killed and robbed Indians, or enslaved them, there was no punishment." Not only were tamemes abused generally by the settlers, but the president and the oidores themselves exploited the carriers—as well as Indians from encomiendas—using them to carry supplies to the mines and even renting them to others. In fact, Cerrato declared, the encomienda Indians being used were no better off than slaves, and perhaps in worse circumstances because the provision calling for the liberation of those illegally enslaved made no mention of encomienda Indians.[36]

The first audiencia never had spoken of freeing Indians, preventing the use of tamemes, or revising tributes because, Cerrato said, "they determined to be well-liked by the town and people."[37] The example of the highest officials in the land was inimical to the adherence to the laws. Because, Cerrato asked,

How can Indian slaves be liberated when the oidor himself has 200 or 300 slaves? And how can personal service be taken away when the oidor has fifty Indians in his house, carrying water and wood and fodder and other things? And how can tamemes be taken away by an oidor who has eight hundred tamemes in the mines, and when even his dogs are carried by tamemes?[38]

The character of the first audiencia was to great extent formed by the attitudes of the president, Alonso Maldonado (1544–48). As a member of the Salamancan nobility and one with long experience in the Indies, Maldonado's influence was enhanced by his convenient marriage with doña Catalina Montejo. It was his responsibility to shape the policies of the court while his fellow oidores accustomed themselves to the realities of the New World frontiers. But like many royal officials in the Indies, his own interests became closely identified with the colonists whose actions he was to judge.

Martín de Esquivel, holding the official posts of factor and veedor, complained about Maldonado to the Crown in late 1545. He said that Maldonado had been named president of the Audiencia de los Confines without having had a residencia for the seven or eight years during which he had held authority from time to time in the province, despite the fact that, according to what Esquivel had heard, there were many complaints about him. For example, a few days after Maldonado commenced governing, he married his bastard daughter to don Cristóbal de la Cueva, the royal factor for Guatemala who was formerly a lieutenant of Governor Pedro de Alvarado, and who was also a cousin of Pedro de los Ríos, the treasurer of Nicaragua and son-in-law of Contreras. Furthermore, while Montejo was a *residenciado* under review for his term as governor of Honduras (Higueras–Honduras), Maldonado arranged to marry his daughter before Montejo's residencia for Chiapas and Yucatán. With such intermarriages and connections, these men controlled affairs much as they wished and retained the use of their Indians.[39]

The formation of the new audiencia had as one of its purposes the replacement of the system of independent governors who had served in Guatemala, Honduras, Nicaragua, and Chiapas. Rodrigo de Contreras (1534–44), despite his good relations with Maldonado, was suspended in June 1544, when his residencia was ordered and subsequently taken by licenciado Herrera. The province of Nicaragua was thereafter placed under the direct control of the audiencia judges.

Although the arrival of Maldonado and his fellow oidores in Gracias a Dios meant the end of Montejo's tenure as governor in Honduras and Chiapas, the marriage of the adelantado's daughter to the president of the audiencia must have been a consolation. Montejo was a man of fluctuating fortunes, but he was long a figure of importance in Central America, and remained influential in Yucatán and Tabasco even later. His new relationship with his son-in-law worked to their mutual advantage. Chamberlain writes:

The Montejo and Maldonado families apparently had been closely acquainted in Salamanca, and this family union served the Adelantado well in governmental matters. Although it did not preserve the territory of the Rio de Ulua for him, it did prolong his authority over Tabasco for several years, as well as delay the removal of his encomiendas, as the New Laws of 1542–43 required. These laws included articles prohibiting governors and other high officials from holding encomiendas and thus cut off important revenues.[40]

When Maldonado first went to Guatemala in 1536, the arrival of an oidor was welcomed by many, especially those who resented Alvarado. That was certainly true of at least some of the Indians, as indicated in the entry of *The Annals of the Cakchiquels:*

During the year, on the day 11 Noh [May 16, 1536], came the President Mantunalo [*sic*], who came to alleviate the sufferings of the people. Soon there was no more washing of gold; the tribute of boys and girls was suspended. Soon also there was an end to the deaths by fire and hanging, and the highway robberies of the Spaniards ceased. Soon the people could be seen traveling the roads again as it was before the tribute commenced, when the lord Maldonado came, oh, my sons![41]

It appears that it was not until he became president of the audiencia years later that Maldonado became involved in the commercial enterprises that would have evoked a different response from Indians, especially those under his immediate control. There is little doubt that, on the whole, the coming of the royal bureaucracy promised better administration and more justice, and at least in some respects government improved. One might say that his reluctance to apply the New Laws stemmed from a more realistic appraisal of the local situation than that held by the authorities sitting in council in Spain; and that, like Viceroy Mendoza of Mexico, Maldonado, in his wisdom, concluded that enforcement would lead to rebellion. What makes acceptance of that view difficult is the fact that the president was so profitably involved in the status quo. As an encomendero himself, he was hardly an impartial judge or objective advisor to the Crown on the matter of encomiendas and Indian labor in general.

By 1546, a vecino of Gracias a Dios, writing in some apprehension to the Crown, alleged that since Maldonado had found his salary to be insufficient, he had gone into partnership with a sheepherder in Guatemala. The sheepherder, one León, had not served the Crown, yet Alvarado had given him an encomienda, and later Maldonado gave him another. León had, over a period of ten or twelve years, accumulated more than four thousand head of sheep, and Maldonado had profited from the sale of two or three thousand of them. In order to strengthen the partnership, the president awarded León the position of corregidor of the important towns of Totonicapán and Quetzaltenango, for which he received a salary of 100 gold pesos. He used that money to pay the Indians of the two towns who cared for the herds of sheep. All of this was illegal, while there were poor and aged conquistadores struggling to make ends meet with encomiendas of only forty or fifty Indians. In the opinion of the writer, all the oidores should return their salaries to the Crown for not having discharged their obligations.[42]

In Honduras Maldonado was served by four Indian towns, and in addition he had mines with black slaves, as well as herds of livestock.[43] He took over the encomiendas held by Montejo in Honduras and two more belonging to the adelantado in Mexico, the incomes of which he enjoyed throughout his presidency.[44] Eventually Maldonado's assets were impressive: one source said that he and his wife had an income of 5,000 pesos a year from a Mexican encomienda, 4,000 ducats a year coming from investments in Spain, and holdings worth 200,000 pesos.[45] Another, referring to the "adelantado Maldonado," stated that it was well-known that his holdings were worth 200,000 ducats, not counting the houses and other income he had in Mexico worth 100,000 pesos.[46]

Perhaps the most blatant violation was the awarding of an encomienda to Maldonado's infant daughter. Indians of Tapixulapa belonging to Francisco Gil, a vecino of Tabasco, went to his wife and children at Gil's death. Subsequently Gil's survivors were drowned, and Montejo, as governor of Yucatán and Cozumel, put all the Indians in the name of his granddaughter, that is, the daughter of Maldonado, who was then a year and a half old. The income of the pueblo brought Maldonado 600 pesos yearly. When Cerrato arrived, he took Tapixulapa away from the family, writing the king that the Indians should have gone to the Crown.[47]

Nepotism was already well entrenched in the Indies by this time, and Maldonado did nothing to discourage the practice. The best Indians in Guatemala, according to one vecino, belonged to Castillo Maldonado, a relative of the president, who allowed him to trade in Indians.[48] Maldonado's brother, Martín de Guzmán, was given the pueblo of Izalco—which he then sold for 800 pesos—as well as half of the substantial town of Atiquipaque. Following the death of don Pedro de Portocarrero, his encomienda of Zacatepeque and its province went to Maldonado's brother, despite the fact that the town belonged to Portocarrero's widow. When the act was contested, a settlement was made to Martín de Guzmán of 4,600 pesos. The brother also received Zacualpa and Malacatepeque, and when the contador Çurrilla died Guzmán took possession of Zapotitlán and Apinula, while retaining Atiquipaque. Maldonado's first cousin, Juan de Guzmán, who was neither a conquistador nor even a married man, was given the town of Macholoa, which because of the many tamemes it provided was worth 2,000 pesos a year. In addition, the cousin received the tribute and labor of the other town of Izalco (the two Izalcos, side by side, were together called "Los Izalcos"). Other encomiendas were given to different relatives, friends, and servants. Various members of the Montejo clique were allowed by Maldonado to keep their Indians.[49]

Bishop Pedraza of Honduras wrote that the president's Indians were forced to labor excessively, "like branded slaves," from morning until night. Maldonado also, according to the bishop, allowed the Indian women to be rented out. From his encomiendas, which were the best in the land, Maldonado let his Indians be taken from one climate to another, using them as tamemes to carry back and forth to the sea, which had resulted in the deaths of one-third of the men of the town of Comayagua. The carriers were driven by the president's black calpixque, who whipped the Indians and dripped hot lard on them. The calpixque also seized the Indian women, some of whom he sold. Then Maldonado sold the encomienda of Comayagua to a merchant for 2,000 pesos de oro.

As noted previously, Pedraza stated that the president rented out more tamemes than anyone, and that the oidores cooperated. A pueblo in

Yucatán was put in Maldonado's wife's name by an alcalde mayor placed there by the audiencia, the alcalde mayor being a great friend of Montejo. Maldonado and his supporters had the best Indian towns in the district, comprising at least one-third, and perhaps one-half, of all of the natives. Under the circumstances, the president and his fellow judges allowed the encomenderos to break every law. Pedraza, as Protector of the Indians, was prevented from seeing the Indians so that he could not learn the extent of the abuses. Indians were not allowed to go to the bishop's house to discuss their troubles with him and to complain about the cruelties and oppressions they suffered, all of which made the natives desperate.[50]

Quite aside from the observations of the bishop of Honduras, other prelates gave much the same testimony: Bartolomé de Las Casas, bishop of Chiapas, Francisco de Marroquín, bishop of Guatemala, and Antonio de Valdivieso, bishop of Nicaragua, got together to draft a report very similar in its contents. They were joined by one of Maldonado's fellow judges, the irascible Diego de Herrera. Upon receiving word of their action, the president wrote the Council of the Indies to ask for a copy of the document so that he could respond to the charges. He said that he had served the Crown with so much goodwill and so cleanly that there would be no lack of witnesses to clear him of the allegations. He welcomed the opportunity to refute the accusations.[51]

Later testimony prejudicial to Maldonado came when he and his wife filed a suit to gain control of Yucatán and Tabasco, as the heirs of Montejo. In accordance with Crown policy to take control away from strong individuals, the attacks on both Montejo and Maldonado served the royal interest—although in the light of subsequent developments, the wisdom of future appointments is questionable.[52] While the testimony in the documents may well have exaggerated the actions of Montejo in particular, it is likely that the abusive collusion between the two powerful men is essentially accurate in the details. In the opinion of one writer, Maldonado, being wealthy, should have contented himself with what he had, since the Crown did not owe him the *adelantazgo* of Yucatán, either by inheritance or by any agreement. Moreover, the suit made no sense, nor was it justified in view of the cruelties and excesses of his father-in-law. Neither Maldonado nor his relatives should be allowed to return to the Indies because they were rich and powerful, and their presence would only upset the colonies.[53]

The conclusion of one modern historian is that Maldonado ruled "with wisdom and prudence," and he mistakenly follows the failing memory of Bernal Díaz, who was of the opinion that when Maldonado left the presidency of the Audiencia de los Confines he had resigned at the death of his father-in-law to press his wife's claims in Yucatán.[54] That version is incorrect on two counts: Cerrato was clearly appointed to replace Maldonado, who had no choice in the matter; and Montejo did not die until the autumn of 1553.[55] To Bernal Díaz, the residencia of Maldonado taken by Cerrato established that the first president had been "a very good judge"—very good no doubt for the vested interests of the encomenderos.[56]

Because of his many years in the service of the Crown and his influence in Spain, Maldonado emerged unscathed from the charges.[57] If he was unsuccessful in securing the adelantazgo of Yucatán, he was appointed president of the Audiencia of Santo Domingo. The case of Alonso Maldonado goes a long way to explain why administration in the Indies was inefficient. Not only could officials fail to enforce unpopular laws, but they could violate the same laws themselves with virtual impunity, if they did not go too far. The final irony was that after Cerrato's and Maldonado's exchange of positions, Cerrato, who took the residencia of Maldonado in 1548, found his own tenure as president of Santo Domingo being judged by Maldonado in 1552.[58]

Maldonado outlived his older adversary by many years, leaving behind progeny who did very well for themselves.[59] As a man who had considerable power and influence on the affairs of Mexico, Central America, and Santo Domingo during two crucial decades, it is curious that historians generally have made only passing references to him.[60] It is not proposed here that future histories refer to Maldonado as "el malo"; probably he was neither worse nor better than the general run of sixteenth-century judges facing similar pressures. But let us desist from referring to him as "el bueno." If he was that to the Spanish vecinos, most assuredly the Indians would have reserved that designation for his successor, licenciado Alonso López de Cerrato.

Maldonado was to have been replaced by Cerrato regardless of the findings of the residencia, but the other oidores' continuance as members of the court depended on the outcome of the charges posted against them. Of these oidores, licenciado Pedro Ramírez de Quiñones (1544–59) seems to have been the one of greatest merit, and he continued in the service of the Crown for many years. Although Cerrato condemned the first audiencia as a body, Ramírez appears to have abused his position less than the others. He was, for example, the only one of the judges who did not maintain a cuadrilla working mines.[61] He later stressed in a letter to the king that while his colleagues were enriching themselves, he was not.[62]

Still, the first impression he made on the puritanical Cerrato was negative. While all the oidores came in for censure because of their private

142   FORCED NATIVE LABOR

conduct, Ramírez seems to have ranged farther than the others, carrying on affairs with no less than three married women, a situation complicated by the fact that the judge was a married man whose wife waited in Spain.[61] "He would like to go for her," Cerrato wrote, "because everyone is gossiping about it." The Crown had ordered that wives join their husbands in the Indies, and Cerrato added with a hint of sarcasm that "it seems to me that he should go for her, because it is not just that such provision be made for others and not for the oidor."[64]

Aside from his indiscreet personal life, Ramírez proved to be one of the most reliable oidores of sixteenth-century Central America. Far from being merely a courtroom judge, he was a vigorous man of action who apparently enjoyed the rigors of the field. First ordered to travel to Chiapas to reassess the tributes for that province, Ramírez was diverted to Nicaragua to deal with rebels from Peru. In 1546, he quieted down the mischief caused by Captain Melchor Verdugo (Berdugo) with forceful persuasion, and also dealt with Captain Juan Alonso Palomino, who had been sent by Gonzalo Pizarro. Ramírez was then ordered to Peru to assist Pedro de la Gasca against the rebellion of Gonzalo Pizarro. Leading a group of two hundred men from Central America, Ramírez distinguished himself as one of the five captains in the royal forces. He participated in the battle of Xaquixaguana, which resulted in the capture of Pizarro, after which the royal judge returned finally to Central America in the year 1549.[65]

He was absent while Cerrato was taking the residencia of the audiencia, but the new president subsequently reappointed him to the court. Ten years later Ramírez again took up arms when the Crown ordered a Spanish force to move against the Lacandón Indians who had attacked many Christian towns to the north. To punish the Lacandones, their enslavement was authorized. In 1559, Ramírez led an expedition against them, subduing the rebels after an exhaustive campaign. In one region a priest had been killed, as a result of which eighty principales were hanged. The Spaniards returned to Guatemala with 150 captives.[66] While Ramírez was not always in complete agreement with Cerrato, it must be said that on the whole he worked with the president.

Some evidence of the licenciado's impetuous nature is evident in this cryptic entry in the Annals of the Cakchiquels: "One month and five days after the bronze bell came, the Lord Licenciate Ramírez wished to kill the Lord Bishop in Pangán [Santiago], while the Lord Cerrado [sic] was there. Ramírez entered the house of God. This happened on Tuesday, the 2 Can [January 17, 1553]."[67] The biographer of Bishop Marroquín entitles his version of the incident, "The oidor Ramírez wants to kill the bishop."[68]

When the bishop interceded on behalf of an escaped prisoner, Ramírez became incensed and approached the scene with a sword. He squabbled with the fiscal, from whom he took the staff and broke it over his head. Then he swung his sword at the bishop, cutting his habit and scratching his arm. Ramírez called for a harquebus and, according to the bishop, was preparing to put the fuse to it when someone snatched it from his hand. Whether the judge would actually have fired on Marroquín we may leave to conjecture; but the affair caused a great scandal.[69]

In 1555, Ramírez wrote to the king asking for consideration because he had brought his wife and his brother over at considerable expense, as a result of which he was in financial straits. He had served thirteen years, he said, while others with far less service had been given permission to return to Spain or were promoted to better posts. Although Cerrato had received credit for reforms, Ramírez said that he got little even though he helped execute them. While the other oidores were building their assets he was pacifying the land and dealing with rebellions.[70]

Cerrato died in 1555 while his residencia was being taken by his replacement, Dr. Antonio Rodríguez de Quesada. As traditional accounts have it, Quesada died in 1558, after which Ramírez, as "oidor decano," assumed the presidency, a position he held for more than nine months until the arrival of licenciado Juan Núñez de Landecho.[71] There is, however, sufficient documentary evidence showing that Quesada actually died in October, 1555, and that Ramírez acted as president of the audiencia, apparently until the arrival of Landecho in 1559.[72]

That same year Landecho took the residencia of Ramírez, which was remarkably free from charges against the oidor's service. Witnesses had little to say about any scandalous relations with women, even Bernal Díaz, who could usually be relied upon for spicy details.[73] Finally, in 1559, Ramírez was promoted and ordered to the city of La Plata de los Charcas in Peru at the good salary of 5,000 pesos annually.[74] Despite his militant manner, he had served long and well during some turbulent years in Central America.

Licenciado Juan Rogel (1544–50) was a man of less substance, but one whose character and service merit a brief glance here. Compared to Ramírez, his duties were more prosaic, and he was a man whose interests lay more with his bank account than with feats of arms. He maintained the "best" blacks in Honduras in a cuadrilla exploiting the mines. According to one Spaniard, those slaves numbered more than those held by fifty conquistadores.[75]

Rogel was a philanderer whose conduct was the subject of gossip. During his residenica, an *alguacil mayor* deposed that the judge was going around publicly and "dishonestly" with a married woman, and another witness told how it was common knowledge that Rogel had an "amiga." Gonzalo de Alvarado confirmed the relationship with the married woman, "with whom he slept many nights."

The liaison brought grief to all concerned because licenciado Rogel, according to one witness, thrashed the unfortunate woman until she screamed. The cuckolded husband complained bitterly about the arrangement and was, at least on one occasion, reduced to tears. As some of the citizens complained publicly about the scandal, one of them discussed Rogel's notoriety with him, assuring the oidor that there was a lot of whispering about the affair. To that, the unkind judge remarked that, "in a word, she was a bad woman who gave her body to whomever wanted it." (The statement was apparently accurate enough, however, for witnesses said that her favors were shared by a fellow oidor, Diego de Herrera; and others believed that President Maldonado had made love to her as well, although they added that he had been very discreet and that it had happened before he married Montejo's daughter.)

Rogel was also in love with a young maiden, whose reputation was ruined by his improper attentions.[76] The judge could hardly excuse his indecorous conduct owing to the passion of tender years; indeed, he was a man past forty. Rogel had said he wanted to go to Spain to marry, and Cerrato's suggestion that the king give him license to do so was no doubt best for the domestic tranquility of the community.[77]

In all fairness to the first audiencia, it should be observed that some attempt, however modest, was made to rectify abuses of the natives. It fell to Rogel to carry out what was perhaps the most significant reform of their period in the province of Chiapas. In 1546, the oidor traveled to Chiapas to revise the tributes to a more equitable assessment. He took away much of the personal service that the Indians had contributed to mine labor, sugar mills, the care of livestock, and domestic service in Spanish homes. He forbade, under grave penalty, the use of any Indian inside a sugar mill, working a press or in any other capacity; however, they were allowed to work outside carting firewood or cane.

According to Remesal, he also took away the greater part of the tamemes, and allowed no carrying by humans for more than fifteen or twenty leagues from their region. These changes alleviated the burden on the Indians, but the reforms were not complete enough to satisfy them or the Dominican friars. The encomenderos, however, felt that the oidor had gone too far, and in 1547, thirty-five vecinos, keenly resenting the loss of tamemes, put their signatures to a protest.[78] While Rogel was in Ciudad Real he also took the residencia of Francisco de Montejo.[79]

Licenciado Juan Rogel has had few defenders, although the generous Remesal gave the opinion that is best known: "He was a wise and educated man, a friend of peace and justice; and although he wanted to do more than he did, it was not in his power to go forward because of finding himself in such dangerous times."[80] There was bad blood between Rogel and.Bishop Marroquín, who leaves us with quite a different impression of the judge.[81] As we shall see, Cerrato's assessment of Rogel's character was little different from that of the bishop; nevertheless, he reappointed the oidor out of necessity. Much to the relief of Cerrato, the Crown moved to replace Rogel a little more than a year later.[82] Rogel returned to Spain with the intention of never returning to the Indies.[83]

The remaining judge of the audiencia was licenciado Diego de Herrera (1544–48), considered by Las Casas and Bishop Valdivieso the only one of the oidores fit to serve.[84] Cerrato, on the other hand, thought Herrera the worst of the lot.[85] Cerrato's opinion might have been otherwise, because in a sense Herrera was the conscience of the first audiencia, frequently at odds with his fellow judges. But his commercial interests and personal life made him unfit to be an oidor, in Cerrato's view. Perhaps most notable among his various charges was taking the residencia of Rodrigo de Contreras, who governed the province of Nicaragua autocratically. The results of the inquiry were inconclusive, but Herrera felt that he had incurred the enmity of the governor.

In the preliminary investigation carried out (the *pesquisa secreta*) under Cerrato, as well as in the public residencia, Herrera had been found "very culpable." The most serious charge against him was his dealing in black slaves, acquired from a priest in a mining enterprise. Despite Herrera's objections, Cerrato felt that the oidor could make no effective defense because of his greed.[86] The case against Herrera was, in Cerrato's words, one of "great importance."[87] Moreover, aside from taking his pleasure with Rogel's married girl friend, Herrera also kept an Indian girl, a naboría of generous spirit known to the oidor as "doña Ysabelica" in tender moments.[88]

While reappointing Ramírez and Rogel with misgivings, Cerrato would not return the staff to Herrera with his suit pending. The president wrote the king that,

Licenciado Herrera goes around complaining about me because I did not return the staff of office to him; and it seems to me that he has no reason to do so, because aside from what is in the residencia, I convicted him for a mine that he took by force from a priest, and more than seven or eight thousand castellanos, and the tribute of forty Negroes that he also took in a certain manner. And although he appealed all of it [and] I assigned the appeal to him, he did not want to follow up on it, and he made an agreement with the party [the priest]. And this, together with the rest, seemed to me to be enough reason for him not to remain here as oidor because, in addition, he is so troublesome and greedy that he is not suitable for an oidor, at least not in this province. And it seems to me that he should be satisfied, because it is well known that in a little over four years he made twenty thousand ducats. He has made it public that he will come back to take my residencia. If he takes it with the same will that I took his I would rejoice in it.[89]

Herrera also wrote Charles V to give his version:

After he had taken our residencia . . . licenciado Cerrato readmitted licenciados Ramírez and Rogel to their official capacities and left me out; and I have felt this because I have a right. The cause that moved him [to this action] will be given by him. What I suspect is that licenciado Maldonado and Rodrigo de Contreras, who was governor of Nicaragua, felt for sure (and they have publicized it) that I am party to taking away the Indians that their wives and children had. And thus, in the residencia, they sought to do me all the harm they could, especially Rodrigo de Contreras, who sent his sons here to post against me seventy accusations of guilt. And they will solicit others to bring suit, offering money to anyone who might help them in the prosecution of their passion. It is said that they spent a thousand castellanos; and among others who, at their entreaties, brought charges was a clergyman from whom I had bought the third part of a cuadrilla of twenty nine Negroes who together, without having been divided, discovered a rich mine. This clergyman made a claim in the residencia for this part of the mine that I had, because of my Negroes; and claiming that the Negroes that he sold me were sold at a price lower than their worth. For that he [Cerrato] convicted me, [claiming] that I should pay for each Negro, in fulfillment, a hundred and forty pesos, having bought them at a hundred and thirty. It seemed to me that he had abused me, and I said that I was thinking of claiming abuse in the residencia because of the charges and claims that, more than anything, made me lose my position.[90]

Herrera had some reason for suspecting vengeance on the part of Contreras, because it was Herrera who condemned the governor harshly for his treatment of the Indians in Nicaragua.[91] The judge later went even further by writing the Crown that officials should not have any Indians, nor should Indians be assigned to any of their relatives or servants, a most unpopular suggestion which, if adopted, would have seriously affected the other oidores. Furthermore, he recommended that government be in the hands of one person only and that that person visit the provinces personally.

He requested permission to return to Spain: "I fear this land very much," he wrote, adding that he was ill and wanting to seek a cure in his native land.[92] Perhaps he was ready to retire, for to Cerrato's estimate of the judge's wealth, Bishop Marroquín added that few men had gone to the Indies who, in such a short time, had been so avaricious as Herrera and

Rogel.[93] According to witnesses, both had used Indians from crown towns to build their residences.[94]

Apparently the Crown had not anticipated that Cerrato would find the oidores so reprehensible, because no provision had been made to replace any one of them, aside from the president. As it turned out, Cerrato would have preferred replacing all of them. The immediate dilemma facing him was that there were no other qualified men available, and he could not manage alone. Consequently, he contemplated retention of the oidores whose record he found so shockingly remiss.

Finishing the residencia quickly, he wrote the king four months after his arrival, on September 28, 1548, to report his predicament. After reviewing the abuse of the Indians, he said that for him to remain quiet would be to act "worse than Mohammed." The oidores had created an intolerable situation that he could not handle without help. He could not take on Herrera, although he said he would have had it not been for the lawsuit pending against him. He did reappoint Rogel, but Ramírez had not yet returned from Peru. Given a choice, he said he would return the office to none of them, "nor would it be suitable for them to be here because they have threatened everyone, and even me as well, in a manner not lacking passion."[95]

He very shortly regretted having given Rogel his post back; within three months Cerrato wrote the king, saying that the oidor was so passionate with those who had testified against him in the residencia and so vengeful that he could not depend on his judgments. The Crown appointed licenciado Tomás López to travel to Central America to replace Rogel,[96] who would finally leave in 1550.

Other charges of misconduct were brought against the oidores in the residencia trial, but the foregoing is sufficient to indicate the difficulty of establishing a court to command the respect and obedience of the rambunctious vecinos. To Cerrato's mind, the first audiencia represented inefficiency, disorder, and immorality. The judges were lacking in the dignity and integrity demanded by their offices. For the colonists, however, the court had been easy to live with, for if the oidores themselves set bad examples they could hardly expect the others to do better. The legal informalities to which the settlers had become accustomed made it exceedingly difficult for Cerrato when he attempted to impose the full weight of the laws on a hostile community. Moreover, he found it necessary to do so in the company of judges in whom he had little confidence and for whom he entertained scant respect.

Cerrato looked to the reformation of the audiencia district, a task for which he could use the services of ten oidores, or so he informed the king.[97] With the residencia completed in Gracias a Dios by late September 1548, he liberated the Indian slaves held illegally by the few settlers and moved across to San Salvador.[98] In that city, the second largest settlement in the province of Guatemala, the judges found the Indians suffering from the unreasonable tributes they were forced to pay, a situation they remedied to the accompaniment of loud complaints from the encomenderos.[99] Shortly after his arrival there Cerrato freed the slaves, and even though they had been taken illegally from encomiendas, the Spaniards blamed the officials for their losses. In San Salvador about five hundred Indians were taken from some forty vecinos.[100] Later Cerrato explained how the Indian men and women were liberated:

It was ordered that they [the slave holders] show the titles indicating how they held the slaves justly. No one produced them, nor did they even try, because in truth all of them were from encomienda pueblos, and none was taken in just war or any kind of war. And thus, conforming to the law that disposes in such cases, all of them were freed, the parties being called in and heard.[101]

The cabildo of Santiago elaborated on Cerrato's pithy version by noting that, in San Salvador,

The first thing he did was to have it announced that all those who had slaves should bring them before the Audiencia, under a certain penalty which he imposed. And later when the vecinos brought them he ordered that the Indians be freed.

And the vecinos asked the Audiencia by what authority they wished to free them. And licenciado Cerrato said that he brought a cédula from Your Majesty whereby he freed those of Santo Domingo, and also by the law given by Your Majesty regarding the making of slaves.

And notwithstanding that the vecinos claimed to have had the slaves for a long time in this area, possessing them as slaves who were branded with the iron of Your Majesty; and having bought them at public auctions (and other places as well), and having engaged in exchanging them, one for another, as is done with slaves; and that many of them are from the slaves that the officials of Your Majesty sold from the [royal] quintos—without any one of those Indians asking for liberty (because they had no reason to ask for it), licenciado Cerrato ordered them set free. And he, with the authority of the said Audiencia, (and as the Audiencia), gave the order and they were marked [branded] "free" on their arms, and they were free.[102]

The plight of the Spaniards was exemplified in the petition made by the conquistador Diego Holguín. He explained that the fifty slaves he had held were all he had to sustain him because they had furnished his food. He had purchased the Indians for more than 3,000 pesos de oro, and Cerrato had taken them away, as well as his lands and buildings.[103] Many of the vecinos had large sums of money invested in their slaves, and since there was no recompense the loss was severe in many instances.

Leaving San Salvador and its forlorn vecinos, Cerrato turned northward to Santiago de Guatemala, which had become the most important Spanish settlement in Central America. Arriving there about the first of 1549, the audiencia presently established quarters in the largest and best house in the city, the residence of Bishop Marroquín.[104]

When Cerrato was still in Gracias a Dios, Marroquín and two representatives of the Franciscans and Dominicans had traveled to meet with the new president to beg him to go to Santiago to remedy the misfortunes of the miserable Indians. In Guatemala, and Nicaragua and Chiapas as well, they said, the judges of the first audiencia had done nothing to help the natives.[105]

Once in Santiago, Cerrato moved swiftly to set free those slaves held illegally, and again the protestations were heard. The president's own accounts of his actions are sententious, observing merely that the audiencia freed the slaves according to law and punished those culpable.[106] The cabildo of the city complained that Cerrato ordered all slaves brought before him within ten days. Then, they said, without even giving a fair hearing to the vecinos, he freed the Indians. The numbers liberated made up fifty cuadrillas of slaves who were taking gold and silver out of the mines, so that the king lost a great deal of money from his share.[107]

Affairs in Chiapas were a subject of concern, because the reforms made in 1546 by licenciado Rogel had not been observed. There, as in Guatemala, "the great number of slaves they made is incredible," according to a report by Las Casas.[108] The Council of the Indies appointed Diego Ramírez, then residing in Mexico, *visitador* and *juez pesquisidor* to investigate the circumstances surrounding the protests in Chiapas. The judge, called "very virtuous and zealous of justice" by Fray Francisco Ximénez, arrived at Ciudad Real in June 1548, a month or so after the arrival of Cerrato in Gracias a Dios. He found that those Indians not actually enslaved were suffering under such excessive tributes that they were reduced to circumstances little better than slavery. Although Ramírez was properly distressed by conditions in Chiapas, his influence there remained only as long as his presence. At his departure affairs reverted to their former status.[109]

Cerrato sent another investigator in 1549, his cousin Gonzalo Hidalgo de Montemayor, and the results appear to have been somewhat more fruitful. Hidalgo was armed with the authority of a royal judge and invested with broad powers to liberate the slaves and to reassess the tributes. Arriving at Easter, he freed the Indian slaves as well as the naborías.[110] There was great jubilation on the part of the Indians and Dominican friars alike, as the procedure assumed a ceremonial aspect.

The formal declaration of the new order of things was scheduled for the day of San Bartolomé, the significance of which was not lost on the Spaniards, who blamed Las Casas for the turn of events. Their grumblings caused the act to be postponed until the next day, a Sunday. A witness said that a platform was erected in the plaza on which sat Hidalgo and his officials, the bishop, various Dominicans, and some of the branded slaves. The laws were then proclaimed and spoken by interpreters so that Indians of all tongues would understand. The next day tributes were lessened and alguaciles were named to execute all the laws. The witness said he had never seen so many Indians in the city and that there were tears of joy along with singing.[111]

In his version of the event, Remesal notes that losing their Indians cost the Spaniards not only their food and investments, but also their authority and honor. Labor was taken from households, cattle ranches, farms, and sugar mills. From that day, according to the chronicler, there were no more tamemes and no Indians gave personal service. The Spaniard who had in his house forty or fifty servants (when perhaps four or five would have been too many), along with Indians doing other work, was left without help. Within two days the Spaniards began to beg Indian men to carry water and firewood for pay, and the same was true when they tried to get the women to make bread.[112] Remesal, who arrived in Central America sixty-five years later, might have added that those happy circumstances did not last. But as a Dominican and an admirer of Las Casas, he no doubt felt compelled to savor the victory.

The same year Cerrato arrived, the Crown issued new legislation repeating the order that no slaves could be made and that those held illegally were to be freed, thereby reinforcing the actions of the new president.[113] Within a few months Indian labor practices in Central America were drastically revised. Tributes were cut significantly, slaves were freed, naborías were taken from masters, and the use of tamemes was curtailed. On the Chiapas frontier where rebellious Indians had given cause for taking prisoners, Spaniards were forbidden to obtain any more in that manner—either slaves of war or rescate.

A more general cédula forbade any "entradas rrancherias," that is, raids for the purpose of making slaves, the penalty for which was death and loss of assets.[114] And the Crown approved of the expedition sent by Cerrato under the command of licenciado Ramírez to the province of Verapaz to expel troops of the adelantado Montejo who were there to gather more Indians.[115]

Then, in 1549, a very significant law was issued forbidding the commutation of tribute to personal service, even if caciques and maceguales were agreeable. It had become common practice in many areas for the encomenderos to require their villagers to perform labor in lieu of tribute. Since some of them demanded tribute that was not common to the region—such as cacao—Indians had to travel long distances to trade what they produced for the cacao, cotton, or whatever. This was illegal, but common practice nevertheless. Moreover, for various reasons, the Indians were sometimes not always able to meet their tribute requirements and so performed some kind of personal service. Thus, in some towns tribute commitments were met almost exclusively by labor contributions. Particularly valuable for the encomenderos was the use of tamemes, who were often rented out to merchants and others, and by this law a lucrative aspect of the encomienda was abolished.[116]

Another development was viewed with some apprehension by vecinos of Santiago de Guatemala—the removal of the seat of the Audiencia de los Confines to their city, as a consequence of which it would gradually be referred to as the Audiencia de Guatemala. Under ordinary circumstances such a distinction would be much desired by the status-conscious settlers, but the prospect of Cerrato's ominous presence in their own community was seen as a mixed blessing. The transfer made perfectly good sense because of the size and importance of Santiago and because of its geographical situation.

In contrast, the original site of Gracias a Dios was, even by the account of the town's cabildo, "the most abject and needy" settlement in the Indies. There had been about thirty vecinos there but most had died. The Indian towns nearby were in crown hands, and even they gave pitiful returns, the best one yielding only about 100 pesos, which was in turn used to pay the corregidor whose duty it was to administer the village. The other towns paid only about 60 pesos in tribute. Since the remaining vecinos had little with which to sustain themselves, there was no excuse for the existence of the city except that the audiencia was there. It was satisfactory for the oidores who had their cuadrillas working their mines and who also had cattle ranches and other business enterprises. The poor vecinos could not even purchase a Castilian shirt without sacrificing.[117]

When Cerrato arrived a few months later he found the settlement with only eighteen vecinos and without the services of a physician, surgeon, or druggist. Its isolation and location in a mountainous area discouraged any from traveling there to seek justice, and in his four months there Cerrato said there had been only one appeal to be considered. Moreover, he noted that there was very little in the way of food, even fodder for horses. There was no inn where a plaintiff could stay and, he added, "everything that has been spent, and is being spent, on this Audiencia will be thrown in the sea if it is not moved from here." The only reason it had remained there was because President Maldonado had four Indian villages serving him and because the investments of the oidores paid them more than their salaries, which could be saved. There was the added advantage for them of not having official matters getting in the way of their commercial interests.[118]

Licenciado Herrera opposed moving the audiencia seat without crown approval, but in June 1548, the Crown authorized Cerrato to transfer the court to any place he deemed most suitable. After he effected the change in 1549, he received royal approval.[119]

Finally, after a quarter century of having things pretty much their own way, the encomenderos felt the long arm of Spanish bureaucracy closing in on them. Somewhat to their disbelief, the jaded conquerors of the Maya-Quiché saw an elderly judge methodically destroying what was to them the natural order of things in their small corner of the world. The consequences were to place in jeopardy the social and economic status of the distraught encomenderos. But the drama was not yet over, and they were not disposed to submit without a fight.

9

Reaction to the Reforms

THE REFORMS IMPLEMENTED in Central America in the months following were viewed by the vexed colonists as no less than draconian. And there was no question in their minds that it was all the fault of Alonso López de Cerrato; for, after all, he was for the most part enforcing the New Laws that had lain dormant for years. Even the Crown had been reasonable enough in its attitude toward the loose administrations of various governors and the first audiencia, and it was natural enough to assume that without the rude intrusion of the new president affairs would have continued as before.[1]

Bearing in mind the violent character of that society, Cerrato was a most unlikely figure to effect such momentous changes in the threatening atmosphere that prevailed. A year after his arrival in Santiago, Cerrato wrote the king that he was in no condition for the Indies nor did he have the disposition to continue. He felt it would be in the best interests of the Crown for him to leave. "I am old," he said, "now that I am approaching sixty. I have no teeth left nor any hair, my whiskers are gray, and I have insufficient strength for so much work." After seven years in the New World he wanted to return to his homeland to die as a Christian.[2] In addition to those infirmities of age, the judge suffered from a painful kidney stone that kept him in bed for protracted intervals.[3] Even before the rain of abuse descended upon him he had notified the king that it was all too much for a man of his years, especially in a land of such unruly people.[4]

But if the president was no robust, brawling type, the avuncular image presented by his self-effacing remarks is belied by the boldness and energy with which he pursued his aims. The wonder is, given the temper of the times and the passion generated by his actions, that he was not assassinated. Apparently there was such a plot, but he survived seven years of threats to die a natural death.[5]

Fierce reaction on the part of the colonists was both predictable and immediate. What was, indeed, a *fait accompli* represented to the vecinos a challenge equal to that presented earlier by the New Laws, but perhaps no more hopeless. Prior to Cerrato's arrival the Crown had retreated before the dire predictions of those in the colonies. The difference was that while previous officials of the Crown had deliberated over implementation of the laws, Cerrato had moved quickly to apply them.

The settlers had been defensive about their use of Indian labor for years, for they were well aware of the Crown's uneasy stance on the issue of slavery and other forms of forced labor. Their reasoning, however spurious at times, deserves a hearing if one is to understand the heated exchanges and the attitudes of the vecinos; for it was to a considerable extent the early policies of the Crown that allowed circumstances to develop which were ultimately unfair to some of the conquerors. Because they faced the practical realities of frontier life, far removed from the comfortable quarters of those who addressed themselves to philosophical considerations, the case of the vecinos is of some interest.

Bernal Díaz, reflecting on the Córdoba expedition to Mexico prior to the conquest of Cortés, noted piously that when Governor Velásquez of Cuba wanted members of the expedition to take slaves from the islands off Honduras, "we soldiers knew that what Diego Velásquez asked of us was not just, we answered that it was neither in accordance with the law of God nor of the king, that we should make free men slaves."[6] But that was written years after the liberation of Indian slaves and in no way represented the thoughts of most Spaniards during the early decades.

From the beginning it was a convenient pretext to consider the inhabitants of the New World as subhuman, and opinions to that effect from men of the Church had significant influence on the formation of Crown Indian policies. Pagan customs shocked the Christian sensibilities of the ethnocentric Spaniards. Bishop García de Loaysa, president of the Council of the Indies, commented that the Caribs of the islands had been enslaved because of their sins of sodomy, idolatry, and cannibalism.[7] Fray Juan de Quevedo, the bishop of Darién, stated at the junta of 1519 at Barcelona:

I am of the opinion that the Indians were born to be slaves and only by enslaving them can they be made to behave properly. Let us not deceive ourselves; we must unfailingly give up the conquest of the New World and the profits of the New World if we grant the barbarous Indians a liberty that would prove disastrous to us. . . . If any people ever deserved to be treated harshly, it is the Indians, who resemble ferocious beasts more than rational creatures. . . . What does the Christian religion lose by losing such subjects? We seek to make them Christians, when they are hardly men. . . . I maintain that slavery is the most effective and indeed the only means that can be used with them.[8]

Fray Tomás Ortiz, asked in 1525 to state his position on the justification for enslaving the Caribs of Tierra Firme, answered,

That they ate human flesh; that they were sodomites more than any other people; and they had no justice among them; that they went about nude and had no shame; they were like silly asses, reckless and unwise, and they gave no thought to killing themselves or others; they were inconstant; they did not know what advice was; ungrateful in the extreme and friends of novelties; that they boasted of being drunkards and had wines of diverse fruits, roots, and grains; they intoxicate themselves with smoke. . . .[9]

In referring to the habits of the natives, the chronicler Remesal wrote:

The state in which the Dominican fathers found them was most miserable, both in the soul and in the body, because the latter was ordinarily naked as they were born from their mothers. They covered themselves only with a band four fingers wide called *mastel* wrapped around them, which was small observation of modesty. They painted themselves with a bitumen, either red or black, dirty and loathsome. The hair that is naturally black and thick was curled or entangled on their heads like hemp because they did not comb it; the fingernails were long and dirty like those of a sparrow hawk, because, purposely, they never cut them, and they are shortened only by being worn down by the use of their hands. In their personal needs they had less instinct than dogs or cats, because in front of each other they urinated sitting down as they were in conversation; and the first times they went to sermon they left all the ground wet and muddy, no less than a corral of sheep.[10]

They sacrificed animals and birds for the slightest occasion, and they worshiped idols. While they retained their old vices, particularly those of sensuality, they also added the vices of the Spaniards. If, Remesal wrote, after baptism an Indian began to steal, swear, lie, kill, and steal women, he would say, "I am getting to be a little like a Christian." The caciques no longer had absolute control over the Indians, and the Spaniards cared little about their habits so long as the tributes were paid. The Indians continued to have different women, and the religious indoctrination they received was little understood by them. Yet baptism was desirable to many of them because they considered that it made them like "a person of Castile," which gave them more favor with the Spaniards. Indians referred to their purchase of baptism, and because many of them forgot the Christian names given them by the priests, they returned a second or third time to pay the fees and be baptized.[11]

These are views of well-educated men of the Church. The attitudes of the rough conquistadores can only be imagined. Perhaps the chronicler

Oviedo summed up their feelings: "Who will deny that to use gunpowder against pagans is to offer incense to the Lord?"[12]

Both Crown and Church adopted a paternalistic attitude toward the Indians, and the settlers were quick to see that the policy was to their advantage. They feigned concern for the natives' welfare and became solicitous, arguing that both body and souls of the Indian would be saved through enslavement. The procurador of the city of Santiago, Gabriel de Cabrera, pointed out that slaves were better off under the Spaniards than under their native lords, because they would not be sacrificed; on the contrary, they would be instructed and indoctrinated in matters of the faith. The queen agreed.[13]

In 1531, a survey was made to determine, among other things, if slaves were actually being instructed in the faith, and several witnesses swore that they had slaves who had become Christians. While some slaves had come to know God, they said, those who remained out of contact with Spaniards continued in their infidel ways. One witness stated that he had seen sacrificed Indians on the roads and at places of pagan worship with fresh blood spread on the idols.[14] Aside from the salvation of their souls, it was pointed out that if all Indians could be enslaved in hostile encounters, including women and boys under fourteen, more care would be taken to spare their lives. Slavery, it was noted matter-of-factly, was preferable to death.[15]

In 1545, vecinos of San Salvador justified their treatment of the Indians by explaining that after the conquest the Indians pretended to be peaceful; but subsequently they rebelled and killed Spaniards with the objective of driving them out so that they could return to their sinful ways. For rebellion, considered as treason, the rebels deserved death, and many of the Indians, seeing they would be killed in combat, agreed to surrender as slaves. Not only was enslavement a more humane punishment, but the Indians would also become Christians, thereby saving their souls. In fact, a Spaniard stated, trying to avoid killing the rebels in order to enslave them prolonged the pacification, and some of the soldiers wanted to kill them in battle in order to end the fighting.

In any event, the vecinos said that when the Spaniards first arrived in San Salvador it was customary among the natives to have slaves who could be bought and sold. Alvarado and his successors gave license for the Spaniards to buy and trade slaves, after inspection by the governor and bishop to verify that they were truly slaves. Before the Spaniards came the Indians had made war on each other for very little cause, stealing women, children, and property. Spaniards stopped all that, keeping them occupied and cared for, with the result that the slaves of the Christians were more content than the other natives. They were eager to fight against their former Indian adversaries. Finally, the vecinos related, the Indian slaves were better off because they were not under the control of their oppressive caciques.[16]

Aside from such expressions of concern for the natives' welfare, there was the case for discipline. Even this was coated with apparent sentiments of altruism, for it was observed that the Indians needed to be restrained for their own good. As an example, the slaves of Jorge de Bocanegra were cited. When Bocanegra died, his slaves, according to his will, were to have been set free. But Bishop Marroquín, an executor of the estate (and Protector of the Indians), told Alvarado that it seemed to him that the Indians should be deposited with some person who would bring them together and instruct them to prevent their lounging about and becoming scoundrels who harmed other Indians. Accordingly, Alvarado, "seeing that the opinion of the said Señor Bishop was good and holy," gave them to the veedor as naborías.[17]

The arguments were presented on a practical plane as well, that is from the viewpoint of the well-being of the Spaniards. The conquistadores had incurred large expenses in fitting out themselves for the campaigns; hence, they expected to get back their investments plus profits for their sacrifices. Testifying on that point, Antonio de Salazar said that most of the Spaniards were in debt and that he alone owed more than 700 pesos de oro which had been spent for a horse and equipment. Don Pedro de Portocarrero stated that he had bought horses, some of which had died in the conquest, and he had other expenses amounting to more than 3,000 pesos de oro, one third of which he still owed.[18]

After the initial conquest the pacification continued as native uprisings occurred sporadically. Many of the soldiers were disillusioned over the pittances they had realized from their labors and were no longer receptive to promises of wealth. At least in the first entradas they had been sustained by fables of great native wealth, but later many looked to Peru or other lands. There had been some rewards during the earlier hostilities because of the slaves they captured; however, with royal provisions restricting that practice, Spaniards lost interest in taking the field against the enemy.

Typical of the attitudes was that of Diego de Rojas, who had commanded troops. His men waged war more effectively when there were profits to be made from slaves; but without that incentive they did not want to leave their homes, and either refused to fight or did so with ill will. In his opinion the land would never be pacified until the captains allowed their men to enslave rebellious Indians.

Testifying at the same time, Portocarrero told of going with Alvarado to

subdue the Chontales of Naco in 1536, where "they branded slaves to give
some profit to the Spaniards who went along to make war, which they
made better, being motivated by the interest in slaves." The land was in
rebellion, he continued, and many Spaniards had been killed; however,
no Spaniards would take the field without the promise of slaves because of
the rough terrain and "because the Indians were indomitable and merciless in their treatment of the Spaniards that they have killed."

Marco Ruyz swore that to make slaves and crude warfare against the
natives was the only way to impose peace, and for that reason—and "to
give some profit to the *compañeros*"—slaves had to be taken.[19] Since they
received no pay for their fighting, even if they were allowed to enslave
captives the rewards were slight—a half dozen slaves or so with which to
pay for what they had spent on the campaign. Especially in the case of
fighting the fierce Chontales, according to Pero Rodríguez de Carmona,
"without making slaves the Spaniards would not go to conquer them,
because they go for profit; otherwise they do not wish to serve against the
indomitable and sly natives."[20]

It was generally felt that punitive measures were necessary to discourage rebellion in the provinces; therefore, some pointed out that the
prospect of slavery for rebels was a deterrent. Rojas said that the Indians of
Central America had less reason and more resistance than any natives he
had seen in the islands or in New Spain. Because of their ill manner and
wickedness, he was of the opinion that they should be chastised. Those
views were substantiated by Portocarrero, who added that war was en-
demic in those parts and that it was necessary for soldiers to take up arms
every summer in order to maintain some semblance of peace.

It was commonly felt that it was preferable for the Indians to be terrified
of their masters in order to uphold Castilian dignity and respect; otherwise, Francisco López indicated, the natives would not obey. When he
ordered some of his Indians to carry food to the mines, they laughed at him
and taunted him, so that he feared for his life.[21]

All those reasons notwithstanding, it is probable that uppermost in the
mind of the king and his council was the threat of losing the colonies
through a general exodus of the settlers, who constantly decried the
poverty of Central America and remarked on the numbers of Spaniards
who had already left the region. The most serious dilemma was the
inability to work the mines without slave labor, a matter of grave concern
to the royal treasury.[22] Juan Ruano, the treasurer in Honduras, wrote the
Audiencia of Mexico that in spite of the rich gold mines in that province,
there were few Spaniards with which to conquer and sustain the land, one
reason being that they had no slaves with whom to work the mines. Only

with one thousand to two thousand slaves could the land be sustained, in his estimation.[23]

"The Indians of the land are so contumacious and of such little reason . . . [and such] liars," according to one witness, that it was almost impossible to obtain tribute from them. The only thing of value was the precious metal, which could not be mined without slaves. He said not only would the Spaniards leave without rewards, but also crown incomes would be lost, and no churches, monasteries, or hospitals could be built. Several Spaniards elaborated on the same theme.[24] When Alvarado was called to account for illegally enslaving some Indians in San Miguel and Puerto de Fonseca, he stated very candidly that he had given the slaves to deserving vecinos because they were so poor. They requested the slaves in order to support the villa of San Miguel and as rewards for their military services.[25]

These were the main reasons given prior to the coming of Cerrato to convince the Crown of the necessity of making slaves. The arrival of the second president of the audiencia gave new impetus to the continuing campaign of the conquerors to maintain the labor system, and the nature of their arguments reflected the very real desperation they felt.

As the audiencia represented, at least in theory, the conscience and interest of the sovereign, so did the cabildos make a case for the vecinos. Because the latter stood to lose everything, the cabildos were active in their protestations to Spain. Their propositions rested on two dubious theses: Cerrato's iniquitous character; and the harm to the Indians posed by his reforms. Since the president's reformation embraced not only the liberation of slaves, but also the qualified use of personal service and lightened tribute assessments, the protests derived from the general losses of labor and tribute.

In the beginning the cabildo of Santiago sought to persuade the president to assess the situation carefully before freeing the Indians. While Cerrato was still in Gracias a Dios taking the residencia of the first audiencia, the regidores sent him the following entreaty:

This city has learned of your Lordship's commission concerning the slaves. . . . We have also heard that your Lordship has not been well informed in the matter and we are convinced that in a project of such moment and difficulty you will wish to consider, weigh, and think over the consequences. And, if you do so, you will abandon the project, because your Lordship will discover that the whole well-being of these parts lies in the contentment and permanent establishment of the Spaniards and in the small amount of silver and gold that is being mined, and not in the contentment and opinion of the religious. Their zeal may appear to be holy and good, but it does not contribute to the support of the republic in these parts. Who doubts that the words *let the Indians be free*, when spoken by the religious sound holy and good? And if they should say *his Majesty desires his vassals to be free from tribute*, it would sound the same, whether or not it were necessary for the well-being and universal peace and contentment, and, consequently, for the support of the Faith.

But it is not clear [to us] as it is to the religious and we beg your Lordship, as our Governor and President, our Father and Lord, in the name of his Majesty, with your great prudence, learning, and zeal, to consider the support and good government of all those whom his Majesty has entrusted to you. And bear in mind, your Lordship, that we are Christians and that we consider ourselves loyal vassals of our Prince, as we have proved ourselves to be, in war and peace, and that we wish to save ourselves and to clear our consciences. And know, your Lordship, that the discharge of his Majesty's conscience, and yours in his name, and the good government of these parts, do not consist in freeing these Indians who are called slaves, because their number is as nothing, as compared with the rest. At present it is better for them to remain in our company than out of it, because we consider most of them as though they were our own children. And, if in times past there was some carelessness in their treatment, it is no longer true—rather, they are beholden to us for having reared them.

The point is that they are in the mines, and for that reason your Lordship . . . should consider what we have said, that is, that a great part of our well-being and contentment hangs upon this bit of gold. Consider also that his Majesty has never completely clarified the matter [of the liberation of the slaves]. When he, as our Lord, commands that it be done, then let it be done and we shall humbly obey.[26]

The new president was not moved by their specious reasoning, and the cabildo's correspondence soon lost its supplicatory tenor. "The president," the cabildo of Santiago wrote later, "is so rigorous and unpleasant, and he gives us such bad responses, that we are afraid and terrified, and he has us in his grasp." They would have more license before the king himself, they said.[27] Later the regidores wrote that Cerrato was "so wild, so coarse and ill-bred that no one can stand him or give him recognition because of what he says and does"; and no one wanted to trade or bring goods to Santiago because the city was ruined. The reputation of the land was such that ships from Peru and New Spain, even Spain itself, no longer put in at their ports out of fear of the president.[28]

From the correspondence of the vecinos, one gains the impression of Cerrato as a boorish and arbitrary tyrant. Moreover, he was represented as being unfit because of senility. He countermanded his own orders the same day he issued them, to suit his caprice. He insulted the Spaniards, calling them traitors, thieves, "and other ugly names that cannot be repeated." He was so unrefined that,

If he invites someone to eat who is not married, he says, "Get married;" and if the guest answers that he does not have the means, but that if Cerrato would provide them he would marry, Cerrato answers that he does not have charge of such things. And if some married conquistador or *poblador* is invited by Cerrato to dine, Cerrato asks, "Why did you get married?" And he adds that Your Majesty owes him nothing.[29]

The cabildo complained that the president bothered everyone with orders and edicts, taking away everything they had, which he declared publicly was his intention. People avoided seeking justice, fearful that appearance in his courtroom would only result in their being insulted and dishonored. "He does not treat us as vassals of Your Majesty, but as if we were of some other, foreign king."[30] Cerrato, they said, had even intimidated the members of the cabildo. On his orders one of the regidores, an aged and honored conquistador, was put in irons, "and for this reason the city does not dare to form a cabildo, nor gather together as was the custom for the well-being of the republic, as Your Majesty orders."[31]

In addition to the protests by the cabildos, private individuals also wrote to the king or the Council of the Indies. Increasingly, over the years, there would be many such complaints, which usually took the form of appeals, either for an encomienda or a position in the bureaucracy. One example will suffice to indicate the nature of their complaints. Cristóbal Lobo, an old conquistador and one of the first vecinos, had lived in the province of Guatemala for about twenty-five years. After Cerrato's reforms he found himself with six children and few resources. The audiencia, he said, for all practical purposes consisted of Cerrato alone, and the president hated him because he had complained to the Council of the Indies about Cerrato's practice of nepotism. Consequently, the president took away his cuadrilla of forty slaves who had been mining more than 1,000 pesos de oro a year. He requested compensation for the slaves, or at least some consideration. He had only a few Indians in encomienda, and the president would not give him any support, not even a *corregimiento*. But while Lobo's family was suffering, Cerrato's relatives were prospering. Encomiendas were being granted to favorites, "as if they were the patrimony of the president." Lobo, who claimed to be representing thirty encomenderos, wrote that Cerrato made matters worse by calling conquistadores "robbers" and other insulting names. In sum, the president was so severe and impetuous that the encomenderos called for his residencia as soon as possible.[34] These were sentiments shared by most of the vecinos.

Cerrato's reception by men of the Church was not unmixed. So far as the hierarchy was concerned, his policies were in line with those espoused by

Las Casas, the absent bishop of Chiapas, Bishop Pedraza of Honduras, and Bishop Valdivieso of Nicaragua. Like Las Casas, Valdivieso instructed priests not to absolve anyone who illegally held Indian slaves, which led several Spaniards to come forward and free their Indians so held. Furthermore, he forbade any Indian to serve a priest or friar.[35] By 1551, with Las Casas in Spain and Valdivieso dead, Cerrato said that the prelates opposed him, maintaining that his policies were badly implemented. They acted, in his words, "like popes and kings."[36]

Of all the Central American bishops, the one who had the most pervasive influence was don Francisco Marroquín, the first bishop of Guatemala. Marroquín was a man held in high esteem by his contemporaries, and historians have recorded few discordant notes concerning this most important figure of early Guatemalan history.[37]

Aside from his religious duties, he served prominently in secular affairs, at one time sharing the governorship of the province, following the death of Alvarado. Probably more than any other individual in sixteenth-century Central America, he approached the status of a statesman. Although as Protector of the Indians he took a sincere interest in the welfare of the natives, Marroquín was also keenly aware of the complicated nature of the relationship between Spaniards and Indians, and the implications it had for the Spanish empire. He was sensitive to the oppression of the natives; yet, he was sympathetic to Alvarado, Maldonado, and the plight of the encomenderos. The bishop was a man of reasoned considerations, but that very moderation inevitably led him into confrontation with Las Casas and Cerrato. While he was on record against the enslavement of the Indians,[38] he feared the reaction, perhaps violent, that might attend a radical and sharp break with established custom; and persuaded by that conviction, he enjoined all to pursue a compromise solution to keep the peace.

With his humanitarianism tempered with realism, Marroquín had every reason to welcome the new president who, in light of his administration in the Antilles, could be expected to ameliorate the conditions of the natives. At first the relationship was harmonious, but subsequently his modest proposals were too much at variance with the uncompromising resolve of Cerrato.

Bancroft was of the opinion that hard feelings existed between them as early as 1548, and to substantiate that view he cites a report of Cerrato written on November 3 of that year in which it is mentioned that the tributes assessed by the bishop and ex-president Maldonado were intolerable.[39] Yet five months later Cerrato wrote Charles V that he was well impressed by Marroquín's service to the Church, noting that the bishop was spending all he had—and some he didn't have—to support it.[40] Trouble between the two grew as the bishop began to offer unsolicited advice to the president.[41] When his counsel failed to alter Cerrato's course, Marroquín began writing the Crown about the president's errors, as well as signing some of the cabildo correspondence in which Cerrato was taken to task.

But the Crown stood behind the president, rebuking Marroquín by writing that, "we are astonished at your bad opinions of what licenciado Cerrato has accomplished," and reminding him that, as pastor to the flock, he was charged with their well-being, and that his duties did not include the disapproval of what the Crown decreed for their benefit. The King emphasized that he considered Cerrato's performance a service, and that Marroquín was to cease his criticism and begin assisting the president in effecting the reforms.[42]

To that point the Crown demonstrated firm commitment to Cerrato's methods, even to the extent of reprimanding the prestigious bishop of Guatemala, who represented the vecinos' cause in relatively moderate terms. Moreover, the prelate was censured in royal correspondence that made reference to the implication that Marroquín was suspected of malfeasance in the spending of Church money without rendering an account, of not cooperating with other officials, and of utilizing Indian slaves for work in the construction of a church. The most painful barb was an order that the matter of financial accounting was to be entrusted to licenciado Cerrato, "of whose rectitude and conscience we are aware." The president was also to take account of the bishop's activities in the collection of rents.[43]

Bancroft writes that "Bishop Marroquin's remonstrances with Cerrato only developed hostile feelings in the latter which were publicly evinced by his absenting himself for a long time from the services of the church, conducted by the prelate."[44] There is another explanation ignored by Bancroft: Cerrato explained later that his absence was owing to a painful kidney stone and an illness of the urine which had confined him to bed for six months. If, however, he missed services, he insisted that Mass had been said daily to him in his residence.[45] Perhaps there was more to it than that, but it is apparent that Cerrato was a devout Christian.

The stance of Marroquín was crucial because of his position in the community. For years the bishop had commanded the respect of his fellow Spaniards and, at least before the arrival of Cerrato, that of the Crown as well. The obtrusive presence of the new president in local affairs not only diminished the prelate's influence in the community, but also caused his loss of prestige at court. Still, Marroquín, backed by the secular clergy and most of the vecinos, was an opponent Cerrato could ill afford.

Cerrato had a special rapport with the Dominicans, but he was often critical of the secular clergy. He was convinced that many of them shirked their responsibilities and that the condition of the land at his arrival was to no little extent their fault. Even though Cerrato seems to have been pious enough, it was alleged that his disdain for the priests resulted in his frequent references to them as "scoundrels, thieves, robbers and similar names." His enemies said that further evidence of Cerrato's disrespect was his entering the church armed, which gave a bad example to Spaniards and Indians alike.[46] It appears, however, that his conflicts with the seculars stemmed from their treatment of the Indians. On one occasion, he said, an Indian woman approached him and the bishop with her mouth bruised and bleeding profusely, complaining that her hair had been pulled as well. The woman said that it was the dean who had maltreated her. And, Cerrato continued,

I asked the Dean why he had done such a cruel thing to the woman, and he said that she had done and said I-don't-know-what. And I answered him that if she had done something [wrong] there was justice to punish her and that he should not be her judge. He replied with much disrespect and little shame, "Such fine justice you would do to me!" And to this I answered that I would give better justice than he deserved, but I did not say any other injurious words.

Following that scene, Cerrato got into an argument with Marroquín because he would not punish his dean. When another clergyman admitted before Cerrato and the bishop that he had beaten an Indian with a stick, the president told him that if the bishop were not present he would put him in the stocks, even though he was a man of the cloth.[47] "And such are the clergymen of this bishopric in other things," Cerrato added,

and they are such tyrants to the Indians that they rob them publicly . . . and they do not want to be in the church, but prefer to go to places of the Indians, where it is well known that they rob them and sell them wine, and take their cacao, and make them give offerings by force. And it is the subject of talk that the priests rob them as much as the encomenderos used to do. And the Indians say they go to look for something for the offering, because they are ordered to give a tostón [half a peso] every feast day; and the one who does not [pay] is slandered for keeping a mistress, or for not going to Mass, and they are whipped and overworked—and this cannot go on without censure. And although the Bishop indicated to the clergymen not to trade with the Indians, that does not stop them from selling wine and other things to them, nor from taking away their cacao and clothes; and the priests do as they wish, committing other outrages by way of bad example for the Indians.[48]

Cerrato conceded, however, that the failure of the priests was not entirely their fault. He made these comments about the obstructions placed by the encomenderos:

There was no doctrine among the Indians, nor friar or religious who dared to preach it nor to enter the towns to do so, because they [the encomenderos] said that it was not necessary for the Indians to know any other "doctrine" except to serve their masters and to pay them their tributes. And in all the ways they could they prevented the Indians from knowing that there was justice or anything else except to serve and pay tribute to their encomenderos. And if some friars or religious went to preach to them or to indoctrinate them, they [the encomenderos] threw them from the pueblo and did not consent. And it happened that while a friar was preaching to the Indians their encomendero (or one of his slaves) entered and with slaps and blows took the Indians out of the church so that they might serve their master and not hear the doctrine.[49]

In Chiapas particularly, Las Casas and his Dominicans exerted considerable pressure in the matter of Spanish-Indian relations, much to the disgust of the encomenderos. Because the friars' attitudes were in concert with those of Cerrato, many perceived a conspiracy against the vecinos. Some went even further by insisting that the president was a tool of the Dominicans and that it was really they who gave the orders. Remesal wrote that Cerrato greatly favored the friars and that he gave great credit to them in everything that touched on the Indians.[50] "This unfortunate city," wrote the cabildo of Ciudad Real de Chiapa, "[has been] persecuted and conquered by friars of the Order of Santo Domingo and the Bishop of this province." And, they said, the friars had taken over the services of the liberated slaves, and that "the justices of Your Highness do not direct Indian affairs, but the friars do; and if the Spaniards do not do many things the friars wish, they told licenciado Cerrato for his report."[51]

Equally incensed were the regidores of Santiago, who wrote that it was the Dominicans who ran things in Guatemala, not the audiencia. Cerrato, solicitous of their support, feared to cross them and so let the friars alone. The Dominicans, so said the cabildo, were determined to "break everything in pieces" rather than let affairs return to their former state; and their position they wanted to defend "with lance and sword, and not as religious, because they have so much ill will for the vecinos of this city." At the same time, the regidores accused the Dominicans of hypocrisy:

If the Spaniards now have no slaves, the friars do have them, and the Indians serve them better than they served their masters before. The Spaniards never had such complete personal service as the friars now have, because they take the service of the Indians as if they were theirs. . . .

Now there are no tamemes, and they have been taken away primarily because of the friars . . . [but] they load as many Indians as they want to without anyone interfering with them; and just a few days ago it happened that from Verapaz, which is very far from this city, there came four hundred Indians loaded down.

And the President and oidores saw them, and since they knew that they were from the friars, they excused it.[52]

The Spaniards were contemptuous of the friars' claim to being "adored" by the Indians. Cerrato was accused of holding the Dominicans to be divine and considering their every action ("although they may make the greatest nonsense") to be holy. The president, they wrote, did not dare to govern because of his fear of the friars, and it was because of them that he freed the slaves. In the vecinos' opinion, the deception of the friars was for the purpose of securing Indian services for themselves. Moreover, they complained that the Dominicans

consider it heresy that they [the Indians] serve us, and holy that they serve them. Certainly we had our consciences with our good intentions and better deeds. If we speak of the assessment of tributes it is a thing of ridicule, and those same villages laugh. What kind of government can there be if it is ruled and governed by the religious?[53]

The regidores' emphasized that the friars had a much different stake in the outcome, and that they would not be affected to the degree, or even in the same manner, as the vecinos:

The religious pretend to be adored. This only incites our contempt and is in much prejudice to the faith and doctrine of Jesus Christ. And since they do not feel pain from either the good or the bad of the land, they content themselves with what is good for them—or what seems good to them—without looking ahead. They have in mind leaving tomorrow, but if they thought about settling here for always they would do things in another way, with more wisdom. This is the truth, Catholic Lord; and it pains us to see the loss of what we have worked for for thirty years, in the service of God and Your Majesty, and they [the friars] think that they gained it [the land] themselves; and, as we say, time will tell.

While those who conquered the land were in poverty, the cabildo affirmed that "there is no poor friar; they can support all the people because they are the lords of the pueblos."[54]

The extent to which the Dominicans influenced Cerrato is debatable;[55] more likely, their views happened to coincide with his. The suggestion that he was solicitous toward the friars to gain favor at court is inconsistent with his behavior. At the same time, many of the charges leveled against the friars, particularly regarding their use of native labor, appear to contain a measure of truth. At their best, the Dominicans were stout friends of the Indians; at their worst, the strong-willed friars did violence to their charges.[56]

Despite the alleged meddling of the Dominicans, however, it was the audiencia that enforced the legislation—or, more precisely, Cerrato. For the Spaniards inferred that the other oidores of the court were little more than creatures of the president, holding their posts at his pleasure. "He does not take into account the oidores," the cabildo stated, "nor does he pay attention to them; and there is no audiencia except the one he wants it to be."[57] Later the regidores of Santiago wrote that Cerrato

orders in such a manner that the oidores cannot do anything except that what he wishes, and this audiencia is nothing more than if he alone were in it. And speaking about this, licenciado Ramírez, who is the one who has resided with him the most, says that he has already told him [so], and that he cannot do any more; and that he does not want to be in bad with him because Cerrato put him in the audiencia, and that he is Cerrato's oidor, not Your Majesty's, and that he can do nothing except what Cerrato orders.[58]

Ramírez had earlier written the Crown acclaiming the good work of the president in accents that give a different impression:

He [Cerrato] has such care and rectitude in complying with what touches on the service of Your Majesty that it seems to me convenient that he alone provide for the affairs of government, and that he be given a private commission; because sometimes matters that need attention await disposition because of not all [the oidores] being present. . . . Nor, even, are they done with such care when charged to many as when the charge is to one only. And even the distribution of the Indians can better be done by him alone than by all. In the visitation of the district it is convenient that the President name the provinces that each oidor has to visit, because each one wants to go to the best land and where there is less expense and less work.[59]

We do not have comments from Ramírez with respect to the regidores' indiscreet reference to his attitude toward the president; but assuming that it was true, it is quite possible that Ramírez gradually became disillusioned. One has the impression that Ramírez, as a demonstrated leader of men, must have chafed a bit under Cerrato's imperious ways. His suggestion that the president rule alone may also have indicated his wish not to be associated with the unpopular reforms—although it must be said that he was willing to take credit for some of them later. While it seems likely that Cerrato did dominate the audiencia, he disclaimed sole responsibility; in fact, he resented the inference that all the reforms were his doing alone. The audiencia's actions, he insisted, derived from consensus, and the votes of Ramírez and Rogel were allowed. Yet all the complaints of the settlers went to him, so that he alone was seen as the enemy.[60]

Much of the criticism of Cerrato concerned his abrasive manner, but his detractors also impugned the president with the charge of nepotism. Cerrato, however, felt little constrained to produce a vigorous defense of the practice, because it was a charge to which almost every high official in the Indies would have to plead guilty. The ubiquitous relatives and retainers gathered for the spoils, and scrupulous as he was in most respects, the president followed custom and dispensed encomiendas and official positions to them.

Perhaps most meaningful is the fact that most of those who censured him for nepotism stressed not so much the principle involved, but rather what they considered to be the disastrous results of his appointments. The cabildo of Gracias a Dios, for example, implored the king to allow only oidores to be visitadores (inspectors), "because many times your President and oidores provide as visitors *personas idiotas* who have eyes only for their own interest and do not provide justice."[61]

It is pertinent to review the comments of the vecinos with regard to nepotism under Cerrato because it was one of the few aspects of his administration subject to proper criticism. Doubtless, the settlers hoped to discredit the president's whole program by placing the man himself in disrepute, failing which there was at least the satisfaction of putting into question his integrity.

The disgruntled Francisco de Bañuelos, whose services had been rejected by Cerrato, sent a dispatch to Charles V in which he made allusion to the impoverished conditions of the conquistadores, noting that others received rewards belonging to them. He left us a detailed account of Cerrato's largess. His charges were substantiated by the cabildo of Santiago, Las Casas, and others.[62]

Colonists were galled by the fact that the brother of the president, Dr. Alonso Cruz Cerrato, was given two important encomiendas (or repartimientos) near Granada in Nicaragua which had belonged to two prominent conquerors, captains Calero and Machuca, distinguished for their exploration of the desaguadero (the San Juan River). Those two pueblos were considered the best in Nicaragua, one of them alone paying 6,500 gold pesos annually in tribute. At least that was the statement of Las Casas; others indicated that their combined income was only a third or a half of the Las Casas estimate for just one. Even so, according to the cabildo of Santiago, their yield was almost as much as all the other tribute-paying towns around Granada together. Moreover, Dr. Cerrato was given a corregimiento which paid him a salary of 150 pesos de oro (or 250 according to one witness), plus an expense account. In what was a clear conflict of interest, he was also made Protector of the Indians. According to the vecinos, Dr. Cerrato arrived poor and became wealthy within a short period of time. As a lawyer, he used his knowledge of the law to his advantage, preventing interested parties from making legal petitions. Worse yet, it was said that he had killed a man in Spain.

President Cerrato gave to Nicolás López, married to Cerrato's brother's daughter, two wealthy towns, one of which was Cegunteacan (or "Sanct Ana"), part of the city of San Salvador. The repartimientos had belonged to Antonio Campos who, in the opinion of Las Casas, must have sold them, perhaps receiving as much as 3,000 castellanos. Because of the cacao yield of the pueblos, it was said that the income was 2,500 pesos de oro a year for each of the towns. [63]

To his son-in-law, Sancho Cano Guerrero, Cerrato gave a large repartimiento in the villa of San Miguel that belonged to a Captain Avilés, an official of that settlement for many years and according to Las Casas, "a very powerful robber." The town was said to pay its encomendero more than 2,000 gold pesos a year.

When the president arrived from Española he had with him some of his retainers from the island who were given rewards. A criado named Fuenmayor received a good town in San Miguel. Another criado named Francisco de Morales was made *relator* of the audiencia, a position worth 600 castellanos a year, in addition to which he was awarded a corregimiento carrying a salary of 150 pesos annually. Another criado, Cristóbal Mexía, was also given a corregimiento; one (Mexía?) was made *portero* of the audiencia with his corregimiento paying 100 pesos. The most notorious case cited involved a friend and criado of Cerrato from Española, Juan Barba Vallezillo, sent by the president to Nombre de Dios and Panama (or the Kingdom of Tierra Firme) as governor and juez de residencia. Bañuelos claimed that in the seven months Vallezillo held office he stole more than 10,000 castellanos. When the Crown appointed Sancho de Clavijo as governor, the charges against Vallezillo during his residencia resulted in his being arrested and put on a ship for Spain. He escaped, apparently at Cartagena, and made his way to Puerto de Caballos (Honduras) and finally made contact with "his great friend" Cerrato. The president not only refused to turn him in, but rather awarded him two repartimientos in the villa of Comayagua that yielded more than 500 pesos de oro in rents.

It was customary as a family obligation, if not a point of honor, for an official to provide for his relatives, and Cerrato favored even those not in his immediate family. His cousin, Gonzalo Hidalgo de Montemayor, "a man of very low manner," was sent to inspect the province of Chiapas with the title of juez de residencia and visitador, receiving a salary of 2.5 pesos (or 3 pesos, according to one source) daily. The cabildo of Santiago informed the king that Hidalgo had removed twenty repartimientos from the conquerors and first settlers, including the best villages in the province. Moreover, one of the encomenderos was fined the large sum of 7,000 pesos, and another was fined 2,500. The heirs of a Spaniard, dead about six years and guilty of some crimes, were deprived of their Indians and fined 800 pesos. In addition, some of the settlers were arrested and taken to Santiago. Bañuelos asserted that Hidalgo personally stole 2,000 pesos from the vecinos of Chiapas. The regidores of Ciudad Real were incensed, writing the Crown that the cousin's appointment was

contrary to what Your Highness has ordered, which is that an oidor go to visit; [but he] is a poor and uneducated man with little understanding and experience. He came to fulfill his needs with our properties, which he took from us, and . . . the rest remained destroyed. . . . And although we have lost from the inspection, we considered it as nothing because Your Highness ordered that it be an oidor who would make the *visita;* for which, in order to see it done [correctly] we beg Your Highness to order that a residencia be taken of licenciado Cerrato and his visitador by one of the oidores of the Audiencia of Mexico [as soon as possible].[64]

One of Cerrato's cousins was made contador of the province of Chiapas and another was given the lucrative post of *visitador de minas,* while yet another relative, Alonso Hidalgo, was given the *contaduría* of Guatemala. To the province of Nicaragua the president sent three investigators, his friends and servants, which added to the unrest in that troubled province. There were many complaints that Cerrato was using his relatives, friends, and criados to make official visits which should have been carried out by judges of the audiencia.

The president's patronage extended to those with friends at court. He gave Indians in encomienda to a brother-in-law of Gregorio López, a member of the Council of the Indies, without the man having been in Central America for a year. A wealthy mine owner, Alonso Bueso, was given Indians in the same city merely because he married a sister-in-law of the influential López.

Cerrato sent a friend as juez de residencia to the province of Yucatán, who, "wishing to imitate the President in cruelty," was so harsh that a royally appointed judge took his residencia and made him prisoner. The talk was that he was sentenced to death.

Finally, the regidores of Santiago said that Cerrato gave to a niece (the daughter of Dr. Cerrato?) Indians who paid tribute of 2,000 pesos a year and wanted to give other Indians who paid the same profit to his daughter.[65] Yet the conquistadores who had no livelihood were forced to ask for favors, in which case the president gave them something that amounted to 50 or 70 pesos.

When these charges were filed against Cerrato later during his residencia he did not deny them, although he did attempt to mitigate the circumstances. He insisted that he had not ignored worthy individuals in awarding encomiendas, and he listed sixteen such recipients, in addition

to twelve married men to whom he had given Indians, including Bernal
Díaz del Castillo, who had disparaged the president. He acknowledged
that he had made provisions for his brother and a Gonzalo López in
Nicaragua, a "sad and dangerous" land. In fact, he added, what he had
given them was actually very little, and owing to the nature of the place
both Dr. Cerrato and his wife had died, as had López. What he gave to
Sancho Cano Guerrero was in San Miguel, "a sad and lonely place," where
Cano, three of his sons, and two nephews died. Nicolás (Nicolao) López
had received his Indians before he married Dr. Cerrato's daughter; in
fact, the family had tried to discourage his attentions to the girl with
a whipping.

In response to the Crown's reprimand, Cerrato answered that what he
had really given his brother and Sancho Cano Guerrero was death.
Moreover, he had seen no provision against the practice of assisting those
close to an official. In his forty-one years in royal service he had observed it
in both Spain and the Indies. Since the time of King Ferdinand he had
never seen nor heard anything to the contrary; rather, royal officials had
always provided for their relatives, friends, and retainers.[65]

The people to whom he had given encomiendas were, for the most part,
those who came with wives and children, with households, prepared to
settle as people of honor. There were repartimientos in Santiago, he said,
which by themselves were worth more than all of those given to his
relatives. According to the Las Casas figures, this was an overstatement;
however, of those "excessive" repartimientos listed by the Dominican in
Guatemala, at least three brought annual incomes of 4,000 pesos or more
and none was a village given by Cerrato. Various others gave 2,000 in
tributes.[66] As further defense, Cerrato went into a long disquisition
concerning the custom of nepotism in Guatemala, beginning with Alvarado and recounting in detail how ex-president Maldonado had parceled
out bounties to those close to him.[67]

It is clear that the president was culpable in the matter of favoritism, but
he was merely indulging in what had become established practice in the
Indies from the beginning of Spanish occupation, and the charges apparently caused no great concern at court.[68] Although governors were enjoined to give preference to the conquerors and married men among the
earliest settlers when dispensing repartimientos and offices, it was customary for favorites of those in power to be favored. Conversely, those at
odds with governors, regardless of their qualifications, were often given
little or nothing.

A change in power ordinarily saw a certain turnover of encomenderos—although in the case of Cerrato this was apparently more lim-

ited than with many other governors. While this was to the detriment of
many deserving Spaniards, it came to be accepted as a matter of course,
as a consequence of practical politics. Cerrato's response to the charge
of nepotism consisted of weak rationalizations, but his record overall
is remarkably free from corruption. It is significant—one might say
extraordinary—that in all of the various complaints posted against him
there was no substantive charge against the president of taking advantage
of his position for personal gain.[69]

We can reasonably assume that much of the invective aimed at Cerrato
was hyperbole; but even conceding that there was substance to the
allegations regarding his idiosyncrasies, the fact remains that much of the
criticism was *ad hominem* and dissimulation irrelevant to the critical
issues. The Crown had issued a fiat liberating all slaves held illicitly, and
the president had executed the mandate with dispatch. There were those
who saw the more rational approach of trying to convince the Crown of the
integrity of two premises: 1) that the slaves were, in truth, not so badly
treated, and that 2) without slavery the king's colony would collapse. If the
court humanitarians evinced skepticism of the first of these, the more
pragmatic advisors could hardly ignore the second.

If conditions had actually been as some colonists stated, policy-makers
in far-off Spain could have easily enough justified perpetual slavery because of the concomitant "benefits" to the Indians; but the speciosity of the
proposition was surely evident to those *indianos* who had seen the reality
of the situation. No doubt there were masters who treated favorite slaves
with kindness or even affection, but the documentation does not support
the thesis of a contented slave class. While there is some manuscript
evidence to the contrary, one must bear in mind the personal stake of the
authors, whose involvement ultimately renders their argument suspect.
The vecinos could, in their fancy, write of the close and amiable relationship that existed between slave and master. "In no manner," the regidores
wrote, "can these [Indians] we have here be called slaves either in esteem
or in treatment. The only ones lacking doctrine are those gathering gold,
and that could easily be remedied." The cabildo went on to say:

Know, Your Majesty, that the slaves of this city and pueblo have been—and
are—so well treated that almost all of them have so much freedom that it is
excessive; because the owners have no accounting of them, other than to see that
they make some plantings for themselves and their masters, with very moderate service.

And they go where they wish and return when it pleases them. They have, and
know, the doctrine in abundance. All this liberty comes because their masters love
them so much, and they are not considered as slaves, but as true sons.

We promise Your Majesty that for no price would the Spaniard give one of them away, because he loves them. And there are many who, if they had wished to sell them, would have had to have seven, or eight, or even ten thousand pesos for them.[70]

When a slave could be purchased for about 50—and certainly not more than 100—pesos, the absurdity of the last remark would have been clear to even the most dedicated *esclavista*. That the regidores, presumably the most distinguished men of the community, were possessed to make such incredible statements to their sovereign illustrates the desperation of the vecinos, seeing the crumbling of their estates.

Later, lamenting that the friars had alienated the affections of the natives for the settlers, the cabildo wrote that "the truth is that we love them [the Indians] very much, more so than they [the friars] do; and we wish them all the good that they could wish for themselves."[71] This affection felt by the Spaniards for the natives had been reciprocal, or so the emperor was informed. But the machinations of the Dominicans, and now the temerity of Cerrato, had spoiled the familial relationship. The friars, according to the cabildo, considered the vecinos as enemies of the Indians, who were themselves convinced by the friars. With the favor shown to the natives by the president, affairs had reached such a state that the Indians were impudent; "they do not recognize us; rather they despise us. How much harm this might be time alone will tell." And, "bad as we are," they wrote, "if we should take ourselves out of the way the friars would see, and everyone would know, how this land and everything else would change."[72]

"Your Majesty will consider for certain," the cabildo continued,

that the principal foundation for the perpetuation of these parts is that we should be good Christians and that we be loved by the Indians; and that, lacking this, we should be feared by them. It seems that the President and oidores understand all of this in reverse, because they have provided—and do provide—that instead of loving us, the Indians abhor us. . . . [The Indians] we considered as our sons, and as such they were treated, wanted, and loved. Such servitude! Liberty was for their souls and bodies. . . . Because of the religious the Indians are our enemies, and the religious make the Indians adore them. Even a blind man could judge if this is the work of God or of Satan.[73]

And they added that the separation of the Indians from the vecinos was a traumatic experience for the natives.

While this line of reasoning was on the whole rather pathetic, there were more rational arguments offered which might have warranted a more gradual transition, as opposed to the abrupt cleavage favored by Cerrato. Even though most of the appeals for moderation derived more from

emotion than logic, the letter of fray Francisco Bustamante, written to the
emperor in 1551, put the matter into a better perspective. He had tried to
convince the president of the need for a more qualified judgment:

Regarding the matter of the slaves, I told him [Cerrato] that to me it seems that
all should not be seen as equal, because in this land of Guatemala there are four
kinds of slaves: 1) some who serve in the mines; 2) others in the *milpas* (fields);
3) others [who are slaves] of the Spaniards who are not artisans; and 4) [those]
others of the artisans.[74]

But Cerrato, Bustamante remarked, came with the idea of liberating all
of them with no distinctions made. While all slaves belonging to Spaniards
had been set free, native caciques were allowed to keep their slaves, the
justification for which was unclear to Bustamante, especially in view of the
fact that many of the slaves held by the vecinos had been purchased from
the caciques. Why, he asked, was it that an Indian who entered the house
of a Spaniard was a slave, but not if he was in the possession of another
Indian?[75] His proposal to the president had been to allow a year or two to
provide for the progressive diminution of slaves in the mines to avoid the
serious economic dislocations that would surely result from immediate
and general manumission. During the phasing-out period black slaves
could be acquired to take over duties of the Indians. In the meantime,
native slaves could be paid for their labor, and it could be seen that they
were well treated and not used in excessively dangerous or arduous work.

Granted that slaves working the mines suffered considerably, those
working in the fields, in Bustamante's view, were in altogether different
circumstances. Those laborers, he observed,

worked the land with the master giving them their own land to till, and in some
cases even a house in which to live. They worked so many days of the week for
themselves and so many for their master. Can these be called slaves, Your
Majesty? I told him [Cerrato] that it appeared to me that they were like the
renteros of Spain, and that it was not slavery; that if the days they worked for their
masters were many, this could be moderated and reduced. But they should not be
taken away. That would be a great harm to the republic because those milpas of
wheat and corn were the principal provision of this city, and if the slaves were to be
taken away there would be no one to plant and harvest.[76]

Indians working in households, Bustamante added, had comparatively
favorable conditions—although in his opinion they should be free and paid
for their labor. But since they did not have excessive work and could
remain with their families, they should be obliged to serve the Spaniards.
If, however, they were mistreated in the future they could be let free to go
wherever they pleased. For the moment, most of them were well treated,
and if they were released it would be difficult to get them to return to work

for the Spaniards. If those Indians were working in surrounding towns it would be worse because of their having to leave their wives and children; moreover, it might require their leaving the milpas at a time when the fields needed care. Finally, he said, "each day the Spaniards had to go around showing one how to curry a horse, and another how to milk the bee and how to make cheese, and other things like that; and just when they have learned, their time of service is finished."

With regard to those Indians serving artisans as apprentices, Bustamante wrote:

I told him [Cerranto] to order an investigation to see how long they had served their masters after they learned the trades. Because it was not right that, having spent three or four years teaching the slave a trade, they [the slaves] were later taken away without any other satisfaction or service; for even the Spaniards, while they are apprentices, give the *maestro* something. And, finally, already having learned the trade, he works some time for the one who taught him.

As one of the few moderate voices, Bustamante's suggestions deserved consideration, but the president would not listen. "All were liberated," the friar lamented, "without condition or examination, with great brevity, making one announcement after the other." He cited the technique used in Mexico, which was like a "dead-smooth file," in contrast to the effect of the "hammer blow" which deafened all in Guatemala. He proposed that Cerrato might follow Mexico's example, and that if necessary, "the screw could be tightened a little later on."[77]

In the meantime, the cabildo wrote, the Indians were alienated, going around like "crazy men," confused and unaware of what was going on. "And if we are discontented," the regidores stated, "much more so are the natives."[78] Worse yet, the disturbing changes were making the Indians insolent, and they had no fear of the Spaniards; the new freedom gave them aspirations and made them shameless.[79] From the standpoint of the friar Bustamante, the changes had obstructed the conversion process. By 1551, he said, the natives had less Christianity than ever, there was less order and more carnality, thievery, and idleness. He went on to say:

Drunkenness is almost continuous and very common in the last two years in this area; and it is the root of all their evil and sins because from this comes idolatry, incest and enormous sins committed with mother, daughter, and sister. . . . And if we tell him [Cerrato] to punish them because it is an infernal vice among them and worthy of great punishment, he replies that the Indians should not enter the faith because of beatings and whippings; and that the Moriscos of Granada also get drunk, as do some Christians.[80]

A persistent charge was that Cerrato favored the Indians to the detriment of the Spaniards. Not only did this result in a lack of respect for, and fear of, the Spaniards, but it led to outright brutality on the part of the Indians toward their former masters—or so said the cabildo of Santiago. They explained that the new liberty had encouraged the natives to maltreat the settlers, imprisoning them and even whipping them. It was claimed that one Spaniard was wounded while being imprisoned by Indians and that another was killed by being cut to pieces.

One of the charges against Cerrato was that when some Indians killed a Spaniard in the pueblo of Caçaguastlán in 1551, one of them was arrested and confined in the public jail. Cerrato released the Indian and did not punish him.[81] According to the regidores, the president remarked that he only went to the colony to favor the Indians and that he did not care what the Spaniards lost. When a revolt of the vecinos was feared, the Franciscans told Cerrato of their apprehensions, but the president merely laughed. When the cabildo members told him to remedy the situation before the land was lost, Cerrato's answer was, they said, that his only concern was the seven pesos he earned every day.[82]

Bustamante informed the king that Cerrato's favoritism toward the natives had emboldened them to the point of withholding food from the religious, until licenciado Ramírez went to the pueblos and ordered them to supply food. Furthermore,

even the boys who we had in the school to teach them to read and write, and to learn the doctrine and afterwards to teach it in their villages, felt so bold because of what had happened that they all left, and no one remained to help with saying the Mass. And speaking of this to your president, he answered that they were free, and that we should not force them. What a condition the faith would be in in New Spain if we had left everything to the wish and decision of the Indians![83]

Leaving aside the many diversionary arguments, the crucial factor was the economic pinch in which the vecinos found themselves. For although Cerrato's principal concern was the liberation of the slaves, his broad reforms also resulted in the downward revision of tribute assessments, as well as limiting the use of tamemes and other forms of personal service. Given the excessive dependence upon the Indians, these changes affected the whole style of life for the Spaniards. It was not simply that their incomes were reduced, drastically in some instances, but also that they could no longer count on the many little services that had lent some air of gentility to their otherwise crude frontier existence. Still, the most stunning blow of all was the abolishment of slavery, because it had the effect of almost halting mining operations, agricultural production, and construction work.

So severe were the economic consequences that, if we can believe the many protests sent to the court, the very life of the colony was in jeopardy. And the complaints rarely omitted reminding the emperor of the losses to the royal coffers. The matter was complicated by the fact that liberated Indians had no desire to work even though they were paid wages, according to regidores of Santiago. Instead, they became vagabonds.[84] Not disposed to work themselves, many Spaniards had indeed packed up to seek opportunities in Peru or other areas, and some lost hope and returned to Spain. Serious depopulation, however, did not result.[85]

The cabildo of Ciudad Real de Chiapa sent a bitter report to the Crown in which it described the result of Cerrato's administration as catastrophic. While slaves still existed in other parts of New Spain, those in Central America had been taken away under the misguided impression of those who governed that the land would not suffer as a result. In actual fact, the regidores contended, such action was incompatible with the royal interests because of the losses sustained in mining, ranching, and farming. There were only a few Negro slaves and they could not do all the work. There was not in Chiapas one black employed in the mines, nor was one available even for household service, with the result that the women remained alone in their houses, "lacking service in all that is necessary." And even if Indian men and women sought, of their own volition, to serve in some homes, the Dominican friars would not allow it.[86]

Not only would gold mining cease, but sugar production would end as well. In Ciudad Real there had been seven sugar mills, which produced more income than any other enterprise. Now those were lost and the owners were deep in debt and not able to recoup their losses. The mills had been operated with Indian slaves primarily, although some encomienda natives had been employed in the carrying of cane, because it was light work. In order to survive the transition of labor, the mill owners wanted to pay the Indians for their labor until they could purchase black slaves to replace them, and thus avoid bankruptcy. But, the regidores complained, the Dominicans would not allow it. The reason for the friars' resistance, they said, was that the Dominicans wanted to gather the Indians close to their monasteries in order to utilize them for their own personal service. Consequently, the sugar industry, from which the owners had flourished, and from which the greater part of the city was sustained and the royal rents augmented, was now a shameful ruin.[87]

In Guatemala farms and mines were neglected and there were no Indians to guard the cattle. Another important consequence was the exodus of badly needed Spanish artisans because they had no help. The

178   FORCED NATIVE LABOR

Indians who had been apprentices were now serving in their trades for
the friars.[88] The bitterness of the vecinos for the Dominicans is very evident in correspondence sent to Spain during these years.

To the vecinos, it seemed that Cerrato went beyond merely applying
the New Laws:

> In this city [Santiago] he took away an *ejido* that had been held more than twenty
> years, where there were many cattle grazing, as well as mares, saying that the land
> belongs to the Indians and not to anyone else. He ordered all the cows and other
> animals killed [because they] did some damage in the [Indians'] milpas. And thus
> the Indians killed a great number of them, from which no little damage has been
> sustained by many persons, and some have even been ruined because of them.
> And the vecinos of this city, not having any other produce, except the cacao which
> is given them as tribute, and which they sell to other areas, were forbidden by
> Cerrato to [sell it outside]. Some who had taken it out were made to return it to the
> city from a long way off, which has cost them dearly.[89]

Since so much depended on the labor of the Indians,[90] the vecinos of
Santiago asked Cerrato to at least put the freed slaves in encomiendas, but
he refused. Moreover, as part of the reforms the president and oidores
prohibited Indians from taking food to the city, as they had been accustomed to doing. When inflation resulted from the shortage of provisions,
the cabildo asked that the law be moderated in order to stabilize prices. It
was also requested that Indians be required to sell food to travelers
because there were no inns. Spanish travelers had relied on the custom of
receiving food from the natives, but when the president ruled against the
practice, the Indians refused even to sell food, as a result of which the
travelers began seizing it. This turn of events, the regidores said, would
produce an Indian rebellion that would lead to indiscriminate killing.[91]
Cerrato, they added, had found Santiago second only to the city of Mexico
in prosperity and good order, but everything had been ruined and the
vecinos had less liberty than those of Guinea.[92]

Perhaps no other document sums up the complaints of the *pobladores*
more comprehensively than the petition presented by Bernal Díaz del
Castillo, acting as procurador for Santiago. Dated February 1, 1549, it
shows that the Spaniards lost no time in making representations to the
Council of the Indies.[93] Nevertheless, in spite of the overwhelmingly
negative reactions expressed to the Crown by almost all elements of
Spanish colonial society, this time the Crown stood firm.

Rarely had a New World official been as disinterested as Cerrato either
in matters of his own financial affairs or in his relationship to his fellow
Spaniards. He had no illusions about his unpopularity, a fact to which he

made frequent reference. When the president first entered Central America and saw conditions, he anticipated public reaction to his plans. In September 1548, Cerrato wrote that complaints about him would probably follow. At Comayagua he had taken away Indians from some vecinos because they were using them illegally to haul supplies to the mines. And his order, "was such a scandal that it was as if I had sold the land to the Turk." But trying to discuss justice with the vecinos, at least insofar as the Indians were concerned, was to hear "the most incomprehensible gibberish."[94] Referring to the double standard of justice, he wrote that, "it is commonly considered no more of a sin to kill an Indian, or a hundred of them . . . than if they were the Turk. Whoever interferes with this is considered a [heretic or traitor]."[95]

Probably the only other person so heartily detested was Bartolomé de Las Casas. Both men were seen as ruinous: the friar for his denunciations that helped bring about the New Laws, and the president for having applied them. Of the two, Cerrato has remained by far the more obscure. Most of his views were contained in official reports to the Crown, uncolored by the drama that characterizes the polemics of the bishop of Chiapas. Cerrato's comments were mundane and concerned with practical matters, while Las Casas drew on spectacular examples and was more preoccupied with philosophical arguments. Nor did Cerrato leave works to be studied by future historians. What writings he did leave in the form of reports, however, are more reliable than those of Las Casas who, while essentially correct in his observations, was prone to hyperbole. The correspondence of Cerrato is characterized by a pithy style, usually devoid of rhetoric, and seldom philosophizing about the moral aspects of slavery. His concern was the enforcement of existing laws.

Aside from the labor and tribute reforms, there were other reasons for vecinos to protest; for, like all officials, Cerrato made some enemies in the course of his administration, and he noted that many of the complaints against him were for personal reasons. In his residencia, following custom, he listed several witnesses whose testimony was suspect. From some he had taken encomiendas; others had been fined for various infractions; one man's wife had been convicted by Cerrato as a procuress and exiled; a clergyman had been imprisoned for whipping an Indian who denied him his daughter; the archdeacon was angry because the president tore up a letter of excommunication directed to him; a vecino threatened to "drink my blood" because he did not receive sustenance, and so on.[96] If the officials of Seville were going to take the word of ill-humored Spaniards returning to Spain, there was nothing left to do, Cerrato said, "but to order me to cut off my head."[97]

Regarding his correction of some of the abuses in Santiago, the president wrote that "this has been seen as such a new and harsh thing here that it is incredible, because this has never been seen or even heard of, and it seems to them a very rough thing." He had, Cerrato insisted, not exceeded one point of the law, and what he did was done with temperance and piety. "God forbid," he wrote, "that Your Majesty order that I ease up in that which gives me no advantage, but rather hard feelings, passions, and complaints. . . ." And, he continued, "there is nothing more odious in these Indies than to want to comply with that which Your Majesty orders, especially if it is in prejudice to their interests. . . ." While there were poor conquistadores, his troubles were with the rich Spaniards, many of whom had never "seen a wild Indian in their whole lives."

To the charge that he was a friend of the extremists, Cerrato answered: The vecinos "were at fault, and it is right that they have been penalized . . . [and] moderation of the laws from now on is something in which I have no part, nor do I have the power [to act in that regard]." In the matter of the slaves, he said,

they were ordered to serve the Spaniards, receiving reasonable pay and indoctrination, as Your Majesty has ordered; and thus they do it, but the Spaniards are not happy with this, and they think the Indians should work for nothing and with the same subjection as before, and this is their complaint.[98]

It is very much thrown in my face [Cerrato noted] that neither this nor anything like it is observed in the Audiencia of Mexico; and so it seems to them that we do them a great damage, and it gives them a great opportunity to complain about us. We humbly request that Your Majesty order what would best serve in a way that the complaints about us would be excused, and that [the laws] be carried out the same in all parts; because there is no reason to do it in one area and not in another.[99]

If the Spaniards in Central America assaulted the character of Cerrato, he replied in kind, labeling them uncouth and unprincipled adventurers whose pretensions to gentility rested squarely on the backs of the native peoples. Thus he excused his own brusque tactics in a situation where tact and reason would have availed little. In his residencia he maintained that

I have always treated everyone well and always had the door open to everyone at all times . . . [but] the people of the Indies are very impudent and rude; and if sometimes I treated some badly or roughly it was suitable because of their impudence and shamelessness, and I could not deal with them in any other way.[100]

There is ample evidence that a prime requisite for leadership in the Indies during the sixteenth century was a dominant personality. This may be noted in Central America in contrasting the singular achievements of Alvarado with the frustrations of the weaker Montejo. The hardy Dominicans opposed the conquistadors with some success, even to the point of imposing their wills on them in some instances. Thus the facets of Cerrato's character brought to bear against him were the very traits which enabled him to dominate an angry and threatening populace. Within two years of his arrival Cerrato was of the opinion that, even though it was difficult for the Spaniards at the time they lost Indian services, afterwards most of them said that it—the reformation—was well done, and that they realized his good intentions.[101] No doubt that version was to solidify his position with the Crown, for the president could hardly have believed it himself. If so, he was gravely mistaken—the vecinos never forgave him, nor did their children and grandchildren.[102]

Support for Cerrato's actions was minimal, but aside from the general concurrence of the Dominicans, it appears that at least a few of the settlers welcomed his arrival. Some had suffered at the hands of the oidores of the first audiencia, and it was reported that certain individuals had been threatened by both Rogel and Ramírez.[103]

Within the audiencia, Cerrato had cooperation from Ramírez, but little from the other judges.[104] The most trouble came from Tomás López, assigned as a replacement in the second audiencia. López left Spain on August 7, 1549, arriving at Puerto de Caballos on November 21, 1549. He got only as far as San Pedro before he fell ill, as a result of which he remained in bed for three months. When he finally arrived in Santiago on March 19, 1550, López found only Cerrato in the audiencia. One of the oidores (Ramírez?) was inspecting the region of Golfo Dulce, and the other (Rogel?) was very ill.

López soon impressed the regidores of the cabildo with his zeal. But it was clear from the outset that the "zeal" was on behalf of the vecinos. The new oidor was quite outspoken in his sympathy for the plight of the settlers, who he said had suffered because of the loss of their slaves and personal service. He was of the opinion that Cerrato's methods were too heavy handed. The president complained to the Crown that the land was in good order until the arrival of López, who was so contrary that he considered all the laws badly executed. López had brought with him a cédula forbidding oidores to have business interests (*granjerías*), but when Cerrato enforced it both Rogel and López were angry. Ramírez agreed that it was a good law.

With López a friend at court, the vecinos were stirred up and encouraged; the rumor spread that an oidor from the audiencia in Jalisco, a licenciado Vena, was going to take Cerrato's residencia and revoke the labor reforms. At that, Cerrato stated, some wanted him quartered, others felt he should be sentenced to the galleys or put in chains to be eaten by lice, while others would simply send him prisoner to Spain. In the president's opinion, López was not only disloyal in his public utterances against Cerrato's administration, but was also uncooperative. On one occasion, to comply with a royal order, one of the judges had to be sent on an inspection tour of Chiapas. Since Ramírez was in Nicaragua, and Rogel had just returned very ill from another tour, López was the indicated man. When López balked at going, the president had to force him, and when the oidor returned he was angry and stubborn, attitudes which invited more criticism from the public.

Later, shortly after Cerrato's death, the other judges (Dr. Quesada, the president, and licenciados Ramírez and Zorita) wrote of their high opinion of López. He came out "so clean" in his residencia that they requested that his suspension be lifted.[105] Alonso de Zorita, appointed to the audiencia in 1553, held views on Indian labor similar to those of Cerrato, and he helped maintain the reforms during his short stay in Central America.[106]

Most importantly, Cerrato's views were sustained by Las Casas, whose opinions did much to offset the attacks leveled at the president. The following letter from the Dominican is a good example of his powerful support:

I kiss the hands of Your Highness and say that I have known that a certain vecino and procurador, who is said to be from the city of Guatemala, has arrived at this court; and he requests (or has requested) of Your Highness certain things in revocation of what licenciado Cerrato has executed in compliance with what Your Majesty has ordered. . . .

First, that the Indians who have been freed (who had been enslaved by the Spaniards) be returned to their owners so that they may serve them with obligation and guarantee; that they will not be taken from the province, nor will they be exchanged or transported, but they will be held in moderate service; because the vecinos are left very much ruined, and their haciendas as well, so that they cannot sustain themselves. And in any other way the land would be depopulated.

Truly, very high lords, procuradores that bring such demands deserve rough reprimand and harsh punishment, because having committed such execrable sins and such very grave violences and tyrannies against God and against the kings of Castile, destroying so many kingdoms and so many people, and notably those of Guatemala, they should have fear and shame to appear before their King and his Royal Council to ask not for mercy and remission, and that their lives might be spared (since each deserves to lose his life ten thousand times), but rather [they ask] that they be allowed to persevere in their cruelties so that they can consume the rest of their slaughter and depopulate the rest of the lands, secure from temporal punishment.

Your Highness can be sure that of all the parts of the Indies where there have been the most excesses and disorder, in committing injustice and iniquities, and wickedly treating the innocent Indian slaves . . . [the worst is] in Guatemala and

Chiapa; because one cannot imagine the ways and cunning manner they used to secure them. And the number of slaves they made is so great that it is incredible.

For, consider, Your Highness, if an infinite number of vecinos, having most iniquitously made very free and innocent Indians into slaves (of which nine-tenths have perished in their infernal work and services), now ask for this, that Your Majesty return them, so that they remain always in mortal sin (as they have always been in it) because they have always usurped liberty and have consumed the lives of so many of their fellow men with their tyranny. What kind of demand is this!

Regarding what they say, that they will leave, may it please God, lords, that none of those who participated in those deeds there may remain; because with what each of them has stolen and usurped, and has today, Your Highness would be able to give to better people and [it would be] more benefit to the land.

Rather, I affirm that it is convenient that none remain there, if the King wishes to have assurance and proof regarding those lands, because never again will Your Majesty be able to placate them, they being so badly accustomed to give orders and to be lords. . . . These, I understand, are the ones who are boasting of being conquistadores to simple people [who are] quiet and not infected with so much spilling of human blood. . . .

They should not astonish you, saying that the Indians will rebel, because it is a falsehood and a great evil, for they [the Indians] are not able to raise their heads, as they [the Spaniards] have oppressed them and annihilated them. They, and not the Indians, are the ones who make disturbances and they force the Indians to make uprisings. And if they revolt it is only to flee the cruelties of their lords and from desperation; and they [the Spaniards] are the cause of all the many evils that have been and are today, and the cause of all the ruin of the Indies.

In the second place, they ask that the prelate of that city tax the Indians because they know very well that he will assess them as he assessed Chiapa, so that in a very few days they would all lose their lives; because the Bishop [Marroquín] has had and has many Indians, [as do] one of his brothers and other relatives and friends as well, as a result of which they have made and caused great losses and calamities in those provinces, and they are destroyed because of the tributes as well as the many slaves that he branded; [he], to whom was entrusted the [branding] iron of the King!

Moreover, he [Bishop Marroquín] asks that the Indians bring the tributes on their backs to the city from thirty to forty leagues, where they perish, because in addition to the loads that they carry of the tributes, they put on top of them the pitiful meals for thirty leagues, and since it can only be a little, they die on the roads. . . .

I hear it said that there are complaints because for very trivial things some are condemned and deprived of the Indians. Your Highness should consider as the truth [the fact that] there are, and have been, so many and such grave and evil vexations, cruelties, and injustices made against the Indians that, before God, I affirm that Your Majesty could justly deprive [even] those who have been least harmful, oppressive, and cruel [many times over].

184   FORCED NATIVE LABOR

For all this, I beg Your Highness to consider it well to see that the Indians are not all obligated to perish and be consumed for supporting the Spaniards. Not because they might be there at their pleasure, that they might triumph, looking for, and carrying along the Indians for the tributes that they might give, forsaken; and in the end their women and children die of hunger. . . . The means is changed by the end, and the end by the means. The presence of the Spaniards in the Indies is the orderly means for the good of the Indians, as the end. Well, if this means has to be for the destruction of the Indians, the Indians will say that God should never have brought to their lands such professors of the law of Christ.

If the tributes of the Indians of the province of Guatemala are not enough for a hundred vecinos of the city of Guatemala [Santiago], nor those of the seventy of the city of Chiapa, [then] let the Spaniards restrain themselves so that there will not be so many who eat and do not work, and so that many will return to their trades (for they used to be craftsmen), and so they might quit being "caballeros" by the sweat and blood of the miserable and afflicted [Indians].[107]

Cerrato had been ready to return to Spain years before, while he was still in Santo Domingo. By 1550, ill and weary of the enmity of the Spaniards, he again sought permission to leave. On May 15, 1551, he repeated the request, which the Crown denied, citing the need for him to remain in Guatemala.[108] Finally, in June 1553, the Crown granted him license to return—following the completion of his judicial review, for which purpose a licenciado del Barco was appointed his judge.[109] Del Barco apparently died in Spain soon after, for in November of the same year Dr. Antonio Rodríguez de Quesada, an oidor in the Audiencia of New Spain, was commissioned as juez de residencia for Cerrato's trial.[110] Quesada arrived in January 1555 ("dia de los reyes"), after a journey of about three months and commenced the trials.[111]

Although, aside from the charge of nepotism, there was little of great substance with which to charge the president, his accusers were vehement in their attacks.[112] Cerrato was bitter about the disfavor shown him during his residencia, after eleven years of service in the Indies and twenty-eight years in the royal service before that. He was, he said, being delivered to his enemies who, "like hungry lions were waiting to drink my blood and eat my flesh." Anxious for his trial to end, Cerrato wrote that "I would rather die of hunger in Spain than to be here with all the treasures of the Indies."[113]

In his final months Cerrato increasingly saw himself as a martyr, and he wrote that if his critics were to be believed he should be drawn and quartered. After he first carried out the reforms, he reminded, they were implemented in Mexico and Peru, so that he was seen by everyone in the Indies as the author, an evil that equated him in their minds with Mohammed.[114]

Cerrato's last years were lonely and full of recriminations from his fellow citizens. In contrast to many contemporary officials, he did not practice selective application of the law, at least insofar as Indian labor was concerned. His friends lost their slaves and personal service along with the rest.[115] To add to his woes, the Crown began to waver in its support of his actions. And even his old friend and champion Las Casas expressed reservations about Cerrato, particularly with regard to favors the president had extended to relatives and friends. Even though, as we have seen, nepotism was common in the colonies, his allies seem to have held Cerrato above such weaknesses. The Dominican friar Pedro de Angulo, commenting that the president had always been so upright, was astonished that he was enriching his relatives with the labor of the Indians.[116]

On May 5, 1555, Cerrato died, a few days before the completion of his *residencia*. His *juez de residencia* and the new president, Dr. Quesada, along with the seasoned judge Ramírez, wrote the Crown that Cerrato was regarded as a wise man, who until his death persevered in his loyalty to the Crown. According to terms of the *residencia*, the services of his relatives were to have been assessed and their encomienda grants moderated. The authors said that most of those involved had already died, but Cerrato left behind other members of his family, and the judges asked that Cerrato's contributions be remembered in the matter of assistance for his daughters and grandchildren.[117] The reformer was, fittingly, buried in Santiago's monastery of Santo Domingo.[118]

Contemporaries of Cerrato who were not directly affected by the changes in Indian labor usually recognized his achievements. The Dominican friar Tomás de la Torre, noted that while Cerrato had his faults as an administrator (and was "muy amigo de sus parientes"), the fact remained that there had never been anyone in Central America who so favored the Indians and who so complied with royal orders. In his opinion, it would have been easier to correct his shortcomings than to try finding someone else as good.[119] And the Milanese chronicler, Girolamo Benzoni, who lived in Santo Domingo and Central America during the Cerrato administrations, wrote:

> I can testify that throughout India [i.e., the Indies] there never was a better judge, nor one who practised good precepts more strictly, obeying the royal commands, always endeavouring that the Indians should not be ill-treated by an Spaniard; and sometimes through the little respect that was shewn him by his countrymen, in consequence of his considering the welfare of the Indians, he used

to pray that God would liberate him from such a bad people; and still more, that if God granted him grace to return to Spain, he would warn the king not to let any priest whatever go over to India, on account of their great dissoluteness; but death intervening, he could not do it.[120]

Appropriately, it was a native chronicler who left the most eloquent tribute:

> When he arrived, he condemned the Spaniards, he cut the taxes [tributes] in two, he suspended forced labor and made the Spanairds pay all men, great and small. The lord Cerrado [sic] truly alleviated the sufferings of the people. I myself saw him, oh, my sons![121]

Though he performed one of the most remarkable feats of administration in the history of the Spanish Indies, Cerrato has remained almost ignored by later historians. Little more than passing reference is accorded the man who was the first to implement the famous New Laws. His actions constituted a significant victory for the Crown in its struggle for control in the New World; it was the first truly effective blow to the conquistador-encomendero establishment.

That such momentous changes first occurred in Central America is curious, especially in view of the relatively weak royal bureaucracy there and its violent history. A good part of the explanation lies in the courage and integrity of Cerrato himself, but there are other considerations which probably had a bearing on his success. The failure to apply the New Laws in Peru may be attributed to the anarchy that prevailed in that kingdom. In Mexico Viceroy Mendoza chose to withhold the legislation, fearing a rebellion; but had he been willing to risk the consequences it certainly would have strengthened royal authority and doubtless would have led to earlier application of reforms in other colonies.

In the instance of the Audiencia of Guatemala, two distinct factors were present which helped Cerrato accomplish his ends. First, his actions came five years after the publication of the New Laws. Following the sudden shock of 1543, other decrees calling for enforcement of the Laws led to a gradual awareness of growing royal concern. It was a policy of gradualism, in which later reforms were not totally unexpected. Second, Pedro de Alvarado had been killed in 1541, and no other strong caudillo type emerged to unite effectively conquistador resistance to the Crown. Had there been such a charismatic individual to lead the vecinos Cerrato very likely would have failed.

Most important, however, was the fact that Cerrato dared to make the attempt where others, understandably, had retreated. By defying almost all segments of Central America's Spanish population, he set a precedent which others followed. It might be argued—as indeed it was at the time—that Cerrato's methods were so harsh and unyielding as to be counterproductive.[122] Would a more moderate approach, such as that suggested by Bustamante, have been more beneficial? Perhaps so. But it depends on whose well-being one is considering. Experience had shown that nebulous rulings invited confusion, delay, and bitter misunderstandings. Taking into account all the various elements that combined to frustrate a just policy for the Indians, a clear and firm imperial policy had to be formed and applied by a resolute official. In Cerrato the Crown found such a man.

By mid-century there was cause for some rejoicing on the part of those proponents of Indian liberties. Tributes had been reduced, there was to be no more personal service in lieu of tribute, and there were restrictions on the use of tamemes and naborías, along with other reforms relating to labor. The most dramatic and clear-cut change was the abolition of Indian chattel slavery. No more was it to be a condition given royal sanction, except in extraordinary, isolated cases. Yet the question persists as to the efficacy of the reforms, particularly in the minds of those who make little distinction between legal slavery and the form of repartimiento labor that evolved. There is no arguing the point that chattel slavery was ended in Central America much sooner than in Mexico.[123]

Certainly, in my opinion, the condition of native laborers generally improved in the second half of the sixteenth century.[124] A close study of the documentation reveals a singular contrast in the nature of Indian complaints before and after 1550. True, there was a growing volume of litigation on their part, but that can be attributed to their increased sophistication in the ways of the legalistic Spanish society. They were becoming, as observers noted, "muy ladino"—that is to say, clever in their use of lawyers to capitalize on the laws that were, at least on paper, much in their favor. More significant, however, is the fact that most of their grievances are relatively petty, certainly in comparison with the poignant relations written in the first twenty-five years following their subjection to Spanish rule.

With the passing of Cerrato from the scene there was some backsliding in the enforcement of the labor provisions as less zealous administrators arrived. Furthermore, the nature of the bureaucracy was such that it was difficult to apply the laws in the more isolated regions, even under the most enlightened administrators. The labor codes had become more stringent, but there were frequent violations. The decline of the encomienda system in the second half of the sixteenth century has been exaggerated, at least with regard to Central America. If they no longer had things completely their way, it is nevertheless true that the old conquerors and their sons still remained a force with which to reckon. But while abuses continued, the "golden age"[125] of slavery was over, atrocities were to a considerable extent curbed, and the oppression occurred in a more subtle and litigious manner. The time when "Spaniards gave no more thought to whipping or killing an Indian than if he were a dog,"[126] gave way to a period during which brutality toward a native often carried with it grave consequences.

PART III

10
Repartimiento Labor

THE ANGRY RESPONSES to the reforms of Cerrato were predicated on the whole question of the labor shortage. In particular, the settlers were irked by the restrictions on some forms of labor that had been free to them. Since the majority of the Indians had not been in the slave category, there was still manpower available, presumably; however, Indians were henceforth to work only of their free will and for pay. Accustomed to having everything done for them at no cost, the vecinos found the new order of things hard to accept. They grumbled that the situation was now impossible, because the Indians would not work voluntarily under any conditions, which compounded the serious labor shortage. There is reason to believe that such a view was exaggerated, and that in fact Indians would frequently offer their labor provided they were paid a decent wage, because tribute demands, church fees, and other expenses required their having cash on occasion.[1] It was true, nonetheless, that a problem existed; and in the end, although it was not precisely slavery, forced labor continued.

The Crown would not countenance idleness on the part of the Indians, all of whom were to be kept occupied in some work contributing to the welfare of the community. The natives would have the freedom to choose their kind of work as well as their employer, and they were not to be coerced. Moreover, they were to receive a just wage and were to be well treated.[2] Unfortunately, this equitable proposal was unrealistic, and what appeared to be a manifestly reasonable solution failed for various reasons.

Central to the idea of the free labor system was the naive assumption on the part of the Crown that the Indians would volunteer for work. In fact, they neither wished to labor for their conquerors nor did their simple needs require much money. "In no way will they serve the Spaniards of their own volition," a contemporary wrote, adding that those who said otherwise were simply deceiving the Crown.[3] The problem arose from a fundamental lack of understanding on the part of administrators in Spain

191

regarding the basic attitudes of the native people. The Indian, uncon-
ditioned by the historical patterns of Europe, was considered by most
Spaniards to be merely indolent; but if he was not in fact "naturally lazy,"
neither was he motivated by the same desires of the European. A capitalist
mentality was not part of his intellectual heritage, and he was concerned
only with his immediate needs, which were quite modest. Fray Miguel
Agia, who had long observed the Indians, wrote that the king and the
Council of the Indies had been persuaded that the Indians, with their new
liberty, would respond to the labor needs of the republic and the
Spaniards. However, he added, long experience in the Indies had proved
that untrue, because:

> For them there is nothing more odious than working, even though it is for
> themselves, besides which the Spaniard and the Indian are two opposites, *ex
> diametro:* because by nature the Indian is not covetous, while the Spaniard is
> extremely greedy; the Indian is phlegmatic, the Spaniard is choleric; the Indian
> humble, the Spaniard arrogant; the Indian slow in everything he does, the
> Spaniard hasty in all he desires; *el vno amigo de mandar, el otro enemigo de seruir.*
> And finally, they are dissimilar in circumstances, life, and customs.[4]

The failure of the Indians to come forward to work not only resulted in
their idleness, but it also posed a serious problem for the maintenance and
growth of the colony in light of the absence of a labor force. It was therefore
necessary to *require* the Indians to contribute their labor under the system
known as the repartimiento de indios, or division of Indians. Very simply,
each native village was notified to send a certain number of men to a
Spanish town every week. They were to assemble in the main plaza each
Monday morning to be assigned for the week's work. The workers were
then divided up according to the labor demands, either for public-works
projects or for the use of individual Spaniards who had submitted requests
for a stated number of laborers. Overseeing the system was a Spanish
official, the *juez repartidor*, but it was the obligation of the Indian officials
in the villages to see that the quotas for their towns were met.

In 1549, the commutation of encomienda tribute to labor was abolished
by law, the observance of which would have eliminated personal service
for all intents and purposes. Instructions to Luis de Velasco, the second
viceroy of New Spain, explicitly stated that personal service as a form of
tribute was prohibited.[5] But Bishop Marroquín of Guatemala counseled
caution. While he had always advocated compensation for the work of
Indians, he considered that it was not worthwhile because even with pay
the Indians did not want to serve. As a result, crops were neglected and
cattle were lost; and in response Cerrato and the friars said the Spaniards
could do the necessary work for themselves. However, the bishop said

that Spaniards did not go to the Indies for that, and such a solution served neither God nor the Crown, and it was neither good for the Spaniards nor the Indians. What mattered for good government was for the Spaniards to be esteemed and for the natives to be instructed and well treated. With those objectives in mind, the Spaniards would not be affronted or embarrassed while the Indians would not be exalted. In effect, he argued for the continuance of personal service.[6]

In practice, personal service continued throughout the sixteenth century; and while the repartimiento system did not become an established system of labor drafts, the simultaneous operation of these two forms of forced labor invites confusion, for one is not always sure in some instances whether a group of Indians worked under the legal system or under the persistent, though illegal, concept of personal service. It is no wonder that there is misunderstanding today, considering that at the time the two were often taken to mean much the same thing. Discussing a royal cédula given in 1601, Agia objected to the lack of clear distinction in the wording—"Having seen and understood how harmful and prejudicial to the Indians is the repartimiento that is made of them for the personal services. . . ." The impression that repartimientos of Indians were given in use for personal service was, in Agia's opinion, "notoriously sinister and directly opposite to the truth." Perhaps it was not all that, but it was misleading.

It was understood in the Indies, he continued, that personal service was labor given to the encomenderos instead of tribute. In earlier years, of course, personal service had been authorized in addition to tribute, but it became common practice to accept labor in lieu of tribute. By Agia's time in the Indies (he arrived in 1563), it had apparently become more or less standardized, though illegal. It was called personal service, he explained, because it was work performed for the encomendero's personal benefit. Repartimiento labor, on the other hand, was understood to be labor for the service of the republic, in cultivating the land, working the mines, or in public-works projects. In this regard, Agia is quibbling, because a Spaniard who requested laborers to work his private fields through the repartimiento was benefiting the community only incidentally, and it is clear enough that he was himself profiting personally. In other respects, Agia saw personal service as an evil, while repartimiento was, in his eyes, an essentially fair system.

Specifically, he makes several distinctions. (1) Personal service was performed without pay, while repartimiento labor carried a wage. (2) Personal service was perpetual, the other temporary. (3) The former was imposed through force and violence, the latter through peaceful public authority. (4) Personal service was harsh "slavery," while repartimiento labor was given with "natural and Christian liberty." (5) The first was tyrannical and cruel because it excused no one, regardless of sex, age, or physical fitness; the other admitted only men of reasonable age and strength, excluding women, children, the elderly, and the infirm. (6) The one was inhumane because not only did Indians under personal service receive no pay, but they had to provide their own food; the other was humane because in addition to wages they were also given meals. (7) Personal service was of no public utility, being solely in the interest of the encomendero, while the other was of great benefit inasmuch as the welfare of the republic depended upon repartimiento labor. (8) The first was completely contrary to the spiritual welfare of the Indians because it left no time for their religious needs, whereas the other labor did not interfere. (9) Personal service as a "hellish" form of labor that kept the submissive, miserable natives in constant desperation, while the other occupied them in moderate tasks for fair pay, keeping them from indolence and idolatry, to which they were very much inclined. (10) While the one was totally contrary to natural, divine, and human law, as it deprived men of their liberty, the other conformed with such laws, since with complete liberty they were able to serve the common good. (11) And finally, personal service had been prohibited since the times of the Catholic kings, but repartimiento labor was legal. Agia could have added with regard to the last point that the Crown had in several official provisions allowed personal service up to the middle of the century.[7]

On being informed that there were many Spaniards as well as Indians lounging around with no trades and no desire to work, the Crown ordered them to work to earn their keep. Indolent Spanish bachelors, seen as potential troublemakers, were to be put out of the colonies, onto ships bound for Spain. Indians who were not working were to take jobs in their trades if they were skilled, and if not, in any kind of work to make a living.[8] A few months later Prince Philip wrote that since the Indians did not want to work at all, which among other problems had led to a food shortage, all Indian artisans were to pursue their trades, and native farmers were to begin cultivating their fields, both for their own sustenance and for the supply of the community. Native merchants were to engage in their trading. Any Indian not occupied in one of the foregoing was to hire himself out to labor in the fields or in public works in the towns. If necessary, they were to be compelled to work, but by officials; private Spaniards were not to force them, even if the Indians in question belonged to the Spaniards' encomiendas.

On their visits to the provinces, oidores were to effect this rule for the outlying areas, as well as for the larger settlements. For their work, the Indians were to be paid personally, and under no circumstances were their wages to be handed over to their caciques, principales, or anyone else. Furthermore, the work they were required to perform was to be moderate, and any violation would carry grave penalties.[9] The order was repeated in early 1553, and the following year the audiencia reported that the law was being enforced, with the result that more Indians were working on farms.[10]

Apparently the effectiveness of the program did not last, because four years later reference was made to an order sent to the viceroy of New Spain, to the effect that much harm derived from the fact that "the Indians are by natural inclination *amigos de holgar*," that is to say, lazy. It was therefore provided once again that in all the provinces of New Spain all Indians were to be engaged in some kind of work, lest they be subject to all the vices common to idlers. The religious were to be charged with persuading the Indians to comply, as were the judges on their inspection tours.[11] But, unfortunately, even if the Indians wanted to work, it was not worthwhile for them. The problem was similar in all parts of greater New Spain. Benjamin Keen, citing a 1552 letter of Fray Pedro de Gante, writes:

> Fray Pedro also called attention to the evils of the emerging institution of repartimiento or labor draft. The Indians from towns within a distance of ten leagues around Mexico City had to come to the capital to be hired by Spanish employers. A common laborer received a wage of 12 maravedis a day. An Indian might spend two days in travel to the capital, and then might have to wait for three or four days for some Spaniard to hire him; during this time he must sell the clothes off his back to keep alive. After being hired he got his 12 maravedis a day, of which 10 or all had to go for food, and so he had served for nothing and had lost his clothing in the bargain.[12]

Subsequently, reviewing the earlier orders with regard to vagabonds, the Crown noted that those types still persisted, especially mestizos, who as "an idle people" were to be made to settle down and take jobs. Moreover, all idlers—Spanish, Indian, and mestizo—were to be brought together in two or three villages or more. Indians were to be settled by themselves, and the Spaniards and mestizos would be put together. In both areas lands were to be given on which they were to grow crops and raise livestock. All necessary support was to be given them. And because in the first years they would need help with such things as seeds for the plantings, and would have to eat until their crops bore fruit, and would have need of livestock and help to maintain their homes, funds were to be taken from the royal treasury as loans to the resettled people, who were to repay them within a specified time period. Franciscan friars were to be sent to minister to the Indian settlements, and some "good" priests to those of Spaniards and mestizos.[13]

Within the context of Spanish colonial policy, it was a reasonable proposition. It was also enlightened self-interest, for footloose men often caused mischief wandering about the provinces, either as marauders or as enlistees in various causes detrimental to Crown stability. If they could be converted to settled citizens the republic would benefit.

At the same time, the Crown referred to another aspect of vagabondage. Citing the 1552 decree, in which all idlers were advised to occupy themselves, the king pointed out a reported abuse. It had been alleged that the audiencia was compelling large numbers of Indians to leave their pueblos to labor in public-works projects and in other tasks; but they were also being distributed to serve individual Spaniards, as designated by the oidores. Those Spaniards were requiring Indians to work excessively hard, and the pay was so little that the laborers could not sustain themselves. Some were being made to travel more than twelve leagues to the city of Santiago, leaving their wives and children without food. It sometimes happened that when they returned they found their families dead.

To remedy this tragic development, a new cédula was given: the audiencia was not to compel Indians, under the pretext of the earlier ruling, to hire out, except in cases of those who were clearly idlers. Moreover, even true loafers were not to be forced to leave their towns except to go to Spanish towns that had no Indians for their needs. In such cases, workers were not to travel more than two or three leagues from their homes. They were to be paid a just wage, according to the view of the audiencia, or one of the justices; and if it was applicable, they could be paid either by contract or by piece work, instead of on a daily wage basis.[14] An admonition to conform to the law was passed the following year, but it appears as if the problem of vagabonds and idlers in the audiencia district largely disappeared in the decades following.[15]

A related problem was that native artisans did not want to pursue their trades because of being forced to leave their families in their villages to travel to Spanish settlements for work. Thus, a carpenter would prefer to become a farmer and plant cacao to be near his family and village. The archdeacon of León protested that the coercion of Indians to work in other areas was unreasonable, especially since there were Spanish and mestizo craftsmen in the Spanish cities to do the work. Indians were in demand only because they could be paid less.[16]

Indian labor, whether forced labor without pay under the concept of personal service, or free conscripted labor for wages (repartimiento), was subject to widespread abuses. The Crown, though unsteadily treading the path between expediency and conscience, sought from the early years to regulate native labor to minimize the hardships. Almost all Indians were liable for labor service, but eventually there were certain limitations on the obligation to work and the type of labor involved. It was ruled in 1552 that Indians condemned to labor in public works were not be given to individual Spaniards owning estancias, sugar plantations, fulling mills (or other mills), or any kind of factory *(obraje)*. No Indian was to be compelled to work at a trade with which he was unfamiliar, and some time later it was ordered that none was to serve mestizos, Negroes, or mulattoes.[17]

The very young and the aged were ordinarily exempt from labor. No ill person was to be required to work, nor was a husband whose wife had recently given birth; since women did not use neighbor women to help or employ the use of midwives, it was necessary for the husband to give assistance. If an Indian could otherwise demonstrate that he had pressing obligations elsewhere for the week he was to be excused from work.[18] Late in the century the Crown ruled that married Indians and their wives were to live in their own towns and that they were not to leave for the service of anyone. The law was, however, not effectively enforced.[19]

Indian officials were exempt from labor, which made those positions much to be desired. A Spanish judge investigating conditions in Soconusco in 1571 noted that many of the natives in that province had successfully avoided all personal service by becoming officials. In every little pueblo of twenty Indians he found six or seven alguaciles, regidores, and governors. In the principal town of Huehuetlán ("Uebetlan") he found twenty-four alguaciles for the 120 vecinos of the settlement. In addition, the Indian governor resided there with another three or four alguaciles.[20]

In a curious letter to the king in 1582, the cabildo *(ayuntamiento)* stated that the audiencia had alloted too many Indians for service among vecinos of the capital, a situation which the Crown ordered corrected.[21] This kind of complaint rarely emanated from the colonies, where there was almost always a great shortage of native labor, or so the vecinos said.

Following the reforms at mid-century, the period of adjustment to the idea of hiring free labor took some time, but after about five years the audiencia had outlined firm guidelines in accordance with the royal will. In each province Indians living closest to a Spanish town would voluntarily hire out by the week in order to provide firewood or fodder, to repair houses, and to perform other necessary tasks of a routine nature—that is, servicio ordinario. Workers were to be paid three reales a week or the just equivalent in cacao, in addition to being given their meals. But no one was to go and take them out of their pueblos. Indians were forbidden to saw wood, carry abodes, and to perform other labor proscribed by law. They were to be paid in the presence of a justice and the local friar or priest in charge of their instruction.

For these jobs Indians within half a day's walking distance of the Spanish settlement were to be used, and the Indians were to be paid for their roundtrip travel. Only a few were to be taken from any village; from a pueblo of 100 Indian vecinos, only 2 a week were to be absent on labor projects for Spaniards. If these regulations were observed, the oidores reasoned, the Indians would not be vexed, and the Spaniards, who had suffered from lack of laborers, would more easily adjust to the loss of slaves and personal service, as well as the reduction of tributes.[22] These provisions were effective only so long as a zealous administration stood guard, a situation often not in evidence.

There were other problems over which the royal officials had little control. There developed in Santiago an unusually plentiful supply of money, oddly enough in the years just following the reforms that were predicted to cause financial collapse. This led to sharp inflation, so that the wages paid the Indians were of scant advantage to them. Clothing and cacao were so expensive and in short supply that the Spaniards scuffled over them, and firewood, maize, and other staples were very costly. Prices had been going up for several years, and they seem not to have been checked by the early 1550s. Consequently, an Indian who previously dressed himself and his family for 10 reales had to spend 100 for the same clothing. The result was that the workers had to charge higher wages in order to survive in the Spaniard's society.[23] The Indian's wages were further reduced by certain deductions for taxes.

By 1559, the Crown was advised that, owing to the inflation and taxes, Indians sometimes asked for such excessive wages that no one would hire them, as a result of which work in the fields and on public buildings occasionally ceased, to the detriment of the colony. When these cases arose, the president was to assess a daily wage to be paid to each Indian, conforming to the going rate and the cost of living, so that the workers could sustain themselves and the necessary work could be accomplished. And it was forbidden to deduct taxes from their pay.[24]

The order to pay Indians for their work explicitly extended to all levels of Spanish society, including high officials such as oidores, who were cautioned to avoid requiring Indians to serve in their households without pay; all Indians without exception were to be paid, in accordance with the rate established by custom and the law.[25]

Abuses of this law by provincial officials became notorious, but examples of cheating were even charged to the judges of the audiencia. Dr. Mexía allegedly sent two Spanish alguaciles to get a supply of fish, utilizing the services of native fishermen. Many Indians were kept occupied in that task during the whole of Lent, after which the fish were sent to Dr. Mexía, while the fishermen were sent home with no compensation whatever. Witnesses in his residencia said this was not the only time it had happened.[26] Those testifying in the residencia of the more honorable judge, licenciado Ramírez, in the same year said that the general picture was that of Indians working voluntarily by the week for pay. Bernal Díaz del Castillo testified that he knew of no Indian serving against his will without compensation. The witnesses, often encomenderos, were not always reliable in their testimony.[27]

An official wrote that all vecinos who had Indians in service were required to bring them in to be registered, and in the process he discovered that most of them had served for five or six years without pay. "As a miserable people," he said, they did not dare ask for their back pay and they were afraid to refuse working. To make matters worse, Spanish judges were not disposed to see justice done, and the writer said that in the future no Spaniard would receive an Indian in his service without first obligating himself before a notary to pay a stipulated wage.[28]

The lieutenant governor in Honduras was accused of using Indians to clear his *milpa de yuca* without paying them in the presence of a justice, as required by law. The official denied the charge, stating that he had Negroes to care for his milpa, and that if he used Indians it was to repair his house, which was permitted by law, provided they were compensated. He admitted that he had used Indian labor, but that was before he held his position, and he insisted that he had paid the workers. As for the rule about paying wages before a justice, he said that applied only to encomenderos.[29]

In 1574, the Crown ordered the audiencia to make no change regarding the custom of neighboring villages giving Indians to the vecinos of Santiago for service, with each worker being paid four reales a week and meals.[30] Because of the law allowing Indians to be distributed for public-works projects, Spaniards continued to abuse the concession and, using it as a pretext, were putting Indians into their fields and occupying them in other tasks, for which the workers were paid the insufficient sum of four reales a week, with no meals or any other consideration offered. Agreeing that Indians could not live on that pittance and support their families, the Crown ordered the practice corrected.[31]

In response to the investigations of the oidor, licenciado Diego García de Palacio, witnesses gave a different version of Indian labor. They agreed that the audiencia had made sure that the workers were protected, in fact more so than the Spaniards at times. One said that he saw Indians of the valley going to hire out for the week in Santiago being paid ahead of time. Skilled workers were being paid at the rate of one real a day, or six reales for the week, while unskilled labor was given five reales for a week. In addition, the workers were given food and were well treated, even if they were late to work.

All of this, the witnesses maintained, was agreed upon beforehand. The same was confirmed by others in what is almost verbatim testimony for all, which renders it rather suspect. They stated further that the labor arrangements were very advantageous to the Indians and their families, because being "idlers by nature" and not wanting to work, they got everything they needed for their livelihood and for the payment of their tributes, not to mention religious instruction in how to live like good Christians, to have charity, and to learn the fear of God.[32]

Fray Gómez de Córdova wrote that in discussions and rulings on personal service several decisions were made, including one to the effect that corregidores should not be giving orders right and left, requiring Indians to work for only four reales a week, or out of "friendship," or for whatever reason.[33] Indications that labor arrangements had deteriorated even further by 1587 are seen in the instruction to President Mallén de Rueda to determine who was maltreating natives by forcing them to work for nothing.[34]

Occasionally a case would be brought to light reminiscent of the early decades. One such was the suit brought against an encomendero named Diego de la Barrera in 1591. He was charged with making Indians of his town of Çanbo carry firewood and fodder for his horses and mules. Women were required to serve as molenderas to grind his corn. Even the native alguaciles were forced to gather chile, tomatoes, fruit, and honey, while others cared for his horses and mules. For this work they received no compensation. Other Indians were compelled to cultivate his large milpa of cotton for little pay. If the villagers did not provide fodder, maize, eggs, and shrimps for Barrera and his criados they were jailed. Three Indians were used daily just in the care of his horses and mules, serving without pay. Tamemes were used by the encomendero with no pay, and if the Indian officials failed to provide the carriers, Barrera called them "cabrones."

Generally he was charged with insulting his people, and as a defamer of honorable married women and men of the church. He allegedly beat Indian men and women and on one occasion stabbed a man. One time he simply seized a young Indian girl and took her for his house for service. Don Domingo Alvarez, an Indian principal, testified that every day six or seven Indians took the encomendero household supplies. Each of those "guaçetones" provided daily thirty cacao beans, an egg, some shrimps, and a small basket of maize for the tortillas. Not one of them was paid. Finally, it was charged that he sold wine to his villagers, including the officials.[35] Although it had been the law for many years, the king found it necessary to emphasize by late in the century that no Spaniard was to receive the services of an Indian without declaring what he was going to pay him, and that his word was to be honored.[36]

It appears that gradually, over the years, the compensation of Indians for their work became the norm, with some exceptions here and there. In a statement of 1598, it was asserted that Indian workers were being paid their wages, and that if any were not being compensated they could complain. If their claims were just, they would be paid and the employer would be punished.[37]

The president of the audiencia informed the king in 1563 that Indians living in the valley of Santiago worked in the plantings close to them and repaired houses, without taking on other work far away. Those living closer to the city performed servicio ordinario, and from pueblos some ten leagues distant men went to work in fields that lay about five leagues from Santiago, that is, half way to the outlying pueblos. Under this system no one had to travel far, and it was not necessary for an Indian to take a turn more than twice a year.[38]

That essentially reasonable arrangement is in sharp contrast to the picture drawn in the province of Soconusco eight years later. There, according to an investigator, all year long maceguales were occupied three days a week for the community, and the other three days working for themselves in order to pay their tributes. For, in addition to paying tribute to the Crown (in lieu of an encomendero), the natives also had to contribute cacao to the community. The ones who were very poor, with little or no property, also had to work for money in order to support their families. As a result, those Indians were constantly kept occupied in making ends meet.

The visiting judge called for abolition of the personal service the maceguales had to contribute every week, but at the same time, he ordered that none of them was exempted from services in building the church and buildings for the justice, nor from work in community milpas. Even so, he estimated that by rotation those community projects could be taken care of without an Indian having to contribute more than six days a year for the community.[39]

Labor obligations eventually became more standardized and the repartimiento de indios system became established, following the practice in New Spain. Under that system villages were required to contribute on a regular basis Indians for a labor pool, from which the maceguales would be delivered to Spaniards for a given period.

An example of the way it operated can be seen from a labor call for the pueblo of Chamula in Chiapas, much of which is written in Nahuatl. Juan de la Tovilla, the *teniente general de alcalde* and the *justicia mayor* of Ciudad Real and its provinces, ordered the Indian governor, the alcaldes, and principales of the pueblo of Chamula to give to Pedro Ortes de Belasco, a Spanish vecino, eight indios naborías to work his fields, each of whom was to be paid four reales a week for his work, according to the provisions of the cabildo of the city. Failure of the Indian officials to supply the workers would cost them a fine of ten *tostones.*

In another order, Paulo Cota Manuel, the alcalde mayor in Ciudad Real and its provinces, instructed the alcaldes of Chamula to deliver six Indians to a Spaniard for the repairing of his house. The workers would be paid a tostón each for the week, which was the customary wage. The Indians were to report for work the following Monday, failing which the alcaldes would be fined ten pesos de oro, and a Spanish alguacil would be sent, at the cost of the Indian alcaldes themselves, to take them prisoners.[40]

Despite frequent admonitions from the Crown and audiencia, abuses of the most extreme nature continued. It was reported in 1581 that Indians in Honduras were forced to travel so far to work that it took them twelve days going and returning, in addition to the eight days they were expected to work. In order to comply, they had to abandon their women and children for twenty days, often leaving them destitute.[41]

Another abuse is illustrated by the appearance of two Indians, regidores and principales of the pueblo of Ystapa, before the audiencia. They submitted a petition in which it was stated that Ystapa, held in encomienda by Luis Destrada, was situated in the lowlands seven leagues from the city of Ciudad Real de Chiapa. Although the law clearly provided that only villages within five leagues of a Spanish settlement were to furnish workers for ordinary service, the Spanish justices had pressured them to send indios de servicio to Chiapa every week. Each week they had sent workers from the hot lands up to the cool highlands, following which those laborers *(tequitines)* became ill. It took them two days to get to the city from their homes.

An order was given that in the future no Indians from Ystapa were to be required to work in the city through any repartimientos, nor was the village to be molested. If labor was necessary it was to come from towns nearby, and anyone who violated the regulation would be fined 200 pesos.[42] About the same time, friars in Guatemala called for limited distances for Indians to travel to work, but they were vague as to what the limit should be.[43]

During the long work periods Indians' homes and their personal effects were lost. Prolonged absences meant virtual abandonment of their families, and it happened all too frequently that both husband and wife ended up taking lovers. An official in Honduras, sensitive to the harm, ordered all married Indians joined together and gathered in their pueblos where they were to remain. This was best for the conservation of the natives, he asserted, because in towns where previously there had been a thousand Indians there were left no more than five or six.

In 1576, the Crown was informed that during the long absences of the husbands the wives sometimes indulged in sinful acts in their own villages. But the husband had little choice about leaving the villages for work; if they failed to appear for work at their assigned places every Monday, alguaciles were sent for them and they were whipped and shorn of their hair, the ultimate insult. The main problem was that often the men worked too far from their own pueblos to return on Sunday, the only free day. Absence of the man of the house invited the attention of mulattoes and mestizos, who from time to time went into villages and assaulted wives and daughters. Thus again, much later, in 1605, it was ordered that all Indians be returned to their pueblos and be left alone.[44]

Even though many of the violations occurred in rather isolated regions distant from the control of the audiencia, the capital itself was by no means free from transgressions. As late as 1593, caciques and other officials from the pueblos of Malacatepeque and Aguacatepeque complained that they were being required to send four to six workers every week to Santiago for labor gangs. In the past they had not been expected to contribute labor to the capital because their towns were very distant. Moreover, their people lived in *tierra caliente*, while Santiago was *tierra fría*, and they were cacao producers, paying high tribute in that product.

In response, the president of the audiencia noted that because Santiago had grown so fast, with more Spaniards settling all the time, there was a need for more Indian workers because some Spaniards had no indios de servicio at all. Consequently, just recently the more distant pueblos were being asked to contribute labor. He added that the pueblos in question were in reality only four and five leagues away, which was not "muy distante," as one of the caciques stated. Furthermore, he said the towns of Malacatepeque and Aguacatepeque were not producing cacao at all.

Alonso de Bargas Lobo, the *procurador síndico*, in attempting to justify the use of the Indians' personal service, noted that other Indians went to Santiago from the hot country and they did not become ill and die. Some traveled to Santiago from distances of more than seven leagues, and Malacatepeque was five leagues at the most. Thus, he said, the Indians had no good excuse, and they were obligated to serve. Regarding the cacao, he said they did not actually produce very much, and their milpas did not require much of their time and labor in any case. The procurador asked that those villagers be required to continue giving "personal service" on a weekly basis—thus indicating that in 1593 personal service, supposedly abolished long before, was being equated with repartimiento labor.[45]

In reference to an order given by President Landecho years before, a witness during an investigation of 1598 said that working conditions for the *jornaleros* (those paid by the day) and Indians who gave servicio ordinario had been made very tolerable because the neighboring villages were only one to six leagues from the city of Santiago, and rarely did an Indian have to travel farther. And, since they were divided up within the pueblos for the ordinary service, going in shifts and taking their turns, it was not a problem for anyone. Each was to work three days a week for pay, and it was not difficult work, consisting of carrying a load of firewood or fodder, fetching water, and other simple, daily tasks. Others labored in the construction of buildings and houses, repairing them, and making corrals or working on estancias. The Indians were always paid for their work, the witness claimed.[46]

In other ways, too, the Crown gave legislation designed to protect the Indians in their work. The physical disorders afflicting Indians from the steamy lowlands when they traveled to the cool highlands was early brought to the attention of the Crown, who decreed in 1538 that Indians were not to be taken from one extreme climate to the other.[47] The law was repeated in 1550, along with the warning that Indians were not to carry fatiguing loads or to be mistreated in any way, either by word or deed.[48] The extent to which these regulations were ignored can be seen by the many similar cédulas over the decades. Even though special officials were appointed with the somewhat pretentious title of "Protector of the Indians," beginning with Bartolomé de Las Casas, these men, usually of noble sentiments, were only partially successful in ameliorating conditions.

A continuing problem throughout the second half of the sixteenth century was the open flouting of the legislation by the highest officials. One oidor, Dr. Mexía, allegedly issued orders during his *visitas* in certain pueblos stating that in order to meet tribute obligations, half of the maceguales of the villages would have to labor in their encomenderos' milpas, estancias, or cacao groves three times a year. They would work three days a week each time, and although the encomendero was expected to pay them, their wages were only one real each for the three days. This was a grave injustice, because over a period of three days an Indian needed two pesos to sustain himself and his family. Worse yet, the obligation meant that some of them would have to journey ten to twelve leagues to the Spaniard's estate.[49]

More than twenty years after the law prohibiting personal service, the practice was being encouraged by Pedro Pacheco, the Spanish governor in Soconusco, under whom local maceguales were forced to work every week.[50] Closer to the seat of government at Santiago, Indians seem to have been comparatively well treated, in conformance with the law. The audiencia reported in the 1570s that maceguales were working the fields, repairing public roads and weeding the streets, while the women were caring for Spanish children. According to the oidores, all their labor was voluntary and for pay. They added that it was necessary for them to live among Spaniards so they could support themselves, because as they were lazy they would not otherwise do so.[51]

Others, however, presented a different picture. Through a "sinister" report to the Crown, with the counsel of the Dominicans, some Indians of the Barrio de Santo Domingo near Santiago, purportedly influenced the Crown to pass a law affecting personal service and day laborers who worked in the fields. The Indians supposedly claimed that they were forced to work for no pay. The procurador of Santiago denied it, insisted that the workers were well compensated prior to beginning their work, and said that without those peones jornaleros the fields could not be cultivated. Now, he said, their use was threatened, "as if there were Spanish peones to take their places, available for hire in the plazas, as in Spain." The procurador warned that more friars were going to Spain to misrepresent the vecinos' case.[52]

President Francisco Briceño, the governor of Guatemala (1564–69), was accused of having violated the law by sending a Spaniard to the pueblo of Çamayaque allegedly to count Indians for their tribute assessment. Instead, he took the villagers to a place on the river six leagues distant where they were required to take out a great quantity of fish —*tepemerhines, vagres,* and other kinds—to send out on the backs of maceguales. In the process, the Indians were made to open a rough road, which in itself occupied a large number of workers. All of this was done against the wishes of the caciques and principales of the town. The road was unnecessary, serving only for that fishing expedition.

Witnesses claimed that it took 400 men eight days to build the road, after which they spent another two or three days catching the fish, which were then carried out for licenciado Briceño. In addition, many women were forced to go along to work in the shacks they built by the river where they fed the workers. Briceño's man also took a large quantity of chickens, tortillas, maize, and fodder for the horses, the supplying of which occupied many more Indians. Other workers were made to tote the baggage of the Spanish party. For all this labor the Indians were paid nothing, and it was done, so the charge stated, with the knowledge and commission of the governor, who failed to punish his agent for the excesses. But whether or not the testimony relative to this alleged gross abuse of labor was distorted, Briceño was absolved of the charge. [53]

The rise in Spanish population was concomitant with the drastic decline of population among the native people, principally owing to the ravaging plagues. As the demand for food rose, the available manpower decreased, with resulting shortages of provisions causing serious inflation. The audiencia wrote in 1559 that because of the high prices of maize, wheat, and other staples, new sites for production should be laid out. Since the region around Santiago was narrow, and because the capital had attracted a number of idlers, the judges proposed that on the outskirts of Sacatepequez (Çacatepeques), five leagues from Santiago, vacant lands be given to Spanish farmers to cultivate and to settle a town. The same should be done on vacant lands near Copanabastla, halfway between Santiago and Chiapas. Both sites had climates even better than that of the capital. There was a great need for a settlement on the road to Chiapas for travelers, and the land was very fertile.

Moreover, the towns were important for the advance of Christianity and the good order of the natives, because there were no towns near the suggested sites, and Indians nearby were being neglected. At the same time, Spanish European settlement would result in the availability of religion, justice, medical attention, and other necessities. The Crown agreed.[54] New settlements meant repartimientos of local Indians, which was to their disadvantage. But it was the general form of labor that prevailed, and under that broad category there were many tasks performed.[55] The dismal aspects of the repartimiento system were set forth in this account by the oidor Zorita:

When they go to the construction projects or other places of labor, they bring from home certain maize cakes or tortillas that are supposed to last them for the time they are gone. On the third or fourth day the tortillas begin to get moldy or sour; they grow bitter or rotten and get as dry as boards. This is the food the Indians must eat or die. And even of this food they do not have enough, some because of their poverty and others because they have no one to prepare their tortillas for them. They go to the farms and other places of work, where they are made to toil from dawn to dusk, in the raw cold of morning and afternoon, in wind and storm, without other food than those rotten or dried-out tortillas, and even of this they have not enough. They sleep on the ground in the open air, naked, without shelter. Even if they wish to buy food with their pitiful wages they could not, for they are not paid until they are laid off. At the season when the grain is stored, the employers make them carry the wheat or corn on their backs, each man carrying a fanega, after they have worked all day. After this, they must fetch water, sweep the house, take out the trash, and clean the stables. And when their work is done, they find the employer has docked their pay on some pretext or other. Let the Indian argue with the employer about this, and he will keep the Indian's mantle as well. Sometimes an enemy will break the jar in which an Indian carries water to his master's house, in order to make him spill the water on the way, and the employer docks the Indian's wages for this.

So the Indian returns home worn out from his toil, minus his pay and his mantle, not to speak of the food that he brought with him. He returns home famished, unhappy, distraught, and shattered in health. For these reasons pestilence always rages among the Indians. Arriving home, he gorges himself because of his great hunger, and this excess together with the poor physical condition in which he returns help to bring on the cámaras or some other disease that quickly takes him off. The Indians will all die out very quickly if they do not obtain relief from these intolerable conditions.[56]

11
Varieties of Forced Labor, 1550-1600

DESPITE SOME CHANGES in labor forms, there was a continuance of many post-conquest varieties of labor into the second half of the sixteenth century. However, the growing Spanish communities required increasing numbers of skilled workers, and arrangements became slightly more formalized.

Contract Labor

At least as early as the 1540s, individual Indians were entering into labor contracts with Spaniards to work for specified periods, lasting anywhere from several weeks to years. The terms of the arrangements were set down in detail by a notary before whom the principals appeared, along with witnesses. Agreement was reached on the length of time involved, the type of work to be performed, and the compensation for the worker. Usually the Spaniard hiring the Indian was obligated to provide food and drink, and often room if it was household service. Invariably it was stated that the worker was to be well treated.

Wages naturally varied according to the years, but the most readily available information appears in the *libros de protocolos*, dated from the 1570s onward. In 1572, to take one example, an Indian signed on to do general work for only three tostones a month (one tostón equaling one-half peso) and his food.[1] But the year 1583 gives a broader sampling. An Indian hired ("en servicio e soldada") by an alcalde mayor to "do as he was told" was paid thirty-two tostones for a year, while another hired out for general service for fifty. Better paid was an Indian who agreed to catch fish and make and repair nets for two years at the pay of eighty-four tostones a year and his food.

Mule drivers *(arrieros)* often signed contracts for seven months (usually for the dry season) at wages varying in 1583 from eight tostones monthly up to twelve tostones for the same period, plus food. One contracted to drive a team to Mexico City and back during a seven-month period for food, drink, and ten tostones a month. But one underpaid *ladino* received only sixty tostones for a year.[2]

Indians signed on as *vaqueros* for Spanish estancias in 1583 for fifty to seventy-five tostones a year, sometimes with meals stipulated.[3] At the same time, the brother of an Indian alguacil, speaking in Nahuatl, agreed to put in a year in a bakery for food and forty-two tostones.[4] Another took work as a wheat farmer for only forty tostones a year, in addition to food and drink.[5] Five years later an Indian agreed to work for a year in the unpleasant occupation of making indigo dye in a Spaniard's *obraje de tinta* for a mere seventy tostones,[6] and a ladino muleteer in 1592 still commanded only twelve tostones a month.[7] But in 1595 an Indian tailor signed on for six months to work for the good wage of sixteen tostones monthly.[8]

Non-Indians, it should be noted, also hired themselves out under the same types of contracts. In 1583, a mestizo agreed to work a year on an estancia and in a fishery for forty tostones a year, to be paid in three equal installments.[9] A mulatto in 1572 put himself under contract for two years, to receive his meals plus five colts each year for his compensation.[10] In 1592, a young free mulatto of sixteen took work for the indigo season (June 20 until the end of September) for the good sum of fifteen tostones a month.[11] Moreover, a number of Spaniards also hired out for the same kind of work as the others, and some of them were vecinos, not just drifters. Usually they were paid more than Indians, but sometimes the difference was not great. In 1583, a Spanish vecino agreed to a contract calling for him to be in service for two years for his meals and 50 tostones annually.[12] Like all others, the Spaniards were required to complete their contracts. In the same year, another Spanish vecino hired out to work in an indigo processing plant for wages of 13 tostones a month, and another agreed to labor in an obraje de tinta for five months for food, drink, and 10 tostones a month.[13] A Spaniard took work as a vaquero for two months to help out on an estancia with the branding and castrating of stock in return for food and 13 tostones a month. Another contracted to do odd jobs for a notary in 1583 for 80 tostones a year, plus a colt.[14] By 1598, wages seem to have generally risen, since a Spanish arriero driving mules for a merchant received 200 tostones a year, plus food and drink.[15]

Indian women also agreed to work under contract, usually in households, and though it gave them a home, the pay was very little. One widow, in fact, apparently received no pay at all: in 1583, she consented to serve for a year for food, clothing, and other necessities, but there is no mention of wages.[16] Another woman, deserted by her husband, contracted in the same year to work with her ten-year-old daughter in a Spanish home, rearing children. At times she was expected to serve as a wet nurse (chichigua). Wages were to be three tostones for the Indian woman and one tostón for the girl, plus their food.[17] To cite another case, fifteen years later an Indian woman agreed to serve a merchant for two years for three tostones a month.[18]

Indian couples frequently hired out together. Again using the year 1583 for purposes of comparison, it is noted that a man and wife entered the service of a Spanish farmer for six months for a combined salary of 35 tostones for the period. The husband was to drive mules and the wife was to make chocolate drinks and meals, and to do other household chores.[19] Another Indian couple did better, earning 110 tostones for a year's service, in addition to food and drink.[20] A different financial arrangement is also shown for the same year, in which both man and wife were to receive food and drink, but the wife was to be paid 4 tostones a month, while the husband was to receive only 3.[21] In 1592, wages for couples were still low; in one case the husband agreed to drive mules, and the wife was to make tortillas and cacao drinks for a six-month period for a combined payment of 54 tostones.[22] And in 1596, a husband was paid 5 tostones a month, while his wife received 3.[23]

It was common for Indian children to be found in Spanish homes as servants, an arrangement that was probably often of mutual benefit. As minors, they were represented by one or both parents, or a guardian, in the case of orphans. The guardian was usually an older brother or sister, aunt, uncle, or some other relative. Occasionally a Spanish official would serve that function. Not infrequently, a young girl of six or seven years was put in a home until she reached marriageable age, that is, about thirteen or fourteen, at which time she would receive a modest cash sum for a dowry to help her find a suitor. In the intervening years, the Spanish family in whose home the girl was to serve, was to provide room, board, suitable clothing, and kind treatment, as well as care during any illness. In addition, her religious instruction was the responsibility of the family.

A young boy often served a Spanish family in much the same way in return for the basic necessities. It was a reasonably fair arrangement, and one apparently not often abused by Spaniards. Particularly was it convenient for orphans or young Indians whose parents could not care for them. In 1583, a seven-year-old girl was put in service by her parents to work in a Spanish woman's household for two years. The first year she was to have only her needs given to her, but the second year the girl was also to receive the sum of twelve tostones.[24] A ladina of eight who had been reared by a

Spanish lady entered into a more formal relationship with a six-year contract that would carry her to marriageable age. She would continue to receive room and board, clothing, and care, but was also to have forty tostones given her at age fourteen for her dowry.[25]

In another instance, an Indian widow let her daughter out to a family for one year, during which time the girl would have her necessities given to her, plus the more equitable pay of twenty-five tostones at year's end.[26] Perhaps in this case, however, the girl was older and had more work to do than the younger girls. A ladina of fifteen contracted to work for three years for her needs and sixty tostones at the end of the period.[27] Less fortunate was an orphan girl of twelve who was signed on for six years, at the end of which she was to receive fifty tostones.[28] Earlier, in 1575, another "yndezuela" of seven was given by her father in contract with wages of twelve tostones for her year of household service, but in 1596 a girl of ten was put into a home by her father for three years with pay of only ten tostones a year.[29] One may observe cynically that the Spaniards were by this system able to have little servants around the house at almost no cost, but I am inclined to believe that this was perhaps the least onerous form of Indian labor. Homeless children, in particular, had little option.

The arrangements for Indians boys were similar. In 1583, a Spanish official, acting as guardian, put an orphan of seven in service for a five-year term. The boy was to receive room, board, clothing, good care, and indoctrination, in addition to a final settlement of 40 tostones in cash.[30] In 1589 an orphan of eleven or twelve years entered service for six years in return for his basic needs and a terminal cash settlement of 100 tostones.[31] These are representative examples. Even boys not under contracts began carrying loads of wood by age eight, at least in Verapaz.[32]

Finally, there were always some who were apprenticed to learn trades. In this "servicio de aprendiz" the Indian boys lived and worked with Spanish artisans for a period of time during which they were taught skills, under an arrangement that was very much like the apprentice programs in Castile and other parts of Europe. Along with room, board, care, and good treatment, the boys received religious training. Ordinarily the native apprentice was to be given his clothing as well; however, apparently he did not receive any pay as a rule, his care and training being considered adequate payment for his labors. At the end of his term of apprenticeship he was often given tools, more clothing, and perhaps a small sum of money.

An early contract, in 1544, shows that an Indian agreed to serve a tailor for three years to learn the trade. He was to receive room and board, in addition to ten pesos de minas a year, but he may have been an adult.[33] In what was probably a more typical arrangement, a 1567 contract had a fourteen-year-old boy apprenticed to a silversmith for four years, at the end of which time he would be given a set of clothing consisting of a kilt-like garment and some breeches, both of which were made of domestic materials, along with a hat, shoes, and two shirts.[34] In 1595, a boy of twelve or thirteen who already had some skill as a tailor's helper went to work for a tailor for one year only, in return for his food and drink, and a final payment of breeches, a cape, two shirts, and a hat. Even though he was somewhat advanced in the trade, he apparently received no wages.[35] In this manner Indian boys learned crafts and supplemented the many others taught by men of the Church, so that by the end of the sixteenth century there was a sizeable corps of indigenous artisans skilled in traditional European trades.

The Hangover of Slavery

Following their liberation slaves tended to congregate together, usually under the care of the Dominicans. In Ciudad Real they moved near the monastery of Santo Domingo, and the Crown was requested to order that the ex-slaves not be molested and that, despite their numbers, they be allowed to stay where they were, to be protected and indoctrinated by the friars. It was so decreed.[36] Many of them also gathered on the outskirts of Santiago. They were given permission by the Crown to have annual elections for their alcaldes and an alguacil in order to have representation. Those Indian officials would be subject to residencias at the end of their terms.[37]

Six years later the Crown noted that in those two cities, as well as in Salvador, the congregations of ex-slaves were still being molested by Spaniards. Although free people, they were being threatened, 'mistreated, and forced to work. A timid people, they were fearful of their situation, as a result of which it was requested that they be put under the direct care of the Crown. In order that they would not be alienated, but rather be treated as vassals, it was to be done.[38] Vecinos had said that since the ex-slaves did not pay tribute they should be forced to labor in public-works projects or for individual Spaniards; the Crown position was that those Indians had been temporarily relieved from paying tribute because of their past suffering. Their forced labor was worse than if they paid tribute like other Indians. The freedmen wanted to pay a moderate tribute, but they were to have three years of exemption, after which a tribute would be assessed. In the meantime they were not to be compelled to work.[39]

Some information on the status of the communities of ex-slaves can be gleaned from the *tasación* of the *barrio* of Santa Inés, near the pueblo of Petapa on the outskirts of Santiago. According to the information gathered by Francisco del Valle Marroquín, a regidor of Santiago appointed royal judge for administration of the Indians, the settlement consisted of many ex-slaves and some naborías. At this time, the word "tributo" was written alongside the names of all Indians except the freedmen. All Indians who had been converted, which is to say practically all within the pale of Spanish society, used Christian first names. Among those in Santa Inés a few retained their native surnames (e.g., Pedro Tzaquimux, Domingo Suchite, and Andrés Cahuti), while others simply took the surnames of their previous Spanish masters. Still others assumed names from their ex-masters' professions: Diego Tesorero had been a slave of the treasurer (tesorero) Francisco Castellanos; Alonso Contador had been a slave of the royal contador Çurrilla (Zorrilla). Several of them were ex-slaves of Castellanos, but only one had his surname. Did Indians need the master's permission to use his name? Was that one a favorite, or perhaps a natural son?

In the list containing forty-six heads of families, twenty-five were ex-slaves and only two are listed as naborías. The others fitted neither category. The alcalde and a regidor were ex-slaves, and another regidor was a naboría. Whether the ex-slaves were there by preference or bureaucratic directive is not completely clear, but it was probably the former.

About half of the Indians listed for the community had houses and milpas; there was a notation in the margin for those who did not with the warning that they should provide them or suffer 100 lashes. There was some prosperity among them, since they had community horses, having purchased twenty-five mares at three and a half pesos each. There were common milpas of both maize and wheat, and the people had the proceeds from forty-nine goats sold to Petapa. There were many of these settlements at the time, with varying degrees of prosperity.[40]

In 1563, the audiencia, referring to a royal order that the Indians who had been slaves be put into crown towns to pay tribute, suggested that all Indians who had no encomenderos and paid no tribute be included, which would bring in 5,000 pesos annually.[41] A month later it was reported that the ex-slaves were being put under the Crown, with their tribute commencing on the day of San Juan in June of 1563. The request by encomenderos that the Indians be assigned in private encomiendas was resisted.[42]

Alluding to the survivors of the slave population in 1574, the Crown noted that there were only a few of them left and that they were old and exempt from tribute.[43] On that matter the Crown was misinformed. Not counting the settlements of ex-slaves in Ciudad Real, Salvador, and any other locations, just around the edges of Santiago there were thirty-one barrios and milpas where they resided. Some of them were classified as ex-naborías, and it is not completely clear that all the rest were ex-slaves, but it appears as if that was the case. The villages made representation to complain of their circumstances, and a number of them submitted information about their general problems, with particular reference to tribute assessments. Nine of the hamlets had tributaries, amounting to a total of around five hundred. The inference is that most of them were ex-slaves.

With the information at hand, I cannot give a total figure for all the thirty-one settlements. Such information is very possibly available in parish records. The community with the largest number of tributaries listed showed 197, while the smallest was only about twenty. It may be speculated that for all of the settlements there were probably at least a thousand ex-slaves, perhaps twice that number. Considering that there were such communities in Chiapas and Salvador (and very likely in other regions), a surprising number of ex-slaves had survived the quarter century since their liberation.

The freedmen represented in the suit lived on the fringes of the Spanish settlement of Santiago, some close to the Dominicans and others a short distance away at "ciudad vieja Tzacualpa almolonga de Santa María Concepción," that is, the site of the earlier city of Santiago demolished in 1541. Others lived on milpas belonging to various Spaniards, including some men of the Church.

In 1559, a royal cédula had given the freedmen exemption from tribute for three more years, during which time they were also not to be compelled to work. Another decree of 1568 imposed a moderate tribute, but they were still exempt from forced labor. In 1575–76, they made petitions in which they stated that the laws were not being observed, that their tributes were exorbitant, and that they were being compelled to work. Indians past the age of fifty-five were not supposed to pay tribute, but they, along with children, were assessed. Moreover, old assessments for those who had died or fled were still on the books and the community had to pay their share. Women were required to live in Spanish homes as wet nurses (chichiguas, chichinas, or chichivas) for a year or two without pay. The ones who ground corn meal and performed other household chores sometimes were paid, but only three reales a week. Men who were farming Spaniards' plots received the same. Children were taken from their parents to work in Spanish houses.

The demands on them were unjust, inasmuch as they were not to be forced to work. It appears, however, that it was the old case of contributing personal service in lieu of tribute. Some of them had land given by the Crown, and more had been purchased by one community—a plot of ground that had belonged to a deceased conquistador was bought at public auction for 210 pesos in 1551. Others said they had no land on which to raise even maize or chickens. Spaniards were trying to take what land they had. Some of them lived six people to one lot, which was crowded. Under the circumstances they could not meet the tribute exactions. From the testimony it does seem that the labor they performed was not onerous. They had to weed crops, sprinkle water on the streets, build stages and decorate with branches for fiestas, sweep buildings, and do other light tasks. Settlements were required to provide "yerbateros" to fetch fodder for the Spaniards' horses, but they were paid usually at the rate of twenty to forty *tapastes* (cacao beans) a load. So it was an annoyance, but nothing like the suffering they had experienced years before.

Many of the ex-slaves seem to have been much under the influence of the Dominicans. After their liberation they were free to return to their native lands, but the Dominicans would not let them go. Still, one gets the impression that the friars were their protectors up to a point and that the Indians accommodated to the Dominican control with good grace. At least in the petitions they did not complain about the Dominicans, while they saw their enemies as Spanish officials and some encomenderos. The ones most abused were the Indian officials who were elected by the ex-slaves and naborías. They were whipped, jailed, or fined if the community quota was not fulfilled. One frustrating example was the demand that for baptisms and *juegos de cañas* trumpeters had to be provided, or the officials would be given lashes. But only the church had trumpets and the Indians apparently could not use them.[44]

Their complaints brought a response from the Crown, ordering the audiencia to see that the earlier cédulas protecting the ex-slaves were observed.[45]

A description of the province of Guatemala in 1594 mentions that by the four monasteries in Santiago there were barrios of ex-slaves, "who were slaves that licenciado Cerrato liberated." It is mentioned that they had trades and were well settled. Twenty-six leagues distant at the pueblo of Çoloma, on the road to Verapaz, a small settlement of about thirty Indian vecinos also consisted of slaves "freed by Cerrato." They had crops and paid a small tribute to the Crown.[46] Given the year, it seems likely that almost all were actually descendants of the ex-slaves, although the wording does not give that impression.

Even though the Indian slaves were liberated under Cerrato at mid-century, the issue of Indian slavery was not completely closed in Central America. At least with some, the idea persisted that Indians who resisted Spanish sovereignty could still be enslaved. A case in point was the intention of Juan Pérez de Cabrera, who in 1551 was planning to leave for the conquest of Nueva Cartago (Costa Rica). He had in mind a violent campaign ("a fuego e a sangre"), in which he would take slaves, a policy resisted by Cerrato.[47] Supporting the plan of Pérez de Cabrera was the fact that rebellious Indians in Mexico were being enslaved off and on.

In 1552, there were still some Indian slaves in Guatemala who had been taken from Jalisco during a rebellion in Nueva Galicia. Prince Philip ordered, however, that they be given a hearing, because some of them may have been enslaved unjustly. If they had been active participants in the rebellion it is apparent that they were to remain slaves.[48] In the same year Philip called attention to the illegal possession of free Indians as slaves by Central American caciques, ordering the audiencia to put a stop to it.[49]

In the district of the Bishopric of Chiapas, the indomitable Indians of Lacandón and Pochutla had successfully resisted Spanish pretensions for years. By the 1550s the problem was viewed as most serious by the Crown, especially because of their attacks on settlements of Christianized natives. In early 1553, the Dominican friars in nearby Verapaz were assigned the task of pacifying them. When their efforts failed, and while the Lacandones and Indians of Pochutla continued their burning of villages and killing other Indians, the audiencia was ordered to investigate and make recommendations.[50]

In March 1558, the Crown authorized a pacification expedition against the rebels. Because the soldiers would not have gone without pay, they were to be rewarded with the tributes that the Indians would pay once they were pacified. Every effort was to be made in the direction of a peaceful settlement, failing which war could be made against the Indians, and those taken could be enslaved, "for their insolence and troublemaking."[51] The expedition from Guatemala was under the command of the energetic oidor, licenciado Pedro Ramírez de Quiñones, who in 1559 successfully brought them to heel. According to an audiencia report, Ramírez captured most of the rebels, but did not make any slaves.[52]

A royal order of 1561 prohibited the sale of Indian slaves.[53] Since at the time there must have been only a few legal slaves introduced from Mexico, the decree has a curious ring, unless the reference was meant to apply to Costa Rica. In that province, which was still largely unpacified, it was reported that caciques were stealing Indians from other groups and enslaving them.[54]

Another plan envisaged the importation of slaves from Mexico. The governor of Soconusco, observing the great richness of the province because of its cacao, also noted the serious lack of population, owing at least in part to the oppressive heat. In 1574, he had suggested that the audiencia could relocate Indians from Verapaz to Soconusco. Furthermore, don Martín Enríquez, the viceroy of New Spain, could move down people from the province of Tehuantepec, which had the same type of climate. At that time he was referring to free Indians—that is, non-slaves, but hardly independent if they could be forced to move from their native lands.

The following year the governor had another idea—Indians who were slaves in various parts of Mexico could be transferred. Every year, he said, more than four hundred Indians were sold into slavery because of grave crimes. Those *Chichimecos* and other delinquents were sold under Crown auspices for no more than thirty pesos each, and they were to remain slaves for eight or nine years. The governor requested that the viceroy and the governor of Guatemala send to Soconusco Indians sold into slavery, along with others who had been exiled for serious crimes. The exiles could take their families with them, and within two years that would repopulate Soconusco, while the four hundred or so Indians who were enslaved every year in Mexico would produce considerable profit for the royal treasury. The Indian slaves from Mexico would be sold to the local natives for their service, and the result would be an extra carga of cacao for each slave taken in. About two thousand more Indians was all the province could support.[55]

Because the Chontal Indians were cannibals who killed and robbed their peaceful neighbors, the audiencia sought permission from the Crown to enslave them. An added reason was that they lived in lands difficult of access, so that added incentive was needed for those who had to pacify them. In his response, in 1580, the king allowed that the Chontales could be forced into service for a certain time period, but they were not to be slaves.[56] About the same time, however, the governor of Cartago in Costa Rica was charged with taking peaceful tributaries, including young boys, from a crown town, and transporting them in chains to Cartago. When two of them died from mistreatment, the governor left them lying in their chains.[57] These are isolated cases, and the evidence is that except in unusual circumstances Indian slavery was for all practical purposes abolished by 1550 in Central America. In Mexico, on the other hand, particularly on the northern frontiers, the enslavement of natives continued for many years.[58]

The Persistence of the Naboría System

In 1549 Cerrato had found conditions of naborías so bad that he asked that their service in private homes be suppressed.[59] That did not come about, but the Crown followed up on another report by ruling that naborías serving in homes, villages, and estancias were to be questioned by the Protector of the Indians or an alcalde to learn whether or not their situation impeded their conversion. The officials were to bring together the naborías and their employers to establish the obligations of both sides, but it was to be emphasized that Indians could change masters if they so chose, and in such case the Protector or alcalde was to help them find new positions, with *wages* established beforehand. It would be further agreed that if a naboría died serving a Spaniard he would be buried in the Spanish church of the village, provided he was a Christian, and was not to be lain to rest in the fields. The employer was to keep accounts of the Indians' wages so that he would know what a deceased naboría left for his heirs, and that amount was to be paid to them.[60]

Some problems still existed for the naborías. Years later, by 1564, the archdeacon of the cathedral church of León, licenciado Juan Alvarez de Ortega, reported to the Crown that encomenderos were using naborías, along with some Indians from their encomienda towns, in their household service, against their wills. Some of the Spaniards had fifteen to twenty of them, and they would not allow them to go to the villages to marry for fear that their services would be lost. Furthermore, they maltreated them and did not even pay them for their work. The *arcediano* suggested that those Indians be made truly free to come and go, and to marry in the villages without any impediment by encomenderos or anyone else, and that they be compensated for their labor.[61]

On the whole, though, such abuses were relatively few in the post-1550 period. The evidence suggests that the status of the naborías was clarified—or more precisely, the designation changed. Those originally classified that way eventually became very few, because the outsiders eventually sank roots. With pacification of the isolated regions, few were taken in that category, and fewer Indians were moved about. The original naborías married, became identified with a Spanish household, or sometimes a pueblo, and found neighbors and friends. Gradually the descendants of the early naborías became merely members of a class of servants working primarily in households, where they received the basic necessities and meager wages. They became, in effect, family retainers in the more modern sense. The system became regularized as they emerged as a less amorphous group.

Legislation had been on the books for years that no one could use an

Indian as a naboría, from which one might conclude that the category itself was abolished by the Crown and that use of the term would disappear. But the point becomes academic, for if the naborías were free and had mobility, if they were cared for and well treated, and if they were paid for their work, then, regardless of what they were called, they were simply servants agreeing to enter the employ of a Spaniard. As it happened, however, most of them became locked in. In the residencia of the oidor Ramírez, one of the better judges in the audiencia during the sixteenth century, he declared in 1559 that he had enforced the law that no Indian could serve as a naboría. A witness verified the statement, but he added that he had seen some Indians serving in that way of their own volition because they needed to earn wages.[62]

Laws to the contrary notwithstanding, we know that the classification of some Indians as naborías persisted through the sixteenth century and into the seventeenth. In 1600, don Jorge de Alvarado, the governor of Honduras, related to the Crown that in the jurisdiction of Olancho warlike Indians had been punished for raiding the villages of peaceful natives, and that they had rescued about five hundred Indians, some of whom had apparently been naborías, "as they had Christian names." The governor sent word for the ex-naborías to be well treated and a clergyman was sent to baptize them. He was sending more expeditions out in the probability of finding more naborías being held by indios de guerra.[63] Thus it appears that by that date the term naboría was applied very loosely.

In drawing up provisions for tribute assessments in 1603, there were included among the tributaries "the Indian naborías not registered in their villages." The designation here applies to those who were not settled citizens of any village. The men, married and bachelors, over the age of eighteen were to pay three tostones, and the single women over the age of sixteen would pay only one tostón for their tribute. Children living with their parents and under their jurisdiction were not obligated to contribute, nor were men over sixty or women over fifty. All tribute-paying naborías were to give an additional tostón to the Crown—two reales for the day of San Juan and two reales for Christmas.[64]

With royal income involved, a close regulation of the naborías resulted. The local official (governor, alcalde mayor, corregidor, or justicia ordinario) was to make a list before a notary within three months' time of the proclamation of the law showing the naborías, as well as the blacks in the province. Each entry was to indicate the birthplace, age, and distinguishing marks of each individual, along with his trade and the employer at whose place the naboría resided. These census lists were to be taken every three years, and were to be kept in books in the possession of the notary.

Whenever one of the naborías, or blacks, wanted to move from the place he had given as his address, or if he wanted to be absent for some time, it would be necessary for him to obtain license from the ranking Spanish official of his area, along with certification that his tribute had been paid. The official of the area to which the naboría was moving was required to help him get settled and inscribed in the local book, while the records were changed in the place he had left. To go for a short stay, the Indian had to check with the justice and tell him why he wanted to leave the area, and then he could have license to leave. If a naboría left without license and certification, he would be subject to 100 lashes and would be returned to his locale at his own expense.[65]

In practice, this system presented difficulties, but it was further evidence that the system had become formalized with a growing bureaucracy, and the trend continued.[66] So the category of naboría persisted, and gradually there evolved the *amo-sirviente* relationship that is prevalent in Latin America today. Documents of the last half of the sixteenth century are much less critical of the system than those of earlier decades, and even Bishop Juan Ramírez, who was very critical of the Spanish exploitation of native labor in the early seventeenth century, did not concern himself with naborías.

Historically, these servants are of some interest, because they may be seen as the forerunners of the modern peones—that is, workers on *fincas* or *haciendas* who are by law free people, but whose families have been associated with the lands and household of the amo's family, in many cases for several generations. They could, if they were not the victims of debt-peonage, seek other situations, but where? The myth of the "free" worker may thus be traced by the thread that goes back 450 years. Independent by law, their mobility has been limited by engrained tradition and social and economic realities, so that over the centuries the naboría mentality has existed.

The Continuing Use of Tamemes

It is not true, as the seventeenth-century chronicler Remesal wrote, that with the coming of Cerrato, "the service of the Indian carriers ceased entirely";[67] but it is fair to assert that his reforms significantly reduced the number of tamemes and abolished many of the abuses of those who continued to carry. The law had not, of course, absolutely ruled out the use of tamemes, but rather decreed a moderation of their use and their treatment. In addition, they were to be paid. The conditions of transportation by mid-century were still such that Spaniards could not get along without them. At the time Cerrato arrived, the cabildo of Gracias a Dios complained that despite the Crown's order that roads be built, nothing had been done by the audiencia, and traveling was so bad that one could hardly walk about. Thus, while the use of tamemes was restricted to instances of absolute necessity, there was little alternative. Still, the regidores said, it was not so bad, because for the tamemes it was customary and natural.[68] Cerrato confirmed that little had been done in the matter of roads, but he was most disturbed about the renting of encomienda Indians as tamemes, who "were like slaves and treated even worse." Cerrato deprived some Spaniards of their Indians for misusing them as tamemes, and the carriers were relieved.[69]

The veedor Hernando de Ugarte informed the Crown that while Cerrato had abolished the practice of forcing pueblos to contribute tamemes, which was well done, the result was to cause food prices to rise because of the resulting shortages of provisions. More often than not, he added, some supplies were unavailable at any price. The Indians who did haul goods on their backs, seeing the lack of roads, and knowing that pack animals could not be used in many instances, had to be coaxed to work, because encomenderos were no longer permitted to rent out their villagers, and there were fewer tamemes to be had. When they did agree to carry, they asked for excessive wages, and the Spaniards paid whatever they charged so as not to lose the merchandise, as had happened. Consequently, the exorbitant wages not only precluded merchants from making a profit, but even resulted in losses. It would be a great help, Ugarte wrote, if the king would order that a standard wage or ceiling be imposed, as the viceroy had done in New Spain. If that were done, the tamemes, knowing they could not make higher wages, would be content to work and would stop trying to charge so much.[70]

One of the more reasonable voices raised in the dispute over Indian labor was that of fray Francisco Bustamante, who usually urged a policy of moderation and common sense. With regard to the controversy over tamemes, he wrote that on a journey one could not manage without the carriers, because he had to take a trunk, his bed, and containers of food, since there were no inns and few settlements. If a Spaniard's business was pressing and he had to wait for pack animals, he would either have to be late, or hire three old nags and a Negro for the round trip, which would cost more than one could afford. Moreover, sometimes it was necessary to go to a village off the road, where animals could not travel.

In any event, he noted, carrying loads was nothing new for the natives because they were used to it. The Indians themselves were not prevented from using those of their own race to carry their goods. Sometimes, he said, tamemes carrying for other Indians were required to pack as much as

75 to 100 pounds; thus the advantage was to Indian traders. Business was lost to Spaniards and given to natives, so that the Indian was the principal merchant and the Spaniard the steward. If there was a limit on the journey, not to exceed four or five leagues, and if the loads were limited to 50 pounds, if tamemes were not taken from the lowlands to the mountains, and if the rich merchants who required many tamemes were made to carry merchandise with animals, then, the friar affirmed, no harm would result.

Rather, it would be a benefit, because with fifteen or twenty days' work a year the Indians could make enough money to pay their tributes. "Do not let them tell Your Majesty," he added, "that it can all be done with pack animals, even with open, smooth roads; because with the bringing of tributes and the carrying of provisions from the ports and with the trade and necessary provisions for the mines and other needs of the land, all the animals of New Spain would not suffice; and it is one thing to see it here and another to make it understood in Spain."[71]

Las Casas, a friar of different outlook, incensed over the use of humans as beasts of burden, was of the opinion that Spaniards should restrain themselves to do without silks and other luxuries, and to content themselves with whatever the unfortunate Indians could offer.[72] But the idealistic friar appealed to an asceticism that was as absent among his countrymen as it is in our own society. Besides, he did not address himself to the real problem: Spaniards might be persuaded to forgo silks, which weighed little; but how many of them would give up their staple provisions of wine, vinegar, and oils, all of which were very heavy? At least Cerrato finally got the Spaniards over their inclination to have their dogs carried by tamemes.[73]

A regidor of Santiago, lamenting the 1549 law restricting the use of tamemes, stressed not only the harm done to Spaniards, but also the damage done to tamemes, who, he claimed, were starving from lack of employment and wanted the liberty to carry as before. If they volunteered and carried moderate weights, there was no need to deprive them of the right to work. Prince Philip did not agree.[74] Writing in two other letters about the same time, Philip said that he was informed that one of the reasons Indians did not volunteer for carrying was the pittance they received for their labors, usually no more than eight and a half maravedís daily, from which they had to buy their food. That was not only too little, in the prince's view, but practically the same as working for nothing. He ordered that when it was necessary for tamemes to be rented they were to be paid a decent wage, from which they could sustain themselves adequately, and be able, in addition, to save some for other necessities.

Aside from all that, Philip said that it was his understanding that the herds of horses, mules, and other beasts of burden had increased to the point where there were sufficient animals to carry all the necessary goods for the land. But, he hedged, since Cerrato was on the spot, and since the Crown had confidence in him, the president could make allowances for the use of tamemes if animals and carts were not available. In villages near Santiago where Indians could be distributed for renting they could be so occupied provided the work was moderate, for a brief time, and involving short distances, and using those whose absence would be felt least. This attitude, as interpreted by Cerrato, did restrict the carrying by Indians, and Philip noted that Francisco Girón, a regidor of the Santiago cabildo, had complained of the limitations. Philip was not disposed to make another exception, leaving discretionary powers in the hands of Cerrato.[75]

Whatever measures Cerrato took, excesses continued. An encomendero was charged with using his Indians to transport sixty fanegas of tribute maize to the city on their backs, and, over a period of years he had paid them only once, when he gave each carrier sixty cacao beans. He said that the oidor licenciado Ramírez had given him the right to let the Indians carry the tribute provided he paid them one half a silver real daily, or the equivalent in cacao.

In his defense, the encomendero, Andrés de Rodas, stated that he was a conquistador of seventy, and that he had been in New Spain, Honduras, and Guatemala for a total of forty years in the Indies. In order to establish his respectability, he noted that he was married to the daughter of another conqueror, was the father of two legitimate sons, fed and housed orphans and maidens, maintained a household, and was ill.

He was tried, nevertheless, and deprived of his encomienda, without which he said he and his family would be destitute. In the end, however, his appeal was successful. He convinced the judge that the Indians who testified exaggerated and distorted the facts, and in the review the audiencia let him off with a fine of seven pesos de oro, which were to be used for the purchase of necessary items for the church of Oçuma.[76]

One of Cerrato's first projects was to attack the basic problem, the lack of roads which made so many carriers necessary. He put idlers to work on them, with the Crown's approval.[77] Early in 1550, he wrote that since his arrival nothing had taken precedence over the opening of roads, and that one had been built between Puerto de Caballos and San Pedro over a formidable mountain. More were under construction connecting San Pedro with Comayagua and Gracias a Dios. Another would be completed from Gracias a Dios to San Salvador and from there to Santiago. To complete the loop, one was being opened from Santiago directly to San Pedro. Finally, a way northward to Chiapas and Mexico would be cleared.

Although not all these roads were finished at that time, beasts were

being driven along all of them. Since merchandise was being carried all
the way from Veracruz in Mexico to provision Santiago, the goods were
very expensive. Hence, it was important that the route from Santiago to
San Pedro, near the port, be cleared, because it was impossible to use pack
animals over the old trail. Cerrato was also exploring the possibilities of
utilizing the Golfo Dulce, only thirty-eight leagues distant from Santiago,
as an alternate route.[78]

To relieve tamemes in the Dominican province of Verapaz, the Crown
ordered, in 1555, that jackasses were to be imported from the islands,
indicating that there was still no real abundance of draft animals in the
audiencia district.[79] Evidently this project bore little fruit, for years later
tamemes were still in widespread use in Verapaz, and the alcalde mayor
claimed there were still no beasts of burden to convey goods.[80] But even
the availability of horses or other draft animals did not always mean that
there was no demand for tamemes; nor, for that matter, did the existence
of flat lands along with beasts lead to the extinction of the use of tamemes.
In Nicaragua, by 1563 the archdeacon of León wrote that the Chontal
Indians around Segovia were carrying maize and other food to the mines in
excessively heavy loads, even though horses were inexpensive. Many of
the Chontales had perished, but they were cheaper than horses.[81]

If, as appears to be the case, the use of tamemes was significantly
reduced during the watchful stewardship of Cerrato, his successors were
less conscientious. In again reminding the audiencia of the 1549 law,
Philip II wrote in 1559 that he was informed that the law was not being
enforced with any vigor. Spaniards continued to use tamemes without
discrimination, roads had not been kept in condition for horses to carry
merchandise, while in all of Mexico pack animals were being used.

The reason for the deviation in Central America, he said, was that
tamemes were simply the least expensive form of transportation—not only
because of the low wages they received, but also because Spaniards thus
avoided paying taxes on other forms of transportation. Moreover, the
officials themselves had the license and first choice in the acquisition of
tamemes, and they were able to send the Indians to the port for merchandise at the wages they wanted to pay. The officials not only broke the law
themselves, but they also allowed their relatives and friends to do the
same, so that no punishment was given and no change occurred. Other
Spaniards, seeing their example, took it as an acceptable practice. Philip
commanded the judges to make amends before the Indians were finished off.[82]

The grand design of Cerrato for a road system was imperfectly developed and maintained over the years. In the 1560s Governor **Briceño**

was called to account for lack of diligence in improving and maintaining the existing network, which led to the continued dependence upon the carrying by humans.[83] Improvement in the roads during the rest of the sixteenth century was apparently slight.

If the tameme system remained entrenched, there was a general lessening of abuses. On the whole, tamemes were paid (though not very much), they usually worked voluntarily (though no doubt out of dire necessity), and carrying was usually restricted to mature adults. One finds, however, indications that this generalization, while essentially true, yields to evidence of grave exceptions. One of the most inhumane of the early practices had been the impressment of women and children in human pack trains. Many of them fell from sheer exhaustion, but an additional tragedy resulted from the breaking up of families, along with the imposition of other social dislocations. And despite reforming laws to the contrary, women were still used on occasion to carry loads.

In 1568, a witness said they were included among a group carrying maize on a journey of three or four days, and that some of the carriers had been maltreated. Allegedly, the women were forced to haul the loads at the behest of the lieutenant of the governor.[84] As late as 1582, it was charged that many Indian women were being broken physically by the heavy loads they were forced to carry. Among those accused were alcaldes mayores and corregidores, but the defense maintained that the guilty officials had been punished.[85]

The illegal use of tamemes by members of the audiencia was the most egregious infraction committed. Their personal involvement mocked royal justice and encouraged violations by all other segments of society. Bureaucracies riddled by corruption became commonplace, all to the detriment of the Indian. At the same time, the fact that even men of conscience used tamemes underscores the dependence on carriers, especially on expeditions.

One gains the strong impression from reading many juicios de residencia and lawsuits that most of the charges against officials were justified, because of the detailed nature of the testimony. At the same time, perjury seems to have been widespread, and it cannot be assumed that all were guilty.

A case in point is the high-minded judge, Alonso de Zorita (Çorita), whose unpopular actions brought many accusations against him. Accused of illegally using tamemes on the journey to his post as oidor, licenciado Zorita, perceiving the charge prejudicial to his reputation, did not wait for it to be brought out later in his residencia, but prepared a probanza for the Consejo de Indias. He stated that his bedding and tablecloths, his Negroes, and his books had all been taken from Puerto de Caballos to the Golfo Dulce in a boat, which had cost him 110 pesos; and from there the bedding was left to be transported by mules and horses. Nothing, he said, was carried by tamemes. His witnesses confirmed his deposition.[86]

Certainly Zorita prosecuted with vigor others who broke the law. Regidores in Santiago complained of what they considered his high-handed methods. One case concerned a "poor conquistador" who used an Indian on a two-day journey from Santiago to carry a six- or eight-pound package of hardtack, which was consumed along the road. Zorita proceeded against him in such a way that the conquistador died saying the oidor was killing him.[87]

One of the more notorious of the audiencia judges was Dr. Antonio Mexía, who not only failed to enforce the laws against the use of tamemes, but also made wide use of them himself. On the long trip from Mexico to Guatemala he allegedly arrived with a human pack train of between fifty and seventy Indians laden with excessively heavy cargoes. When one of them dropped along the way, Mexía's response was to transfer his load to another carrier, leaving the prostrate Indian to his fate. The accusers said that the judge had traveled over roads that merchants took with horses to carry their merchandise. By his action, they said, he had encouraged other Spaniards to follow his example, whereas before they had been afraid to break the law.

When Mexía went on an inspection tour to the coast of Zapotitlán, he took tamemes from various villages along the way, about 190 in all. In Soconusco, where he passed a couple of months, he used more than 30 tamemes without paying them. They carried not only his effects, but also those of his criados and relatives. When he took tropical Indians up to the highlands they suffered physical harm. On his visit to San Salvador, he did more harm than good, witnesses said, because he used tamemes over a period of two months and gave them no compensation. Again, the expedition was over lands flat enough to use horses. There were various other similar charges against him involving tamemes.

In his defense, Mexía said that if he used tamemes it was not to haul merchandise, which was illegal. But, he said, to that point there had been no proceedings against anyone for having used Indians to carry a bed, clothing, or necessary food for a journey, when they worked voluntarily for pay. Anyway, he added, all the oidores took tamemes to carry the necessities for official parties, which included a notary, an interpreter, an alguacil, and others. There was no alternative because of the high mountains; but even when one encountered a good road for part of the journey, there would be other parts where horses could not travel.

Moreover, one could not always find a mule driver with animals, and if one was available he would be loath to go, because on the official inspection tours the oidores did not go directly from one place to another; rather, they would stop at villages for three or four days, depending on the need, all of which was an inconvenience, with less profit, for the arriero. On the other hand, Mexía asserted, carrying was a source of income for the Indians, who were always paid by the visitadores, as, he said, he had paid them.

Regarding his use of tamemes when he came from Mexico, the charge was improper for his residencia, Mexía insisted, because the trial was only to review his acts as an oidor, and at the time he had not assumed his office. Nevertheless, he said he had not used tamemes, since the great part of his effects had gone by sea from Guatulco to Acajutla. Accompanying him on the overland journey was a pack train of fourteen horses, which had cost him dearly.

As to the charge that he used so many tamemes on his visita to the coast of Zapotitlán and other pueblos, this was well known to be false, because when he traveled he took no bed, but only a quilt, a blanket, two sheets, and a pillow, while those in his party took only blankets, in addition to shirts and some preserves, which did not amount to much. Two or three Indians, perhaps a few more, could take those items from village to village, and there was no need for the large numbers of tamemes referred to in the charges. Most of the Indians who testified, he reminded, had admitted that he paid them, and that the two tostones each received was excessive reward.

His protests notwithstanding, Mexía was found guilty by the juez de residencia of using many tamemes and not paying them a single maravedí. He was ordered to pay all the Indians of the several villages named in the various charges a silver real each, amounting to 282 reales for a like number of tamemes. Even those did not include Indians allegedly used on his trip from Mexico, in Soconusco, or in Izalcos, which would have raised the figure another hundred or so. Because he had used those Indians so long, it was difficult to determine who they were and how much was owed, although it was obviously a considerable amount. On that score payment was deferred.

In the end, Mexía was fined 400 pesos, a good sum, but probably only about what he should have paid the tamemes in the first place; hence, although he was forced to make restitution for some of the abuse, he was in fact not ultimately penalized for the infractions. As a consequence, it paid to gamble that one would not be prosecuted, because there was little to lose. [88]

It is a refreshing change to note that over the years at least one of the oidores besides Cerrato, licenciado Pedro Ramírez de Quiñones, a member of the audiencia in Central America for about fifteen years before assuming a presidency in South America, left a distinguished record, his integrity intact. Witnesses in his residencia stated that he had punished those who abused tamemes and removed their Indians from carrying. Ramírez had allowed carriers only where horses could not go, and then only for the transporting of food. In addition he allowed only the use of tamemes who worked in their own interests, for pay.[89]

The alcalde mayor in Honduras was charged with having used tamemes on various occasions, making them carry excessively heavy loads for no pay. He denied the charge, saying that he held his post for only a little more than three months, and of that time he remained in Gracias a Dios for twenty days during that short period. If tamemes carried some of his clothing from Gracias a Dios to San Pedro, it was at the order of the caciques and principales, and it was customary for tamemes to go with alcaldes mayores when they went from village to village, even though it was only three or four leagues. But he took pack horses too, so that there was little for the Indians to carry. They took his bed and a couple of pieces of baggage, wine, and food for the men, without which it was impossible to travel in parts of the country. The rough terrain often prevented the use of animals.

For this comparatively mild charge, he was given the stiff fine of 1,000 pesos de oro, the loss of the merchandise the Indians had carried for him, and was ordered to pay all the tamemes. There were other charges remitted to the Council of the Indies for further consideration. The alcalde mayor admitted that he had ordered the caciques and principales to give traveling Spaniards tamemes, but only in case of dire need, in which case each tameme was to receive one *real de plata* for each day's labor.[90]

Five years later witnesses testified that a high official in Honduras loaded Indians with maize for a journey of three or four days and paid them in cacao worth only half a real.[91] It is clear that despite the royal injunction that all porters be paid, some received nothing, or wages not commensurate with their work and the going rate.[92]

The governor of Honduras supposedly used tamemes and allowed others to do the same. He denied it, explaining that he had no merchandise to transport, and that when he traveled he always took animals, with Indians carrying nothing; nor in his time in office had he heard of anyone else using tamemes. Moreover, he said, the charge against him was absurd, because it was claimed that he used more than two thousand tamemes, while there were not fifteen hundred Indians in the province available to carry. The testimony was, according to his view, vague, and in any event, he said it was legal to use tamemes provided they were not used for carrying merchandise and were traveling where horses could not go.[93]

In Verapaz the alcalde mayor was accused of forcing Indians to carry iron tools and washing troughs, as well as salt and other provisions. He said there was no choice but to use tamemes, and that the Indians were accustomed to carrying and making their livelihoods that way. They were, he said, paid the wages they requested.[94]

Charged with making Indians carry maize, a lieutenant of the governor in Honduras said that he permitted it because in the year 1577 there was such a general hunger in the province that he not only allowed Indians to carry food, but even sent some to Guatemala to get more maize to prevent starvation. It was necessary, because aside from travel on the *caminos reales*, there were places where animals could not negotiate the paths. The shortage of food was so extreme that one fanega of corn went for eight tostones. In his opinion, an official on the spot should be allowed to make judgments of such a serious nature.[95] One of the other lieutenants of the governor of Honduras was found guilty of using tamemes and permitting others to do so. He was fined thirty pesos and suspended from office for two years.[96]

A more aggravated case was that of a corregidor who was said to have used more than 120 tamemes to carry his household effects, and another 10 or 12 to carry his wife around on their shoulders.[97] Perhaps this was an extraordinary instance, for the same year a report instigated at the order of the president of the audiencia indicated that while alcaldes mayores and corregidores did sometimes use tamemes, it was usually only four or five of them to carry food and other necessities. The few who had abused the use of carriers, witnesses said, had been punished.[98] Another investigation dated three days later referred to the same charges, that corregidores and alcaldes mayores had been making illegal use of Indian carriers. Among others, the dean of the cathedral, don Pedro de Liebana, stated in sworn testimony that he had not heard of those officials having used Indians to carry, and he did not believe that they had—except for two cases where the guilty had been punished. Others agreed, including the *maestrescuela*.[99]

Finally the Crown resigned itself to the need of oidores in particular to use tamemes on their inspection tours; however, in order to keep the number of Indian carriers to the minimum, the officials were instructed to restrict the number of Spaniards who went along on the trips.[100] In order to avoid the use of tamemes in the capital city of Santiago, firewood and fodder were taken into the city by carts. Indian household servants then carried the loads the short distances to residences.[101]

While most of Central America was gradually being pacified, the delayed conquest of Costa Rica resulted in scenes reminiscent of earlier decades in other provinces. Per Afán|de Ribera, the governor of Cartago, was accused of putting leading principales in chains to carry baggage, even though the natives of the region had come to him in peace, offering food, cloth, gold, and even tamemes. His son, don Diego, was charged with taking tamemes with him from Nicoya to Cartago, overloading and maltreating them. Needless to say, the carriers were not paid. Some of them ran away, only to be killed by warlike tribes, and of those who remained all became ill, and one of them died.[102]

Some clergymen were concerned about the harm resulting to Indians because of the carrying, but they were largely ineffective in curbing the abuses. Bishop Marroquín presented a petition to the Council of the Indies, saying that many Indians were dying because of hauling, and he requested that it be prohibited altogether. The council took the unwise action of sending the appeal on to the viceroy of New Spain, asking him to consult with the bishop of Mexico and to give an opinion, thus losing more time.[103] The cabildo of Santiago complained that while Las Casas and the other Dominicans were the main reason the use of tamemes had been restricted, the friars themselves were still using them with no interference. The regidores said that a few days before a long train of 400 tamemes had arrived all the way from Verapaz, and though the president and oidores saw them, they excused it because they knew the Indians were carrying for the Dominicans.[104]

The evidence is that village priests used carriers as well. They had Indians carrying chickens, corn, and other goods for no pay.[105] Even the Franciscans, who were relatively inconspicuous compared to the Dominicans, misused Indian labor, according to witnesses. They required the natives to make lime, tiles, and bricks for their monastery in Santiago, after which they required them to carry those materials on their backs more than seven leagues. The most melancholy aspect of their abuses, if the testimony is to be believed, is that those pressed into service included small children. One Spaniard said he saw groups of thirty to fifty of them loaded with lime, bricks, and tiles. The children, in his judgment, could not help being harmed and having their lives endangered, being so young and without sufficient strength for the labor. But the friars, it was said, took no notice and showed no sympathy. To make matters worse, none of the Indians was paid for the work.[106]

Quite late in the century, in 1582, Dominicans were allegedly having large quantities of wine carried to Coban all the way from Puerto de

Caballos on the backs of humans, who were not compensated. The Indians were also required to carry many loads of sarsaparilla over long distances, along with *mantas* (mantles), which the friars sold. Some of the journeys involved distances of twenty leagues or more, from which the Indians profited nothing, at least in any material sense.[107]

By century's end the tameme was still very much in evidence. After all the reports, investigations, royal cédulas, and various injunctions aimed at doing away with the practice, the best one can say is that some of the more brutal aspects associated with post-conquest times were largely eliminated. But carrying heavy loads or light, all too often the Indians were occupied in heavy labor not in their own interest. In 1603, the governor of Soconusco sounded a familiar lament when he wrote that the Crown would be served by issuing a vigorous order to conserve the Indians by not allowing the hauling by tamemes of any kind of cargo, including beds and chests. This prohibition should be made clear to friars and priests who used Indians to carry beds that could easily be transported by horses.

But the priests, so the governor said, wanted the Indians to serve as horses in order to show that their power was stronger than royal justice. He mentioned that he had seen a priest from Tuxtla taking from Tapachula thirteen tamemes, a distance of three leagues, who carried the following: one hauled a bed that was too much for a horse; another took a heavy ornate silver chest with coins inside that the priest usually kept with him; one was used merely to carry an umbrella; another a small chest filled with twenty eggs; two more Indians carried cacao; one led a horse on which a black woman rode; another took a prayer book; one Indian conveyed two straw mats; one a pair of boots; and two more simply walked alongside the priest. It was not uncommon, the governor asserted, for the priest to take a dozen Indians with him, and in that way he let them know that he was powerful.

The governor implored the Crown to instruct Indian governors and alcaldes not to give their Indians as porters to anyone, and to inform the priests that they could purchase horses, since they were rich and were provided with the necessary means for themselves and their servants, which included the owning of horses. If something was not done all the Indians would die from the excessive labor. In the hot lands they bathed in rivers to refresh themselves, then caught colds and fevers, which caused many deaths.[108]

In the same year of 1603, the governor of Guatemala issued an ordinance to the effect that no one in the audiencia district could use tamemes for any cargo, even if the Indians volunteered, not even with the license of any official, including the viceroy of New Spain. Any official who gave such a license was to lose his office for four years, and a fine of 1,000 pesos would be imposed on anyone who used tamemes, even with a license. A person of "quality" who could not afford the fine would be subjected to public disgrace and exile from the Indies.

Indians were not even to carry things for short distances, and specifically it was stated that they were not to carry wheat, flour, and maize, even to take them to the mill; nor to take stones from quarries, nor bricks, nor tiles from tile yards, nor lime from quarries and kilns, nor earth, sand, adobe, straw mats, boxes, and chests. Furthermore, tamemes could not carry firewood, fodder, lumber, or indigo. All this was to be proclaimed publicly in all plazas and markets of all Indian pueblos.[109] But if this ordinance abolished the use of tamemes for all intents and purposes for a while, it was transitory.[110] Indeed, the sight of an Indian bowed under a staggering load is commonplace today.

Mining After Mid-Century

Following the silver strikes in Peru and Mexico during the 1540s, mining in Central America became of less importance in the eyes of the Crown. Although many miners left for the richer fields, mining continued throughout the century in Central America, and important silver strikes in Honduras in the 1570s gave impetus to the industry.

In 1553, Prince Philip recalled that under the old system of commuting tribute to labor, which resulted in the Indians having to work in mines, some of them had been forced to travel as far as fifty leagues, carrying their mantas and what food they could. Lest there be any misunderstanding, he had earlier pointed out that even if caciques and maceguales themselves were in favor of contributing labor in lieu of tribute, it was to cease. Because tribute assessments were often exorbitant, Indians had to work in order to fulfill their obligations, which often meant that they worked in the mines. Philip had ordered a revision downward of the tributes, which had the effect of relieving some of them from that labor.[111]

Little more was reported on the controversy of Indian labor in the mines during the following two decades. The probable explanation is that many mines were inoperative, owing at least in part to the lack of Indian labor, while some mines were simply worked out. The more profitable ones were being mined by black slaves.[112] In 1573, the audiencia initiated a proposal to ascertain the royal attitude toward limited use of native labor in mines once again. Would the Crown allow natives voluntarily to mine gold and silver three or four months a year for wages? If so, the idle mines could be made to pay, giving a lift to Crown revenues as well as those of the depressed province.[113] The king refused to consider the suggestion; in fact, he ordered Franciscan friars in Honduras to watch that Spaniards were not forcing Indians to work the mines.[114]

Trying another tack, the procurador representing the city of Santiago and the miners told the king that Indians were being hurt by not being able to work in the mines, because many of them had earned their livings that way, and they needed the work to sustain their families. The familiar arguments were also trotted out—loss of income to the Crown and the province, and the shortage of black slaves. Again it was requested that Indians be allowed to work voluntarily for pay. This time Philip equivocated. In order to make up his mind, he wanted the audiencia's opinion on the matter (having had it only a few months before), bearing in mind that the natives were free people and were to be well treated. They were to be paid directly, and their health was not to be harmed in any way. In the meantime, however, the oidores could resolve the matter as they thought best.[115]

Not surprisingly, they thought it best to put the Indians into the mines. Replying in 1575, the oidores justified their decision by telling the sovereign of the general good resulting from having given license for voluntary labor in the mines. Satisfied with their report, Philip authorized the audiencia to give the same license to the governor of Honduras, adding that it was to be exercised with care.[116] Even though the rich strikes were made in Honduras about three years later, there is surprisingly little in the way of reported abuses of Indian labor in the mines as a result. Perhaps the reason is that the production of the mines justified the use of many more blacks.

By 1581, Valladolid was the principal settlement in Honduras, the seat of the bishopric, and the location of the cathedral, as well as the residence of the governor. The rise to prominence of that city was due to its proximity to the mines; ten or twelve years earlier a strike had been made at Guaçucaran about fifteen leagues away, and some three years earlier the rich mines of Tegucigalpa had been found. Being so close together, all were in the same jurisdiction under the governor and the alcaldes ordinarios. To assist them, the governor had appointed a lieutenant. Then the audiencia named an *alcalde mayor de minas* with a salary of 600 pesos annually, a move that brought on a jurisdictional conflict. The cabildo of Valladolid said it was an unnecessary drain on the treasury, and that there was overlapping administration because the alcalde mayor de minas had jurisdiction outside the mines. His control extended to an area four to six leagues from Valladolid, where about seven hundred married Indians lived in thirteen or fourteen pueblos.[117]

If this sharing of political power upset the regidores of Valladolid, it seems not to have concerned the governor, whose authority had been vitiated. For the governor, Alonso de Contreras, appears to have gone into business with the alcalde mayor de minas. It was alleged that the two of them illegally had mines being worked for their own profit, an enterprise prohibited for ministers of justice. The audiencia was ordered to investigate when it was reported that the Indians used by those high officials were suffering from excessive labor.[118] The audiencia was also instructed to correct abuses by encomenderos and caciques. The king had been informed that in Honduras and Chuluteca some encomenderos made agreements with miners to rent their pueblo Indians for mining, against the Indians' wishes. Caciques were handing over many of their own people for the same purpose.[119] In response to a petition from the prelate of Honduras, the audiencia issued a provision that no Indians were to go into the mines, but it was not rigidly enforced.[120]

One plan to solve the labor problem in the mines was through importation of Spanish laborers. As it happened, workers from Spain were not especially anxious to labor in the Indies, and the suggestion, made during the years of pacification, had never resulted in bringing more than a handful of them to Central America. Even those workers, however, had certain skills that distinguished them from Indian laborers, so that menial tasks had to be performed by natives in any event. When an alcalde mayor de minas was appointed by the king for Honduras in late 1585, the new official took with him twenty-four Spaniards. They were both married and single, some of them skilled farmers, carpenters, and blacksmiths, and all going for the precise purpose of working in the mining operations. As an inducement, the Spaniards were to be advanced 200,000 maravedís apiece from the royal treasury, with the understanding that they would remain in Honduras for at least eight years. If they left the province before that time they would be obligated to repay the advance.[121]

The plan of using skilled Spaniards to help in the mines apparently had at least some success. In 1600, when the king appointed another alcalde mayor de minas for Honduras, eight more carpenters and blacksmiths went along with their families.[122] The regidores still had to put up with the obtrusive presence of the alcalde mayor de minas, whose powers conflicted with the jurisdiction over Guaçucaran and Tegucigalpa, to which situation the Crown interposed no objection.[123] Helpful as the Spanish craftsmen were, they did not solve the basic labor problem; thus the request was made in 1586 that, because there were too few Indians in the region, 400 to 500 black slaves were necessary in order to work the mines efficiently.[124]

In the last years of the sixteenth century most of the mining activity centered in Honduras. Work inside the mines was done almost exclusively by Negroes, while Spaniards performed the more technical work. Indians were still used in the mining operations, but for the most part they worked outside the mines. President Mallén de Rueda, in naming an alcalde mayor de minas in 1590, gave the official authority to take any Indians necessary from villages to keep the mines in good order.[125] Dr. Criado de Castilla, a later president, said that it was necessary to increase the stability of the mines with the use of more Indians from outside the mining region, where there were too few. He had acceded to a request from Spanish miners to provide more Indian workers, but they were not to enter the mines, and only a small number of them would be allowed to work. The Crown approved his actions.[126]

Building Construction and Shipbuilding

By the 1550s, a sizable corps of native craftsmen had been trained in the building trades, resulting in some remarkable architecture, especially evident in the religious edifices. However, little has survived of sixteenth-century civil architecture when the plateresque style was in flower. There were some residences built in imitation of noblemen's houses in Spain, with adaptations for the frontier. Over the carved façade was raised the owner's coat-of-arms, and above that a window giving on to a balcony. Heavy studded doors added to the fortress-like aspect, which was often relieved by Renaissance details. Perhaps the best example to be seen today is the residence of the adelantado Francisco de Montejo. The "Casa de Montejo," built by the Indians of Mani, and bearing the date 1549, stands in Mérida, Yucatán. In Cindad Real (now San Cristóbal de Las Casas), the house known as that of Luis de Mazariegos seems to be sixteenth century, and is another impressive *casas señorial.*[127] In Antigua may be seen some fine old houses that probably are early seventeenth century.

But most notably, it is the ecclesiastical structures that bear witness to the great skill and artistry of Indian craftsmen working under the direction of Spanish artisans. Aside from the wish to have some measure of elegance, there was also the need to adapt construction to the environment. Buildings had to protect the settlers from the elements, both the heavy downpours of the Central American *aguaceros* and the terrifying earthquakes. Despite the precautions, by the end of the sixteenth century destruction from natural causes had taken quite a toll.

In 1556, the cabildo of Santiago was given the concession to operate for four years two obrajes near Jocotenango for the purpose of making bricks and tiles. The latter were to be sold for four pesos per 1,000, while bricks would be four and a half pesos for the same quantity.[128] A very real danger was fire resulting from lightning, particularly with so many structures built with thatched roofs. In 1575, the president noted that in the pueblo of Osçoques in Chiapas lightning had struck a church full of Indians, and immediately fire swept the straw roof. The blaze consumed 320 persons, most of them women. Another church roof caught fire in Huehuetlán, Soconusco, during a storm; and later just as a new roof was completed lightning started another fire, destroying the roof and killing more worshipers. All the churches were covered with thatched roofs, and the governor wanted them constructed of tiles, at least in the principal settlements. In Huehuetlán, where they had learned the lesson well, tiles and bricks were being made for that purpose, and other regions were following suit.[129]

In addition to work on religious buildings, Indians were also expected to contribute their time to the construction of various governmental buildings and port facilities. In 1552, the audiencia was ordered to establish "ranchos mesones," inns for travelers on roads of the provinces, which would be built and maintained by Indians.[130] As time went by, the system of roadside inns became more extensive and the inns no doubt more commodious. By 1619, officials were rounding up Indians who lived near the road that stretched the sixty leagues from Santiago to the Golfo Dulce in order to put them to work building way stations. These facilities, to be built every four leagues, were primarily for the pack-train drivers. The workers had been receiving no compensation for their labors, although the Crown decreed that in the future merchants and arrieros were to pay for the cost of the stations. The native workers were to be paid and well treated.[131]

Prominent vecinos favored a conspicuous display of wealth. In their probanzas offered in support of applications for Crown favors, Spaniards liked to point with pride to the number of people living in their residences, including Indian servants and black slaves—all connoting a person of substance in the community. We are told that dignitaries, even those in the more remote provinces, built the most sumptuous dwellings that resources could command. Royal officials such as alcaldes mayores and corregidores in the provincial towns usually had very fine houses at the expense of the natives who performed the labor, often without pay. *Escribanos*, alguaciles, and other lower functionaries lived in some luxury, despite the modest salaries they received.[132] All officials, of course, knew how to supplement their incomes, often by exploitation of the natives.

Spaniards in Central America, like those back in Spain, came to develop pride in their own cities, which gave incentive to more extensive development plans. There is little evidence of these creations left today, however, other than the magnificence of Antigua. But the crushed remains of León viejo give some evidence of the ambitious construction in the sixteenth century.[133]

Since the early years following the conquest, an important industry for the Pacific coast had been that of shipbuilding. Alvarado's armadas were constructed there in the 1530s, along with many other vessels. Nicaragua, in particular, was an important region for the trade with Panama and Peru, including the slaving activity. In addition, there was trade northward to Mexico. Since there was almost no sailing around the Horn or through the Straits of Magellan during the sixteenth century, vessels had to be built in yards on the Pacific side.[134] The industry was seriously affected by laws regulating Indian labor, especially one limiting the use of tamemes and prohibiting Indians from cutting timber. Because of those restrictions, the regidores of San Salvador wrote in 1548 that ships would disappear from the South Sea (the Pacific). The old ones would fall apart, and no new ones could be built to replace them without native labor.[135]

A few years later it was reported that Indians were involved in shipbuilding and repair in a different way. Encomenderos in León and other settlements with trade on the coast were using Indians from their encomiendas to make pitch and tar for vessels in the port. The maceguales were ordered to the mountains where they were occupied for many days. Indians were not required by law to do such work in lieu of tribute—it was in fact prohibited—but encomenderos let it be known that the workers went voluntarily and for pay. The worst part of the job was that the pitch and tar had to be packed out of the mountains to the sea on human backs. The rough terrain had caused the crippling or deaths of many Indian porters. Orders to correct the illegal activity had been issued to no avail, but the Crown again forbade it.[136]

In 1578, the royal treasurer in Nicaragua was ordered by the viceroy of New Spain to have wood cut for the construction of two ships destined to sail for the Philippines. The official complied by taking a large group of Indian workers to the mountains outside of León to cut cedar and other woods for the purpose. But he, and other witnesses, told of the many sick maceguales as a result of the sweltering climate.[137] Despite earlier orders against such labor, the cutting of timbers and other heavy work continued on the project. Because of fatigue and the oppressive heat, many Indians were dying, according to information sent to Spain.

It was proposed that if more ships were to be built for the "China" trade.

or for other areas, it would be best to purchase forty black male slaves and twenty females to work in the shipyards. They could spend six months a year at that work and the other half year producing indigo dye, during the season when the leaves flourished. Their labor on the vessels would be preferable because the blacks were better workers than the Indians. Before being convinced of the wisdom of that move, the king wanted complete information on the number of Indians who had been working on the ships, reasons for the causes of the death of any, and the opinion of the governor on the idea of buying Negroes. He wanted to know where they would work and the location of the coastal settlement that would be the most salubrious climate, while still having security.[138] The reference to security stems from the fact that precisely one year earlier (6 September 1578), Drake had sailed into the Pacific through the Straits, and had since run the coast.

In November 1579, the opinion of the cabildo of León was sent to Spain. According to the regidores, both the vecinos and the natives were in misery since work had commenced about a year and a half earlier on the two galleons being built for the voyage to the Islas de Poniente. Licenciado Palacio had come as visitador of the land with a commission authorizing him to see the shipbuilding project through. Because of the hardships imposed on the Indian labor force, the small native population had been further diminished owing to the many deaths in the shipyards, and as a result of the various other excesses in which Palacio was the principal actor and most responsible. Not only was his administration bad, they said, but the officials he had with him caused considerable harm. Local royal administrators did not check Palacio, and it was all a "nightmare" for the residents of Nicaragua. The regidores called for a residencia of the visitador.

Six months later the treasurer wrote to state essentially the same thing, that the land was being ruined.[139] But another Spaniard wrote the Crown that while the Indians had suffered some because of the work, the reports had been exaggerated.[140] Whatever the Crown's ultimate ruling, it is clear that no effective legislation was implemented at the time, for in 1583, Indians in Costa Rica were building ships and gathering *pita* fiber for the rigging. They were forced to work without pay.[141]

The shipyards also gave rise to other commerce in which the Indians played a supporting role. Encomenderos of León used their village Indians to provide fish for crews of ships, under the pretext that it was of the Indians' volition and for pay. Many of the workers ended up crippled or dead.[142] Indians living near the coast were also pressed into service on the ships in menial positions, as well as in combatant roles.

Although Indian allies had made significant contributions in helping the Spaniards during the conquest of Central America, in the years following pacification Indians were discouraged from any activities that might give them the means with which to mount an armed rebellion. Except for some caciques, natives were forbidden to carry arms. But by the end of the century the "amigos" were again in use, particularly on the coast.

In response to a message from the viceroy of Peru that three galleons of pirates were in the South Sea, the defensive units that formed on the beach near Acajutla consisted of 600 Spaniards, 800 Indian *flecheros* (archers), and 50 blacks.[143] Indian soldiers also helped a few soldiers subdue natives in Honduras in 1600 and assisted in their settlement. In the early part of the seventeenth century, the alcalde mayor in San Miguel mobilized 300 flecheros to resist corsairs sighted off the coast of Amapal.[144]

12

Agricultural Labor

AGRICULTURE WAS ALWAYS WORK that kept many Indians occupied laboring merely to provide for the sustenance of Spanish and Indian societies alike. The native maize remained a basic food for the Indians and was increasingly used also by the Spaniards, along with many other foods of the New World. Sugar cane and bananas were introduced from the Canary Islands to supplement the diet, and many other fruits and vegetables were imported as well. Francisco de Castellanos, who arrived from Spain in 1528, was the first to plant wheat in Guatemala. Fernando Cortés took various kinds of livestock to Honduras even earlier, and Hector de la Barreda exported from Cuba to Guatemala the first head of cattle. Soon sheep were grazing in the provinces, along with more horses and mules.[1]

Certainly most Spaniards preferred the quick wealth of the mines to any other economic activity, but the isolation and difficulty of access to many of the mining areas merely complicated the problems arising from the labor shortages. Moreover, equipment and black slaves were expensive, the metal was elusive, and the mining areas were often inhabited by fierce Indians, all of which made mining a dubious venture. It gradually became clear, however, that the provinces yielded other wealth as well. Thus export agriculture, although resulting in slower, more modest profits, came to be a worthwhile enterprise.

Cacao
One of the richest crops that could be taken out of Central America was cacao, a fruit long used by Indians for both food and money.[2] The chocolate drink made from cacao became a favorite beverage of the Spaniards, and eventually cacao was exported to Europe where it caught the fancy of many. The beans of the fruit continued after the conquest to be used as a medium of exchange, and were particularly valued by the natives, who often received wages in cacao.[3]

240

The tree grew in the hot, humid climates along the Pacific coast, and it did particularly well in regions that are today Soconusco in southern Mexico and in El Salvador. The Aztecs had been supplied with cacao from Soconusco prior to the coming of Cortés.[4] With the arrival of the Spaniards, some of the cacao was shipped to Peru in the early decades, but most went to Mexico, either on vessels up the west coast or packed overland. On the Caribbean coast it was usual for two or three ships a year to pull in at Puerto de Caballos once the fleet system was well established. Those vessels parted from the ships bound for Mexico and went to the Central American coast to provision the colonists with merchandise from Spain, and took on some cacao, indigo, hides, sarsaparilla, *cañafístola*, some gold and silver, and various other items of trade in Spain. Much to the disgust of the vecinos, arrival of the ships from Spain was undependable.[5]

Little mention is made of cacao as a significant factor in the economy during the first half of the century. However, in 1552 the king said he understood that most of the pueblos had previously paid their encomenderos cacao for tribute, but that Cerrato had markedly reduced the cacao tributes. The fruit had been worth four and a half to five pesos a *carga* (2 fanegas, or about 3.2 bushels), but with the shortage of the fruit it was now worth ten to eleven pesos. This, so the Crown was informed, was the result of the downward revision of tribute by Cerrato. Subsequently the price dropped to five or six pesos a carga, but it could not be sold even at that price. Despite Cerrato's having lowered the tributes, the encomenderos had recovered because of the high prices they received for their cacao; but with the prices low they were again in trouble. They complained that although the Indians could easily enough have continued paying the old tribute assessments, Cerrato reduced them by half. The vecinos were, consequently, suffering and "dying from hunger," no longer able to maintain arms and horses to protect the land.

The king, who was of the opinion that tribute should not be paid entirely in cacao, but rather in various fruits of the land, instructed Cerrato to do what he thought best for both Spaniards and Indians—thereby handing the president an impossible situation, their interests being mutually exclusive.[6] It was difficult to prevent the encomenderos from insisting that Indians pay their tribute in cacao. The worst part of it was that often the Indians were not even in a cacao area, so that they had to haul maize or other products to the hotlands to trade for cacao, or to take extra work in order to earn the money with which to buy it.

The value of cacao became a political issue as well, not excluding exacerbation of the persistent ill feelings that existed between the reli-

gious orders and the secular priests. Fray Tomás de la Torre wrote the
Council of the Indies that it would "serve the conscience of the Crown" to
expel the priests from Los Izalcos and Tacuxcalco (Tacusçalcos) and to
build either a Franciscan or Dominican monastery, because the tribute of
those pueblos amounted to almost eight thousand pesos. The prosperity
notwithstanding, there was no good order or Christianity. The area contained the richest cacao lands in the Indies, he said. And if only good
administration could be established—the friar added in a flight of
fancy—within six years the area would be "like six Medinas del Campo." It
would be best if so many priests did not pass through there, and those who
did go should help the natives and not capitalize on their positions to make
money, acting like merchants in order to return to Spain quickly.[7]

Three years later a Spaniard wrote that the pueblos of Izalcos and
Tacuxcalco, which lay thirty leagues from Santiago, near the port of
Acajutla, had an abundance of cacao, which was what the Indians desired
above all other things. They used it for money around San Salvador, as
well as in the highlands of Gracias a Dios in Honduras, the Villa de San
Miguel de Guatemala, and in many other areas. Large numbers of people
went to the cacao regions to sell and trade their maize, chickens, fruit, and
other things for cacao, and some went to hire themselves out to work in the
cacaotales (or *cacaguatales*, cacao plantings). But, he added, that land was
a general graveyard for all the Indians who went there, since a great many
of them died, and others forgot their wives, who were left in their villages,
and the children were left fatherless. In the cacao lands the alien workers
were either buried there or they remarried. Other unfortunate problems
resulted to them physically because of the radical change of climate.[8]

Los Izalcos (Yçalcos or Itzalcos) consisted of two principal pueblos, held
in encomienda by Juan de Guzmán and a Spaniard named Girón. Guzmán
had cacao plantations in which he placed his criados and black slaves.
According to the oidor Mexía, Guzmán had Indians working in the cacao
plantations as well, but they were given none of the fruit, and they were
afraid to ask for any. Guzmán earned 5,000 pesos a year off his crop, a
handsome income for a Central American encomendero.

Mexía felt that a visitador should investigate, and that the Crown should
take over the villages, at least Guzmán's, and added that he did not even
know if Guzmán held any title to the cacao milpas.[9] Guzmán's holdings
were exceptionally rich, but many others were much more modest. One
encomendero noted that cacao tribute from his own pueblo was only thirty
xiquipiles (one xiquipil or *jiquipil* equalling 8,000 beans), usually worth
110 to 120 pesos, although that encomienda was apparently in Honduras,

an area not known for rich cacaotales.[10] In fact, it is possible that his tributaries were required to go out hunting for the fruit.

By 1560, the cacao trade was already booming, with some 20,000 cargas (one carga equals three xiquipiles) worth 60,000 pesos being exported annually. That does not take into account the amounts smuggled out. One problem was that instead of paying money for the cacao, the merchants were trading other goods for the fruit. That meant that badly needed silver was not going in to the province, and President Landecho ordered that at least 50 percent of the cacao acquired had to be paid for in cash.[11]

Another problem, at least from the viewpoint of the Crown, was that large shipments of cacao and other goods were leaving the port of Acajutla for Mexico and Peru without payment of duties *(almojarifazgo)*. Merchants took their wares into Soconusco from Mexico with horses and returned loaded with cacao, paying no almojarifazgo.[12] Francisco de Morales noted in 1562 that the 7.5 percent almojarifazgo was charged on 50,000 cargas of cacao, which, he said, was the amount sent to Mexico each year. Moreover, he added that in some years it was double that amount, though in view of Landecho's estimate only two years earlier, Morales's figures may be questioned. He went on to say that, in his opinion, the total value of goods leaving in a year was about 500,000 pesos de oro, principally in cacao. With so much merchandise going into the region, he thought that the almojarifazgo for the ports of Acajutla and Guatulco in Oaxaca, Mexico, would be worth 150,000 ducats annually. But for forty years taxes had been lost because of slipshod collection. He reported that another 3,000 cargas of cacao a year were being taken to Mexico or for sale in Guatemala.[13]

The following year Morales said that in Acajutla and Soconusco the Crown could realize a million *pesos de tipuzque* income, of which 400,000 could be used to sustain deserving Spaniards who had served the king, or would in the future. He agreed with others that the port area was one of the most prosperous and important riches of the world, which was something of an exaggeration. Soconusco, in particular, was potentially very rich for the Crown because all the Indians there were in royal encomiendas.[14] How many Indians were involved in all the cacao production one cannot say, but judging by the volume of the trade, there must have been a great many of them.

In 1570, the Englishman John Chilton spoke of the rich cacao planters in Soconusco, where 4,000 cargas were being exported annually with a value of 21 pesos a carga.[15] Still, the Crown frequently exhorted its officials to look for ways of increasing revenues, and to that end Dr. Antonio González, the president (1569–73), offered the opinion in 1571 that crown income could be raised 8,000 pesos annually by imposing a tostón of tribute on each carga of cacao shipped from Izalcos to Mexico, which money could be used to help poor deserving Spaniards.[16]

Cacao yields in Soconusco were good, but the province was not producing up to its potential. The fiscal, licenciado Arteaga Mendiola, had been sent there to investigate grave charges against Governor Pedro Pacheco and others. After a month he found scarcely two thousand Indian tributaries in the province, which was about 120 miles long. They paid tribute to the Crown in the amount of 400 cargas of cacao annually, plus another 200 cargas for sobras de tributo, some maize, and other food for the priests.

Every day there were fewer vecinos in Soconusco, although many strangers drifted in and out looking for cacao. He was not sure why that was so, because while the land was hot and full of insects, in his opinion the climate was healthful enough and not excessively warm. He believed a principal cause for the sparse population was that the officials and priests of the province were publicly engaged in commerce, being primarily interested in selling clothing and trading in cacao. Indians' crops were being neglected because the maceguales spent their time obtaining cacao to pay the judges and the vicars. The officials were not even careful to see that the Indians planted maize, without which supervision there were shortages. This belief was frequently expressed in sixteenth-century Central America, which leads one to wonder how the natives got along all those centuries without someone telling them to plant crops. Maize ordinarily sold for ten tostones to four reales a fanega, but with the shortages it sometimes reached twenty tostones. Those who had cacao could trade it for maize, but less fortunate Indians ate grass and other things that made them ill and sometimes killed them.

Aside from the impositions and vexations of the caciques and governors, the Indians were also compelled to work three days a week for the community and three more just to sustain their families.[17] At least in their favor was the arrest of governor Pacheco as a result of his maladministration and trading in cacao at the expense of the natives. He was found with 450 cargas of the fruit, worth 6,000 ducats.[18]

In 1574, Governor Ponce de León wrote from Soconusco that much had changed from the old days, with many Indians having died during the period of Spanish occupation. The province at that time had only some twelve hundred Indians (although later he says eighteen hundred). With the land being so extremely fertile and good for cacao, Ponce de León felt that if the Crown would allow the introduction of 3,000 Indians from New Spain and another 1,000 from Verapaz (where, he said, they were idle), within five years—the time new trees needed to bear fruit—the Crown tribute would be augmented by 1,000 cargas of cacao worth 22,000 pesos; whereas at the time of his writing the tribute was no more than 400 cargas worth less than 9,000 pesos. The plan would be very profitable, he explained, because the least productive Indian in Soconusco produced ten times as much tribute as an Indian in Mexico, and others a hundred times as much, depending on the cacao grove.

Ponce de León described the province of Soconusco as being sixty leagues in length and seven or eight leagues wide—that is, about 156 miles by something over 20. An earlier official had estimated its length as about 120 miles. There was a mountain chain running lengthwise, with numerous rivers and a lake filled with alligators that consumed many Indians traveling in canoes. For the most part, the land was flat, at least between the mountains and the sea, and it had many marshes and thick woods through which one could not travel in the wet season. The southern part was very hot and humid, for it rained eight months a year, from March to October, and this was accompanied by much lightning that killed many people and burned straw houses. In 1573, within a space of four months, lightning had destroyed the main church twice, and another three churches in the province were ruined in the same way.

There were forty small Indian settlements, some with as few as ten vecinos or less, most of them situated on the road taken by merchants and other travelers, who provided the needs of the land. The principal town was Huehuetlán, where the governor resided. There were twenty Spanish vecinos and the rest were all Indians. Soconusco had no private encomenderos, all of the villages being crown towns. There were four cattle ranches, but no mines or precious metals in the province. Unfortunately for the cacao business, there were no ports, and the rivers were not navigable, except for canoes.

Tribute gathered by the Crown officials amounted to 600 cargas of cacao, but 200 of those were divided among the Indian communities for religious needs. The province produced a total of 4,000 cargas annually, which amounted to business worth 130,000 pesos for the region, including the imports. Passing through the province from Suchitepéquez were another 1,000 cargas, so that there was a total of 5,000, valued at 100,000 pesos or more, inasmuch as each carga was bringing 20 to 22 pesos. At the same time, more than 30,000 pesos a year worth of merchandise entered, the imports and exports thus amounting to about 130,000 pesos worth of business for Soconusco.

Finally, the governor said that the only salaries paid for the province consisted of the 600 pesos de oro for the governor and 300,000 maravedís for the priests, curates, and vicars, who also received another 50,000 maravedís from the Indians and Spaniards resident there.[19]

Still pressing for more Indians to work the land, Ponce de León noted almost two years later that in Mexico and Guatemala there were many Indians, and that in any given year more than five hundred delinquent Indians, including Chichimecs, were sold for from eight to nine years of labor at low prices, no more than thirty pesos apiece. Those condemned Indians could be sold and exiled to Soconusco, bringing their families with them, and in two years the province would be populated. He added that there were quite a few free blacks and mulattoes, but apparently they seldom hired themselves out for work in the cacao plantations.[20]

The governor repeated his request the following month, asking for condemned Chichimecs or other Indian slaves, either for a few years or in perpetuity. Each one of them, so he said, could produce a carga of cacao annually, which was more than they could do in New Spain. He reported that at the time 6,000 cargas of cacao left the province each year, including the crop from Suchitepéquez, and that did not include the contraband cacao going through from Guatemala (actually, Sonsonate).[21]

Years later the labor shortage still had not been relieved in Soconusco, and with the province in a depressed state, the potential still had not been realized. But in 1585, the Crown stipulated that any Indians who wished to go there from anywhere in New Spain should be given the license to do so, and they would be exempt from tribute for a certain period. The king, apparently not completely convinced of the wisdom of such a move, solicited the audiencia's opinion.[22] Things had deteriorated so much in Soconusco, however, that by 1600 it was suggested that the province be incorporated into the Bishopric of Chiapas, because Soconusco was "finished," owing to the small population. It was no longer a profitable cacao province.[23]

According to Governor Andrés Díaz de Rivadeneyra, Soconusco had gone into decline as a result of the neglect of former governors who had not properly fostered the cacao plantations. Díaz de Rivadeneyra said that he had seen to the planting of more trees, but the Spaniards there kept the few natives so busy with personal service that they had no time left for the care of cacao.[24] Nevertheless, the governor persevered in the contention that the ruined land could be brought back. In order to promote the cacao trade, he wanted to introduce 2,000 Indians for the planting of more trees. It would help, he said, if the Crown would order married Indians who had left the area to return. They had become vagabonds in other regions, but if they were required to resume life with their families Soconusco would be repopulated, and the return of the wayward spouses would stimulate the economy by taking care of the neglected cacaotales.

In the meantime, another problem had arisen because of the marriages of mulattoes and *zambaigos* (Negro-Indian mixed bloods) with Indian women who owned cacaotales. When that happened neither man nor wife would work the plantings, and the same thing resulted if such an Indian woman married a mestizo. In the governor's opinion, mulattoes, zambaigos, and mestizos should not be allowed to marry Indian women with cacao holdings. Spaniards should not be permitted to live among the natives nor be allowed to use them for work, because, he said, they took the Indians to their livestock estancias where they became thieves and highwaymen, going in the company of blacks and mulattoes who taught them evil ways.

The Indians were not, in any case, paid in money, but rather in horses or clothing worth half their just wages. The result was that the Indians were like slaves and the pueblos were depopulated. Indians from other areas used to go to Soconusco to work, but former governors had not allowed them their freedom and they stopped going. Many Indians were needed just to guard the cacao because the fruit was ruined by creatures who ate it, such as parrots and other birds, peccaries *(puercos de monte, peçotes, coatipizotes)*, monkeys, squirrels, and deer. Harm also came from loose livestock that ate the plantings, so much so that they had destroyed the groves of four Indian pueblos.[25]

If Soconusco was not developing as it should have, things were proceeding nicely farther to the south—at least for some. In a suit regarding the tribute of the pueblo of Tecpan Izalco, which was held by don Diego de Guzmán, the tribute assessment made in 1575 by licenciado Palacios was in the generous amount of 1,300 cargas of cacao. Licenciado Espinosa, the fiscal, representing the village, maintained that the assessment was based on the Indians having in their cacaotales more than four million cacao trees, whereas in fact they had not even a fourth part of that. Still, the yield from almost a million trees could have made life quite comfortable for Guzmán, who must have been getting wealthy from the tribute collection based on four million![26]

In the city and port of Acajutla, and surrounding it, were two settlements of Los Izalcos and Naolingo, within an area of four leagues, "with some of the richest land in the world." Every year 250,000 pesos worth of cacao was sent to New Spain. If the almojarifazgo were imposed and collected it would take in 15,000 pesos a year or more for the Crown, according to testimony. The fruit slipped illegally through Soconusco to

New Spain from Guatemala would bring another 6,000 pesos in duties. Fourteen leagues from Santiago was the port of Istapa, three-fourths of which belonged to one encomendero, and the other one-fourth was owned by the Crown. The crown area was almost worthless, but it could be developed with a dozen Negroes to produce more than 1,000 pesos annually, instead of the 20 then being earned in 1574.

Antonio González, the president, was accused of creating on more than one occasion the post of "juez de milpas" in the town of Naolingo to see that Indians cared for their cacao trees. The president allegedly appointed to that post the relative of a priest who was friendly to him, with a salary of 200 pesos a year, which the Indians, poor as they were, had to pay out of their pockets.[27] The practice continued; a decade later President García de Valverde appointed jueces de milpa, who still caused many problems for the Indians. The royal opinion was that such officials were unnecessary because the corregidores and alcaldes ordinarios could administer affairs, and the Crown ordered the office abolished.[28]

By 1576, the area of Los Izalcos, situated precariously on the skirt of a constantly smoking volcano, was extremely rich, producing more than 50,000 cargas of cacao worth 500,000 gold pesos.[29] Because of the cacao wealth the town of Santísima Trinidad was founded in 1578.[30]

But then a decline set in, and by 1598 the province of Guatemala (including present-day El Salvador) was producing only 20,000 cargas worth more than 200,000 pesos a year. Unfortunately, the response to lower production was for Spaniards to ask that the Indians be required to pay more tribute.[31] Since cacao was the most profitable agricultural enterprise, many Spanish merchants, as well as mestizos and free Negroes, went to live in Indian villages to sell them unnecessary items of little value in exchange for cacao. To prevent gullible natives from being done out of their cherished fruit, the Crown finally decreed in 1605 that non-Indians should stay out of the villages during the harvesting and that afterwards they should not be allowed to remain more than three days in any month. They were to sell the Indians only standard goods of wear, and no business could be done on a credit basis.[32]

Ultimately, in an attempt to achieve more organization among the Indians, the president appointed a judge with the title of "reformador de las milpas" with a salary of 1,000 tostones a year to see that natives kept the cacao plantings weeded and to supervise the planting of new trees because of the need to protect such a valuable commodity. The alcalde mayor complained of this to the king, seeing the appointment as an infringement on his jurisdiction, and the Crown asked the audiencia for a justification.[33]

By 1620, the cacao market in Central America was still in some trouble. One reason was that while merchants from Peru formerly had gone up to Central American ports to buy cacao, they had planted so much of their own in Peru that they were taking their fruit to Central America to sell. The result was a surplus.[34] But perhaps such reports were distorted, for Vázquez de Espinosa tells us that prosperity had returned. Although many regions on the west coast were producing cacao by 1620, the richest area was the province of Sonsonate with its towns of Los Izalcos, Naolingo, and Caluco: "Within a district of 2 leagues of these cacao plantations or groves, they harvest 50,000 loads, worth at the very lowest 500,000 ducats." At harvest time, he writes, 200 beans sold for one real or less. For the Diocese of Guatemala (with the chief producers being the provinces of Soconusco, Suchitepéquez, Guazacapán, Sonsonate, Zacatecoluca, and Chiquimula) more than a million and a half ducats' worth of cacao was being produced annually.[35]

Sugar

The cultivation of sugar in Central America was very modest during the sixteenth century. Considerable capital outlay was involved, a good supply of timber was necessary, along with the right climate, and the availability of a sufficient labor force. Very importantly, sugar grown for export required convenient access to shipping. While these demands were met with success in the Antilles and in Brazil, the possibilities in Central America were restricted. Only in Chiapas did the cane assume much importance in early decades.

Regarding Cerrato's earlier letter about the "tyranny" of the sugar planters in that province and his order against the use of encomienda Indians for the work, the Crown agreed with his ruling.[36] Illogically, however, only a month later the emperor instructed Cerrato to lend all support to the establishment of sugar plantations, in spite of the president's explanation of the danger to the natives.[37]

The implementation of the restrictive labor laws in 1549 had the effect, nonetheless, of limiting sugar production. The planters, along with stockmen, farmers, and tradesmen, were, according to the oidor López, on the brink of perdition because they lost slaves and personal service all at once. Many of the sugar men had exhausted their resources in their operations, built in the hope that slavery would last. It would be a great help, López wrote, if the king would authorize the purchase of 300 blacks on credit so that the seven or eight sugar plantations already built could operate. That would certainly benefit Ciudad Real, he added, because its economy was tied to the plantations, and the Crown would profit from the sugar to be sent to Seville.[38]

Diego Vázquez de Rivadeneyra, a vecino of Ciudad Real, informed the king that he had a very good sugar plantation still in the process of construction on the outskirts of the city, but the work had stopped when he lost his slaves. Now he was bankrupt and could not finish the mill, and he requested a loan from the royal treasury in the amount of 3,000 pesos for a period of four years in order to complete the construction and planting. The loan, in his view, would be worthwhile for both the Crown and Chiapas.

The king responded that if Rivadeneyra would obligate himself by putting up legal collateral in writing, and if he promised to pay back the loan within four years, he could have the money. But it would be necessary to mortgage his plantation with all the documentation placed in the royal chest (arca de los tres llaves). Transcripts were to be validated by the royal accountant and sent to Spain.[39]

Crown interest in promoting the sugar industry in Central America is manifest also in the request of a Juan Ortiz de Gatica for a loan. He had gone to Spain to get his wife and children, and was returning to Honduras with the intention of laying out a sugar plantation. Lacking sufficient capital to complete the project, Ortiz de Gatica asked for a loan of up to 3,000 pesos for four years. He was authorized a loan of 2,000 pesos, provided he gave good collateral, and if he agreed to invest a total of 6,000 ducats in a water mill, not a trapiche, that is a mill powered by beasts or men. He, too, was to mortgage everything and repay the loan within four years.[40]

On the scene in Guatemala, a member of the audiencia, licenciado Jufre de Loaisa, suggested that conditions in Verapaz were good for the production of sugar. He noted that the Indians there gave no tribute to the Crown. The audiencia had no authority in that Dominican province, but in the oidor's opinion, there should be a Spanish town there to give the area more security, and the sugar would produce additional revenues for the royal treasury.[41]

Few references to sugar appear in Central American documents for the rest of the century, from which one may conclude that sugar never developed on a large scale, certainly not to the extent of cacao or indigo. But the plantations did continue to exist. The king remarked in 1581 that, according to information passed to him, the alcalde mayor de minas in Honduras was taking thirty to forty Indians from La Chuluteca each week to work in sugar mills under oppressive circumstances.[42]

After the turn of the century, in 1603, President Criado de Castilla related to the king the illegal activity of corregidores in the valley of Santiago, Izquintepeque, and Guazacapán who were giving Indians for work on the sugar plantations. He passed an ordinance against that practice with a fine of 500 pesos and suspension from office for those who violated the law. The president also emphasized that sugar planters were to use Spanish laborers, blacks, mulattoes, or mestizos, but no Indians.[43] Yet, it is clear that the president's decree had little lasting effect, for Indians were still being pressed into labor on the sugar works well into the seventeenth century, and no doubt far beyond that.[44]

By 1620, Vázquez de Espinosa noted that Jesuits and other religious orders had sugar mills, and that at Amatitlán there was a large operation. Others were located in Sonsonate and in Nicaragua near Granada and León.[45] The Englishman Thomas Gage, who resided for many years in Central America during the 1630s, knew a Spaniard who had made a large stake through his teams of draft animals. He developed a rich *ingenio de azúcar*, built "a princely house," and shipped a lot of sugar to Spain. The planter kept at least sixty black slaves on his plantation and was thought to be worth more than half a million ducats. His holdings were located near Petapa, about five leagues from Santiago. Not far away, Augustinian friars had a smaller mill, a trapiche operating with twenty slaves. At Amatitlán was the largest of the sugar operations:

This ingenio seemed to be a little town by itself for the many cottages and thatched houses of Blackamoor slaves which belong unto it, who may be above a hundred men, women and children. The chief dwellinghouse is strong and capacious, and able to entertain a hundred lodgers. These three farms of sugar standing so near unto Guatemala [Santiago] enrich the city much, and occasion great trading from it to Spain.

In Verapaz, Gage noted the mill of the Dominican cloister, "which indeed goeth beyond that of Amatitlan, both for abundance of sugar made there and sent by mules to Guatemala over that rocky mountain, and for the multitude of slaves living in it under the command of two friars." He noted some trapiches of sugar in San Salvador as well.[46]

Indigo

Traditionally, woad was imported to Spain from France and Portugal for the purpose of dyeing Spanish cloth blue. As the textile industry boomed in Spain as elsewhere, the volume of trade made it more than ever desirable for Spain to find its own source of dye. Philip II was informed that in Central America there was a kind of plant, or earth, that gave off the same effect as woad, and that it was used to dye cotton and wool made by the natives of the Indies. A Portuguese had reported to the sovereign that a plant of the East Indies could also be cultivated in the New World for the same purpose; but if such a dye already existed, it would be very important to use it instead of the imported woad.

The king, characteristically, wanted the most detailed information about the quality of the dye, the quantity available, whether it grew wild in the fields or needed to be cultivated, or whether it was in fact a lode. He asked if it would be good for dyeing cloth in Spain, and exactly how the dyeing process occurred. Philip asked the audiencia to supervise experiments, using the dye both fresh and aged, and to send a quantity of it, along with the judges' opinion as to the cost of exporting it in quantity, the best way to send it, and as to its benefits to the Indians. [47]

The king referred of course to indigo, called by the Indians *xiquilite* (*jiquilite*) and by the Spaniards *añil (añir)*. Surprisingly, little mention is made of the dye until many years later. After two decades, the treasurer in Nicaragua notified Philip that for the past two years vecinos had been producing the añil, which was of considerable importance, because in the year just past they had produced over a hundred *quintales* (a quintal was 46 kilos, or 101.2 lbs.). However, no duties had been paid on it. [48]

About the same time the bishop of Nicaragua wrote that while the indigo being produced was profitable for the royal treasury, it was not healthful for the royal conscience because it was produced at the cost of the miserable Indians' sweat. The encomenderos did not pay them for their labor, or at least gave them so little that, "like innocent sheep before the shearers, they do nothing but give a bleat toward the heavens." Because of the strenuous labor involved, the natives were dying, and their families were left destitute because the men were working in the indigo when they should have been cultivating their crops to maintain a supply of maize. The audiencia had been informed of these excesses, but the judges, so the bishop said, were too interested in getting rich and marrying off their relatives to take notice and remedy the situation. [49]

Working with the añil was very unpleasant: the plant burned the skin, it had a noisome odor, and it attracted bothersome insects. Given the danger to the health of the Indians, it was proposed that for Nicaragua forty Negro men and twenty Negro women be purchased. They could work six months a year with the indigo while the leaves lasted, and the rest of the year in the shipyards. It was estimated that in half a year's time they could produce thirty quintales worth 3,000 ducats. [50] Shortly thereafter the regidores of León also urged the Crown to send blacks, asking for 100 of them to work the indigo. The province of Nicaragua was very poor, they said, but things would be much improved if they could properly exploit the profitable dye industry. [51]

The audiencia had written the Crown of the benefits resulting from xiquilite leaves which were produced in abundance in the warm regions. Indians gathered the leaves and processed them, but the work proved so harmful to them that they would be "finished off" in a few years if they continued to do so. Accordingly, the judges prohibited them from working in the dye processing, even if they volunteered to do so, and the judges added that they felt it necessary to extend the ruling.

The Crown, convinced that the labor was manifestly dangerous and a risk to the natives' lives, upheld the audiencia decision and declared its intention to decree the same law for Yucatán. The king made the decision, "desiring the well-being and conservation of the natives more than the profit that results from their work."[52] The Dominicans asserted that it was at their entreaty that the audiencia had made the rigorous provision that no Indians be taken to obrajes de tinta, "where they would surely die."[53] The royal declaration putting the welfare of the Indians before profits no doubt had a hollow ring to some, but in this instance, leaving aside infrequent violations, it appears that the law was generally enforced, at least for the remainder of the century.[54]

With the order against Indian labor for indigo implemented, the governor in Nicaragua protested that the province was in great need because there was no gold or silver, and about the only thing of value was the dye. The Spaniards were not able to harvest much of that because it was illegal to use the natives, and it was impossible for them to buy blacks. He requested the Crown to allow at least those Indians serving in Spanish households to produce some añil, without taking any people from their pueblos. He did not specify exactly how this would be less harmful to the natives, but he stated that the land would not suffer. On the contrary, he maintained that there would be very great profit, even though there were no mines or cacao, and the Crown income would be augmented. The other solution was to send a couple hundred blacks, whose cost could be repaid within two or three years. Their presence would be no threat to the maintenance of the Indians, since there was usually plenty of food in Nicaragua, produced with little work.[55]

The cabildo of León followed up the governor's request three years later, noting to the Crown that they and others had written several times asking for 100 Negroes for the indigo works, which were the principal industry of Nicaragua. The whole economy was faltering because they could not use Indians, and they were willing to be obligated to reimburse the Crown for the blacks within four years.[56]

Finally, in 1587, the Crown responded to the governor's suggestion that half of the añil be produced by household servants—or at least that 200 Negroes be introduced. Instead of taking decisive action, Philip

merely requested an opinion from the oidores, cautioning them to keep
the welfare of the natives in mind.[57] Whatever happened to the proposals
for black slaves does not appear in documents known to me, but by the
turn of the century it was again reported that in Nicaragua, the vecinos,
encomenderos, and the justices were forcing excesses on the Indians.
According to the fiscal, Bartolomé de la Canal de la Maduz, even women
and children were being taken from their homes and forced to work in the
obrajes de tinta, where many of them died from the exhausting labor.[58]

Although officials often became illegally involved in all sorts of commercial enterprises, they seem not to have been much involved in indigo
during the sixteenth century. An exception may be noted in the accusation
in 1583, that the alcalde mayor of Trinidad had a factory for making the
dye, at a time when a quintal was valued at 300 tostones in Nicaragua. The
accused, Captain Juan de Torres, allegedly delivered a great number of
Indians to work in the obraje de tinta belonging to his mistress. In no
instance, apparently, were the Indians even paid.[59]

By the early seventeenth century the collusion of royal officials appears
to have been more common. Indian leaders in Nicaragua complained that
the governor and other officials were demanding that their women work
on indigo plantations, as well as in tobacco fields, which was unjust
because their village regularly gave servicio ordinario.[60] Whatever the
labor situation in the early seventeenth century, it is apparent that the
indigo business was thriving, because the Crown gave an order for the
purchase of 2,000 arrobas of the dye in 1618.[61]

Evidence that Indian policy under King Philip III (1598–1621) de-
clined, at least in some respects, from that of his predecessor (in spite of
the comprehensive reforms on paper in 1609), can be observed in the
correspondence of the king to the president of the audiencia. He noted
that some poorly informed persons had given different judgments about
the value of indigo and the red cochineal dyes, holding them to be of
little profit. Philip III requested the president to give an opinion to the
viceroy of New Spain, and to send a transcript of it to Spain.

In the meantime, the president was instructed to motivate the natives
in the harvesting of both indigo and cochineal (cochinilla). He also requested a report with details of how the crops were exploited, as well as
information on the management of the industries, and the utility and gain
for the natives to be derived therefrom. It was then made clear that what
he really wanted to know was if it would be profitable for the Crown to
consider managing and controlling the dyes in the universal market. He
solicited an opinion on the ways and means by which this monopoly could
be effected. After then commending the president, a kinsman of his, the

king said it was understood that in the transactions involving the dyes there had been some carelessness and that the Crown had been shortchanged, because excessively high prices were paid by royal agents, and because mule drivers were acting as middlemen and taking an extra profit.[62] One does not find in the communication any compassion shown for the Indians; on the contrary, the sovereign encourages their participation in the indigo production.

A few months later, word came from another source in Guatemala that the area was suffering because of the declining value of its products. As one example, the price of a pound of indigo which had formerly been eleven reales had dropped to four or five. The solution proposed was that if part of the taxes owed by the colony to the Crown could be paid in choice añil, worth only five reales in Central America, the dye could be sold later in Seville for at least eleven reales a pound. If it went without duties and shipping charges, both the colony and the Crown would benefit. A further inducement to that remedy would be that some silver would remain in the provinces, whereas under the system then operating silver was leaving and there was a shortage of it for commerce.[63] There were undoubtedly more blacks involved in the indigo production than earlier, but it seems that Indians were no longer excluded from the work that was so dangerous to them.

By 1620, there were numerous indigo operations, many of them small. In Tecpan Atitlán the dye was being sold for four reales an arroba. Seven leagues from Santiago in the corregimiento district of Izcuintepeque there were more than forty indigo obrajes, considered by Vázquez de Espinosa as "the best in the Indies." The corregimiento of Guazacapán had more than sixty obrajes de tinta, and at the village of San Jacinto, near the city of San Salvador, there were more than two hundred of them, with many more in adjacent areas. He reported other indigo processing plants in Nicaragua and around San Miguel.[64]

Sarsaparilla

Sarsaparilla was a plant used in the preparation of a cooling beverage and for medical purposes. In the Dominican province of Verapaz, and to some extent in Honduras, the root of the sarsaparilla was exploited for profit. By 1574, it was reported that sarsaparilla was being processed in five villages in Verapaz, as well as in surrounding mountains. But the roots were two or three days off the road in distant areas. Although merchants in Seville questioned its value, sarsaparilla was much esteemed in Central America.[65]

The friars had the Indians of Verapaz gathering the root and carrying it to markets, taking large quantities to Santiago and other centers. Near Cobán and other villages more than three hundred arrobas were collected and later sold by Dominicans in Golfo Dulce. Another three hundred arrobas were taken to Jocolo and sold for one peso an arroba. From the villages of Cahabon and San Agustín, Indians were sent by friars to search out roots in the mountains so far away that it took them two weeks just going and returning. The cargo then had to be transported on the backs of Indians twenty leagues to the freshwater gulf, for which the Indians received no pay.

Over a period of time, according to one witness, Indians had given the friars about fifteen hundred arrobas of sarsaparilla without receiving any compensation. One of the principal buyers was a procurador in the city of Santiago, a good distance away. A witness said that he had collected in person 200 tostones for sixty arrobas that he sold for a fray Francisco Viana.[66] A report not long afterward mentions that vecinos of Honduras around the port of Trujillo were living in poverty, supporting themselves with only cows and sarsaparilla.[67] But it is clear that the root did not become an important aspect of the economy in sixteenth-century Central America, and very few Indians were involved in its harvesting.

By 1620, it was reported that around the city of Trujillo, Honduras, "they raise much sarsaparilla in this city and region, of the best quality to be found in the Indies; every year they load quantities of it on ships for Spain." The author also mentions that around the city of Cartago, Costa Rica, they were also harvesting "the best sarsaparilla in all the Indies."[68]

Cochineal

In addition to the blue indigo dye, the Crown also had an interest in the production of the reddish cochineal dye, taken from the insect that was found in the nopal cactus. The dye did not have the great importance in Central America that it had in parts of Mexico, but rather late there was interest in fostering its production as a stimulant to the economy. In 1573, the president wrote Philip II that in the region of Santiago Indians grew *tunas* (edible cactus fruit) from which the cochineal insects were taken to dye their mantas and for use in their paintings. He suggested that it could be grown commercially to the profit of the natives, who might use the dye as part of their tributes. This would necessitate the planting and care of the cactus, but it would be worthwhile because the only other thing they had to offer as tribute was cacao, which had been failing for the past two or three years owing to the poor land.[69]

In acknowledging receipt of the president's letter, the Crown approved the intensification of cochineal production.[70] Villalobos followed up by writing that the Indians were planting many "tunas de grana" in the hills where they grew best. He explained that the only other thing the Indians had to grow was corn, but because the tribute was assessed in cacao, Indians had to carry the corn down to the hotlands to exchange for the fruit. It was hoped that the red dye would replace the need to seek out cacao.[71]

The extent to which those *nopaleras* thrived is uncertain, for there is little more said about them in correspondence, although presumably there was modest production of the insect. Many years later the Crown asked for more specific information on the value of cochineal, adding that the president should encourage the natives to produce more of it. Royal interest in the dye was part of the plan to control the universal market in indigo as well.[72]

Salt

The Crown was also interested in the potential for salt production. In 1553, the king wrote seeking information about what profits might accrue to the Indians from the exploitation of the salt beds on the Pacific coast.[73] Evidently little was done about the matter for many years, but after the Crown again instructed the audiencia to pursue the possibilities of salt in 1575, ordering the oidores to prepare salt works "like those of Spain," the audiencia responded that it was hardly worth the effort. Such an operation had been started by a Spaniard at Istapa, about twelve leagues from Santiago. Sifting the salt had not turned out well, because although the Indians scratched *salitre* from the coast, boiled it, and strained it, finally putting it in trays where it solidified in the sun, not enough salt was produced to make it worth the effort. The president said that he would send expeditions along the coast to search for a more favorable site.[74] The search was not very productive, and Central America did not develop any export business in salt that I am aware of.

In 1603, the king ordered the president to report on the saltworks in Nicaragua. The president wrote back that he had made a careful personal inspection tour and had found no *salinas* established, but only a few places where they took salt out for local consumption. The two principal settlements, Granada and León, were both by freshwater lakes, and Indians had to travel to the coasts to get salt for their own use and for tribute. They could go either to the Mar del Sur (Pacific) or the Mar del Norte (Caribbean), each of which was only three or four leagues distant. The procedure was still very primitive: Indians took seawater in casks and boiled it until the water evaporated, leaving some salt deposits, but only in small amounts.[75] For all their travail, the Indians at least did not have to put up with toil in saltworks.

Livestock

As in other parts of the Indies, settlers in Central America saw the introduction of livestock as fundamental to the development of the colony. For several years, however, the increase in the number of draft animals was agonizingly slow. The immediate demand was for warhorses during the conquest and pacification, as well as the continuing defense of the land, during which time almost any horse brought a very high price. Eventually they were worth comparatively little. From the first there was almost a desperate need for beasts of burden to relieve the Indians from the grueling task of carrying everything on their backs—at least in the view of humanitarians. As it turned out, many years would pass before there were sufficient draft animals to replace the work of men. Horses and mules were needed to form pack trains, and oxen were desirable for plowing and powering mills. Both were in demand to haul carts. The Spaniards, accustomed to a European diet, wanted meat from domestic animals, creating a market for cattle, swine, sheep, and goats.

The care of the herds naturally fell to the Indians, who were, in the beginning, often frightened of the larger animals. Herders were always required, since there were no large enclosures and many of the beasts were not branded. Not only was it necessary to keep track of the animals, but they had to be kept out of planted fields, where they often ruined crops. There was no great problem getting workers for the estancias when maceguales worked for nothing, but after the liberation of the slaves and labor reforms of Cerrato, a critical situation developed, as herds went wild. The representatives of the villa of Valladolid, Honduras, implored the king to require some Indians to guard the livestock, and he ordered the audiencia to enforce the rule stipulating that all Indians were to occupy themselves with work.[76] In order for that to be effective, however, the Indians would have to volunteer.

One reason that work on the estancias was not attractive to the Indians was that they often belonged to an encomendero who placed one of his non-Indian criados to serve as estanciero in managing the stock farms. If the estanciero was a Spaniard, he was often of the lower class. Not infrequently the position was filled by a mestizo or a mulatto. Since they were usually in isolated regions, far removed from officers of the law, the

Indian workers were often treated with brutality, with no recourse. Later, at least in some provinces, the abuses were curbed by more official control. The governor of Honduras, for example, had flat land outside Trujillo cleared so that animals could forage close to town. This resulted in less work for the *criados de ganado* and produced a better meat supply for the vecinos. [77]

Loose cattle were especially destructive in the cacao country, where they caused great damage and loss of profit. They invaded the plantings and ate young trees, in one case destroying the livelihood of four villages. By the turn of the century, livestock had become big business as the herds proliferated. In 1603, it was reported that one cattle estancia ran 18,000 head, in addition to 2,000 to 3,000 mares. The havoc caused by their indiscriminate feeding prompted the governor of Soconusco to request a royal order giving license to kill loose livestock with impunity in order to protect the cacaotales. [78]

In the meantime, another threat to the cattle herds was developing. A Spaniard informed the king that animals were becoming scarce and that prices had risen dramatically. Beef had been selling for forty pounds for one real, but it had gone up to only fourteen pounds for a real. The shortage was such that cattle were being taken into Honduras from other provinces. The principal cause of the shortage, so the writer contended, was that many free blacks and mulattoes roamed the countryside on old nags, slaughtering cattle for their hides and tallow. Beef owners did not take proper care of their herds, not bothering to brand them or to castrate any of them. Apparently Indians were not available for use as herdsmen, and the free mulattoes and blacks would agree to work only for exorbitant wages, with the result that the herds were unmanageable without any help.

It was proposed that the cattlemen be made to take better care of their beef, under pain of loss of the cattle and ranches. At the same time, blacks and mulattoes should not be allowed to ride around on horses, subject to fines of 200 lashes and ten years in the galleys. With that threat they would then agree to serve at moderate wages, and owners of estancias would improve their management so there would again be an abundance of beef. The Crown deferred a ruling, asking the audiencia to check into the problem and to give an opinion. [79] The work of caring for livestock in the second half of the sixteenth century was not a source of great concern to Indians, despite some minor complaints.

PART IV

PART IV

13
The Native Aristocracy under Spanish Rule

THE ADVENT OF SPANISH DOMINATION led to consequences more shatter-
ing for the Indian aristocracy than any other group in native society. For
while the lower classes found themselves subjected to a regimentation
probably exceeding that of their pre-conquest roles, and while they were
often brutally exploited, the evidence suggests that their condition had
been deplorable in many respects even in prehispanic times. It is true that
the circumstances of many of them worsened under the conquerors, but it
was a matter of degree. For the native nobility, however, the Spanish
conquest was their world turned upside down.[1]

Unfortunately, the historian has little concrete source material from
which to construct an accurate picture of upper-class society before the
coming of the white man. The accounts we have were filtered through
those who may well have distorted the picture. It should be borne in mind
that it was men of the Church who most often recorded such matters; and
while on the one hand one must recognize their achievements, it is well to
remember that for the most part they were committed to the denigration
of pagan ethics. Consequently, with few exceptions, one cannot trust their
objectivity in treating the subject.

Others referred to prehispanic society, but seldom in much detail. And
even they represented attitudes colored by ethnocentrism, logically
enough. Nevertheless, the weight of evidence, such as it is, indicates
rather strongly that the idyllic scenes painted by Las Casas were as
misleading as those of the opposite view, that of a society without redeem-
ing qualities.[2]

What is quite clear is the fact that following the conquests the Indian
elite class experienced a radical change in its status. Though much in
decline from the earlier centuries, there remained at point of Spanish
contact a certain magnificence evident in native royal courts. It was a
society not without dignity, a sense of justice, and a system of order and

tradition that had survived for centuries. Within those civilizations society seems to have been every bit as stratified as among those in other parts of the world at the time; indeed, more so than in Europe. The labored concept of the divine right of kings notwithstanding, monarchs of Europe were not held to be demi-gods, as was the case among many New World societies. On the other end of the scale, the most ignoble Spanish peasant enjoyed a far better status than the hapless slave among the Indians. Perhaps the pre-conquest societies are better compared to those of the Orient.

In general usage, members of the native elite were called by the Spaniards "principales," and while that term denoted a member of the upper class, there were rankings within. Leaders of Indian communities were also designated caciques, señores, and *tlatoque,* often with little distinction. The highest of the order were usually called caciques (chiefs), a word picked up by the Spaniards in the Antilles and applied generally throughout New Spain. Spaniards sometimes used the term loosely, imputing that status to some more accurately designated as principales. And even among the cacique class there were rankings. Cerrato, referring to pre-conquest times, made this observation:

> What I have been able to ascertain is that in this land there were four lords: one they called Çinaca, who was lord of the Utlatecas; and another, Sacachul of the Guatemaltecas; and another of Comalapa; and another of Gilotepeque, although the last two acknowledged the other two. Many pueblos served these, but they did not give them tribute nor ordinary service, except that which was necessary. With those were twenty-four deputies who were learned in affairs of government and justice, and they were influential enough so that if the most powerful lord did some unlawful thing they cut off his head. Those señores principales put caciques in all the villages that were subject there, whom the Indians also served in the planting of crops and in hauling wood and water and in making their houses and giving what was necessary.[3]

Thus, according to Cerrato's understanding, there were two dominant caciques and two lesser caciques in the highest rank. The twenty-four "deputies" were also among the exalted, but the confusion is evident in Cerrato's designation of "señores principales" having appointed caciques for the villages. It is apparent that most villages had at least one local ruler with the status of cacique, and that large settlements had more than one. Edward Calnek writes that in Chiapas the aristocracy included three ranks among the rulers: *señores naturales* (caciques), principales, and *principales del común.* He elaborates as follows:

> Civil authority at Zinacantan . . . seems to have been shared by three or four principales, probably drawn from each of the most noble lineages of the pueblo.

. . . The majority of the highland provinces . . . appear to have been governed by a single cacique, who resided permanently at the *cabecera*, and held the office for life. The rulers of important subject towns were also called *caciques*, though obviously of subordinate status.

Calnek adds that at Tuni the cacique during the sixteenth century met with principales for consultation on important decisions. "The cacique was much respected, but evidently could not make important decisions on his own initiative."[4]

Licenciado Zorita, a contemporary of Cerrato, elaborated on pre-conquest rulers and their subsequent decline:

The province of Utlatlán borders on Guatemala. When I was an oidor in Guatemala, I made a visit of inspection to this province. Through the services of a religious of the Dominican Order . . . I learned with the aid of paintings that they had which recorded their history for more than eight hundred years back, and which were interpreted for me by very ancient Indians, that in their pagan days they had three lords. The principal lord had three canopies or mantles adorned with fine featherwork over his seat, the second had two, and the third one.

I saw their lords at that time in the town of Utlatlán (from which the whole province takes its name). They were as poor and miserable as the poorest Indian of the town, and their wives fixed their tortillas for dinner because they had no servants, nor any means of supporting them; they themselves carried fuel and water for their houses. The principal lord was named Don Juan de Rojas, the second, Don Juan Cortés, and the third, Domingo. They were all extremely poor; they left sons who were all penniless, miserable tribute-payers, for the Spaniards do not exempt any Indians from payment of tribute. . . .

There were many large *cúes* or temples to their idols in Utlatlán. I saw some of them, and they were of marvelous construction, though in a very ruined state. Neighboring towns also had their cúes there, and the most important of these was the cúe of a town named Chiquimula. The Indians regarded this town of Utlatlán as a sanctuary, and that is why there were so many important cués there. The lord of Chiquimula used to have many towns and vassals, but when I saw him, he was very poor and miserable.[5]

How numerous the noble class was we may leave to speculation, but as a curious observation, one of the conquerors of Costa Rica, which was not heavily populated in comparison with other areas of Central America, was met by eighty "caciques señores," who came forward to submit peacefully.[6] Nor is it possible, from the manuscripts I have consulted, to determine a general pattern of the ratio of principales to maceguales.[7]

Again, to cite Calnek:

Principales—men and women—could be distinguished through their exclusive use of certain kinds of clothing and ornaments. . . . The elegant *penacho* [head-dress] made from the precious feathers of the quetzal and other birds, was also worn by the nobility. Commoners, by contrast, either went naked, or used some type of loincloth and cloak.

While the maceguales occupied crude huts, "the highest ranking *principales* at Zinacantan occupied adobe houses."[8]

It remains to be noted that the terms "cacique mayor" and "cacique principal" were occasionally employed after the conquest to distinguish among the native rulers.[9]

Although, as Cerrato mentioned, even the highest caciques were subject to certain laws and could be punished for violations, they were held in awe by their subjects, who considered them not as men but as gods.[10] At the time of the Spanish invasion the impoverished descendants of the brilliant Mayas ruled over much smaller kingdoms, and the empire had disintegrated. Rulers were not surrounded by the opulence familiar to Moteczuma and Atahualpa. Still, they enjoyed semi-divine status, power, wealth, and prestige, however modest in comparison with the emperors of Mexico and Peru. The Central American noblemen received the tribute of their vassals, owned property, including slaves, and maintained concubines.[11] They carried the staffs of office and held absolute power over their subjects, who were often oppressed. Since warfare had become a commonplace, they were also commanders of large armies.[12]

The dramatic reversal of their fortunes followed the fall of the Aztec confederacy to the north. In subsequent months, some lords of Central America sent emissaries to the Spaniards, assuring the conquerors of their submission. Ordinarily chiefs who chose to submit without resistance fared better than those who defended their lands, particularly since the Crown enjoined its captains to treat with leniency those who recognized the sovereignty of the king of Spain. Caciques who did not deliver their people to the invaders were considered traitors and rebels, and the Spaniards proceeded against them as such. Later, when Alvarado was called to account for his treatment of caciques during the conquest, he recounted how some native lords had dined at his table one evening, after which they rebelled. In his words, they made "very crude" warfare, covering deep pits with sharp stakes in the bottom, on which many Spaniards and their horses were impaled.[13] In other reports the adelantado told of the "treachery" of the Indian leaders.

Caciques were sometimes tortured to make them reveal the location of treasure. In a suit to recover his position years later, don Juan Cortés, the heir to the *cacicazgo* of Utatlán and its subject towns, said that he was the legitimate son of don Juan Chicuet-Quiagut and the grandson of Yeymasate, the former lords of the region. When Yeymasate was conquered,

Alvarado burned him alive because he did not give the conqueror gold. Thereafter Alvarado deprived don Juan Chicuet-Quiagut of almost all the province.[14]

Alvarado did not, however, routinely treat all caciques with cruelty and contempt. If on occasion he made threats to them and punished some by pulling their hair, it was, he contended, in order to teach them to behave for the good of the land and so they would serve the Spaniards to whom they were given in encomienda. That was sometimes necessary, in his view, because the Indians were indomitable and without reason or judgment.[15] The treasurer, Francisco de Castellanos, testified that he had seen Alvarado treat a lord of Guatemala and other principales badly at times, giving them kicks. In other instances the adelantado had treated the same Indians with kindness, making gifts to them of merchandise from Castile, such as swords, clothing, and other items. Castellanos felt that Alvarado acted as he did of necessity.[16]

Remesal recounts an instance in which Bartolomé de Las Casas took a cacique into Santiago. The cacique, don Juan, made a good impression on Alvarado, who wanted to favor the Indian. He did so by offering him what was closest to hand, his red taffeta hat, fitted with plumes. He placed the hat on don Juan's head, which greatly honored and pleased the cacique; but the gesture evoked murmurings from the adelantado's men, both captains and soldiers, "because they said it was wrong that a lieutenant of the Emperor, King of Castile, should take the hat off his head and put it on that of an Indian dog."

Alvarado and the bishop took the day off to show the visitor their city, and Alvarado ordered the merchants to select their best silks and other stuffs, and to display their finest and most interesting merchandise in their shops for the cacique's appraisal. Silversmiths were told to take out their best work so that don Juan could admire them. The bishop ordered the artisans to offer the guest anything that caught his eye, and for them to insist that he accept gifts, for which the bishop would pay later. To the astonishment of the Spaniards, "the barbarian" observed it all with a grave demeanor, as unimpressed "as if he had been born in Milan!" And much as various gifts were pressed on him, he refused all. According to Remesal, the cacique's only interest was in an image of the Virgin, which he accepted with veneration.[17] Such consideration for a native chief was unusual, although it is no doubt true that observers were more apt to comment on the negative and dramatic rather than the prosaic and positive.

Perhaps the executions of Cuauhtémoc and Atahualpa could be viewed as extreme measures taken in perilous situations, but the Crown did not condone the killing of Indian nobles. Especially with the brutal cases in Mexico of don Carlos Chichimecatecuhtli of Texcoco, the Calzontzin of Tzintzuntzan, and the excesses of Bishop Landa in Yucatán, royal directives sought to protect caciques and principales. But it was allowed that under some circumstances one of them might have to be executed, "by way of justice."[18] Even though the terrorizing of the native elite had no official sanction, instances of cruelty toward them continued in the years following the initial conquest. Sometimes the torture of nobles took on the perverse nature of sadistic sport.

The chronicler Oviedo relates that he was present in Nicaragua during 1528 when such a gory spectacle occurred. Pedrarias Dávila, governor of Castilla del Oro, ordered sixteen or seventeen caciques who were considered troublemakers brought forth for punishment. On Tuesday, June 15, he records precisely, the chiefs were brought out separately to test themselves against Spanish dogs. The Indian was given a club and instructed by an interpreter to defend himself, after which five or six whelps, still in training, were loosed on their victim. The inexperienced dogs circled the cacique, doing little but barking, so that they could be fended off with the club. When it appeared to the cacique that he had successfully survived the ordeal, the Spaniards slipped one or two of the mature dogs, probably greyhounds or mastiffs. They quickly bowled over each Indian in turn and the rest of the dogs closed quickly, disemboweling and consuming the Indian on the spot. In that way, Oviedo said, eighteen of the caciques from the valley of Olocoton and its environs were killed.[19]

In 1527, when Diego López de Salcedo, the royal governor in Honduras, seized tamemes to take to Nicaragua, those taken included many señores and principales bound in chains with iron collars on their necks. Most of those nobles died from fatigue under heavy loads, or from maltreatment. Those who escaped to return to their native lands were hanged by orders of the governor.[20] Andrés de Cerezeda, who became acting governor in Honduras, personally chained caciques. The son of the cacique Antonio from the pueblo of Roata, on the island of Guayava, had gone to Trujillo to serve his encomendero, but instead was chained by the hands with a ring around his neck and taken along with others.[21]

On one occasion when Indians attacked Spaniards, two of the principales were captured and their right hands were cut off, after which they were hanged as an example to others.[22] The atrocities committed by Francisco Gil and Lorenzo de Godoy, as reported by the cabildo in Chiapas, which resulted in the burning of at least twenty-one nobles and the mutilation of others, have already been noted in an earlier chapter.

In 1529, a cacique of Nicaragua brought suit against a Spanish vecino of

León, charging him with seizing his wife, and other women from his household, along with nephews, and branding them as slaves. The same happened to various principales. The cacique was whipped on three occasions in order to force him to give more slaves, and in one instance salt was rubbed into his cuts. Principales were given lashes as well. The Spaniard responded by saying that he treated Indians like his own sons, that the cacique was a "bellaco" who slept with women he took from other Indians. In the end, his defense was not very convincing.[23]

In Costa Rica, Hernán Sánchez de Vadajoz complained that after he had pacified areas of that territory, having gained the goodwill of the caciques, Rodrigo de Contreras, the governor of Nicaragua, invaded and caused great harm. Accompanying Contreras as allies were cannibalistic Indians who consumed many Costa Ricans with the consent of the governor— or so it was alleged. Contreras arrested the peaceful cacique Coasta (or Coaça), put him in chains, and gave his women to the governor's Negroes and grooms.

Vadajoz admitted that he had himself put Coasta under house arrest, since he thought it best for the pacification of the land; however, he said that the cacique was treated as a noble, eating at the same table with Vadajoz, drinking twice as much Castilian wine as his captor, and joking and gambling with the Spaniards, so that he did not feel like a prisoner. Contreras wanted to burn Coasta, but the cacique screamed and struggled so much that other Spaniards present were moved to compassion and tried to prevent it. Contreras, according to witnesses, spoke with "great arrogance," saying, "let me burn this cur . . . and if you do not let me burn him I will throw him to the dogs." Nevertheless, Contreras relented for the time being. Another witness noted that Coasta was further humiliated by having to carry sick Spaniards around on his back, and he was later jailed with another cacique called Tariaca, a "gran señor," until they both starved to death.

The cacique who ranked just below Coasta was Xele (or Coxele), who was face down in a hammock when Contreras first addressed him. Without raising his head, the cacique inquired what the Spaniard wanted, whereupon Contreras, furious at the lack of respect shown him, kicked the cacique and thrashed him until the Indian's scanty clothing fell off. Later Xele was bound and taken with a rope around his neck by a Spaniard to search for yuca. Along the way he was whipped, but he eventually escaped and rallied his people to rebellion, which, according to testimony, caused the loss of 400,000 ducats worth of gold.[24]

The principales of Honduras were terrorized by the expedition of a Miguel Díaz. He and his men entered the pueblo of Çacatoa and demanded slaves for working in the mines, and when the principales did not deliver a sufficient number, Díaz ordered his blacks to kill the caciques. They were hanged, after which their houses and grain supplies were put to the torch. Later the expedition continued to the village of Catao, where three more caciques principales were hanged. Other nobles were among those loaded with heavy cargoes and marched more than sixty leagues to the mines of Cuyapeque, as a result of which many died.[25]

In spite of royal wishes as to treatment of the native patrician class, the matter of justice was to a considerable degree dependent upon the whim of local powers. Chamberlain notes a case in which a Spanish prisoner on his way to being tried for having clubbed to death five principales was set free by followers of Alvarado.[26] Be that as it may, colonists were sometimes tried for extreme abuses resulting in the deaths of caciques, as in the case of one Alonso López of Tabasco, who was charged with killing a cacique named don Francisco by kicking and beating him with a club. A criminal proceso against López was sent to the Council of the Indies. The case was then sent to the Audiencia of New Spain and then returned to Spain, before it was finally forwarded to the audiencia in Guatemala for disposition. It was a delicate situation in one sense: López, a vecino of La Vitoria, was the brother-in-law of Montejo, who was the father-in-law of Maldonado, the president of the audiencia.[27] What the final judgment was I cannot say.

Those with political influence often literally got away with murder, and royal officials sometimes hesitated with good reason to move against them. Pedro Xuárez de Toledo, the alcalde mayor of La Trinidad, investigated charges that a prominent vecino named Gómez Díaz de la Reguera was responsible for the death of a cacique. Later the alcalde mayor died, a persecuted man in trouble with the Inquisition, a result, so his daughter charged, of his having proceeded against one with political connections.[28]

As a final example, we may refer to the later case of don Diego, son of Per Afán de Ribera, governor of Cartago (Costa Rica). When don Diego was on his way to the Caribbean shore, having encountered good cooperation from Indians along the way, he finally arrived at the province of Pocoçi, where a cacique greeted him in peace. The ruler gave 300 tamemes, after which he and his father went along with the Spaniards to guide them to the province of Avyaque, where don Diego ordered the cacique to summon all the local caciques and people to come to serve the Spaniards. They were promised freedom to return to their homes afterward. First two caciques came before don Diego, appearing anxious to be elsewhere, and when one of them actually bolted, a collar was put around his neck. Because of that display of reluctance on the part of the chiefs, the

Spaniard took an old Indian and scorched him. The two caciques of Avyaque were then burned alive. A witness to the scene testified later that another reason for their murders was that they did not give enough gold to the Spaniards. Far from having the effect of intimidating the natives, the atrocity provoked a rebellion and impeded the advance of the Spaniards when they found roads blocked and bridges cut.[29]

With the exception of the last incident, all of the atrocities cited above occurred during the first years of conquest and pacification. Perhaps most noteworthy is the fact that the perpetrators of the cruelties were all men of power and position, so that the killing of caciques could not be excused as the work of mere ruffians or outlaws. Nor are these the only examples: it would be tedious to relate details of other cases that are so appallingly similar, but the skeptical reader will find numerous instances in the manuscripts.

Following the initial conquests there remained a social turbulence in the Indies which the Crown anxiously sought to dispel. In the uneasy post-conquest years a few Spaniards lived in a sea of native peoples who still retained a considerable measure of respect for their own leaders. For practical reasons if nothing else, Spanish policy aimed at preserving at least some of the traditional authority of the "natural lords" (señores naturales) with a view toward maintaining harmony through them in the Indian communities. Thus the Crown hoped to see the emergence of a well-ordered society, with the conquered race living in *policía*, as *gente política*.

Given the traditional power of the native aristocracy over the commoners, it was natural enough that royal policy aimed at utilizing the nobles as culture brokers through whom the natives could be controlled. Leaving aside the clash of cultures, there was the initial practical problem of communication. While many of the Indians of Central America spoke "Mexican" (Nahuatl), a tongue with which Spanish veterans of New Spain were familiar, a number of the native groups spoke other languages, and even the most assiduous of friars could hope to learn no more than two or three of them. Therefore, it was reasoned that the native nobility should serve as the catalyst between the two cultures. They would be taught Spanish to act as purveyors of European civilization to their people. This was the plan of the Crown, although implementation was less than perfect.

Royal advisors saw very early the wisdom of gaining the goodwill of the principales, and in 1529, the emperor issued an order pertaining to the good treatment of the nobles in New Spain. According to the spirit of that cédula, it would be best for the Indian leaders to retain a measure of their traditional status so that, conceded some power, they could compel their own people to work the fields and not live in idleness. They should be allowed to keep some power of jurisdiction in the governing of the maceguales because, with the advice and instruction of the Spaniards, the caciques could do it better and more to the liking of the Indians.

The practical nature of the provision becomes more clear when it was also specified in the document that the lords should be induced to persuade their subjects to undertake certain moderate tasks, such as working in the mines in teams on occasion, with the labor divided so as not to work a hardship on them. The Indians could keep the gold they took out, from which they could pay the king his share, buy things they needed, and still have enough left to help pay their tribute to the Crown.[30]

Provided that the native aristocracy could be preserved and the privileges and powers pertaining to it recognized, the more immediate problem was that of communication and education. It was apparent that the transition would pose difficulties owing to the drag of custom and habit, the language barriers, and the resistance, however subliminal, of the ruling class, all of which conspired to subvert the insinuation of Castilian practices.

The clear solution for the long-range conversion lay in the instruction of the future Indian nobles. To that end, Crown policy would be to indoctrinate the sons of principales in the new ways. In 1537, a royal decree was issued to that effect.[31] In a less formal way, the policy was already in operation: about 1534, when the Mercedarians went in as the first permanent religious order, the comendador Sanbrana, the founder, took special care to gather a large number of the sons of caciques and principales. At least a hundred of the boys were taught to read and write, to sing in church, to serve at the altar, and to perform other duties. After their instruction they were sent out to spread the faith and, incidentally, Hispanic culture.[32]

Men of the Church were the only ones who could feasibly undertake the program of instruction, which in large measure accounts for the extent of clerical influence over the nobles, and by extension, over the native masses. One of those most active in this regard was the enlightened bishop of Honduras, Cristóbal de Pedraza. Chamberlain notes that Pedraza maintained such a school for the sons of caciques in his residence in Gracias a Dios. When the good bishop left in late 1539 or early 1540, the school unfortunately functioned only a short while longer.[33]

One gains the impression that the imperial plan for the education of young nobles was indifferently carried out, for the oidor Herrera wrote Spain in 1545, recommending that the sons of caciques and principales be gathered together in a school where a religious could educate them, with expenses to be met by the fines imposed during inspection tours of the villages.[34] At least some such schools continued to operate, and in 1552 it was reported that the boys were being taught Spanish and other subjects so they could pass them on to the maceguales. Even though many Spaniards felt that all of the Indians should learn to speak and understand Spanish, some of the Franciscans were of the opinion that if any maceguales did not want to learn it they should be taught Nahuatl, because it was a general tongue in the land.[35]

While a new generation of Indian leaders was being trained, the adult members of the aristocracy were to be treated with consideration and respect. A number of caciques journeyed to Spain and were presented at court, and they felt free to write the king and to institute suits, in which litigation they pressed the advantages they had as a privileged group. The caciques at the top of the native nobility were to be addressed as "don," a privilege accorded very few Spaniards. In 1542, fray Pedro de Angulo requested that the Crown reward four caciques who had been helpful in the spiritual conquest.[36] It is perhaps significant that about the same time the New Laws were being drawn up and that one of the prime movers behind the legislation, Las Casas, favored the proposal of his fellow Dominican.

In 1543, a cédula was issued in which reference was made to the contributions of don Juan, cacique of Atitlán, and don José, don Miguel, don Gaspar, and the cacique of Sacatepequez, who had assisted Angulo and other Dominicans in attracting to the faith Indians of the troublesome areas of Teculutlán and Lacandón. Angulo had also requested that their villages be made crown towns, with reduced tributes. Because half the pueblo of Atitlán belonged to Sancho de Barahona, and the villages of the other caciques cited belonged to other encomenderos, those Spaniards were to be compensated with other encomiendas. As an alternative, they could keep the tributes of those towns, but were not to enter them.[37] However, those caciques and others who helped the Dominicans were apparently not given much special consideration, since the Crown had to issue another order on their behalf later.[38]

In the meantime, the emperor authorized the granting of coats of arms to don Pedro and don Diego, caciques of Sacatepequez in the province of Guatemala. Far from being simple, rustic creations, they were invested with all the familiar devices of heraldry: the *escudos* were to have two castles, one gold and one silver, and between them there was to be a gold key and a sword with a blue banner with letters of gold spelling "Ave María." Those figures would be on a red field with four blue keys on the edges with four red insignias on a field of gold, with a closed helmet; and from a fist would appear a red flag, a sword, and a key, on top of which would be an insignia in gold, along with other keys of blue, red, white, and gold.[39]

Rank had its privileges in other respects as well. As in Spanish society, Indians of the upper class fared better in courts of law. Indian nobles, like prosperous Spaniards, usually paid a fine when found guilty of some infraction, while the lower classes in both societies took lashes or a term in jail. No doubt the Crown would have preferred having fines from all, but the impecunious masses were usually in no position to comply. For more serious crimes the disparity of justice was even greater, certainly insofar as the natives were concerned. At least in some instances, the sons of caciques found guilty of sodomy got off with a whipping; for the same offense maceguales died by fire. When, however, the stepson of Montejo tried to sodomize the adelantado's page, the matter was disposed of quickly. The intended victim complained to Montejo's wife, who told the page to keep quiet or he would burn, as a result of which he left the territory forthwith.[40]

It appears that at times the caciques were required to pay tribute to the Crown just like the maceguales. This seems to have been the case around mid-century, when reference was made to their payments, but in 1561, the Crown requested information from the audiencia as to the wisdom of having the caciques and principales pay.[41] Later they were relieved of the obligation. At the same time, the nobles received tribute from maceguales. However, in 1553, the Crown asked for detailed information regarding the customs of tribute in prehispanic times, and wanted to know what tribute was being paid to the caciques and principales, and if it came to about what they had been paid before the Christians arrived.[42]

The extent to which caciques were allowed to act in administrative capacities among their own people varied considerably, and even as late as 1560, the king had reservations about the native philosophy of government. In that year he wrote to the president of the audiencia, observing that a cacique named don Juan governed in the province of Verapaz by royal provision; but since the Indian manner of governing and executing justice was different and "somewhat false according to the requirements of Christianity," it would be well to order that, in matters of government, a "virtuous and prudent" Spaniard assist don Juan as *asesor* and coadjutor in the administration. The appointment should be made in consultation with fray Pedro de Angulo, with a proper salary offered. It should be done, the king cautioned, without any harm to the caciques and principales.[43]

In other ways the traditional customs of the nobility had to be curtailed, especially that of holding their own people as slaves, a practice then reserved (before 1548) for Spaniards. As late as 1546, reference was made to complaints that some Indians were raiding other villages and stealing women and children who were sold as slaves.[44] In the minds of some Spaniards a curious double standard prevailed. The chronicler Herrera, perhaps with conscious sarcasm, relates that in early Nicaragua the Indians had enslaved other free people, and for that reason the guilt of the Castilians was not so great, because the slaves of rescate they acquired were already in that condition. The Protector of the Indians there, Bishop Diego Alvarez Osorio, and Pedrarias Dávila spoke to the caciques, decrying the evil committed by them in enslaving their own, because no one should be deprived of his liberty.[45] At least as early as 1536, a royal cédula forbade caciques to hold slaves, and another order a year and a half later prohibited caciques and principales from making any new slaves.[46]

In late 1538, a similar decree was issued for New Spain, forbidding the nobles to reduce Indians to slaves or to buy and sell them. The custom had been, as the Crown observed, for the nobility to enslave their subjects for very slight causes and to trade them to other Indians or Spaniards. Because of the resulting harm, and since all of the natives were to be considered subjects and vassals of the Spanish emperor, continuation of the practice was strictly forbidden.[47] Such admonitions notwithstanding, some caciques persisted in making slaves and holding them, apparently even after Indian slaves belonging to Spaniards had been liberated.[48]

It seems probable that caciques under Spanish domination lost their slaves, for the most part, when the Spaniards gave them up. Caciques and principales of Atitlán lamented that Cerrato took away their slaves, without whom their fields were ruined. At the same time, Cerrato lightened the tribute loads of their villages. President Landecho raised them again, and when the caciques complained to President Briceño he raised them even more. By 1571, they were given more consideration by the audiencia, but they protested their situation nevertheless. Their fathers had been generous in helping Alvarado and cooperated with other Spaniards, but now they were being used like the slaves their fathers used to have. And since they were not accustomed to serving, their numbers were diminishing.[49]

Instructions given to an alcalde mayor in 1557 indicate some of the other restrictions imposed on caciques. If they were found guilty of selling wine, arms, horses, dogs, or Castilian clothing to Indians they would be fined ten pesos. For the second offense the cacique or principal would again be fined ten pesos, and in addition he would be exiled for six months.

Furthermore, he would have to present himself before the audiencia for further consideration. At the same time, the orders also show that special consideration was given to the native aristocracy. While the maceguales were not to drink wine, because they were immoderate in its use and could not cope with it, provision was made for some "wealthy" caciques and principales "of good sense" to take wine on occasion, but not often and only in moderation. For their own use they could, with the license of the alcalde mayor, buy horses and clothing made in Spain.[50]

One alcalde mayor, who said that it was the custom to give Indian governors some wine on certain feast days, was charged with arresting the same caciques for being drunk. He admitted that he had arrested them for drunkenness on various occasions. Found guilty of the charge, he was fined four pesos.[51]

Enterprising alcaldes mayores found ways to exploit those privileges for their own profit. In Nicaragua they sold licenses to caciques allowing them to ride horses with saddles and bits for the price of a peso or two. When new alcaldes mayores were appointed they said the old licenses were invalid, and the caciques would have to purchase new ones. In that way the Indian nobles paid time and again, along with their sons and grandsons.[52]

The fact that caciques even had horses and arms, however, is evidence of a relaxed policy, since for years earlier they were denied both. Reference was made in 1535 to the many Spanish arms in the hands of señores and principales, sold to them by "bad Christians." It was forbidden then because of fear of a native uprising.[53] But the danger of generalizations is again illustrated, because years later the president of the audiencia was found guilty in his residencia for having allowed an Indian named don Luis Bonifacio to wear a sword and dagger.[54]

It was recognized that caciques required discipline to curb abuses, but their punishment was to be executed with discretion. A judge wrote the following at mid-century:

Indians can be whipped, and even if the punishment is harsh they are satisfied, provided their guilt is clear. A good example is given by public punishment, as is customary. The principales ask the judges to hear their cases with patience and to listen to their long arguments and complaints; and if they are not heard with understanding, or if the judge's responses are harsh, the principales never return to seek justice, even though their own interests are at stake. The judges should listen dispassionately and punish the principales in such a manner that the maceguales and subjects do not lose respect for their leaders, which is of great importance among the principales and the maceguales, so that they understand that they can freely seek justice and to seek to correct abuses of them by their caciques and principales.[55]

As it happened, such care was not always taken to protect the prestige of the nobles, with the inevitable result that their position in the eyes of the maceguales deteriorated. Because of the restrictions placed on the caciques and their indifferent treatment by Spaniards, their status had sunk to a low level by 1551. They were, it was reported, very poor, and they suffered more than the other Indians of their pueblos. The very name of cacique had come to mean little more than "tribute collector," and all who came in contact with them were contentious. The Crown ordered that they be provided with sufficient food and that they be restored to the rights and privileges consistent with their cacicazgos.[56]

A contributing cause to the decline of the caciques was the difficulty on the part of Spaniards in ascertaining exactly who the legitimate caciques were. The disruptions subsequent to the conquest and pacification saw various caciques killed, enslaved, uprooted and displaced, while some of them simply ran away to the wilds. With the line of succession broken it was not always easy to establish the legitimacy of the heirs. Under some circumstances Indians were allowed to elect their own caciques. To complicate the situation, there were false claims to cacicazgos by pretenders with little or no valid proof. Moreover, while there was a defined line of succession among the nobility, the tradition was sometimes disregarded when a royal official, an encomendero, or even a clergyman, arbitrarily appointed an Indian as chief.

In some instances encomenderos displaced caciques and señores principales, and named in their positions teamsters or naborías from their household staffs, either to increase production or to please the villagers. Losing their privileges, the deposed nobles often ended up with the status of maceguales, sometimes serving in humble trades. The same happened to their sons and grandsons, and the archdeacon of León asked the Crown to make restitution to them.[57]

The crown attitude toward political power for the Indian nobles was to some extent conditioned by, and predicated upon, their traditional roles, which was still not entirely clear many years after the seating of Spanish hegemony. A cédula of 1547 cautioned the alcaldes mayores and corregidores not to deprive caciques of their jurisdictions, and reminded officials four years later that all necessary guarantees for the nobles were to be observed.[58]

In the meantime, the audiencia was ordered to inquire into the manner and custom of inheriting rule among the Indian rulers. The king was to know about the way in which caciques were elected and named prior to the conquest, as well as the relationship to their cacicazgos. Did they succeed to the cacicazgos through inheritance, or did the people nominate them? The sovereign also wished to know what they had received in the way of tribute, as well as the exact nature of their rights.[59]

Although some encomenderos were appointing native alcaldes ordinarios as caciques in their villages, it was done without royal sanction. Cacicazgos were being taken from those who had legitimate claims to them and given to others who did not, all of which provoked great disorder. To remedy that development, the Crown called for an examination to determine who were the true caciques and who were the false pretenders, with the admonition that the rule be given to the deserving Indians. If it happened that there was no legitimate claimant, the natives should be allowed to elect their own cacique, as well as alcaldes ordinarios and alguaciles. Furthermore, tributes should be provided for the caciques, and salaries for the Indian officials so that they could sustain themselves. The audiencia was instructed to prepare a detailed report and to render an opinion.[60]

The confusion was not only in the minds of the king and his advisors. Frequently those on the spot were equally perplexed. When a cacique in Nicaragua was deprived of his señorío by an encomendero the case came up in the governor's residencia, at which time the judge wanted to know if the caciques of Nicaragua inherited their cacicazgos or whether they were made caciques by the señores of the pueblos. And, more specifically, had the encomendero installed that particular cacique in his position? A witness testified that some succeeded their antecedents who were caciques, and that others were put in and taken out at the pleasure of their encomenderos. In the case before the court, he said that the cacique had been put in by a former encomendero, but he did not know if the title was legitimately his through rights of succession.[61]

In 1553, the Crown again instructed the audiencia to determine which of the señores had the señorío through succession of blood and which ones through election by the Indians subject to them. And, again, the judges were to report on the jurisdiction formerly exercised by the caciques over their subjects as compared to the present, as well as what benefits were accruing to them from having the señorío. Their method of government was also to be examined.[62]

It appears, out of all the obfuscation, that in pre-conquest days caciques inherited through blood lines in some regions and that in other areas they were elected, a circumstance the Crown was apparently willing to recognize. It approved the unanimous election, "in the old custom," of don Juan Apobazt, the cacique mayor of the pueblo of San Juan de Hamelco, as governor and cacique principal, because he was a man of authority and good sense, and particularly since he had assisted the religious in the territory. Don Juan was confirmed in that position for life by the king, who added that the old customs were to be observed.[63]

About the same time, nonetheless, that order was being violated. The cabildo of Santiago wrote to Spain that the oidor licenciado Alonso de Zorita—generally regarded by historians as an enlightened judge—with his brothers had removed many caciques and principales from their cacicazgos and señoríos in a high-handed fashion. Those were nobles who had held their positions from olden times, according to the regidores, and Zorita had not even given them a hearing, all of which caused a great commotion.[64]

Referring to such cases, the king noted that some Indians who had been caciques and lords of pueblos in the time of their "infidelity" were dispossessed of their ranks without cause. Those nobles should not lose their rights or be in a worse position, the sovereign stated, for having converted to Christianity, and he ordered that those descended from legitimate caciques be given justice through a hearing immediately.[65] But by that time some prominent Indian nobles had been dispossessed for more than thirty years, that is, dating back to the conquest.

When Alvarado and his lieutenants deprived don Juan Chicuet-Quiagut, the cacique mayor of Utatlán, of most of his province, the pueblos were given to the soldiers in repartimientos. The encomenderos then made caciques of whomever they wished, which is to say, those of whom they could take most advantage. When don Juan died, his son, don Juan Cortés, was a mere boy and was not obeyed by the people or allowed to be señor and cacique as his antecedents had been. Even though the Indians asked the encomenderos to allow the boy to be lord, the Spaniards replied that he was not to be a señor of so many pueblos, nor were the Indians to obey him. Don Juan Cortés then appealed to the justices to no avail, as a result of which he lived in hardship. When he appealed to the Crown, arguing that the king was not well served by the situation, which was causing considerable damage, he asked to be restored as cacique of Utatlán and all the subject pueblos, as his forefathers were. The audiencia was ordered to examine the case and report to Spain.[66]

It was reiterated in 1558 that those caciques who had been deprived of their rights and alienated from their people should be restored, and the king again remarked that it made no sense for them to be worse off as Christians than they had been in pagan times, and that such abuses were to cease. But while the Crown thought it wise to allow the nobles to retain their traditional ranks and privileges, that was to be so only insofar as it comported with Castilian practices. It has been observed that caciques and principales were no longer to have slaves, and the Crown added that they were not to have jurisdiction in any punishment of Indians that involved mutilation of limbs or execution.[67] While this was a humanitarian law, it further reduced the authority of the nobles. Thus, in these and other ways the customary powers of the caciques were circumscribed.

According to one source, by 1582 the province of Chiapas had no cacique whose ancestors held señoríos in pre-conquest times, and there was the persistent suspicion that Dominican friars had suppressed the succession because native lords enjoyed the affection of the Indians and defended them from the friars. Apparently not all pueblos had caciques, for the audiencia determined to find out which towns had them and when others stopped having them. The judges also wanted to know if it was owing to the fault of succession or because cacicazgos had been taken away. If there were deposed caciques who had legitimate claims through direct descent or cross descent they should appear before the audiencia to present evidence. The procedure was given crown approval.[68]

The question of succession among the nobility was never completely clarified during the sixteenth century. As late as 1598, the Crown still wanted to know about the custom among Indians regarding the succession of cacicazgos and if it was the same all over. The audiencia was to give its opinion as to whether or not it would be convenient for the purpose of better government to give another order concerning succession.[69]

In such matters caciques were to follow the Spanish pattern of establishing one's claim to privilege. In 1610, a procurador submitted a probanza for an Indian named Pérez, in which he sought to prove that the parents and grandparents of Pérez were principales of good lines and customs, and that they had met the obligations of being good Christians. The probanza stated further that Pérez himself, being of noble blood, had sought since childhood to live in peace and quiet without involving himself in discordant suits, that he was never seen intoxicated, and that he had faithfully discharged his duties and offices in the Church in his pueblo, and that in all he had acted with rectitude and integrity.[70]

The ambivalence of the Crown and the lack of any firm laws executed by dedicated judges encouraged what would have been in any event a loose interpretation of the royal intent. On the local level royal officials often treated with the native nobility according to demands of local exigencies, or in line with the particular caprice of the Spaniard on the spot. This is not to say that the importance of the caciques was always ignored by administrators. When Governor López de Salcedo of Honduras died, the cabildo of Trujillo sought a replacement. The regidores rejected the contador, Andrés de Cerezeda, since he had arrived only four months before from Nicaragua and had no familiarity with the señores naturales of the land.

Instead, they elected as justicia mayor Vasco de Herrera, who, it was stressed, had a good knowledge of the lords of the land, knew very well their language and how to deal with them, and who enjoyed the esteem of the caciques.[71] However, that was in 1530, at a time when there was still danger from Indian rebellions.

In other ways the residual control of the chiefs over the maceguales was recognized. When Alvarado was planning his expedition to Quito, he intended to take all the señores and principales with him so that the leaderless natives would not dare rebel. The treasury officials, on the other hand, felt that such action would have quite the opposite effect, and that the Indians, seeing their leaders taken from them, would rise up in protest. Therefore, they made a strong request that Alvarado be prohibited from taking any Indian noble away.[72]

In other instances, arbitrary actions of Spanish officials indicated their lack of regard for the utility of the caciques. Some of the chiefs complained that tributes imposed by encomenderos were excessive and that they had trouble with the religious who went to their villages. Because of the resulting disagreements, both the encomenderos and the religious had made unjust charges against the caciques to the alcaldes ordinarios who, to please the Spaniards, illegally deprived the lords of their cacicazgos. The Crown reaction was to order the alcaldes ordinarios not to interfere in such matters under pain of loss of office and a fine of 50,000 maravedís, adding that only the audiencias had the power to deprive a cacique of his inheritance.[73]

Quite aside from the abuse of caciques by encomenderos, the same treatment was often accorded them by the mayordomos of crown towns who were sometimes taskmasters no less harsh than those managing the estates of private individuals. In both types of villages, it was the caciques and other Indian officials who were held responsible for the collection of tributes. Although they were given the responsibility for the delivery of the village assessment of tribute and workers, the nobles' power of enforcement had been vitiated.

The extent to which caciques should have power and privileges was disputed by many Spaniards, and even the enlightened and pro-Indian Cerrato had strong reservations. He forwarded his opinion to the king, as follows:

I am very tired of the religious, especially the Dominicans, saying that free rule of the Indians should be left to the caciques, and that they should have the jurisdiction that they had in olden times, and that they [the Indians] should serve them and give them tribute as they were accustomed, and other things of this kind. . . . When the Spaniards came to this land they killed some caciques and took away the cacicazgos from others, in such a manner that in all this province there is hardly a natural, or legitimate, cacique. And if tribute is given to them as before, and more tribute [is given] to the encomenderos, it implies a great contradiction to what Your Majesty has ordered; because in a cédula of Your Majesty it is clear: that the Indians [are to] pay less tribute to the encomenderos than they used to pay to their caciques. And if they have to pay the tribute to the encomenderos and more to the caciques they could not endure it. There is another great damage, because the justice that they [the caciques] dispensed (in times past) was by their will, without legal procedure or any reason; and for very slight causes they hanged whomever they pleased, and they took his children and wife for slaves and perpetrated insults, which if allowed now would be a very great hardship. Now it is to be understood that their cacicazgos will be returned to many of the old lords and their sons. But, ultimately, although some of them deny it, most of them still act like tyrants, and if they have to assess ten maravedís of tribute [for encomenderos] they assess twenty, and the lords take it [the difference] for themselves, and only God has the power to remedy it. It would certainly be a convenience if Your Majesty would make a declaration about this.

Also, there are complaints from the Dominicans that the Indians do not have the reverence for the caciques that they used to have, because in olden times they did not consider them [simply] as lords nor have reverence for them as men, but as gods. And now, since the Indians commonly see the [bad] treatment that the caciques receive, and the liberty that they themselves have, they boast a lot about being vassals of the Emperor, and they do not have that obedience they used to have. And some Spaniards, and even some religious, have the opinion that this is not inconvenient for the land; because if they had the reverence and obedience of old they would be in the hands of the caciques to make an uprising any time they wished, which they cannot do as things are now.[74]

Cerrato's letter is of some interest because of his hostile remarks regarding the Dominicans with whom he had worked so closely, and because he indicates that the friars were supporting the power of the caciques, a view contrary to that noted previously in this chapter.

One of the difficulties involved in the relationship between royal representatives and the native rulers was the infrequent communication resulting from the scattered demographic pattern and the distances between settlements. When Spain requested information from the caciques regarding the pre-conquest tribute system, the audiencia replied that it could not gather the information in time to send on the next ship because it was necessary to summon caciques and principales from thirty, forty, or even eighty leagues distant.[75] The end result of such poor communication was that oidores had to rely on the judgment of minor provincial officials to implement policy, a task for which many of them were poorly suited. In that context, it should be noted, however, that the judges of the audiencia themselves were not always above exploiting the nobles.[76]

In general, Indian leaders fared best at the hands of high officials who had no regional interests, such as the royal visitors. It sometimes happened that those judges favored the caciques at the expense of local Spaniards, as well as the maceguales.[77] Local Spanish officials, as might be expected, took excessive liberties in the more remote provinces. Caciques in the small isolated province of Soconusco, testifying in Nahuatl, said local Spanish officials imposed special taxes on them and beat them. If tribute quotas were not met they were imprisoned. Moreover, the officials, including the alcalde mayor, were merchants who forced the Indians to buy their merchandise. Their wives and daughters were taken from them, and they could get no satisfaction from either the bishop or President Landecho of the audiencia. For those reasons, they petitioned the Crown to return them to the jurisdiction of Mexico instead of Guatemala.[78] Two years later the caciques complained that the governor of Soconusco was treating them like slaves and that he threatened them with the pillory or hanging if they attempted to appeal to higher authority.[79]

Officials found other ways to exploit the native rulers. Hortun de Velasco, alcalde mayor and corregidor of Zapotitlán, was charged with fining don Domingo, governor of the pueblo of Çamayaque, nine tostones and keeping the money instead of giving it to royal treasury officials. In addition, he was accused of fining the caciques and principales of the village of Cuyotenango eighty-two tostones, the partial proceeds of which were to go to buy wax for village fiestas, but which he kept for himself instead.[80]

It is understandable that Indian officials feared the encomenderos, most of whom, at least for many years, were tough conquistadores; but even some royal officials assumed pompous and threatening airs, which intimidated natives and Spanish vecinos alike. Pedro Girón de Alvarado, the alcalde mayor of San Salvador in the late sixteenth century, walked about preceded by a mulatto and flanked by two blacks, each of whom was armed with two swords. His lieutenant was accused of whipping and clubbing native alguaciles mayores and molesting the women of an Indian alcalde's family.

Girón de Alvarado's judicial review revealed abuses that were commonplace many years before; however, coming at the end of the century, they represent what was probably by then an extreme case. When he went to the pueblo of Çacatecoluca he ordered an Indian alguacil to bring him a beautiful Indian woman for the night. When the alguacil showed reluctance to procure for the alcalde mayor, Girón tied him up and whipped him so badly that the Indian had to stay in bed. On another afternoon he ordered the same Indian and another alguacil to bring a beautiful *mulata* named Catalina Chirinos to him. When they did not deliver her, the Spanish alguacil of Girón tied the Indian officials and whipped them cruelly, causing great unrest in the village, according to later testimony.

That same night Girón's Negro slave took the mulata to him. One of Girón's companions ordered another Indian to fetch him an Indian woman, and when the alguacil mayor of the village asked that the Indian be paid for his trouble, because he was to go outside to another village, Girón said that he would pay the Indian personally. He then had the Indian official seized, tied to a pillory, and given 100 lashes, from which the victim passed out. Later, when the same alguacil mayor refused to bring an Indian medicine man to cure a Spaniard's wife, he was given more stripes.[81]

In the region of Chiquimula a principal over sixty was summoned by the corregidor to deliver himself as prisoner. The Indian did not want to go because it was close to Christmas, but he finally relented. After traveling for ten leagues to town he was jailed for six days. He denied that he was guilty of any infraction, but witnesses for the corregidor said he was a troublemaker, arrogant, and disobedient. Among other things, he had denied that the corregidor had a proper commission. Some felt that he deserved 100 lashes, but owing to his age he was fined nine tostones and released.[82]

Despite occasional instances involving royal officials in the mistreatment of the nobles, there are indications that there were far fewer extreme cases as the decades passed. While it is commonly understood that the corregidores placed over crown towns were perhaps the greatest oppressors of Indians, residencias of those officials by late in the century reveal fewer abuses than earlier. At the same time, the residencia testimony could be misleading because those testifying were, for the most part, Indian officials. They had little bad to say about the corregidores, which could imply that at least the native leaders were better treated (and perhaps involved in collusion with corregidores in exploiting the maceguales) or that they were too intimidated to speak out. Whatever the reasons, there is, at least on paper, quite a contrast to the testimony of earlier years.[83]

However well-intentioned and practical the royal policy for preserving the relative influence and dignity of the Indian nobles, on the frontiers the mere fact that they were natives put them in an inferior position vis-à-vis the Spaniards. There were numerous white men of the lower social and economic class, but there is little doubt that the most degraded of them considered himself superior to any cacique. Conquistadores and first settlers, soon joined by royal bureaucrats and other professionals, formed the basis of New World aristocracy, in which there was no convenient place for Indian nobles. Caciques and principales, accustomed to the reverence due demi-gods, found themselves humiliated, a circumstance precluding their maintaining the haughty dignity that characterized their behavior before the coming of the Christians. There were implicit contradictions in the Crown's intent, for many of the pre-conquest practices of the ruling class in Central America were inconsistent with Spanish social and legal behavior. Beyond that, there was a studied contempt on the part of many Spaniards for the pretensions of the caciques. And even among those white men inclined to abide by the royal policy, there was uncertainty about the manifestations of that philosophy. An influential friar wrote to the Council of the Indies:

The King has ordered many times that the caciques be honored, and that their rights be preserved [but] it would be well for the Crown to define the rights that are to be observed; because the caciques are called thieves for receiving from their people even a fowl or a load of firewood. And the audiencia will not allow them to give even a flick of the finger [*papirate*] to an Indian for whatever happens. And many things occur that need remedy, but the audiencia is far away from many pueblos and nothing is done to correct the situation, as a result of which much harm derives.[84]

Aside from the restricted authority imposed by law, the prestige of the native aristocracy was diminished in other, more personal ways in which they were insulted by officials of the Crown. An alcalde mayor in La Trinidad allegedly went to the encomienda pueblo of Izalco, belonging to Juan de Guzmán, to collect his own salary, and there dishonored don Pedro, the Indian governor of the town, calling him "perro puto" (sodomite dog), and knocking him into a wall. In his defense, the Spanish official stated that don Pedro said that he did not want to pay the salary and that he spoke disrespectfully in other ways, for which he gave the Indian a shove or two, but nothing else.

The alcalde mayor was also charged with insulting don Juan Chiame, governor of Tacuxcalco (Tlacucalco). According to the charge, the native governor had appeared before the alcalde mayor to seek justice because a prominent Spaniard named Gómez Díaz de la Reguera had pulled his whiskers and beaten him, in addition to other mistreatment. The alcalde mayor, being a friend of Gómez Díaz, gave the Indian no satisfaction; on the contrary, instead of consoling the cacique, he affronted him by calling him a "perro borracho" (drunken dog), as a result of which the cacique ceased to seek justice. Moreover, it was charged, Gómez Díaz was not punished. In rebuttal, the alcalde mayor said only that he had ordered the arrest of Gómez Díaz.

The royal official was also accused of demeaning the dignity of the caciques, principales, and the native alguaciles by giving them a quantity of money, some clothing from Yucatán, wine, and wax for them to trade among the various pueblos for cacao to be delivered to him. Finally, it was stated that the alcalde mayor implored the caciques of the town of Caluco and other villages not to post charges against him in his residencia, and they did not. The alcalde mayor denied the charges and said that the witnesses from the community were "dastardly drunkards and of vile opinion."[85]

Insults and physical abuse of Indians were imputed to even Francisco Briceño, the governor of Guatemala and president of the audiencia. It was charged that when don Diego, the cacique principal of the pueblo of Misco, the encomienda of Alvaro de Paz, went to complain of an injustice involving community lands, Briceño called him "perro" and slapped him, almost knocking him down. Apparently, however, the evidence did not convince the judge, because Briceño was absolved of the charge.[86]

Dr. Villalobos noted in 1573 that when he journeyed from New Spain to Santiago he passed through the province of Soconusco, where he saw that caciques and principales were still being wronged by officials. He reported that for ten years they had suffered at the hands of the alcaldes mayores, adding that because of the disorder and greed the Indians were poor and the area was depopulated. Soconusco, he reported, was once one of the best provinces, but had deteriorated because of the exploitation of the alcaldes mayores. There were only eighteen hundred natives left in the province.[87]

If the royal officials demeaned the native aristocracy, it is no surprise that the encomenderos were extreme in their behavior toward them. While the former were usually men of some education—certainly those in the higher echelons of the bureaucracy—and men responsible for carrying out royal directives, the encomenderos were frequently rude, illiterate adventurers with little regard for social amenities and with an arrested sense of justice. Moreover, they were often isolated from officers of the Crown; hence, they exerted great authority in the pueblos assigned to them.

At least in the first few decades, the objective of many of them was to accumulate sufficient wealth to enable them to return to Spain, retired as gentlemen of leisure, and toward that end they sought by every means at their disposal to hasten the process. The tribute and labor supplied by the villagers usually did not provide enough profit to enable the encomenderos to realize their dreams. Consequently, they sought to supplement their income through the acquisition of precious metals, slaves, or through commercial activities.

In order to obtain the desired wealth it was logical for the encomenderos to work through the caciques. As a result, Spaniards sometimes mistreated the nobles in order to exact more treasure from them, even when the caciques had already given gold and jewels.[88] Encomenderos on occasion simply appropriated Indians to work their fields or mines. When Alvarado was settling his milpa of Jocotenango he called in the caciques of his various encomienda towns and ordered each to give him so many Indians from their villages, along with their principales. When they arrived, most of the Indians were unjustly branded as slaves.[89]

Gold was of course the preferred commodity, but it was in short supply. Accordingly, many of the encomenderos went into the business of slave trading, and in order to gather slaves they pressured the Indian rulers. Some of the Spaniards were relentless in their demands for slaves, even when the supply was exhausted, and their threats to the caciques could lead to dire social consequences. A treasury official who resided in Honduras during the early years of Spanish occupation stated that it was customary for Spaniards to mistreat caciques and principales to induce them to supply Indians for branding as slaves. And sometimes, after receiving shameful torments and severe beatings, the nobles gave their own sons, saying that they were their slaves. The writer felt that an order should be given against asking caciques for slaves, and that each district should have an official traveling around eight months a year (that is, during the dry season), going from cacique to cacique, seeing that they were well treated so the Indians would know they had a protector.[90]

On other occasions encomenderos provided caciques with cacao and other goods with which to trade for slaves with other Indians.[91] Las Casas wrote that the worst pestilence in Nicaragua was the license conceded to the Spaniards to ask caciques for slaves, as a result of which in a period of fourteen years so many Indians had died that only four or five thousand of them remained.[92] Some caciques reacted to the pressures of encomenderos to furnish slaves by running away to the mountains, and while presumably most of them simply wanted to be left alone, others went on the offensive and became bandits.[93]

In 1536, the Crown issued an order prohibiting the extortion of caciques for the purpose of acquiring slaves. It was sent to the governor of Nicaragua, where the abuse was extreme, stating explicitly that guilty

Spaniards were to be punished.[94] The governor, Rodrigo de Contreras, was aware of the problem. He wrote the king that one encomendero was in the habit of asking his cacique for slaves from those the cacique held before the conquest, and if the cacique said he had none to give, the encomendero told him to look for some or he would kill him. The unfortunate chief, afraid not to comply, took free Indians from his own village to trade for others from a neighboring cacique. The free Indians he got in trade were then delivered to the Spaniard as slaves.[95]

Even though the cacique was too ashamed to give his own people into slavery directly, it is likely that they were traded as slaves in the pueblo to which they were delivered. At best, their whole social orientation to family, friends, and village was dislocated. Contreras reminded the king, however, that such unjust enslavement of their fellow Indians was common enough in days before the white man arrived.[96] It should be observed, in addition, that some caciques were apparently all too willing to trade their own slaves (as well as some free Indians) to the Spaniards, albeit at reduced prices. The Crown ordered such practice to cease, even though the caciques were willing partners.[97]

Encomenderos further vitiated the prestige of the nobles by forcing caciques and principales, as well as their wives and children, to perform menial tasks. In the early days of conquest such nobles were sometimes enslaved or drafted as tamemes, but later they were further debased by having to serve as grooms for Spaniards' horses, and acting in other capacities usually reserved for slaves and naborías. Their children and wives were used as house servants, to carry needs for making huts, and to haul firewood. Such humiliations occurred, according to a royal official, despite the fact that encomiendas were granted in the royal name with the provision that caciques, principales, and their families were not to perform manual labor.

One of the most prominent offenders in that regard was Pedrarias Dávila, but there were others who used nobles held in encomienda in the same way, including royal officials and clergymen. And, the writer said, it was customary in a repartimiento of, say, 1,000 Indians to take all of them, from the cacique to the youngest children, to the mines, forcing them to travel for forty leagues with four arrobas (100 pounds) on their backs, over trails where the Christians could not even go without loads.[98] Encomenderos and their criados around León compelled the sons and grandsons of caciques to clear land, plant crops, and work the fields.[99]

Indian nobles had little choice but to submit to the orders of the Spaniards or face the consequences. Jorge de Alvarado, brother of the adelantado, was accused of frightening many señores and principales into serving his friends and relatives who held nobles in encomiendas.[100] When the principales of Huehuetenango refused to serve Juan del Espinar, their encomendero, Jorge de Alvarado gave the encomendero license to convince them otherwise by putting them in chains. Later those señores took revenge by burning some houses in the pueblos of Espinar.[101]

Encomenderos also sought to obtain land from the nobles without paying or else offering very little. The Crown issued an order in 1549 to the effect that if an encomendero wanted lands belonging to his Indians he should negotiate with the caciques and principales, and if they were willing to sell, the Spaniard would be required to pay what they asked.[102]

The Indian rulers were responsible for the maintenance of justice and order among the villagers, and to see that they tended their crops to avoid a shortage of food. As far as the encomenderos were concerned, however, their prime function was to see that the tribute quotas were met. If the collection was short, even by one real or the equivalent value in maize or cacao, the caciques were put in jail. The punishment was the same even in crown encomiendas.[103] Royal officials enforced the policy under the most trying circumstances: because of a serious pestilence in Verapaz, the Indians could not deliver the tribute quota owed to the Crown, and the alcalde mayor himself jailed the principales.[104] And as Spanish demands gradually increased, the diminished native population became even more hard pressed.

Encomenderos did not always exploit the Indian nobles with impunity, and there are numerous cases recorded in which royal officials took their encomiendas away from them. One suspects, however, that the motivation was more often politics than a sense of justice. Officials found it convenient to have vacant encomiendas because there were always relatives, friends, and supporters to be rewarded. Nonetheless, knowing that some governors awaited a pretext, encomenderos were no doubt held somewhat in check by the threat of losing their means of income.

When the governor of Nicaragua took away the encomienda from the window of an encomendero, he said it was done because she and her late husband had mistreated a cacique. Specifically, the encomendero, Mateo de Lescano (who had previously been accused of mistreating the cacique Xele in Costa Rica) and his wife, Luisa de Santiago, allegedly took the pueblo of Çindega from the señorío of the cacique don Diego. Furthermore, they took away the services he had received from his people, sequestered his goods, and finally made him a cow herder. A witness added that Lescano had frequently beaten the cacique. Mateo de Lescano was made a prisoner in his house where he remained until he died, after which Luisa lost the encomienda.[105] Of course there are many cases of encomenderos losing their encomiendas for various other reasons besides mistreating caciques.

Encomenderos and owners of estancias were forced to restrain themselves more during the second half of the century, and the killing or mutilating of a cacique became unusual by 1600. Cheating and mistreatment of them, however, did continue in different ways. More than a century following the conquest, in 1631, four principales, one of whom was an alcalde and the others *cabezas de calpul*, from the pueblo of Nuestra Señora de la Visitación, estancia of Santiago Atitlán, complained that don Gaspar de Argueta, the owner of an estancia ten leagues from their village, habitually went to pressure them into giving him Indians to work his estancia. He also demanded horses and loads of maize. Because they sometimes excused themselves from contributing, explaining that they did not have what he wanted, and also because he never paid them, Argueta beat them. The alcalde said that Argueta kicked him and punched him in the face, knocking him to the ground, and that the same treatment was given to Diego Quehu of his village. Argueta also asked them for presents of honey and chickens, which greatly irritated the principales. The Indians asked that the corregidor be advised to prevent the injustices.[106]

The role of the Church in the treatment of the Indian aristocracy is as controversial as its part in other aspects of Spanish-Indian relations. One finds both extremes. Since most of the early histories of Central America were written by churchmen, we have detailed chronicles of the many good works of clergymen, whose significant contributions are not questioned. As the preceding pages suggest, however, their presence in some instances was not an unmixed blessing. A study of Indian labor would be incomplete without making reference to some individuals in the Church whose indecorous conduct is usually not discussed in detail by the religious chroniclers. The record of the achievements of outstanding men of the Church (some of whom are discussed in the present work) are well known; to afford some balance and to arrive at a picture as representative as possible within the limited context of this essay, the negative side must be shown as well, citing specific documentation.

Some of the earliest conflicts between caciques and clergymen arose because of the intrinsic incompatibility of pagan and Christian standards of morality. Native societies were not without a sense of morality, but what seemed acceptable social behavior to them often offended the Christian sensibilities of the churchmen, who felt it incumbent upon them, in good conscience, to correct the "errors" of the Indians. It sometimes happened that the zealous friar or priest went to extremes, and others became involved in matters having little to do with the teaching of the faith.

The custom of Indian nobles having more than one woman was to be eradicated; but the caciques were reluctant to conform, and it was a troublesome issue for years. Two decades after the initial conquest, in Zinacantlán during Easter of 1546, the Dominicans insisted that baptized caciques and principales give up their mistresses, thus precipitating an unpleasant and arduous campaign.[107] Shortly thereafter Indian nobles from Chiapas testified that the friars had interfered in their lives in an offensive manner, causing great scandals. The Dominicans, they said, went to their houses and threatened them, laid hands on their persons, whipping and beating them like slaves. Those grievous affronts to the nobles were observed by the maceguales under their jurisdiction, making the treatment all the more humiliating.[108]

A notorious affair occurred in Chiapas about the same time, in which caciques found themselves in the center of a controversy between the encomenderos and the Dominicans. In 1548, don Diego Ramírez conducted an inquiry into alleged persecutions of the friars by the encomenderos, and what emerged from the testimony has a bearing on the subject at hand. Don Pedro, cacique of Chiapas, held in encomienda by Baltasar Guerra, protested that, although he was a good Christian and a friend of the Dominicans, he was unjustly accused by some of the friars who were moved by passion. As a result he was deprived of his cacicazgo by the alcalde, and was persecuted in other ways.

Another cacique of Chiapas named don Juan complained to Gonzalo de Ovalle, the alcalde, that fray Pedro Calvo had whipped him so badly that his back was full of cuts. Worse, the lashes were administered in front of the native villagers who were very upset by the scandalous treatment of their leader. The alcalde told him to return to Chiapas, and the cacique was so offended by the whole affair that he mounted an unruly horse to ride away and was thrown and dragged to death. The shocked villagers fled to the mountains.[109]

In 1546, according to the testimony of an Indian merchant, Joan Martínez, the majordomo of Baltasar Guerra in the pueblo-encomienda of Chiapas, had told don Juan, some principales, as well as maceguales, that they could only go to church once a day, whereas before they had gone at least twice. Furthermore, Martínez told the Indians to ignore the friars and not to give them any food. In that instance, as in others, the Indians were being caught in the quarrel between the Dominicans and the encomenderos over control of the natives. That was seen as background to

the incident of the whipping of the cacique, but another witness said that
Calvo had punished don Juan because the cacique had taken some fodder
to the sugar mill of Guerra, which the friar said was not an obligation of the
Indians, and that he ordered don Juan not to do it again. But when the
witness, a Spanish vecino, remonstrated with Calvo over the disagreement, the friar answered that the whipping was for a very different reason
and that the cacique had given him good reason for punishment. Calvo
added that the encomenderos were using the affair as a pretext for having
him thrown out of the village.

When the alcalde Gonzalo de Ovalle, who was also the encomendero of
Zinacantlán, ordered don Cristóbal and other principales not to give food
to the Dominicans and not to obey them, the nobles agreed out of fear.
The royal oidor Rogel went to Chiapas to reassess the tributes, which he
cut in half. As soon as he departed, Ovalle's wife, Ana de Torres, called in
don Cristóbal and told him that Rogel's action meant nothing, and that
now he was gone the Indians were to revert to the former tribute quota.
The cacique reported her orders to the friars, who told him that the
Indians were not to pay more than the revised assessment. In that bewil-
dering situation the Indians had no place to turn.

Miguel Naca, a principal of the pueblo of Chiapas, said that in 1545,
Guerra had summoned him and told him to let the alcaldes of Ciudad Real
know that the Indians did not want the friars because they ate too many
chickens, eggs, and fish. Guerra said that two Dominicans would suffice to
serve all their needs. The principal replied innocently that the friars were
of Guerra's own kind and that the encomendero himself had given the
friars the lots for their buildings, and that now he wanted them to leave.
Guerra apparently took that for impertinence and kicked the cacique and
cuffed him about. Then Guerra called the *naguatato* (interpreter), Antonio Notoya, and in Naca's presence ordered him to go to the pueblo of
Chiapas and tell the other principales that Naca was a friend of the friars
and that they should send to the city another Indian "de mas conçon"
(probably for *cónsone*, harmonious).

But the other caciques did not want to evict the friars either. The
interpreter (Chiapenecan to Mexican) stated that Guerra told him and
Naca to call their alcaldes to tell them that two friars were enough (when
there were at least six of them), and that all of them were eating too much.
They replied that they did not want to go before the alcaldes because they
did not know the wishes of the caciques and principales of the pueblo of
Chiapas. It was at that point that the encomendero began knocking the
principal Naca about and calling him "perro." The next day Guerra told
Notoya to do what he had asked Naca to do, and the witness replied that
he was unsure of the will of the principales.[109]

There were other feuds in which the caciques were the victims, particularly in cases where they were inclined to favor one faction over the other. The friars had ways other than physical means to punish the caciques. When a Dominican ordered that no Spaniards were to live in a village, a sixty-five-year-old native regidor rented a house to a Spaniard. With the assistance of the corregidor, the friar had the regidor jailed in the cell of a monastery for three days, after which he was displayed in the pulpit of the church. He stood with a cord around his neck, holding a candle in his bound hands during the Mass, and remained that way later while the friar inveighed publicly against the Indian's crime.[110]

Conflict between caciques and clergymen was by no means the rule. On the contrary, there was often close cooperation and good feelings. As noted previously, Indian leaders could be most helpful in the conversion of scattered Indian groups, and caciques frequently indicated their contentment under the Church.[111] A cacique who had helped the Dominicans in converting natives in Verapaz was thanked by the king, who then ordered the chief to perform the same service in Nicaragua.[112]

Churchmen were well aware of the value of the Indian nobility as an agent through which religion and culture could be transmitted to the Indian masses. Fray Tomás de la Torre, one of the most astute Dominicans, wrote that "we are very certain that the door through which the faith has to enter the Indians is the caciques and the elders."[113] Assuredly, that door was not wide open because of the depressed circumstances of the caciques, which often embittered them and caused them to lose respect among their peoples. The maceguales, without firm guidance from their traditional leaders, became idle or went into trading to the neglect of their fields. More to the point here, the lessening authority of the caciques rendered them less effective as conduits of the faith.

The clergymen, for their part, did not always serve the cause well. Eighteen months after the foregoing report, Tomás de la Torre, acting as visitador general, investigated the behavior of priests, revealing that some men of the cloth had contributed in personal ways to the fallen status of the native aristocracy.[114] He found that one village priest had demanded payments of cacao and then whipped caciques because they did not deliver enough of the fruit. Another cacique's wife was molested by the priest while the cacique was absent from the village, and the woman finally had to leave until her husband returned. The priest was also in the habit of putting caciques in the pillory, sometimes for a couple of nights. When another cacique hesitated to pay money over and above the demand for cacao, the priest hit him, bloodying his nose, and afterwards pulled his hair.

The report revealed that another priest whipped a noble because he did not give the priest some vinegar he asked for. A dean of the church was accused of selling watered wine to a cacique for exorbitant prices. The diluted grape was apparently strong enough, for the cacique was said to be continuously drunk, even during visits to the dean's residence, where he dined frequently. At the same time, the dean was carrying on an affair with the cacique's wife, one María of "mala fama," and finally the cacique simply gave his woman to the dean, after which she became his mistress, living openly in his house.

Also recorded was the case of a vicar who slept with the married daughter of a cacique, and when the girl's husband went to look for her, he caught the couple in *flagrante delicto* ("vio al dicho padre sobre su muger."). The affair lasted for some time. The vicar summoned the cuckold several times, and when he refused to appear, the vicar mistreated him.

Another priest was angry because the Indians of a village did not give enough contribution for a fiesta. He confronted about twenty principales in the church and beat them with the bridle from his horse, blaming them for the poor offering of the village. Other cases are documented in the inquiry showing that priests had allegedly beaten native señores, who were always expected to contribute more than the maceguales, even though in some cases they were poor. For example, when a cacique married, the priest demanded six times the fee of a commoner's marriage.

Francisco Quicaxcoyol testified that when a padre arrived in the village on one occasion the people were not gathered to greet him because they were out of town. Nevertheless, the witness and a principal were stripped of their shirts and whipped with a leather strap. The same priest on another occasion entered the house of a deceased cacique and forcibly took his pleasure with the frightened widow, all of which was admitted by the woman and was public knowledge. When the same cleric had sexual relations with two virgins from among those he was teaching in the church, a cacique took the two girls before the vicar and related the circumstances of their defloration by the priest. The cacique was told to hold his tongue. The priest was also charged with kicking various principales and breaking sticks over their heads for not taking him enough food. On one occasion, for what the priest considered insolence, he tied a principal's hands, tore his shirt to shreds, and beat him in the face until his nose bled. Then he kicked him, reducing him to tears in the presence of a cacique, another principal, and some Spaniards. When the principal complained later he was punished again

Various other priests were accused of intimidating caciques by threatening them with hanging, beatings, or imprisonment. Out of fear of the priests, they were coerced into providing goods, services, and money.

It may be observed that there was rivalry and bitterness between seculars and the friars, particularly where the Dominicans were involved. Well aware of the delicate nature of his task, the visitor general summoned three Dominicans and made them swear that they had done nothing to prejudice the case of the priests by inducing the caciques and principales to give false testimony. One of them said that, on the contrary, he stopped one Indian from testifying because he had received abuses and that his testimony would be distorted because he was clever in the ways of litigation ("era muy ladino para se saver quexar"). The witnesses had been cautioned that it was a sin to perjure themselves to the detriment of a priest. Other matters were not delved into because of the nature of certain secret and religious aspects of the investigation: ("no se llamaron mas testigos por ser cosas secretas y tocantes a sacerdotes").[115]

Royal policy did not always help the relationship of the Indian nobles with clergymen, and sometimes the caciques were put in difficult positions. Because the priests were said to be demanding too much food and service from the Indians, a standard list was drawn to which each priest was to adhere. The audiencia required that the caciques and principales, along with native alcaldes, were to be responsible for enforcing the order, under pain of losing their cacicazgos. That put the Indian nobles in direct confrontation with the *clérigos*, inviting disharmony, even though the intent may have been to shore up the prestige of the caciques. In fact, it was another, perhaps inevitable, situation in which the authority of priests was being challenged by traditional native order, a conflict which should have been clear by the time of the ruling, in 1561. The order not only listed the food to be given, but specified that an "old woman" should make bread, and that an Indian should carry fodder. Indians were not to pay any money to priests, nor to pay them for services incurred on their inspections.[116]

Village priests of strong character often dominated Indian leaders, but it was the Dominicans who were most forceful and influential. The president of the audiencia stated that in the Dominican stronghold of Chiapas the caciques made their judgments based on what the friars ordered.[117] Usually the friars punished their charges with impunity, but not always. In Nicaragua fray Juan Piçarro went to a crown town, without any soldiers for a guard, to spread the gospel. For some reason, he whipped publicly the brother of a cacique, along with two principales, all of whom were Christians. At that point the cacique and principales seized fray Juan and three Indian boys who were in his party, and rose up in rebellion.[118]

Because of their pervasive influence on Indian affairs, the Dominican activities in Central America merit a complete and scholarly examination based on thorough examination of the manuscripts.

While the native aristocracy was broken and reduced to a miserable state compared to the high station it enjoyed in previous times, one must not lose sight of the fact that its prehispanic role was in several respects tyrannical. It·may be argued that the Spaniards, to considerable extent, released the maceguales from the grasp of their native rulers, except that the Spanish solution was a dubious improvement. It is probably fair to say that *eventually* the condition of the commoners improved over their situation at the point of conquest, but when that time arrived is debatable. Caution in making such conclusions is advisable, however, for Professor Gibson, writing of pre-conquest Aztec laborers, refers to a sense of joy involved in much of their work.[119] Perhaps such sentiments were also prevalent before the arrival of the Spaniards in Central America. And the possibility must be admitted that the reverence, perhaps affection, of the maceguales for the caciques outweighed the negative aspects of their rule.

In spite of Spanish stewardship, many caciques continued to abuse their own people in a variety of ways. At times it was indirect—that is, caciques allowed others to extort villagers when they probably could have prevented it. To illustrate, a long-time resident of Santiago stated that some Indians from Tlaxcala and other parts of Mexico went to some of the local villages where, with the consent of the caciques, they mistreated the macegual farmers, eating their food like the retainers of a lord "in the seignioral town," and doing other damage. "It would be enough," the observer said, "for the Indians to pay their tributes to their cacique and to the señor who held them in encomienda without their having other *señorejos* to give them orders and to take what they have."[120] While Indian leaders were often powerless to prevent misdeeds by Spaniards, they should have been able to check the Indians from Mexico.

In a more direct form of abuse, caciques rounded up vagabond Indians who went from village to village scrounging food, and sold them as slaves to other Indians.[121] Testimony for a lawsuit arising out of a conflict of interest during the conquest of Costa Rica illustrates the callous disregard for human life on the part of one cacique. A rebellious Indian slave girl owned by a Spaniard ran away and took some other girls with her. Soldiers pursued and captured them in the house of a cacique and returned them to the Spanish camp. The cacique Coasta, under whose jurisdiction she came, was angry because the Spaniards had not killed her as soon as they found her. According to the cacique, the girl was a chronic troublemaker who would entice all the other women to leave the camp and would cause great trouble if they did not kill her. It was customary among the Indians themselves, Coasta said, to punish offenders of her sort with a cruel death, such as burning or drowning. One witness affirmed that the cacique then ordered her burned in conformity with their customs, and Coasta was present while she was tied up on a *barbacoa*. A fire was lighted beneath her and she was burned alive.[122]

Although his view was self-serving, a Spaniard testifying about the conquest of Salvador said that with the pacification of the land, the Indians had more freedom than before and more security. They were no longer subject to attacks by their ancient enemies, and less obligated to their caciques and principales, "each of whom was lord."[123]

A frequent cause of mistreatment of villagers by their native officials was the shortage of tribute. Since the officials themselves would be punished if the quota was not fulfilled, they in turn castigated the maceguales who were short in their payments, or who in any way caused trouble.[124] However, caciques often cheated their own people in the collection of tributes, and the Crown ordered that, to prevent the practice, villagers should know precisely what they owed so that their leaders would not defraud them.[125]

A few days later the Crown elaborated on the problem in new instructions, noting that the caciques and señores naturales were so oppressive toward the Indians of their cacicazgos that they made them serve in everything they wished, and demanded more tribute than they could pay, so that they were fatigued and vexed. Just as the natives were assessed for tribute paid to Spaniards, so should there be an assessment for tributes owed to caciques. Moreover, there should be a classification of the service and vassalage owed to the nobles by the commoners. The audiencia was ordered to determine if what the Indians were giving was based on customs of antiquity inherited from their ancestors, by justice and law, or whether it was imposed tyrannically against reason and justice. If the latter, it was to be corrected.[126]

Despite the royal injunction, the abuse continued. In 1563, the audiencia said that it had always attempted to identify natural caciques and to make sure they had enough for their sustenance, without their provisions being part of the regular tribute, because it would give rise to the robbing of the tribute-paying maceguales by the caciques.[127]

Miguel Agia, having spent many years in Guatemala, had a low opinion of the caciques, whom he thought were more cruel and tyrannical than the worst Spanish tyrant in the world. And he warned that the commoners should be paid directly for their work, because if their wages were given to their caciques they would never receive them.[128]

In Honduras some encomenderos made agreements with miners to the effect that they would provide Indian laborers from the encomiendas in return for money, and the caciques joined in those enterprises, selling the maceguales' labor. Informed of the illicit practice, the Crown ordered the grievances remedied, but, even at the late date of 1581, the order of Philip II did not have an emphatic ring about it.[129] Furthermore, notwithstanding the royal order against it, caciques were imposing special taxes on their people in the form of money and goods.[130] Extortion of the maceguales by their own leaders continued; by the turn of the century a Spanish official reported that the Indian governor and other principales of the pueblo of Çamayaque were accepting wine from the alcalde mayor as a bribe for helping him cheat the maceguales in a transaction concerning cacao.[131] Petty graft was evidently widespread among Indian officials.

Although native leaders were to bear much of the responsibility for governing the Indians, they often did so in a lordly manner reminiscent of their pre-conquest attitudes. When Spanish officials tried to oversee their conduct in the matter of government, the caciques frequently regarded the supervision as interference and protested. That was the case when in 1568 an alcalde mayor sent his lieutenant to live in a village because the cacique was not maintaining order and good morals.[132] In a more specific instance, the alcalde mayor exiled a cacique for a year and deprived him of his position of governor of the pueblo of Çamayaque for two years for having cruelly whipped an Indian woman.[133]

The extent to which Spanish officials curbed the caciques depended naturally enough on their own personal qualities and abilities. Corregidores placed in Indian communities to see to their good order were often appointed with little regard to their qualifications. Indeed, the audiencia did not consider the position of much importance, and rather saw the post as one to be given as a reward in lieu of an encomienda or a pension. In 1572, however, the Crown instructed the oidores to take the charge more seriously, and among the corregidores' obligations was that of seeing that maceguales were not mistreated by their own caciques.[134]

The excesses of caciques could be contained to some degree when more important Spanish officials were in the vicinity, but there was, for example, no alcalde mayor in Chiapas for some time; consequently, the caciques-gobernadores were oppressing the Indians with impunity, since the audiencia was eighty leagues distant.[135]

Investigations of caciques were carried out during the regular visitas of judges of the audiencia. When licenciado Diego García de Palacio undertook a *visita general* to certain pueblos in Nicaragua he found Pedro Ximénez, the native governor of Poçolteguilla, guilty of crimes, as was the cacique don Juan. In addition, the cacique of Guaçama and the cacique and alcalde of Agangasca were charged with wrongdoing. All of them were imprisoned.[136]

Government officials within the pueblos were usually from the traditional ruling class of the natives, except in those cases where others were imposed by Spaniards. Some idea of the structure of village governments in Central America can be gathered from a suit of 1587 against the towns of Tecpan Atitlán and Quetzaltenango regarding alleged overdue tribute for the Crown. The corregidor, don Fernando de Ayala, was instructed to take the testimony of the governor of Tecpan Atitlán, along with the alcaldes, regidores, *calpuleros*, and other principales. Of twenty-one principales named, only eleven could sign their names, which indicates that the earlier plans to educate the native aristocracy had met with indifferent success. Titles mentioned were the governor, two alcaldes, five regidores, one alguacil mayor, and one escribano. Of those the only one addressed as "don" was the governor, but five others of the twenty-one were also given that honor, suggesting that a total of six were actually caciques, while the others were apparently of a slightly lower rank. The group as a whole is described as being "todos yndios principales y cabeças de calpul."

All the Indians lived in sections that were called variously barrios, *parcialidades*, or calpules. Sometimes Spaniards called the *cobradores* (tribute collectors) calpules, but the proper term for them was calpuleros or cabezas de calpul. The cobradores were to gather tribute from the sections for which they had responsibility and to deliver the goods to the alcaldes and regidores. It was emphasized that the placing of the calpuleros was done by the Indians, not by Spaniards. The testimony of Diego Ramírez, the contador of the audiencia, affirmed that it was certain that the *concejos*, alcaldes, and regidores of the pueblos, who were called tlatoque, appointed the collectors. The Spanish treasurer noted that the calpuleros were assigned, not by the encomenderos or royal officials, but by the tlatoque, and one of them kept a book of accounts, noting who had paid and when. A representative of the treasurer said that neither the calpuleros nor the principales had ever been empowered by the treasurer to collect the tribute from the maceguales and the community. Rather, the calpuleros were named by the maceguales themselves.

The calpuleros took the tribute to the *casa de comunidad* of the pueblo where it was given to the governor and alcaldes, and they in turn took it to the royal officials in the case of a crown town, or to the encomendero. Officials issued a *carta de pago* as a receipt when the tribute was delivered.

The treasurer said that on several occasions when back tribute was not paid he put the caciques and alcaldes in jail, but that the audiencia had ordered them released. In his opinion nothing more could be done about it than to imprison the tlatoque, because it was well known that the individual Indian had nothing but a small hut, a grinding stone and an axe.

Since the native leaders were threatened with imprisonment if the quota was not met, they pressured the commoners to meet village tribute obligations. A Franciscan friar testified that caciques jailed some of the maceguales, but that he did not know whether or not it was done at the behest of royal officials.

In a power of attorney dated before the corregidor in 1592, the crown town of Tecpan Atitlán showed a list of principales and cabezas de calpul. There were fifty-one names shown, of whom eight were addressed as "don." In a similar document for Quetzaltenango about the same time, twelve principales were named, four of whom were given the same designation. Those examples indicate that there was considerable variation in the percentage of the principales who were apparently caciques.[137]

As much as possible, the Indians were expected to govern themselves, under the watchful eyes of the padres and royal officials. A royal order of 1549 stated that Indians should be brought together gradually in large settlements in whatever locations they chose, so that they could more conveniently be indoctrinated and governed. They would be given the faculty of electing their own officials, as it was being done in Tlaxcala.[138] The Indians were to provide for alcaldes ordinarios who would oversee justice in civil matters, as well as municipal council members (regidores cadañeros) to be elected annually by the Indians, who would be charged with maintaining the community welfare. In addition, towns were to have alguaciles and other officials to keep order, along with jails. All pueblos were to have community corrals for livestock, at least for sheep and swine, and merchants should be resident to provide for the needs of travelers. Work horses should also be available for rent.[139]

It has already been noted that Indians were anxious to be officials (at least by 1571 in Soconusco) because of exemption from tributes; however, because of restrictions imposed by the Spanish bureaucracy, being an official was often a dubious distinction, except for the local prestige and some authority. Aside from the responsibilities for providing laborers and delivering the full tribute quotas, failure of which led to severe punishment, there was only a small salary attached to the positions. It varied with the post of course. Generally speaking, being Indian governor carried worthwhile perquisites. Alcaldes, on the other hand, were elected annually and had to report to Spanish authorities for confirmation in their posts every year. That sometimes meant traveling as far as thirty leagues, the cost of which was often more than the salaries they received for the year.[140]

In 1559 the Crown referred to the same vexation faced by Indian alguaciles who had to appear before the audiencia for confirmation. In addition to the expense and lost time, officials sometimes fell ill on the journey and occasionally some of them died. Moreover, their appearance served no purpose other than to pay two reales for each confirmation to the escribano of the audiencia. Consequently, it was ordered that the requirement be abolished and that escribanos in other respects had better moderate their whole scale of fees.[141]

It comes as no great surprise that the firm order was not observed; many years later, in 1585, the audiencia commented that the cost and inconvenience involved in the officials traveling to Santiago for confirmation was too much. An added problem was that assumption of their duties was deferred by the long journey. Henceforth, the judges ruled, only those Indian officials within a radius of five leagues would be required to go, and the basic charge would be only two tostones for each cabildo. Other more distant pueblos would have their officials confirmed with the closest royal official within five leagues, that is, a Spanish governor, alcalde mayor, or corregidor. In those instances where the village was more than five leagues from any Spanish official, a special commission would be given to the tlatoque and cabildos to pass on the staffs of justice to the elected officials.[142]

In spite of the network of native officials and the supervision of the clergy and Spanish bureaucrats, there was often great disorder in the Indian settlements.[143] The audiencia judge Ramírez wrote that in the vicinity of Santiago the encomenderos were not abusing the Indians, but their own officials were. There was no justice, he wrote, and widows and poor people in particular were being robbed and put upon as their lands and goods were being stolen by other Indians. There was no protection for orphans who were losing all goods left them by their parents because their nearest relatives and neighbors were simply taking them. But the worst offenders, Ramírez said, were the caciques and principales in the villages.

There were very great public sins being committed among the villagers, he went on, and most of them went unpunished because they never came to the attention of the audiencia; and although royal policy had made provisions for Indian alcaldes to maintain order, they themselves were the greatest offenders. Not only did they neglect their responsibilities, but their positions gave them more authority with which to steal from their fellow Indians. Ordinances had been given to instruct them about their behavior, but the alcaldes neither understood nor observed them. It did not help much that oidores visited pueblos because there were so many settlements covering great distances that the native officials knew that a visiting judge would be in their villages only two or three days, or eight at the most, and after the inspection they did not have to worry about another one for two years. The judges did not have time to visit even a tenth of the villages, nor all the Spanish towns for that matter. Accordingly, the maceguales were afraid to complain to the investigators, knowing that when the judge left there would be retribution. Around Santiago at least, the writer asserted, Indians were well treated by Spaniards because of the proximity of the audiencia, but even Indians in nearby villages were mistreated by their own administrators.

Ramírez recommended that for four or five large Indian towns a Spanish official be appointed to check constantly on their affairs, and to teach the Indians how to elect their alcaldes and regidores and what to discuss in their cabildo meetings so that they could live in the manner of Spanish communities. He suggested that there were many Spaniards who could and would undertake such tasks for little salary. Certainly the audiencia judges could not by themselves regulate the villages, or even know what was going on, nor were there enough of the religious to do the work.[144]

The suggestion of Cerrato years before did not anticipate the problems of communication with the audiencia. He had ordered that Indian alcaldes were to have administrative independence from the Spanish alcaldes ordinarios in order to avoid the pressures and abuses that often resulted. The alcaldes ordinarios sometimes had conflicts of interest, and many were less than dedicated officials. But Cerrato's instruction for the Indian alcaldes to be responsible only to the audiencia was impractical; and years later the audiencia revoked the provision and made the Indian officials subject once again to the alcaldes ordinarios. In turn, that led to new vexations and prejudices against the Indians, as a result of which the king ordered the audiencia to inform him fully on the matter.[145]

The judges responded many months later, stating that they had in fact forbidden alcaldes ordinarios from being involved in Indian affairs, but that the native alcaldes had been made subordinate to the alcaldes mayores of the province. If, however, some alcaldes ordinarios had involved themselves it was because their areas had no alcaldes mayores, and there were minor matters which the audiencia could not deal with because of being so far away.[146]

The alcaldes mayores were often at odds with the Indian officials. The alcalde mayor of Zapotitlán wrote that all the Indian governors were generally harmful to their own people, because they stole not only community properties but those of individuals as well. They extorted the maceguales in a variety of ways. He noted that the viceroy of New Spain had removed Indian officials, an act of which the alcalde mayor approved.[147]

An obvious detriment to good order was the fact that so many people gave orders to Indian officials—they were ordered about by encomenderos, priests, friars, and various Spanish officials. Moreover, in their own communities the native hierarchy limited them even more. The Indian governor, as well as various caciques and principales, could check them. As one example, the alcaldes and regidores were charged with seeing that milpas of maize and wheat were planted and harvested, and that none of the grain was sold without the permission of the governor or judge, under pain of privation of office, 200 lashes, and perpetual banishment.[148]

The real authorities among the Indians were their governors, who were usually caciques as well, and they administered justice, often without much consideration of the alcaldes.[149] The Crown noted in 1582 that Indian governors in pueblos of Chiapas were superior to the alcaldes and that most of the alcaldes were not elected, but rather named by the Dominican friars. The audiencia was ordered to remove the alcaldes and to give an opinion as to whether it would be convenient to retain Indian governors, or to determine who could best serve that function. Whatever may have been the temporary measure, neither of the Indian positions was long removed.[150]

The depreciation of the status of native lords by the Spanish occupation inevitably had very serious consequences for Indian society. The breakdown of the lords' authority and prestige led to confusion and disorder on the part of the maceguales, who served many masters. Moreover, the humiliation of the native aristocracy was an abasement of all Indians. Of those caciques and principales who survived the violent years, a few resisted and paid the price, while others became willing satraps. A number of them were able to maintain some semblance of respectability, and a few were able to live in ease, if not in splendor.[151] But in all too many cases, the dignified and haughty nobles of times past were reduced to pathetic sycophants.

14

Indian Women and the Spaniards

NATIVE WOMEN, like the nobility, formed a discrete segment of the community, requiring separate discussion here. The arrival of the Spaniards in Central America had a more varied effect on Indian women than on any other group in native society. The traditional family unit was often destroyed when the conquerors demanded the women's labor and their bodies as well. The result frequently was a social dislocation of tragic dimensions. Yet indias born into the nobility (sometimes loosely designated *cacicas*) or fortunate enough to be endowed with pleasing physical features sometimes found themselves in favorable circumstances. As concubines or, occasionally, wives they bore the children of Spaniards and reared them, and thus as a privileged minority led lives of leisure, enjoying consideration and often affection from the Europeans. For many Indian women of different social strata life did not change substantially from their pre-conquest roles. But for a sizable number of them life under the Spaniards was one of great hardship and anguish.

It would be misleading to ignore the fact that there was considerable diversity in the social and economic conditions of indias before the conquest as well as after. While those of the elite class led lives of comparative luxury, the indias of lower strata often suffered hardship and sometimes misery. At the point of European contact some were slaves, others also put in long days of hard labor, and many were left orphans or widows because of the frequent warfare. High infant mortality was general. Nor should one conclude that the morals of an idyllic society were corrupted without bearing in mind that in the native culture prostitution was common and that restraints on sexual behavior were often slight, marriage was often inclined to informality, and concubinage was widespread.

In sum, while the conquerors rearranged things somewhat and did violence to the traditional positions of many women, it was a question of degree rather than kind in many instances. As in most other societies of

304

the age, women, excluding the pampered noblewomen or favored courtesans, were given little consideration.[1]

Indian women of the macegual or sub-macegual classes were probably treated no worse than their counterparts in many contemporary Oriental societies, and of course even European women were subjected to indignities that were barbarous by our lights. If marriages were arranged in other contemporary societies with little voice in the matter by the women, it does not then seem so strange that Indians frequently treated their women as property. Prominent Spanish conquerors like Cortés and Alvarado were given maidens as gifts by Indian rulers who sometimes offered their own daughters. Caciques of Indian villages continued for some time to give indias to importunate Spaniards, although often under duress. But there is evidence to suggest that many Indian rulers put little value on females and often used them as commodities to be traded for favors from the conquerors. As noted above, caciques frequently mistreated women and cruelly punished female transgressors.

In the first instance indias were the objects of the invaders' lust. That did not necessarily degrade the relationship. We are assured that Cortés treated with respect doña Marina, who bore a son recognized by the conqueror. Pedro de Alvarado had as his concubine doña Luisa, daughter of the powerful Tlaxcalan cacique Xicotencatl, who bore his children and was held in affection. There were many other less celebrated relationships that produced offspring, and while documentation for such an assumption is scanty, it seems safe to say that some women no doubt achieved a level of domestic bliss.

In the early years of conquest and pacification the sexual liaisons were more likely to be ephemeral, owing at least in part to the nomadic habits of the conquerors. While the indias were often raped, without doubt on many occasions sexual acts were entered into with the consent of the woman, since Indian attitudes were less inhibited by moralistic preachments or legalities than the Spanish. It is well not to generalize too much regarding sexual practices because of the diversity of customs among the tribes encountered in Central America, but puritanical attitudes seem to have been largely absent. Indian prostitutes could make the transition from Indian men to Spaniards with relative ease; the daughter of a cacique was more commonly reserved for a white man of substance, as befitted her exalted rank. For indias of the general macegual class the adjustment was more difficult.

Concubinage began with the first contact of the two races.[2] Indias, taken by force, given by caciques, or simply attracted by baubles offered by the conquerors, shared not only the Spaniards' beds, but their hardships as well. Following the Spaniards on campaigns, they prepared food, drew water, dressed wounds, carried baggage, and bore children. Some of them did not survive such rigors, and those who did had no security; often they were sent away or abandoned when they became pregnant, or when a Spaniard found another more to his liking. Eventually their men usually married Spanish women more suitable for community status, or the wives of the married men arrived from Spain. Nonetheless, as the lands were ultimately pacified and most of the men settled, a good number maintained the relationship with their indias.

The prevalance of those arrangements was such that Bishop Pedraza of Honduras wrote in shocked terms to the Crown by 1547 that, in his estimation, there were not ten Spaniards in the province who did not have mistresses (some of whom it must be remarked were Spanish women and mestizas). The practice was so entrenched, he said, that the Spaniards knew no other way of life and did not know how to live without their illegal women.

The vices began, according to the bishop, when the Spaniards were mere boys coming to the Indies, and he requested that youths and other bachelors be prevented from going to the colonies because they were corrupted by the licentious milieu. As a result of their loose living, one saw boys of thirteen or fourteen dead from consumption or venereal diseases which manifested themselves by pus-filled tumors (bubas). Others presented the piteous sight of fleshy growths under their chins. The young men became vagabonds interested only in war, rebellion, and uprisings, because they had no wives or children, nor anything to lose. Those drifters came and went, committing crimes and insults. Only married Spaniards should be allowed, in the prelate's opinion, and they should bring their wives with them so that they would not take concubines. Callow youths picked up dirty vices, especially those involving "cosas de carnalidad," because of the easy access to so many Indian girls, who were themselves corrupted since childhood, or so the bishop said. Consequently, even boys of ten and twelve years were as debauched and vice-ridden as many of the older men.

In Honduras many of the boys were crippled and covered with pustules, dying from ulcers and consumption. No doubt with some exaggeration, Pedraza remarked that all of the indias were born with bubas. He said that he had baptized many recently-born girls and that they were covered with the tumors. Indians told him that most, if not all, of the girls were born that way because they contracted the affliction in their mothers' wombs. Few of the male babies, however, were infected. Spaniards, especially those much given to "esta fruta carnal de las yndias," contracted the disease. Footloose youths in particular, free from parental and other restraints, spent a good deal of their time pursuing Indian girls in one village after another.

The moral suasion of the Church was ineffective, the bishop admitted, because the Spaniards did not fear God, the clergymen, censure, or even excommunication—on the contrary, they ridiculed them. Nor was secular pressure of any use, primarily because the officials themselves were keeping concubines. The alcalde of Trujillo had three or four Indian women in his house, and so did the alguacil. When a vecino lodged a complaint about the immorality of the settlers, the officials laughed. Witnesses were not only scorned, but threatened as well. Another alcalde kept three indias publicly as his mistresses, and he had children by all of them. One of the oidores of the audiencia maintained two Indian women, one of whom was married. In the view of the bishop, those who kept women should be put in pillories or chains and exiled from the land, but the very ones obligated to execute such punishment were guilty of the same transgressions. They did not believe such conduct was sinful.[3]

The bishop was surely aware that the most flagrant offenses involving concubinage were committed by members of the clergy. Many dedicated ecclesiastics deplored that aspect of clerical behavior, not only from the moral considerations, but also because it caused a loss of respect among the Indians for the Church, which did incalculable damage to the conversion process. One such high-minded person was fray Tomás de la Torre, who reported scandalous incidents. He recounted that on one Sunday as Indians were leaving Mass they came across padre Francisco Pacheco near the orchard by the Dominican monastery lying on his habit with a woman. Indian alguaciles tried to seize him, but the padre mounted a horse and escaped punishment.[4]

The investigation undertaken by Tomás de la Torre and another Dominican by the name of Cárdenas revealed that many of the clérigos kept women, in addition to engaging in other kinds of dissolute behavior. The report is very damaging, but Torre, Provincial of the Order of Santo Domingo, was a man of integrity and more credible than most, and the investigation was based on testimony of the many witnesses.[5]

From the standpoint of the indias concerned, life in the household of a clergyman was often quite comfortable, and on the whole they seem to have been treated well, if for no other reason than to avoid scandal. Vicars and other religious frequently traveled to visit Indian villages with retinues that included their Indian women, and in such instances it was alleged that some of the indias were criminally treated and died or ran away to the hills.[6]

Obviously the treatment of indias by men of the Church depended upon the individual and the personal relationship. On the whole, it is probably true that the women were molested less by ecclesiastics than other groups, except when they were charged with some violation, such as witchcraft.[7] While it was not a rarity for priests to have affairs with Indian women, they were usually discreet, avoiding incidents involving forcible access. Exceptions are noted, such as the case of padre Sebastián de Morales, who took an india named Catalina from the house of a Spaniard in Huehuetlán. When she resisted his advances, he whipped her into submission and had his way with her. His alleged protector in this case was none other than the roguish Dr. Mexía, who was supposedly informed of the misdeed, but did nothing because of his friendship for the priest.[8] Mexía was not always so cooperative with the friars, however. Some Dominicans had been putting indias in jail, and one of them complained to the oidor that she was unjustly jailed. Mexía freed her, for which reason the bishop excommunicated him, or so Mexía said.[9]

The presence of women in the quarters of ecclesiastics did not necessarily indicate immoral behavior, but it invited comment. The Crown observed that friars of the Order of Merced kept in their houses "suspicious indias," which was giving a bad example to the natives. That was to cease, and the Mercedarians were to keep no indias as naborías or in any other category in their establishments.[10] Perhaps the Mercedarians conformed to the regulation, but some Dominicans continued to keep indias, at least in their kitchens.[11] A later order repeated that ecclesiastics were forbidden to have any women around their quarters, except for those who did the cooking. Even then, it was specified that the cook would be an "old" woman, who was to be replaced at the end of each week.[12] Although perhaps not directly involved in consorting with indias, one clergyman was accused of keeping in his house Spaniards with their Indian mistresses, by whom they had children.[13]

Indian women were kept by some of the most prominent men in the land, beginning with Alvarado and continuing with later royal officials, as in the case of the oidor Herrera of the first audiencia. Among others, the tradition continued with the priapic Dr. Mexía, also an audiencia judge. He was involved in scandalous love affairs with various women, and he discriminated against no racial or social group in pursuit of his interests. Mexía regularly took to his house indias, as well as mestizas and mulatas, all of which excited murmurings among the citizens. He had a trapdoor where he sometimes concealed the women, but on fiesta days they could be seen at his windows during the celebrations, thereby eliciting more commentary. It was noted that one day during such festivities, Mexía, "lacking the decency, circumspection, and honesty consistent with the office of royal oidor," waited on the indias, serving them supper with his own hands. He was accused of keeping the girls around his house when he went out, as well as when he had business within.[14]

Mexía's conduct was exaggerated for an oidor, but he was by no means unusual in his social conduct measured by other standards. The governor of Honduras, although he denied it, was charged with having sexual relations with Indian maidens, as well as with a married india.[15] Far from effectively checking concubinage, royal officials even fostered it to some extent by allowing indias, mulatas, and other women to live at or near the mines, which was illegal.[16] With no serious opposition from the government, Spaniards openly kept mistresses of diverse racial types. Of the lack of Spanish morals, Pedraza said the Spaniards were like "Moors without a king," with some settlers keeping two or three indias in their houses. He knew of one Spaniard who had for five years slept with his two concubines at the same time.

The officials, he said, were the worst offenders, and far from doing anything about correcting the immoral situation, they made light of it.[17] The alcalde mayor of San Salvador allowed his mulatto alguacil to keep an india as his concubine. The official was in no position to moralize, since it was his habit to demand beautiful young women for the night when he stayed over in an Indian village. Nor could he object strenuously to the scandalous behavior of his lieutenant, Joan de Hojeda, who forced a comely widow to sleep with him.[18] High officials sometimes raped Spanish women as well, even married ones,[19] though to be sure that was far less common than assaults on indias and other women of color. And while the former was a serious crime, the mistreatment of Indian women was by no means condoned; some corregidores were at pains to establish that indias were well treated under their administrations.[20]

Whatever may have been the harm issuing from the moral aspect of such relationships, the more serious consideration was the dislocations in native society. So long as indias were willing partners, the problem was minimized, but there were tragic consequences involved in the frequent practice of taking women by force. Rape is common enough in the history of conquering armies, although it usually subsides with pacification. In Central America it continued for many years, albeit on a reduced scale.

Indias who were slaves had almost no rights, so that Spaniard and Indian alike did as they wished with them. They were bartered freely like property, and at least on one occasion an esclava was a Spaniard's stake in a card game, being valued at seventy pesos.[21] To make matters worse, free indias were sometimes sold as slaves; the lieutenant of the alcalde mayor of Nicaragua was charged with selling a free woman to a sailor for seventy pesos de oro and with giving another india to the escribano público in Granada for thirty pesos to settle a debt. The accused maintained that the women involved were "esclavas de guerra." The alcalde mayor himself admitted that he bought a woman slave, "muy buena," from the treasurer, who was returning to Spain, for sixty pesos.

Castañeda was accused of selling a free india, allegedly from an encomienda, for thirty pesos. Another testified that the girl, Elvira, had belonged to Pedrarias, and later went to another's repartimiento. A criado of Pedrarias gave her to Castañeda, who in turn sold her for fifty pesos to one Ayala, who took her to Peru. The girl seems to have been traded often because of careless personal grooming ("hera la dha. yndia suzia lo qual este testigo sabe por q. los dhos licenciados e diego de ayala le dezian"). Castañeda maintained that the girl was a slave of war, and although she was not branded as such, she could be traded as a slave, according to the custom in Nicaragua. He insisted that he had purchased her from a criado of Pedrarias for thirty pesos.[22]

As alcalde mayor (and later governor) of Nicaragua, Castañeda was in an advantageous position to profit from slavery. Many ships left from that province for Peru, and he issued the licenses necessary for the transporting of slaves. He was charged with having sold an india to a Spaniard for 200 pesos, when she was worth only 40, the reason being, according to his accuser, that for such a price the alcalde mayor readily gave a license to take her out of the region. Castañeda denied the charge, adding that if he sometimes sold slaves at high prices it was because they were very valuable at the time. He complained that the slaves were sold on credit and that he had not been reimbursed. In a similar case, it was alleged that he sold another india worth 25 pesos for 200, including the license. Two others were sold for 200 and 300 pesos. He was absolved of all those charges.[23] The significant point of these cases is that Castañeda was accused merely of overpricing; there was little apparent concern that the highest official in Nicaragua was in the business of selling slaves.

Indias were also rented to sailors for the journey to Peru and back, usually for a period of two to three months, or to others who had just arrived in the province of Nicaragua. Those involved were engaged in illicit business because the women were often from encomiendas, rented out by their encomenderos or estancieros. Encomienda Indians of course had the status of free persons.[24] The worst offenders were the calpixques (majordomos), who seized wives and daughters of Indians, and either sold them outright or rented them as concubines to Spaniards taking ship southward. Girls rented out for only a peso a month were called "alvahacas" (basil, or *albahaca*); the more attractive ones, the "rosas" (roses), brought two pesos monthly; and the most desirable indias were known as "clavellinas" (pinks), going for three pesos a month.[25]

Calpixques were inclined to brutality toward all Indians, but especially toward the women. In Honduras, the bishop wanted Indians of the town of Talua placed under the care of the Crown because the president of the audiencia had put a Negro calpixque in charge of them. He had mistreated them in many ways, including raping some indias.[26] In Nicaragua Indian women were regularly whipped along with the men for little cause, and a number of them were seduced, attacked, and tortured in various ways.[27] An estante in Nicaragua tried to rape an india, and because she defended herself the Spaniard set fire to her hut, burning her alive. Even though the governor proceeded against the culprit, the punishment for his atrocity was only five pesos de oro. In that instance the queen demanded a full account of the crime, with the proceedings and statement of punishment forwarded to the Council of the Indies for investigation.[28] A Spanish woman accused of killing an india "in a cruel manner" received special consideration when her husband allegedly bribed the alcalde mayor.[29]

On several similar occasions, however, justice of a sort was done. When a criado of the governor of Nicaragua killed an india, he was imprisoned for several months until he was taken to trial. In another instance one of the governor's estancieros was put in chains for raping a cacique's woman.[30] Some men attached to the adelantado Montejo stole a cacique's wife in Verapaz, and Cerrato sent licenciado Ramírez to bring them to justice.[31] Attacks on women of the nobility were taken more seriously than if an india of the macegual class was involved, while little concern was shown over the mistreatment of an esclava.[32]

Still, a mestizo official late in the century whipped three indias, wives of principales, simply because they were short a chicken or two in their offerings, a punishment that was common, but usually reserved for men.[33] About the same time and place, a lieutenant of the alcalde mayor forced his way into the house of an Indian alcalde one night under the pretext of checking to see if any indias were sleeping with lovers. Later he took one of the girls for his own mistress, or so it was reported.[34]

Cerrato, who was genuinely incensed about the treatment of the natives, wrote that Spaniards traveling about the countryside felt free to collect Indian women who caught their eyes in the pueblos. Calpixques in encomienda towns demanded all sorts of services from the women.[35] Dr. Mexía, a judge of lesser character, was accused of picking up some "yndias frescas hermosas" that he found in certain pueblos during an official visitation. He took them, along with a loose mestiza, and deposited them in quarters near his house.[36]

It was said that the governor of Honduras had forced indias to go on entradas to Taguzgalpa, which resulted in some of their deaths. One of the Spaniards on the expedition illegally took an india from his encomienda, and another of the men was charged with hitting an Indian in the head and carrying off his daughter.[37] An alcalde mayor allegedly failed to punish a Spaniard who raped an Indian woman, and he was charged with being remiss in not bringing to justice another who made a girl pregnant and then sent her back to her village.[38] When an official went to check on the tribute at Tztuncalco, the encomienda of don Francisco de la Cueva, he asked the village elders to give him an india for his service, and out of fear they gave him a macegual girl. The official then took her back to Santiago, a distance of more than thirty leagues. In his trial, the governor was absolved of charges that he had not punished the offending official.[39]

The mulatto interpreter of an alcalde mayor was said to have stolen a married india and kept her hidden for many days. It was alleged that the alcalde mayor knew of the crime, and that despite an appeal made to him, he did not want to prosecute the culprit. The alcalde mayor defended himself by saying that the only witnesses were "two lying Indians," who were angry because he had punished them.[40] Encomenderos felt even fewer restraints and simply took Indian women, including those who were married.[41]

While cases involving Spaniards of some position in society who had mistreated Indian women were common enough, one can only imagine the widespread abuses of indias by the lower strata of society that do not appear in surviving records. But it is clear enough that especially in isolated regions the Indian girls were molested with frequency. Mestizos, mulattos, blacks, and some Spaniards as well, were in the habit of lounging around fountains or rivers where the indias went to get water and do their washing. There the women were enticed, deceived, and mistreated. To check the problem, the king ordered local alguaciles to be responsible for patroling those places and to arrest any male seen talking to an india.[42] Such a law was difficult to enforce, and many years later another order was issued directing blacks and mulattos to stay away from Indians because they were mistreating them and teaching them bad habits. But they continued to steal the Indian women.[43] And in 1605, the audiencia alluded to the fact that mulattos and mestizos in Nicaragua were still entering Indian towns, taking girls and married women from their homes, offending their husbands and fathers.[44]

From the first, Indian women were needed by the Spaniards to prepare their food. Maize had to be ground and prepared in a variety of ways, and a Spaniard needed an india just for the purpose of making tortillas two or three times daily.[45] The Crown observed as early as 1528 that encomenderos were also taking women from their villages to make tortillas for slaves who worked in the mines. Other indias were forced to be house servants and were treated like slaves themselves. All of them involved in such work were kept from their husbands and children, which led to great harm. It was ruled that the practice was to cease, even though the indias went voluntarily for pay. Despite the stiff penalty of 100 pesos for each woman used for that work, the infractions continued.[46]

Being kept apart from their husbands so much, it was difficult for the Indian women to be good wives. Usually they married very young, a custom encouraged by the encomenderos who hoped thereby to increase their rents with the larger population. Finally the Crown issued an order against forcing girls to marry at a tender age.[47] It happened frequently that recently-married Indian girls who had just become mothers were drafted for their milk. Pregnant Spanish women were in the habit of taking ten or twelve women from Indian pueblos into their homes to help with the birth of a Spanish baby and to nurse it. During those long periods of time the husbands of the indias remained in their villages. In the houses of the Spaniards the wet nurses often became mistresses of other Indians or Negroes who worked there, while the Indian husbands took other women back in the village. Spanish women customarily used as many girls as they wished for other work, and Cerrato stated that in Spanish households there were two or three indias for every task. When he tried to restrict the number used for service the Spanish women complained and said it was "treason."[48]

Although many Indian couples were forced apart, it appears that they readily assumed liaisons with new partners, an informal regard for the marriage vows that Spaniards, and more precisely ecclesiastics, were supposed to correct. The archdeacon in León noted that when merchants took women, as well as men, from Nicaragua to provinces as distant as Mexico, they remarried, abandoning their families. Perhaps it was because they despaired of ever returning to their homeland, but the inference is that they adjusted with relative ease to the separations.[49]

Whatever the sentiments of the adults, the implication for their children is clear. Most Spaniards seem not to have concerned themselves with such arrangements and perhaps even encouraged them. Baltasar Nieto, the encomendero of Çacatequienca in San Salvador, kept in his house an Indian named Juan Quitapot who had one of Nieto's criadas as his concubine, while his legal wife was mistreated by him. To make matters worse, Quitapot had been exiled for witchcraft.[50]

Indian women, both married and single, were used for all sorts of tasks, including heavy labor. A common forced occupation for them was the spinning of cloth, for which work they were often taken from their homes. The governor of Nicaragua saw the harm that resulted from that procedure and ruled that for four months a year the women should remain at home in order to make clothes for their husbands and children.[51] The Crown issued a more generous law prohibiting married indias working in a Spaniard's house from being away from home for more than a month, and they were never to be gone while the husband was away, because with both of them away there would be no one to watch their houses and orchards, both of which might be pre-empted by someone else. Unfortunately, the custom of allowing both to be gone at the same time was so ingrained a practice that the new law was very difficult to enforce.[52]

Family life was further interrupted by the forced moving of Indian towns, especially with the husbands gone. Friars complained of the oidor licenciado Alonso Zorita, who moved natives to new sites. It was, they wrote, a painful sight to see indias tied as prisoners, with their small children on their backs, marched along the roads in the rainy season, separated from their men.[53]

Aside from the demands of personal service, Indian wives often disappeared while their husbands were gone as a result of being seized and carried off simply because they appealed to their abductors. The oidor Dr. Mexía, who had, it appeared, given himself over largely to pleasures of the flesh, took two beautiful young indias from San Salvador, one of whom was married, and put them in a house near his own that belonged to his fellow audiencia judge, licenciado Loaisa. When the husband of the one came looking for his wife, the judges would not release her. Because of the rigors of the journey, traveling from the hot, humid lowlands to the cool altitudes, the husband suddenly became ill and died. Mexía was also accused of taking another married india from her husband and giving her to a Spaniard against her will, an act that contributed to his excommunication by the bishop. Mexía denied the truth of the allegation.[54]

It was asserted that the governor of Costa Rica forcibly took an india from her husband and gave her to another man. When the husband asked for his wife back he was refused and mistreated.[55] Other complaints were made that corregidores, alcaldes mayores, and their followers were taking maidens and married indias who appealed to them, "as if they were lords."[56]

Indian women raped by blacks, mulattoes, and mestizos often became their concubines and sometimes married them. This was particularly true of girls who had been orphaned and had lost ties with their communities.[57] Negroes, both free and slave, often married indias because of the shortage of their own women, but also because of certain other incentives. They tried to maintain not only that their mixed children (zambaigos) could not be slaves, since their mothers were free, but that they were not really Indians and so did not have to pay tribute. That posed an interesting question indeed and one that puzzled the audiencia.[58] The Crown resolved the judges' doubts by ruling that the zambaigos were to pay tribute like Indians.[59]

Even though it was natural enough that indias and Negroes would be thrown together under the system of forced labor, the Crown tried to prevent their mixing. But since some of the women worked near the cattle herds which were tended by blacks, illicit unions were formed. And blacks sometimes forcibly took married women after first mistreating their husbands. Accordingly, the king forbade indias from serving near the herds.[60] In cacao regions a number of mulattos and zambaigos married Indian women who owned cacaotales. Those men were mostly free herdsmen who, with their new economic status, did not expect to have to contribute labor in public-works projects. The governor of Soconusco argued that they were not in a better position than Indian men in the same category who did the work. The governor requested that mestizos not be allowed to live in native villages and was of the opinion that mestizos married to Indian women should be expected to pay tribute.[61]

Perhaps the greatest social evil emerging from the debased position of Indian women was the impact on native children. One obvious result of separated couples and excessive labor was a lowered rate of reproduction.[62] Some of the indias even as late as the 1580s were being broken physically, their insides literally bursting in some instances from the heavy loads they had to carry. Unable to endure more, some of them committed suicide by hanging, starving themselves, or by eating poisonous herbs. Encomenderos forced them to work in open fields where they tried to care for their children. They slept outside and there gave birth to and reared their babies, who were often bitten by poisonous insects. Mothers occasionally killed their offspring at birth to spare them future agonies.[63]

Neglect of the children was the inevitable consequence of broken

homes, and evidence indicates that abandoned or orphaned children were
not given much attention by relatives or friends of the parents. Whereas
Indian mothers often carried their babies on their backs as they labored,
that was not always feasible, especially if there was more than one child to
be cared for. Accordingly, children were often left in the care of a neighbor
who usually had only the most meager provisions for her own children.
Working mothers present a poignant image when we hear of them returning home after weeks or months of separation from their children, only to
find that they had died or had been taken away.

Witnesses testified that in the early years of pacification babies were
taken from their mothers' breasts and tossed aside.[64] Even though that
brutality stopped after a while, the general neglect of children continued
to result in distressing circumstances. All of those factors help explain the
fact that on tribute rolls married couples were frequently entered as
having no children at all or only one, and seldom more than two.[65]

There was a scarcity of Spanish women in the provinces for several
years, as a consequence of which the preponderance of conquerors and
early settlers were not established in a tranquil domestic setting. Some of
them had Spanish wives in Spain or elsewhere, while others had put off
marrying in the hope of returning to Spain to marry a woman worthy of
their new status. Whatever the individual reasons, the fact remains that
there were many bachelors in Central America, which accounts for the
prevalence of concubinage. The Crown was anxious for settlers to marry
and take root, particularly in view of the persistence of violence and
turmoil in the Indies, and to that end the marriage of the colonists and
Indian women was encouraged.[66]

Spaniards who remained single gave the excuse that there were no
women available for them who were acceptable, by which they meant
Spanish women.[67] Ignoring (but no doubt understanding perfectly) what
was implicit, the bishop of Honduras said that was a pretext because there
were Castilian women present and more arriving all the time. Moreover,
there were also mestizas, daughters of established Spaniards, some of
whom were hidalgos. But he was writing in 1547, by which time a good
number of españolas had indeed been introduced to the frontier. Many of
the Spaniards had sisters, nieces, and other female relatives who needed
husbands, and the women were brought over for the purpose of finding
them. By that time, too, a good number of the mestiza daughters, the
great majority of whom were illegitimate, were of marriageable age. The
bishop added that the Spaniard wishing to marry could, after all, marry an
Indian woman, because there were indias of intelligence.[68]

But even though the Spaniards were in no way inhibited about cohabiting with native women, it was quite another matter to enter into the formal and permanent institution of marriage with women who were considered their social inferiors. Some of the vecinos did eventually marry indias, either because they despaired of marrying an acceptable Spanish woman, or because they loved the india who was usually the mother of their children, who would otherwise virtually be abandoned by the father. Usually those who did, however, were Spaniards of the lower social and economic classes who entertained little hope of upward social mobility. The generalization must be qualified somewhat, because there were indias of the native aristocracy who offered promise.[69]

Bartolomé de Las Casas wrote that he saw in the villa of Verapaz in Española a population of sixty Spanish vecinos, most of whom were hidalgos and married to beautiful Indian women. It is very questionable that most of them were hidalgos and that most of the encomenderos were married to natives—in fact, Simpson shows that the number was only six married to indias.[70] Las Casas speaks highly of the native women of the Indies, and the graceful Indian women of Central America today suggest that their forebears must have been physically desirable.

A Spaniard of modest birth and limited economic circumstances could enhance his position—provided he had abandoned hopes of returning to Spain—by marrying a cacique's daughter, for she often brought a very respectable dowry of one sort or another. To take one example, in 1537, the king wrote to the Protector of the Indians in Nicaragua recommending the bearer of the letter. She was doña Ana, daughter of Taugema, the cacique of the pueblos of Maçatega and Tecolotega, who was returning to her homeland from Spain with the wish to marry and remain in Nicaragua. And since the king was informed that she was a good Christian, he ordered that doña Ana be favored in all ways. She was not to be given to an encomendero, but was to be free because she had the preparation to bring other Indian women into the faith. The Protector was also enjoined to help her find an honorable Spaniard and to encourage him to marry her; but it would be best for them not to have her father's village among their encomiendas. Although not specifically ordered, it is certainly made clear that her husband was to be an encomendero, in which case an honorable but perhaps impecunious settler might have to be given a village.[71]

A Spaniard who married a cacique's daughter was in a good position to have some consideration, if not as the recipient of an encomienda, at least in the form of an official position. For example, a Spaniard who married the daughter of a cacique in Soconusco and had children by her received no encomienda, because there were none there for individuals; he was, however, named to the post of corregidor in Quetzaltenango.[72]

Offspring of a racially-mixed union, sanctified by marriage or not,

318   FORCED NATIVE LABOR

sometimes achieved prominence in the case of a mother of the native
nobility or a Spanish father of importance. Obvious examples coming to
mind are illegitimate mestizo children of Cortés, Alvarado, and Pizarro.
Even among children of less prominent fathers, if the mother was from the
Indian elite class, special consideration was usually accorded the children.
The Crown was anxious for daughters of caciques to be converted to
Christianity and Hispanicized as examples to the native commoners, and
they were consequently given special treatment. A notable exception was
the kidnaping of two daughters of a cacique, one of whom was given, along
with her children, to some Spanish soldiers, while the other was turned
over to a Spanish captain as his slave. But that was a serious crime and one
that was investigated with vigor.[73]

William Schurz passes on an episode related by Garzilazo that illustrates the difficulty of matchmaking on the frontier. When Alvarado
returned to Santiago in 1538 he was accompanied by his second wife, doña
Beatriz de la Cueva, niece of the Duke of Alburquerque, along with a
grand company of nobles and their ladies. And, Schurz writes:

There were Doña Ana Fadrique and eight other young ladies of good family and
marriageable age. The return of Alvarado and his train to Guatemala was celebrated with a round of festivities that lasted for several days. At one of these affairs,
the local contingent of ex-conquistadores was present en masse. Sitting in stiff-
backed chairs along the walls of the sala of the governor's palace, as millions of
other Spanish-Americans have sat since then, the veterans must have been ill-at-
ease in the presence of all the new finery from Spain. They were gnarled and
battle-scarred, and their party manners had never been very good anyhow. Stout
Bernal Díaz, chronicler of the Conquest, who had settled in Guatemala, was
probably one of the guests; but it was some anonymous spectator who served as
society reporter of that afternoon's function.

While the aging veterans were herded into the big hall, the damsels who had
come from Spain watched them through a door at one end of the room. One of
them spoke up and remarked to the other: "They say we are to marry these
conquistadors!" Another added: "Do they mean that we are to marry these
broken-down old men? The rest of you can do what you like, but I do not intend to
marry any of them. To the devil with them! They must have escaped from hell,
they look so crippled. Some of them are lame and others are one-armed. Some
have lost an ear and others an eye. Some of them have only half a face and the best
of them have long scars across their faces." Then the first answered: "We are not
marrying them for their elegance, but for their Indians. Since they are old and
worn out they will soon be dead. Then we can have the young husbands that we
want. It will be like changing a broken old bottle for a strong new one."

One of the old conquerors who was sitting close to the door overheard the
conversation and, turning on the young ladies, poured out all his scorn on them.

Then he told his companions what he had heard and said to them: "Marry these dames and you will see how they repay the favor you do them!" "At this," says Garcilaso, "he went to his house and called a priest, and was married to a noble Indian woman, by whom he already had two natural children. He wished to legitimize them, so that they could inherit his Indians, and not some *señora*, who would enjoy what he had earned by his labors, and who would treat his children as servants and slaves."[74]

Much less consideration was given to a woman from the macegual class, or to her Spanish husband. In the early years especially it was considered not quite respectable for a European to marry a native, and certainly not an Indian commoner. Nonetheless, increasingly a fairly good number of Spaniards defied conventions and took the commoners as wives, which led to some social ostracizing as well as financial complications for the families. When an encomendero of Nicaragua died, his Indian wife claimed his encomienda. The governor refused to let her keep it, saying that the encomendero had married the india just before he died, "estando articulo mortis." Curiously, the governor did not deny her outright on the grounds of her race.

There had been a controversy about even Spanish widows succeeding to encomiendas because holders of encomiendas were charged with defending the land. A similar case in Nicaragua caused even more talk: Alonso Bibas, an encomendero of Granada, had married an india who had been his slave. Again the governor did not let the woman keep the encomienda, arguing that the encomendero had married the girl on his deathbed, and witnesses had confirmed that he was out of his mind at the time ("muy enfermo de la cabeça e casi loco").[75]

There was soon a large number of the new racial type of mestizo because of the mix of the conquerors with the Indian women. They were more often than not illegitimate, so that the term mestizo was almost the equivalent of bastard in the sixteenth century. They were caught between the cultures and not quite acceptable in either, but it made considerable difference whether or not the father abandoned them. The mestizo child of a commoner mother and an absent father tended to be more Indian in outlook because of the mother's influence on him, and the child's prospects were therefore dim. If the mother was of the native nobility it helped the child somewhat in Indian society, and if the Spanish father was a prominent man many social barriers could be overcome in white society.

Mestiza daughters of prominent conquistadores often married very respectably, not only because of the social standing of the fathers, but also because there was apt to be a good dowry involved. Both sons and daughters of the conquerors and first settlers were given special consideration when encomiendas and official positions were distributed. Therefore, a man married to the mestiza daughter of a distinguished Spaniard would be in line for an encomienda, a corregimiento, or some kind of pension, with the possibility of inheriting his father-in-law's encomienda some day.

Likewise, the mestizo son of an important conqueror was often rewarded. It was a matter of some importance whether or not the mestizo children lived in the fathers' households and were recognized by them. When the Crown created the title of *alférez mayor* for Central America, which was for sale and inheritable, it was specified that a son could succeed his father in the post, "even though his mother be Indian."[76] Mestizos who were recognized direct descendants of conquerors or first settlers had an obvious advantage, and in the late part of the century some of them who were grandchildren of such men claimed privileges. Other mestizos without distinguished lineage fared poorly: the son of a tailor who had arrived, say, in 1550, and a macegual india had little opportunity other than to learn his father's trade—provided the father recognized him.

Most mestizos had little social standing and were, in fact, often grouped legally with blacks and mulattoes. Yet, the Crown could see the advantages to society in terms of social stability if some attention was given to them. Accordingly, the governor of Guatemala was instructed to establish a school for the education of sons of Spaniards and indias.[77] It appears, however, that the plan had very limited success, and mestizos remained in a low category.

It was almost unheard of for an Indian male to marry a Spanish woman and very unusual for one to even marry a mestiza, especially if she lived in a Spanish settlement. Moreover, a mestizo youth had limited prospects of marrying an española, and usually had to settle for a mestiza or an india, unless he was rich or prominent. Mestizas, on the other hand, had better opportunities for marrying a Spaniard, so that their social status could rise and often did. But if a mestizo married an Indian woman, their children would have to pay tribute, being considered Indians.[78]

Mestizos would eventually become the dominant racial types in Central America and the most dynamic members of society, but at least during the sixteenth century they were held in low esteem generally. Whether or not they turned to European or Indian styles of life depended to great extent on the interest shown in them by their fathers, which was often minimal.

During the conquest and pacification years Indian women were often subjected to the same brutal treatment accorded Indian men. They were frequently killed in the fighting, and some of the conquerors' vicious dogs were set on indias.[79] Aside from the social contact with Spaniards that quickly developed, the women played a significant role in the system of forced labor. They were enslaved as indiscriminately as men during the early years, as has been noted here earlier.

One does find examples of compassion shown, and the chronicler Bernal Díaz put himself in that company. During the conquest of Chiapas by Luis Marín the Spaniards took "muy buenas indias" as prisoners, and one of the Spaniards suggested that they be branded as slaves in retaliation for the warlike stance of local warriors. Díaz portrays himself as the defender of the indias, claiming that he opposed the suggestion to the point of getting into a knife fight, from which he and his opponent both emerged wounded. Marín, because he was "very good and not malicious, and saw that it was unjust," agreed to release the women.[80]

Although it was not long observed, a decree of 1534 forbade the enslavement of women (or children under fourteen) taken in just war. They could be used as naborías. In practice, women continued to be branded.[81] It was later ruled that indias were not to be utilized as naborías or tapias, but the president and oidores continued to use them in that capacity without paying them, and they allowed the vecinos to do likewise.[82] Vecinos in Honduras said that since Indian men slaves ran away and rebelled, they needed female slaves to supply the needs of labor. They added that it was better for the women to be enslaved than killed in war.[83]

In certain specific cases it appears that women were given more consideration than male slaves. A royal order in 1548 instructed the first lady of Central America, doña Catalina Montejo, daughter of the adelantado and wife of Alonso de Maldonado, the president of the audiencia, to free her slave Leonorica, since it was forbidden for indias to serve in that status.[84] As in the case of the men, free Indian women were treated in many cases little better than chattels. In Honduras it was reported that girls from encomiendas were made to work for Spaniards without pay, and that they were whipped and aggrieved in other ways, as if they were slaves.[85]

Early provisions were made to protect women in the Laws of Burgos, 1512. After four months of her pregnancy an Indian woman was not to work in mines or in the fields; however, those held in encomienda were expected to do light work in the kitchen or weeding. Moreover, new mothers were exempt from work in the mines or fields, until their children reached the age of three.

The Laws of Burgos were modified in 1513, with more protective legislation for indias. Married women were no longer obligated to serve in the mines or anywhere else, unless they volunteered, or unless their husbands took them along. They could, however, be compelled to work in their own fields (milpas) or those of the Spaniards provided that in the latter case a wage was agreed upon by the women or their husbands. Pregnant women were exempt. Unmarried girls were to work with their parents on their own lands, or if their parents consented they could work on other lands. Single indias not living with their parents were to work with other Indians on lands in order to avoid becoming vagabonds.[86]

As we have seen, those humane laws were not enforced, and the extent to which that early compassion cooled is illustrated by Bishop Marroquín's recommendation many years later that pregnant women be allowed a mere month's rest before birth and only a month and a half after giving birth.[87]

Of all the labor performed by indias, the most damaging was that of serving as tamemes. It was bad enough that esclavas were forced into carrying, but the law was broken with frequency by the use of free women held in encomienda, and officials were lax in punishing offenders. A witness said that he and the alcalde mayor of Nicaragua, Castañeda, were on the road once when they saw many indias loaded down with maize, some of them carrying their children on their backs as well. He told Castañeda that the women were from the encomienda of the notary public, but when the alcalde mayor did nothing, the witness spurred his horse toward one of the women, causing her to drop her cargo and return to her house.[88] Yet Castañeda had written the king earlier that while he had indeed found indias being used as tamemes, he had given an order against it.[89] Later, when Rodrigo de Contreras arrived in Nicaragua, he confirmed that although women had been used to carry, he had stopped the practice and punished those responsible.[90] Witnesses testified that Contreras discovered an estanciero who was one of his criados making Indian women haul maize and that the governor had indeed punished his own man.[91]

In the mining districts of Honduras indias were forced to carry maize to the mines, a distance of fifty to seventy leagues.[92] When the men were pressed into labor gangs in the hotlands the indias had to carry water to them over three or four leagues. The water jugs weighed more than an arroba, and they often carried babies on their backs, in addition to two gourds for their own drinking water. Even though the Crown ordered an end to that kind of work for the women, it continued.[93] Certainly as late as

1568, women in Honduras were still carrying loads on journeys of three or
four days, for little pay and much suffering.[94] And the evidence is that the
abuse continued for many years: reference is made in the 1580s to the
ruining of the health of female tamemes who were physically broken by
carrying heavy cargoes over rough terrain, in heat and cold rains.[95]

Somewhat more fortunate were those women who worked in Spanish
households. In Santiago, in particular, there was a large number of mature
indias in the service of Spaniards.[96] Encomenderos made indias stay in
their houses without pay.[97] For example, the oidor of the audiencia,
licenciado Loaisa, was allegedly guilty of forcing indias from Ciudad Vieja
to be servants in his Santiago home without paying them.[98] Cerrato wrote
that Spaniards kept many Indian women around their houses for service,
and, "when their wives were pregnant they sought the most attractive
indias for housekeepers and took them from their husbands, and thus took
them to their houses. And the indias, as they are [people of] little reason,
became mistresses of some Indian or Negro, and their husbands stayed in
their villages and took concubines there. They married with other women,
which resulted in much damage and inconvenience." The president said
that he had stopped the practice of taking women from their villages
for service.[99]

Household work did separate the women from their families in many
instances, but at least the physical aspect of their duties was far less
strenuous. All households, including those of ecclesiastics, had *panaderas*
who made tortillas and whose work was little different from that to which
they were accustomed at home. Those who seem to have had the least
difficult duties were the wet nurses (chichiguas) and nanas. In 1578,
Diego García de Palacio made a detailed inquiry into the treatment of
indias who cared for Spanish children to find out, among other things, if
they were paid and if they took the work willingly, as some women did
in Castile.

Witnesses testified that the Indian women offered their services, seeing
the advantages to be derived. They were well fed and well dressed, and
according to testimony, always very well treated. One witness went so far
as to say that chichiguas were treated better than the lady of the house
because they had the master's children at their breasts. He said that he
knew it to be so based on his observation of them for thirty-seven years,
and that the truth could be measured from the comments of the indias
themselves.[100] Indias becoming so intimately involved in households
resulted in the mistress taking a proprietary interest in them, often to the
point of considering them permanent servants. It was alleged that the

governor in Costa Rica ordered indias to take care of the baby of a lady friend of his, and that a year later she took the native nurses with her to the town of Nicoya against their will.[101]

On the whole, however, according to other investigations and general opinion, indias who reared Spanish children were comparatively well paid and well treated, they volunteered for the work, and enjoyed some measure of freedom.[102] Nevertheless, as Cerrato noted years before, the fact remained that Indian women were taken by encomenderos to raise Spanish children, while the indias' own families were broken up and their children abandoned.[103] In some instances the situation was alleviated, either because the women lived nearby and could go home at nights or with frequency, or because the Indian family lived on the Spaniard's premises with the man and wife, and sometimes children, performing tasks.

Indias were widely used for the purpose of spinning cloth, for which there was a good and steady market. Here again, the work itself was not so much different from traditional occupations, except that the Spaniards often forced the indias to work, sometimes without pay, and kept the women from their homes. In Nicaragua the alcalde mayor reported that indias were gathered at the houses of Spaniards to work all day spinning cotton without even being given any food. The estancieros took any women they wanted. It was ruled that the women were not to do that work in Spaniards' houses, but in their own places. The only ones who were to go to Spanish dwellings were those given by the caciques.[104] Evidently the order was not observed, for when Governor Contreras arrived later he said that it had been the custom for encomenderos to take women to their houses to spin, and he reissued the law that indias could spin only in their own homes.[105]

In Guatemala and Nicaragua indias were being locked up in houses on the estancias of encomenderos while they made cloth, and they were kept there for a month or two without their being able to leave to go to their homes during all that time to see their hungry children or to tend their crops. And if an india did not have food to take with her she went hungry, because the estancieros gave the workers nothing to eat.[106] As an example, Luisa de Santiago, wife of the encomendero Mateo de Lescano, illegally took indias from their pueblo of Gualteveo and made them spin cloth at another of their encomiendas (Çindega), a distance of six leagues.[107]

By 1549, it was fairly common in the various provinces for encomenderos to be in the habit of taking Indian women from their villages and enclosing them in corrals where they were forced to spin and weave cotton and woolen clothing to be used as tribute. Once again the order was given, this time from the king, that such work was to be done only in the houses of the women, and that they were not to be abused in any way.[108]

The Dominican friars were actively engaged in the cloth trade as well, and in Verapaz they forced indias to make *huipiles* ("guaypiles") for them. Women with special skills, the *maestras*, made huipiles that sold for two or three tostones. Each of the pueblos under the Dominicans in that area made thirty to forty of the blouses a year, in addition to *ropa de manta*. The friars sent their majordomos to sell them in Los Suchitepéquez, Sonsonate, or Santiago, the profits being kept by the friars and the indias receiving no pay.[109] When their production lagged, the women were sometimes punished harshly.

The encomendero Baltasar Nieto of San Salvador was found guilty of flogging more than thirty indias for tardiness in delivering *naguas* (petticoats) for their tribute. There were other charges of which he was found guilty, yet he was fined only 100 tostones—half of which went to the pueblo concerned—plus the pay for the investigators and other court costs.[110]

The work assigned to women was greatly varied, and those who were drafted for labor were referred to by the general term *tezines;* and although it was more specifically applied to molenderas, those who ground maize on stone metates into a paste or *masa*, the word came to have a wider application. One of the most unpleasant and harmful tasks was work in the obrajes de tinta making indigo dye. The alcalde mayor of La Trinidad was accused of taking Indian girls from the pueblo of Naolingo and giving them to Spaniards for their service, to use them as they wished; but more damaging was the specific charge that he was sending at least two or three indias a week to make dye.[111] It is true that the Crown decreed that the dangerous work in the dye industry was prohibited for Indians, that labor being restricted to blacks. Nevertheless, as late as 1607 (and no doubt much later) Indians complained that their women—single, married, and widows—were being taken to *xiquilicales* where the xiquilite, or indigo, was gathered.

The same categories of women were taken to estancias de ganado (cattle ranches) in contravention of an earlier law, as well as to *tabacales* (tobacco works) and other industries. In those places indias were compelled to remain and to marry black slaves, free mulattos, and assorted criados. At least for the village from whence the complaint issued, Masaya, Nicaragua, it was ordered that no Indians of either sex could be taken out for labor without an order from the president of the audiencia, under pain of a fine of 200 pesos. Previously there had been a quota by which the village of 100 adult Indians was to contribute for service 14 indios and 7 indias a week. Again, the governor prohibited their labor in indigo works.[112]

In Honduras, because of the shortage of Indian laborers, free indias had been taken from their pueblos and forced to labor in the mines.[113] Women frequently helped in the mining operations in a supportive role, such as drawing water, gathering wood, and making meals. On occasion they were forced into hard labor. Governor Cerezeda of Honduras wrote that he saw a cuadrilla of slaves from Guatemala which included twenty men and forty women, the indias laboring in the mines right along with the men.[114]

The Crown reproved the governor of Nicaragua because indias and their small boys and girls were sent out to gather fodder for the Spaniards' horses, and because the women were being rented out for two or three months or longer for "dishonest" (sexual) purposes. If the indias resisted any of those demands they were mistreated and vexed in various ways by the encomenderos or their estancieros.[115] The governor testified later that he had, among others, issued ordinances against the use of indias in the clearing and weeding of plantings.[116] A list of the common duties which indias had to perform would be a long one, not counting special projects. The alcalde mayor of Chiapas was found guilty of compelling Indian widows to make him a bed with a canopy of damask cloth, and then not paying them. His judge ordered him to pay the women 120 tostones.[117]

Despite a gradual improvement in the treatment of women in the decades following the first few years of confrontation, certain abuses remained. Well over a century after the conquest the familiar and increasingly dismal order was given that indias were under no circumstances to be obligated to leave their houses for any kind of work, and that those who had been taken away were to be returned.[118]

Finally, some attention should be given to two alienated groups of females—orphans and widows. Because of the early deaths of parents, or because of forced separation resulting in practical desertion, there were many young orphan girls with no one to care for them, which made them particularly vulnerable. Those *huérfanas* were often taken into homes where they were held virtually as bond servants, though one should not exclude the instances of altruism that surely figured into some cases. The alcalde mayor of La Trinidad, who was accused of giving Indian girls to Spaniards, admitted only that he had given an orphan girl of seven who had been separated from her province to a Spaniard and his wife to be cared for until she married.[119]

It has been observed above that orphans were sometimes put to work in

Spanish homes under contract arrangements. Others became child brides
of mulattoes and Negroes, and while many of them married Indians, it
often happened that they were from other regions so that it was not easy
for them to adjust to different foods and customs, with the result that it was
difficult for them to satisfy their husbands. Indeed, it appears that other
Indians were not especially sympathetic to the orphan girls. An official
commented that even though girls were often taken into other Indian
homes, there was little charity involved and they were given a place only
because they could be exploited for their labor. But, he added, they did
not get many years of work from them because girls ordinarily married at a
tender age.[120]

The number of Indian widows was large because so many men died in
fighting, at least in the early years, and because of ill treatment and
excessive labor. In the first two decades many Indians were shipped off to
other lands, or to distant mines, which left their wives widows for all
intents and purposes. Widows were more likely to be drafted into labor
than other women, and they seldom got any special consideration. Quite
the contrary, for although they had no husbands, widows were required
for several years to pay tribute. The audiencia had ruled that they would
be exempt from payments, but the Crown nullified that in 1571.[121] A
couple of years later it was decreed that those *indias viudas* would pay
tribute at a flat rate of five reales annually.[122] Eventually, however, a law
freed them from payment altogether.[123]

As women alone, they were subject to molestation and harassment from
all elements of society. Without protection and security, often with children to care for, the widows faced a grim situation, especially in view of the
fact that there seems not to have been a closeknit extended-family concept
so familiar in Latin American society today, wherein relatives make provision to ease the circumstances of unfortunate members of the family.

Postscript

SLAVES, TAMEMES, NABORÍAS, FORCED LABOR, AND TRIBUTE all existed in Central America before the advent of the Spaniard. Prehispanic times saw a stratified society in which a native aristocracy enjoyed status and luxury at the expense of the maceguales and the sub-macegual class. In a variety of ways some Indians were brutalized by others. When the Spaniards became the new masters, many of the native practices were retained with some adaptations, while new forms of labor were introduced. There were, however, surprisingly few changes in the basic labor structure, which continued much as it had for centuries.[1]

Without more knowledge of pre-conquest labor practices in Central America, it is difficult to make comparisons and contrasts between Indian and Spanish systems. It may well be that the lower classes under their native rulers had a completely different attitude toward their labors. It is possible, certainly, that they willingly performed their work with a sense of commitment and satisfaction. It may well be that the requirements were moderate, that tributes were light, and that laborers were not pushed beyond the limits of endurance. Perhaps there were few social dislocations resulting, so that families were seldom separated. Few Spaniards in Central America wrote about conditions before the conquest, and from those who did we have conflicting versions. No information I have seen gives substantial evidence supportive of one position or the other.[2]

At the same time, we do have considerable knowledge about postconquest labor systems. Spaniards were cautioned to exact no more tribute and labor than the Indians gave in heathen times, but those injunctions were frequently breached. Spaniards were at pains to point out that conditions improved with them because the Indians' souls were saved, that some were rescued from the sacrificial altars, and that there was a higher morality and better order. Although the new masters were uncon-

328

scionable in their demands, they said the native principales were as bad or worse.

During the years of pacification many Indians were killed; however, Spaniards maintained that before they arrived there was almost constant warfare among many of the tribes. It is true that the conquerors did away with cannibalism, human sacrifice, and frequent, if not continuous, warfare. Nevertheless, in other respects the lot of the Indians worsened under the Europeans. A discussion of the broader Spanish role in the New World would be superfluous here, since it has been dealt with by many others more qualified than I.[3]

Spanish treatment of Indians for the first two decades in Central America was clearly dreadful, so much so that conditions could only improve. It is indisputable that the natives were better off in 1600 than they were in 1530. But except for the high point of Cerrato's administration, the changes were not dramatic. The concrete achievement of that president was that he abolished chattel slavery, with rare exceptions.[4] His other reforms relative to lightened tribute loads and generally better treatment for tamemes and other laborers were less definable in the long run; only infrequently were there zealous officials ready to enforce them.

The year following the death of Cerrato in 1555, the Spanish prince took the crown as Philip II, and as Benjamin Keen has pointed out, the Lascasian movement, to which Cerrato largely subscribed, went into decline.[5] The new king's desperate financial situation dampened royal enthusiasm for reforms. Silver production by the mid-1550s was such that it discouraged the easing of Indian labor requirements. Keen's point is buttressed by the distinctly cool attitude of the Crown toward Cerrato following his actual implementation of Indian legislation. His death was seen as a blessing by many, perhaps including the Crown and officials of the exchequer. Aside from the aged Las Casas, there seemed to be few prepared to carry on the struggle. Perhaps discouraged humanitarians accommodated to what was becoming an accepted condition for the Indians.

Still, the state of native labor was changing perceptibly over the decades. Using 1550 as a pivotal year, by which time the Cerrato reforms were in force, treatment of the natives had improved sufficiently to note the clear contrast between the first generation of Spanish occupation and the following two. Familiarity with the documentation for the second half of the century reveals a noticeable decline in the frequency of complaints, and assuredly in the nature of them. While the first quarter century witnessed many atrocities and truly inhumane labor practices, the complaints after 1550 generally are of a much less serious nature.

There is reason to believe that at least in some cases there came to be exaggeration in some of the Indian pleas for relief. Spaniards argued that the Indians were no longer so innocent; that in fact some of them had become "muy ladino" in the manner in which they filed their suits, hoping to catch the sympathetic notice of a reforming friar, or even a bishop. In this they were apparently encouraged by the lawyers who flocked to the Indies. It appears that some of the more clever Indian leaders may have occasionally represented minor grievances in querulous terms inconsistent with the realities of the situation, resorting to a casuistry which Spaniards considered "sinister."

The work performed by some of the natives was indeed grueling, and the attendant evils of humiliation, cruelty, separation from families, and the lack of pay, among others, were unjust. One does find such cases reported, but many others were of a much milder nature. Disgruntled groups began to lament their having to provide fodder for Spanish horses, to sweep streets, to carry firewood, or to guard sheep, none of which was, *per se*, particularly fatiguing. Considering that they may have been unjustly required to perform those tasks, their complaints seem legitimate enough to us; but in the context of the times, and certainly in contrast to earlier years, to the Spanish vecinos they appeared petulant and carping. The Spaniards complained that the Indians would not work at all, regardless of good conditions and pay. The workers, seeing little recompense, and still resisting regimented labor, were loath to aid in the advance of their masters' ambitions.

One example will serve to illustrate the nature of a number of the suits. Over the years there had been many Indian complaints about the requirement to clean the streets, which led to an investigation by the royal oidor, licenciado Palacio, in 1578. Spanish witnesses said that it was a very old custom of the Indians of the milpas and barrios to clean the streets of Santiago. It was not done often, they added, but only at the time of general processions, such as Corpus Christi and Holy Thursday. According to the testimony, it was not very hard work with so many Indians participating, so that it was "almost like playing." One described the work as simply using a wooden hoe which was used to give two or three strokes to a clump of grass, after which the worker moved on, working his way along the street.

Other witnesses explained the background to the custom. When Alvarado conquered the land he gave the outlying fields to the city, provided for in an edict in the old archive of the cabildo, and verified by the conquistadores. The ejidos and uncultivated fields within a five-league radius of Santiago belonged to the city. Permission was given to Indians to live on those lands, but those who inhabited the milpas of the valley and the barrios of the city of Santiago had to have license. The right was granted on condition that they would clean the streets on certain occasions and build barriers for the bull fights. With that understanding, the Indians had been given the lots and allowed to build their houses on municipal property, which they had done for years.

Indians were also required to keep clear the road from Santiago to Golfo Dulce, from which port many goods from Spain were eventually brought. That task had to be performed only infrequently, witnesses claimed, and it was no vexation for the Indians because it was not difficult. In any case, they added, the workers took little care to do a good job, and since the Indians hauled goods over the road it was in their interest to have it clear. [6]

Therefore, some distinctions have to be made, and as some clear-thinking Spaniards had counseled over the years, it was not necessarily true that all forms of the labor system were inherently evil (though they were exploitative), but it was rather the abuse of those forms that made them odious.

While in the second half of the sixteenth century one does find examples of clearly abusive, and sometimes cruel, treatment, the extreme cases are appreciably less common. This may be seen, for example, in the nature of the charges brought out in residencias. At the same time, it happened that while the encomendero group was more restrained, the worst offenders after mid-century were the officials. Minor judges, notaries, and various petty functionaries, including some clergymen on the village level, imposed all sorts of extra burdens on the Indians. However vexing those impositions, they tended more to a nonviolent character; for while the bureaucrats did not scruple to cheat the natives, they were as a group less prone to brutality than the conquistadores had been.

Moreover, the colony was changing in character for various reasons. As the conquerors and first settlers acquired property and positions of prestige in the communities a measure of self-restraint evolved. Even the simple footsoldier had a certain aura of heroic status which imposed responsibilities. Most of them had been born around 1500 or earlier, and by the 1550s they were getting old and tired, a few more dying every year. Jaded warriors, no doubt feeling the heat of the next world, had softened. One imagines those patriarchal figures content to sit in the sun telling tales of the conquests to their grandchildren, some of whom carried the blood of the vanquished in their veins.

The conquerors' sons, beneficiaries of their fathers' hardships, enjoyed the perquisites of the well-born, such as they were on the frontier. The second generation may have held the natives in low esteem, but few had fought Indians and, consequently, had no reason to hate them. Some of the conquerors' progeny were themselves mestizos, and if not, it was likely that they had half-brothers and sisters, cousins, or close friends who were. *Mestizaje* itself was a phenomenon of great social import, for one finds it difficult to be prejudiced against part of oneself, although some manage to be.

Those who were *criollos*, or creoles, may well have found it expedient to hold themselves above mestizos and Indians, but their association with them could hardly have passed without some softening in their attitudes. If they held those of color to be socially inferior, they were fully aware of the similarity to themselves of mestizos and acculturated Indians (ladinos), who were essentially Spanish in almost all respects save physical features.

The creole, waited upon by Indians since infancy, was accustomed to regarding them as servants, but frequently it was an intimate relationship; more often than not he had been suckled by a chichigua and grew up playing with mestizo and Indian children of the household. His first sexual contact was most likely with one of the Indian servant girls, and the chances are that he had fathered mestizo children. In brief, unlike his peninsular, conquistador father, the second generation creole knew nothing but a racially mixed, culturally divided, pluralistic society. While it is true that those same elements had been traditional in Spanish society of times past, the conquerors grew up in a Spain that was to a great extent culturally homogeneous.

Within Central American society the creole well knew that class lines were to a considerable degree based on race. But already there existed distinctions to be made among the native peoples—there were Hispanicized "ladinos," and there were unacculturated "indios." The latter, along with blacks, could be held in contempt with little conflict of conscience. The increasingly meliorative attitude of the second generation does not make a case for them as having necessarily more noble instincts than their fathers; indeed, owing to the circumstances of their births, many of them were immoral, as well as spoiled, lazy, spiteful, and effete. Certainly they mistreated Indians, but they were less likely to kill them.

By a natural process, towns became more civilized as they took on the trappings of European culture. As the provinces began to see the influx of more stable persons, among them royal officials, more clergymen, and professionals of every category, the educational level inevitably rose somewhat. A few schools were established, so that sons of the conquerors probably became more literate than their fathers. Ineluctably, society became more civil with increasing numbers of Spanish women arriving and as men became resigned to a more domestic mode of life. The building of more churches and monasteries, the arrival of more of the religious orders, the establishment of schools, hospitals, orphanages, and the erection of impressive public buildings and handsome dwellings, all promoted a sense of civic pride which was less inclined to indulge barbarisms. At least to some extent, the formal establishment of the Holy Office of the Inquisition doubtless acted as a rein on the more blatant moral excesses.[7]

As it gradually became likely that there were no more Mexicos or Perus (even though some held out faint hope for El Dorado or Nuevo México), a less adventurous type migrated to the Indies. The more sedentary Spaniards of the later sixteenth century accepted the increasingly mundane colonial existence, and the fortunate few who had good cacao encomiendas were greatly outnumbered by those who had to settle for a life of modest ease. It is apparent that a good many Spaniards left Central America beginning in the 1570s, and those who remained resigned themselves to genteel poverty. Still, most of them were better off than they would have been in Spain. Spaniards of almost any socioeconomic level were in an elevated position within the motley Central American society, and they had servants to await their orders. It was nonetheless true that more and more Spanish immigrants of the lower class found it difficult to maintain themselves in any style. Many of them remained artisans of limited means, while others managed only to eke out a living as impoverished employees of their better-established countrymen.

The more stable milieu was also the outgrowth of a changing economy in which it became difficult to make a quick fortune. The days of the Indian slave trade were gone, and it became evident that large deposits of precious metals were few. Consequently, there was more diversification of the economy, with more Spaniards occupied in the prosaic business of agriculture, both for domestic consumption and export. Among the latter products were cacao, sarsaparilla, liquidambar, naval stores, sugar, cochineal, and indigo. There was always some production of silver. Internal food requirements stimulated the cultivation of a variety of fruits and vegetables, both native and imported. There was considerable growth in the raising of cattle, sheep, goats, horses, and mules, animals whose hides and tallow could be exported. With all this there was a corps of artisans —tailors, masons, shipwrights, cobblers, blacksmiths, bakers, and the whole run of tradesmen that one would find in almost any European settlement of the time. Merchants abounded, both those who traveled about, still bilking the artless natives, and those who established themselves in urban shops.

All this is not to suggest that Central America was a booming, prosperous colony; as MacLeod has convincingly demonstrated, the last quarter of the century saw the onset of depression. But that in itself had a sobering, and perhaps settling, effect on the colony, one that encouraged adventurers to move on. Nor is it meant to imply that the society had been transformed into a scene of domestic tranquility. On the contrary, it was still a society of considerable violence, immorality, and injustice, turbulent and crude in many respects. Change was a matter of degree, in the tradition of frontier settlements. It was irresistible and it was mostly positive.

How did the Indian fare in this modest transition? The obvious and inevitable change was his gradual assimilation into a Europeanized society. The process of Hispanicization was hastened by all of the factors mentioned above. The Indian's fundamental role was that of supplying labor, a part he still resisted. That situation, so frustrating to the Spaniards, was exacerbated by the growing shortage of native laborers, especially following the pestilences of the 1570s. The labor crisis forced competition for Indian services, which was conducive to somewhat more favorable working conditions. However, as they were absorbed more into Spanish society, new generations of urban Indians caught at least some of the spirit of capitalism, leading gradually to more willingness to work for just wages.

While the Indian of the sixteenth century was not obsessed with materialism (nor is he today), ladinos were often attracted to European products, for which money was required. Commerce remained mostly a system of barter among the Indians, but they knew the value of cash. One of the more tragic social consequences of Spanish occupation was the availability of wine and other intoxicating beverages to which many Indians had little resistance. Unfortunately, all too often their willingness to work was to enable the purchase of drink.

Those Indians living in remote areas were often less harassed by repartimiento drafts, and although they had to pay tribute, the demands for their labor were far less frequent than for those in proximity to Spanish towns. The clergy exercised great control over many native pueblos, and to some degree the inhabitants were protected as a result. Relatively few of the rural natives had learned the Spanish language, and their acculturation consisted primarily of a smattering of Christianity.

Life was still grim for those who continued to serve as tamemes or miners, and in certain other occupations. The lot of those who had trades or who worked as household servants was much easier. It is difficult to generalize about conditions in the second half of the sixteenth century because so much depended upon the nature of the work performed and the character of the taskmaster under whom one labored. On the whole, it is fair to say that those working within the scrutiny of royal officials were usually given more consideration than those in outlying regions, who were more likely to be mistreated by some estanciero or calpixque. Laws for the protection of Indians were observed more than in the early decades, although society was far from law-abiding. And the extent to which conditions for most Indians changed was due more to the developmental factors mentioned above than to any conscious crown policy.

The foregoing observations are adduced from a familiarity with the documentation of the period; and while such matters are rarely dealt with in specific details of the time, a number of random comments have been stitched together to present a view of some changing social patterns that had a bearing on the relationship between the races.

Now if, as asserted here, the treatment of the Indians was perceptibly improved by the end of the sixteenth century, it must nevertheless be stressed anew that their condition was still lamentable in many respects. No comprehensive report is conveniently available to provide a description of Indian life under the Spaniards in 1600, although some discuss the situation in years before and after. Again, there is some conflict in versions presented.

Although his picture of leisurely and prosperous native villages is highly suspect, if not preposterous, the account of Juan Pineda, written in 1594, is of some interest because it is evidence of the type of information that continued to confuse the Crown and Council of the Indies as to the true state of affairs.[8] He noted that while years before, in 1557, almost all Indians went about naked, in 1594 they were well dressed. They were shod in boots or shoes, wore hats of taffeta or felt, and had Spanish shirts, trousers of linen, and capes. "All of them have horses," he wrote, and they used them to take their goods to market or to ride out to their fields to inspect the crops, which they sold to the Spaniards for good profit. Some of the Indians, according to Pineda, owned two or three horses, if not more. All the people were clean and neat, and they had plenty of good food. Some of them, he maintained, even had Negroes for servants. He does mention, offhandedly, that while those Indians did not work, others from the mountains hired out to work the fields and to perform other tasks. Even though he does not say so, he is surely writing only of some native principales, and it may well be questioned how many, if indeed any, of them lived quite so well. Yet, for village after village his remarks are almost the same.

The point of his view becomes clear when it is realized that he is writing about crown towns, which, Pineda indicated, were paying far too little tribute, offering less than the contributions to private encomenderos. The residents of Yztapan, for example, were able to pay four times their assessment. His distortions were apparently for the purpose of increasing royal revenues, a result that could only enhance his position at court.

Evidence that the Pineda report should not be accepted is seen in the royal legislation issued in 1601 reiterating previous decrees and acknowledging that crown cédulas in favor of the Indians were still being ignored.[9] Further indication of the need for reforms is enunciated in the comprehensive labor laws given in 1609.[10]

There is yet more explicit commentary on the persistent exploitation of Indian laborers in the letters of the reforming bishop of Guatemala just after the turn of the century, fray Juan de Ramírez.[11] The unjust aspects of repartimiento labor were of particular concern to the prelate. Tequitines, those Indians required to work by the week, were forced to labor against their will when they should have been tending their own milpas, were paid insufficient wages, and were often made to walk to work farther than the six-league limit imposed by law. The provision that no more than 10 percent of the adult males of a pueblo could be absent at any time was being violated. If the workers failed to appear for work they were whipped, subjected to various ignominious treatments, and fined, regardless of the excuses they offered. The tequitines were paid so little that they lost money because of having to purchase their own food for the work week.

Indian women continued to fare badly, according to the bishop. Village indias who were forced to leave home for work grinding corn, weaving, or whatever, left behind their children and husbands, with grave social consequences. Those tezines sometimes returned to find their children badly neglected or abused, if not dead, and the mothers themselves sometimes expired in grief and despair. Aside from the tasks that kept women away from home for about ten days at a time, other indias were forcibly taken to serve in Spanish homes as servants. They were separated from their husbands, and sometimes they saw their young daughters taken away. Under those circumstances girls, as well as married women, often ended up as concubines of Spanish overseers, mestizos, or Negroes.

Widows, because they had no husbands to raise a clamor, were most often taken away to serve Spaniards; and despite their condition and having to support children, they were required to pay tribute. Young Indian women were sometimes overtly kidnaped by both encomenderos and alcaldes mayores, among others, and taken to Spanish homes or to obrajes where they languished in conditions of servitude little different from that of slavery. The more attractive women were, not surprisingly, in the most danger of being taken.

There had been since the early years following the conquest young native boys called teupantlacas serving in the churches, singing, playing musical instruments, and performing all the duties of priests, except to say Mass. For those time-consuming tasks they received no pay, but at least in the past they had been exempt from paying tribute. By the early seventeenth century, and perhaps even earlier, they no longer had even that consideration. On the contrary, Spanish officials often humiliated them publicly, despite the honored place they were supposed to have in the community.

Bishop Ramírez alludes to the mortification of Indian officials, the persistence of personal service, and the defrauding of Indian artisans. Tributes were still excessive, and the natives were harassed by scheming peddlers called *quebrantahuesos* and by plagues of Spanish officials, all of whom seemed determined to exact some profit from the hapless Indians. Although the most insignificant officials were the worst offenders, even alcaldes mayores were guilty of the same extortion.[12]

A valuable and much quoted account is the comprehensive report on the Indies written by Antonio Vázquez de Espinosa, a Carmelite friar who was in parts of Central America between 1610 and 1620.[13] Unlike the comparatively short Pineda report, Vázquez de Espinosa's treatise is very extensive, being primarily concerned with matters other than the conditions of the Indians; but his remarks in that regard are more credible than those of Pineda. He depicts a thriving economy with many caravans of mules taking goods up into Mexico. He writes with admiration of the Indians of Chiapas, who were "all well disciplined and intelligent. They are very skillful and ingenious, and quickly learn any trade that requires artistry; they are very gentlemanly, courteous, and well brought up, and the great majority are excellent horsemen and so they have very good horses and fine rodeos." At the same time, he offers a seemingly realistic description of Indian dress, noting that those in Guatemala wore full trousers, undershirts, and blankets *(escapapules)* used as capes. In hot country they wore *tilmas* of cotton or linen, and only the principales used sandals *(ojotas)*.

Though the author gives an overall impression of order and prosperity, occasional remarks indicate that there was a survival of the ill-treatment of natives. He saw them loaded down "like donkeys," and, "in most cases they are treated harshly and are belabored and kicked and beaten, with-

out turning against those who maltreat them."[14] He speaks of the same
being true in other provinces, among which he specifies Honduras
and Nicaragua.

The apostate friar, Thomas Gage, lived in Central America for several
years and left an impression of life there during 1627–37. Among his more
pertinent recollections are those on the numbers of pack animals in use.
Just in the valley of Mixco in Guatemala there were twenty teams of mules
containing more than 1,000 animals used by merchants of the province for
their commerce. In an Indian town in Nicaragua Gage saw in one day six
recuas entering, accounting for at least 300 mules.[15]

The great numbers of beasts and better roads suggest less dependence
on human carriers than formerly, especially on the long hauls that had
been so fatiguing for the carriers. The author does, however, go on to say
that Indians were used to carry trunks for travelers, sometimes having to
carry a hundred pounds for two or three days; "then at journey's end he
[the Spaniard] will pick some quarrel with them, and so send them back
with blows and stripes without any pay at all." If mules and carts could be
used on main roads between Spanish settlements and important Indian
pueblos, it was also true that many native villages were isolated except for
crude trails. Merchants, priests, and officials visiting those places would
have used tamemes, who were still required to carry loads in town streets
and between fields and the community, bearing wood, fodder, and produce. Indians of course continued to carry loads of their own goods.

Forced labor was still a fact of daily life in Gage's time, and his poignant
descriptions of it have a familiar ring. The Englishman's explicit discussion
of the functioning of the repartimiento system indicates that little had
changed in that respect over the years. And at least on one occasion he
alludes to extreme violence toward Indians.[16]

Gage's authority as an on-the-spot observer notwithstanding, it should
be borne in mind that he had personal reasons for presenting the picture of
a depraved Spanish colonial society in which the Indians were ripe for
rebellion, and consequently it is to be suspected that he may have exaggerated in some respects, particularly with regard to physical abuses.

In sum, while it is manifest that unjust exploitation continued in a
familiar vein until at least a century following the conquest, the vicious
atrocities and chattel slavery of the early decades after the conquest were
far less in evidence.

There is good reason to believe that the character of native labor
discussed here did not differ materially from that in other Spanish colonies. In most of them the disposition of affairs was much the same, the

economies were similar, and royal legislation applied to all regions pretty generally. Local conditions certainly resulted in some variations, and always the treatment of Indians depended upon the vagaries of particular authorities. It is pertinent to inquire if the situation in Central America during the sixteenth century was measurably better or worse than in other audiencia districts. In his time Las Casas alleged that Chiapas and Guatemala were the scenes of the most brutal treatment of natives. If that was so, did those provinces remain the worst over the decades?

In order to answer that question with any degree of satisfaction, substantial research will have to be undertaken into the system as it operated in other kingdoms. We do have, for the moment, informed comparisons written by Miguel Agia, who had spent some three decades in Central America and Peru when he wrote his account in the early seventeenth century. While one should not place too much reliance on the views of one man, his notes are persuasive and interesting as a starting point.

Agia, who is generally very critical of Spanish labor practices, notes that there was considerable difference between regions with regard to the repartimiento system. In New Spain generally, but especially in Guatemala where he had lived for some years, the work week consisted of five days—from Mondays at the hours of vespers until five o'clock on Saturday afternoons. The farthest Indians had to travel to work was seven leagues, without having to take along their women, children, or horses. Nor did they have to pass from one extreme climate to another. Moreover, in the space of a year's time, no Indian had to work more than fifteen to twenty days total. Their turns were broken up into three or four periods of five days each.

Workers were paid five reales for the week's work, which was better compensation than Indians received at Potosí or any other part of the Indies, especially taking into account the abundance (and therefore lower prices) in Central America compared with the penury of Peru. In the former, one real would buy five or six pounds of bread or twenty-five pounds of beef, while in Peru a real bought much less. Agia said that he considered the pay in Central America good, considering the little work they did, especially those who worked for officials, or females who worked as water carriers (like "moças de cantaro en Castilla"), or household servants. Under the eyes of the audiencia judges, they were well treated.

When Indians returned to their homes they found them as they left them, without discovering their wives and children dead, as used to happen in other places. For those reasons, the native populations of Guatemala and Chiapas were increasing; although he added that in Comayagua (Honduras), Nicaragua, and Costa Rica, their numbers had diminished because of personal service. The same was true for Soconusco as a result of seventy years of the Indians having to carry cacao the long distance to Mexico. In Guatemala poor Spaniards were sustained by the work of one or two Indians, which Agia felt was a benefit to the land. If Indians were to be assigned, they should be given first to the poor Spaniards, not to the rich.

Later Agia moved to Peru, where (in Trujillo) Indians were required to travel thirty leagues for their work on occasion, even though the legal limit was twenty-five. A sixth part of the population of pueblos served at a time, and the length of their turn (*mita*) was twenty days. The pay for the period of work was food and twenty-five reales, but as he noted before, the money did not go as far as in Guatemala.

In Lima the work period was a month, and the pay was two reales daily, with food. Since this was a later time, inflation may have forced wages up in Guatemala as well. The general mita lasted six months; however Indians rotated so that a worker had to put in only a month for the year. Contrary to the custom in Guatemala, the Indians were not assigned to Spanish urban dwellers. In the Audiencia of Santa Fe de Bogotá, conditions were worse: workers served for forty days, being forced to walk as far as thirty leagues, with their wives and children, and having to go from one climate to another.

The nature of the work itself was worse in Peru than in Central America because, Agia writes, the mining at Potosí was extremely arduous and dangerous. To send the Indians to work in the mercury mines was to give them a death sentence. Indian miners had to travel great distances, and their turn in the mines was long. Compared to the work in the textile factories (*obrajes de paños*) in Guatemala, where workers sat down all day in the shade, the workers of Peru were much worse off.[17]

Agia not only distinguishes the degree of evils in various kingdoms, but like his fellow Franciscan of earlier years, the moderate Francisco de Bustamante, he cautions against generalizing about labor conditions. In particular, the law abolishing repartimientos altogether should be reconsidered because obrajes and ingenios were not uniformly destructive of the Indians.

If the obrajes de paños were relatively harmless in Guatemala, he writes that the obrajes de tinta, of which there were many in Central America, were without question harmful. For although the season was no more than four months, the labor of cutting and hauling the plants in the sun and the corruption of the solution in the troughs was fearful. Few Indians in that work escaped death from the burning fevers they contracted. Consequently, in the years during which he was living in Guatemala, the presidents of the audiencia forbade the use of native laborers in the dye works, except for some of them who had grown up with it and were resistant to its virulence.

The same distinctions should be made for ingenios. Some were the trapiches and others were the big mills, some driven by water, others by men or beasts—"vnos son de agua, y otros son de sangre." There was a vast difference between the water-powered mills used for sugar in Central America and the *ingenios de metales* in use at Potosí and other mining areas. But the worst conditions he had seen were in Mexico, where in mines and textile obrajes Indians labored behind locked doors. They were put in with Negroes, but the Indians always ended up with the worst work, Agia states, because the owners would rather see ten Indians dead than one black who had cost them money.

Referring to the weaving generally done by Indian women, he was of the opinion that it was reasonable labor. They worked much as women did in Spain, seated in the shade. Many of the indias finished their work before noon, having earned about a real and a half, depending on their skills; and there were some so dexterous that they could finish two or three tasks daily, and were paid accordingly. They were not forced to do more than one assigned task, however, and the women had liberty to return to their houses as they wished, giving them time to tend their crops or take care of other necessities. Agia concludes that labor in the obrajes de paños of Central America was moderate and profitable for all, including Indian children. If his description is accurate, it is in stark contrast to reports of the same activity in Mexico, as he acknowledges.[18]

In various parts Agia had observed the excesses of the tameme system, which ruined the Indians more than anything else. In some areas, specifically Peru, they had to haul corn to the mines for distances of up to forty leagues. Again, he had seen the many deaths caused by that labor in Soconusco, Zapotitlán, and Suchitepéquez in Central America, but apparently the worst excesses there had moderated. In other parts of the Indies old people and pregnant women ("con la barriga a la boca que dizen") were forced to tote burdens of corn of up to seventy-five pounds into the mountains, "as if they were horses in a drove." But the custom in Guatemala was so strongly ingrained by prehispanic times that the Indians carried everything for themselves on their backs, and it would be impossible to prevent the practice.

Agia's three *pareceres* were written in response to the labor legislation of 1601, and with his experience of some thirty years residence in the Indies, the writings carry some force. In the end, despite his concern with making proper distinctions, most importantly because of the error in equating personal service with repartimiento labor, he is critical of labor policies, and suggests many reforms.[19] In May 1603, a royal cédula was issued, perhaps in response to the reports of Agia, directing Bishop Ramírez, and others, to do away with the abuses of personal service.[20]

Many of the Spanish labor policies that became widespread in the Indies had their origins in early years when the only Spaniards in the New World were the relatively few in the Antilles. Certain precedents were established, and the weight of custom encouraged their continuance. The astounding discoveries and conquests of the 1520s and 1530s must have had an overwhelming effect on a crown that was so absorbed with other pressing matters in the Old World that it could not readjust rapidly enough to the momentous unfolding of events in the New World. Mexico and Central America were already conquered by the time the Council of the Indies began effectively to function. In the confusion, the humane Laws of Burgos seemed forgotten.

There is no thread running so consistently through Spanish documents of the sixteenth century as the question regarding treatment of the conquered natives. Given that fact, it may be accepted that the Crown had a genuine concern for their welfare. But one of the thorniest problems in formulating policy was in determining the true state of affairs in America. Views on the nature of the Indians and the manner in which they were, and should be, treated covered the broadest spectrum. Opinions were offered by almost every segment of Spanish society in the colonies, and with few exceptions they were colored by personal interests. It was not simply that arguments of the conquistador-encomendero faction contributed to the irresolute attitude of the Crown; their stake in the outcome was all too obvious, which debased their position. The problem was that salaried crown officials of the highest rank, who were presumably disinterested, often corroborated the points made by encomenderos. Even bishops disagreed among themselves in the strongest terms about Indian policy.

For every voice raised in defense of the Indians, there were many others who contradicted it. While Las Casas and Cerrato catalogued the horrors of the Indies, other men of prominence called the two hysterical and distorted in their accounts. Leaving aside some members of the religious hierarchy who were clearly against a liberal policy, there were others known to be sympathetic to the Indian cause, such as Bishop Marroquín of Guatemala, and Motolinía and Vasco de Quiroga in Mexico, who counseled moderation.

With the many aspects of the dilemma to be taken under advisement, no clear and firm policy emerged. For while the New Laws were issued, one of the most fundamental articles—that limiting the succession of encomiendas—was soon abrogated because of encomendero reaction. That same year, 1545, the great silver strike at Potosí occurred, followed shortly by the discovery of rich deposits at Zacatecas and Guanajuato. Under the circumstances, a rationale for gradualism in the matter of Indian policy was desirable. No wonder then that the Crown came to regard the reforms initiated by Cerrato with mixed emotions. It must not be overlooked that he was allowed to proceed; but if the slaves were subsequently freed, the repartimiento system was the answer to forced labor for the mines and other necessary enterprises.

It is sometimes argued that, given the multiple considerations involved in the complex Indian question, implementation of laws on the books was neither realistic nor feasible. The frailties of that apologia bear examination. The root of the problem was that the Indies were conquered by adventurers, not by paid soldiers of the Crown. Hence, the king was in considerable debt to them and obligated to reward them. To deny those hardbitten veterans would almost certainly have meant rebellion and probable loss of the new territories. Even after being awarded Indians in a limited way, the unruly vecinos presented a vexing problem with their further demands. Considering the times and circumstances, the encomienda system and repartimiento labor would not have to be considered so oppressive had the regulations been observed. That they were not was the fault of local officials in the royal bureaucracy; however, the ultimate blame, it appears to me, attaches to the Crown and Council of the Indies for encouraging the abuses by their failure to crack down on negligent and corrupt officials.

In apprehension of the power and prestige of Cortés, and to provide better for royal administration, an audiencia was created. That disgraceful court, presided over by Nuño de Guzmán, was replaced with the appointment of judges of a higher caliber. Much has been written of the intelligent selection of the second audiencia in New Spain, with its men of integrity and humanitarian principles, remembered for having accomplished notable feats of administration. But how closely has their rule been examined for its Indian policy? The most celebrated of them, Vasco de Quiroga, became an advocate of moderation. Alonso Maldonado, at least in later years, exploited the Indians as much as the encomenderos (of whom he was one). There are indications that Juan de Salmerón urged caution in labor policies. I have not examined the attitudes of President Sebastián Ramírez de Fuenleal and Francisco Ceynos, but if they favored significant labor reforms it was hardly manifest.

Nor did the distinguished first viceroy, Antonio de Mendoza, usually seen as a wise and humane administrator, effect fundamental changes for Indian labor. Perhaps his decision to suspend implementation of the New Laws in face of menacing encomenderos is understandable. It was apparently for the same reason that he forbade Las Casas to introduce a discussion of Indian slavery at an assembly of bishops convened in 1546 for the precise purpose of examining Indian legislation. The viceroy's explanation was that it was "for reasons of state," which probably reflected the royal wish. It is thus all the more remarkable that Cerrato liberated the slaves in Central America only two years later under similarly threatening conditions.

In Central America proper, the behavior of a few of the highest authorities has been studied here. How typical were they of crown judges in the Indies? Some study of the later oidores in the audiencia leads me to the conclusion that there was an appalling lack of conscience among the majority of them; yet even when found guilty of egregious misconduct in office, a great percentage of them remained in the colonial bureaucracy, going from one audiencia to another, often with promotions.

Many appointees were men who had distinguished themselves in Spain, and the bland assumption was made that they would continue to do so in the Indies. It may be said that the Crown appointed good men who succumbed to the temptations of the frontier colonies; but once it was known that they had gone astray, the king and council were reluctant to recall them. It is apparent that an important consideration was that of the individual's connections at court. How else is the long tyranny of Pedrarias explained? It took years to get Nuño de Guzmán back to Spain, and the same was true in the case of Contreras and others with influence. It has been noted that Alonso Maldonado perpetuated his own power through his noble origins and marriage to the daughter of Montejo. Dr. Antonio Mexía, an oidor of scandalous morals, held on for many years in audiencias of Mexico and Guatemala, and became president in Santo Domingo.[21]

In this regard, consider the case of Alvarado. His prestige at court was earned through his daring exploits, then strengthened by charm. If others drew their advantage from birth, Alvarado is a good example of the incipient New World aristocracy. To a considerable extent his extraordinary tenure can be explained by his position at court: twice he married nieces of the Duke of Alburquerque, girls who were also related to the powerful Francisco de los Cobos, secretary to Charles V. A favorite at court, Alvarado became a business partner of Dr. Diego Beltrán of the Council of the Indies. Three days after signing a contract with Beltrán to market Negro slaves in America, Alvarado was appointed adelantado, governor of Guatemala, and a commander in the prestigious Order of Santiago.[22] No doubt these factors explain in large measure his independence of action, which was usually detrimental to the Indians. Many examples similar to those above could be cited, and it appears that the Crown was hesitant to punish men of prominent families or those who had distinguished themselves in the conquests.

Judges engaged in illegal commercial activities, more often than not including the use of Indian labor, protested that their salaries were too low to allow them a decent standard of living. Perhaps the Crown overlooked their illicit enterprises rather than raise their pay. If salaries were insufficient for oidores, they were niggardly for lower officials. Corregidores in Central America were often paid 150 pesos a year or less, certainly a meager income that encouraged their supplementing it, usually at the expense of the natives. Moreover, the position of corregidor came to be very much like a pension in lieu of an encomienda for impoverished conquerors or first settlers, many of whom were wholly without qualifications for a position so crucial for Spanish-Indian relations. Alcaldes mayores were paid somewhat more, and they were on the whole men of higher quality. Even so, their salaries were much too low. At the same time, the officials actually lived well, having the opportunity to extort their native charges.

The Spanish system of checks and balances notwithstanding, few officials were sufficiently punished for their transgressions. Visitas and residencias, laudable as they were in conception, were not very effective in the final event. Witnesses and judges could be suborned or intimidated, and perjury was commonplace. Even though the detailed testimony of several witnesses was often in substantial agreement, enough so that an official could be judged guilty beyond a reasonable doubt, the residenciado could usually controvert the charges through his own witnesses. Or, by offering examples to demonstrate that he was a just official, he would usually attempt to vitiate the charges, even though his defense did not directly confute them. Because most officials practiced selective enforcement by not applying the laws to persons close to them, while they were enforced for others, examples of their having implemented legislation could be shown.

Even when the residenciado was found guilty of a charge, the punishment was more often than not very light. The imposition of a 100-peso fine for illegal activity that had netted the official or his relative thousands of pesos in profit was hardly a deterrent. For serious crimes an official was sometimes deprived of office for two or three years, but charges of a very grave nature were referred to Spain for disposition. Because of appeals, many of the charges went unresolved for years, and many an official died with his case pending. Thus one could indulge in corruption with relative impunity. In a few residencias it can be seen that a guilty official received a harsh sentence, but that seems to have been the exception. Consequently, those high functionaries who were responsible for the good treatment of the Indians abused their positions, and by its complacence, the Crown invited the excesses. Spanish law expressed the Christian ideal; but neither the imperial exigencies at court nor the social and economic ambitions of the colonists permitted its execution.[23]

Appendix A
Indian Populations of
Central American Provinces

THE AUDIENCIA DISTRICT

Year	Figures	Source	Comments
ca. 1500	2,225,000 to 5–6 million and upwards	Rosenblat, 1:303–6.	Many estimates are given, some of which are probably far too high.
1550s probably	65,000 "yndios"	Estimate of Juan Estrada, clérigo, vecino de Guadalajara (n.p., n.d.), Archivo General de Indias, Seville (AGI), Indiferente General 857.	He mentions Francisco de la Cueva and Gómez Díaz de la Reguera, both with grown sons, as good men to settle Costa Rica. The information appears incomplete and is no doubt considerably below the true count.
1571–74	ca. 120,000 tributaries (i.e., 480,000 Indians, using a ratio of 1:4)	López de Velasco, p. 283.	They lived in about 1,000 pueblos and were distributed in 900–1,000 encomiendas, of which about ⅓ were located in Guatemala (excluding San Salvador).

347

Province of Guatemala (Including San Salvador)

Year	Figures	Source	Comments
1545	12,000 "indios" for San Salvador only	"La información q hizo sanct saluador" (Villa de San Salvador: 20 April 1545), Archivo General de Centro América (AGCA), Al. 28, leg. 2335, exp. 17305.	Held in encomienda by 44 Spaniards.
1550s?	26,000 "indios" (Santiago and its jurisdiction)	Estimate of Juan Estrada (n.p., n.d.), AGI, Indiferente General 857.	Almost certainly much too low.
	7,000 "indios" for San Salvador	Ibid.	San Salvador 1,000 San Miguel 4,000 La Chuluteca 2,000 (Xerez de la Frontera)
1571–74	22,000 tributaries	López de Velasco, p. 286	There were 130–140 villages and 70 encomenderos.
	15,000 tributaries (San Salvador)	Ibid., pp. 292, 297.	The city of San Salvador had 10,000 tributaries, San Miguel 5,000. No figure is given for La Chuluteca. The Indians of La Trinidad were assigned to encomenderos of Santiago.
	40–45,000 tributaries for the province of Guatemala (including San Salvador). That is, at 1:4, between 160–180,000 Indians	Ibid., p. 284.	The Indians of the province were apportioned to more than 300 encomenderos. There were about 300 native pueblos.
1575	56,000 "yndios casados" (i.e., tributaries)	Dr. Villalobos to the Crown (Santiago, 15 March 1575), AGI, Guatemala 39.	"Discrepción de los corregimientos que a de auer en la gouernacion de guatimala."

CHIAPAS

Year	Figures	Source	Comments
1550s?	15,000 "indios"	Estimate of Juan Estrada (n.p., n.d.), AGI, Indiferente General 857.	A low count.
1571–74	26,000+ "indios"	López de Velasco, p. 304.	
1575	24,000 "yndios casados" (tributaries)	Dr. Villalobos to the Crown (Santiago, 15 March 1575), AGI, Guatemala 39.	They lived in 80 pueblos. This is probably a fairly reliable count of Indians.
1581	40,000+	"Testimonio de la Ciudad . . . Real de Chiapa" (Chiapas, 11 September 1581— presented at court, Madrid, on 17 January 1583), AGI, Guatemala 44. Testimony of Lucas Camargo, royal notary (Madrid, 4 January 1583), AGI, Guatemala 966.	All were reported baptized.
1619	100,000+	Crown to the bishop of Chiapas (Madrid, 12 December 1619), AGI, Guatemala 386, lib. Q-2.	There were 180 pueblos listed for the bishopric.

HONDURAS

Year	Figures	Source	Comments
1524	400,000 (tributaries?)	MacLeod, *Spanish Central America*, p. 59, citing Benzoni	Benzoni's work is not always reliable.
ca. 1525	As heavily populated as "Mexico" and "Peru"	Companions of Cortés and Gil González, as reported in Pedraza to the Crown (Trujillo, 1 May 1547), AGI, Guatemala 164. Pedraza to the Crown (Gracias a Dios, 18 May 1539), AGI, Guatemala 9.	
ca. 1538	30,000 "indios"	Pedraza to the Crown (n.p., n.d.), AGI, Indiferente General 1206 ("Expedientes, Ynformaciones y probanzas, 1539–1541").	
1539	c. 15,000 "indios"	Pedraza to the Crown (Gracias a Dios, 18 May 1539), AGI, Guatemala 9.	
1541	8,000+ (tributaries)	MacLeod, *Spanish Central America*, p. 59, citing Benzoni.	
1550s?	6,000 "indios"	Estimate of Juan Estrada (n.p., n.d.), AGI, Indiferente General 857.	
1567	ca. 1,500 "indios"	Lic. Alonso Ortiz de Elgueta, alcalde mayor of Honduras (1567), AGI, Justicia 314.	This figure is without doubt grossly deflated. The author was accused of using 2,000 tamemes for his own ends.
1571–74	8–9,000 tributaries (i.e., 32–36,000 Indians at 1:4). Local figures for tributaries were: Valladolid 2,600 Gracias a Dios 3,000 San Pedro 700	López de Velasco, p. 306–13.	There were 220–30 pueblos. 56 pueblos 61 pueblos 30 pueblos

HONDURAS (cont'd)

Year	Figures	Source	Comments
	Puerto de Caballos		No Indian villages
	Trujillo 600		24 pueblos
	San Jorge de Olancho (see comments)		"En la jurisdicción y comarca de este pueblo hay como diez mil indios tributarios." This is obviously an error.
1582	5,840 tributaries distributed as follows:	Bishop of Honduras to the Crown (Trujillo, 10 May 1582), AGI,	
	Trujillo 590	Guatemala, leg. 164.	Of the Trujillo count,
	Puerto de Caballos 120		150 were on offshore islands.
	San Pedro 330		
	Comayagua (Valladolid) 1,800		
	Teguzigalpa 200		
	Agalteca 300		
	Gracias a Dios 2,100		
	San Jorge de Olancho 400		
1582	5,106 tributaries distributed as follows:	"Relación hecha a su Majestad por el gobernador de Honduras, de todos los pueblos de	
	Valladolid 1,723	dicha gobernación.—Año	
	Gracias a Dios 1,769	1582," *Boletín del Archivo General del Gobierno*	
	Trujillo 413	*(BAGG)* (Guatemala),	
	San Pedro 415	11 (1946): 5–19.	
	San Juan P. de Caballos 60		
	San Jorge de Olancho 726		
ca. 1590	4,864 tributaries	MacLeod, *Spanish Central America*, p. 59.	
1600	5,786 tributaries, of which 4,998 were distributed as follows:	Chamberlain, *Conquest and Colonization of Honduras*, p. 245.	Using a ratio of 1:5, Chamberlain postulates the total number of Indians in the province in 1600 at 36,000.

HONDURAS (cont'd)

Year	Figures		Source	Comments
	Valladolid	1,666		
	Gracias a			
	Dios	1,888		
	San Jorge			
	de Olancho	464		
	Trujillo	500		
	San Pedro	376		
	Puerto de			
	Caballos	104		

NICARAGUA

Year	Figures	Source	Comments
At Spanish contact	600,000 "yndios" (total?)	Lic. Herrera to the Crown (Gracias a Dios, 24 December 1544), AGI, Guatemala 9.	This was the estimate given to Herrera by conquerors. He was not present at that time.
ca. 1538	300,000 "indios" (total?)	Bishop of Nicaragua to the Crown (León, 17 January 1578), AGI, Guatemala 161.	This was according to information passed on to him. It is probably too high a figure.
1544	30,000 "indios" (tributaries only?) (total) of 120–150,000?)	Lic. Herrera to the Crown (Gracias a Dios, 24 December 1544), AGI, Guatemala 9.	In "Ynformacion de Gregorio Lopez," AGI, Patronato 231, ramo 4, it is stated that between 1539–43 over 14,000 Indians were missing in "aquellas provincias."
1548	11,137 tributaries	MacLeod, Spanish Central America, p. 53.	MacLeod takes the figure from the assessment of 1548–51 (AGI, Guatemala 128), which is fairly complete and reliable. The total would be slightly higher.
1553	ca. 7,000 "indios"	Fr. Tomás de la Torre to Council of the Indies (Santo Domingo de Coban, la Verapaz, 22 May 1553), AGI, Guatemala 8.	Tributaries only?
1550s?	3,000 "indios"	Estimate of Juan Estrada (n.p., n.d.), AGI, Indiferente General 857.	The figure is much too low, unless it refers to tributaries only.

NICARAGUA (cont'd)

Year	Figures	Source	Comments
ca. 1560*			
1571–74	12–12,500 tributaries; (48–50,000 total Indians?)	López de Velasco, pp. 318–31.	He lists more than 100 pueblos for León with 5,500 tributaries; and 100 pueblos for Granada with 6,500–7,000 tributaries. He gives no figures for areas of the five other Spanish towns. Hence, the figure is low.
1574?	6,650+ "vezinos naturales"	D. Pedro del Pazo, dean de León, "Lista del obispado de Nicaragua" (n.p., n.d.) AGI, Guatemala 167.	A breakdown of tributaries by areas is given. MacLeod, *Spanish Central America*, p. 58, assigns this to the probable date of 1560, which may well be correct.
1578	ca. 8,000 "indios"	Bishop of Nicaragua to the Crown (León, 17 January 1578), AGI, Guatemala 161.	This was the account according to the *padrones* of the priests and vicars.

SOCONUSCO

Year	Figures	Source	Comments
Pre-conquest	20,000 "indios"	López de Velasco, p. 302.	According to the author, Moteczuma sent an army of 800,000 to take the cacao-rich Soconusco province.
Pre-conquest	30,000 tributaries	MacLeod, *Spanish Central America*, p. 71.	
1524–26	15,000 tributaries	Ibid.	
1550s?	2,000 "indios"	Estimate of Juan Estrada (n.p., n.d.), AGI, Indiferente General 857.	
1563	1,600 tributaries	MacLeod, *Spanish Central America*, p. 71.	
1571–74	2,000 "indios"	López de Velasco, p. 302.	There were 33 hamlets, no encomiendas.
1573	1,800 "indios"	Dr. Villalobos to the Crown (Santiago, 15 May 1573), AGI, Guatemala 9.	

SOCONUSCO (cont'd)

Year	Figures	Source	Comments
1574	1,200 or 1,800 "indios"	D. Luis Ponce de León to the Crown (Soconusco, 19 January 1574), AGI, Guatemala 40.	The author gives both figures in the same letter. The Indians lived in 40 hamlets, some containing only 10 people.
1576	1,800 tributaries	MacLeod, *Spanish Central America*, p. 71.	
1609	2,000 tributaries	Ibid.	

LA VERAPAZ

Year	Figures	Source	Comments
1544	12–14,000 tributaries	MacLeod, *Spanish Central America*, p. 93.	
1561?	6,000+	Viceroy Velasco to bishop of La Verapaz (n.p., n.d.), AGI, Guatemala 965.	MacLeod, *Spanish Central America*, p. 93, suggests the date.
ca. 1565	13,000 "indios"	Bishop of La Verapaz to the Crown (Santiago, 13 December 1582), AGI, Guatemala 156; bishop of La Verapaz (La Verapaz, 1583?), AGI Guatemala 163.	Reference is made back to about ca. 1565, and is no doubt a rough figure.
1566	3,856 tributaries	MacLeod, *Spanish Central America*, p. 93.	
1571	3,135 to 3,329 tributaries	Ibid.	A low figure.
1571–74	ca. 4,000 tributaries	López de Velasco, p. 305.	There were about 17 pueblos, but no Spanish town. The area was opened up by Dominicans, to the exclusion of encomenderos.
1573	3,864 "indios"	Dr. Villalobos to the Crown (Santiago, 15 May 1573), AGI, Guatemala 9.	
1575	3,125 "yndios casados"	Dr. Villalobos to the Crown (Santiago, 15 March 1575), AGI, Guatemala 9.	There is mention of 15 pueblos.

La Verapaz (cont'd)

Year	Figures	Source	Comments
1582	3,000 "indios"	Bishop of La Verapaz to the Crown (Santiago, 13 December 1582), AGI, Guatemala 156.	
1583–84	3,000 tributaries	MacLeod, *Spanish Central America*, p. 93.	
1598	3,000 "indios"	D. Juan fray Rosillo, bishop of La Verapaz, to the Crown (Santiago, 10 January 1598), AGI, Guatemala 163.	They lived in 11 pueblos.
1598	1,948 "indios"	"Memoria de los yndios tributarios de la provincia de la Verapaz . . ." by the alcalde mayor (Santiago, 10 April 1598), AGI, Guatemala 966.	There were 12 pueblos, all paying tribute to the Crown.
1600	fewer than 1,800	D. Juan fray Rosillo to the Crown (Santiago, 2 March 1600), AGI, Guatemala 966.	

Appendix B
Spanish Vecinos in
Central America During the
First Century of Colonization

THE AUDIENCIA DISTRICT

Year	Figures	Source	Comments
1570	2,000+	Lic. Arteaga, fiscal, to Crown (Santiago, 16 December 1570), AGI, Guatemala, leg. 9.	Described as 2,000 "con casas pobladas."
ca. 1572–73	2,200–2,300	López de Velasco, p. 283.	900–1,000 of them were encomenderos. Of the 19 Spanish settlements, 14–15 were ranked as *ciudades*.
ca. 1575	1,090	"Relación . . . que sacada de un libro que tiene el Presidente Villalobos," AGI, Indiferente General, leg. 1528. See also Sanchíz Ochoa, *Los hidalgos*, p. 27.	This count, ordered by President Villalobos, includes 16 Spanish towns. In 14 there were encomenderos, totaling 416. This count compared with that of López de Velasco, which was taken about the same time, but showing more than twice the number of vecinos and encomenderos, illustrates the unreliability of censuses of the time.

THE AUDIENCIA DISTRICT (cont'd)

Year	Figures	Source	Comments
1594	1,760+	Pineda, "Descripción."	The source lists 16 Spanish settlements.
ca. 1620	2,840+	Vázquez de Espinosa, *Description.*	The source lists 15 Spanish settlements.

PROVINCE OF CHIAPAS

Year	Figures	Source	Comments
Ciudad Real (San Cristóbal de los Llanos)			
ca. 1555	50–60	Las Casas to Council of the Indies (n.p., n.d.), AGI, Patronato, leg. 252, ramo 9.	Under Cerrato's early administration 20 encomiendas were taken from some of these vecinos. Cabildo to Crown (Santiago, 24 January 1550), AGI, Guatemala, leg. 41.
1555	50	Las Casas to Fr. B. Carranza de Miranda, *Colección de documentos inéditos relativas al descubrimiento . . . de las antiguas posesiones españoles de America . . . (DII),* 7:332–33.	
1571	150 "casas"	Dr. Antonio González to Crown (Santiago, 2 March and 15 March 1571), AGI, Guatemala, leg. 9.	Of the vecinos, 60–70 of them were encomenderos.
ca. 1572–73	200–250	López de Velasco, p. 304.	
ca. 1575	108	"Relación . . . Villalobos," AGI, Indiferente General, leg. 1528.	47 encomenderos
1581	80	Lucas de Camargo, testimony (Madrid, 4 January 1583), cabildo report of 11 September 1581, AGI, Guatemala, leg. 966.	

PROVINCE OF CHIAPAS (cont'd)

Year	Figures	Source	Comments
1582	80	"Testimonio de la . . . Ciudad Real de Chiapa (presented at Madrid, 17 January 1583), AGI, Guatemala, leg. 44.	
1583	100	Pedro Castillo to Crown (1583), AGI, Guatemala, leg. 966.	
1587	80–100	"Testimonio de la . . . Ciudad Real de Chiapa" (1587), AGI, Guatemala, leg. 44.	
1594	200	Pineda, "Descripción," pp. 557–59.	
1600	120	"Memoria de los pueblos y beneficios que ay en el obispado de Chiapa" (Chiapas, 22 February 1600), AGI, Guatemala, leg. 966.	"Gente de toda broça y toda bien pobre."
ca. 1620	250+	Vázquez de Espinosa, p. 204.	"The great majority of noble rank."

PROVINCE OF SOCONUSCO

Year	Figures	Source	Comments
ca. 1572–73	60	López de Velasco, p. 302.	For many years the province had no truly Spanish town. There were merchants living in Indian settlements and traveling about. Many of the merchants had families, most of whom were settled in the principal town of Huehuetlán, where the Spanish governor resided. There were no encomenderos.
1574	20	Gov. Ponce de León to Crown (Soconusco, 19 January 1574), AGI, Guatemala, leg. 40.	
1594	50+	Pineda, "Descripción."	

PROVINCE OF GUATEMALA

Year	Figures	Source	Comments
Santiago			
1524	99	Remesal, *Historia general* (1964–66), 1:83.	These were the first vecinos inscribed.
1529	150	Bancroft, *History of Central America*, 2:120, n. 37.	
1531	100	Sherman, "Indian Slavery," p. 89.	
1541	78	Pardo, *Prontuario*, p. 2.	Perhaps not the total number; after the destruction of the second Santiago (Ciudad Vieja) 78 vecinos attended the *cabildo abierto*. Some had been killed during the flood.
1548	ca. 40	Cerrato to Crown (Santiago, 3 November, 1548), AGI, Guatemala, leg. 9.	
1549	100	Cabildo to Crown (Santiago, 30 April 1549), AGI, Guatemala, leg. 41.	80 of them were encomenderos.
ca. 1550?	100	Las Casas to Council of the Indies (n.p., n.d.), AGI, Patronato, leg. 252, ramo 9.	
1555	100+	Las Casas to Fr. B. Carranza de Miranda, *DII*, 7:332–33.	
1562	200–250	Probanzas of Juan de Guevara and Juan de León (Santiago, 16 November 1562), AGI, Guatemala, leg. 111.	Both were escribanos.
1563	300	Antonio Rosales to Crown (Santiago, 1 February 1563), Guatemala, leg. 44.	
ca. 1572–73	500	López de Velasco, p. 286.	70 were encomenderos. The province of Guatemala (including San Salvador) had 1,300 Spanish vecinos, of which 300 were encomenderos.

PROVINCE OF GUATEMALA (cont'd)

Year	Figures	Source	Comments
ca. 1575	227	"Relación . . . Villalobos," AGI, Indiferente General, leg. 1528	77 encomenderos
1570s	500	"Los pueblos despañoles sujetos a esta gouernacion . . ." (n.d.), AGI, Patronato, leg. 20, no. 5, ramo 21.	
1585	700	"Los encomenderos que hay . . ." (Santiago, 1585), AGI, Guatemala, leg. 966.	The number "800" was crossed out.
1594	500+	Pineda, "Descripción."	
1620	1,000+	Vázquez de Espinosa, p. 216.	
San Salvador			
1529–30	60	Çurrilla and Castellanos to Crown (Santiago, 20 August 1530), AGI, Guatemala, leg. 9.	
1532	51+	"El Licenciado Francisco de Marroquín y una descripción de El Salvador, año de 1532," *Anales de Sociedad de Geografía e Historia de Guatemala (ASGH)* 41 (1968): 199–232.	There were 51 listed as encomenderos.
1545	44	"La informacion q. hizo sanct saluador . . ." (San Salvador: 20 April 1545), *AGCA* Al.28, leg. 2335, exp. 17305.	
1551	50	Barón Castro, *La población de El Salvador*, p. 198.	With 50 vecinos in San Salvador and 30 in San Miguel, the author figures a total of 400 Spaniards for what is today El Salvador.

Spanish Vecinos 361

PROVINCE OF GUATEMALA (cont'd)

Year	Figures	Source	Comments
ca. 1555	50	Las Casas to Council of the Indies (n.p., n.d.), AGI, Patronato, leg. 252, ramo 9.	
1555	50	Las Casas to Fr. B. Carranza de Miranda, *DII*, 7:332–33.	
ca. 1572–73	150	López de Velasco, p. 292.	There were 60–70 encomenderos.
ca. 1575	130	"Relación . . . Villalobos," AGI, Indiferente General, leg. 1528.	42 encomenderos.
1594	60	Pineda, "Descripción"	Most of them were encomenderos.
ca. 1620	200+	Vázquez de Espinosa, p. 229.	
San Miguel			
1535	70	Montejo to Crown (Gracias a Dios, 1 June 1539), AGI, Guatemala, leg. 9.	Montejo notes that Cristóbal de la Cueva refounded San Miguel with 70 men. How many of them remained as vecinos is uncertain. Originally established in 1530 by Luis de Moscoso, it was depopulated in 1534 with the Alvarado expedition to Peru.
1551	30	Barón Castro, *La Población*, p. 198.	
1555	25–30	Las Casas to Fr. B. Carranza de Miranda, *DII*, 7:332–33.	
1555?	25–30	Las Casas to Council of the Indies (n.p., n.d.), AGI, Patronato, leg. 252, ramo 9.	
ca. 1572–73	130	López de Velasco, p. 297	About 60 were encomenderos.
ca. 1575	60	"Relación . . . Villalobos," AGI, Indiferente General, leg. 1528.	33 encomenderos.

PROVINCE OF GUATEMALA (cont'd)

Year	Figures	Source	Comments
1594	60	Pineda, "Descripción."	Almost all were encomenderos.
ca. 1620	100+	Vázquez de Espinosa, p. 231.	

La Trinidad (Sonsonate)

Year	Figures	Source	Comments
1557	100+	"Probanza de Méritos y Servicios de Francisco de Valle Marroquín. Año de 1557," *Anales* 36:373-79.	Settlement founded by lic. Pedro Ramírez.
1558	150 "casas"	Audiencia to Crown (Santiago, 22 February 1558), AGI, Guatemala, leg. 9.	150 "casas todas de mercaderes y tratantes."
ca. 1572-73	400	López de Velasco, p. 296.	No encomenderos.
ca. 1575	66	"Relación . . . Villalobos," AGI, Indiferente General leg. 1528.	No encomenderos.
1594	300+	Pineda, "Descripción."	
ca. 1620	200	Vázquez de Espinosa, p. 226.	

Xerez de la Frontera (Chuluteca)

Year	Figures	Source	Comments
1544	15-20	Lic. Herrera to Crown (Gracias a Dios, 24 December 1544), AGI, Guatemala, leg. 9.	
ca. 1572-73	30	López de Velasco, p. 300.	
ca. 1575	24	"Relación . . . Villalobos," AGI, Indiferente General, leg. 1528.	18 encomenderos.
ca. 1620	60	Vázquez de Espinosa, p. 233.	

PROVINCE OF HONDURAS

Year	Figures	Source	Comments
Gracias a Dios			
1548	18	Bancroft, *Central America*, 2:326.	
1550	29–35	MacLeod, *Spanish Central America*, fig. 15.	
ca. 1572–73	50	López de Velasco, p. 309.	There were 35 encomenderos.
ca. 1575	42	"Relación . . . Villalobos," AGI, Indiferente General, leg. 1528.	18 encomenderos.
1582	30	"Relación hecha a Su Majestad por el Gobernador de Honduras, de todo los pueblos de dicha Gobernación. —año 1582," *BAGG* 11:5–19.	22 encomenderos.
1594	70+	Pineda, "Descripción."	
ca. 1620	60	Vázquez de Espinosa, p. 242.	
Trujillo			
1540	18	Relación of bishop of Honduras (1544), *Colección de documentos inéditos relativos al descubrimiento . . . de las antiguas posesiones españoles de Ultramar (DIU)* 14:385–434.	
1542	20–25	Chamberlain, *The Conquest and Colonization of Honduras*, p. 244.	
1544	50	Relación of bishop of Honduras (1544), *DIU*, 14:385–434.	
1544	14–15	Lic. Herrera to Crown (Gracias a Dios, 24 December 1544), AGI, Guatemala, leg. 9.	

PROVINCE OF HONDURAS (cont'd)

Year	Figures	Source	Comments
1547	25+	Bishop to Crown (Trujillo, 1 May 1547), AGI, Guatemala, leg. 164.	
1547	50+	Bishop to Crown (Trujillo, 25 June 1547), AGI, Guatemala, leg. 164.	
1548	45+	Bishop to Crown (Trujillo, 22 December 1548), AGI, Guatemala, leg. 164.	
ca. 1572–73	100	López de Velasco, p. 311.	Only 3–4 were encomenderos. "La mayor encomienda no pasa de doscientos ducados de valor."
ca. 1575	39	"Relación . . . Villalobos," AGI, Indiferente General, leg. 1528.	8 encomenderos.
1582	30	Bishop to Crown (Trujillo, 10 May 1582), AGI, Guatemala, leg. 164.	Reference is to 30 "vezinos casados."
1582	20	"Relación" of the governor, *BAGG* 11:5–19.	9 encomenderos. Report dated 20 April; cf. preceding entry.
1594	25	Pineda, "Descripción."	
ca. 1620	100+	Vázquez de Espinosa, p. 243.	

Puerto de Caballos

Year	Figures	Source	Comments
1547	25–30	Bishop to Crown (Trujillo, 1 May 1547), AGI, Guatemala, leg. 164.	
1561?	10–12	"Memoria de Alberto de Melgar," AGI, Guatemala, leg. 44.	Re: "San Juan de Puerto de Caballos."
ca. 1572–73	20 "casas"	López de Velasco, pp. 310–11.	"Todas casi son de factores de mercaderes y negros de servicio."

PROVINCE OF HONDURAS (cont'd)

Year	Figures	Source	Comments
ca. 1575	55	"Relación . . . Villalobos," AGI, Indiferente General, leg. 1528.	20 encomenderos.
1582	19	Bishop to Crown (Trujillo, 10 May 1582), AGI, Guatemala, leg. 164.	Puerto de Caballos and San Pedro were dismantled in 1604 in favor of the port facilities of Amatique (Santo Tomás de Castilla). Vázquez de Espinosa, pp. 242–43.
1582	8	"Relación" of the governor, *BAGG* 11:5–19.	2 encomenderos.

Comayagua (Valladolid)

Year	Figures	Source	Comments
1539	60	Cabildo to Crown (Comayagua, 5 September 1539), AGI, Guatemala, leg. 43.	
1542	39	"Relacion de los oficiales del tesorero" (San Pedro, 17 February 1542), AGI, Guatemala, leg. 965.	
1550	29	MacLeod, *Spanish Central America*, fig. 15.	
ca. 1572–73	100	López de Velasco, p. 307.	
ca. 1575	70	"Relación . . . Villalobos," AGI, Indiferente General, leg. 1528.	25 encomenderos.
1582	50 "vecinos casados"	Bishop to Crown (Trujillo: 10 May 1582), AGI, Guatemala, leg. 64.	
1582	70	"Relación" of the governor, *BAGG* 11:5–19.	22 encomenderos.
1594	100+	Pineda, "Descripción."	
ca. 1620	200+	Vázquez de Espinosa, p. 240.	

PROVINCE OF HONDURAS (cont'd)

Year	Figures	Source	Comments
San Pedro			
1542	32	"Relacion de los oficiales del tesorero" (San Pedro, 17 February 1542), AGI, Guatemala, leg. 965.	
1547	25–30	Bishop to Crown (Trujillo, 1 May 1547), AGI, Guatemala, leg. 164.	
1550	32	MacLeod, *Spanish Central America*, fig. 15.	
ca. 1572–73	50	López de Velasco, p. 310.	
ca. 1572–77	40		
ca. 1575	40	"Relación . . . Villalobos."	18 encomenderos.
1582	20	Cabildo to Crown (San Pedro, 20 April 1582), AGI, Guatemala, leg. 44.	
1582	11–12	Bishop to Crown (Trujillo, 10 May 1582), April 1582), Guatemala, leg. 164.	
1582	20	"Relación" of the governor, *BAGG* 11:5–19.	12 encomenderos.
1594	30	Pineda, "Descripción."	
San Jorge (de Olancho)			
1542–43	25	Chamberlain, *The Conquest of Honduras*, p. 244.	
1544	50	Relación of bishop of Honduras (1544), *DIU* 14:385–434.	
ca. 1572–73	40	López de Velasco, p. 313.	19 encomenderos.

PROVINCE OF HONDURAS (cont'd)

Year	Figures	Source	Comments
ca. 1575	26	"Relación . . . Villalobos," AGI, Indiferente General, leg. 1528.	16 encomenderos.
1582	25	"Relación" of the governor, *BAGG* 11:5–19.	19 encomenderos.
1582	28	Bishop to Crown (Trujillo, 10 May 1582), AGI, Guatemala, leg. 164.	The reference is to "vecinos casados."
1620	40+	Vázquez de Espinosa, p. ñ43.	

PROVINCE OF NICARAGUA

Year	Figures	Source	Comments
León (viejo)			
ca. 1527–30	200+	Oviedo, 4:35.	
1535	150	Lozoya, p. 24	About 100 were encomenderos.
ca. 1572–73	150	López de Velasco, p. 318.	There were still 100 encomenderos.
1574?	60	D. Pedro del Pazo, dean of León, "Lista del obispado de Nicaragua" (n.p., n.d.), AGI, Guatemala, leg. 167.	
ca. 1575	62	"Relación . . . Villalobos, AGI, Indiferente General, leg. 1528.	37 encomenderos.
1580s?	150	"Los pueblos despañoles . . . ," AGI, Patronato, leg. 20, no. 5, ramo 21.	
1594	120	Pineda, "Descripción."	
ca. 1600	500	Vázquez de Espinosa, p. 256–57.	According to Vázquez de Espinosa, León had reached 500 vecinos by late

PROVINCE OF NICARAGUA (cont'd)

Year	Figures	Source	Comments
			century. The city was destroyed by volcanic eruptions and quakes in 1605–1606. The new León was settled 6 leagues away and had 80 vecinos by about 1620. But in view of Pineda's figure of 120 vecinos in 1594, Vázquez de Espinosa very likely had an inflated estimate.
ca. 1620	80 (Léon *nuevo*)	Ibid.	At the new location, the site of modern León.
Granada			
1535	200	Lozoya, p. 30.	About 100 were encomenderos.
ca. 1572–73	200	López de Velasco, p. 321.	There were still about 100 encomenderos.
1574?	60	D. Pedro del Pazo, "Lista . . . " (n.p., n.d.), AGI, Guatemala, leg. 167.	
ca. 1575	65	"Relación . . . Villalobos, AGI, Indiferente General, leg. 1528.	35 encomenderos.
1583	ca. 200	Gov. Casco to Crown (Granada, 17 February 1583), AGI, Guatemala, leg. 40.	" . . . es pueblo donde abra ducientos españoles aunque muchos dellos son mestiços."
1570s?	200	"Los pueblos despañoles . . . " AGI, Patronato, leg. 20, no. 5, ramo 21.	
1594	120+	Pineda, "Descripción."	
ca. 1620	250+	Vázquez de Espinosa, p. 258.	

PROVINCE OF NICARAGUA (cont'd)

Year	Figures	Source	Comments
Realejo			
ca. 1572–73	30	López de Velasco, p. 327.	
1574?	25	D. Pedro del Pazo, "Lista . . ." (n.p., n.d.), AGI, Guatemala, leg. 167.	
ca. 1575	50	"Relación . . . Villalobos," AGI, Indiferente General, leg. 1528.	No encomenderos listed.
1570s?	80	"Los pueblos despañoles . . . ," AGI, Patronato, leg. 20, no. 5, ramo 21.	
1594	30	Pineda, "Descripción."	
ca. 1620	100	Vázquez de Espinosa, p. 250.	
Nueva Segovia			
ca. 1572–73	40	López de Velasco, p. 326.	
1574?	24	D. Pedro del Pazo, "Lista . . ." (n.p., n.d.), AGI, Guatemala, leg. 167.	
ca. 1575	26	"Relación . . . Villalobos," AGI, Indiferente General, leg. 1528.	20 encomenderos.
1570s?	40	"Los pueblos despañoles . . ." AGI, Patronato, leg. 20, no. 5, ramo 21.	
1594	15	Pineda, "Descripción."	
Santa María de Esperanza			
1531	70	Cabildo to Crown (Léon, 1531), AGI, Guatemala, leg. 43.	Apparently all 70 were given encomiendas in this short-lived town.

PROVINCE OF COSTA RICA

Year	Figures	Source	Comments
Cartago			
1571	30	Dr. Antonio González to Crown (Santiago, 2 March and 15 March 1571), AGI, Guatemala, leg. 9.	
ca. 1572–73	60	López de Velasco, p. 331.	
1573	40	Dr. Villalobos to Crown (Santiago, 15 May 1573), AGI, Guatemala, leg. 9.	
1574?	50	D. Pedro del Pazo, "Lista . . . " (n.p., n.d.), AGI, Guatemala, leg. 167.	The reference is to "hombres."
1594	80+	Pineda, "Descripción."	
ca. 1620	100+	Vázquez de Espinosa, p. 262.	
Aranjuez			
ca. 1572–73	3–4	López de Velasco, p. 331.	
1573	15	Dr. Villalobos to Crown (Santiago, 15 May 1573), AGI, Guatemala, leg. 9.	
1573	16 "casas"	Dr. Villalobos to Crown (Santiago, 10 October 1573), AGI, Guatemala, leg. 9.	
1574?	10	D. Pedro del Pazo, "Lista . . . " (n.p., n.d.), AGI, Guatemala, leg. 9.	The reference is to "hombres."
1580s?	3–4	"Los pueblos despañoles . . . " AGI, Patronato, leg. 20, no. 5, ramo 21.	

Notes

Introduction

1. President Alonso López de Cerrato to the Crown (Santiago, 8 April 1549), Archivo General de Indias, Seville (hereafter cited as AGI), Guatemala, leg. 9. A league was 2.6 miles.

2. For a discussion of the various estimates, see Angel Rosenblat, *La Población Indígena y el Mestizaje en América, 1492–1950*, 2 vols., 1:303–6.

3. Those native auxiliaries were not, as is often stated, automatically free from paying tribute. See William L. Sherman, "Tlaxcalans in Post-Conquest Guatemala," *Tlalocan* 6 (1970): 124–39.

4. See, e.g., the comprehensive assessment made between 1548–51, AGI, Guatemala, leg. 128.

5. Juan López de Velasco, *Geografía y descripción universal de las Indias, desde el año de 1571 al de 1574*, p. 283.

6. See, e.g., Charles Gibson, *Tlaxcala in the Sixteenth Century*, p. 139. Conditions in Tlaxcala may well have altered the case.

7. "Ynformacion hecha por mando del muy ilustre señor licenciado garcia de valverde . . . año 1582" (Santiago, 7 November 1582), Archivo General de Centro América, Guatemala (hereafter cited as AGCA), A3.16.40.478, leg. 2799.

8. Murdo J. MacLeod, *Spanish Central America*, p. 41. MacLeod has an excellent discussion of the epidemics and pandemics.

9. Probanza de servicios de Francisco Sánchez (Santiago, 21 February 1551), AGI, Guatemala, leg. 52.

10. Cabildo to the Crown (León, 1531), AGI, Guatemala, leg. 43.

11. Alfonso Argüello Argüello, *Historia de León Viejo*. See also *Breve Guía de León Viejo*.

12. MacLeod, *Spanish Central America*, p. 205. This loss of life is not uniformly detectable in my figures for Indian population, except in the case of Honduras. More than anything else, that is perhaps a reflection on the paucity of accurate records.

13. Bishop Francisco Marroquín to the Crown (Santiago, 20 February 1542), AGI, Patronato, leg. 184, ramo 35, in writing of his late friend said, "solo su nombre bastava para sustentarla [tierra] y tenerla pacifica."

14. See William L. Sherman, "A Conqueror's Wealth: Notes on the Estate of Don Pedro de Alvarado," *The Americas* 26 (October, 1969): 199–213.

15. The career of Pedrarias is discussed in some detail by Kathleen Romoli, *Balboa of Darién*.

16. Pedrarias planned his daughters' marriages well. When death ended Balboa's betrothal to one daughter, the girl was then betrothed to Contreras. Another daughter married Hernando de Soto.

17. See the scholarly study by Robert S. Chamberlain, *The Conquest and Colonization of Honduras, 1502–1550.*

18. Lesley B. Simpson, *Studies in the Administration of the Indians in New Spain. 1. The Laws of Burgos of 1512*, pp. 18–21. Walter V. Scholes, *The Diego Ramírez Visita*, p. 26. See also Roland D. Hussey, "Text of the Laws of Burgos," *Hispanic American Historical Review* 12: 301–27.

19. *Recopilación de Leyes de los Reynos de las Indias* [1681], 4 vols. Vol. 2, book 6, título 2 ("De la libertad de los Indios"). Those cédulas of Charles V were dated as follows: Granada, 9 November 1526; Madrid, 2 August 1530; Medina del Campo, 13 January 1532; Madrid, 5 November 1540; Castellón de Ampurias, 24 October 1542; and Valladolid, 21 May 1543.

Chapter 1

1. Hubert H. Bancroft, *Native Races of the Pacific States of North America*, 5 vols., 2:649. The author writes that "slavery was an institution of all the nations in the sixteenth century, and had been traditionally for some centuries. . . . In the annals of . . . Maya nations [excluding Yucatán] no time seems to be noted when slaves were not held." For comparison with Mexican slavery, see Carlos Bosch García, *La esclavitud prehispánica entre los aztecas.*

2. Rodolfo Barón Castro, *La Población de El Salvador*, p. 98. Sylvanus G. Morley, *The Ancient Maya*, p. 149, gives the traditional Maya classifications: "the nobility (Maya *almehenob); the priesthood (ahkinob); the common people (ah chembal uinicob); and the slaves (ppencatob)."

3. El Capitán Gonzalo Fernández de Oviedo y Valdés, *Historia General y Natural de las Indias, islas y tierra-firme del mar océano*, 4 vols., 1:204.

4. Bancroft, *Native Races*, 2:651.

5. Letter from the caciques and principales of Santiago de Atitlán (Guatemala, 1 February 1571), published in Henri Ternaux-Compans, ed., *Voyages, Relations et Mémoires originaux pour servir à l'histoire de la Découverte de l'Amérique*, 20 vols. (Paris: Bertrand, 1837–41), 10:415–28, cited in Silvio Zavala, *Los esclavos indios en Nueva España*, p. 80, n. 26.

6. Barón Castro, *La Población*, p. 98.

7. Bancroft, *Native Races*, 2:260.

8. Edward E. Calnek, "Highland Chiapas before the Conquest" (Ph.D. diss., University of Chicago, 1962), pp. 81, 83, 100.

9. France V. Scholes and Ralph L. Roys, *The Maya Chontal Indians of*

Acalan-Tixchel, p. 56. While slavery was common in Yucatán, Ralph L. Roys, *The Indian Background of Colonial Yucatán,* pp. 34–35, found "no evidence of breeding slaves for profit."

10. Fray Juan de Torquemada, *Los veinte i vn libros rituales i Monarchia Indiana, con el origen y guerras, de los Indios Ocidentales, de sus Poblaciones, Descubrimiento, Conquista, Conuersion, y otras cosas marauillosas de la mesma tierra, distribuydos en tres tomos.* (Hereafter cited as *Monarquía Indiana.*) 3 vols., 1:335.

11. F. V. Scholes and Roys, *The Maya Chontal,* pp. 30, 58–59, note that "there was an extensive trade across the base of the Yucatan Peninsula with the northern coast of what are now Guatemala and Honduras" that included slaves. See also Roys, *The Indian Background,* pp. 34, 53, 65, and Bancroft, *Native Races,* 2:649.

12. Bancroft, *Native Races,* 2:649, 723, 747.

13. Fray Francisco Ximénez, *Historia de la Provincia de San Vicente de Chiapa y Guatemala de la Orden de Predicadores,* 3 vols., 1:92, 94.

14. Torquemada, *Monarquía Indiana,* 2:386–88; and Bancroft, *Native Races,* 2:650–51. See also Capitán D. Francisco Antonio de Fuentes y Guzmán, *Recordación florida del reyno de Guatemala,* 3 vols., 1:13.

15. Torquemada, *Monarquía Indiana,* 2:390.

16. Bancroft, *Native Races,* 2:650–51.

17. Ibid., 2:386.

18. Ibid., 2:390.

19. Diego de Landa, *Landa's Relación de las Cosas de Yucatán,* Alfred M. Tozzer, trans. and ed., p. 95. Tozzer is citing Oviedo, who for purposes of comparison added that a rabbit sold for ten beans and a prostitute charged eight to ten beans.

20. Torquemada, *Monarquía Indiana,* 2:387, 391.

21. Ibid., p. 391. Morals were strict among the native societies in some respects. Among the laws affecting "gente fornicaria" was one that compelled a young man to marry a maiden with whom he had had sexual relations. However, in the case of a girl recently married to another when she committed the act, her husband would not accept her, and he took back everything of value that he had contributed to the marriage.

22. "Relación hecha por el Licenciado Palacio al Rey D. Felipe II, en la que describe la Provincia de Guatemala, las costumbres de los indios y otras cosas notables" (Guatemala, 8 March 1576), *Anales de la Sociedad de Geografía e Historia de Guatemala* (hereafter cited as *ASGH*) 4 (Sept., 1927): 71–92. The same document is available in Diego García de Palacio, *Carta Dirigida al Rey de España, por el Licenciado Dr. Don Diego García de Palacio, Oydor de la Real Audiencia de Guatemala: Año 1576,* p. 80. Cf. Antonio de Herrera y Tordesillas, *Historia general de los hechos de los castellanos en las islas i tierra firme del mar océano,* 4 vols., 1: década 4, book 8, ch. 10, who seems to have taken some material from the Palacio report cited above and who in turn was copied by others. See also Bancroft, *Native Races,* 1:651.

23. Ximénez, *Historia*, 1:98. Roys, *The Indian Background*, p. 27, states that among the Maya of Yucatán children of a noble and a slave seem to have been sold into slavery upon the father's death, and that on occasion they were sacrificed.

24. Torquemada, *Monarquía Indiana*, 1:341. Ximénez, *Historia*, 1:95.

25. Ephraim G. Squier, *The States of Central America*, p. 334. Bancroft, *Native Races*, 1:729, adds that among the Indians of Honduras, "the adulterer caught in the act had his ear-rings forcibly torn out; then he was whipped by the relatives of the injured. The woman went free on the supposition that she, as the weaker party, was not responsible."

26. Roys, *The Indian Background*, pp. 34–35, 53. Among the Aztecs, the author tells us, "slave dealers were among the most highly honored members of the merchants guild." On p. 68, Roys suggests that perhaps slaves taken from neighbors in warfare were often sold, and that they purchased slaves for themselves "from more distant regions, who could less easily escape to their homes." See also Bancroft, *Native Races*, 2:650; F. V. Scholes and Roys, *The Maya Chontal*, pp. 30, 58–59. The merchants of Acalán were wide-ranging, the authors note, and there was an important slave trade, "but whether they were largely captured in their wars with neighbors is hard to tell. Since slaves were brought to Tabasco by the Aztecs and to northern Honduras from Yucatan, it might well be inferred that the Acalan acquired most of their slaves by capture, employing some at home and exporting the surplus."

27. Fray Diego Durán, *The Aztecs*, p. 147.

28. Spaniards frequently alluded to the fact that prior to their arrival the Indians had enslaved their own kind for little cause. See, e.g., "La Informacion q. hizo sanct saluador ante la justicia hordinaria . . . " (Villa de San Salvador, 20 April 1545), AGCA, Al. 28, legajo (hereafter abbreviated as leg.) 2335, expediente (hereafter abbreviated as exp.) 17503. Torquemada, *Monarquía Indiana*, 2:563–67, offers a detailed account of prehispanic slavery, with particular reference to Mexico. See also Eric R. Wolf, *Sons of the Shaking Earth*, pp. 142–44, for a discussion of the servile group *tlacotli* in *Mexica* society.

Chapter 2

1. For a discussion of slavery in the Antilles under Isabella and Ferdinand, the reader is referred to the absorbing account of Lesley Byrd Simpson, *The Encomienda in New Spain*. On p. 15, Simpson suggests that Isabella ultimately put Crown interests above humanitarian considerations. Cf. Silvio Zavala, "Los Trabajadores Antillanos en el Siglo XVI," *Revista de Historia de América* 2 (June, 1938), and 3 (Sept., 1938): 31–68, 60–88.

2. For slavery legislation see *Recopilación de leyes de los Reynos de las Indias*. See also Ruth Kerns Barber, *Indian Labor in the Spanish Colonies*.

3. Much has been written on this theme. Standard works in English are Lewis Hanke, *The Spanish Struggle for Justice in the Conquest of America*, and by the same author, *Aristotle and the American Indians*. See also Silvio Zavala,

Servidumbre natural y libertad cristiana, según los tratadistas españoles de los siglos XVI y XVII.

4. Herrera, *Historia general*, vol. 1: déc. 3, book 8, ch. 10.

5. See, e.g., Torquemada, *Monarquía Indiana*, 2:560–67.

6. Because of continuing resistance of the Indians, Charles V, in 1527, reiterated that those who persisted could be enslaved. Royal cédula (hereafter cited as R.C.) (Valladolid, 16 March 1527), AGI, Guatemala, leg. 402, lib. 1, fols. 53v–54v.

7. See Lewis Hanke, "The 'Requerimiento' and its Interpreters," *Revista de Historia de América* 1 (March, 1968): 25–34. Examples of the document appear in Charles Gibson, ed., *The Spanish Tradition in America*, pp. 58–60, and in Herrera, *Historia general*, vol. 1: déc. 1, book 7, ch. 14, who repeats the one issued in 1510 by Alonso de Ojeda. See also *La Muerte de Tecun Uman: Estudio Crítico de la Conquista del Altiplano Occidental de la República* (Guatemala: Editorial del Ejército, 1963), pp. 125–34.

8. Hubert H. Bancroft, *History of Central America*, 3 vols., 1:623. Unless otherwise noted, I am following Bancroft's account of the conquest. See also the following: Adrian Recinos and Delia Goetz, trans., *The Annals of the Cakchiquels;* S. W. Miles, "Summary of Preconquest Ethnology of the Guatemala-Chiapas Highlands and Pacific Slopes," in *Handbook of Middle American Indians*, vol. 2, part 1, pp. 276–87.

9. See Francis Gall, *Título del Ajpop Huitzitzil Tzunún.*

10. See Jorge A. Guillemin, *Iximché, Capital del Antiguo Reino Cakchiquel.*

11. Sedley J. Mackie, ed., *An Account of the Conquest of Guatemala in 1524 by Pedro de Alvarado*, p. 53.

12. José Fernando Remírez, ed., *Proceso de Residencia Contra Pedro de Alvardo, 1529*, pp. 7, 48, 77–78.

13. Ibid., p. 79.

14. Mackie, *An Account of the Conquest*, p. 64. Ramírez, *Proceso Contra Alvarado*, pp. 8, 58, 79–80. In Ramírez, p. 141, it states that a witness said that the horse was run to death in the encounter. Regardless of the cause, the Indians were blamed, and the loss of a war horse was serious. Under the circumstances no more could be acquired, but even a later replacement could cost from 500 to 800 pesos.

15. Ramírez, *Proceso Contra Alvarado*, pp. 80, 101, 116. See also residencia of Pedro de Alvarado (Santiago, 1535), AGI, Justicia, leg. 296.

16. Ramírez, *Proceso Contra Alvarado*, pp. 8, 29, 58, 80–81.

17. Mackie, *An Account of the Conquest*, pp. 77–78, 83–84, 85.

18. Ramírez, *Proceso Contra Alvarado*, pp. 8, 9, 82.

19. Mackie, *An Account of the Conquest*, p. 131, citing Las Casas.

20. Alvarado to the governor's lieutenants in the City of Mexico (Santiago, 5 June 1525), Archivo General de la Nación, Mexico (hereafter cited as AGN), Hospital de Jesús, leg. 271, exp. 14:1. I am indebted to Professor France V. Scholes for the transcript of this document.

376 *Notes*

21. Ramírez, *Proceso Contra Alvarado*, pp. 8, 29, 58, 102, 162.
22. Residencia of Alvarado (Santiago, 1535), AGI, Justicia, leg. 296.
23. Mackie, *An Account of the Conquest*, p. 132.
24. Bancroft, *History of Central America*, 1:614.
25. MacLeod, *Spanish Central America*, p. 41, is of the opinion that one-third of the population of highlands Guatemala died of plagues following Spanish contact.
26. For the best treatment of these early years in Honduras see Robert S. Chamberlain, *The Conquest and Colonization of Honduras*.
27. Probanza de Hernán Cortés contra Moreno (Trujillo, 23 October 1525), AGI, Patronato, leg. 170, ramo 23. See also Bancroft, *History of Central America*, 1:372, 536.
28. Bancroft, *History of Central America*, 1:577–94.
29. Diego López de Salcedo to Crown (Trujillo, postrero de 1526), AGI, Guatemala, leg. 39.
30. Crown to governor of Honduras-Higueras (Valladolid, 16 March 1527), AGI, Guatemala, leg. 402, lib. 1, fols. 53v–54v.
31. Noting the abuses, the Crown acted to stop enslavement (Medina, 2 August 1530) cited in *provisión* (Toledo, 20 February 1534) AGCA, A.1, leg. 4575, fols. 18v–23.
32. Andrés de Cerezeda to Crown (Trujillo, 24 April 1533), AGI, Guatemala, leg. 49.
33. Cerezeda to Crown (Puerto de Honduras, 14 June 1533), AGI, Guatemala, leg. 49.
34. Juan Ruano to Audiencia of Mexico (Trujillo, 14 April 1533), AGI, Guatemala, leg. 49.
35. General provision for the Indies (Toledo, 20 February 1534), AGCA, A.1, leg. 4575, fols. 18v–23.
36. Diego García de Celis to the Crown (Puerto de Caballos, 20 June 1534), AGI, Guatemala, leg. 49.
37. Francisco de Barrientos to the Crown (Trujillo del Pinar de Puerto de Honduras, 25 July 1534), AGI, Guatemala, leg. 49.
38. Residencia of Alvarado, AGI, Justicia, leg. 296, citing royal cédula given in Toledo, 20 February 1534.
39. Cabildo to the Crown (Puerto de Caballos, 12 August 1536), AGI, Patronato, leg. 20, no. 4, ramo 5.
40. Jerónimo de San Martín, lieutenant of the treasurer Celis, to the Crown (San Pedro de Puerto de Caballos, 23 April 1537), AGI, Guatemala, leg. 49.
41. This was true of other provinces as well. For example, José Joaquín Pardo, *Prontuario de Reales Cédulas, 1529–1599*, p. 59, R.C. of 2 August 1530, states that only Indians making war were to be reduced to slavery; ibid., R.C. of 20 July 1532, gives Alvarado the power to enslave Indians who resist recognizing the crown of Castile; licenciado Francisco Castañeda to the Crown (León, 1 May 1533) AGI, Guatemala, leg. 9, states that it would be well if the Chontales, an especially

fractious group of Indians who preferred to fight than work, were shipped out so that the mines could be worked by Negroes; and a later R.C. of the queen (Valladolid, 9 September 1536), AGCA, A.23, leg. 4575, fol. 42, allowed that Indians taken in just war could be enslaved, owing to the unsettled state of the land.

42. Castañeda to the Crown (León, 5 October 1529), AGI, Guatemala, leg. 9.

43. "Los cargos que se hazen a don xpoval de la cueba capitan y teniente de gouernador que fue de la villa de san miguel de la pesquisa secreta que le fue tomada por mandado de su magt. por el licdo. maldonado," in residencia of Alvarado (Santiago, 1535), AGI, Justicia, leg. 296. See also "Testimonio de ciertos robos q. hizieron la gente de don Xpoval de la Cueba a los mensageros del Governador de Honduras" (Buena Esperanza, Honduras, 29 January 1535), signed by Governor Cerezeda, AGI, Patronato, leg. 180, ramo 62. Cristóbal de la Cueva, sent either by Alvarado or his brother Jorge, entered Higueras and branded peaceful Indians, contrary to a royal cédula prohibiting the enslavement of Indians in that province. From the pueblo of Yamala alone they took sixty Indians, according to testimony.

44. Montejo to the Crown (Salamanca, 10 August 1534), AGI, Patronato leg. 184, ramo 25; R.C. of 10 March 1548, AGI, Guatemala, leg. 393, lib. 3; Montejo to the Crown (Gracias a Dios, 15 August 1539), AGI, Guatemala, leg. 9; Montejo to the Crown (Gracias a Dios, 31 December 1545), AGI, Guatemala, leg. 9; "Segunda memorial . . . " (n.p., n.d.), AGI, Guatemala, leg. 965. Montejo's disclaimers notwithstanding, Cerrato reported that it was said that the adelantado took more than two thousand Indian slaves in fighting in Yucatán, and that for his sugar plantation at Champotón (Campeche) he seized Indian lands and more than five hundred slaves to work the mill. Perhaps of more concern to the Crown, it was alleged that Montejo cracked the royal treasure chest in Tabasco, taking 1,350 pesos and some documents. Cerrato to the Crown (Santiago, 8 April 1549), AGI, Guatemala, leg. 9.

45. Chamberlain, *The Conquest of Honduras*, p. 121. Because of certain evidence against Montejo, some of which is discussed at more length later in these pages, I am inclined to view him in harsher terms than Dr. Chamberlain, who is nonetheless the authority on the adelantado.

Chapter 3

1. See, e.g., Rodrigo de Contreras to the Crown (León, 25 June 1537), AGI, Guatemala, leg. 43.

2. "Carta de H. Cortes a Hernando de Saavedra su lugarteniente en Truxillo. Sin firma, 1525," *Colección de documentos inéditos relativos al descubrimiento, conquista, y organización de las antiguas posesiones españoles de América y Oceanía*, 42 vols. (hereafter cited as *DII*), vol. 26, pp. 185–94.

3. Diego López de Salcedo to the Crown (Trujillo, 31 December 1526), AGI, Guatemala, leg. 39.

378   *Notes*

4. "Ordenanças que se dieron a Diego Mendez cuando fue por lugarteniente a la villa de Trugillo . . . por mando del gobernador . . . " (León, 20 August 1527), AGI, Guatemala, leg. 965. Licenciado Diego de Herrera to the Crown (Gracias a Dios, 10 July 1545), AGI, Guatemala, leg. 9.

5. R.C. (Toledo, 20 February 1534), AGCA, A1.23, leg. 4575, exp. 39528, fols. 18v–19.

6. R.C. (Medina del Campo, 20 July 1532), AGI, Guatemala, leg. 393, fols. 42–43.

7. R.C. (Toledo, 20 February 1534), AGCA, A1.23, leg. 4575, exp. 39528, fols. 18v–19.

8. Zavala, *Los esclavos indios en Nueva España*, p. 80, n. 26.

9. Residencia of Pedro de Alvarado (Santiago, 1535), AGI, Justicia, leg. 296. "Informacion de Hernan Mendez" (Santiago, 28 May 1531), AGI, Guatemala, leg. 110.

10. Francisco del Paso y Troncoso, ed., *Epistolario de Nueva España, 1505–1818* (hereafter cited as *ENE*), 16 vols., 3:88, 107, 117.

11. A royal cédula (Madrid, 12 July 1530) for New Spain included these comments: "Y porque somos informados que los yndios entresi tienen por ley y costumbre de hazer esclauos, ansi en las guerras que vnos conotros muy particularmente, y prouereys en ellos lo que os pareciere que segun justicia y razon se deue proveer: esto se entiende para entre los mesmos yndios." Vasco de Puga (comp.), *Prouisiones, cédulas, instrucciones de Magestad. . . .* 2 vols., 1:64.

12. R.C. of 20 February 1534, *Colección de documentos inéditos relativos al descubrimiento, conquista y organización de las antiguas posesiones españolas de Ultramar* (hereafter cited as *DIU*), 25 vols., 10:192–203. R.C. (Valladolid, 9 September 1536), AGCA, A1.23, leg. 4575, fol. 42. R.C. (Toledo, 31 January 1538), AGCA, A.1, leg. 4575, fols. 43–43v. R.C. (Toledo, 31 March 1539), AGCA, A1.23, leg. 4575, exp. 39528, fols. 40–41. R. C. (Toledo, 7 June 1539), AGI, Guatemala, leg. 402, lib. 1, fols. 239–40. Diego de Encinas, comp., *Cedulario Indiano*, 4 vols., 4:367, citing R.C. (Fuensalida, 26 October 1541).

13. Cabildos of Santiago, Ciudad Real, San Salvador, and San Miguel to the Crown (Santiago, 22 January 1539), AGI, Guatemala, leg. 41.

14. Bishop Marroquín to the Audiencia of Mexico (Santiago, 1 October 1539), AGI, Guatemala, leg. 9. See also, "La informacion q. hizo sanct saluador ante la justicia hordinaria . . . " (Villa de San Salvador, 20 April 1545), AGCA, A1.28, leg. 2335, exp. 17503.

15. Rodrigo de Contreras, governor of Nicaragua, to the Crown (León, 25 June 1537), AGI, Guatemala, leg. 43.

16. Royal officials to the Crown (Ciudad de Guatemala, 28 September 1531), AGI, Guatemala, leg. 45. The officials were Çurrilla, the contador; Castellanos, the *tesorero;* and Ronquillo, the factor.

17. Zavala, *Los esclavos indios en Nueva España*, p. 43, citing B. M. Biermann, "Zwei Briefe von Fray Bartolome de las Casas, 1534–1535," *Archivum Fratrum Praedicatorum* 4 (Rome, 1934): 211 ff.

Chapter 4

1. Royal provision to Cerezeda (Madrid, 22 April 1535), AGI, Guatemala, leg. 402, lib. 1, fols. 158–60.

2. Pardo, *Prontuario*, p. 59, R.C. of 13 February 1531; R.C. (Medina del Campo, 24 May 1532), AGI, Guatemala, leg. 393, R-1, fols. 15–15v; and ibid., p. 59, R.C. of 5 June 1532.

3. Pardo, *Prontuario*, p. 59, R.C. of 1 March 1535, and repeated on 1 November 1535; ibid., p. 121, R.C. of 30 March 1536; R.C. (Valladolid, 29 January 1538), AGI, Guatemala, leg. 402, lib. 1, fols. 209v–10; and Provisión general del Consejo de las Indias (Valladolid, 28 September 1543), AGI, Patronato 231, ramo 2.

4. "Probanza de H. Cortes vs. Moreno" (Trujillo, 23 October 1525), AGI, Patronato, leg. 170, ramo 23. Herrera, *Historia general*, déc. 3, book 10, ch. 11.

5. Herrera, *Historia general*, déc. 4, book 1, ch. 7.

6. *DII*, 1:450–55.

7. "Declaracion" (28 July 1530), AGI, Patronato, leg. 246, ramo 2, no. 14. See also, Hayward Keniston, *Francisco de los Cobos, Secretary of the Emperor Charles V*, pp. 105–6.

8. Bernal Díaz del Castillo, *The True History of the Conquest of New Spain*, 3 vols., 5:328–29. The best study of early Spanish Honduras is Chamberlain, *The Conquest of Honduras*.

9. Herrera, *Historia general*, dec. 3, book 9, ch. 10.

10. Chamberlain, *The Conquest of Honduras*, p. 120. Montejo's career in Yucatán can be traced through the excellent work of Robert S. Chamberlain, *The Conquest and Colonization of Yucatán, 1517–1550*. See also by the same author, *The Governorship of the Adelantado Francisco de Montejo in Chiapas, 1539–1544*.

11. Information of Andrés de Cerezeda (31 March 1530) AGI, Guatemala, leg. 491.

12. Cabildo to the Audiencia of Mexico (Trujillo, 20 March 1530), AGI, Guatemala, leg. 44.

13. Cerezeda and Herrera to the Crown (Trujillo, 20 March 1530), AGI, Guatemala, leg. 49. Francisco de Barrientos to the Crown (Trujillo, 29 March 1530), AGI, Guatemala, leg. 49.

14. "Informacion Contra los gobernadores que fueron de la ciudad de Truxillo en Honduras, Diego Lopez de Salzedo y Andres de Zerezeda, levantados estos contra el capitan Hernando de Sayavedra puesto alli por Hernan Cortes luego que la pacifico. . . . Pedimiento y ynterrogatorio . . . Presentado por lic. Pedraza" (12 November 1539), AGI, Patronato, leg. 170, ramo 45. See also, Pedraza to the Crown (Trujillo, 1 May 1547), AGI, Guatemala, leg. 164. This was not an isolated instance, as seen in a letter from Francisco de Castañeda, governing in Nicaragua, who wrote that "a la menor provocación e incluso sin provocación alguna, los españoles, montados a caballo, derribaban a los indios, incluyendo

mujeres y niños, y los lanceaban," cited in Bartolomé de las Casas, *Historia de las Indias*, 3 vols., 1: xvi.

15. Las Casas, *Historia*. Fallen Indians were decapitated by others also, as in the expedition of Martin Estete to Chorotega: Francisco Castañeda to the Crown (León, 5 October 1529), AGI, Guatemala, leg. 9.

16. F. Castañeda to the Crown (León, 5 October 1529), AGI, Guatemala, leg. 9.

17. Ibid.

18. Rodrigo del Castillo, tesorero juez de Honduras, to the Crown (Seville, 1531), AGI, Indiferente General, leg. 1092. The writer comments that the dogs were specially trained to hunt down and kill Indians, and that they were worth fifty castellanos or more. At the ruins of León viejo one can still see the footprints of one of these animals that stepped on a wet brick in the doorway of the cathedral. Fierce dogs were also used by Ponce de León and Pedrarias, among others. See Romoli, *Balboa of Darien*, pp. 71, 161, 188, 286, 311.

19. Royal provision (Medina, 24 May 1532, AGCA, A1.23, leg. 4575, exp. 39528, fol. 23.

20. Cerezeda to the Crown (Valle de Naco, 31 August 1535), José Antonio Saco, *Historia de la esclavitud de los indios en el Nuevo Mundo*, 2 vols., 1:160.

21. "Informacion Contra los gobernadores . . . por Pedraza," AGI, Patronato, leg. 170, ramo 45.

22. Ibid.

23. Ibid.

24. Ibid.

25. Ibid.

26. Ibid.

27. Ibid.

28. "Informacion de Hernan Mendez" (Santiago, 28 May 1531), AGI, Guatemala, leg. 110.

29. Diego García de Celis to the Crown (Buena Esperanza, 10 May 1535), AGI, Guatemala, leg. 49. Andrés de Cerezeda, governor of Honduras, to the Crown (Naco, 31 August 1535); Saco, *La esclavitud*, 1:160. Chamberlain, *The Conquest of Honduras*, p. 33.

30. Licenciado Cristóbal de Pedraza to the Crown (Gracias a Dios, 18 May 1539), AGI, Guatemala, leg. 9. At one time, according to Pedraza, Alvarado had from two thousand to three thousand of the Achies under his command. Within the hour that an enemy Indian was captured, "they sacrificed him and cut him into pieces and ate him, half cooked, still running blood," and they would take a child, "even though he was at the breast of his mother, and put him alive in an oven and [then] eat him." A witness told Pedraza that he had counted at one time some thirty *asaderos*, with a child cooking in each one, in addition to which there were more than twenty or thirty persons sacrificed, after which they were cut up and divided to provide food on the road. During the dangerous Indian revolt in Honduras in 1537, Montejo tried unsuccessfully to have some Achies sent

from Guatemala to help subdue the rebels. Chamberlain, *The Conquest of Honduras*, p. 123.

31. Chamberlain, *The Conquest of Honduras*, p. 123.

32. Ibid. When Pedraza speaks vaguely of one encomendero in New Spain having more than the fifteen thousand Indians he estimates were in Honduras, he probably had in mind the extensive holdings of Cortés.

33. Chamberlain, *The Conquest of Honduras*, p. 123. Pedraza's humanitarian proposal had scant prospect of success and the danger to himself in trying to take slaves away from conquistadores is clear. His suggestion that Spaniards who illegally held slaves be excommunicated anticipated similar action by Las Casas in Chiapas a few years later. A royal cédula (Valladolid, 7 July 1536), AGI, Guatemala, leg. 402, lib. 1, fols. 171–71v, directed the Audiencia of Santo Domingo to appoint a reliable person to liberate slaves unjustly enslaved in Honduras and sold to Cuba and other regions. This was probably designed to check the extensive slave trading that developed under Salcedo and Cerezeda. They allowed free people to be shipped out as slaves to Santo Domingo, Cuba, San Juan de Puerto Rico, and Jamaica. Others were sent to Nicaragua for shipment to Panama and Peru. Pedraza to the Crown (Trujillo, 1 May 1547), AGI, Guatemala, leg. 164.

34. A very damaging account of his activities, in "Memoria para el illmo. señor Bisorrey de la nueva spaña sobre lo tocante a los puntos y auisos en la prouança que haçe doña catalina de montejo hija del adelantado don francisco de montejo sobre la gobernacion de yucatan" (n.p., n.d., probably ca. 1563), AGI, Guatemala, leg. 965, includes the following:

Lo que hiço la primera bez que entro en yucatan fue matar gran cantidad de yndios y catibar y hacer esclauos en grande numero dellos los quales se sacaron en cantidad e [en] nabios herrados por su abtoridad por tales esclauos que fueron mas cantidad de cinquenta mill animas de cuya causa aquellas provincias quedaron muy despobladas y los yndios mui amedrentados y mal tratados y los esclauos que hicieron los llebaron a honduras a las minas y a las yslas y a mexico y a otras partes a bender de abonde hubieron gran aprovechamiento y con que se sustentaban el adelantado y su gente y andaban rricos.

Que siendo el adelantado montejo gobernador de honduras y teniendo en ella muchas quadrillas de yndios esclauos naturales que sacauan oro de las minas y teniendo en aquella gobernacion muchos yndios de rrepartimiento y ganados huertas labranças e otros aprobechamientos que le davan los naturales. . . .

Que todo el tpo. de la conquista lleuo en cada un año mas de cinco mill pesos de oro de rrenta de los yndios de su rrepartimiento que tubo en mexico aunque no rresidio en ellos ni los probeyo de dotrina y lo demas necesario antes llebandoles el y doña catalina su hija [the wife of licenciado Alonso Maldonado, first president of the Audiencia de los Confines] muchos trebutos y servicios demas de la tasa que los aprobechamientos que los yndios de yucatan tienen.

See also royal provision of 10 March 1548, AGI, Guatemala, leg. 393, lib. 3, fols. 72v–73.

35. Montejo to the Crown (Salamanca, 10 August 1534) AGI, Patronato, leg. 184.

36. Montejo to the Crown (Pueblo de Naco, Higueras, 28 July 1537), AGI, Guatemala, leg. 9.

37. Chamberlain, *The Conquest of Honduras*, pp. 121–22. Montejo's restrictive policies and ineffective leadership resulted in the vecinos' requesting the intervention of Pedro de Alvarado. Cabildo to the Crown (Gracias a Dios, 21 December 1536), AGI, Guatemala, leg. 44.

38. Chamberlain, *The Conquest of Honduras*, pp. 121–22. Montejo seems later to have reverted to his earlier policies. He and his captains allegedly made slaves on various entradas, during which there was much violence and theft. "Segunda memorial . . . " (n.p., n.d., but following the New Laws of 1542–43), AGI, Guatemala, leg, 965.

39. Montejo to the Crown (Gracias a Dios, 1 June 1539), AGI, Guatemala, leg. 39. Montejo to the Crown (31 December 1545), AGI, Guatemala, leg. 9.

40. "Fiscal contra Miguel Diaz" (14 August 1543), AGI, leg. 393, lib. 21, fols. 206–206v.

41. Cabildo to the Crown (Trujillo, 12 March 1540), AGI, Guatemala, leg. 44.

42. Diego de Herrera to the Crown (Gracias a Dios, 24 December 1545), AGI, Guatemala, leg. 9.

43. Castañeda apparently sailed for the Indies in 1527, appearing on the register for November 8 of that year. *Catálogo de Pasajeros a Indias Durante los Siglos XVI, XVII y XVIII, 1 (1509–1533)*, p. 376.

44. Castañeda to the Crown (León, 5 October 1529), AGI, Guatemala, leg. 9.

45. "Proceso hecho en Nicaragua contra Rodrigo Nuñez vecino de la ciudad de Leon por haber herrado ciertos indios por esclavos siendo libres" (León, 19 March 1529), AGI, Patronato, leg. 231, no. 4, ramo 2. A copy of this document was made available through the courtesy of the Library of Congress.

46. Bancroft, *History of Central America*, 1:608–609.

47. Castañeda to the Crown (León, 30 May 1531), AGI, Guatemala, leg. 9.

48. Cabildo to the Crown (León, 1531), AGI, Guatemala, leg. 43.

49. Raúl Porras Barrenechea, ed., *Cartas del Perú (1524–1543)*, 24 (cited hereafter as *Cartas del Perú*).

50. Ibid., pp. 40, 43, 55.

51. Castañeda to the Crown and council (León, 1 May 1533), AGI, Guatemala, leg. 9. "Interrogatorio," residencia of Alonso López de Cerrato, et al., 1553–55, AGI, Justicia, leg. 301.

52. Cabildo to the emperor (Granada, 30 July 1535), *Cartas del Perú*, pp. 169–70.

53. R.C. (Toledo, 20 February 1534), AGI, Justicia, leg. 296.

54. Francisco de Barrionuevo to the emperor (Panama, 19 January 1534), *Cartas del Perú*, p. 96. However, this estimate is probably exaggerated; other accounts, including those in the residencia of Alvarado, AGI, Justicia, legs. 295–96, say the adelantado took about one thousand Indians. Perhaps the distinction was that one thousand of them were free Indians taken illegally, while the remainder were actually slaves.

55. Francisco Sánchez to the Crown (Granada, 2 August 1535), AGI, Guatemala, leg. 52.

56. Herrera, *Historia general*, déc, 4, book 3, ch. 2.

57. Residencia of Francisco de Castañeda (1536), AGI, Justicia, leg. 293.

58. Ibid.

59. "Cargos contra Fernando de Alcantara Botello, teniente por el lic. Castañeda e del tpo. que fue alcalde hordinario" (1536), AGI, Justicia, leg. 294.

60. "Cargos contra Luis de Guevara, teniente de governador, Nicaragua" (1536), AGI, Justicia, leg. 298.

61. "Cargos contra Pedro de los Rios" (1535–36), AGI, Justicia, leg. 298.

62. *Cartas del Perú*, pp. 284–85.

63. R.C. (Talavera, 31 May 1541), AGI, Guatemala, leg. 401, lib. S-3, fols. 84v–86. Pedro de Alvarado had been directed to pay for the return of the 1,000 Indians he took illegally to Peru, at the rate of 100 pesos apiece. Perhaps it was no coincidence that the amount of 100,000 pesos was the sum he reportedly received when he sold his equipment to Pizarro and Almagro, though in fact the silver was mixed with copper. Apparently he never complied with the order. See Sherman, "A Conqueror's Wealth," p. 210.

64. "Informacion Contra el Governador Rodrigo de Contreras," for the Council of the Indies (n.d.), AGI, Guatemala, leg. 52; and "Pleito de Hernan Sanchez de Vadajoz, Governador y Capitan General de Costa Rica con Rodrigo de Contreras, Gouernador de Nicaragua" (1543–54), AGI, Justicia, leg. 1164, ramo 3. For detailed treatment of Contreras, see Marqués de Lozoya, *Vida del Segoviano Rodrigo de Contreras, Gobernador de Nicaragua (1534–1544)*. Political developments in Nicaragua are fully discussed in Carlos Molina Argüello, *El Gobernador de Nicaragua en el Siglo XVI*. Although various expeditions entered Costa Rica earlier, the effective conquest was not undertaken until the 1560s under the command of Juan Vázquez de Coronado. The reform legislation with regard to conquests, the smaller Indian population, and, at least to some extent, the more humane policies of the commander, resulted in a less violent clash. See Victoria Urbano, *Juan Vázquez de Coronado y su ética en la conquista de Costa Rica*.

65. Martín de Esquivel to the Crown (Nicaragua, 30 December 1545), AGI, Guatemala, leg. 50.

66. AGI, Justicia, leg. 297.

67. Royal provision (Segovia, 25 June 1548), AGI, Guatemala, leg. 401, lib. S-3, fols. 154–54v; and R.C. (Valladolid, 1 September 1548), AGI, Guatemala, leg. 402, lib. T-2.

68. Çurrilla and Castellanos to the Crown (Santiago, 20 August 1530), AGI, Guatemala, leg. 45.

69. Saco, *La esclavitud*, 1:191.

70. Çurrilla et al. to the Crown (Santiago, 28 September 1531), AGI, Guatemala, leg. 45.

71. Montejo to the Crown (Gracias a Dios, 1 June 1539), AGI, Guatemala, leg. 9.

72. AGI, Justicia, leg. 295.

73. Ibid. About 500 Spaniards accompanied Alvarado, of whom 170 were horse and about 340 foot or seamen. Horsemen were allowed three slaves, black or Indian, though some apparently were permitted only two. If three, one was usually a female. Foot soldiers took one, some of them two. Alvarado took for himself twenty to twenty-five Indian men and women, of whom only seven or eight returned. Of the more than one thousand Indians taken from Guatemala, Mexico, and Nicaragua, most died or remained in Peru. Some were slaves, others were free Indians.

74. Ibid.

75. "Ynformacion de Gregorio Lopez," (Madrid, 30 June 1543) AGI, Patronato, leg. 231, ramo 4.

76. Cabildo to D. Antonio de Mendoza, viceroy of New Spain, and the Audiencia of Mexico (San Cristóbal de los Llanos, 4 June 1537), AGI, Guatemala, leg. 110. Despite some variation in details presented by witnesses, there is consensus on the main outlines of the events. Lucas de Beneçiano, one of the participants, said that "fifty or a hundred" Spaniards were involved, and that they spent six months on the expedition.

77. Ibid.

78. Occasionally a lax official was brought to justice. Francisco de Castañeda, who governed in Nicaragua, was convicted and fined the substantial sum of 500 pesos. Residencia of Castañeda, AGI, Justicia, leg. 293.

Chapter 5

1. Puga *Prouisiones*, 1:29. The loss of property added to the death penalty was not so gratuitous as it may seem. In effect, it impoverished the condemned man's family, a prospect that was in itself a strong deterrent. Two years later a similar cédula was issued omitting, however, the death penalty as a consequence of infraction. R.C. (Madrid, 19 September 1528), AGI, Patronato, leg. 170, ramo 34, and repeated in R.C. (Toledo, 20 November 1528), AGI, Patronato, leg. 180, ramo 21.

2. Antonio de Remesal, *Historia general de las Indias Occidentales, y particular de la gobernación de Chiapa y Guatemala*. 2 vols. (1932), 2:57.

3. Rodrigo Contreras to the Crown (León, 25 June 1532), AGI, Guatemala, leg. 43. Herrera, *Historia general*, dec. 5, book 2, ch. 8. More precisely, it was ruled (Medina del Campo, 13 January 1532), that no slave was to be branded, even if he was a slave, without Crown permission. Encinas, *Cedulario*, 4:366. Zavala, *Los esclavos indios en Nueva España*, p. 77, n. 6, writes that Indian accounts mention that some were branded on the lips, some near the mouth, and others on the cheek.

4. Francisco de Barrientos, veedor, to the Crown (Trujillo, 29 March 1530), AGI, Guatemala, leg. 49.

5. Licenciado Diego de Herrera to the Crown (Gracias a Dios, 10 July 1545),

AGI, Guatemala, leg. 9. But Donald E. Chipman, "The Traffic in Indian Slaves in the Province of Pánuco, New Spain, 1523–1533," *The Americas* 23 (October, 1966): 149, states that an upper case "R" was an abbreviation for "Real Marca." In Pánuco that brand was applied to the left side of the face.

6. Residencia of Francisco de Montejo (1544), AGI, Justicia, leg. 300. Witnesses in this document relate the brutality of the expedition. See, e.g., the testimony of Francisco del Ojo (fol. 30 ff.) in which descriptions are given of Indians being thrown to the dogs, burned alive, and having their hands cut off. Bernal Díaz del Castillo wrote that he had once broken a branding iron in an attempt to prevent the branding of more slaves. Herbert Cerwin, *Bernal Díaz, Historian of the Conquest*, p. 73. It may be remarked, however, that the chronicler himself held a number of slaves in later years.

7. The queen to lic. Cristóbal de Pedraza (Valladolid, 30 January 1538), AGI, Guatemala, leg. 402, lib. 1, fols. 221–21v. See also, Agustín Millares Carlo and J. I. Mantecón, *Indice y extractos de los Protocolos del Archivo de Notarias de México*, 2 vols.

8. R.C. to the Audiencia de los Confines (Guatemala, 1552) AGCA, A1.23, leg. 1511, fols. 186–87.

9. Zavala, *Los esclavos indios en Nueva España*, pp. 4–5. The drawings here are taken from Zavala's reproductions from Bernal's manuscript. Ruth Pike, "Sevillian Society in the Sixteenth Century," *Hispanic American Historical Review* 47 (August, 1967): 344–59, commenting (p. 348) on slaves, both black and white, in Seville, writes that, "the most frequent brand consisted of an S and a line *(clavo)*, standing for esclavo, on one cheek and the owner's initial or mark on the other. But several other kinds were also in use. In 1500, for example, we have mention of a slave branded with fleur-de-lis on one cheek and a star on the other. In another instance, a slave bore the full name of his owner on his face." Referring to the latter (n. 21), Pike states that "the slave's face bore the following inscription: 'Francisco de Aranda en Sevilla 29 de mayo de 1539.'"

10. Bernal Díaz del Castillo, *La Conquista de Nueva España*, 2 vols., 2: tomo 3, ch. 143. Diego López de Salcedo to the Crown (Trujillo, postrero de 1526), AGI, Guatemala, leg. 39.

11. General Cédula for the Indies (Madrid, 19 September 1528), AGI, Patronato, leg. 170, ramo 34. R.C. (Toledo, 20 November 1528), AGI, Patronato, leg. 180, ramo 21.

12. R.C. (Toledo, 20 February 1534), AGCA, A1.23, leg. 4574, exp. 39528, fols. 8v–19. Some were not prompt in giving the Crown's share, but a royal provision allowed them two years within which to pay. Provision (Medina, 24 May 1532), AGCA, A.1, leg. 4575, fol. 23.

13. Puga, *Prouisiones*, 2:9–10 (R.C. of 14 February 1549).

14. Residencia of Alvarado (Santiago, 1535), AGI, Justicia, leg. 295.

15. Francisco de Castañeda, the alcalde mayor, to the Crown (León: 5 October 1529), AGI, Guatemala, leg. 9.

16. Cabildo to the Crown (Granada, 30 July 1535), AGI, Guatemala, leg. 44.

17. AGI, Justicia, leg. 295.
18. Residencia of Alvarado (Santiago, 1535), AGI, Justicia, leg. 296.
19. Pardo, *Prontuario*, p. 122 (R.C. of 23 September 1552).

Chapter 6

1. Owing to shortages, prices of all goods were very high during the early years, and they remained exorbitant because of the influx of more Spaniards. In 1549, a xiquipil of cacao (8,000 beans) was worth a peso and a half, whereas six years later it had a value of four pesos. During the same period the cost of a length of cloth (manta) rose from eight reales to forty. Residencia of Alonso López de Cerrato (Santiago, 1552–55), AGI, Justicia, leg. 301.

2. "Probanza de don Pedro de Portocarrero" (9 August 1531), AGI, Guatemala, leg. 110. See also Ramírez, *Proceso*, pp. 151–52.

3. Lawsuit of Pedro de Alvarado against Fernando Cortés regarding the spoils of Tututepeque and Soconusco (Madrid, 1528–29), AGI, Justicia, leg. 1031. Six or seven years later, while the price of slaves rose somewhat, the value of swine dropped to two pesos apiece. "Juan de Espinar contra Alvarado" (Santiago, 1537), AGI, Justicia, leg. 1031.

4. Diego López de Salcedo to the Crown (Trujillo, 31 December 1526), AGI, Guatemala, leg. 39.

5. Espinar contra Alvarado, AGI, Justicia, leg. 1031.

6. "Declaración" of Pedro de Alvarado (28 July 1530), AGI, Patronato, leg. 246, ramo 2, no. 4.

7. "Fray Jacobo Testera y otros religiosos de la orden de San Francisco de México a Carlos V" (31 July 1533), in Paso y Troncoso, *ENE*, 3:97.

8. President of the Audiencia of Mexico to the empress (Mexico: 8 August 1533), Paso y Troncoso, *ENE*, 3:117. But cf. "Libro de Quentas," 1528–31, AGI, Audiencia de México, leg. 1841, which shows some Indian slaves selling for from 2 to 10 pesos. At the same time, a black sold for 158 pesos.

9. Saco, *Historia*, 1:180–81.

10. Royal provision (3 April 1534), AGI, Guatemala, leg. 393, lib. 2, fol. 102.

11. "Relacion de la Probança hecha por parte de Sancho Barahona en el pleito que en la residencia trato contra . . . Alvarado," AGI, Justicia, leg. 295. However, the plaintiff Barahona, who had reason to exaggerate, claimed that slaves were then worth ten to twelve pesos each. Studies on Indian slavery in Mexico show only slight variations from Central American prices. Jean-Pierre Berthe, "Aspects de l'esclavage des indiens en Nouvelle-Espagne pendant la premiére moitié du XVI$_e$ siécle," *Journal de la Société des Américanistes*, 2 (1965): 193–95, 203–5, notes that slaves taken in the province of Tepeaca during the year 1520 included a lot of 13,500, based on the assumption they sold for 2 pesos each. In the years 1528–29, slaves taken in Tututepec brought 2 or 3 gold pesos *(de oro común)*. Mining slaves on one occasion in 1527–28 sold for up to 10 pesos, but the average price seems to have been 4 to 5 pesos apiece. They were sold in groups of 20 to

150, along with their few tools. By 1531, 10 pesos was a common price, and from 1536–38, the price varied between 26 and 78 pesos, or about 50 pesos on the average. Few Indians were being sold by 1550, and those that were available were bringing up to 200 hundred pesos, which was about the price of the more desirable black slaves.

Silvio Zavala, in *Los esclavos indios en Nueva España*, pp. 11, 66–75, indicates somewhat higher prices, showing that unskilled slaves sold in lots during the 1520s went for 3 to 7 pesos, while individual slaves, who were often skilled, brought as high as 75 pesos de oro. The price for female Indian slaves in Mexico varied between 10 and 100 pesos, and black slaves were worth between 100 and 200. White female slaves (*moriscas* or *berberiscas*) seem to have been most in demand, one of them bringing 330 pesos de oro. By the mid 1530s prices for mining slaves had risen to 25 pesos and sometimes more than 100 pesos each. This is much in contrast to prices in the province of Pánuco under Nuño de Guzmán in 1527, when the price of mining slaves was fixed at 4 pesos each. Previous to that time as many as a hundred slaves were traded for a horse, but it was ruled that no more than fifteen could be given in such a transaction. For a discussion of slaving activities in that region see Donald E. Chipman, *Nuño de Guzmán and the Province of Pánuco in New Spain, 1518–1533*, and by the same author, "The Traffic in Indian Slaves," p. 142–55.

12. "Informacion de Pedro Calçada" (Trujillo, 2 February 1540), AGI, Guatemala, leg. 110.

13. Francisco de Barrientos to the Crown (Trujillo del Pinar del Puerto de Honduras, 25 July 1534), AGI, Guatemala, leg. 49.

14. Probanza of Juan de Aragón (Guatemala, 1551), AGCA, A1.29.1, leg. 1, exp. 11, fol. 11 ff.

15. Rodolfo Barón Castro, *Reseña histórica de la villa de San Salvador, desde su fundación en 1525 hasta que recibe el título de ciudad en 1549*, pp. 45–46. In 1546 or 1547, black slaves in New Spain were valued at eighty to ninety pesos, but Indians always sold for much less. "Información" (Valladolid, 9 May 1556), AGI, Patronato, leg. 170, ramo 60.

16. Probanzas of Andrés and Juan de la Tovilla (Ciudad Real de Chiapa, 1579–1601), AGI, Guatemala, leg. 966.

17. "Los cargos q. de la pesquisa secreta se hazen quenta al lic. Castañeda del tpo. q. fue alcalde mayor en Nicaragua," and "Cargos contra Luys de Guibara lugarteniente q. fue del lic. Castañeda en la cibdad de Granada" (1535–36), AGI, Justicia, leg. 293. Castañeda and his cronies grumbled that they had sold Indians on credit and had trouble collecting their money. They also gave out licenses for the transporting of blacks and horses, which allowed more extortion. It was noted that a black suffering from hemorrhoids sold for only 200 pesos, but one in prime condition could bring 500. Although he fled to Peru, Castañeda was eventually brought to justice and went to prison in 1540. Lozoya, *Vida del Segoviano*, p. 27.

18. Çurrilla et al. to the Crown (28 September 1531), AGI, Guatemala, leg. 45. According to Bernal Díaz, during the conquest of Mexico, Cortés set aside

one-fifth of the slaves for the king, another fifth for himself, and divided the rest among the men, which led to some discontent among those who were left with old, worn-out women. Customarily a captain took only one-seventh or one-tenth for his share, but Cortés had made the agreement for a one-fifth share (after the king's *quinto* was taken out) before the conquest began. Zavala, *Los esclavos indios en Nueva España*, p. 2. France V. Scholes, *The Spanish Conqueror as a Business Man*, p. 18, writes: "It would be difficult to estimate how many slaves Cortés owned at any given time, but certainly he had no less than 3,000 after the conquest of Mexico, of whom two-thirds or more died from hard labor or neglect in placer mining. At his death in 1547 he still owned more than four hundred."

19. Eduardo Guerra, "Quito y Pedro de Alvarado," ASGH 25 (Sept. 1951): 288–90. For a fuller discussion of Alvarado's slaves, see Sherman, "A Conqueror's Wealth," pp. 199–213.

20. "Relacion sacada de la probança hecha por parte de Sancho Barahona . . ." AGI, Justicia, leg. 295.

21. Espinar contra Alvarado, AGI, Justicia, leg. 1031. Because of conflicting testimony, perhaps only half of those were actually slaves. Espinar, although rumored to be a hosier by trade, distinguished himself in the conquests of Mexico and Guatemala. His success is evident not only by his acquisition of the encomienda of Huehuetenango, but also because he was able to afford losing 20,000 pesos de oro gambling.

22. Remesal, *Historia general* (1932), 1:465. Barón Castro, *Reseña histórica*, pp. 45–46.

23. "Testimonio" of the audiencia (Santiago, 22 March 1551), AGI, Guatemala, leg. 965. Later, in Cristóbal Lobo to the Council of the Indies (Santiago, 1 July 1553), AGI, Guatemala, leg. 52 the writer states that forty mining slaves were taken from him, and that they had produced more than a thousand pesos de oro a year.

24. Probanza de méritos of Lorenzo de Godoy (Santiago, October, 1560), AGI, Escribanía de Cámara, leg. 332.

25. "Informacion acerca del tesorero" (n.d., n.p., but probably 1540s), AGI, Indiferente General, leg. 855.

26. Residencia of lic. Pedro Ramírez de Quiñones (Santiago, 1559), AGI, Justicia 308.

27. R.C. of 11 August 1544, Pardo, *Prontuario*, p. 59.

28. "Informacion de Hernan Mendez" (Santiago, 28 May 1531), AGI, Guatemala, leg. 110.

29. Ibid. An observer noted that for about two years no one had wanted to go to the province. On the contrary, Spaniards were leaving.

30. Juan de Lerma to the Crown (Puerto de Caballos, 1 June 1537), AGI, Guatemala, leg. 52.

31. Pedraza to the Crown (Gracias a Dios, 18 May 1539), AGI, Guatemala, leg. 9. Three thousand other Indians were taken in non-slave categories, he said, and only fifteen thousand Indians remained in the province.

32. Don Antonio de Salazar and the contador, Francisco Castellanos to "Muy Magnífico Señor" (n.p., n.d.), AGCA, A-1, leg. 2198, exp. 15793, fols. 255–55v. This document came to my attention through the kindness of Christopher Lutz.

33. This information comes from two documents, one from Seville and the other from Guatemala. They are similar, with some of the material duplicated. Again I am indebted to Mr. Lutz for supplying information from the "Libro de la tesoreria de su magestad de la quenta y razon q. della tiene yo el tesorero francisco de castellanos tesorero en esta provincia de guatemala." The document is in the AGCA, but at this writing it has recently been discovered and as yet has no archival classification. The Seville manuscript is classified as "Libro de Cargo y Data del Comendador de Guatemala, 1529–1536," AGI, Patronato, leg. 180, ramo 34. It is signed by treasury officials Çurrilla and Castellanos, as well as licenciado Maldonado.

34. Ibid.

35. Ibid.

36. Alonso López de Cerrato to the Crown (Santiago, 3 November 1548), AGI, Guatemala, leg. 9.

37. Licenciado Pedro Ramírez to the Crown (Santiago, 20 May 1555), AGI, Guatemala, leg. 9. Lending credence to that figure is the complaint that fifty cuadrillas were liberated in 1549 in Guatemala. Cabildo to the Crown (Santiago, 24 January 1550), AGI, Guatemala, leg. 41.

38. Pedraza to the Crown (Gracias a Dios, 18 May 1539), AGI, Guatemala, leg. 9. In "Ynformacion de Gregorio Lopez" (testimony of 23 June 1543), AGI, Patronato, leg. 231, ramo 4, some fourteen thousand Indians were reported "missing" in the province, but the witness does not elaborate.

39. Licenciado Alonso López de Cerrato to the Crown (Santiago, 22 September 1548), AGI, Guatemala, leg. 9.

40. Henry R. Wagner and Helen R. Parish, *The Life and Writings of Bartolomé de las Casas*, p. 82. Francis A. MacNutt, *Bartholomew de Las Casas*, p. 340. Regarding the behavior of Spaniards in Nicaragua, Las Casas wrote (MacNutt, p. 340) the following:

> By such conduct from the year 1523 to 1533, they ruined all this kingdom. During six or seven years, five or six vessels carried on this traffic taking . . . Indians to sell them as slaves in Panama and Peru, where they all died. . . . In this way they have carried off more than five hundred thousand souls from this province making slaves of people who were as free as I am.
>
> In their infernal wars and the horrible captivity into which they put the Indians up to the present time, the Spaniards have killed more than another five or six hundred thousand persons, and they still continue. All these massacres have occurred in the space of fourteen years. At present they kill daily in the said province of Nicaragua, from four to five thousand persons, with servitude and continual oppression; it being, as was said, one of the most populous in the world.

It is regrettable for historians that the impassioned friar, who wrote so extensively and in so much detail, resorted to such extravagance, depriving us of a wealth of reliable statistics.

41. MacLeod, *Spanish Central America*, p. 52.

42. Esquivel to the Crown (Nicaragua, 30 December 1545), AGI, Guatemala, leg. 50.

43. Ships in the trade from Seville to the Indies averaged only about 110 tons in 1526, but by 1550 there were many of more than 200 tons and some up to 400. Pierre and Huguette Chaunu, *Seville et l'Atlantique*, 8 vols. 2:162–453.

44. José Antônio Gonsalves de Mello, *Tempo dos Flamengos: Influencia da ocupação holandesa na vida e na cultura do Brasil* (Rio de Janeiro: Editora José Olympio, 1947), p. 209; and by the same author, "A Situação do Negro sob o Dominio Hollandez," in *Novos Estudos Afro-Brasileiros* (Rio de Janeiro: Civilização Brasileira, 1937), both cited in Geraldo Cardoso da Silva, "Negro Slavery in the Sugar Plantations of Veracruz and Pernambuco, 1550–1680." Herbert S. Klein, "North American Competition and the Characteristics of the African Slave Trade to Cuba, 1790 to 1794," *William and Mary Quarterly*, 3d. ser., 28 (January, 1971): 97–101.

45. James Lockhart, *Spanish Peru, 1532–1560*, p. 117.

46. Woodrow Borah, *Early Colonial Trade and Navigation between Mexico and Peru*, pp. 4–5. For more on the subject, see David R. Radell and James J. Parsons, "Realejo: A Forgotten Colonial Port and Shipbuilding Center in Nicaragua," *Hispanic American Historical Review* 51 (May, 1971): 295–312.

47. Borah, *Early Colonial Trade*, pp. 4–5.

48. Licenciado Espinosa to the emperor (Panama, 10 October 1533), *Cartas del Perú*, p. 70.

49. Barrionuevo to the Council of the Indies (Panama, 19 January 1534), *Cartas del Perú*, p. 97.

50. Francisco Sánchez to the Crown (Granada, 2 August 1535), AGI, Guatemala, leg. 52.

51. Zavala, *Los esclavos indios en Nueva España*, p. 43. But what seems exaggeration on the part of Las Casas was also reflected in the letter of Francisco Sánchez cited above, in which he said that only one of twenty survived the voyage to Panama or Peru.

52. Royal provision (Valladolid, 9 September 1536), AGI, Guatemala, leg. 401, lib. S-2, fols. 177–78v.

53. Lockhart, *Spanish Peru*, p. 200.

54. Barrionuevo to the emperor (Panama, 8 April 1534), *Cartas del Perú*, p. 106.

55. Francisco Sánchez to the Crown (Granada, 2 August 1535), AGI, Guatemala, leg. 52.

56. Licenciado Diego de Herrera to the Crown (Gracias a Dios, 24 December 1545), AGI, Guatemala, leg. 9.

57. Cabildo to the Crown (Santiago, 1 June 1550), AGI, Guatemala, leg. 9.

58. Espinosa to the emperor (Panama, 10 October 1533), *Cartas del Perú*, p. 70.

59. Alvarado to the emperor (Puerto de la Posesión, 18 January 1534), ibid., p. 94.

60. Martin de Paredes to the treasurer Martel de la Puente (San Miguel de Piura, 15 December 1534), ibid., p. 99.

61. It was startling, however, to read in Professor Bowser's work that Indian slaves in Peru during the late 1530s sold for 50 to 150 pesos and that skilled Indians could sell for twice those amounts. If that was indeed the general level of prices paid, this aspect of my argument would probably be invalid. Frederick P. Bowser, *The African Slave in Colonial Peru, 1524–1650*, p. 11.

62. Lockhart, *Spanish Peru*, p. 115, writes: "In 1562, after what can be imagined to have been a slow, steady increase, a group of experienced masters agreed that between fifty and sixty ships were navigating the Pacific coast." Ships were, however, not infrequently lost in wrecks or ruined by shipworms, consequently the building activity was more than might appear to be the case.

63. Barrionuevo to the officials of Seville (Panama, 23 October 1536), *Cartas del Perú*, p. 224.

64. MacLeod, *Spanish Central America*, p. 52.

65. Torquemada, *Monarquía Indiana*, 1:329. He writes: "Hacense aqui [Nicaragua] muchos Navios. En el Año mil quinientos y quarenta y quatro, se hecharon à la Mar seis Navios, que son, ò valen tanto, como sesenta en Vizcaia. Navio avia, que llevava mas de noventa Caballos, porque como en España cuentan por Toneles, àca contaban por Caballos."

66. Fernand Braudel, *The Mediterranean and the Mediterranean World in the Age of Philip II*, 2 vols., 1:297–98. Braudel observes that even in Europe in the last half of the sixteenth century, "a ship of 1000 tons was a giant and a rarity." He cites an astonished traveler in 1597 who had seen an "enormous" ship of about 750 tons.

67. Espinosa to the emperor (Panama, 5 August 1532), *Cartas del Perú*, p. 28. Espinosa to the emperor (Panama, 10 October 1533), ibid., p. 70.

68. Barrionuevo to the emperor (Panama, 19 January 1534), ibid., p. 96.

69. Alvarado to the emperor (Santiago de Guatemala, 1 September 1532), ibid., pp. 31–33.

70. Alvarado to the emperor (Puerto de la Posesión, 18 January 1534) ibid., p. 93.

71. Espinosa to the emperor (Panama, 10 October 1533), ibid., p. 70.

72. Sherman, "A Conqueror's Wealth," p. 208.

73. Alvarado to the emperor (Santiago, 18 November 1539), *Cartas del Perú*, pp. 376–77.

74. Martin Esquivel to the Crown (Nicaragua, 30 December 1545), AGI, Guatemala, leg. 50.

75. Lesley B. Simpson, *Studies in the Administration of the Administration of the Indians of New Spain, IV, The Emancipation of the Indian Slaves and the Resettlement of the Freedmen, 1548–1553*, p. 17.

76. Juan Comas, "Historical Reality and the Detractors of Father Las Casas," in *Bartolomé de Las Casas in History*, eds. Juan Friede and Benjamin Keen, pp. 502–504, discusses this tendency of sixteenth-century Spaniards in the Indies to use grossly inflated figures and descriptions.

77. Even in the audiencia district of Mexico only three thousand or so slaves were freed in the middle of the sixteenth century. See Silvio Zavala, *La filosofía política en la Conquista de América*. Las Casas, in referring to Mexico, Coatzacoalcos, Pánuco, Jalisco, Chiapas, Guatemala, Honduras, Yucatán, Nicaragua, the coast of San Miguel, and Venezuela, stated that three million ("tres cuentos") Indian slaves had been made. In another place he claimed that it was four million. Fray Toribio Motolinía, a contemporary who sought to discredit the figures of Las Casas, said that the numbers of slaves taken in those provinces would not reach two hundred thousand. Fray Toribio Motolinía, *Carta al Emperador*, pp. 91–92. Berthe, "Aspects de l'esclavage," p. 193.

With regard to the enslavement of Indians in Mexico, the comments of George Kubler, *Mexican Architecture in the Sixteenth Century*, 2 vols., 1:134–35, are of some interest:

> The role played by slavery was negligible, although it has often been overestimated. . . . That such a slave class existed in Mexico cannot be denied, but it was formally abolished in 1569, in consequence of the movement for emancipation that had been under way since 1530. The practical abolition of Indian slavery was virtually completed by 1561 in New Spain. Indeed, in 1555, Motolinía estimated that but a thousand Indian slaves remained to be manumitted. For that matter, the class had never been very numerous. Fewer than four thousand cases of slavery were handled during the period 1552–61 in the Audiencia and peripheral provinces. This figure, however probably represents but a part of the slave population that was emancipated, for the records deal only with cases upon which individual review was necessary, and the total number of emancipations was certainly much larger.

While the importance of Indian slavery in Central America has also been embellished on occasion, my belief is, accepting Kubler's assessment, that it was of more importance in Central America than in Mexico.

Chapter 7

1. Alonso de Zorita, *Life and Labor in Ancient Mexico*, pp. 194–95. It is not clear if Zorita refers specifically to Central America or Mexico, but it is likely that the situation applied to both.
2. Simpson, *The Encomienda*, pp. 8–9.
3. W. V. Scholes, *The Ramírez Visita*, p. 29, n. 47.
4. Ibid., p. 30.
5. Charles Gibson, *The Aztecs Under Spanish Rule*, p. 221.
6. W. V. Scholes, *The Ramírez Visita*, p. 34.
7. See, for example, Silvio Zavala, *Contribución a la historia de las instituciones coloniales en Guatemala*. In that study, Dr. Zavala, who has made important contributions to our knowledge of the encomienda and labor systems, presents quite a different view on personal service from that shown here.
8. José Miranda, *El tributo indígena en la Nueva España durante el siglo XVI*, pp. 263–64.

9. Fray Miguel Agia, *Servidumbres Personales de Indios*, pp. 36–41. Agia seems to have gone to the Indies in 1563, spending several years in Guatemala before moving to Peru. His work was first published in Lima in 1604. Cf. Silvio Zavala, "Los Trabajadores Antillanos," pp. 31–68, 60–88.

10. Remesal, *Historia general* (1932), 1:74.

11. Simpson, *The Encomienda*, p. xiii.

12. This was enunciated as early as 1503 in a communication of Ferdinand and Isabella for Santo Domingo. Ibid., p. 13.

13. Chamberlain, *The Conquest of Honduras*, p. 124.

14. Cristóbal de Pedraza to the Crown (Trujillo, 1 May 1547), AGI, Guatemala, leg. 164.

15. Ibid.

16. Royal provision (Medina del Campo, 4 November 1531), AGI, Guatemala, leg. 402, lib. 1, fols. 83–83v.

17. Chamberlain, *The Conquest of Honduras*, p. 238.

18. See, e.g., Sherman, "Tlaxcalans in Post-Conquest Guatemala."

19. "Quenta de Chimaltenango," taken by Francisco del Valle Marroquín, regidor and *juez administrador* (Chimaltenango, 20 February 1562), AGI, Guatemala, leg. 45.

20. "Quenta de Çunpango," by Francisco del Valle Marroquín (Zumpango, 20 February 1562), AGI, Guatemala, leg. 45.

21. Espinar contra Alvarado, AGI, Justicia, leg. 1031.

22. Licenciado Juan Nuñez de Landecho to the Crown (Santiago, 3 February 1563), AGI, Guatemala, leg. 9.

23. Royal provision (Valladolid, 16 March 1556), AGI, Guatemala, leg. 402, lib. T-3, fol. 144v.

24. R.C. (13 February 1531), Pardo, *Prontuario*, p. 74.

25. Residencia of Alonso López de Cerrato (Santiago, 1553–55), AGI, Justicia, leg. 301.

26. Remesal, *Historia general* (1932), 1:422, 465.

27. Crown to Alonso López de Cerrato (Valladolid, 29 April 1549), AGI, Guatemala, leg. 402, lib. T-3, fols. 27v–33.

28. Pedraza to the Crown (Trujillo, 1 May 1547), AGI, Guatemala, leg. 164.

29. Cerrato to the Crown (Santiago, 3 June 1549), AGI, Guatemala, leg. 9.

30. Oviedo, *Historia General*, vol. 1, book 4, ch. 3.

31. Royal provision (Madrid, 31 January 1552), AGI, Guatemala, leg. 386, lib. Q-1, fol. 23v.

32. Rafael de Arévalo, *Libro de actas del ayuntamiento de la ciudad de Santiago de Guatemala, desde la fundación de la misma ciudad en 1524 hasta 1530*, pp. 53–54.

33. Remesal, *Historia general de las Indias Occidentales, y particular de la gobernación de Chiapa y Guatemala* (1964–66), 2 vols., 1:102. See also, Pedro Pérez Valenzuela, *Ciudad Vieja*, pp. 50–54.

34. Sherman, "Tlaxcalans"; and R.C. of 20 July 1532, Pardo, *Prontuario*, p. 74.

35. R.C. of 25 February 1538 and R.C. of 4 August 1550, Pardo, *Prontuario*, pp. 75, 78.

36. See Verle L. Annis, *The Architecture of Antigua Guatemala, 1543–1773;* and Sidney David Markman, *Colonial Architecture of Antigua Guatemala.*

37. Bancroft, *History of Central America*, 2:322.

38. Cabildo to the Council of the Indies (San Salvador, 3 February 1548), AGI, Guatemala, leg. 43.

39. The conquerors wasted no time in putting Indians to work washing for gold. According to one historian, while Alvarado was still at Patinamit in 1526, he demanded 200 youths for that purpose, each of the Indians being obligated to collect the amount of one castellano de oro weekly. This author, Ximénez, cites Fuentes de Guzmán for the information, as well as Vázquez, whose version was that the conqueror forced 400 youths and 400 girls to work every day, under the threat of enslavement, and that each was required to turn in gold filling a container the size of the little finger. Their discontent contributed to the rebellion of the region. Ximénez, *Historia* 1:150, citing Fuentes y Guzmán, *Recordación florida*, and R.P. Fray Francisco Vázquez, *Crónica de la Provincia del Santísimo Nombre de Jesús de Guatemala*, 4 vols.

40. The queen to Marroquín (Valladolid, 10 February 1530), AGI, Guatemala, leg. 393, lib. R-2, fols. 7–11. The order was repeated on 26 February 1538, AGI, Guatemala, leg. 393, lib. 2.

41. "Informacion de Hernan Mendez" (Santiago, 28 May 1531), AGI, Guatemala, leg. 110. Chamberlain, *The Conquest of Honduras*, p. 25.

42. Montejo to the Crown (Naco, 28 July 1537), AGI, Guatemala, leg. 9. The adelantado added that each Indian mined four to six reales "por ordinario." Mining was not always so lucrative, however. Aside from the labor shortages and attacks by hostiles, as well as rebellion of the Indian miners, the yield was sometimes low. In 1531, it was noted that it could cost 300 pesos or more just to maintain a cuadrilla, which sometimes did not pay for its keep. Another lamented that he had invested more than 800 pesos, while his profit was less than 200. "Informacion de Hernan Mendez" (Santiago, 28 May 1531), AGI, Guatemala, leg. 110. In 1532, Alvarado wrote Charles V that because of an epidemic of measles that was sweeping Guatemala, he ordered Indians out of the mines to prevent more deaths, as a result of which production had fallen off. Alvarado to the Crown (Santiago, 1 September 1532), AGI, Guatemala, leg. 9. When the plague hit Nicaragua it carried off more than 6,000 Indians by 1533, which put the mining operations in jeopardy because of the few Indians in mining cuadrillas. Castañeda to the Crown (León, 1 May 1533), AGI, Guatemala, leg. 9.

In Marroquín to the Crown (Santiago, 20 February 1542), AGI, Patronato, leg. 184, ramo 35, the bishop reports the Indians' fear of Alvarado: "Solo su nombre bastava para sustentarla [tierra] y tenerla pacifica." Yet, in "autos hechos en Santiago de Guatemala sobre la tasacion de los Yndios de aquella provincia" (Santiago, 6 October 1535), AGI, Patronato, leg. 180, ramo 64, one reads that the natives were in rebellion and would not even obey Alvarado. They refused to carry food to the slaves in the mines, which held down production.

43. Chamberlain, *The Conquest of Honduras*, p. 124. The vecinos of Gracias a Dios were sorry to see Alvarado replaced by Montejo. In cabildo to the Crown (Gracias a Dios, 10 August 1539), AGI, Guatemala, leg. 44, the regidores noted the benefits resulting from Alvarado's arrival in May 1536, both in terms of the pacification of the land, as well as the exploitation of the mines by the cuadrillas brought from Guatemala. In the first demora of nine months, gold had been smelted in the amount of 60,000 gold pesos. Montejo, however, had impeded the mining, with the result that the miners returned to Guatemala with their cuadrillas. By 1538, the total value of gold taken out was only 8,000 pesos de oro, whereas if the Guatemalan Indians had remained they could have taken out in the two seasons more than 150,000.

44. Cabildo to the Crown (León, 1531), AGI, Guatemala, leg. 43.

45. Queen to officials (Medina del Campo, 15 July 1532), AGCA, A1.23, leg. 4575, exp. 39528, fols, 17v–18.

46. The Chontales, often called "perverse" by the Spaniards, left a lingering impression. Torquemada, *Monarquía Indiana*, 1:335, said that Spaniards called some Indians Chontales, "queriendo decir Boçal, ò Rustico"; and Antonio Vázquez de Espinosa, in his *Description of the Indies (c. 1620)*, wrote that in the Nicaraguan province of Los Chontales the Indians "are the most unsophisticated of all those provinces, to such a degree that in the other provinces when they want to call someone an offensive name, they tell him he is a Chontal, which amounts to saying he is a dumb animal."

47. Early legislation made provision for special treatment for Indians engaged in mining. In 1509, Ferdinand ruled that mine owners were to be given preference in the allotment of Indians in encomienda. In 1511, it was ordered that Spaniards having Indians in Española and Puerto Rico were to keep a third of them occupied in mining. At the same time, Indians in mining were to have meat twice daily—or fish on days of abstinence—while Indians occupied in other labor were to receive meat once a day. Provision was even made for mining Indians to have "beds"—which no doubt meant mats or hammocks. Silvio Zavala, *Estudios indianos*, pp. 160–62. The Laws of Burgos (1512) stipulated that mining Indians were to have a pound of meat a day, and on meatless days a pound of fish. In addition, they were to be given tortillas and chile. Encomenderos were to be allowed the use of their Indians in mining five months a year, after which the Indians were to rest for forty days. During that rest period slaves could be kept working. Simpson, *Studies in the Administration . . . I*, and *II*, pp. 15, 16.

48. Francisco Castañeda to the Crown (León, 1 May 1533), AGI, Guatemala, leg. 9. Similar sentiments were expressed by the treasurer in Guatemala, Çurrilla, to Francisco de los Cobos, secretary to Charles V (Santiago, 15 September 1531), AGI, Guatemala, leg. 45. When he arrived in Guatemala from Mexico he found "la cosa mas perdida y mas pobre del mundo y q. no avia persona q. aqui quisiese bibir y de nosotros se burlaban en mexico por q. beniamos a tal tierra. . . ." Despite the

rich mines they had discovered, the making of slaves was illegal. If that order were not changed the king would have nothing in the territory but its name. He seemed to think that enslaving the Indians would mean their survival: "estos pocos q. agora ay se acabaran muy presto por ser gente muy miserable y de poco mantenimiento y q. naturalmente biben muy poco q. por marabilla ay entre ellos honbre viejo y esto no piense vra sa. q. es de agora o q. por q. los cristianos los traten mal syno q. en hecho de verdad biben poco. . . ." In 1539, the factor in Honduras said that because of the lack of slaves there was little mining and all the Spaniards had their feet in the stirrups, ready to ride off. Juan de Lerma to the Crown (San Pedro del Puerto de Caballos, 31 October 1539), AGI, Guatemala, leg. 49.

49. Governor Rodrigo de Contreras to the Crown (León, 6 July 1536), AGI, Guatemala, leg. 40.

50. Residencia of Pedro de Alvarado, AGI, Justicia, leg. 295.

51. Diego García de Celis to the Crown (Buena Esperanza, 10 May 1535), AGI, Guatemala, leg. 49.

52. Governor Andrés de Cerezeda to the Crown (Buena Esperanza, 1 December 1535), AGI, Guatemala, leg. 49.

53. Cerezeda to the Crown (Puerto de Caballos, 14 August 1536), AGI, Guatemala, leg. 49.

54. Chamberlain, *The Conquest of Honduras*, pp. 237–39.

55. Montejo to the Crown (Gracias a Dios, 1 May 1542), AGI Patronato, leg. 184, ramo 25. Chamberlain, *The Conquest of Honduras*, p. 224, states that by 1543 there were about fifteen hundred blacks in the mines of Olancho, Honduras.

56. "Ynformacion de Gregorio Lopez" (Seville, 1543), AGI, Patronato, leg. 231, ramo 4.

57. Licenciado Diego de Herrera to the Crown (Gracias a Dios, 10 July 1545), AGI, Guatemala, leg. 9.

58. Alonso de García to the Crown (Gracias a Dios, 1 February 1546), AGI, leg. 9.

59. R.C. (Madrid, 5 July 1546), AGCA, A1.23, leg. 1511, fol. 40. Some of the mining slaves got little rest. Although slaves were supposed to have Sundays and fiesta days free, some of them got time off on those days only for religious services. The gold taken out on those days was used for the construction of the church. The Crown was upset and suspicious of fraud because its 20 percent was not being paid on the yield. Crown to the officials of Guatemala (22 December 1539), AGI, Guatemala, leg. 393, lib. 2, fol. 95. Later, the bishop of Honduras ordered that all slaves, Indian and black, along with naborías, were to attend religious instruction on Sundays and fiestas, under pain of excommunication for masters who were remiss. Provision of don Cristóbal de Pedraza (San Pedro, 9 July 1552), AGI, Guatemala, leg. 168.

60. Zavala, *Estudios indianos*, p. 152.

61. Simpson, *The Encomienda*, p. 10.

62. Zavala, *Estudios indianos*, pp. 153–54.

63. While naboría is the most common designation, it is occasionally written as *naburía, naborío,* or *laborío.* Another term, apparently signifying the same, is tapia, variations of which are *tlapis* and *tapis.*

64. Provision of the audiencia (Santiago, 15 October 1603), AGCA, A1.23, leg. 4588, fols. 99–102. See also, Remesal, *Historia general* (1964–66), 1:391.

65. Zavala, *La filosofía,* p. 57. Zavala, *Los esclavos indios en Nueva España,* pp. 77–78, n. 13, presents the following definitions of naborías:

Acerca de la significación del término naboría, de origen antillano, decía el clérigo Luis de Morales, en una información promovida en Sevilla el 20 de junio de 1543 por el licenciado Gregorio López: "ques un vocablo paliado para servir contra su voluntad casi como esclavos aunque no se bendian y es desta manera que los tenian depositados personas para servirse dellos en las minas y en sus haziendas y si se querian ir algun cabo no podian porque se llamaban naborias." A.G.I., Patronato, 231, Num. 1. Ramo 4. Fol.I. Las Casas dice en su *Tratado de la esclavitud de los indios,* Sevilla, 1552, fol. IV: "naboria quiere decir: que les sirve continuamente en casa de la misma manera que esclavo, sino que pública ni secretamente los pueden vender sin pena." Véase también *RHA,* 3 (Septiembre 1938), pp. 61–63. Otras referencias que concuerdan con las anteriores recoge Georg Friederici, *Hilfswörterbuch für den Amerikanisten,* Halle, Verlag von Max Niemayer, 1926, pp. 68–69: "Indio libre, pero de servicio perpetuo; naboria es un indio que no es esclavo, pero está obligado a servir aunque no quiera; naboria es el que ha de servir a un amo aunque le pesse; e él no lo puede vender ni trocar sin expresa liçençia del gobernador; pero ha de servir hasta que la naboria o su amo se muera, acabado es su captiverio; y si muere su señor, es de proveer de tal naboria al gobernador, y dála a quien él quiere. E estos tales indios se llaman naborias de por fuerça e no esclavos; pero yo por esclavos los avria, queanto a estar sin libertad (Oviedo)."

For those interested, Zavala provides other authorities cited.

Remesal, *Historia general* (1964–66), 1:391, adds:

Este vocablo naboria que es usado asi en los libros de cabildo de la ciudad de Santiago de los Caballeros, como en estos de Ciudad Real, y otras villas y ciudades, trajéronla a estas partes, dice el señor obispo de Chiapa en su historia, los españoles que estuvieron en la isla de Santo Domingo, adonde era muy usado y quiere decir, *criado:* y dábanle a los indios que servían y no eran esclavos. Al principio que los indios se encomendaban a los españoles, sujetábanlos o oprimíanlos tanto con la falsa opinión que tenían de que no eran hombres, ni tenían dominio de sus cosas más que las bestias del campo, que totalmente les prohibían el comprar y vender y tratar y contratar, asi con los demás españoles como entre sí mismos. Sin esperar los regidores de Ciudad Real el breve que el Papa envió sobre esto, tenían remediada semejante tiranía, según parece por el cabildo que se tuvo a 16 de noviembre de 1537 en que se manda: *Que los naturales libremente puedan comprar y vender, tratar y contratar entre sí y los españoles y que sus amos o encomenderos no se lo impidan.*

For further discussion of the naborías in the Antilles, see Simpson, *The Encomienda,* p. 178, n. 15. John H. Parry, *The Audiencia of New Galicia in the Sixteenth Century,* pp. 56–57, equates the *mayeques* or *tlalmaites* of prehispanic Mexico with the naborías who worked for the Spaniards.

66. Ramirez, *Proceso Contra Alvarado,* p. 101.

67. Arévalo, *Libro de actas del ayuntamiento de la ciudad de Santiago de*

Guatemala, desde la fundación de la misma ciudad en 1524 hasta 1530,
pp. 110, 140–41.

68. Remesal, *Historia general* (1932), 1:391. "Fiscal contra Miguel Diaz" (14 August 1543), AGI, Guatemala, leg. 393, lib. 2, fols. 206–206v.

69. "Ordenanças que se dieron a Diego Mendez cuando fue por lugarteniente a la villa de Trugillo" (León, 20 August 1527), AGI, Guatemala, leg. 965.

70. Cerrato to the Crown (n.p., n.d., probably 1546), AGI, Audiencia de Santo Domingo 49, ramo 1.

71. R.C. (Toledo, 20 February 1534), cited in residencia of Pedro de Alvarado (Santiago, 1535), AGI, Justicia, leg. 296. The decree was proclaimed in Santiago in February, 1535.

72. In a royal provision, note was taken of the illegal transfer of slaves and naborías out of Nicaragua, and it was decreed that all those not branded were to be free, indicating that there were by that time unbranded Indians being forced to serve as naborías. Prince Philip to Cerrato (Segovia, 25 June 1548), AGCA, A1.23, leg. 1511, fol. 72.

73. Residencia of Francisco de Montejo (Gracias a Dios, June, 1544), AGI, Justicia, leg. 300.

74. Diego García de Celis to the Crown (Puerto de Caballos, 20 June 1534), AGI, Guatemala, leg. 49.

75. Residencia of the first audiencia (Gracias a Dios, 1547), AGI, Justicia 299.

76. Diego García de Celis (Puerto de Caballos, 20 June 1534), AGI, Guatemala, leg. 49.

77. Francisco de Barrientos to the Crown (Trujillo del Pinar del Puerto de Honduras, dia de Santiago, 25 July 1534), AGI, Guatemala, leg. 49.

78. Residencia of Alvarado (Santiago, 1535), AGI, Justicia 295.

79. Crown to Cerrato (Valladolid, 15 December 1548), AGCA, A1.23, leg. 1511, fols. 91–92.

80. "Ynformacion de Gregorio Lopez" (Seville, 1543), AGI, Patronato 231, ramo 4.

81. Andrés de Cerezeda to the Crown (Naco, 31 August 1535), AGI, Guatemala, leg. 39.

82. Montejo to the Crown (Gracias a Dios, 1 June 1539), AGI, Guatemala, leg. 9.

83. "Ynformacion de Gregorio Lopez" (Seville, 1543), AGI, Patronato, leg. 231, ramo 4. As early as 1539 there were complaints from other areas because they were not allowed to use naborías in mining. Concejos of Santiago, Ciudad Real, San Salvador, and San Miguel to the Crown (Guatemala, 22 January 1539), AGI, Guatemala, leg. 41.

84. Residencia of first audiencia, AGI, Justicia, leg. 299.

85. Royal cédulas of 20 March 1536 and 28 January 1586, Pardo, *Prontuario*, pp. 75, 83.

86. Residencia of Rodrigo de Contreras (Nicaragua, 1544), AGI, Justicia, leg. 297.

87. Residencia of Alvarado, AGI, Justicia, leg. 295.

88. R.C. (Valladolid, 29 January 1538), AGI, Guatemala, leg. 402, lib. 1, fols. 211–11v.

89. R.C. (Valladolid, 24 November 1537), AGI, Guatemala, leg. 401, lib. S-3, fols. 22–22v.

90. Residencia of Francisco Castañeda (Granada, 1535–36), AGI, Justicia, leg. 293.

91. Residencia of Contreras, AGI, Justicia, leg. 297.

92. Concejos of Santiago, Ciudad Real, San Salvador, and San Miguel (Guatemala, 22 January, 1539), AGI, Guatemala, leg. 41.

93. Crown to governor of Guatemala (Madrid, 23 November 1540), AGCA, A.1, leg. 4575, fol. 49v; and proclamation of Diego García de Celis (San Pedro: 26 December 1541) AGI, Guatemala, leg. 965. Pedraza wrote that encomenderos were not only selling Indians from their villages, but were also selling naborías from other provinces, both openly and through deceit. They traded their own naborías for those of other Spaniards, and sometimes they exchanged a naboría for a pig, a sheep, a cheese, vinegar, oil, or other merchandise. As a result, many naborías ran away to the wilderness or hanged themselves. Spaniards would not permit their naborías to attend church services nor to learn the Christian doctrine; "y las açotavan y maltratavan peor que si fuesen mill vezes sus esclavos." Robert S. Chamberlain, "Un documento desconocido del licenciado Cristóbal de Pedraza, Protector de los indios y Obispo de Honduras," *ASGH* 20 (March, 1945): 33–38.

94. R.C. (Valladolid, 28 August 1543), AGCA, A1.23, leg. 1511, fol. 17.

95. Pedraza to the Crown (Trujillo, 1 May 1547), AGI, Guatemala, leg. 164.

96. Licenciado Francisco Castañeda to the Crown (León, 30 May 1531), AGI, Guatemala, leg. 9.

97. Cabildo to the Crown (San Pedro del Puerto de Caballos, 1 November 1539), AGI, Guatemala, leg. 44.

98. Cabildo to the Crown (Gracias a Dios, n.d., but apparently the early 1540s), AGI, Guatemala, leg. 44.

99. Alonso de Baldes et al. to the Crown (San Pedro Puerto de Caballos, 15 May 1542), AGI, Guatemala, leg. 49.

100. Residencia of the first audiencia, AGI, Justicia, leg. 299.

101. Licenciado Castañeda to the Crown (León, 1 May 1533), AGI, Guatemala, leg. 9.

102. The term comes from the Nahuatl *tlameme*. R.P. Fray Tomás de la Torre, *Desde Salamanca, España, hasta Ciudad Real de Chiapas*, p. 179, notes that the carriers were called *tlamemeque*, a term corrupted by the Spaniards to tamemes. There is abundant evidence of the widespread use of the tamemes in native societies. See, e.g., Calnek, "Highland Chiapas," p. 44, who writes of the "large numbers of tlamemes . . . at the disposal of the rulers of Zinacantan."

103. For a view of prehispanic routes see Pedro Zamora Castellanos, "Itinerarios de la conquista de Guatemala," *ASGH* 20 (March, 1945): 23–32. On

400 *Notes*

the state of roads in 1539, see Robert S. Chamberlain, "Plan del siglo XVI para abrir un camino de Puerto Caballos a la bahía de Fonseca en sustitución de la ruta de Panamá," *ASGH* 21 (March, 1946): 61–66. See also by the same author, "Ensayo sobre el Adelantado don Francisco de Montejo y sus proyectos para el desarrollo económico de la provincia de Honduras e Higueras," *ASGH* 20 (September, 1945): 209–16.

104. As early as 1505, the use of Indian carriers was put into question. The king wrote Governor Ovando of Española of the great labor involved with transporting supplies to the mines and merchandise from the ports to the interior. Accordingly, it had been ordered that 150 asses, of which 50 were to be jackasses, be sent to alleviate the situation. In 1511, the use of tamemes was prohibited owing to the diminution of the natives. Those who violated the law were to lose their Indians. From Puerto Rico (San Juan) came word that because of the rough terrain and the lack of roads it was necessary to use human carriers; but Indians were to carry only thirty pounds at a time while roads were being laid out. The Crown lowered the legal weight to twenty-five pounds and ordered completion of the roads. Zavala, *Estudios indianos*, pp. 158–60. The Laws of Burgos (article 11), issued in 1512, prohibited Indians from carrying anything but their own baggage or provisions. Spaniards who forced Indians to carry anything else were to be fined two pesos, a sum not calculated to be a very effective deterrent. Simpson, *Studies in the Administration . . . I*, p. 14.

105. Puga, *Prouisiones*, 1:122–23. This cédula (Toledo, 4 December 1528) stated that violators would be fined 100 pesos for the first infraction, 300 pesos for the second, and loss of all the offender's property, including encomiendas.

106. An interesting exception was observed in Yucatán where some of the Maya natives, through "passive resistance," refused to deliver tamemes or to perform personal service, a posture they maintained with a good measure of success. Chamberlain, *The Conquest of Yucatán*, p. 172.

107. Ramírez, *Proceso contra Alvarado*, pp. 22, 29. Nuño de Guzmán, traditionally seen as the scourge of the Indians of New Spain, saw the need for tamemes, but issued restrictive orders: "A mounted soldier could have six; a foot soldier, three. Those employing slaves in their mining enterprises could use them as burden bearers; however, no slave was to carry more than an *arroba* . . . of cargo plus his food ration, and this for a distance not to exceed thirty leagues." Chipman, *Nuño de Guzmán and Pánuco*, p. 179.

108. Residencia of Alvarado, AGI, Justicia 295.

109. Cabildo of Trujillo to the Council of the Indies (Trujillo, 20 March 1530), AGI, Guatemala, leg. 44.

110. Saco, *La Esclavitud*, 1:173.

111. Cabildo to the Audiencia of Mexico (San Cristóbal de los Llanos, 4 June 1537), AGI, Guatemala, leg. 110.

112. R.C. for the governor of Guatemala (Talavera, 28 January 1541), AGCA, A.1, leg. 4575, fol. 50; and R.C. for the governor of Nicaragua (Talavera, 31 May 1541), AGI, Guatemala, leg. 401, lib. S-3, fols. 86–86v.

113. "Ynformacion de Gregorio Lopez" (Sevilla, 1543), AGI, Patronato, leg. 231, ramo 4; and R.C. to the governor of Guatemala (Talavera, 28 January 1541), AGCA, A.1, leg. 4575, fol. 50.

114. Simpson, *The Encomienda*, p. 141, writes that, "The New Law concerning Indian carriers was soon modified [1549] to permit their use where there was a shortage of pack animals, but their loads were to be moderate and their journeys short. The Council [of the Indies] also decided that the present wage of carriers amounted to their working for nothing, for they received 8½ maravedís (equivalent to ¼ real, or 1/32 peso) a day. It reminded the Audiencia that it was the ultimate purpose of the Crown to abolish personal services entirely."

115. Representatives of Santiago, San Salvador, and San Miguel to the Crown (Gracias a Dios, 9 June 1544), AGCA, A.1, leg. 2198, exp. 15793; and same to same (Gracias a Dios, 14 June 1544), A1.2.5, leg. 2363, exp. 17869.

116. Licenciado Herrera to the Crown (Gracias a Dios, 10 July 1545 and 24 December 1545), AGI, Guatemala, leg. 9.

117. R.C. to the audiencia (Madrid, 5 July 1546), AGCA, A1.23, leg. 1511, fol. 40.

118. Cabildo to the Crown (Gracias a Dios, 6 September 1547), AGI, Guatemala, leg. 44.

119. Audiencia to the Crown (Gracias a Dios, 23 September 1547), AGI, Guatemala, leg. 9.

120. Residencia of the first audiencia, AGI, Justicia, leg. 299.

121. Alonso López de Cerrato to the Crown (Santiago, 27 August 1554), AGI, Guatemala, leg. 9.

122. Cerrato to the Crown (Santiago, 27 August 1554), AGI, Guatemala, leg. 9.

123. Remesal, *Historia general* (1932), 1:75.

124. Bancroft, *History of Central America*, 2:237, n. 10.

125. J. Joaquín Pardo, *Efemérides de la Antigua Guatemala, 1541–1779*, p. 3.

126. R.C. of 26 March 1546 and R.C. of 17 April 1553, both in Pardo, *Prontuario*, pp. 76, 78.

127. Fr. Francisco Bustamante to the Crown (Santiago, 22 May 1551), AGI, Guatemala, leg. 168. Interestingly enough, the specific charge in this instance was that native principales were guilty of overloading other Indians.

128. Residencia of the first audiencia, AGI, Justicia, leg. 299.

129. Paso y Troncoso, *ENE*, 2:116–17.

130. Fr. Bartolomé de Las Casas to the Council of the Indies (n.p.,n.d.), AGI, Patronato, leg. 252, ramo 9.

131. R.C. (Talavera, 28 January 1541), AGCA, A1.23, leg. 4575, exp. 39528, fol. 50.

132. Ibid.

133. Residencia of the first audiencia, AGI, Justicia, leg. 299.

134. Residencia of Alonso López de Cerrato (Santiago, 1553–55), AGI, Justicia, leg. 302.

135. Residencia of the first audiencia, AGI, Justicia, leg. 299.

136. Remesal, *Historia general* (1932), 1:281.

137. Paso y Troncoso, *ENE*, 2:116–17. The order is dated at Mexico, 30 March 1531.

138. "Libro de cargo y data del comendador de Guatemala [Alvarado], 1529–1536," signed by Çurrilla, Maldonado, and Castellanos, AGI, Patronato, leg. 180, ramo 34. Interesting comparisons can be seen in G. Micheal Riley, "Labor in Cortesian Enterprise: The Cuernavaca Area, 1522–1549," *The Americas* 28 (January, 1972): 274–75. Noting that Fernando Cortés usually paid his tamemes, Riley adds that the Marqués del Valle used them to carry goods to the city of Mexico, to the mines, and to Acapulco. From the information gathered by Riley, it appears that Cortés used between 12,000 and 24,000 tamemes a year and that they were generally paid at the rate of one tomín (about $.48) for every 145 miles.

139. Residencia of first audiencia, AGI, Justicia, leg. 299.

140. Hernando de Ugarte, veedor, to the Crown (Santiago, 12 April 1549), AGI, Guatemala, leg. 41.

141. Cabildo to the Crown (León, 1531), AGI, Guatemala, leg. 43.

142. Fr. Bartolomé de Las Casas to the Council of the Indies (n.p., n.d.), AGI, Patronato, leg. 252, ramo 9.

143. Juan de Lerma to the Crown (San Pedro de Puerto de Caballos, 31 October 1539), AGI, Guatemala, leg. 49.

144. Petition of Antón de la Torre, *síndico procurador* of San Cristóbal (San Cristóbal de los Llanos, 3 April 1534), AGI, Indiferente General, leg. 1204.

145. Pedraza to the Crown (Seville, 28 July 1544), AGI, Guatemala, leg. 164.

146. Residencia of Rodrigo de Contreras, AGI, Justicia, leg. 297.

147. R.C. (Madrid, 26 March 1545), AGCA, A.1, leg. 4575, exp. 39528, fols. 76v, 88v–89. See also AGI, Guatemala 393, lib. R-3, fols. 10v–11.

148. Treasury officials to the Crown (Gracias a Dios, 20 September 1547), AGI, Guatemala, leg. 49.

149. The Crown to Cerrato (Valladolid, 15 December 1548), AGCA, A1.23, leg. 1511, fols. 91–92.

150. Alvaro de Paz to the Crown (San Pedro de Puerto de Caballos, 1 August 1549), AGI, Guatemala, leg. 49.

151. Pardo, *Prontuario*, p. 28.

152. Crown to the audiencia (Valladolid, 28 August 1543), AGCA, A1.23, leg. 1511, fol. 17v.

153. Licenciado Herrera to the Crown (Gracias a Dios, 10 July 1545), AGI, Guatemala, leg. 9.

154. Representatives of Santiago, San Salvador, and San Miguel to the Crown (Gracias a Dios, 9 June 1544), AGCA, A.1, leg. 2198, exp. 15793; and same to same (Gracias a Dios, 14 June 1544), AGCA, A1.2.5, leg. 2363, exp. 17869.

155. The queen to Bishop Francisco Marroquín (Valladolid, 10 February 1530), AGI, Guatemala, leg. 393, lib. R-2, fols. 7–11.

156. Residencia of Castañeda (Granada, 1535–36), AGI, Justicia, leg. 293.

157. Rodrigo de Contreras to the Crown (León, 25 July 1537), AGI, Guatemala, leg. 43.

158. Montejo to the Crown (Gracias a Dios, 1 May 1542), AGI, Patronato, leg. 184, ramo 25.

159. The queen to Bishop Marroquín (Valladolid, 10 February 1530), AGI, Guatemala, leg. 393, lib. R-3, fols. 7–11.

160. Diego García de Celis, treasurer, to the Crown (Buena Esperanza, 10 May 1535), AGI, Guatemala, leg. 49.

161. R.C. of 26 February 1538 and R.C. of 28 January 1540, Pardo, *Prontuario*, p. 121.

162. Bancroft, *History of Central America*, 2:237–38.

163. Paso y Troncoso, *ENE*, 2:116–17. This is dated 30 March 1531.

164. The queen to Bishop Marroquín (Valladolid, 10 February 1530), AGI, Guatemala, leg. 393, lib. R-3, fols. 7–11.

165. Cabildo to the Crown (Gracias a Dios, 16 February 1548), AGI, Guatemala, leg. 44.

166. Las Casas himself, however, had no recourse but to use tamemes; Motolinía observed that the famed Dominican used 120 tamemes on one occasion, adding that most of what the Indians carried consisted of Las Casas's writings against Spaniards' abuses of Indian labor. Motolinía, *Carta al Emperador*, pp. 61–62.

167. Arévalo, *Libro de Actas*, p. 40.

168. Residencia of Alvarado, AGI, Justicia, leg. 296.

169. Andrés de Cerezeda to the Crown (Puerto de Caballos, 14 August 1536), AGI, Guatemala, leg. 39.

170. Contreras to the Crown (León, 25 June 1537), AGI, Guatemala, leg. 43.

171. Audiencia to the Crown (Gracias a Dios, 23 September 1547), AGI, Guatemala, leg. 9.

172. Residencia of the first audiencia, AGI, Justicia, legajo 299.

173. Herrera to the Crown (Gracias a Dios, 29 January 1546), AGI, Guatemala, leg. 9.

174. Residencia of the first audiencia, AGI, Justicia, leg. 299.

175. Herrera to the Crown (Gracias a Dios, 24 December 1545), AGI, Guatemala, leg. 9.

176. Pedraza to the Crown (Trujillo, 1 May 1547), AGI, Guatemala, leg. 164.

Chapter 8

1. R.C. (Valladolid, 28 August 1543), AGCA, A1.23, leg. 1511, fol. 15v. See also, Remesal, *Historia general* (1964–66), 1:292–93.

2. Crown to Maldonado (Valladolid, 7 September 1543), AGCA, A1.23, leg. 1511, fol. 14.

3. Pardo, *Efemérides*, p. 5.

4. Ignacio Rubio Mañé, "Alonso de Maldonado, Primer Presidente de la

Audiencia de Guatemala," *ASGH* 2 (1964):163–65. Rubio Mañé states that Maldonado's first appointment was as "Captain General" for Charcas, South America. But Maldonado arrived in Mexico in April 1530, and he wrote to the king on December 18, 1544, that he had served fourteen years in the Indies. Maldonado to the Crown (Gracias a Dios, 18 December 1544), AGI, Guatemala, leg. 9.

5. Maldonado to the Crown (Gracias a Dios, 18 December 1544), AGI, Guatemala, leg. 9.

6. Ibid.

7. R.C. (Madrid, 27 October 1535), AGI, Justicia, leg. 232, fols. 24, 27v–28. Domingo Juarros, *Compendio de la historia de la ciudad de Guatemala*, 2 vols., 1:253–54.

8. André Saint-Lu, *La Vera Paz*, p. 452.

9. Pardo, *Efemérides*, pp. 3–4.

10. Maldonado to the Crown (Gracias a Dios: 18 December 1544), AGI, Guatemala, leg. 9.

11. Bancroft, *History of Central America*, 2:301, erroneously concludes, on the basis of one document, that the audiencia first met in 1545. He probably took his information from a letter dated 30 December 1545, sent to the king and signed by all four of the judges (AGI, Guatemala, leg. 9). They wrote that Herrera and Rogel had arrived on March 15, and that on May 15 they convened. Since it was dated the end of the year, it seems likely that the scribe anticipated the coming year, putting 1545, when it was really still 1544. Writing to the Crown from Gracias a Dios on 22 May 1544, licenciado Herrera (AGI, Guatemala, leg. 9) says quite clearly that he and Rogel arrived at Puerto de Caballos on March 16, and "el primer dia q. hizimos audientia fue a quinze de mayo." Pardo, *Efemérides*, p. 5, gives the first day as May 14.

12. Cited in Crown to Audiencia de los Confines (Valladolid, 28 August 1543), AGCA, A1.23, leg. 1511, fol. 17 ff. Antonio Muro Orejón (ed.), *Las Leyes de 1542–1543*. See also, Simpson, *The Encomienda*, pp. 123–44. For another view of this important legislation, see Lewis Hanke, "The New Laws—Another Analysis," in *Indian Labor in the Spanish Indies*, ed. John Francis Bannon, pp. 55–64.

13. "La supplicacion de las hordenanças q. interponen los pueblos en la audiencia real y la respuesta" ("Probança de los esclavos hechos") (Gracias a Dios, 14 June 1544), AGCA, A1.2.5, leg. 2363, exp. 17869.

14. Maldonado to the Crown (Gracias a Dios, 18 December 1544), AGI, Guatemala, leg. 9.

15. AGI, Justicia, leg. 331.

16. Simpson, *The Encomienda*, pp. 132–33, makes this note: "The Crown did not entrust the execution of these unpopular laws to the existing authorities in New Spain and Peru, where opposition was the strongest. Four men were commissioned to enforce them: Blasco Núñez de Vela [who lost his life as a result], for Peru; Francisco Tello de Sandoval, for New Spain; Miguel Díaz Armendariz, for Tierra Firme; and Alonso López de Cerrato, for the Antilles and the Pearl Coast."

17. Oviedo, *Historia General*, 1:158.

18. Díaz del Castillo, *The True History*, 2:323. Marroquín wrote in February, 1548, that Cerrato was a priest, although he had not yet met him. I have no evidence that he was, though he may have been a lay brother. Carmelo Sáenz de Santamaría, *El Licenciado Don Francisco Marroquín, Primer Obispo de Guatemala (1499–1563)*, pp. 122, 217, and 223.

19. José María de la Peña y de la Cámara, *A List of Spanish Residencias in the Archives of the Indies, 1516–1775*, p. 2.

20. Licenciados Cerrato and Grajeda to the Crown (Santo Domingo, 24 April 1545), AGI, Santo Domingo, leg. 49, ramo 1.

21. Tomás de la Torre, *Desde Salamanca*, pp. 94–95.

22. *DII*, 7:431–37.

23. Cerrato to the Crown (Santo Domingo, 19 March 1547), AGI, Santo Domingo, leg. 45, ramo 5.

24. Prince Philip to Cerrato (Valladolid, 24 April 1545), AGI, Santo Domingo, leg. 868, lib. 2, fols. 244–45 and again (Madrid, 13 December 1545), AGI, Santo Domingo, leg. 868, lib. 2, fols. 278v–79v.

25. Cerrato to the Crown (Santo Domingo, 19 March 1547), AGI, Santo Domingo, leg. 49, ramo 5.

26. Cerrato to the Crown (Santo Domingo, 18 December 1547), AGI, Santo Domingo, leg. 49, ramo 5. The Crown approved Cerrato's liberation of the Indian slaves who had been "sold like Negroes from Guinea." Crown to Cerrato (14 July 1548), Pardo, *Prontuario*, p. 59.

27. R.C. (Madrid, 21 May 1547), AGCA, A1.23, leg. 1511, fols. 55–55v. AGCA, A1.23, leg. 4575, fols. 141v–42. His annual salary was to be 750,000 maravedís, beginning when he left Espánola.

28. Cerrato to the Crown (10 January 1548), AGI, Santo Domingo, leg. 49, ramo 5.

29. Cabildo to the Council of the Indies (Santo Domingo, 22 December 1547), AGI, Santo Domingo, leg. 73.

30. Cerrato to the Crown (Santo Domingo, 29 July 1546), AGI, Santo Domingo, leg. 49, ramo 5.

31. Oviedo, *Historia General*, 1:158.

32. Ibid. AGCA, A1.23, leg. 4575, fol. 142.

33. Pardo, *Efemérides*, p. 6.

34. Ibid.

35. Cerrato to the Crown (Santiago de Guatemala, 8 April 1549), AGI, Guatemala, leg. 9.

36. Ibid.

37. Cerrato to the Crown (Gracias a Dios, 28 September 1548), AGI, Guatemala, leg. 9.

38. Cerrato to the Crown (Santiago, 26 January 1550), AGI, Guatemala, leg. 9. This comment was in response to the royal order given on September 16, 1549, that the president and oidores of audiencias were to have no commercial interests. Pardo, *Prontuario*, p. 122. Cerrato had suggested that the king make such a provision in a letter of November 9, 1548.

39. Martin de Esquivel to the Crown (Nicaragua, 30 December 1545), AGI, Guatemala, leg. 50.

40. Chamberlain, *The Conquest of Yucatán*, p. 183. The relationship between the families remained strong. On p. 308, Chamberlain notes that in 1551 Montejo was presenting an appeal to the royal court and was aided by Maldonado who was then president of the Audiencia of Santo Domingo. "Maldonado seems to have enjoyed high favor at Court and his influence helped the Adelantado."

41. Recinos and Goetz, *The Annals of the Cakchiquels*, pp. 130–31. It appears that Maldonado did free some slaves when he visited San Salvador, probably in 1538. AGI, Guatemala, leg. 393 (26 June 1539), fol. 55v.

42. Alonso García to the Crown (Gracias a Dios, 1 February 1546), AGI, Guatemala, leg. 9. In García's opinion, things had not changed much from the administration of Maldonado's father-in-law, about whom he commented: "Y digo que esta provincia esta perdida y los conquistadores della acavsa de aber sido vro gobernador Montejo y su muger tan tiranos como an sido porque ella es la que governaba y desgovernaba y aqui es ella queria que su marido les quitase los yndios sin raçon." On the encomiendas given to León, see also Cerrato to the Crown (Santiago, 27 August 1554), AGI, Guatemala, leg. 9.

43. Cerrato to the Crown (Gracias a Dios, 28 September 1548), AGI, Guatemala, leg. 9.

44. Cerrato to the Crown (Santiago, 27 August 1554), AGI, Guatemala, leg. 9.

45. Francisco de Morales to the Crown (Mexico, 1 October 1563), Paso y Troncoso, *ENE*, 9:242–48.

46. "Memoria para el illmo. señor Bisorrey de la nueva spaña," AGI, Guatemala, leg. 956. According to *Cartas de Indias*, pp. 792–93, Maldonado died in 1560, being governor of Yucatán, and holding the title of adelantado by virtue of his marriage to doña Catalina de Montejo.

47. Cerrato to the Crown (Santiago, 16 July 1549), AGI, Guatemala, leg. 9. R.C. of 20 September 1548, cited in Crown to the audiencia (Valladolid, 15 January 1549), AGCA, A.23, leg. 4575, exp. 39528, fols. 116–17. Cerrato to the Crown (Santiago, 27 August 1554), AGI, Guatemala, leg. 9, in which Cerrato says that Maldonado put the encomienda in his daughter's name at her birth.

48. Alonso García to the Crown (Gracias a Dios, 1 February 1546), AGI, Guatemala, leg. 9.

49. Cerrato to the Crown (Santiago, 27 August 1554), AGI, Guatemala, leg. 9. On Juan de Guzmán, see "Cargos" of the residencia of Francisco de Magaña, alcalde mayor (La Villa de la Trinidad del Puerto de Acaxutla, 1568), AGI, Justicia, leg. 312.

50. Cristóbal de Pedraza to the Crown (Trujillo, 1 May 1547), AGI, Guatemala, leg. 164.

51. Maldonado to the Crown (Gracias a Dios, 20 September 1547), AGI, Guatemala, leg. 9.

52. See F. V. Scholes and Eleanor Adams, *Don Diego Quijada, Alcalde Mayor de Yucatán, 1561–1565*.

53. Francisco de Morales to the Crown (Mexico, 1 October 1563), Paso y Troncoso, *ENE*, 9:242–48. See also, Robert S. Chamberlain, "El último testamento y mandato de don Francisco de Montejo, Adelantado de Yucatán, 1553," *ASGH* 20 (June, 1945): 83–90, which discusses the dealings in black slaves between Montejo and Maldonado. "Memoria para el illmo. señor Bisorrey de la nueva spaña," AGI, Guatemala, leg. 956.

54. Rubio Mañé, "Alonso de Maldonado," pp. 163–65.

55. Chamberlain, "El último testamento," and Chamberlain, *The Conquest of Yucatán*, p. 310.

56. Díaz del Castillo, *The True History*, 2:323.

57. Montejo was not quite so fortunate. Although he avoided serious punishment, he was found guilty in his 1544 residencia for Honduras-Higueras of being remiss in the matter of protection and care of the Indians. As a result, he was suspended from holding office in the Indies for six years. Chamberlain, *The Conquest of Yucatán*, p. 309.

58. Peña, *List of Spanish Residencias*, p. 3.

59. Rubio Mañé, "Alonso de Maldonado." This short article contains errors and omissions, but there is an interesting discussion of the descendants of the president. Rubio Mañé writes that Maldonado was drowned in 1560, but it appears from the language of the reactions to his suit for Yucatán, cited above, that he was still alive in 1563. Bancroft, *History of Central America*, 2:309, certainly errs in asserting that Maldonado died a couple of years after his 1548 residencia. More reliable is Maldonado's widow, doña Catalina, who wrote the king from Mexico on November 21, 1565 (Paso y Troncoso, *ENE*, 10:79–82), pointing out that her husband had drowned along the coast of Tabasco and Yucatán the year before after having served in the Indies for thirty-four years. After leaving Central America he functioned as president of the Audiencia de Santo Domingo for nine years, but the widow lamented that the family Indians had been taken away and she said she was destitute, with two daughters and a son.

60. Despite his important role in early Spanish government in Mexico, he is not even listed in the monumental *Diccionario Porrúa de Historia, Biografía y Geografía de México*.

61. Cerrato to the Crown (Santiago, 8 April 1549), AGI, Guatemala, leg. 9.

62. Ramírez to the Crown (Santiago, 20 May 1555), AGI, Guatemala, leg. 9.

63. Residencia of the first audiencia, AGI, Justicia, leg. 299. Ramírez to the Crown (Santiago, 20 May 1555), AGI, Guatemala, leg. 9.

64. Cerrato to the Crown (Santiago, 8 April 1549), AGI, Guatemala, leg. 9.

65. Maldonado to the Crown (Gracias a Dios, 20 November 1546), AGI, Guatemala, leg. 9. R.C. (Zaragoza, 30 June 1547), AGI, Guatemala, leg. 402, lib. 2, in Federico Argüello Solórzano and Carlos Molina Argüello, *Monumenta Centroamericae Histórica*, pp. 699–700. Remesal, *Historia general* (1964–66), 2:53–54. The chronicler calls Ramírez an "hombre de valor, diligente y de todo cuidado, en lo que se le encomendaba, y algo inclinado a cosas de guerra, por cuya causa aceptaba siempre de buena gana estos embites." In a letter from Bernal Díaz

del Castillo to the emperor (Santiago, 22 February 1552), it is noted that Ramírez was later sent back to Nicaragua to maintain order after the murder of Bishop Valdivieso, at a salary of seven and a half pesos per day in expenses, plus his food and keep. At the time of the writing, Díaz said that Ramírez was preparing to go to Castile. *Cartas de Indias*, pp. 38–44, 830.

66. Remesal, *Historia general* (1964–66), 2:310–13. *Cartas de Indias*, p. 830.

67. Recinos and Goetz, *Annals of the Cakchiquels*, pp. 137–38.

68. Sáenz de Santamaría, *Marroquín*, pp. 81–82. The author describes the encounter in some detail.

69. A different version of the incident may be seen in Ramírez to the Crown (Santiago, 20 May 1556), AGI, Guatemala, leg. 9. Marroquín's account of the scandal is a harsh indictment of Ramírez, but later (1556), when the judge was acting president of the audiencia, Marroquín had kind words for him. Sáenz de Santamaría, "Vida y escritos de don Franciso Marroquín, primer Obispo de Guatemala, 1499–1563," ASGH 36 (1963): 256–57. The bishop had trouble with the audiencia, and he particularly disliked Rogel. He had a better opinion of Ramírez a couple of years before the oidor attacked him, but he was aware of his hot temper even then. Comparing Ramírez to Rogel, he wrote: "Ramirez mas hombre es y es studiante, tiene mucha colera y poco cuidado de la justicia. . . ." Marroquín to the Crown (Santiago, 20 March 1551), Sáenz de Santamaría, *Marroquín*, p. 266.

70. Ramírez to the Crown (Santiago, 20 May 1555), AGI, Guatemala, leg. 9.

71. Pardo, *Efemérides*, pp. 8–9.

72. See, for example: Cabildo to the Crown (Santiago, 1 December 1555), AGI, Guatemala, leg. 41. Cabildo to the Crown (Puerto de Caballos, 29 May 1556), AGI, Guatemala, leg. 49. Diego de Robledo to the Crown (Santiago, 10 April 1556), AGI, Guatemala, leg. 9. Audiencia to the Crown (Santiago, 21 April 1556), AGI, leg. 9. Various friars to the Crown (Guatemala, 18 October 1556), AGI, Guatemala, leg. 52. Crown to the audiencia (Valladolid, 22 December 1556), AGI, Guatemala, leg. 386, lib. Q-1, fols. 202–202v. In R.C. (Valladolid, 11 April 1559), AGI, Guatemala, leg. 386, lib. 1, in Argüello Solórzano and Molina Argüello, *Monumenta Centroamericae*, pp. 700–701, the princess notes: " . . . me ha sido hecha relación que de tres años a esta parte, que es después que fallesció el doctor Quesada, él ha seruido de Presidente en la dicha Audiencia. . . ." Pardo, *Efemérides*, p. 8, indicates, erroneously, that Quesada died on 28 November 1558, and that Ramírez assumed power as president at that time. Even more confusing than most accounts is that in *Cartas de Indias*, p. 830 ("Datos Biográficos"), which states that after defeating the Lacandones at Pochutla, Ramírez returned to Guatemala in the spring of 1559, and "en premio de sus servicios y por muerte del doctor Quesada, fue ascendido Ramirez a presidente de aquella Audiencia en 1565, desde donde se le trasladó después a la de Lima." In fact, he was sent as regent and oidor of the Audiencia de la Plata de los Charcas, although he would act as president when the viceroy was not present. Carta de oficio to Ramírez from the Crown (Valladolid, 4 March 1559), AGI, Guatemala, leg. 386, lib. 1, in Argüello Solórzano and Molina Argüello,

Monumenta Centroamericae, pp. 597–98. Clarence H. Haring, *The Spanish Empire in America*, p. 93, states that in 1563 Ramírez was invested with the rank of president outright.

73. Residencia of licenciado Pedro Ramírez de Quiñones (Santiago, 1559), AGI, Justicia, leg. 308.

74. R.C. (Valladolid, February, 1559), AGI, Guatemala, leg. 386, lib. Q-1, fols. 259–60. He stood for his residencia as president of the Audiencia de la Plata (Charcas) in 1579. Peña, *List of Spanish Residencias*, p. 64. To that point he had served about thirty-six years as a crown judge, during which he was presiding for some twenty-nine years.

75. Alonso García to the Crown (Gracias a Dios, 1 February 1546), AGI, Guatemala, leg. 9.

76. Residencia of the first audiencia, AGI, Justicia, leg. 299.

77. Cerrato to the Crown (Santiago, 8 April 1549), AGI, Guatemala, leg. 9.

78. Remesal *Historia general* (1964–66), 2:54, 59, 69–70.

79. Ibid. Chamberlain, *The Conquest of Yucatán*, p. 309.

80. Remesal, *Historia general* (1964–66), 2:69–70.

81. Sáenz de Santamaría, *Marroquín*, notes in his index several references by the bishop to Rogel. On p. 244, he cites one of the letters, which includes these comments: "Si el [Cerrato] hubiera echado de su compania al liçdo Rogel no le faltaba nada; en verdad, que no conviene que un honbre tan deshonesto y ruin este en audiencia. Remitome a su residençia. Ahora va a visitar, echarlo han por cargo, y va a ver sus negros questan en las minas y de camino por que parezca que haze algo lleva poder para visitar y por enmendar lo passado no tiene lastima de destruir al que puede, y que suene su voz." Bernal Díaz del Castillo wrote the Crown (Santiago, 22 February 1552) making reference to Rogel's illicit business affairs: "Sepa V.M. la manera que a tenido é tiene en dar estos yndios que e dicho: para que allá V.M. crea que son bien dados por bia de Avdiençia Real, procuró de admetyr en esta Real Avdiençia á un Juan Rogel por oydor, por tenelle de manga . . . puesto que aquel Rogel le avía desechado desta Avdiencia Real quando le tomó residencia, e oydo dezir que por tenelle para aqueste efeto desimuló con él muchas cosas, diziendo 'azme la barva.' " *Cartas de Indias*, p. 40.

82. Crown to Cerrato (Valladolid, 16 September 1549), AGCA, A1.23, leg. 1511, fol. 125.

83. Crown to Cerrato (Monzón, 11 July 1552), AGI, Guatemala, leg. 386, lib. Q-1, fols. 45v–46.

84. Las Casas and Valdivieso to Prince Philip (Gracias a Dios, 25 October 1545), *Cartas de Indias*, p. 25. Herrera returned their confidence in them by refusing to sign an audiencia letter that was detrimental to the two bishops. The judge was reprimanded, because he was supposed to go along with the majority, although he could write the Crown separately to express his dissent. Crown to Herrera (Guadalajara, 10 September 1546), AGI, Guatemala, leg. 402, lib. 2, in Argüello Solórzano and Molina Argüello, *Monumenta Centroamericae*, pp. 596–97.

85. Cerrato to the Crown (Santiago, 8 April 1549), AGI, Guatemala, leg. 9.

86. Cerrato to the Crown (San Salvador, 3 November 1548), AGI, Guatemala, leg. 9.

87. Cerrato to the Crown (Gracias a Dios, 28 September 1548), AGI, Guatemala, leg. 9.

88. AGI, Justicia, leg. 299. According to a witness, "Una yndia naboria de un vecino desta cibdad que se llama po. de orellana se fue a casa del dho licdo. herrera la qual le pidio el dho po. de orellana muchas vezes y no se la quiso dar aunq tenia necesidad su muger del dho orellana della porq dezian quel dho licdo. se hechava con la dha yndia y la llamava doña ysabelica en la cama y esto oyo dezir a una persona que se hechava con la dha yndia que se llamava villalobos [Martin de Villalobos, the alguacil mayor?]."

89. Cerrato to the Crown (Santiago, 8 April 1549), AGI, Guatemala, leg. 9.

90. Herrera to the Crown (Gracias a Dios, 9 May 1549), AGI, Guatemala, leg. 9.

91. *DII*, 24:397–420.

92. Herrera to the Crown (Gracias a Dios, 24 December 1545), AGI, Guatemala, leg. 9.

93. Marroquín to the Crown (Santiago, 20 September 1547), Sáenz de Santamaría, *Marroquín*, p. 220.

94. AGI, Justicia, leg. 299.

95. Cerrato to the Crown (Gracias a Dios, 28 September 1548), AGI, Guatemala, leg. 9.

96. Crown to Cerrato (Valladolid, 16 September 1549), AGCA, A1.23, leg. 1511, fol. 125.

97. Cerrato to the Crown (Santiago, 8 April 1549), AGI, Guatemala, leg. 9.

98. Residencia of Cerrato (Santiago, 1553–55), AGI, Justicia, leg. 301.

99. Cerrato and Ramírez to the Crown (Santiago de Guatemala, 21 May 1549), AGI, Guatemala, leg. 9. Cerrato to the Crown (Santiago, 8 April 1549), AGI, Guatemala, leg. 9.

100. Cerrato to the Crown (San Salvador: 3 November 1548), AGI, Guatemala, leg. 9.

101. Cerrato and Ramírez to the Crown (Santiago, 21 May 1549), AGI, Guatemala, leg. 9. Cerrato to the Crown (Santiago, 8 April 1549), AGI, Guatemala, leg. 9.

102. Cabildo to the Crown (Santiago, 30 April 1549), AGI, Guatemala, leg. 41.

103. Barón Castro, *La Población*, p. 46.

104. Cerrato to the Crown (Santiago, 8 April 1549), AGI, Guatemala, leg. 9. Pardo, *Efemérides*, p. 7.

105. Cerrato to the Crown (Gracias a Dios, 28 September 1548), AGI, Guatemala, leg. 9.

106. Cerrato to the Crown (Santiago, 8 April 1549), AGI, Guatemala, leg. 9. See also the president's testimony in AGI, Justicia, leg. 301.

107. Cabildo to the Crown (Santiago, 24 January 1550), AGI, Guatemala, leg. 41. Perhaps the mention of fifty cuadrillas represented the number of

slaving gangs taken away over a period of time, or maybe the *regidores* were simply exaggerating. Earlier, about four months after the arrival of Cerrato, they wrote that "forty and some cuadrillas" had been lost. Cabildo to the Crown (Santiago, 30 April 1549), AGI, Guatemala, leg. 41.

108. Bartolomé de Las Casas to the Council of the Indies (n.p., n.d.), AGI, Patronato 252, ramo 9.

109. Ximénez, *Historia*, 1:463. Bancroft, *History of Central America*, 2:333. For a broader discussion of the career of Diego Ramírez, see Walter V. Scholes, *The Diego Ramírez Visita.*

110. AGI, Justicia, leg. 301. See also Remesal (1932), 2:237.

111. Ximénez, *Historia*, 1:480.

112. Remesal, *Historia general* (1932), 2:237.

113. See, e.g., R.C. of 25 June 1548, Pardo, *Prontuario*, p. 59, calling specifically for the liberation of slaves in Nicaragua.

114. Pardo, *Prontuario*, p. 43. R.C. (Valladolid, 31 December 1549), AGI, Guatemala, leg. 402, lib. T-3, fols. 60–60v.

115. R.C. of 4 August 1550, Pardo, *Prontuario*, p. 8.

116. This important legislation, given on February 2, 1549, is discussed in Prince Philip to the audiencia (Madrid, 12 April 1553), AGCA, A1.23, leg. 4575, fol. 123.

117. Cabildo to the Crown (Gracias a Dios, 6 September 1547), AGI, Guatemala, leg. 44.

118. Cerrato to the Crown (Santiago, 8 April 1549), AGI, Guatemala, leg. 9. Bancroft, *History of Central America*, 2:326. Cerrato to the Crown (Gracias a Dios, 28 September 1548), AGI, Guatemala, leg. 9.

119. Herrera to the Crown (Gracias a Dios, 9 May 1549), AGI, Guatemala, leg. 9. Pardo, *Efemérides*, p. 7. Crown to Cerrato (Valladolid, 7 July 1550), AGI, Guatemala, leg. 393, lib. 2, fol. 165. Cerrato to the Crown (21 May 1549), AGI, Guatemala, leg. 9.

Chapter 9

1. Parts of this chapter appeared in my article, "Indian Slavery and the Cerrato Reforms," *Hispanic American Historical Review* 51 (February, 1971): 25–50.

2. Cerrato to the Crown (Santiago, 26 January 1550), AGI, Guatemala, leg. 9. Barón Castro, *La Población*, pp. 189–90, attributes to Cerrato almost the same words in a letter written on April 1, 1549.

3. AGI, Justicia, leg. 301. The assertion of the regidores of Santiago that no one dared oppose Cerrato, who allegedly said he would stab the first to do so, credits the president with a physical vigor which was probably lacking. The original remark to that effect seems to have come from licenciado Ramírez, who, on the other hand, was himself quick to pull a blade.

4. Cerrato to the Crown (Gracias a Dios, 28 September 1548), AGI, Guatemala, leg. 9.

412

Notes

5. AGI, Justicia, leg. 301, 302. Cerrato testified that in order to frustrate the application of the laws, Spaniards had spread rumors of rebellions, circulating bad news out of Peru and Mexico, and worse,

que me avian de matar y aun hasta españa e servieron que me avian muerto en una batalla en la nueva españa e servieron que me avia perdido y no parescia y otros dixeron que me avian benido a matar desde mexico e que en un dia nos avian de matar a mi y al señor visorrey don luys de velasco e que echo un clerigo fama que por cinquenta pesos e un caballo se obligava una a matarme e antes de la navidad pasada del año de cinquenta e quatro al principio del vyno una persona de muncha calidad e nos hablo a mi e al licenciado Çorita oydor en gran secreto y con juramento que primero nos tomo que no le descubriesemos nos dixo q thenian concertados de nos matar o prender a mi e al licenciado çorita la justicia e regimiento desta ciudad todo a fin que no se tasen ni visitasen la tierra como su magt tiene mandado y ansy agora se an juntado e hecho liga los alcaldes e regidores e procuradores que son Santos de Figueroa e joan perez dardon alcaldes e don francisco e francisco lopes e al fator ovalle e alonso gutierrez e xpoval lobo e bernal diaz del castillo regidores e joan bazquez procurador e juramentaron sobre ello de me seguir en esta resydencia e destruyrme a efeto que los juezes que de aqui adelante fueren no osen hazer cosa alguna contra ellos. . . .

6. Díaz del Castillo, *The True History*, 1:12.
7. Herrera, *Historia general*, vol. 1:dec. 1, book 7, ch. 14.
8. Friede and Keen, *Las Casas*, p. 517.
9. Herrera, *Historia general*, vol. 1:dec. 1, book 7, ch. 14.
10. Remesal, *Historia general* (1932), 1:430.
11. Ibid.
12. Friede and Keen, *Las Casas*, p. 517.
13. R.C. (20 July 1532), AGI, Guatemala, leg. 393, lib. 2, fols. 42–43.
14. "Informacion de Hernan Mendez" (Santiago, 28 May 1531), AGI, Guatemala, leg. 110.
15. Cabildos of Santiago, Ciudad Real, San Salvador, and San Miguel to the Crown (Guatemala, 22 January 1539), AGI, Guatemala, leg. 41.
16. "La informacion q. hizo Sanct Saluador" (Villa de San Salvador, 20 April 1545), AGCA, A1.28, leg. 2335, exp. 1705. See also, "La supplicacion de las hordenanças q. interponen los pueblos en la audiencia real y la respuesta" (Gracias a Dios, 14 June 1544), AGCA, A1.2.5, leg. 2363, exp. 17869; and a similar response (Gracias a Dios, 9 June 1544), AGCA, A.1, leg. 2198, exp. 15793.
17. AGI, Justicia, leg. 295.
18. "Informacion de Hernan Mendez," AGI, Guatemala, leg. 110.
19. Ibid.
20. Ibid.
21. Ibid.
22. Çurrilla to Francisco de los Cobos (Santiago, 15 September 1531), AGI, Guatemala, leg. 45.
23. Juan Ruano to the Audiencia of Mexico (Trujillo, 14 April 1533), AGI, Guatemala, leg. 49.
24. "Informacion de Hernan Mendez," AGI, Guatemala, leg. 110.

25. AGI, Justicia, leg. 295.

26. Simpson, *Studies in the Administration* . . . *IV*, pp. 6–7.

27. Cabildo to the Crown (Santiago, 6 May 1549), AGI, Guatemala, leg. 41.

28. Cabildo to the Crown (Santiago, 29 January 1550), AGI, Guatemala, leg. 9.

29. Cabildo to the Crown (Santiago, 24 January 1550), AGI, Guatemala, leg. 41. Bernal Díaz del Castillo wrote the Crown from Santiago on February 22, 1552 (*Cartas de Indias*, p. 40), complaining about Cerrato: "Pues más sepa V.M., que quando algun prove [pobre] conquistador biene á él á le de mandar que le ayude á se sostentar para sus hijos é muger si es casado . . . les responde [Cerrato] con cara feroz y con una manera de meneos, en vna silla, que avn para la avtoridad de vn onbre que no sea de mucha arte no conbiene, quanto más para vn presidente, y les dize: ¿"quien os mandó benir á conquistar? ¿mandoos S.M.? mostrá su carta: andá, que basta lo que aveys robado."

30. Ibid.

31. Cabildo to the Crown (Santiago, 30 April 1549), AGI, Guatemala, leg. 41. Pardo, *Efemérides*, p. 6, notes that a royal edict of 21 October 1547, ordered the cabildo to meet once a week, and (p. 8) that on 15 March 1555, the audiencia instructed the regidores to meet every Tuesday and Friday.

32. Cabildo to the Crown (Santiago, 10 March 1551), AGI, Guatemala, leg. 41.

33. Ibid.

34. "Christoval Louo vezino de Santiago de Guatemala por si y en nombre de varios descendientes de conquistadores antiguos sobre ser preferidos a otros mas modernos en las provisiones de encomiendas" to Council of the Indies (Santiago, 1551), AGI, Guatemala, leg. 53. Cristóbal (Xpoval) Lobo to "muy poderoso señor" (Santiago, n.d.), AGI, Guatemala, leg. 52. Cristóbal Lobo to the Council of the Indies (Santiago, 1 July 1553), AGI, Guatemala, leg. 52. Crown to the audiencia (Madrid, 5 April 1552), AGI, Guatemala, leg. 386, lib. Q-1, fols. 30–30v. Lobo was also angry because Cerrato had called him a "porquero." AGI, Justicia 302.

35. Probanza of Bishop Valdivieso (Madrid and León, Nicaragua, 1547–49), "Probanzas de religiosos," no. 11, AGI, Guatemala, leg. 965. Although it does not conform to other information, Cerrato made the curious statement that when he first arrived no priest or friar was confessing or absolving anyone who had a slave. Thus, while almost all had freed their slaves voluntarily, their losses were blamed on him. Cerrato to the Crown (Santiago, 15 March 1551), AGI, Guatemala, leg. 9. Unfortunately, there are no records to my knowledge to indicate how many slaves might have been manumitted in response to pressures from men of the Church. Lacking vecinos' complaints, which would have been voluminous, it must be concluded that very few slaves were liberated for such reasons.

36. Cerrato to the Crown (Santiago, 18 March 1551), AGI, Guatemala, leg. 9.

37. A notable exception is the late Spanish historian, Manuel Giménez Fernández, who referred to Marroquín as "opportunistic," "venal," and "the scheming politician." But it must be remembered that the author was a fervent admirer of Las Casas, with whom Marroquín had bitter disputes. Manuel

Giménez Fernández, "Fray Bartolomé de Las Casas: A Biographical Sketch," in *Bartolomé de Las Casas*, eds. Friede and Keen, pp. 67–126.

38. See Ernesto Chinchilla Aguilar, "El Obispo Marroquín y Las Leyes Nuevas de 1542," *ASGH* 36 (1963): 35–41. Lázaro Lamadrid, O.F.M., "Bishop Marroquín, Zumárraga's Gift to Central America," *The Americas* 5 (January, 1949): pp. 331–41, assigns to the prelate a greater role in the liberating of the Indians than I am willing to concede. The author questions the view, held by some, that Alvarado brought Marroquín to the New World. There is no question, however, that the two were close. Furthermore, Sáenz de Santamaría, *Marroquín*, p. 112, points out that the bishop and Alonso Maldonado were close, old friends.

39. Bancroft, *History of Central America*, 2:327.

40. Cerrato to the Crown (Santiago, 8 April 1549), AGI, Guatemala, leg. 9. Marroquín was visiting Gracias a Dios, perhaps not coincidentally, when Cerrato first arrived, and the bishop formed a good opinion of the new president. Sáenz de Santamaría, *Marroquín*, p. 234. Cerrato was initially well impressed by the bishop; in fact, he proposed in August, 1548, that he be appointed archbishop of Mexico to succeed the deceased Zumárraga. Sáenz de Santamaría, "Vida y escritos," p. 219. By May 4, 1549, Marroquín still had a favorable view of Cerrato as an administrator, with some reservation; the president was "un poco precipitado," and his abrupt liberation of the slaves was benefitting no one, in the bishop's view. In other correspondence in 1549, the prelate increasingly criticized Cerrato's methods and the influence of the Dominicans on him. While the president was, in his eyes, a very honorable man and a good judge, the Spaniards were very discontented. Writing to Las Casas in 1550, Marroquín said that Cerrato had been excessively zealous, and he urged moderation. By March 1551, Marroquín was openly against Cerrato, writing that he was not a good governor and that he had not had oidores to advise him. Tomás López, who opposed Cerrato's methods, did, however, impress the bishop. Marroquín added that, while he had not specified it before, Cerrato, having begun well, ultimately could not resist rewarding all of his relatives. Sáenz de Santamaría, *Marroquín*, pp. 234, 242–43, 247, 252, 263. It is worth noting, however, that in the years following Cerrato's reforms Marroquín had relatively little to say about the abuse of the Indians.

41. Francisco de Bañuelos to the Crown (Santa Fe de Guatemala, 15 June 1550), AGI, Guatemala, leg. 45.

42. "Respuesta al obpo. de guatimala" (4 August 1550), AGI, Guatemala, leg. 393, lib. 3, fol. 172.

43. Royal provision (18 August 1550), AGI, Guatemala, leg. 393, lib. 3, fols. 181v–82.

44. Bancroft, *History of Central America*, 2:327. Bancroft very likely based his statement on a letter in which the officials of Santiago mention that Marroquín reprimanded Cerrato from the pulpit, as a consequence of which Cerrato became his enemy and did not attend Mass at the *iglesia mayor* for several days. Officials to the Crown (Santiago, 10 March 1551), AGI, Guatemala, leg. 52.

45. Residencia of licenciado Alonso López de Cerrato (Santiago, 1553–55), AGI, Justicia, leg. 301.

46. Ibid.

47. Ibid.

48. Ibid.

49. Ibid.

50. Remesal, *Historia general* (1932), 2:203.

51. Cabildo to the Crown (Ciudad Real de Chiapa, 1 May 1550), AGI, Guatemala, leg. 44.

52. Cabildo to the Crown (Santiago, 1 June 1550), AGI, Guatemala, leg. 41.

53. Cabildo to the Crown (Santiago, 15 September 1549), AGI, Guatemala, leg. 41.

54. Ibid. Four months later the regidores repeated many of the same charges, adding that Cerrato was especially influenced by three or four Dominicans, men "of little wisdom, but much ambition, friends of their own interests," who were humored because they wrote good things about him to the king. Cabildo to the Crown (Santiago, 24 January 1550), AGI, Guatemala, leg. 41.

55. According to officials of Santiago, Cerrato deceived the friars with his "furious zeal" because he was old and astute. Officials to the Crown (Santiago, 10 March 1551), AGI, Guatemala, leg. 52.

56. Beatings of the natives by Dominican friars are documented in various places. See, for example, friars Cárdenas and Torre to the Crown (Estancia de Çoncocuyloco, 12 November 1552), AGI, Guatemala, leg. 168.

57. Cabildo to the Crown (Santiago, 15 September 1549), AGI, Guatemala, leg. 41.

58. Cabildo to the Crown (Santiago, 24 January 1550), AGI, Guatemala, leg. 9.

59. Ramírez to the Crown (Santiago, 25 May 1549), AGI, Guatemala, leg. 9.

60. AGI, Justicia, leg. 301. See also, Cerrato to the Crown (Santiago, 8 April 1549), AGI, Guatemala, leg. 9.

61. Cabildo to the Crown (Gracias a Dios, 10 April 1551), AGI, Guatemala, leg. 44.

62. Unless otherwise noted, the following discussion of Cerrato's nepotism is based on these sources: Francisco de Bañuelos to the Crown (Santa Fe de Guatemala, 15 June 1550), AGI, Guatemala, leg. 45; cabildo to the Crown (Santiago, 24 January 1550), AGI, Guatemala, leg. 41; cabildo to the Crown (Santiago, 1 September 1549), AGI, Guatemala, leg. 41; cabildo to the Crown (Ciudad Real de Chiapa, 1 May 1550), AGI, Guatemala, leg. 44; and a letter written by Las Casas, cited in Marcel Bataillon, "Las Casas et le Licencié Cerrato," *Bulletin Hispanique* 55 (1953): 79–87. Bataillon refers to "Juan" López Cerrato, but he surely means Alonso López de Cerrato.

63. Bataillon, "Las Casas et le Licencié Cerrato," p. 82. According to Las Casas, Nicolás López "lo querría tanta allá como a Tordesillas acá, que no se puede dezir la felicidad suya y de la tierra que tiene alrededor." In this letter Las Casas refers to López having married Cerrato's granddaughter, but Cerrato

in his residencia refers to the girl as the daughter of his brother, Dr. Alonso Cruz Cerrato.

64. Cabildo to the Crown (Ciudad Real de Chiapa, 1 May 1550), AGI, Guatemala, leg. 44.

65. Bernal Díaz wrote in February 1552 (*Cartas de Indias*, pp. 40–43), that Cerrato would claim that the repartimientos he gave to his relatives were not worth much; but, he said, they were the best, and the least of them was comparable in Central America to one worth 10,000 pesos in Peru. Dr. Cerrato had died, but his daughter had just arrived and would receive her father's income of 3,000 pesos a year. "No sabemos," he added, "quando verná otra barcada de Çerratos á que les den yndios."

66. AGI, Justicia, leg. 301.

67. Bataillon, "Las Casas et le Licencié Cerrato."

68. AGI, Justicia, leg. 301. While there is no question that Maldonado and his associates held many Indians, the allegation of Las Casas and the bishop of Nicaragua that they had 60,000 of them is almost certainly an exaggeration. MacNutt, *Bartholomew de las Casas*, pp. 255–56.

69. It is true, however, that Prince Philip, in 1552, sent a provision in which he noted the encomiendas given to Dr. Cerrato and Cano, with the admonition that conquistadores and married pobladores be given first consideration. At the same time, he cautioned the president to be more moderate in the language he used with merchants. Philip to Cerrato (Monzon, 11 June 1552), AGI, Guatemala, leg. 386, fols. 44–44v.

70. Among other complaints, regidores stated that Cerrato had ordered a vecino jailed because he would not lend tools to be used for making a road, although finally Cerrato yielded to the entreaties of "some good people." It was also charged that he put a merchant in jail because he would not give him some linen. It was further alleged that Cerrato jailed a Spaniard in a scandal over the counterfeiting of maravedís, in which the president was purportedly involved. Cabildo to the Crown (Santiago, 6 May 1549), AGI, Guatemala, leg. 41.

71. Cabildo to the Crown (Santiago, 15 September 1549), AGI, Guatemala, leg. 41.

72. Ibid.

73. Ibid.

74. Fray Francisco Bustamante, "Comissario General," to the Crown (Santiago, 22 March 1551), AGI, Guatemala, leg. 168.

75. Ibid.

76. Ibid.

77. Ibid.

78. Cabildo to the Crown (Santiago, 15 September 1549), AGI, Guatemala, leg. 41.

79. Cabildo to the Crown (Santiago, 6 May 1549), AGI, Guatemala, leg. 41.

80. Bustamante to the Crown (Santiago, 22 March 1551), AGI, Guatemala, leg. 168.

81. Residencia of Cerrato and judges of the audiencia, AGI, Justicia, leg. 302.

82. Cabildo to the Crown (Santiago, 24 January 1550), AGI, Guatemala, leg. 41.

83. Bustamante to the Crown (Santiago, 22 March 1551), AGI, Guatemala, leg. 168.

84. Cabildo to the Crown (Santiago, 24 January 1550), AGI, Guatemala, leg. 41. But see Severo Martínez Peláez, *La Patria del Criollo*.

85. In 1551, officials of Santiago assured the king that because of conditions in Central America all the pominent and wealthy men had left, or would soon leave. Officials to the Crown (Santiago, 10 March 1551), AGI, Guatemala, leg. 52. There was a very real precedent for such a turn of events in the drastic decline of population in the Antilles. The islands were depopulated, despite severe restrictions on emigration, owing to the discoveries of the rich civilization in Mexico and Peru. By 1551, rumors to the contrary, there was little evidence to suggest that ready wealth awaited the adventurous. As early as 1549, in response to predictions of an exodus of the prominent vecinos, Cerrato said they only made him laugh. He added that the poor Spaniards prayed that the rich ones would become so angry that they would leave. Perhaps four Spaniards in the province would leave, he said, and there were four hundred just as good as they to take what they would leave behind. Cerrato to the Crown (Santiago, 16 July 1549), AGI, Guatemala, leg. 9.

86. Cabildo to the Crown (Ciudad Real de Chiapa, 1 May 1550), AGI, Guatemala, leg. 41.

87. Ibid.

88. Cabildo to the Crown (Santiago, 15 September 1549), AGI, Guatemala, leg. 41.

89. Cabildo to the Crown (Santiago, 24 January 1550), AGI, Guatemala, leg. 41.

90. I cannot agree with Murdo J. MacLeod, *Las Casas, Guatemala, and the Sad but Inevitable Case of Antonio de Remesal*, p. 53, that "Indian slavery as an institution was almost dead by 1543. . . ." There were still many thousands of slaves laboring for the Spaniards at that time. The assertion of the vecinos of Guatemala in a letter to the king, 1 August 1549, that "no slaves have been taken for the past fifteen years," is patent nonsense. Cited in Simpson, *Studies in the Administration . . . IV*, p. 8.

91. Cabildo to the Crown (Santiago, 30 April 1549), AGI, Guatemala, leg. 41.

92. Cabildo to the Crown (Santiago, 15 September 1549), AGI, Guatemala, leg. 41.

93. Reproduced in Simpson, *Studies in the Administration . . . IV*, pp. 32–36.

94. Cerrato to the Crown (Santiago, 28 September 1548), AGI, Guatemala, leg. 9.

95. Cerrato to the Crown (Santiago, 25 May 1552), AGI, Guatemala, leg. 9.

96. AGI, Justicia, leg. 301.

97. Cerrato to the Crown (Santiago, 8 April 1549), AGI, Guatemala, leg. 9.

98. Ibid.

99. Cerrato and lic. Ramírez to the Crown (Santiago, 21 May 1549), AGI, Guatemala, leg. 9.

100. AGI, Justicia, leg. 301.

101. Cerrato to the Crown (Santiago, 26 January 1550), AGI, Guatemala, leg. 9.

102. Licenciado Cavallón, a close relative of Cerrato, wrote that despite the president's great services, his enemies were still trying to discredit him after his death. Cavallón to the Crown (Santiago, 14 April 1556), AGI, Guatemala, leg. 52. For the next half century Spaniards continued to lay the blame for their misfortunes on Cerrato. While such sentiment was widespread, a sampling of the correspondence from Chiapas will illustrate the nature of their complaints. Juan de la Tovilla, in 1601, traced his family's decline back to the liberation of their slaves, most of whom had been purchased at prices of seventy to eighty pesos each. Thereafter, the family mining interests were ruined, their wheat was lost, their livestock strayed and became wild. The freed Indians refused to work for pay. Tovilla had ten legitimate children and was in financial stress. Probanza of Juan de la Tovilla (Ciudad Real de Chiapa, 1601), and citing that of his father, Andrés de la Tovilla (Ciudad Real de Chiapa, 1579), AGI, Guatemala, leg. 966. Representations of the city of Ciudad Real were presented in the 1580s in which it was stated that there were 80 to 100 vecinos, all conquistadores or their children, and all poor because their slaves had been taken away many years before. Using that as a pretext, they went on to explain that because of their poverty their daughters had no dowries; and since they could, accordingly, not marry, the citizens requested 500 pesos yearly from the Crown to support a nunnery for the girls, to be built at royal expense. "Testimonios" of the city of Ciudad Real de Chiapa, 1583 and 1587, AGI, Guatemala, leg. 8. And in 1591, the regidores of the city wrote that the original settlers had high hopes, with mines and forty-seven encomiendas dispensed to the conquerors. Then the slaves were freed and the mining ceased, a blow from which they had not recovered. Cabildo to the Crown (Ciudad Real de Chiapa, 28 November 1591), AGI, Guatemala, leg. 44.

103. Cabildo to the Crown (Santiago, 24 January 1550), AGI, Guatemala, leg. 41.

104. Ramírez ably assisted the president in the implementation of the laws, in fact "demasiado" in the opinion of Bernal Díaz del Castillo, testifying in Residencia of Pedro Ramírez de Quiñones (Santiago, 1559), AGI, Justicia, leg. 308.

105. Tomás López to the Crown (Santiago, 9 June 1550), AGI, Guatemala, leg. 9. Cabildo to the Crown (Santiago, 1 June 1550), AGI, Guatemala, leg. 41. "Cargos contra licenciado Thomas Lopez . . . Pesquisa Secreta" (Santiago, 1555), AGI, Justicia, leg. 302. Cerrato to the Crown (Santiago, 15 March 1551), AGI, Guatemala, leg. 9. Quesada and Ramírez to the Crown (Santiago: 28 May 1555), AGI, Guatemala, leg. 9. Because of his outspoken criticism of Cerrato, López was reprimanded by Prince Philip on November 30, 1551, for showing disrespect. Argüello Solórzano and Molina Argüello, *Monumenta Centroamericae*, pp.

302–303. Like other encomenderos, Bernal Díaz liked López, whom he characterized as a man of "good conscience" with zeal to apply laws. Díaz noted that López opposed giving Cerrato's brother a repartimiento. Bernal Díaz to the Crown (Santiago, 22 February 1552), *Cartas de Indias*, p. 40.

106. Zorita went to the Audiencia of Santo Domingo in 1548, as Cerrato left for Central America. Appointed oidor for Guatemala in 1553, he was ordered to New Spain in 1556. Zorita, *Life and Labor in Ancient Mexico*, pp. 21, 33, 36. For a detailed treatment of the career of Zorita, see Ralph H. Vigil, "Alonso de Zorita, Crown Oidor in the Indies, 1548–1556" (Ph.D. diss., University of New Mexico, 1969).

107. "Sobre la libertad de los indios esclavos que poseian los españoles en la provincia de Guatimala," B. de las Casas al Consejo de Indias (n.d.), AGI, Patronato, leg. 252, ramo 9. Schäfer lists it as "1555 ca., Valladolid." In the *DII* it is shown as "Representación de Fr. B. de las Casas al Consejo de Indias: Contra las pretensiones del procurador de Guatemala, recién llegado, sobre los servicios de los indios," *DII*, 7, pp. 167–72. A note adds: "Este documento no tiene fecha y está firmado de mano del P. Las Casas desprendiéndose de su contexto que fue presentado después de su último regreso a España en principios de 1547." It would of course have to have been written after Cerrato's arrival in Central America in 1548. Very likely the document refers to the representation of Bernal Díaz del Castillo, dated February 1, 1549, when he acted as procurador for Santiago.

108. Cerrato to the Crown (Santiago, 26 January 1550), AGI, Guatemala, leg. 9; and Cerrato to the Crown (Santiago, 12 June 1550), AGI, Guatemala, leg. 9. "Respuesta a Cerrato" (Madrid, 9 December 1551), AGI, Guatemala, leg. 386, lib. Q-1, fol. 13v.

109. Crown to the audiencia (Madrid, 9 June 1553), AGI, Guatemala, leg. 386, lib. Q-1, fols. 90–91. Licenciado del Barco (Varco) was at the time "Colegial del Colegio de Sant Bartolomé de la Ciudad de Salamanca."

110. Royal provisions (Valladolid, 17 November 1553), AGI, Guatemala, leg. 386, lib. Q-1, fols. 108–10, 114, 116. He was further instructed to take the residencias of Rogel and Herrera, both of whom died in the meantime. Tómas López was also to be tried before he took his new appointment as oidor in New Granada. In the case of Ramírez, if nothing notable was found against him, he was to be returned to office.

111. "Probanza de gastos" of Quesada (Santiago, 18 July 1555), AGI, Guatemala, leg. 52. He said that he left Mexico City about the middle of October, 1554.

112. Alonso Ydalgo (Hidalgo) to the Crown (Santiago, 14 April 1556), AGI, Guatemala, leg. 52. The writer was a relative of Cerrato.

113. Cerrato to the Crown (Santiago, 27 August 1554), AGI, Guatemala, leg. 9.

114. Ibid.

115. Hernando Méndez de Sotomayor, elected procurador general for San-

tiago (in which capacity he traveled to Madrid to request the residencia of Maldonado), was a "great and intimate" friend of Cerrato; yet the president took from him many slaves in his mines of La Acensión at San Miguel de la Frontera. Nonetheless, according to the son of Méndez de Sotomayor, his father remained close to the president and spent much time in his house. "Peticion de una merced para d. Bernabe Cerrato de Carvajal . . . " (Guatemala, 6 June 1613), AGI, Patronato, leg. 83, ramo 1, fols. 15–46v. This part of the testimony was given in 1596.

116. Fr. Pedro de Angulo to the Crown (April, 1552), cited in Saint-Lu, *La Vera Paz*, p. 457.

117. Quesada and Ramírez to the Crown (Santiago, 28 May 1555), AGI, Guatemala, leg. 9. Cerrato apparently left three daughters, along with nieces and other relatives, most of whom seem to have married well and achieved some prominence. See, e.g., "Peticion de una merced para d. Bernabe Cerrato de Carvajal. Adjunta los meritos y servicios en Guatemala de su bisabuelo el licenciado Alonso Lopez Cerrato" (Guatemala, 6 June 1613), AGI, Patronato, leg. 83, ramo 1, fols. 15–46v. Don Alonso de Acuña, governor of Soconusco, to the Crown (Soconusco, 30 October 1585), AGI, Guatemala, leg. 40. Francisco de Morales to the Crown (Mexico, 9 April 1562), Paso y Troncoso, *ENE*, 9:234–48.

118. "Peticion de una merced para d. Bernabe Cerrato de Carvajal . . . " (Guatemala, 6 June 1613), AGI, Patronato, leg. 83, ramo 1, fols. 15–46v.

119. Fr. Tomás de la Torre to the Council of the Indies (Sancto Domingo de Coban, 22 May 1553), AGI, Guatemala, leg. 8, fols. 41–41v.

120. Girolamo Benzoni, *History of the New World*, p. 168.

121. Recinas and Goetz, *Annals of the Cakchiquels*, pp. 136–37.

122. Cerrato was, for the most part, simply applying the laws without discretion. One may see some validity in the charges of extremism in the statement that slave holders were to bring in their slaves within three days, under pain of death. "Peticion de una merced para d. Bernabe Cerrato de Carvajal . . . " (Guatemala, 6 June 1613), AGI, Patronato, leg. 83, ramo 1, fols. 15–46v. While the death penalty was laid down from time to time for seemingly unjustifiable reasons, offenders were seldom executed, except in cases of rebellion or other acts of treason. At least some flexibility is seen in Cerrato's statement that he felt obliged to compensate an owner for a slave held legally—but he assured the king that not one such claim would be made, implying that no slave was held under lawful circumstances. Cerrato to the Crown (Santiago, 15 March 1551), AGI, Guatemala, leg. 9.

123. While Indian slaves were almost all freed in Central America by 1551, it took much longer for the process of manumission in Mexico. Berthe, "Aspects de l'esclavage," pp. 203–205, notes that between 1551 and 1561, the Audiencia of New Spain liberated at least 3,105 ("3,205") slaves.

124. Most of those who have touched on Cerrato's career—his contemporaries and a few later historians—have agreed that Cerrato's reforms were indeed far-reaching. One modern authority, however, sees it quite differently. MacLeod,

Las Casas, p. 57, opposes the view that Cerrato "played a major part in an improvement of the conditions of the Indians."

125. In referring to the Spaniards' yearning for former times, Cerrato testified that "llaman al tienpo pasado quando ellos hazian lo que querian la hedad dorada lo qual agora lloran." AGI, Justicia, leg. 301.

126. Cerrato to the Crown (Santiago, 26 January 1550), AGI, Guatemala, leg. 9.

Chapter 10

1. Benjamin Keen is of this opinion. In a personal note to me (30 April 1974), he observes that Zorita wrote that Indians were willing to hire themselves out at a rate twice that of the repartimiento wage; and that in his recent work, Martínez Peláez cites evidence that Indians were glad to work for a wage slightly higher than the repartimiento rate.

2. In 1550, in Panama, colonists wanted to continue using the services of slaves freed by Governor Sancho de Clavijo. He agreed, provided that Indians were paid fourteen pesos de oro annually. Simpson, *The Repartimiento*, p. 17.

3. Agia, *Servidumbres personales*, p. 57.

4. Ibid., pp. 55–56.

5. W.V. Scholes, *The Ramírez Visita*, pp. 45–46. See also Miranda, *El Tributo Indígena*, pp. 108–9.

6. Marroquín to the Crown (Santiago, 3 February 1550), Sáenz de Santamaría, *Francisco Marroquín*, p. 258.

7. Agia, *Servidumbres personales*, pp. 52–55.

8. R.C. (Toro, 18 January 1552), AGI, Guatemala, leg. 386, lib. Q-1, fol. 21v.

9. Prince Philip to the audiencia (Monzón, 11 July 1552), AGI, Guatemala, leg. 386, lib. Q-1.

10. R.C. of 20 January 1553, Pardo, *Prontuario*, p. 72. Audiencia to the Crown (Santiago, 6 September 1554), AGI, Guatemala, leg. 9.

11. R.C. (Valladolid, 10 April 1557), AGI, Guatemala, leg. 402, lib. T-3, fols. 168-168v. The order was in specific response to the report of a procurador of Honduras, who said that because the Indians refused to guard the cattle, herds were being lost and were in danger of extinction.

12. Keen's introduction in Zorita, *Life and Labor*, p. 65.

13. R.C. (Valladolid, 28 November 1558), AGI, Guatemala, leg. 386, lib. Q-1, fols. 240–40v.

14. Ibid., fols. 241v–43.

15. R.C. (Valladolid, 21 January 1559), AGI, Guatemala, leg. 386, lib. Q-1, fols. 252–52v. The subject of vagabonds is discussed in detail in Norman F. Martin, *Los Vagabundos en la Nueva España, Siglo XVI*. See also Magnus Mörner, *La Corona Española y los Foráneos en los Pueblos de Indios de América*, pp. 75–80.

16. Lic. Juan Albarez de Ortega to the Crown (n.p., n.d., but apparently 1563), AGI, Guatemala, leg. 965.

422   *Notes*

17. R.C. of 23 September 1552, Pardo, *Prontuario*, p. 43; R.C. of 21 July 1552, in ibid., p. 78; and R.C. of 25 November 1578, in ibid., p. 82.

18. Fray Gómez de Córdova to the Crown (Santiago, 12 November 1582), AGI, Guatemala, leg. 156.

19. R.C. tô Gerónimo Carranza, governor of Honduras (Soria, 7 December 1592), AGI, Guatemala, leg. 402, lib. T-3 (segunda parte).

20. Arteaga Mendiola to the Crown (Soconusco, 30 March 1571), AGI, Guatemala, leg. 9.

21. R.C. of 20 May 1582, Pardo, *Prontuario*, p. 82.

22. Quesada and Ramírez to the Crown (Santiago, 28 May 1555). AGI, Guatemala, leg. 9.

23. AGI, Justicia, leg. 301.

24. R.C. to President Landecho (Valladolid, 21 January 1559), AGI, Guatemala, leg. 386, lib. Q-1, fols. 248–48v.

25. R.C. of 23 September 1552, Pardo, *Prontuario* (A1.23.–1511.–186).

26. Residencia of Dr. Antonio Mexía (Santiago, 1559), AGI, Justicia, leg. 309. In 1562, Mexía's representative stated that he had served with complete rectitude for more than ten years. Because he had applied laws detrimental to the interests of the encomenderos, some of them testified against him in the residencia. Furthermore, don Carlos de Arellano, Pedro Tellez, and many of their companions tried to assassinate Mexía, which resulted in the wounding of two of the judge's relatives. Two other encomenderos threatened to kill him. The Crown wrote to warn against any such recurrence. Argüello Solórzano and Molina Argüello, *Monumenta Centroamericae*, pp. 321–23.

27. Residencia of lic. Ramírez (Santiago, 1559), AGI, Justicia, leg. 308.

28. Unsigned, undated document entitled, "Las cosas que sean remediado en el govierno de honduras," AGI, Guatemala, leg. 44.

29. Residencia of Pedro Romero, teniente general de governador for licenciado Hortiz de Elgueta, governor of Honduras (San Pedro, 1568), AGI, Justicia, leg. 315.

30. Royal provision of 21 April 1574, Pardo, *Prontuario*, p. 81.

31. Crown to the audiencia (Madrid, 27 November 1576), AGI, Guatemala, leg. 386, lib. Q-2.

32. Investigation of lic. Diego García de Palacio (Santiago, 11 March 1578), AGI, Guatemala, leg. 41.

33. Fray Gómez de Córdova to the Crown (Santiago, 12 November 1582), AGI, Guatemala, leg. 156.

34. Crown to Mallén de Rueda, 26 September 1587, Pardo, *Prontuario*, p. 83.

35. "Autos del ffiscal desta rreal audiencia contra Diego de la barrera sobre las cosas que se le opone aver cometido en la costa de suchitepeques," 1591, AGCA, A1.30, leg. 4697, exp. 40631.

36. Crown to Gerónimo Carranza, governor of Honduras (Soria, 7 December 1592), AGI, Guatemala, leg. 402, lib. T-3 (segunda parte).

37. "Informacion sobre la falta de medios para que vivan los pobladores de la provincia de Guatemala" (Santiago, 1598), AGCA, A1.29, leg. 4677, exp. 40238.

38. Licenciado Landecho to the Crown (3 February 1563), AGI, Guatemala, leg. 9.

39. Licenciado Arteaga Mendiola to the Crown (Soconusco, 30 March 1571), AGI, Guatemala, leg. 9.

40. "Repartimiento de Indios, Chiapa. Mandamiento a los justicias del pueblo de Chamula, jurisdicion de la alcaldia" (Ciudad Real de Chiapa, 6 March 1580 and 13 March 1579), AGCA, A-3, leg. 2896, exp. 42979, pp. 228–36.

41. Crown to president of the audiencia (Lisbon, 13 November 1581), AGI, Guatemala, leg. 386, lib. Q-2.

42. Ordinance of chanciller Juan de Victoria to the alcalde mayor of Ciudad Real de Chiapa and other officials (Santiago, 12 November 1582), AGI, Guatemala, leg. 966.

43. Fray Gómez de Córdova to the Crown (Santiago, 12 November 1582), AGI, Guatemala, leg. 156.

44. Undated, unsigned document entitled "Las Cosas que sean remediado en el govierno de honduras," AGI, Guatemala, leg. 44. Crown to the audiencia (Madrid, 27 November 1576), AGI, Guatemala, leg. 386, lib. Q-2; audiencia to the Crown (Santiago, 11 February 1604), AGI, Guatemala, leg. 40.

45. "Autos de los yndios del pueblo de Malacatepeque sobre que se agrabian mandar que del pueblo den cinco yndios para el servicio ordinario desta Ciudad (Santiago, 10 September 1593), AGCA, A1.31, leg. 2774, exp. 40024.

46. "Informacion sobre la falta de medios para que vivan los pobladores de la provincia de Guatemala" (Santiago, 1598), AGCA, A1.29, leg. 4677, exp. 40238. For purposes of comparison, note the wages paid in Mexico in the latter years of the century, in Silvio Zavala and María Castelo, eds., *Fuentes para la historia del trabajo en Nueva España* [1575–1805], 8 vols., 3:75–118.

47. R.C. of 26 February 1538, Pardo, *Prontuario*, p. 75.

48. R.C. of 4 August 1550, ibid.

49. Crown to the audiencia (Valladolid, 27 December 1558), AGI, Guatemala, leg. 386, lib. Q-1, fols. 247–47v.

50. Arteaga Mendiola to the Crown (Soconusco, 30 March 1571), AGI, Guatemala, leg. 9.

51. Audiencia to the Crown (Santiago, no date, but apparently the 1570s), AGI, Guatemala, leg. 41.

52. "Ynstrucion y memoria de la ciudad de santiago de la probincia de Guatemala de lo que se a de negociar y suplicar a su magt en su rreal consejo de las yndias por el señor alonso de herrera en nonbre de la dicha ciudad despachada en su cabildo y ayuntamiento . . ." (Santiago: 24 March 1579), AGI, Guatemala, leg. 41.

53. Residencia of licenciado Francisco Brizeño (Santiago, 1569–70), AGI, Justicia 316, 317.

54. Crown to the audiencia (Madrid, 18 July 1560), AGCA, A1.23, leg. 4575, fol. 199, duplicated in AGI, Guatemala, leg. 386, lib. Q-1, fols. 349–53.

55. For a discussion of the evils of the system, see Richard Stafford Poole, "The Franciscan Attack on the Repartimiento System (1585)," in *Indian Labor in the*

424 *Notes*

Spanish Indies, ed. John Francis Bannon, pp. 66–75. The functioning of the repartimiento system in Mexico is discussed with clarity and detail in Gibson, *The Aztecs*, pp. 220–56. Many examples of specific work assignments are given in Simpson, *The Repartimiento*.
  56. Zorita, *Life and Labor*, pp. 214–15.

Chapter 11

  1. Libro de Protocolos de Bernabé Pérez, año 1572, AGCA, A1.20, leg. 1169, fols. 51–51v. For a view of contract labor elsewhere, see Gibson, *Tlaxcala*, 155–57.
  2. Libro de Protocolos de Luis Aceituno Guzmán, año 1583, AGCA, A1.20, leg. 422, fols. 1–1v, 18–18v, 22–23v, 60–71, 96v–97.
  3. Ibid., fols. 53–53v, 58–58v.
  4. Ibid., fols. 40–40v.
  5. Libro de Protocolos de Cristóbal Aceituno Guzmán, año 1583, AGCA, leg. 422, fols. 127–28.
  6. Libro de Protocolos de Fernando Niño, año 1588, AGCA, A1.20, leg. 1127, no. fol.
  7. Ibid.
  8. Libro de Protocolos de Sebastian Gudiel, año 1595, AGCA, A1.20, leg. 810, fols. 42–42v.
  9. Libro de Protocolos de Luis Aceituno Guzmán, ibid., fols. 25–25v.
  10. Libro de Protocolos de Bernabé Pérez, ibid., fols. 21–21v.
  11. Libro de Protocolos de Fernando Niño, ibid., no fol.
  12. Libro de Protocolos de Luis Aceituno Guzmán, ibid., fol. 43.
  13. Ibid., fols. 37–37v. Libro de Protocolos de Cristóbal Aceituno Guzmán, ibid., fols. 138–38v.
  14. Libro de Protocolos de Cristóbal Aceituno Guzmán, ibid., fols. 101v–102v.
  15. Libre de Protocolos de Marcos Díaz, año 1598, AGCA, A1.20, leg. 786, fols. 13–13v.
  16. Libro de Protocolos de Luis Aceituno Guzmán, ibid., fol. 47.
  17. Libro de Protocolos de Cristobal Aceituno Guzmán, ibid., fols. 106v–107.
  18. Libro de Protocolos de Marcos Díaz, ibid., fols. 13–13v.
  19. Libro de Protocolos de Luis Aceituno Guzmán, ibid., fol. 19.
  20. Libro de Protocolos de Cristóbal Aceituno, ibid., fols. 131v–132v.
  21. Ibid., fols. 129–30v.
  22. Libro de Protocolos de Fernando Niño, ibid., no fol.
  23. Libro de Protocolos de Sebastian Gudiel, ibid., fols. 79v–80v.
  24. Libro de Protocolos de Luis Aceituno Guzmán, ibid., fols. 2–2v. A decree of 1513, revising the Laws of Burgos, stated that children under fourteen were to serve only in work suitable for their strength, such as weeding their parents' crops.

Those over fourteen would remain with their parents until they were of legitimate age, or when they married. If they had no parents, they were to be cared for by a guardian, given some work by the advice of Spanish officials, and provided food and pay. If they wanted to learn trades they could do so, and they would not be compelled to work at something else. Zavala, *Estudios indianos*, p. 169.

25. Libro de Protocolos de Cristóbal Aceituno Guzmán, AGCA, A1.20, leg. 810, fols. 86–87.

26. Ibid., fols. 98–99.

27. Ibid., fols. 99v–100.

28. Ibid., fols. 107–107v.

29. Libro de Protocolos de Pedro Grijalva, año 1574, AGCA, A1.20, leg. 807, fols. 181v–82, and Libro de Protocolos de Sebastian Gudiel, año 1596, ibid., fols. 88v–89v.

30. Libro de Protocolos de Luis Aceituno Guzmán, ibid., fol. 29.

31. Libro de Protocolos de Fernando Niño, año 1589, ibid., no fol.

32. Fray Francisco Montero de Miranda, "Descripción de la Provincia de la Verapaz" [1575], *ASGH* 27 (1953–54): 342–58.

33. Libro de Protocolos de Juan de León, año 1544, AGCA, A1.20, leg. 732, fol. 82v.

34. Libro de Protocolos de Luis Aceituno, año 1567, AGCA, A1.20, leg. 1111, fol. 495.

35. Libro de Protocolos de Sebastian de Gudiel, ibid., fol. 37v–38.

36. Crown to the audiencia (Madrid, 17 April 1553), AGI, Guatemala, leg. 386, lib. Q-1, fol. 78.

37. Crown to the audiencia (Madrid, 6 May 1553), AGI, Guatemala, leg. 386, lib. Q-1, fols. 82v–83. López de Velasco, *Geografía y descripción*, p. 287, adds the following: "Cuando se mandaron poner en libertad los indios hizo el licenciado Cerrato un pueblo junto á la ciudad, de los que habia en ella, que se llama *Santa Fé*, en que habrá como ochocientos vecinos indios, todos oficiales de diferentes oficios, muy españolados y ladinos y útiles y provechosos para la república; los euales [cuales] en agradecimiento de haber conseguido libertad por mano del dicho licenciado, le han instituido una capellanía en el monesterio de Santo Domingo, donde está enterrado, y le hacen cada año unas solemnes exequias." He was writing of the early 1570s.

38. Crown to the audiencia (Valladolid, 5 June 1559), AGI, Guatemala, leg. 386, lib. Q-1, fols. 295v–96.

39. Royal provision (Valladolid, 17 June 1559), ibid., fols. 296–97.

40. Tasación del pueblo de Petapa (Petapa, 1 February 1562), AGI, Guatemala, leg. 45.

41. Audiencia to the Crown (Santiago, 6 January 1563), AGI, Guatemala, leg. 9.

42. Antonio de Rosales to the Crown (Santiago, 1 February 1563), AGI, Guatemala, leg. 45. It was almost immediately suggested that the new source of tribute income go to support a home for young maidens founded by the bishop.

Lic. Juan Cavallon to the Crown (Santiago, 7 February 1563), AGI, Guatemala, leg. 9.

43. Reply to the audiencia (Madrid, 24 December 1574), AGI, Guatemala, leg. 386, lib. Q-2.

44. "Los indios que eran esclavos en la provincia de Guatemala en solicitud de que sean asistidos para todos sus negocios por los religiosos de Santo Domingo," 1575, AGI, Guatemala, leg. 54. A copy of this important document was made available to me through the kindness of Mr. Christopher Lutz. Regarding the Dominican influence, there is included an earlier letter in which the Indians state they do not want a secular priest, because priests were merchants who sold wine to Indians. They used to insult Indians, they said, and they did not know the Indian tongues. They would not marry Indians without a fee, and if the Indians did not give offerings on Sundays the priests would whip them.

45. Crown to the audiencia (El Pardo, 24 October 1576), Encinas, *Cedulario Indiano*, 4:379–80.

46. Juan de Pineda, "Descripción de la provincia de Guatemala, año de 1594," *Revista de los Archivos Nacionales* 3 (1939): 557–79. A copy of this published document was made available through the courtesy of Sr. Victor Rojas and Sr. Ramón Luis Chacón of San José.

47. Cerrato to the Crown (Santiago, 15 March 1551), AGI, Guatemala, leg. 9.

48. Prince Philip to the audiencia (1552), AGCA, A1.23, leg. 1511, fols. 186–87.

49. Prince Philip to the audiencia (Toro, 18 January 1552), AGI, Guatemala, leg. 386, lib. Q-1, fols. 22–22v.

50. R.C. of 20 January 1553, and R.C. of 22 January 1556, Zavala, *Los esclavos indios en Nueva España*, p. 180.

51. Royal provision (Valladolid, 16 March 1558), AGI, Guatemala, leg. 386, lib. Q-1, fols. 229–31.

52. Audiencia to the Crown (Santiago, 22 August 1559), AGI, leg. 9. Saco, *La esclavitud*, 1:201, states that the Spaniards enslaved two hundred Indians and took them to Santiago. Saco cites Villagutierre, *Historia de la Conquista de la Provincia de Itzá*. For additional study of the Lacandón problem see Saint-Lu, *La Vera Paz*, and El Capitán don Martín Alfonso Tovilla, *Relación Histórica Descriptiva de las Provincias de la Verapaz y de la del Manché* [1635], . . . pp. 255–62. The Lacandones destroyed fifteen Christian Indian villages, killing many people and taking others as captives. Most repugnant was their practice of sacrificing children on altars at the foot of the cross in churches, at which time they taunted, "Christians, tell your God to defend you!" As the company of Ramírez entered their territory, the Lacandones captured a black slave, who was sacrificed to bring them luck in battle.

53. R.C. of 15 September 1561, Pardo, *Prontuario*, p. 60.

54. Lic. D. León Fernández, ed., *Colección de documentos para la Historia de Costa Rica*, 5 vols., 4:212–23.

55. Don Luis Ponce de León to the Crown (Soconusco, 15 December 1575),

AGI, Guatemala, leg. 40. Essentially the same in content is Ponce de León to the Crown (Soconusco, 16 January 1576), AGI, Guatemala, leg. 40.

56. R.C. (Badajoz, 26 May 1580), AGI, Guatemala, leg. 386, lib. Q-2. Pardo, *Prontuario*, pp. 15, 60, erroneously notes that by this document the Crown authorized the enslavement of Chontales.

57. 'Capitulos contra per afan de rribera gouernado de cartago" (Cartago de Costa Rica [1583?]), AGI, Guatemala, leg. 49.

58. In 1587 there was still an illegal traffic in Indian slaves from Nuevo León. Zavala and Castelo, *Fuentes para la Historia*, 3:12–13.

59. Pardo, *Prontuario*, p. 77.

60. R.C. (Valladolid, 7 June 1550), AGCA, A1.23, leg. 4575, exp. 39528, fol. 107v.

61. Crown to the governor of Nicaragua (Barcelona, 3 March 1564), AGI, Guatemala, leg. 401, lib. S-3, fols. 22–22v. Alvarez de Ortega to the Crown (n.p., n.d., but apparently 1563), AGI, Guatemala, leg. 965.

62. AGI, Justicia, leg. 308.

63. Jorge de Alvarado to the Crown (Trujillo, 15 May 1600), AGI, Guatemala, leg. 39.

64. Provision of the audiencia (Santiago, 15 October 1603), AGCA, A1.23, leg. 4588, fols. 99–102. It is an interesting point that the naborías were assessed less than the free blacks: Negroes, mulattoes, and zambaigos were to pay four tostones and the single women had to give two. A decade earlier naborías, free blacks, and mulattoes all paid just one tostón a year. Residencia of Pedro Giron de Alvarado, alcalde mayor of San Salvador (San Salvador, 1593–98), AGCA, A1.30, leg. 297, exp. 3730.

65. Provision of the audiencia (Santiago, 15 October 1603), AGCA, A1.23, leg. 4588, fols. 99–102.

66. See provision of the audiencia (Santiago, 8 February 1611), AGCA, A1.2, leg. 2245, exp. 16.190, fols. 186–86v.

67. Remesal, *Historia general* (1932), 2:237.

68. Cabildo to the Crown (Gracias a Dios, 16 February 1548), AGI, Guatemala, leg. 44.

69. Cerrato to the Crown (Santiago, 8 April 1549), AGI, Guatemala, leg. 9.

70. Hernando de Ugarte to the Crown (Santiago, 12 April 1549), AGI, Guatemala, leg. 41. As early as 1531, the second audiencia in Mexico established a flat rate of payment for tamemes at 100 cacao beans (about one real) daily. They could carry no more than fifty pounds, and they were not to travel more than a day's journey from their villages. In 1543, standard rates were fixed for specific distances between towns. Simpson, *The Repartimiento*, pp. 67–68, 70. On February 28, 1558, the Audiencia of Guatemala ruled that tamemes in Yucatán were to be paid a silver real for carrying manta cloth and wax for five leagues; and for carrying maize or other food for the same distance half a real. F. V. Scholes and Adams, *Don Diego Quijada*, 2:1078. These two volumes contain extremely important information on native labor in Yucatán.

71. Fr. Francisco Bustamante to the Crown (Santiago, 22 March 1551), AGI, Guatemala, leg. 168.

72. Fr. Bartolomé de Las Casas to the Council of the Indies (n.p., n.d.), AGI, Patronato, leg. 252, ramo 9.

73. AGI, Justicia, leg 302.

74. Prince Philip to the audiencia (Madrid, 17 April 1553), AGI, Guatemala, leg. 386, lib. Q-1, fols. 80v–81.

75. Prince Philip to the audiencia (Madrid, 12 April 1553), AGCA, A1.23, leg. 4575, exp. 39528, fol. 123; and Prince Philip to the audiencia (Madrid, 17 April 1553), AGCA, A.1. leg. 2195, exp. 15749, fols. 89–90.

76. "Pleito criminal que es entre partes de la una Joan de Argujo, fiscal, y de la otra, Andres de Rrodas vezino desta cibdad de Santiago de Guatemala . . . que se le acusa aver hecho a los yndios y naturales de Oçumba . . . " (Santiago, 25 September 1554), AGCA, A3.16, leg. 2797, exp. 40667.

77. Respuesta a Cerrato (Valladolid, 27 April 1549), AGI, Guatemala, leg. 402, lib. T-3, fols. 27v–33.

78. Cerrato to the Crown (Santiago, 26 January 1550), AGI, Guatemala, leg. 9.

79. Crown to the audiencia (Valladolid, 3 August 1555), AGI, Guatemala, leg. 386, lib. Q-1, fols. 157–57v.

80. Residencia of Alonso de Paz, alcalde mayor of La Verapaz (Cobán, 1568), AGI, Justicia, leg. 313.

81. Crown to the governor of Nicaragua (Barcelona, 3 March 1564), AGI, Guatemala, leg. 401, lib. S-3, fols. 22v–23.

82. Crown to the audiencia (Valladolid, 21 January 1559), AGI, Guatemala, leg. 386, lib. Q-1, fols. 248–49.

83. AGI, Justicia, legs. 316, 317.

84. Residencia of Hernando Bermejo, "teniente de Governador e visitador general que fue en esta provincia por el liçenciado Hortiz [de Elgueta] governador que fue [Honduras]" (San Pedro, 1568), AGI, Justicia 315.

85. "Ynformacion hecha por Mando del muy ilustre señor licenciado garcia de valverde . . . presidente" (Santiago, 7 November 1582), AGCA, A3.16, leg. 2799, exp. 16478; and "informacion hecha sobre lo contenido en dos cedulas rreales de su mag, de que todo lo en ellas contenido fue falsa rrelacion q se hizo a su rreal consejo. . . " (Santiago: 10 November 1582), AGI, Guatemala, leg. 966.

86. "Probanza hecha en esta real avdiencia a pediminto del Licençiado Alonso de Çorita sobre dezir q. no cargo ciertos yndios" (Santiago, 6 August 1554), AGCA, A1.29, leg. 4678, exp. 40245.

87. Cabildo to the Crown (Santiago, 1 December 1555), AGI, Guatemala, leg. 41.

88. "Los capitulos de la cibdad de santiago de guatemala sobre la resydencia q. pide a los oydores de los confines y a los demas oficiales" (Santiago, 10 December 1557), AGI, Guatemala, leg. 111; and residencia of Dr. Antonio Mexía (Santiago, 1559), AGI, Justicia, legs. 309, 310.

89. Residencia of Ramírez, AGI, Justicia, leg. 308. Although the provincial

officials were usually the ones who most abused the regulations, some of them did keep record books to demonstrate that tamemes were being paid. See, e.g., "Residencia of Gonzalo de Ocampo Saavedra, corregidor del cerro e valle de ciudad Real" (Chiapas, 1577), AGCA, A1.30, leg. 182, exp. 1411.

90. Residencia of Pedro de Salvatierra, alcalde mayor of Honduras (San Pedro, 1563), AGI, Justicia 311.

91. Residencia of Hernando Bermejo, AGI, Justicia, leg. 315.

92. See, e.g., Crown to the audiencia (Aranjuez, 29 May 1571), AGCA, A.6, leg. 1512, fol. 379, where it is noted that some tamemes were still receiving no pay whatsoever.

93. Residencia of Alfonso Ortiz (Hortiz) de Elgueta, governor of Honduras (San Pedro, 1567), AGI, Justicia 314.

94. Residencia of Alonso de Paz, alcalde mayor of La Verapaz, AGI, Justicia, leg. 314.

95. Residencia of Hernando Bermejo, AGI, Justicia, leg. 315.

96. Residencia of "Johanes de Debaide, el moço, teniente general que fue de governador de esta provincia por el licenciado Hortiz governador que fue en ella" (San Pedro, 1568), AGI, Justicia, leg. 315.

97. Crown to the audiencia (Lisbon, 27 May 1582), AGCA, A1.23, leg. 1513, fol. 608.

98. "Ynformacion hecha por Mando del muy ilustre señor licenciado garcia y valverde . . . " (Santiago, 7 November 1582), AGCA, A3.16, leg. 2799, exp. 40478.

99. "Informacion hecha sobre lo contenido en dos cedulas rreales de su mag. de que todo lo en ellas contenido fue falsa rrelacion q. se hizo a su rreal consejo . . . " (Santiago, 10 Nov. 1582), AGI, Guatemala, leg. 966.

100. R.C. of 17 July 1589, Pardo, *Prontuario*, p. 124.

101. Lic. Arteaga Mendiola to the Crown (Santiago, 16 December 1570), AGI, Guatemala, leg. 9.

102. "Capitulos contra per afan de rribera gouernador de cartago" (Cartago de Costa Rica, 1583), AGI, Guatemala, leg. 49.

103. Crown to don Antonio de Mendoza (Talavera, 28 January 1541), Puga, *Provisiones*, I:437–38.

104. Cabildo to the Crown (Santiago, 1 June 1550), AGI, Guatemala, leg. 41.

105. Friars Torre and Cárdenas to the king and council, "Ynformacion . . . sobre la vida y costunbres de los clerigos deste obispado de guatemala" (Tecpan Izalco: 12 November 1552), AGI, Guatemala, leg. 168.

106. Testimony regarding abuses by friars (Santiago, 20 November 1562), AGI, Guatemala, leg. 45.

107. "Sobre las mantas e otras cosas de la Verapaz" (Santiago, 13 February 1582), AGI, Guatemala, leg. 966.

108. Governor Andrés de Rivadeneyra of Soconusco to the Crown (Santiago, 5 February 1606), AGI, Guatemala, leg. 40.

109. Ordinance of Dr. Alonso Criado de Castilla, governor of Guatemala, to the

Crown (Santiago, 23 November 1603), AGCA, A-1, leg. 1751, fols. 93v–94, duplicated in AGCA, A-1, leg. 4588, fols. 97v–98.

110. Speaking primarily of Mexico, however, Simpson, *The Repartimiento*, p. 70, writes: "It is noteworthy that complaints concerning the use of carriers cease with the sixteenth century. The reason for this I suspect is that heavy freighting by that time was being handled by mule trains, except in remote districts, and that in these latter places the use of carriers had become regulated by custom."

111. Prince Philip to the audiencia (Madrid, 12 Apr. 1553), AGCA, A1.23, leg. 4575, exp. 39528, fol. 123, ff. The vecinos protested, but Philip would not relent. Similar reactions came from miners in New Spain; however, one writer contended that the laws were just because Indians had not only been mistreated in the mines, but were also contaminated by noxious fumes which caused the deaths of many. As in Central America, the labor shortage slowed down the production, and the writer said that Negroes were priced at 200 pesos or more. With no workers, more than a hundred mines were not being worked. "Informacion" regarding the mining (Valladolid, 9 May 1556), AGI, Patronato 170, ramo 60.

112. To avoid the use of Indians in mines and public works, the sale of more blacks was authorized in 1561. R.C. of 15 September 1561, Pardo, *Prontuario*, p. 60. This was apparently in response to a report of the president of the audiencia that the colony was very poor because Indians could not be used in the mines. New silver mines had been discovered near San Miguel, and he asked the Crown to make provision for 2,000 Negro slaves. Lic. Landecho to the Crown (Santiago, 16 July 1560), AGI, Guatemala, leg. 9.

113. Audiencia to the Crown (Santiago, 22 October 1573), AGI, Guatemala, leg. 9.

114. R.C. of 21 April 1574, Pardo, *Prontuario*, p. 100.

115. Crown to the audiencia (Madrid, 2 May 1574), AGI, Guatemala, leg. 386, lib. Q-2.

116. Crown to the audiencia (Madrid, 27 April 1575), ibid.

117. Cabildo to the crown (Valladolid del Valle de Comayagua, 17 April 1581), AGI, Guatemala, leg. 43.

118. Crown to the audiencia (Lisbon, 13 November 1581, AGI, Guatemala, leg. 386, lib. Q-2.

119. Crown to the audiencia (Lisbon, 13 November 1581), AGCA, A1.23, leg. 4575, fol. 401.

120. Fray Gómez de Córdova to the Crown (Santiago, 12 November 1582), AGI, Guatemala, leg. 156.

121. Crown to the audiencia and officials of the Casa de la Contratación at Seville (Binesa, 6 December 1585), AGI, Guatemala, leg. 402, lib. T-3 (segunda parte). The royal appointee as alcalde mayor de las minas was Juan Núñez Correa. Like one of his predecessors, he went into business for himself once in the colonies, and the cabildo, no doubt with some satisfaction, informed the king that Núñez had been expelled from the land by the justices for being a merchant, as well as being licentious and indiscreet. Crown to the audiencia (Madrid, 20

January 1587), AGI, Guatemala, leg. 386, lib. Q-2. There is a discussion of Spanish workers in the New World in Zavala, *Estudios indianos*, pp. 183–96.

122. Crown to the audiencia and officials at Seville (Toledo, 4 March 1600), AGI, Guatemala, leg. 402, lib. T-3 (segunda parte), fols. 61v–62.

123. Crown to Dr. Alonso Criado de Castilla (El Pardo, 20 November 1599), AGI, Guatemala, leg. 386, lib. Q-2.

124. Francisco Romero to the Crown (Puerto de Caballos, 29 April 1586), AGI, Guatemala, leg. 49.

125. Zavala, *Contribución a la historia*, p. 77.

126. Dr. Alonso Criado de Castilla to the Crown (Guatemala, 29 October 1598), AGI, Guatemala, leg. 39; and Crown to Criado de Castilla (El Pardo, 20 November 1599), AGI, Guatemala, leg. 386, lib. Q-2.

127. Manuel Toussaint, *Colonial Art in Mexico*, pp. 122–25. It is a hotel today.

128. R.C. of July 1556, Pardo, *Efemérides*, p. 8; and see also Pardo, *Prontuario*, p. 98.

129. Dr. Pedro de Villalobos to the Crown (Santiago, 15 March 1575), AGI, Guatemala, leg. 39. In Alvaro de Paz et al. to the Crown (Puerto de Caballos, 27 April 1551), AGI, Guatemala, leg. 8, it is noted that fire had destroyed half the town of San Pedro which was built of reeds and straw.

130. R.C. of 21 July 1552, Pardo, *Prontuario*, p. 79.

131. Crown to the audiencia (Madrid, 12 December 1619), AGI, Guatemala, leg. 386, lib. Q-2.

132. Crown to the audiencia (Lisbon, 27 May 1582), AGCA, A1.23, leg. 1513, fol. 608.

133. For literature relating to construction in the sixteenth century, the reader is referred to the following: Kubler, *Mexican Architecture;* Annis, *The Architecture of Antigua Guatemala;* Sidney D. Markman, *San Cristóbal de Las Casas;* Markman, *Colonial Architecture of Antigua Guatemala;* and Argüello Argüello, *Historia de León Viejo.*

134. On this subject, see Borah, *Early Colonial Trade.* For a discussion of the important Nicaraguan trade, see Radell and Parson, "Realejo," pp. 295–312.

135. Cabildo to the Council of the Indies (San Salvador, 3 February 1548), AGI, Guatemala, leg. 43.

136. Crown to the governor of Nicaragua (Barcelona, 3 March 1564), AGI, Guatemala, leg. 401, lib. S-3, fols. 23v–24.

137. "Prouança y testimonio de juan moreno aluarez de toledo thesorero de su magestad de las prouincias de Nicaragua para el Real y Suppremo consejo de las Yndias" (Realejo, 7 February 1579), AGI, Guatemala, leg. 50.

138. Crown to governor of Nicaragua (San Lorenzo el Real, 6 September 1579), AGI, Guatemala, leg. 401, lib. S-3, fols. 117v–18.

139. Cabildo to the Crown (León, 12 November 1579), AGI, Guatemala, leg. 43. Juan Moreno de Alvarez to the Crown (Realejo, 24 May 1580), AGI, Guatemala, leg. 50.

140. Diego de Artieda to the Crown (Granada, 18 March 1582), AGI,

Guatemala, leg. 40.

141. Antonio de Cabrillo to the Crown (Cartago de Costa Rica, 20 February 1583), AGI, Guatemala, leg. 49.

142. Lic. Juan Albarez de Ortega, archdeacon of León, to the Crown (n.p., n.d. but apparently 1563), AGI, Guatemala, leg. 965.

143. "Ynterrogatorio de Dn. Geronimo de Santiago y Chaves" (San Salvador, November, 1587), AGI, Escribanía de Cámara, leg. 332.

144. Hierónimo Sánches de Carrança to the Crown (Comayagua, 18 December 595), AGI, Guatemala, leg. 39. Dr. Alonso Criado de Castilla to the Crown (Santiago, 15 May 1600), AGI, Guatemala, leg. 39. "Libro de Pareceres de la Real Audiencia de Guatemala," AGCA, A1.29, leg. 2033, exp. 14.084, fol. 73.

Chapter 12

1. Adrian Recinos, "La expansión hispánica en la América Central durante la primera mitad del siglo XVI," ASGH 31 (1958): 73–79.

2. An informative discussion of the importance of cacao prior to the advent of Spanish rule is found in John F. Bergmann, "The Distribution of Cacao Cultivation in Pre-Columbian America," *Annals of the Association of American Geographers* 59 (March, 1969): 85–96.

3. According to François Chevalier, *La Formación de los Grandes Latifundios en México*, p. 61, there was a move to establish an official rate of 1,120 cacao beans to one peso.

4. Robert H. Barlow, *The Extent of the Empire of the Culhua Mexica*, p. 98. There are many good studies of cacao. See especially the extensive treatments in MacLeod, *Spanish Central America;* René F. Millon, "When Money Grew on Trees," (Ph.D. diss., Columbia University, 1955); Manuel Rubio Sánchez, "El Cacao," ASGH 31(1958): 81–129: and Anne C. Chapman, "Port of Trade Enclaves in Aztec and Maya Civilizations," in *Trade and Market in Early Empires*, eds. Karl Polanyi, Conrad M. Arensberg, and Harry W. Pearson, pp. 114–53.

5. By November, 1582, not a single ship had put in for that year, which caused great inconvenience. The cabildo of Santiago asked the king to order that two or three ships a year call consistently so that trade would not be lost. It was said that the cause of the trouble was a merchant in Seville who had impeded the trade in order to guard his own private interests. Cabildo to the Crown (Santiago, 11 November 1582), AGI, Guatemala, leg. 41.

6. Crown to Cerrato (Monzón, 21 July 1552), AGI, Guatemala, leg. 386, lib. Q-1, fols. 49–50. Prices rose again, and by 1558–59, cacao was valued at eleven pesos a carga. Crown to the audiencia (Valladolid, 17 June 1559), AGI, Guatemala, leg. 386, lib. Q-1, fols. 297–98.

7. Fr. Tomás de la Torre to the Council of the Indies (Santo Domingo de Cobán, Verapaz, 22 May 1553), AGI, Guatemala, leg. 8, fols. 40–41v.

8. Diego de Robledo to the Crown (Santiago, 10 April 1556), AGI, Guatemala, leg. 9.

9. Dr. Mexía to the Crown (Santiago, 30 July 1557), AGI, Guatemala, leg. 9. As noted above, Juan de Guzmán was a cousin of ex-president Maldonado. If charges lodged against Mexía himself the same year had any substance at all, the oidor was guilty of the finest hyprocrisy. It was alleged that the oidor was speculating in cacao to be shipped to Mexico. "Los capitulos de la cibdad de santiago de guatemala sobre la resydencia q. pide a los oydores de los confines y a los demas oficiales" (Santiago, 10 December 1557), AGI, Guatemala, leg. 111. According to Bishop Marroquín, Guzmán's encomienda of Izalco was the best in the territory. Sáenz de Santamaría, p. 308.

10. Crown to the governor of Honduras (Madrid, 18 November 1564), AGI, Guatemala, leg. 402, lib. T-3, fols. 251–51v.

11. Ordinances of President Núñez de Landecho (Santiago, 7 February 1560), Pardo, *Efemérides*, p. 10.

12. Treasury officials to the Crown (Santiago, 17 July 1560), AGI, leg. 41.

13. Francisco Morales to the Crown (Mexico, 9 April 1562), Paso y Troncoso, *ENE*, 9:149, 155.

14. Francisco de Morales to the Crown (Mexico, 1 October 1563), ibid., 9:239.

15. Chevalier, *La Formación*, p. 61.

16. González to the Crown (Santiago, 2 March 1571), AGI, Guatemala, leg. 9.

17. Lic. Arteaga Mendiola to the Crown (Soconusco, 20 March 1571), AGI, Guatemala, leg. 9.

18. Audiencia to the Crown (Santiago, 6 September 1571), AGI, Guatemala, leg. 9.

19. Don Luis Ponce de León, governor of Soconusco, to the Crown (Soconusco, 19 January 1574), AGI, Guatemala, leg. 40. Another Spanish official described the climate in other cacao areas, where the heavy downpours of rain and the loud thunderclaps and menacing rays of lightning made living there a frightful experience. "Descripción de la Provincia de Zapotitlán y Suchitepéques, año de 1579, por su Alcalde Mayor Capitán Juan de Estrada y el Escribano Fernando de Niebla," ASGH 28 (1955): 68–84.

20. Ponce de León to the Crown (Soconusco, 15 December 1575), AGI, Guatemala, leg. 40.

21. Ponce de León to the Crown (Soconusco, 16 January 1576), AGI, Guatemala, leg. 40. Crown to don Martín Enríquez, viceroy of New Spain (Aranjuez, 21 May 1576), AGI, Guatemala, leg. 386.

22. Crown to the audiencia (Monzón, 1585), AGI, Guatemala, leg. 386, lib. Q-2.

23. "Memoria de los pueblos y beneficios que ay en el Obispado de Chiapa" (Chiapa, 22 February 1600), AGI, Guatemala, leg. 966. The historical development of Soconusco is treated in a scholarly article by Francis Gall, "Soconusco (Hasta la época de la Independencia)," ASGH 35 (1962): 155–68.

24. Crown to Dr. Alonso Criado de Castilla (Tordesillas, 22 February 1602), AGI, Guatemala, leg. 386, lib. Q-2.

25. Díaz de Rivadeneyra to the Crown (Soconusco, 5 February 1603), AGI, Guatemala, leg. 40.

26. "Autos del Consejo en la Audiencia de Guatemala sobre el pleito de don Diego de Guzman" (Guatemala, 1587), AGI, Guatemala, leg. 966.

27. Residencia of Dr. Antonio Gonzalez (Madrid, 1574), AGI, Justicia, leg. 320.

28. Crown to the audiencia (Barcelona, 8 June 1585), AGI, Guatemala, leg. 386, lib. Q-2.

29. "Relación hecha por el Licenciado Palacio al Rey D. Felipe II, en la que describe la Provincia de Guatemala, las costumbres de los indios y otras cosas notables" (Guatemala, 8 March 1576), ASGH 4 (1927): 71–92.

30. Vázquez de Espinosa, *Description of the Indies*, p. 226.

31. "Informacion sobre la falta de medios para que vivan los pobladores de la provincia de Guatemala" (Santiago, 1598), AGCA, A1.29, leg. 4677, exp. 40238.

32. R.C. to the audiencia (Valladolid, 22 December 1605), AGCA, A.1, leg. 1514.

33. Crown to the audiencia (San Lorenzo, 21 July 1611), AGI, Guatemala, leg. 386, lib. Q-2.

34. Don Jaime de Portillo, chantre de Guatemala, to "Illustrisimo Señor" (Guatemala, 21 May 1620), AGI, Guatemala, leg. 165.

35. Vázquez de Espinosa, *Description of the Indies*, p. 225.

36. R.C. to the audiencia (Valladolid, 7 June 1550), AGCA, A1.23, leg. 4575, exp. 39528, fol. 103.

37. R.C. of 7 July 1550, Pardo, *Prontuario*, p. 91.

38. Lic. Tomás López to the Crown (Santiago, 18–25 March 1551), AGI, Guatemala, leg. 9.

39. Crown to treasury officials in Guatemala (Madrid, 31 January 1552), AGI, Guatemala, leg. 386, lib. Q-1, fol. 23v.

40. Crown to treasury officials in Honduras (Madrid, 12 May 1552), AGI, Guatemala, leg. 402, lib. T-3, fols. 103v–104.

41. Lic. Jufre de Loaisa to the crown (Santiago, 22 August 1559), AGI, Guatemala, leg. 9.

42. Crown to the audiencia (Lisbon, 13 November 1581), AGI, Guatemala, leg. 386, lib. Q-2.

43. Ordinance of Dr. Alonso Criado de Castilla (Santiago, 1603), AGCA, A-1, leg. 4588, fol. 97v.

44. Provision of the audiencia (Santiago, 14 October 1640), AGCA, A.1, leg. 4647, exp. 39627. In this document reference is made to the royal cédula of 29 April 1549 in response to Cerrato's claim that one ingenio de azúcar was enough to kill 2,000 Indians a year. Following that, the Crown had given Cerrato the authority to do what he thought best about the renting of Indians from encomiendas for sugar work. Don Alvaro de Quiñones Ossorio, caballero of the Order of Santiago, president of the audiencia, governor, and captain general, among other titles, provided on 2 April 1636 that no Indian men or women were obligated to contribute personal service, in conformance with cédulas of the Crown. In 1640 Dr. don Pedro Vázquez de Velasco, the fiscal, presented a petition of two Indian

officials of the pueblo of San Bartolomé in the province of Chiapas, the encomienda of don Acasio de Solórçano, in which it was stated that it was forbidden for Indians to work on sugar plantations or to give personal service. Francisco de Ayllón, the owner of the sugar mill near their pueblo, had forced them to work for him under the pretext that the former owner of the mill had possessed a provision allowing him Indian service. The Indian representatives said that the maceguales were harshly pressed into labor and maltreated, as if they were slaves. They were whipped cruelly and not paid for their work. The village, described as "generous," was being consumed, while Ayllón got rich with their labor and sweat, and the Indians could tolerate no more. The local officials had done nothing to prevent the abuse, the representatives claimed, because the sugar families were so intermarried with the officials. It was again requested that the law against Indians working in sugar or giving any personal service be enforced.

45. Vázquez de Espinosa, *Description of the Indies*, pp. 218, 222, 226, 248, 251.

46. Thomas Gage, *Thomas Gage's Travels in the New World*, pp. 203–4, 211, 305.

47. Crown to the audiencia (Valladolid, 14 July 1558), AGI, Guatemala, leg. 386, lib. Q-1, fols. 232v–33v. For a good discussion of indigo in Central America, see Manuel Rubio Sánchez, "El añil o xiquilite," *ASGH* 26 (1952): 313–49. Chevalier, *La Formación*, p. 62, notes that in Mexico it was believed that "the first inventor" of indigo was a Spaniard who produced it in 1561—or so the viceroy informed the emperor. Chevalier adds that in Mexico the production of indigo dye was strictly a Spanish enterprise. By 1577, there were forty-eight "ingenios de añir" in Yucatán that had cost 2,000 to 3,000 pesos each to construct. Each had its water wheel, turned by mules, along with boilers. The leaves were harvested four times a year, and by 1576, 600 arrobas were produced for export. In 1609, the production was such that 11,660 arrobas worth the great sum of 546,562 pesos left Veracruz.

48. Juan Moreno Alvarez de Toledo to the Crown (León, 27 February 1578), AGI, Guatemala, leg. 50.

49. Bishop of Nicaragua to the Crown (León, 7 April 1578), AGI, Guatemala, leg. 161.

50. Crown to the governor of Nicaragua (San Lorenzo el Real, 6 September 1579), AGI, Guatemala, leg. 401, lib. S-3, fols. 117v–18.

51. Cabildo to the Crown (León, 12 November 1579), AGI, Guatemala, leg. 43.

52. Crown to the audiencia (Tomar, 15 May 1580), AGI, Guatemala, leg. 386, lib. Q-2.

53. Fray Gómez de Córdova to the Crown (Santiago, 12 November 1582), AGI, Guatemala, leg. 156.

54. Haring, *The Spanish Empire*, p. 65n., citing the *Recopilación*, is somewhat vague when he states: "From the reign of Philip II it was absolutely forbidden to use Indians in the cultivation of indigo in Central America and Yucatan, even

on a voluntary basis." To be more precise, the order followed the audiencia action in 1579.

55. Governor Casco of Nicaragua to the Crown (Granada, 17 December 1582), AGI, Guatemala, leg. 40.

56. Cabildo to the Crown (Leon, 22 January 1586), AGI, Guatemala, leg. 43.

57. Crown to the audiencia (Madrid, 20 June 1587), AGI, Guatemala, leg. 402, lib. S-3, fols. 154–54v.

58. Audiencia to the Crown (Santiago, 11 February 1605), AGI, Guatemala, leg. 40.

59. Residencia of Captain Juan de Torres, alcalde mayor of Trinidad (1583), AGI, Escribanía de Cámara, leg. 344-A.

60. Testimony of Indian alcaldes and regidores in the pueblo of Masaya (Granada, 2 April 1607), AGI, Guatemala, leg. 40.

61. Crown to don Antonio Cuello de Portugal, the fiscal (Madrid, 19 December 1618), AGI, Guatemala, leg. 386, lib. Q-2.

62. Crown to "Conde de la Gomera pariente capitan general de la provincia de Guatimala y presidente de mi audiencia real" (Madrid, 12 December 1619), AGI, Guatemala, leg. 386, lib. Q-2.

63. Lic. don Jaime de Portillo to the Crown (Santiago, 21 May 1620), AGI, Guatemala, leg. 165.

64. Vázquez de Espinosa, *Description of the Indies*, pp. 223–24, 230–31, 254. In pp. 235–37, the author gives a good description of the plant and its processing. See also the extended treatment in MacLeod, *Spanish Central America*, pp. 178–80.

65. "Relación de la Verapaz hecha por los religiosos de Santo Domingo de Cobán, 7 de diciembre de 1574," *ASGH* 28 (1955): 18–31.

66. "Sobre las mantas e otras cosas de la Verapaz" (Santiago, 13 February 1582), AGI, Guatemala, leg. 966.

67. Royal provision for Honduras (El Pardo, 8 October 1584), AGI, Guatemala, leg. 402, lib. T-3, fols. 375v–76.

68. Vázquez de Espinosa, *Description of the Indies*, pp. 244, 263.

69. Dr. Pedro de Villalobos to the Crown (Santiago, 15 May 1573), AGI, Guatemala, leg. 9.

70. Crown to the audiencia, 23 March 1574, and again on 3 May 1575, Pardo, *Prontuario*, p. 108.

71. Dr. Villalobos to the Crown (Santiago, 15 March 1575), AGI, Guatemala, leg. 39.

72. Crown to Conde de la Gómera (Madrid, 12 December 1619), AGI, Guatemala, leg. 386, lib. Q-2.

73. Crown to the audiencia, 13 May 1553, Pardo, *Prontuario*, p. 85.

74. Dr. Villalobos to the Crown (Santiago, 15 March 1575), AGI, Guatemala, leg. 39.

75. Alonso de Lara de Córdova to the Crown (Provincia de Chinandega, Nicaragua, 27 July 1604), AGI, Guatemala, leg. 40. About 1620, Gage described

the processing of salt at Amatitlán: "This town also getteth much by the salt which here is made, or rather gathered by the lake side, which every morning appeareth like a hoary frost upon the ground, and is taken up and purified by the Indians, and proves very white and good. Besides what they get by the salt, they also get by the *recuas* of mules in the valley, and about the country, which are brought to feed upon that salt earth a day, or half a day, until they be ready to burst (the owner paying sixpence a day for every mule), and it hath been found by experience that this makes them thrive and grow lusty and purgeth them better than any drench or blood-letting." Gage, *Travels in the New World*, p. 204.

76. Crown to the audiencia (Valladolid, 10 April 1557), AGI, Guatemala, leg. 402, lib. T-3, fols. 168–68v.

77. Crown to Gerónimo Carranza, governor of Honduras (Soria, 7 December 1592), AGI, Guatemala, leg. 402, lib. T-3 (segunda parte).

78. Andrés Díaz de Rivadeneyra to the Crown (Santiago, 5 February 1603), AGI, Guatemala, leg. 40.

79. Crown to the audiencia (Valladolid, 22 December 1605), AGCA, A.1, leg. 1514.

Chapter 13

1. For the limited purposes of this essay, the terms *nobility, elite,* and *aristocracy* are used interchangeably to denote those above the macegual class. There are fine distinctions to be made among them, but they are superfluous here, and I follow Charles Gibson, "The Aztec Aristocracy in Colonial Mexico," *Comparative Studies in Society and History*, vol. 2, no. 2, pp. 169–96.

2. For some Indian accounts, see Adrian Recinos, *Crónicas Indígenas de Guatemala*. A detailed Spanish version appears in Torquemada, *Monarquía Indiana*, 2:338–45.

3. Cerrato to the Crown (Santiago, 25 May 1552), AGI, Guatemala, leg. 9. Zorita, *Life and Labor*, p. 89, states that, as in Utatlán, other provinces had three, sometimes four, lords. "There were also inferior lords, whom they commonly call caciques," he adds, indicating that those rulers were in a higher, separate category from those referred to as caciques.

4. Calnek, "Highland Chiapas Before the Conquest," pp. 78, 90–94.

5. Zorita, *Life and Labor*, pp. 271–73.

6. "Pleito de Hernan Sanchez de Vadajoz, Governador y Capitan General de Costa Rica con Rodrigo de Contreras, Gouernador de Nicaragua" (1534–54), AGI, Justicia, leg. 1164, R. 3.

7. The ratio of nobles to commoners no doubt varied considerably as to size of the town, among other factors. As a matter of related interest, Professor Gibson, *Tlaxcala*, p. 143, estimates on the basis of his findings that Tlaxcala had about one principal for every seventy-five maceguales in 1541. In the same author's "The Aztec Aristocracy," p. 184, other examples are given. Dave Warren, "Some Demographic Considerations of the *Matrícula de Huexotzinco*," *The Americas* 27

(January, 1971): 256–57, refers to the subject: "The ratio between total principal and total commoner elements is 1:6.7," for Huexotzinco in 1560. He reveals other figures indicating the difficulty of defining terms: "The *Matrícula* provides further information on various sub-classifications of nobility. For example, of the total number of tributary *principales* appearing in the document, 1,088, some 65 are identified as caciques, a number that represented about 5.0% of the total nobility. . . . For the element indicated as *principales*, 850 (78.0%), were reported among the nobility. Another sub-group of the nobility, the *pilli*, were identified in the census and reported as 169 tributaries, about 14.6%, with four other tributaries or .3% making up the remainder of the nobility section."

Although it may well have been true in Central America, as in Huexotzinco, that not all principales were part of the traditional native nobility. I use the latter term loosely to apply to those Indians in the post-conquest period who were in ruling positions. Moreover, included is a discussion of Indian officials who in some instances surely had no claim to noble lineage, again grouping them together as a matter of convenience. It may be fair to say that all of those in the various categories could be considered part of the post-conquest Indian aristocracy, regardless of their antecedents. See also Dave Warren, "The Nobility Element of the Matrícula de Huexotzinco," *Actas y Memorias*, XXXVII Congreso Internacional de Americanistas, vol. 3 pp. 155–73. A related article is Pedro Carrasco, "Documentos sobre el rango de tecuhtli entre los nahuas tramontanos," *Tlalocan* 5 (1966): 133–60.

8. Calnek, "Highland Chiapas Before the Conquest," p. 90. He quotes Tomás de la Torre on the subject: "Los principales traen unos que llaman huepiles, que les cubre todo el cuerpo a manera de sobre pelliz de Clérigo, sin mangas sino unas aberturas para los brazos. Son blancos y sembrados de rosas coloradas o amarillas, es hábito hermoso; los principales traen pr. calzado unas suelas como de alpargates, con cuello por detras muy pintado y labrado y presas por delante unas sintas coloradas y un botón, pareceles bien."

9. See, e.g., Crown to the audiencia (Valladolid, 3 August: 3 August 1555), AGI, Guatemala, leg. 386, lib. Q-1, fols. 156–56v.

10. Cerrato to the Crown (Santiago, 25 May 1552), AGI, Guatemala, leg. 9.

11. ". . . los prencipales deste pueblo en su gentilidad cada uno de ellos tenía a quatro y cinco e seys mujeres, y los *maceuales* tenían dos y tres mujeres y a la primera respetaban las demás." "Descripción de San Bartolomé, del Patido de Atitlán año 1585," ASGH 38 (1965): p. 270.

12. "Las ynsignias que los caçiques y señores deste pueblo trayan en sus dibisas en las guerras unas águilas y otros de tigre y otros otras figuras de animales, de manera que por las dichas dibisas e insignias eran conocidos los tales señores y la gente prencipal de cada reyno y probincia.

"El traje e vestido que estos en su ynfidelidad vestían eran unos *xicoles* que en su lengua materna llamaban *xahpot*, a modo de una chamarra sin mangas que a los señores y caçiques les daba en el medio del muslo. E a los *macehuales* por baxo del ombligo. Y trayan puestos por pañetes unos masteles de algodón a manera de venda con que se cubrían sus vergüenças." Ibid., p. 271.

13. Ramírez, *Proceso contra Alvarado*, p. 102.

14. Crown to the audiencia (Valladolid, 30 November 1557), AGI, Guatemala, leg. 386, lib. Q-1, fols. 224–24v. For more information on this important cacique and a scholarly discussion of the nobility, see Pedro Carrasco, "Don Juan Cortés, Cacique de Santa Cruz Quiché," *Estudios de Cultura Maya* 6 (1967): 251–66.

15. Residencia of Alvarado, AGI, Justicia, leg. 296. It was also charged that in Huehuetenango Alvarado had a native lord thrown to the dogs because he was obstreperous. "Juan el Espinar contra Alvarado" (Santiago, 1537), AGI, Justicia, leg. 1031.

16. Residencia of Alvarado, AGI, Justicia, leg. 295.

17. Remesal, *Historia general* (1964–66), 1:238–39.

18. Discretionary power in such matters was given to Alvarado in the contract for his projected conquest of the Spice Islands and "China." Paragraph 28, treating the division of spoils, states in part that, "en caso quel dho cacique o señor principal matare em batalla o despues por via de justicia o en otra qualquier manera q. en tal caso de los tesoros y bienes susodhos q. del se hoviere justamente ayamos la mitad lo qual ante todas cosas cobren los nros oficiales sacando primeramente nro quinto." If a chief had to be executed, the Crown wanted its share of his property. *Capitulación* between the Crown and Pedro de Alvarado (Valladolid, 16 April 1538), AGI, Indiferente General, leg. 417.

19. Oviedo, *Historia General*, lib. 42, cap. 11.

20. Cabildo to the Crown (Trujillo, 20 March 1530), AGI, Guatemala, leg. 44. See also, Rodrigo del Castillo, tesorero juez for Honduras, to the Crown (Seville, 1531), AGI, Indiferente General, leg. 1092.

21. "Informacion contra los gouernadores que fueron en la ciudad de Truxillo en Honduras . . . " (Trujillo, 13 November 1539), AGI, Patronato, leg. 170, R. 45.

22. Andrés de Cerezeda to the Crown (Naco, 31 August 1535), AGI, Guatemala, leg. 39.

23. "Proceso hecho en Nicaragua contra Rodrigo Nuñez veco. de la ciudad de León por haber herrado ciertos indios por esclavos siendo libres" (León), 19 March 1529), AGI, Patronato, leg. 231, no. 4, R. 2. A copy of this document was made available through the courtesy of the Library of Congress.

24. "Pleito de Hernan Sanchez de Vadajoz . . . con Rodrigo de Contreras . . ." 1534–54, AGI, Justicia, leg. 1164, R. 3.

25. "Fiscal contra Miguel Diaz" (14 August 1543), AGI, leg. 393, lib. 2, fols. 206–6v.

26. Chamberlain, *The Conquest of Honduras*, p. 158.

27. Prince Philip to the audiencia (Madrid, 14 February 1546), AGCA, A1.23, leg. 1511, p. 219. Pardo, *Prontuario*, pp. 28–29, citing from the same document, reads the year as 1556 and says that López was a criado of Montejo. F. V. Scholes

and Roys, *The Maya Chontal*, pp. 30, 132, 146, write that he was a brother-in-law, who acted as Montejo's agent, and had been charged with extorting caciques before.

28. AGN, Inquisición, tomo 212, no. 11 (May, 1572). For similar cases, see Ernesto Chinchilla Aguilar, *La inquisición en Guatemala.*

29. "Capitulos contra per afan de rribera" (Cartago de Costa Rica, 1583?), AGI, Guatemala, leg. 49.

30. Remesal, *Historia general* (1964–66), 1:27.

31. R.C. (Valladolid, 24 November 1537), AGI, Guatemala, leg. 401, lib. S-3, fol. 31.

32. "Probanza . . . a pedimiento de la cassa e monesterio de nuestra señora de las mercedes" (Santiago, 17 October 1551), AGI, Guatemala, leg. 168.

33. Chamberlain, *The Conquest of Honduras*, p. 238.

34. Herrera to the Crown (Gracias a Dios, 24 December 1545), AGI, Guatemala, leg. 9.

35. Fr. Juan de Mansilla to the Crown (Sant Francisco de Guatemala, 30 January 1552), AGI, Guatemala, leg. 168.

36. Fr. Pedro de Angulo to the Crown (Guatemala, 19 February 1542), AGI, Guatemala, leg. 168.

37. R.C. (Barcelona, 1 May 1543), AGI, Guatemala, leg. 393, lib. R-2, fol. 108v.

38. R.C. (Alcalá de Henares, 29 December 1547), AGCA, A1.23, 306, leg. 1511. Those mentioned were don Gaspar and don Francisco, caciques of Tecuzistlán; don Juan, cacique de Atitlán, don Jorge, cacique of Tecpan Atitlán; and don Miguel, cacique of Çinastinango. Although those villages were "in the corona real" (crown towns), they had not been favored, especially in the matter of tribute. Because of the New Laws, and because they had served the Dominicans so well, it was ordered that they be well treated.

39. R.C. (Valladolid, 30 June 1534), AGI, Guatemala, leg. 393, lib. R-2, fols. 203v–204v. Referring to the Crown's intention to grant the caciques certain privileges, including the use of arms, Angulo and other friars answered that because of the treatment they were receiving from Spaniards, the caciques sought no consideration but wanted only to die. Angulo et al. to the Crown (Provincias de Teculutlan, 5 July 1545), AGI, Guatemala, leg. 168.

40. Residencia of Francisco de Montejo (Gracias a Dios, 1543–44), AGI, Justicia, leg. 300.

41. R.C. (Valladolid, 1549), AGI, Guatemala, leg. 402, lib. T-3, fols. 51–52, and Crown to audiencia, 1561, Pardo, *Prontuario*, pp. 28–29.

42. Crown to the audiencia (Valladolid, 23 December 1553), AGI, Guatemala, leg. 386, lib. Q-1, fols. 121–23.

43. Crown to President Landecho (Toledo, 16 September 1560), AGCA, A1.23, leg. 1512, fol. 279.

44. Crown to the audiencia (11 October 1546), AGI, Guatemala, leg. 393, lib. 3, fols. 25v–26.

45. Herrera, *Historia general*, dec. 4, book 3, ch. 2.

46. R.C. (Valladolid, 9 September 1536), AGI, Guatemala, leg. 393, fols. 178–79. R.C. of 31 January 1538, Pardo, *Prontuario*, pp. 28–29.

47. R.C. (Toledo, 6 December 1538), AGI, Patronato, leg. 275, R. 37.

48. Proclamation of Diego García de Celis, justicia mayor and captain general of Honduras (San Pedro, 26 December 1541), AGI, Guatemala, leg. 965; Diego García de Celis, treasurer, to the Crown (San Pedro de Puerto de Caballos, 14 March 1542), AGI, Guatemala, leg. 49: Prince Philip to the audiencia (Villa de Cigales, 21 March 1551), AGCA, A1.23, leg. 4575, exp. 39528, fols. 119–19v; and R.C. (Toro, 18 January 1552), AGI, Guatemala, leg. 386, lib. Q-1, fols. 22–22v.

49. "Relación de los caciques y principales del pueblo de Atitlán, 10. Febrero del Año 1571," ASGH 26 (1952):435–48.

50. "Memoria para el alcalde mayor e ynstrucion de lo que a de hazer para la buena gouernacion de los pueblos de los Yçalcos y Tacuzcalcos y de los demas de su jurisdicion" (La Villa de la Trinidad, 1557), AGCA, A.1, 38.3.21, leg. 356, exp. 4042, fols. 18–29v.

51. Residencia of Captain Juan de Torres, alcalde mayor of La Trinidad (Santiago, 1583), AGI, Escribanía de Cámara, leg. 344-A.

52. Lic. Juan Albarez de Ortega to the Crown (Leon, n.d., probably 1563), AGI, Guatemala, leg. 965.

53. R.C. (Madrid, 13 March 1535), AGI, Guatemala, leg. 393, lib. 2, fol. 125v.

54. Residencia of Dr. Antonio Gonzalez, president of the Audiencia of Guatemala (Madrid, 1574), AGI, Justicia, leg. 320.

55. "Relacion y forma quel licençiado Palacio oydor de la Real Audiencia de guathemala hizo para los que obieren de bisitas contar tasar y Repartir en las provinçias deste Distrito" (Guatemala, 1548–51), AGI, Guatemala, leg. 128 ("Libro de Tasacion").

56. R.C. (Madrid, 14 December 1551), AGCA, A1.23, leg. 4575, exp. 39528, fols. 115–15v. Despite royal concern for the poverty of the caciques, the Crown apparently felt by 1559 that it could exact money from them. In trying to raise money through the sale of offices and loans from Spanish vecinos and merchants, the king inquired of the audiencia if the caciques and señores naturales could also make loans to the treasury without causing inconvenience to them. Crown to the audiencia (Valladolid, 24 June 1559), AGCA, A1.23, leg. 1512, fol. 253.

57. Lic. Juan Albarez de Ortega to the Crown (León, n.d., but probably 1563), AGI, Guatemala, leg. 965.

58. R.C. of 26 August 1547, Pardo, *Prontuario*, pp. 28–29, and R.C. of 14 December 1551, ibid.

59. R.C. (Valladolid, 21 January 1551), AGCA, A1.23, leg. 4575, exp. 39528, fols. 11v–112; and Pardo, *Prontuario*, pp. 28–29. Zorita, *Life and Labor*, pp. 272–73, makes these comments.

The Indians' rule of succession and government was that each lord rose from grade to grade to the next dignity and insignia, and the lord who was always chosen anew was the third lord, whose insignia was one mantle. The election was made in the same way as in Mexico and in Matlalcinco. The principales chose the best-qualified son or brother of the lord who had died, and in the absence of such they chose a close relative of his. In short, it was done in the same way as in New Spain.

The lords appointed governors over their subject towns. If a governor died, the lord chose the best-qualified son or brother of the deceased to succeed him, and in the absence of such, some qualified relative. These governors were always principales and kindred of the lords.

The tribute these Indians gave their lords consisted of labor on maize fields and fields planted to other things they eat. They also made a field for the governor in each town. All was done in a very orderly manner, and the lords ruled their people wisely and meted out justice.

60. R.C. (Valladolid, 9 October 1549), AGCA, A1.23, leg. 4575, exp. 39528, fol. 111; duplicated in AGI, Guatemala, leg. 402, lib. T-3, fol. 55v.

61. Residencia of Rodrigo de Contreras, AGI, Justicia, leg. 297.

62. R.C. (Valladolid, 23 December 1553), AGI, Guatemala, leg. 386, lib. Q-1, fols. 121–23.

63. "Aprovacion de la elecion de don Juan Cacique por governador" (Valladolid, 3 August 1555), AGI, Guatemala, leg. 386, lib. Q-1, fols. 156–56v, and R.C. (Valladolid, 6 August 1555), AGI, Guatemala, leg. 386, lib. Q-1, fols. 161–61v. Regarding the traditional succession in Chiapas, Calnek, "Highland Chiapas Before the Conquest," p. 104, writes: "Advancement through the ranks of nobility depended on achievement, but was limited by genealogical prerequisites for advancement to the highest offices. Thus, the *tlatoani* could be elected only from a group of four 'señores,' each closely related to the previous ruler, and the next highest ranking functionaries of the state."

64. Cabildo of Santiago to the Crown (Santiago, 1 December 1555), AGI, Guatemala, leg. 41.

65. R.C. (Valladolid, 18 November 1556), AGI, Guatemala, leg. 386, lib. Q-1, fols. 197v–98.

66. Royal provision (Valladolid, 30 November 1557), AGI, Guatemala, leg. 386, lib. Q-1, fols. 224–24v.

67. R.C. (Valladolid, 21 November 1558), AGI, Guatemala, leg. 386, lib. Q-1, fols. 239–39v.

68. Crown to the audiencia (Lisbon, 13 November 1582), AGI, Guatemala, leg. 386, lib. Q-2.

69. Crown to the audiencia (San Lorenzo, 5 September 1598), AGI, Guatemala, leg. 386, lib. Q-2.

70. Probanza of Pérez, a native of Santiago Tejutla, corregimiento of Quetzaltenango, 1610, AGCA, A1.29-7, leg. 5923, exp. 51528.

71. Cabildo of Trujillo to the Crown (Trujillo, 20 March 1530), AGI, Guatemala, leg. 44.

72. Treasury officials to the Crown (Santiago, 28 September 1531), AGI, Guatemala, leg. 45.

73. R.C. (Monzón de Aragón, 26 August 1547), AGCA, A1.23, leg. 1511, fol. 59; and R.C. (Monzón de Aragón, 14 September 1547), AGCA, A1.23, leg. 4575, exp. 39528, fols. 142–43.

74. Cerrato to the Crown (Santiago, 25 May 1562), AGI, Guatemala, leg. 9.

75. Audiencia to the Crown (Santiago, 21 April 1556), AGI, Guatemala, leg. 9.

76. See, e.g., residencia of Dr. Mexía (Santiago, 1559), AGI, Justicia, leg. 309. Mexía, a judge of the audiencia, was accused of selling a fifteen-peso horse on credit to don Baltasar, cacique of the pueblo of Acapellavatl, in Soconusco, for five cargas of cacao worth seventy-five pesos. It was forbidden to trade with natives on the installment plan, but the oidor was in no case to be excused for engaging in trade, much less exploiting an Indian.

77. See, e.g., Bartolomé Bermúdez to the Council of the Indies (San Salvador, 12 April 1542), AGI, Guatemala, leg. 52.

78. "Memoria de lo que los yndios de la provincia de Soconusco piden a Su Magt" (Soconusco and Santiago, 1561), AGI, Guatemala, leg. 52.

79. "Carta del señor principal y . . . alcaldes caciques de la provincia de Soconusco, al licenciado Francisco Briceño, visitador y juez de residencia de la Audiencia de los Confines, quejandose de los malos tratamientos que les hacía el gobernador Pedro Ordoñez; suplican que escriba a su majestad paa que ponga remedio y dicen que el dean había hecho falsas informaciones en favor de Pedro Ordoñez" (San Pedro Huehuetlan, 22 February 1563), Paso y Troncoso, *ENE*, 10:62. This Nahuatl document was translated by Professor Wigberto Jiménez Moreno.

80. Residencia of Hortun de Velasco (Çamayaque, 1567), AGI, Justicia, leg. 313.

81. Residencia of Pedro Giron (Xiron) de Alvarado (San Salvador, 1593), AGCA, A1.30, leg. 296, exps. 3725, 3728, and leg. 297, exp. 3730.

82. Residencia of Per Afan de Rivera, corregidor of Chiquimula (Chiquimula de la Sierra, 1599), AGCA, A1.30, leg. 4697, exps. 40633, 40634.

83. See, e.g., residencia of Bartolomé de Salas Abiasido, corregidor of Tecpan Atitlán, 1589, AGCA, A1.30, leg. 4696, exp. 40629; and residencia of don Luis de la Cerda, corregidor of Guazacapan, 1591, AGCA, A1.30, leg. 4697, exp. 40632. See also residencias of Mateo Blandin and Alonso Hernández Alconchel, corregidores of Çacaloaque, Nicaragua (1604), AGCA, A1.30, leg. 266, exp. 2081.

84. Fr. Tomás de la Torre to the Council of the Indies (Santo Domingo de Cobán, Verapaz, 22 May 1553), AGI, Guatemala, leg. 8, fols. 40–41v.

85. Residencia of Francisco de Magaña, alcalde mayor of La Villa de la Trinidad y del Puerto de Acajutla (La Trinidad, 1568), AGI, Justicia, leg. 312.

86. Residencia of licenciado Francisco Briceño (Brizeño) (Santiago, 1569–70), AGI, Justicia, legs. 316, 317.

87. Dr. Villalobos to the Crown (Santiago, 15 May 1573), AGI, Guatemala, leg. 9.

88. See, e.g., treasury officials to the Crown (Santiago, 20 August 1530), AGI, Guatemala, leg. 45.

89. Remesal, *Historia general* (1932), 1:262–63.

90. Rodrigo del Castillo, tesorero juez of Honduras, to the Crown (Seville, 1531), AGI, Indiferente General, leg. 1092.

91. Residencia of Alvarado, AGI, Justicia, leg. 295.

92. Saco, *La Esclavitud*, 1:174–75.

93. Diego García de Celis, treasurer, to the Crown (Puerto de Caballos, 20 June 1534), AGI, Guatemala, leg. 49. The writer reported that the governor had sent him with thirty-six Spaniards to travel twelve or fifteen leagues after the most important cacique in the province, whom the Indians called "el grand mercader Çocimba." Çocimba had robbed a captain Juan Cabrera, killed some Spaniards, and holed up in a very strong fort made of thick wood and surrounded by covered pits. His position could be approached only by crossing a river, because it was situated near a ravine.

94. R.C. to governor of Nicaragua (Madrid, 26 May 1536), AGI, Guatemala, leg. 401, lib. S-2, fols. 174v–75.

95. Rodrigo de Contreras to the Crown (León, 25 June 1537), AGI, Guatemala, leg. 43.

96. Ibid.

97. R.C. (Talavera, 31 May 1541), AGI, Guatemala, leg. 401, lib. S-3, fols. 84v–86.

98. Rodrigo de Castillo to the Crown (Seville, 1531), AGI, Indiferente General, leg. 1092.

99. Juan Albarez de Ortega to the Crown (León, n.d., probably 1563), AGI, Guatemala, leg. 965.

100. Residencia of Alvarado, AGI, Justicia, legs. 295, 296.

101. "Juan del Espinar contra Pedro de Alvarado" (Santiago, 1537), AGI, Justicia, leg. 1031.

102. R.C. (Valladolid, 29 April 1549), AGCA, A1.23, leg. 4575, exp. 39528, fol. 103v, duplicated in AGI, Guatemala, leg. 402, lib. T-3, fols. 27v–33 (to Cerrato), and on fol. 37 to Honduras.

103. R.C. (Valladolid, 9 October 1549), AGI, Guatemala, leg. 402, lib. T-3, fols. 59v–60.

104. "Testimonio de las sentencias de pleyto de los yndios de la berapaz sobre la Esterilidad" (Santiago, 13 March 1578), AGI, Guatemala, leg. 966.

105. Residencia of Rodrigo de Contreras, AGI, Justicia, leg. 297.

106. Petition of principales (Santiago, 20 April 1631), AGCA, A3.12, leg. 2724, exp. 30031.

107. Remesal, *Historia general* (1932), pp. 117–18.

108. Information of the cacique, principales, and señores de calpules (Ciudad Real, 16 September 1547), AGI, Guatemala, leg. 110.

109. Inquiry conducted by don Diego Ramírez into alleged persecutions of Dominicans in Chiapa, 1548, AGI, Justicia, leg. 331. Copies of this document were made available through the courtesy of the Library of Congress. Remesal, *Historia general* (1964–66), 2:120–22, gives a somewhat different version. The Dominican chronicler puts the blame for the accident on the Indians and describes what was a bizarre and horrible death for the cacique. When the nervous horse was spurred he began to buck,

y con una furia extraña como si fuera un león, con los dientes le arrancó las partes viriles, y mientras las cobía [comía?] o tragaba, con los pies y manos le quebró y molió todo el cuerpo, como si le hubieran metido en una atahona, volviendo a comer de él, como si fuera yerba del cacmpo [campo?], que con ese gusto le engullía. Fue todo esto tan de presto, y la ferocidad del caballo tanta, que habiendo allí mucha gente, y todos deudos y parientes suyos, nadie osó ni pudo socorrerle, y el desventurado cacique de Chiapa quedó tal que en una banasta [canasta?] le llevaron a enterrar, porque ni aun la cabeza le quedó entera. No paró en esto solo en enojo que Dios quiso mostrar con él.

110. Inquiry of don Diego Ramírez, AGI, Justicia, leg. 331.

111. See, e.g., Cerrato to the Crown (Santiago, 16 July 1549), AGI, Guatemala, leg. 9.

112. R.C. (Toledo, 23 February 1560), AGI, Guatemala, leg. 401, lib. S-3, fols. 248v–49.

113. Fr. Tomás de la Torre to the Council of the Indies (Sancto Domingo de Vahtemala, 15 March 1551), AGI, Guatemala, leg. 168.

114. Fr. Tomás de la Torre and Fr. Cárdenas, "Ynformacion . . . sobre la vida y costunbres de los clerigos deste obispado de guatemala," for the Council of the Indies (Tecpan Izalco, 12 November 1552), AGI, Guatemala, leg. 168.

115. Ibid.

116. "Treslado de la real auto de la comida de los clerigos" (Santiago, 16 June 1561), AGI, Guatemala, leg. 41.

117. Dr. Villalobos to the Crown (Santiago, 15 May 1573), AGI, Guatemala, leg. 9. Priests also interfered in the matter of justice in villages, often reducing the effective role of the native officials. In La Trinidad a priest physically mistreated and insulted Indian alcaldes and broke their staffs of office. "Informacion contra francisco vargas cura del pueblo [La Trinidad] por haber maltratado de palabra y obra la justicia alcaldes y regidores [indios]," AGN, Inquisición, tomo 44, Honduras, no. 9, año 1568.

118. Diego de Artieda to the Crown (Granada, 18 March 1582), AGI, Guatemala, leg. 40.

119. Gibson, *The Aztecs*, pp. 220–56.

120. "Ynformacion de Gregorio López" (Seville, 1543), AGI, Patronato, leg. 231, R. 4. The witness had left Guatemala about nine months before after a residency there of twelve or thirteen years.

121. Cabildo to the Crown (San Pedro de Puerto de Caballos, 30 July 1540), AGI, Guatemala, leg. 49.

122. "Pleito de Hernan Sanchez de Vadajoz, Governador y Capitan General de Costa Rica con Rodrigo de Contreras, Gouernador de Nicaragua" (1534–54), AGI, Justicia 1164, R. 3. As recounted earlier in this chapter, Coasta narrowly escaped dying by fire himself.

123. "La Informacion q. hizo sanct saluador ante la justicia hordinaria . . ." (Villa de San Salbador: 20 April 1545), AGCA, A1.28, leg. 2335, exp. 17503.

124. This continued to be the case at least well into the seventeenth century. See, e.g., audiencia to the Crown (Santiago, 17 September 1641), AGCA, A1.2.4, leg. 2245, exp. 16190, fol. 182.

125. Crown to the audiencia (Toro, 18 January 1552), AGI, Guatemala,

leg. 386, lib. Q-1, fols. 19v–21. Walter Scholes, *The Diego Ramírez Visita*, p. 16, writes that because of the same abuse by caciques in Mexico, "each Indian was given a picture of what he must give in tribute during the year. To make certain that the Indians understood, Ramírez explained the picture by means of an interpreter."

126. R.C. (Madrid, 31 January 1552), AGI, Guatemala, leg. 386, lib. Q-1, fol. 24, duplicated in AGCA, A1.23, leg. 4575, exp. 39528, fol. 117.

127. Audiencia to the Crown (Santiago, 20 January 1563), AGI, Guatemala, leg. 9.

128. "Y para vsar el dicho ministerio entre los indios [collecting tribute], tengo sin comparacion por mas crueles y tiranos a sus mismos caçiques que el mas tirano español del mundo: del qual si les haze agrauio se quexan con libertad lo qual no osan hazer de sus caçiques, por la cruel vengança que toman dellos." Wages should be paid directly to maceguales, "porque si se da a los Caçiques y principales quedense con ello, sin remedio pues no ay Caco como muchos dellos." Agia, *Servidumbres personales*, pp. 78, 86.

129. Crown to the president of the audiencia (Lisbon, 13 November 1581), AGCA, A1.23, leg. 1513, fol. 598.

130. AGI, Indiferente General 1092 (n.d., n.p., no signature).

131. "Peticion de don Agustin de Medinilla, capitan de ynfanteria por su magestad y alcalde mayor en esta provincia de Çapotitlan . . . " (Çamayaque, 7 July 1603), AGCA, A1, leg. 5532, exp. 47.8828.

132. Residencia of Alonso de Paz, alcalde mayor of La Verapaz (Cobán, 1568), AGI, Justicia, leg. 313.

133. Residencia of Captain Juan de Estrada, alcalde mayor of the Costa de Zapotitlán (Suchitepeques . . . 1584), AGI, Escribanía de Cámara, leg. 344-A.

134. "Respuesta a la Audiencia de Guatemala" (Madrid, 13 May 1572), AGCA, A1., leg. 1512, fol. 416. See also Diego de Robledo to the Crown (Santiago, 10 April 1556), AGI, Guatemala, leg. 9; and President Landecho to the Crown (Santiago, 1 February 1563), AGI, Guatemala, leg. 9.

135. Dr. Antonio González to the Crown (Santiago, 2 March 1571), AGI, Guatemala, leg. 9. See also the reference to abuses by caciques, in Crown to the audiencia (Madrid, 18 May 1572), AGCA, A1.23, leg. 1512, fols. 416–17.

136. "Testimonio de Culpa" from the investigation of licenciado Diego García de Palacio, oidor of the Audiencia of Guatemala (Realejo, 3 January 1580), AGI, Guatemala, leg. 966.

137. "Informaciones y probanzas de varios caciques de Tecpan Atitlan, Atitlan y Quetzaltenango, para que no se le tase tributo" (1587–88, 1591–92), AGCA, A3.16, leg. 2800, exp. 40485.

138. Apropos the Crown's observation, a detailed treatment of Indian government under Spanish rule in Tlaxcala is included in Gibson, *Tlaxcala*, pp. 89–123.

139. R.C. (Valladolid, 9 October 1549), AGCA, A1.23, leg. 4575, fol. 110, duplicated in AGI, Guatemala, leg. 402, lib. T-3, fol. 57.

140. Crown to the audiencia (Valladolid, 16 March 1556), AGI, Guatemala, leg. 402, lib. T-3, fol. 143v.

141. R.C. (Valladolid, 21 January 1559), AGI, Guatemala, leg. 386, lib. Q-1, fols. 249v–50.

142. "Sobre las elecciones" (Santiago, 26 February 1585), AGCA, A1.2, leg. 2245, exp. 16.190, fols. 183–83v.

143. With poor administration and lack of justice, some of the desperate Indians became bandits, assaulting travelers on the roads. According to one source, between the settlements of San Salvador and San Miguel, Indians killed more than thirty Spaniards, one by one, in the year 1538. Bartolomé Bermúdez to the Council of the Indies (San Salvador, 12 April 1542), AGI, Guatemala, leg. 52.

144. Lic. Ramírez to the Crown (Santiago, 20 May 1556), AGI, Guatemala, leg. 9.

145. Crown to the audiencia (Madrid, 15 September 1561), AGCA, A1.23, leg. 4575, exp. 39528, fol. 244.

146. Audiencia to the Crown (Santiago, 20 January 1563), AGI, Guatemala, leg. 9.

147. Diego Garces to the Crown (Santiago, 31 November 1570), AGI, Guatemala, leg. 9.

148. Tasación del pueblo de Petapa, AGI, Guatemala, leg. 45.

149. See, e.g., León Páez Chumor(?) de Sotomayor, governor of Soconusco, to the Crown (Huehuetlan ["Huebletlan"], 12 March 1582), AGI, Guatemala, leg. 40.

150. Crown to the audiencia (Lisbon, 13 November 1582), AGI, Guatemala, leg. 386, lib. Q-2. By 1603, Governor Andrés Díaz de Rivadeneyra wrote to the Crown (Santiago, 5 February 1603), AGI, Guatemala, leg. 40, remarking that the priests in Soconusco retained great influence over Indian alcaldes and other authorities. The prospect of importing Indians to Soconusco was still under consideration, and the governor said that it would be better for Indian government if some of the principales of the outsiders were named governors.

151. Gage, *Travels in the New World*, p. 202, writing in the 1630s, commented on the Indian governor in the Guatemalan village of Petapa: "This Governor hath many privileges granted unto him (though not to wear a sword, or rapier, as may the Governor of Chiapa of the Indians), and appoints by turn some of the town to wait and attend on him at dinner and supper. He has others to look to his horses, others to fish for him, others to bring him wood for his house spending, others to bring him food for his horses. Yet after all this attendance, he attends and waits on the friar that lives in the town. . . ." Crown policy in general toward caciques over the decades can be traced in detail through the various studies by Simpson cited in the bibliography. For the subject of caciques in Mexico, see the works of Gibson, Zavala, and Zorita cited. Also of interest are Parry, *The Audiencia of New Galicia in the Sixteenth Century*, pp. 56–59, 71; Ralph L. Beals, "Acculturation," in *Handbook of Middle American Indians*, vol. 6, pp. 449–68; and

Robert Chamberlain, "The Concept of the *Señor Natural* as Revealed by Castilian
Law and Administrative Documents," *HAHR* 19 (1939): 130–37.

Chapter 14

1. As usual, one can find exceptions to the generalization. William Lytle
Schurz, *This New World*, p. 278, observes that "there were true matriarchies, in
which the women were the bosses and the men were underdogs, as around Lake
Nicaragua, where husbands were cowed and often beaten by their wives."

2. Simpson, *The Encomienda*, p. 10, makes this note: "Native women were
much in demand. A woman was worth a hundred *castellanos*, reported Columbus,
as much as a farm, and even girls of nine and ten had their price. There was a
market for women of every age, he added, and many merchants were doing a
profitable business trafficking in them."

3. Bishop of Honduras to the Crown (Trujillo, 1 May 1547), AGI, Guatemala,
leg. 164; and bishop of Honduras to the Crown (Trujillo, 25 June 1547), AGI,
Guatemala, leg. 164.

4. Fr. Tomás de la Torre to the Council of the Indies (Santo Domingo de
Guatemala, 16 August 1554), AGI, Guatemala, leg. 168.

5. Friars Torre and Cárdenas to the king and Council of the Indies (Tecpan
Izalco: October–November 1552), AGI, Guatemala, leg. 168.

6. Royal provision (Madrid, 15 January 1569), AGI, Guatemala, leg. 402,
lib. T-3, fols. 275–75v. It was common for Spaniards going on journeys, both
by sea and overland, to take indias along. Bancroft, *History of Central America*,
1:577, notes that when Pedro de Garro traveled from Nicaragua to Honduras his
retinue included many servants and beautiful Indian women. When Governor
Castañeda left precipitously for Peru, although he was in flight, he took two free
indias named Susana and Isabel from the village of Mistega. Residencia of
Castañeda, AGI, Justicia, leg. 293.

7. The bishop of Verapaz found his bishopric permeated with "diabolical witchcraft," whose adherents communicated with the devil on the most familiar terms,
and, with their sorcery, were killing many people. The Inquisition was formally
established by then, and the audiencia condemned five of the witches to be
hanged. It is not entirely clear, but apparently they were Indian women. Fray
Antonio de Ervias, bishop of Verapaz, to the Crown (Verapaz, 1583?), AGI,
Guatemala, leg. 163.

8. Residencia of Dr. Antonio Mexía (Santiago, 1561), AGI, Justicia, leg. 301.

9. Mexía to the Crown (Santiago, 30 July 1557), AGI, Guatemala, leg. 9.

10. Prince Philip to the audiencia (Valladolid, 13 September 1543), AGI,
Guatemala, leg. 401, lib. S-3, fol. 117.

11. Tomás López to the Crown (Santiago, 18–25 March 1551), AGI,
Guatemala, leg. 9.

12. "Treslado de la real auto sobre la comida de los clerigos" (Santiago, 16 June
1561), AGI, Guatemala, leg. 41.

13. "Informacion . . . por el licenciado don Christoval de Pedraza . . . contra el

Bachiller Juan Alvarez clerigo . . . " (Gracias a Dios, 10 February 1539), AGI, Justicia, leg. 1031.

14. Residencia of Mexía (Santiago, 1561), AGI, Justicia, leg. 301.

15. Residencia of lic. Alonso Ortiz de Elgueta (San Pedro, 1567), AGI, Justicia, leg. 314.

16. "El capitan don Pedro Martinez Clavijo, Governador y Capitan General de la ciudad de la Concepcion de Veragua, presento en grado de apelacion de la sentencia dada por don Luis Briceño su successor . . . " (Concepción de Veragua, 28 March 1583), AGI, Escribanía de Cámara, leg. 344-A.

17. Bishop of Honduras to the Crown (Trujillo, 1 May 1547), AGI, Guatemala, leg. 164.

18. Residencia of Pedro Girón de Alvarado (San Salvador, 1593–98), AGCA, A1.30, leg. 296, exps. 3729, 3730.

19. See, e.g., residencia of Antonio de Valderrama, corregidor of Quetzaltenango (Quetzaltenango, 1587), AGCA, A1.30, leg. 4762, exp. 41112.

20. See, e.g. residencia of Alonso de Barrientos, corregidor of Caçauastlan (Caçauastlan or "Acaçevastlan," 1586), AGCA, A1.30, leg. 4696, exp. 40627.

21. "Cargos contra Fernando de Alcantara Botello del tpo. q. fue teniente por el lic. Castañeda e del tpo. que fue alcalde hordinario" (Santiago, 1536), AGI, Justicia, leg. 294. On one occasion female Indian slaves were given as rewards for Spaniards who helped put down a rebellion of Spaniards. Crown to Andrés de Cerezeda, governor of Higueras-Honduras (Madrid, 22 April 1535), AGI, Guatemala, leg. 402, lib. 1, fols. 158–60.

22. Residencia of Castañeda as alcalde mayor of Nicaragua, along with "cargos contra Luys de Guibara [Guebara], lugarteniente q. fue del lic. Castañeda" (León and Granada, 1535–36), AGI, Justicia, leg. 293. Esclavas were worth considerably more than male slaves. While indias frequently sold for 60 or 70 pesos, men were selling for as little as 12 to 15 pesos. At the same time Castañeda said he paid 200 pesos for a Negro. For a horse he had just given 300 pesos.

23. Ibid. The licenses were needed for the removal of black slaves, as well as horses, so that Castañeda could inflate their sale prices as well. He admitted that he had sold a horse for 400 pesos and that Negroes were sold for 300 to 500 pesos.

24. R.C. (Talavera, 31 May 1541), AGI, Guatemala, leg. 401, lib. S-3, fols. 86–86v.

25. Residencia of Cerrato, AGI, Justicia, leg. 301.

26. Bishop of Honduras to the Crown (Trujillo, 1 May 1547), AGI, Guatemala, leg. 164.

27. Crown to Cerrato (Valladolid, 19 February 1550), AGI, Guatemala, leg. 402, lib. T-3, fols. 67–67v.

28. Queen to the governor of Nicaragua, "De officio contra un hombre q. forço una yndia" (Valladolid, 9 September 1536), AGI, Guatemala, leg. 401, lib. S-2, fol. 176v.

29. Residencia of Pedro Girón de Alvarado (San Salvador, 1593–98), AGCA, A1.30, leg. 297, exp. 3730.

30. Residencia of Rodrigo de Contreras, AGI, Justicia, leg. 297.

31. R.C. (Valladolid, 4 August 1550), AGCA, A1, leg. 1511, fols. 150–50v.

32. When the oidor licenciado Herrera was in Nicaragua to take the residencia of Rodrigo de Contreras, an Indian slave girl belonging to the governor's niece came to Herrerá bleeding profusely from cuts suffered from a whipping, and, the judge wrote, "si no fuera por un cirujano q. la sangro y curo muriera de los açotes porq. estuvo a punto de muerte." Herrera took the unfortunate girl with him when he returned to Honduras, but his fellow judges ordered the girl returned to her owner. Licenciado Herrera to the Crown (Gracias a Dios, 25 December 1544), AGI, Guatemala, leg. 9; and Herrera to the Crown (Gracias a Dios, 10 July 1545), AGI, Guatemala, leg. 9. It is likely that the slave girl suffered such a fate because of Herrera's problems with the other oidores. Moreover, Governor Rodrigo de Contreras was a personal friend of Alonso Maldonado, president of the Audiencia.

33. Residencia of Pedro Girón de Alvarado, AGCA, A1.30, leg. 297, exp. 3730. It is evident from his judicial review that Girón de Alvarado allowed many abuses.

34. Residencia of Pedro Girón de Alvarado, AGCA, A1.30, leg. 296, exp. 3725.

35. Residencia of Cerrato, AGI, Justicia, leg. 301.

36. "Los capitulos de la cibdad de Santiago de Guatemala sobre la resydencia q. pide a los oydores de los confines y a los demas oficiales" (Santiago, 10 December 1557), AGI, Guatemala, leg. 111.

37. Residencia of Alonso Ortiz de Elgueta, governor of Honduras, AGI, Justicia, leg. 314.

38. Residencia of Alonso de Paz, alcalde mayor of La Verapaz (Coban, 1568), AGI, Justicia, leg. 313.

39. Residencia of Francisco de Brizeño, governor of Guatemala (Santiago, 1569–70), AGI, Justicia, legs. 316, 317.

40. Residencia of Francisco Magaña, alcalde mayor of La Trinidad (La Trinidad, 1568), AGI, Justicia, leg. 312.

41. "Autos del ffiscal . . . contra Diego de la Barrera sobre las cosas que se le opone aver cometido en la costa de Suchitepeques," 1591, AGCA, A1.30, leg. 4697, exp. 40631. See also "Proceso hecho en Nicaragua contra Rodrigo Nuñez veco. de la ciudad de Leon por haber herrado ciertos indios por esclavos siendo libres" (León, 19 March 1529), AGI, Patronato, leg. 231, no. 4, ramo 2, for an example of the way in which one encomendero seized a cacique's woman and various female relatives.

42. R.C. for the governor of Honduras (Madrid, 19 June 1569), AGI, Guatemala, leg. 402, lib. T-3, fol. 243. For more on this subject see Magnus Mörner, "La Política de Segregación y del Mestizaje en la Audiencia de Guatemala," *Revista de Indias* 95–96 (July–December, 1964): 137–51.

43. Crown to the audiencia (Badajoz, 28 September 1580), AGCA, A1., leg. 1513, fol. 579; and Crown to the audiencia (San Lorenzo, 2 September 1587), AGCA, A1., leg. 1513, fol. 676. An ordinance of 1551, although concerned specifically with Lima, is of interest because it illustrates the difference in the

status of a free *versus* a slave woman, and also the seriousness with which the Crown viewed the harsh treatment of Indians by blacks. Referring to the bad treatment of indias by blacks who often held them as concubines, blacks, both free and slave, were prohibited from using any services of any Indians: ". . . so pena al negro que fuere hallado tener India y seruirse della, le sea cortada su natura: y se siruiere de Indios, les sean dados cie[n] açotes, publicamente: y si fuere esclaua, por la primera vez les sea dados cien açotes, y por la segunda cortadas las orejas: y si fuere libre, por la primera vez le sean dados cien açotes: y por la segunda, destierro perpetuo destos Reynos. . . ." Encinas, *Cedulario*, 4:388. Castration for rebellious blacks had been prohibited by the Crown in 1540.

44. Audiencia to the Crown (Santiago, 11 February 1605), AGI, Guatemala, leg. 40.

45. City of Panama to the emperor (Panama, 4 September 1531), *Cartas del Perú*, p. 24.

46. R.C. (Toledo, 4 December 1528), Puga, *Prouisiones*, p. 122.

47. R.C. of 17 April 1581, Pardo, *Prontuario*, p. 57. With regard to customary marrying ages, the following comment of interest appears in "Descripción de San Bartolomé," pp. 262–75: "Dizen estos viejos que en tiempo de su gentilidad los dichos yndios bibian mas sanos y rezios que no en este tiempo porque no bibian con tanta ociosidad porque a la sazon quando se venian a casar los varones pasaban de quarenta años, lo qual es agora al contrario porque antes que lleguen a la edad de quynze años e doze andan persuadiendo y molestando al sacerdote y religioso que los case."

48. Cerrato to the Crown (Santiago, 15 March 1551), AGI, Guatemala, leg. 9.

49. Lic. Juan Albarez de Ortega (León, n.d., but probably 1563), AGI, Guatemala, leg. 165.

50. "Testimonio de la culpa que resulto contra baltasar nieto y la sentencia que contra el dio el señor lic. Palacio" (Santiago and Tequiluca, March–October, 1575), AGI, Guatemala, leg. 966.

51. Rodrigo de Contreras to the Crown (León, 25 June 1537), AGI, Guatemala, leg. 43.

52. Anonymous, n.d., n.p., AGI, Guatemala, leg. 39.

53. Various friars to the Crown (Santiago, 1 January 1556), AGI, Guatemala, leg. 168.

54. "Los capitulos de la cibdad de Santiago de Guatemala sobre la resydencia q. pide a los oydores de los confines y a los demas oficiales" (Santiago, 10 December 1557), AGI, Guatemala, leg. 111.

55. "Capitulos contra per afan de rribera" (Cartago de Costa Rica, 1583?), AGI, Guatemala, leg. 49.

56. Crown to the audiencia (Lisbon, 27 May 1582), AGCA, A1.23, leg. 1513, fol. 608.

57. Licenciado Arteaga de Mendiola to the Crown (Santiago, 16 December 1570), AGI, Guatemala, leg. 9.

58. Audiencia to the Crown (Santiago, 6 September 1571), AGI, Guatemala, leg. 9.

59. "Respuesta a la Audiencia de Guatimala" (Madrid, 13 May 1572), AGCA, A1., leg. 1512, fol. 416v.

60. R.C. (Viana de Navarra, 15 November 1592), AGI, Guatemala, leg. 402, lib. T-3 (segunda parte), fol. 39.

61. Andrés Díaz de Rivadeneyra to the Crown (Santiago, 5 February 1603), AGI, Guatemala, leg. 40.

62. Lic. Castañeda to the Crown (León, 30 May 1531), AGI, Guatemala, leg. 9.

63. "Ynformacion hecho por mando del muy ylustre señor lic. garcia de valverde del consejo de su magt su presidente en la audiencia real de guatemala governador y capitan general en su distrito" (Santiago, 7 November 1582), AGCA, A3.16, leg. 2799, exp. 40578; and bishop of Honduras to the Crown (Valladolid del Valle de Comayagua, 20 April 1584), AGI, Guatemala, leg. 164. Montero de Miranda, "Descripción de la Provincia de la Verapaz," pp. 342–58.

64. Rodrigo del Castillo to the Crown (Seville, 1531), AGI, Indiferente General, leg. 1092. Zorita, *Life and Labor*, p. 210, relates one of the most callous examples: "In Guatemala I heard a prosecutor for the Audiencia say that when he was a soldier on some incursion or conquest, he saw another soldier drop his dagger in the marsh they were crossing, where it sank. An Indian woman bearing a load and an infant at her breast happened to pass, and since it was growing dark he took the child from her and set it in the marsh where the dagger had fallen. The next day he returned to look for his dagger, saying he had left the child as a marker."

65. See, e.g., "Un Libro de Tasaciones de los Naturales de las Provincias de Guatemala, Nicaragua, Yucatan y Pueblos de Comayagua, año de 1548 a 1551," AGI, Guatemala, leg. 128.

66. Very early, at least by 1503, the Crown tried to promote interracial marriages, and a law of 1514 forbade any discrimination against those who married Indian women. Simpson, *The Encomienda*, pp. 9–12. Bishop Marroquín strongly urged the Crown to order all Spaniards, particularly those in the royal service, to marry Indian women, because only in that way would the natives be better treated. J. Fernando Juárez y Aragón, "En el homenaje de la Municipalidad de Antigua al Obispo Marroquín," *ASGH* 36 (1963): 52–56.

67. There was pressure on the encomenderos to marry in order to retain their villages. A royal order required them to take wives within three years, which prompted this response: "Otrosi suplicamos a V. Mt. que la provision que v. mt. fue servido mandar dar para que los vecinos desta governacion se casen dentro de tres años nos mande prorrogar el termino por otro tres o por el tiempo que vra mgt fuere serbido por hecho y hazen es por falta de mugeres y por no tener posibilidad para yr a castilla o a otra parte a lo buscar y v.mt. no sera serbido de mandar casar a ninguno con quien no conosçe pues el matrimonio a de ser para servir a dios o como fuere la merced de vra magt." Concejos of Santiago, Ciudad Real, San Salvador, and San Miguel to the Crown (Santiago, 22 January 1539), AGI, Guatemala, leg. 41.

68. Bishop of Honduras to the Crown (Trujillo, 1 May 1547), AGI, Guatemala, leg. 164.

69. James Lockhart, *The Men of Cajamarca*, p. 229, points out that of the 168 conquerors at Cajamarca during the conquest of Peru, apparently only one of them married an Indian woman, and she was of the nobility. However, their circumstances were unusual because of their wealth, which opened up greater opportunities than for other Spaniards. A great many of them had children by their native concubines, as would be expected.

70. Cited in Torquemada, *Monarquía Indiana*, 2:583. Simpson, *The Encomienda*, p. 177, n. 3. By 1514, almost 10 percent of the Española encomenderos had native wives, many of whom were, according to a contemporary, "persons of little esteem and consequence."

71. Crown to the Protector of the Indians in Nicaragua (Valladolid, 3 February 1537), AGI, Guatemala, leg. 401, lib. S-2, fols. 183-83v, 185.

72. Audiencia to the Crown (Santiago, 15 February 1563), AGI, Guatemala, leg. 9.

73. "Fiscal contra Miguel Diaz" (14 August 1543), AGI, Guatemala, leg. 393, fols. 212v-13.

74. Schurz, *This New World*, pp. 291-92.

75. Residencia of Contreras, AGI, Justicia, leg. 297; and Cerrato to the Crown (Santiago, 5 August 1548), AGI, Guatemala, leg. 9. Regarding the status of lower-class Indian women married to Spaniards, with specific reference to those who were naborías, as early as 1518 the question was posed by a friar: If a female naboría married a Spaniard, what was her legal position? Did she remain in servitude? Zavala, *Estudios indianos*, p. 152.

76. Pardo, *Prontuario*, p. 113.

77. R.C. of 29 July 1565, ibid., p. 57.

78. R.C. of 11 May 1587, ibid., p. 99.

79. Celis to the Crown (Buena Esperanza, 10 May 1535), AGI, Guatemala, leg. 49.

80. Bernal Díaz del Castillo, *Historia Verdadera de la Conquista de la Nueva España*, 2 vols., 2:147.

81. Residencia of Alvarado, AGI, Justicia, leg. 296.

82. Residencia of the first audiencia, AGI, Justicia, leg. 299. A century after the conquest it was the custom for villages to provide Indians for service to corregidores, although sometimes they received wages. Women worked as molenderas, grinding corn and making tortillas. It was asserted, however, that such work took only an hour in the morning and another in the afternoon, while the indias could be in their homes the rest of the time. Residencia of Amador Alvarez, corregidor of Açaçeguastlan, 1623, AGCA, A1.30, leg. 4699, exp. 40642.

83. Jerónimo de San Martin, lieutenant of the treasurer Celis, to the Crown (San Pedro de Puerto de Caballos, 23 April 1537), AGI, Guatemala, leg. 49.

84. R.C. of 29 July 1565, Pardo, *Prontuario*, p. 57. Sancho Clavijo, the governor of Castilla del Oro (Panama) said that he had taken young indias who had

been sold as slaves and put them in homes to serve "honest" Spanish women, while proclaiming the death penalty for enslaving any more Indians. Crown to Clavijo (Valladolid: 4 September 1549), AGCA, A1.23, leg. 1511, fols. 124–25v.

85. R.C. (Valladolid, 16 March 1556), AGI, Guatemala, leg. 402, lib. T-3, fols. 144–44v.

86. Simpson, *Studies in the Administration* . . . *I*, p. 18. Zavala, *Estudios indianos*, pp. 168–69.

87. Rodolfo Quezada Toruño, "Oración fúnebre del Ilustrísimo y Reverendísimo Señor Obispo Licenciado Don Francisco Marroquín, en el IV Centenario de su fallecimiento," *ASGH* 36 (1963): 385–91.

88. Residencia of Castañeda (León and Granada, 1535–36), AGI, Justicia, leg. 293.

89. Castañeda to the Crown (León, 30 May 1531), AGI, Guatemala, leg. 9.

90. Contreras to the Crown (León, 25 June 1537), AGI, Guatemala, leg. 43. See also, residencia of Contreras, AGI, Justicia, leg. 297.

91. Ibid.

92. Montejo to the Crown (Gracias a Dios, 1 May 1542), AGI, Patronato, leg. 184, ramo 25.

93. R.C. (Valladolid, 19 February 1550), AGI, Guatemala, leg. 402, lib. T-3, fols. 67–67v.

94. Residencia of Hernando Bermejo, lieutenant governor (San Pedro, 1568), AGI, Justicia, leg. 315.

95. "Informacion hecha sobre lo contenido en dos cedulas rreales de su mag. de que todo lo en ellas contenido fue falsa rrelacion q. se hizo a su rreal consejo . . . " (Santiago, 10 November 1582), AGI, Guatemala, leg. 966. See also "Ynformacion hecha por mando del muy ilustre señor lic. Garcia de Valverde . . . " (Santiago, 7 November 1582), AGCA, A3.16, leg. 2799; and bishop of Honduras to the Crown (Valladolid del Valle de Comayagua, 20 April 1584), AGI, Guatemala, leg. 164.

96. Lic. Arteaga Mendiola to the Crown (Santiago, 16 December 1570), AGI, Guatemala, leg. 9.

97. See, e.g., "Testimonio de la culpa que resulto contra baltasar nieto y la sentencia que contra el dio el señor lic. Palacio" (Santiago and Tequiluca, March–October, 1575), AGI, Guatemala, leg. 966.

98. "Los capitulos de la cibdad de Santiago de Guatemala sobre la resydencia q. pide a los oydores de los confines y a los demas oficiales" (Santiago, 10 December 1557), AGI, Guatemala, leg. 111.

99. Residencia of Cerrato, AGI, Justicia, leg. 301.

100. Investigation of lic. Diego García de Palacio, oidor (Santiago, 11 March 1578), AGI, Guatemala, leg. 9.

101. "Capitulos contra per afan de rribera, gouernador de cartago" (Cartago de Costa Rica, 1583?), AGI, Guatemala, leg. 49.

102. Audiencia to the Crown (n.p., n.d., but apparently Santiago in the 1570s), AGI, Guatemala, leg. 41.

103. Cerrato to the Crown (Santiago, 27 August 1554), AGI, Guatemala, leg. 9.

104. Lic. Castañeda to the Crown (León, 30 May 1531), AGI, Guatemala, leg. 9.

105. Contreras to the Crown (León, 25 June 1537), AGI, Guatemala, leg. 43.

106. R.C. to governor of Nicaragua (Talavera, 31 May 1541), AGI, Guatemala, leg. 401, lib. S-3, fols. 84v–86.

107. Residencia of Contreras, AGI, Justicia, leg. 297. Lescano, mentioned above in connection with the mistreatment of a cacique in Costa Rica, and his wife Luisa not only lost their pueblos, but were jailed by Governor Contreras. Luisa had been a criada of doña María de Peñalosa, wife of the governor, brought from Spain and later married to Lescano in Nicaragua. A witness stated that it was certain that Contreras would have given her the encomienda Indians, or at least most of them, at her husband's death had it not been for her generally bad treatment of the natives.

108. "Que no consientan q. se encierre en corrales a las yndias a hilar sino en sus casas" (Valladolid, 9 September 1549), AGCA, A.1, leg. 4575, fols. 108v–9. R.C. (Valladolid, 9 October 1549), AGI, Guatemala, leg. 402, lib. T-3, fols. 54v–55.

109. "Sobre las mantas e otras cosas de la Verapaz" (Santiago, 13 February 1582), AGI, Guatemala, leg. 966.

110. "Testimonio de la culpa que resulto contra baltasar nieto y la sentencia que contra el dio el señor lic. Palacio" (Santiago and Tequiluca, March–October, 1575), AGI, Guatemala, leg. 966.

111. Residencia of Captain Juan de Torres, alcalde mayor of La Trinidad, 1583, AGI, Escribanía de Cámara, leg. 344-A.

112. Testimony of Indian alcaldes and regidores of the pueblo of Masaya (Granada, 2 April 1607), AGI, Guatemala, leg. 40.

113. Montejo to the Crown (Gracias a Dios, 1 May 1542), AGI, Patronato, leg. 184, ramo 25.

114. Governor Andrés de Cerezeda to the Crown (Puerto de Caballos, 14 August 1536), AGI, Guatemala, leg. 49.

115. R.C. to the governor of Nicaragua (Talavera, 31 May 1541), AGI, Guatemala, leg. 401, lib. S-3, fols. 84v–86.

116. Residencia of Contreras, AGI, Justicia, leg. 297.

117. "Testimonio de las sentencias contra don garcía de padilla, alcalde mayor que fue de la ciudad real de chiapa" (Guatemala, 1 May 1591), AGI, Guatemala, leg. 966.

118. Provision of the audiencia (Santiago, 14 October 1640), AGCA, A.1, leg. 4647, exp. 39627.

119. Residencia of Captain Juan de Torres, 1583, AGI, Escribanía de Cámara, leg. 344-A.

120. Lic. Arteaga Mendiola to the Crown (Santiago, 16 December 1570), AGI, leg. 9.

121. R.C. of 24 June 1571, Pardo, *Prontuario*, p. 146. It was reported in 1574 that there was a serious shortage of women in the region of La Verapaz, "por ser ellas mas flacas y morir mas a menudo." In view of the lack of Spaniards in that area it is a curious observation. Montero de Miranda, "Descripción de la Provincia de la Verapaz," p. 356.

122. R.C. of 26 May 1573, ibid.

123. "Informacion hecha sobre lo contenido en dos cedulas rreales de su mag. de que todo lo en ellas contenido fue falsa rrelacion q. se hizo a su rreal consejo . . ." (Santiago, 10 November 1582), AGI, Guatemala, leg. 966.

Postscript

1. See Robert S. Chamberlain, "Pre-Conquest Labor Practices," in *Indian Labor in the Spanish Indies*, ed. J. F. Bannon, pp. 1–10. and Robert S. Chamberlain, *The Pre-Conquest Tribute and Service System of the Maya as Preparation for the Spanish Repartimiento-Encomienda in Yucatan*.

2. In a letter to me, dated 30 April 1974, Benjamin Keen observes that, while there are differing versions regarding the treatment of laborers in Mexico prior to the advent of the Spaniards, "I am convinced that Spanish demands for labor and tribute were immeasurably greater than before the Conquest, simply, aside from other reasons, because pre-Conquest tribute demands were limited by the capacity of the native ruling classes to consume the fruits of tribute and labor, whereas the Spanish demands, aimed at the accumulation of wealth in monetary form, were quite unlimited." Labor and tribute before Cortés are treated in Friedrich Katz, *Situación social y económica de los Aztecas durante los siglos XV y XVI*. Certainly there were regional differences, but one would expect that treatment of the macegual class was similar in Central America and Mexico.

3. See, in particular, the stimulating exchanges between Lewis Hanke and Benjamin Keen in *The Hispanic American Historical Review*. Hanke, "More Heat and Some Light on the Spanish Struggle for Justice in the Conquest of America," *HAHR* 44 (1964): 293–340; Keen, "The Black Legend Revisited: Assumptions and Realities," *HAHR* 49 (1969): 703–19; Hanke, "A Modest Proposal for a Moratorium on Grand Generalizations: Some Thoughts on the Black Legend," *HAHR* 51 (1971): 112–27; Keen, "The White Legend Revisited: a Reply to Professor Hanke's 'Modest Proposal,'" *HAHR* 51 (1971): 336–55.

4. It has been observed here previously that rebellious Chichimecas from Mexico were kept in slavery in Soconusco, and that the continued resistance of the Lacandones led to authorization of their enslavement in 1558. When in the 1620s and 1630s the Lacandones, along with Yole and Agitzaes Indians, were in rebellion, the 1558 decree was extended to allow their capture as esclavos de guerra. Doris Z. Stone, "Some Spanish Entradas, 1524–1695," *Middle American Research Series* 4 (1932): 213–96.

5. Keen, "Introduction: Approaches to Las Casas, 1535–1970," in Friede and Keen, *Bartolomé de Las Casas*, p. 5.

6. Investigation of licenciado Diego García de Palacio (Santiago, 11 March 1578), AGI, Guatemala, leg. 41.

7. The role of the Holy Office is discussed in Ernesto Chinchilla Aguilar, *La inquisición en Guatemala.*

8. Pineda, "Descripción de la Provincia de Guatemala," pp. 557–79.

9. The 1601 laws are reproduced in Richard Konetzke (ed.), *Colección de documentos para la historia de la formación social de Hispanoamérica,* 1493–1810, 4 vols., 2 primero tomo, pp. 71–85.

10. These laws, issued at Aranjuez, May 26 1609, appear in AGI, Guatemala, leg. 386, lib. Q-2. They are summarized in translation in Lesley Byrd Simpson, *Studies in the Administration of the Indians in New Spain. III. The Repartimiento System of Native Labor in New Spain and Guatemala,* pp. 12–17, with the full text in his Appendix VI. Simpson adds (p. 17) that they were not well implemented, and an enabling act of 1624 was given as an admonition.

11. His observations are dealt with at length in William L. Sherman, "Abusos contra los Indios de Guatemala (1602–1605). Relaciones del Obispo," *Cahiers du Monde Hispanique et Luso-Brésilien. Caravelle* 11 (1968): 5–28.

12. See, for example, the residencia of don Juan de Medrano, alcalde mayor of Zapotitlán in the year 1616: AGCA, A1.30, leg. 4698, exp. 40639. Some of the material refers to conditions back to 1589. Medrano illegally traded in cacao with the Indians, sold his chickens to them, imposed illegal taxes on them, and cheated them in the sale of clothing. He was also convicted of making illegal use of tamemes. Found guilty, Medrano was given some fairly stiff fines.

13. Vázquez de Espinosa, *Description of the Indies.*

14. Ibid., pp. 18–19.

15. Gage, *Travels in the New World,* pp. 198, 200, 203, 211, 309.

16. Ibid., p. 199.

17. See also Garci Diez de San Miguel, *Visita Hecha a la Provincia de Chucuito por Garci Diez de San Miguel en el año 1567.*

18. See Richard E. Greenleaf, "Viceregal Power and the Obrajes of the Cortés Estate, 1595–1708," *Hispanic American Historical Review* 47 (1969): 365–79.

19. Agia, *Servidumbres Personales,* pp. 58–65, 88, 91–92.

20. "Recopilación de las Reales Cédulas que goviernan en el Supremo Tribunal de la Real Audiencia de Guatemala dispuesta y ordenada en virtud de comisión del mismo Tribunal, por don Miguel Ygnacio Talavera—Año de 1603," *Boletín del Archivo General de la Nación* (Guatemala) 1 (1967): 19–20.

21. According to Molina Argüello, *El Gobernador de Nicaragua,* p. 249, this is the record for Mexía: after serving in the Audiencia of Mexico, he was oidor in Guatemala from 8 September 1555 to 1564; oidor in Panama, 1564–69; and named president of the Audiencia of Santo Domingo on 18 March 1569.

22. Sherman, "A Conqueror's Wealth," pp. 199–213.

23. Frank Jay Moreno, "The Spanish Colonial System: A Functional Approach," *Western Political Quarterly,* 20 (1967): 306–20, makes this observation: "A law which is out of tune with that reality which it is supposed to regulate, is a law

which has to be violated, unless, of course, the coercive power of enforcement is strong enough to prevent such violation. But the Spanish colonial system did not have such coercive forces at its disposal. Thus, the laws Spain enacted for the government of her colonies were subjected to almost constant violation.

"Colonial laws were confined to the domain of the ethically correct and the spiritually pure. They indicated how the loyal and Catholic subjects of the Crown *should* behave. Such regulations were not only violated—they *had* to be disobeyed by less-than-perfect colonists."

Bibliography

MANUSCRIPT SOURCES

Archivo General de Indias (Seville)

Audiencia de Guatemala

Leg. 8. Un libro de cartas a S.M. por varias personas seculares y eclesiásticas, 1549–1570.

Leg. 9. Audiencia de Guatemala: Cartas y expedientes del presidente y oidores de dicha Audiencia: año de 1529 a 1573.

Leg. 39. Cartas y expedientes de los gobernadores de Costa Rica y Honduras, 1526–1699.

Leg. 40. Cartas y expedientes de los Gobernadores de Soconusco y Nicaragua: Soconusco, 1565–1686; Nicaragua, 1539–1692.

Leg. 41. Cartas y expedientes del cabildo secular de Guatemala, 1534–1689.

Leg. 43. Cartas y expedientes de los cabildos seculares de León de Nicaragua, San Salvador y Comayagua, 1539–1689.

Leg. 44. Cartas y expedientes de varios cabildos seculares del distrito de la Audiencia, 1530–1695.

Leg. 45. Cartas y expedientes de los oficiales reales de Guatemala, 1530–1698.

Leg. 49. Cartas y expedientes de oficiales reales de Valladolid de Comayagua en Honduras, 1530–1697.

Leg. 50. Cartas y expedientes de oficiales de Nicaragua, 1533–1697.

Leg. 51. Cartas y expedientes de oficiales de la Villa de Sonsonate, 1579–1688.

Leg. 52. Cartas y expedientes de personas seculares del distrito de la Audiencia de Guatemala, 1526–1561.

Leg. 53. Cartas y expedientes de personas seculares del distrito de la Audiencia de Guatemala, 1562–1571.

Leg. 54. Cartas y expedientes de personas seculares del distrito de la Audiencia de Guatemala, 1572–1576.

Leg. 110. Ynformaciones de oficio y parte del distrito de la Audiencia, 1526–1551.

Leg. 111. Ynformaciones de oficio y parte del distrito de la Audiencia, 1552–1569.

Leg. 128. Un libro de tasaciones a los naturales de las Provincias de Guatemala, Nicaragua, Yucatán y Comayagua, 1548–1551.

Leg. 156. Cartas y expedientes de los Obispos de Guatemala, 1536–1639.

Leg. 161. Cartas y expedientes de los Obispos de Chiapa, 1541–1699.

Leg. 162. Cartas y expedientes de los Obispos de León de Nicaragua, 1544–1685.

Leg. 163. Cartas y expedientes de los Obispos de Vera Paz, 1570–1604.

Leg. 164. Cartas y expedientes de los Obispos de Valladolid de Comayagua en Honduras, 1541–1700.

Leg. 165. Cartas y Expedientes del Cabildo Ecco. de Guatemala, 1551–1636.

Leg. 167. Cartas y Expedientes de los Cabildos Eccos. de Chiapa, León de Nicaragua y Valladolid de Comayagua, 1539–1699.

Leg. 168. Cartas y expedientes de personas eccas. del distrito de dicha Audiencia, 1600–1605.

Leg. 386. Registros de oficio: reales ordenes dirigidos a los autoridades del distrito, 1551–1647.

Leg. 393. Registros de partes: reales ordenes dirigidos a los autoridades corporaciones y particulares del distrito, 1529–1551.

Leg. 401. Registros: Nicaragua: reales ordenes dirigidos a los autoridades y particulares de aquella provincia, 1529–1604.

Leg. 402. Registros: Honduras e Higueras: reales ordenes dirigidos a los autoridades y particulares de aquella provincia, 1525–1605.

Leg. 965. Papeles por agregar, 1527–1571.

Leg. 966. Papeles por agregar, 1578–1599.

Audiencia de Santo Domingo

Leg. 45. Confirmaciones de encomiendas de indios del distrito de esta audiencia, 1667.

Leg. 49. Cartas y expedientes remitidos por la Audiencia de Santo Domingo, 1530–1561.

Leg. 73. Cartas y expedientes remitidos por el Cabildo Secular al Consejo, 1530–1560.

Leg. 868. Oficio y reales ordenes, 1535–1605.

Audiencia de México

Leg. 1841. Libro de Quentas, 1528–1531.

Escribanía de Cámara

Leg. 332. Inbentario de los Pleytos de la Real Audiencia de Guatemala, etc., 1564–1594.

Leg 344-A. Residencia de Juan de Torres, alcalde mayor de la villa de la Trinidad, 1583.

Residencia de Capitan Juan de Estrada, alcalde mayor de la Costa de Çapotitlan, 1583–1584.

Indiferente General

Leg. 417. Registros Reales Ordenes y Capitulaciones sobre la expedición de Alvarado y venta de su Armada, 1538–1540.

Leg. 855. Papeles y borradores del Consejo.

Leg. 857. Papeles y borradores del Consejo, Siglos XVI–XVII.

Leg. 1092. Cartas remitidas al Consejo, 1519–1541.

Leg 1204. Expedientes, ynformaciones, y probanzas, 1533–1535.

Leg. 1206. Expedientes, ynformaciones y probanzas, 1539–1541.

Leg. 1528. Descripciones, poblaciones, y derroteras de viajes, 1521–1818.

Justicia

Leg. 293. Residencia. Lic. Francisco de Castañeda, alcalde mayor de Nicaragua; por Rodrigo de Contreras, gobernador de dicha provincia, 1534–1536.
Cargos contra Luys de Guibara [Guebara], lugarteniente q. fue del lic. Castañeda, 1535–1536.

Leg. 294. Continuation of Castañeda residencia.
Cargos contra Fernando de Alcantara Botello del tpo. q. fue teniente por el lic. Castañeda e del tpo. que fue alcalde hordinario, 1536.

Leg. 295. Residencia tomada el año de 1535 al Adelantado Dn. Pedro de Alvarado Governador que fue de la provincia de Guatemala y a sus tenientes por el Licdo. Alonso Maldonado oidor de la Audiencia de México, 1535.

Leg. 296. Continuation of preceding.

Leg. 297. Residencia. Rodrigo de Contreras, governador de Nicaragua; por el lic. Diego de Herrera, oidor de Guatemala, 1543.

Leg. 298. Residencia. Cargos contra Pedro de los Rios, teniente de gobernador (Contreras).
Cargos contra Luis de Guevara, teniente de governador.

Leg. 299. Residencia tomada el año de 1547 a los Licdos. Alonso de Maldonado, Pedro Ramírez de Quiñones, Diego Herrera y Juan Rogel, Presidente y Oidores de la Audiencia de Guatemala, por el Licdo. López Cerrato juez nombrada para este efecto, 1548.

Leg. 300. Residencia tomada a el Adelantado Dn. Francisco Montejo Governador que fue de las provincias de Chiapa, Yucatán, Tabasco y Cozumel y a sus tenientes, por el Licdo. Juan Rogel Oidor de la Audiencia de Guatemala, juez nombrado para este efecto. 1553. Rogel al adelantado Montejo de la governación de Honduras . . . 1544.

Leg. 301. Residencia tomada el año de 1553 a los Licdos. Alonso López Cerrato, Tomas López, Diego Herrera y Juan Rogel, Presidente y oidores de esta Audiencia de Guatemala, por el Doctor Don Antonio Rodríguez de Quesada Oidor de la Nueva España, juez nombrado para este efecto, 1552 [1553–55].

Leg. 302. Continuation of the preceding.

Leg. 308. Residencia. Lic. Pedro Ramírez de Quiñones, oidor de la Audiencia de los Confines; por el lic. Juan Núñez de Landecho, presidente de ella, 1559.

Leg. 309. Residencia. Dr. Antonio Mexía, oidor de Guatemala; por el lic. Juan Núñez de Landecho, presidente de ella, 1559–1560.

Leg. 310. Continuation of the preceding.

Leg. 311. Residencia. Pedro de Salvatierra, alcalde mayor de la provincia de Honduras; por el lic. Alonso Ortiz de Elgueta, 1562–1563.

Leg. 312. Residencia. Francisco de Magaña, alcalde mayor de la Villa de la Trinidad y del Puerto de Acaxutla, 1566–1568.

Leg. 313. Residencia. Alonso de Paz, alcalde mayor de la provincia de la Verapaz; por Pedro de Casa de Avante y Gamboa, 1567–1568.

Residencia de Hortun de Velasco. 1567–1568.

Leg. 314. Residencia. Lic. Alonso Ortiz de Elgueta, gobernador de la provincia de Honduras; por don Juan de Vargas Carvajal, 1567.

Leg. 315. Residencia. Johanes de Debaide, el moço, teniente general que fue de governador de esta provincia [Honduras] por el licenciado Hortiz [Ortiz], 1568.

Residencia. Hernando Bermejo, teniente de Governador e visitador general que fue en esta provincia por el liçenciado Hortiz governador que fue, 1568.

Residencia. Pedro Romero, teniente general de governador por el licenciado Hortiz de Elgueta, 1568.

Leg. 316. Residencia. Lic. Francisco Briceño, governador de la provincia de Guatemala; por el doctor Antonio González, presidente de la Audiencia, 1569–1570.

Leg. 317. Continuation of the preceding.

Leg. 319. Residencia. Dr. Antonio González, presidente, y licenciados Valdés de Cárcamo, oidor, y Arteaga de Mendiola, fiscal de la Audiencia de Guatemala; por el doctor Pedro de Villalobos, presidente de ella, 1572–1574.

Leg. 331. Comisión dada por Rl. cédula del año de 1547 a Dn. Diego Ramírez para averiguar los malos tratamientos que havían hecho en la provincia de Chiapas a los Religiosos de la orden de Sto. Domingo, 1547.

Leg. 1031. Pedro de Alvarado contra Fernando Cortés, 1528–1529.

Juan de Espinar contra Alvarado, 1537.

Leg. 1164. Pleito de Hernán Sánchez de Vadajoz, Governador y Capitán General de Costa Rica con Rodrigo de Contreras, Gouernador de Nicaragua, 1543–1554.

Patronato

Leg. 20. Descubrimientos, descripciones, poblaciones, conquistas y pacificaciones hechos en las Indias.

Leg. 83. Ibid.

Leg. 170. Papeles tocantes al buen gobierno de las Indias en general, 1480–1556.

Leg. 180. Papeles sobre el buen gobierno [Nueva España], 1519–1540.

Leg. 184. Papeles y cartas de buen gobierno [Nueva España], 1525–1572.

Leg. 231. Papeles pertenecientes a la libertad de los Indios, su doctrina, buen tratamiento y modo de encomendarlos, 1512–1679.

Leg. 246. Materias diversas.

Leg. 252. Historia de las Indias: Papeles escritos por Fr. Bartolomé de Las Casas acerca de la historia de las Indias, 1516–1561.

Leg. 275. Copias de minutas de Reales Cédulas, de sentencias en varias residencias, de despachos y provisiones de enplazamiento despachados por el Consejo y
Cámara de Yndias pertenecientes al buen gobierno de aquellos dominios,
1511–1586.

Archivo General de la Nación (Mexico).

Inquisición. Tomo 44. Honduras, no. 9, 1568.

Inquisición. Tomo 212, no. 11.

Hospital de Jesús. Leg. 271.

Archivo General de Centro América (Guatemala)

Residencias (A1.30 series)

Leg. 182. Gonzalo de Ocampo Saavedra, corregidor del cerro e valle de ciudad
real [Chiapa], 1563.

Leg. 266. Mateo Blandin, corregidor de Çacaloaque [Nicaragua], 1604.

Alonso Hernández Alconchel, corregidor de Çacaloaque, 1604.

Leg. 296. Pedro Girón de Alvarado, alcalde mayor de San Salvador, 1593–1598.

Leg. 297. Continuation of the preceding.

Leg. 4696. Alonso de Barrientos, corregidor de Çacauastlán, 1586.

Bartolomé de Salas Abiasido, corregidor de Tecpanatitlán, 1599.

Leg. 4697. D. Luis de la Cerda, corregidor de Guaçacapán, 1591.

Per Afan de Rivera, corregidor de Chiquimula, 1599.

Leg. 4698. D. Juan de Medrano, alcalde mayor de Zapotitlán, 1616.

Leg. 4699. Amador Alvarez, corregidor de Acaçeguastlán, 1623.

Leg. 4762. Antonio de Valderrama, corregidor de Quetzaltenango, 1587.

Libros de Protocolos (A1.20 series)

Leg. 422. Cristóbal de Aceituno.

Leg. 706. Marcos Díaz.

Leg. 797. Marcos Díaz.

Leg. 732. Juan de León.

Leg. 733. Juan de León.

Leg. 807. Pedro Grijalva.

Leg. 808. Pedro Grijalva.

Leg. 809. Pedro Grijalva.

Leg. 810. Sebastián Gudiel.

Leg. 1018. Diego Jacome.

Leg. 1043. Miguel Monte Verde.

Leg. 1111. Luis Aceituno Guzmán.

Leg. 1127. Fernando Niño.

Leg. 1128. Fernando Niño.

Leg. 1129. Juan Martínez de Soria.

Leg. 1169. Bernabé Pérez.

Leg. 1433. Francisco Valle de Quejo.

Leg. 1489. Various.

Leg. 1507. Francisco Valle de Quejo.
Leg. 4553. Prudencio Pérez.

Miscellaneous Legajos

1 (A1.29.1); 356 (A.1); 1511 (A1.23); 1512 (A.6); 1513 (A1.23); 1514 (A.1); 1751 (A.1); 2033 (A1.29); 2198 (A.1); 2245 (A1.2.4); 2335 (A1.28); 2363 (A1.2.5); 2724 (A3.12); 2774 (A1.31); 2797 (A3.16); 2799 (A3.16); 2800 (A3.16); 2896 (A.1); 4575 (A.1); 4588 (A1.23); 4647 (A.1); 4677 (A1.29); 4678 (A.129); 5532 (A1.); 5723 (A1.29.7); Uncatalogued: Libro de la tesoreria de su magestad de la quenta y razón q. della tiene yo el tesorero francisco de castellanos tesorero en esta provincia de guatemala.

PRINTED SOURCES

Adams, Eleanor B. *A Bio-Bibliography of Franciscan Authors in Colonial Central America*. Washington, D.C.: Academy of American Franciscan History, 1953.
Agia, Fray Miguel. *Servidumbres Personales de Indios*. Edición y estudio preliminar de F. Javier de Ayala. Seville: 1946 [Lima, 1604].
Aguirre, P. Gerardo G., OCD. *La Cruz de Nimajuyú: Historia de la Parroquia de San Pedro la Laguna*. Guatemala: n.p., 1972.
Alvarado, Pedro de. *An Account of the Conquest of Guatemala in 1524*. Edited by Sedley J. Mackie. New York: The Cortés Society, 1924.
Annis, Verle L. *The Architecture of Antigua Guatemala, 1543–1773*. Bilingual edition. Guatemala: Universidad de San Carlos, 1968.
Arévalo, Rafael de. *Libro de actas del ayuntamiento de la ciudad de Santiago de Guatemala, desde la fundación de la misma ciudad en 1524 hasta 1530*. Guatemala: Tipografía Nacional, 1932.
Argüello Argüello, Alfonso. *Historia de León Viejo*. León, Nicaragua: Editorial Antorcha, 1969.
Argüello Solórzano, Federico, and Carlos Molina Argüello. *Monumenta Centroamericae Histórica: Colección de Documentos y Materiales para el Estudio de la Historia y de la vida de los pueblos de la América Central*. Seville: Universidad Centroamericana (Managua, Nicaragua), 1965.
Arriola, Jorge Luis. *Pequeño diccionario etimológico de voces guatemaltecas*. 2d ed. Biblioteca de Cultura Popular, vol. 50. Guatemala: Editorial del Ministerio de Educación Pública, 1954.
Asturias, Miguel Angel. *El problema social del indio*. Paris: Centre de Recherches de l'Institut d'Etudes Hispaniques, 1971.
Ayala, Manuel Josef. *Notas a la Recopilación de Indias*. Transcripción y estudio preliminar de Juan Manzano. 2 vols. Madrid: Ediciones Cultura Hispánica, 1945–46.
Bancroft, Hubert H. *History of Central America*. 3 vols. San Francisco: The History Company, 1882–87.
———. *Native Races of the Pacific States of North America*. 5 vols. San Francisco: D. Appleton and Company, 1875–78.

Bannon, John Francis., ed. *Indian Labor in the Spanish Indies. Problems in Latin American Civilization.* Boston: D. C. Heath and Company, 1966.

Barber, Ruth Kerns. *Indian Labor in the Spanish Colonies.* Historical Society of New Mexico Publications in History, vol. 6. Albuquerque: University of New Mexico Press, 1932.

Barlow, Robert H. *The Extent of the Empire of the Culhua Mexica.* Ibero-Americana, no. 28. Berkeley and Los Angeles: University of California Press, 1949.

Barón Castro, Rodolfo. *La Población de El Salvador: Estudio acerca de su desenvolvimiento desde la época prehispánica hasta nuestros días.* Madrid: Consejo Superior de Investigaciones Científicas Instituto Gonzalo Fernández Oviedo, 1942.

———. *Reseña histórica de la Villa de San Salvador, desde su fundación en 1525 hasta que recibe el título de ciudad en 1549.* Madrid: Ediciones Cultura Hispánica, 1950.

Bataillon, Marcel. "Las Casas et le Licencié Cerrato," *Bulletin Hispanique* 55 (1953): 79–87.

Beals, Ralph L. "Acculturation," *Handbook of Middle American Indians,* vol. 6, pp. 449–68. Austin: University of Texas Press, 1967.

Benzoni, Girolamo. *History of the New World.* Translated and edited by Rear-Admiral W. H. Smyth. The Hakluyt Society, series 1, vol. 21. London: The Hakluyt Society, 1857.

Bergmann, John F. "The Distribution of Cacao Cultivation in Pre-Columbian America," *Annals of the Association of American Geographers* 59 (1969): 85–96.

Berthe, Jean-Pierre. "Aspects de l'esclavage des indiens en Nouvelle-Espagne pendant la première moitié du XVIe siècle," *Journal de la Société des Américanistes* 2 (1965): 189–209.

———. "Xochimancas: Les travaux et les jours dans une hacienda sucrière de Nouvelle-Espagne au XVIIe siècle," *Jahrbuch für Geschichte von Staat, Wirtschaft und Gesellschaft Lateinamerikas* 3 (1966): 88–117.

Borah, Woodrow. *Early Colonial Trade and Navigation between Mexico and Peru.* Ibero-Americana, no. 38. Berkeley and Los Angeles: University of California Press, 1954.

Bosch García, Carlos. *La esclavitud prehispánica entre los aztecas.* Mexico: El Colegio de México, 1944.

Bowser, Frederick P. *The African Slave in Colonial Peru, 1524–1650.* Stanford, Calif.: Stanford University Press, 1974.

Braudel, Fernand. *The Mediterranean and the Mediterranean World in the Age of Philip II.* Translation by Sîan Reynolds. 2 vols. New York: Harper and Row, 1972.

Breve Guía de León Viejo. León: Editorial de la UNAN, n.d.

Bunzel, Ruth. *Chichicastenango, A Guatemala Village.* Seattle: University of Washington Press, 1967.

Calnek, Edward E. "Highland Chiapas Before the Conquest." Ph.D. dissertation, University of Chicago, 1962.

Cardoso da Silva, Geraldo. "Negro Slavery in the Sugar Plantations of Veracruz and Pernambuco, 1550–1680: A Comparative Study." Ph.D. dissertation, University of Nebraska, 1975.

Carmack, Robert M. *Quichean Civilization: The Ethnohistoric, Ethnographic, and Archaelogical Sources*. Berkeley and Los Angeles: University of California Press, 1973.

Carrasco, Pedro. "Documentos sobre el rango de tecuhtli entre los nahuas tramontanos," *Tlalocan* 5 (1966): 133–60.

———. "Don Juan Cortés, Cacique de Santa Cruz Quiché," *Estudios de Cultura Maya* 6 (1967): 251–66.

Cartas de Indias. Madrid: Ministerio de Fomento, 1877.

Cartas del Perú. See Porras Barrenechea, Raúl.

Castellanos, Rosario. *Balún Canán*. Mexico: Fondo de Cultura Económica, 1957.

Catálogo de la Colección de don Juan Bautista Muñoz: Documentos interesantes para la historia de América. Madrid: La Real Academia de la Historia, 1954–1956.

Catálogo de Pasajeros a Indias durante los siglos XVI, XVII v XVIII. 3 vols. Madrid: Ministerio de Trabajo y Previsión, 1930, 1940–46.

Cerwin, Herbert. *Bernal Díaz, Historian of the Conquest*. Norman: University of Oklahoma Press, 1963.

Chamberlain, Robert S. "The Concept of the *Señor Natural* as Revealed by Castilian Law and Administrative Documents," *Hispanic American Historical Review* 19 (1939): 130–37.

———. *The Conquest and Colonization of Honduras, 1502–1550*. Washington, D.C.: Carnegie Institution of Washington, Publication 598, 1953. Reprinted New York: Octagon Books, 1966.

———. *The Conquest and Colonization of Yucatan, 1517–1550*. Washington, D.C.: Carnegie Institution of Washington, publication 582, 1948.

———. "Un documento desconocido del lienciado Cristóbal de Pedraza, Protector de los indios y Obispo de Honduras," *Anales de la Sociedad de Geografía e Historia de Guatemala* 20 (1945): 33–38.

———. "Ensayo sobre el Adelantado don Francisco de Montejo y sus proyectos para el desarrollo económico de la provincia de Honduras e Higueras," *Anales de la Sociedad de Geografía e Historia de Guatemala* 20 (1945): 209–16.

———. *The Governorship of the Adelantado Francisco de Montejo in Chiapas, 1539–1544*. Washington, D.C.: Carnegie Institution of Washington, publication 574 (Contributions to American Anthropology and History, no. 46), 1958.

———. "Plan del siglo XVI para abrir un camino de Puerto Caballos a la bahía de Fonseca en sustitución de la ruta de Panamá," *Anales de la Sociedad de Geografía e Historia de Guatemala* 21 (1946): 61–66.

———. *The Pre-Conquest Tribute and Service System of the Maya as Preparation for the Spanish Repartimiento-Encomienda in Yucatan.* University of Miami Hispanic-American Studies, no. 10. Coral Gables, Fla.: University of Miami Press, 1951.

———. "El último testamento y mandato de don Francisco de Montejo, Adelantado de Yucatán, 1553. *Anales de la Sociedad de Geografía e Historia de Guatemala* 20 (1945): 83–90.

Chapman, Anne C. "Port of Trade Enclaves in Aztec and Maya Civilizations," In *Trade and Market in Early Empires: Economies in History and Theory*, edited by Karl Polanyi, Conrad M. Arensberg, and Harry W. Pearson, pp. 114–53. Glencoe, Ill.: The Free Press, 1957.

Chaunu, Pierre and Huguette. *Seville et l'Atlantique.* 8 vols. Paris: Colin, 1955–59.

Chevalier, François. *La Formación de los Grandes Latifundios en México: Tierra y Sociedad en los Siglos XVI y XVII.* Mexico: Problemas Agrícolas e Industriales de México, 1956.

Chinchilla Aguilar, Ernesto. *La inquisición en Guatemala.* Publicaciones del Instituto de Antropología e Historia. Guatemala: Editorial del Ministerio de Educación Pública, 1953.

———. "El Obispo Marroquín y Las Leyes Nuevas en 1542," *Anales de la Sociedad de Geografía e Historia de Guatemala* 36 (1963): 35–41.

Chipman, Donald E. *Nuño de Guzmán and the Province of Pánuco in New Spain, 1518–1533.* Glendale, Calif.: Arthur H. Clark, 1967.

———. "The Traffic in Indian slaves in the Province of Pánuco, New Spain, 1523–1533," *The Americas* 23 (1966): 142–55.

Colección de documentos inéditos relativos al descubrimiento, conquista, y organización de las antiguas posesiones españoles de América y Oceanía. 42 vols. Madrid, 1864–84.

Colección de documentos inéditos relativos al descubrimiento, conquista y organización de las antiguas posesiones españoles de Ultramar. 25 vols. Madrid, 1885–1929.

Colección de documentos para la historia de Costa Rica. Compiled by León Fernández. 5 vols. Paris: Imprenta Pablo Dupont, 1881–1907.

Colección Somoza: Documentos para la historia de Nicaragua. Edited by Andrés Vega Bolaños. 17 vols. Madrid, 1954–57.

Comas, Juan. "Historical Reality and the Detractors of Father Las Casas." In *Bartolomé de Las Casas in History: Toward an Understanding of the Man and His Work*, edited by Juan Friede and Benjamin Keen. DeKalb: Northern Illinois University Press, 1971.

Conzemius, Eduard. *Ethnographical Survey of the Miskito and Sumu Indians of Honduras and Nicaragua.* Smithsonian Institution, Bureau of American Ethnology Bulletin 106. Washington, D.C., 1932.

Denevan, William, M., ed. *The Native Population of the Americas in 1492.* Madison: University of Wisconsin Press, 1976.

"Descripción de la Provincia de Zapotitlán y Suchitepeques, año de 1579, por su Alcalde Mayor Capitán Juan de Estrada y el Escribano Fernando de Niebla," *Anales de la Sociedad de Geografía e Historia de Guatemala* 28 (1955): 68–84.

"Descripción de San Bartolomé, del Partido de Atitlán, año 1585.," *Anales de la Sociedad de Geografía e Historia de Guatemala* 38 (1965): 262–75.

Diaz del Castillo, Bernal. *La Conquista de Nueva España.* 2 vols. Mexico: Compañía Editorial Continental, 1955.

———. *Historia Verdadera de la Conquista de la Nueva España.* 2 vols. Mexico: Editorial Porrúa, 1955.

———. *The True History of the Conquest of New Spain.* Translation by A. P. Maudslay. 3 vols. London: The Hakluyt Society, 1908–16.

Díaz Ovalle, Tte. J. Lizardo, ed. *La Muerte de Tecún Umán: Estudio Crítico del Altiplano Occidental de la República.* Guatemala: Editorial del Ejército, 1963.

Diccionario de la Lengua Española. 18th ed. Madrid: La Real Academia Española, 1956.

Diccionario Porrúa de Historia, Biografía y Geografía de México. Edited by Angel Ma. Garibay K. 2d ed. Mexico: Editorial Porrúa, 1965.

Diez de San Miguel, Garcia. *Visita Hecha a la Provincia de Chucuito por Garci Diez de San Miguel en el año 1567.* Documentos Regionales para la Etnohistoria Andina, no. 1. Lima: Ediciones de la Casa de la Cultura del Perú, 1964.

DII. See *Colección de documentos inéditos relativos al descubrimiento, conquista, y organización de las antiguas posesiones españolas de América y Oceanía.*

DIU. See *Colección de documentos inéditos relativos al descubrimiento, conquista, y organzación de las antiquas posesiones españoles de Ultramar.*

Durán, Fray Diego. *The Aztecs: The History of New Spain.* Translation and notes by Doris Heyden and Fernando Horcasitas. New York: Orion Press, 1964.

Encinas, Diego de, comp. *Cedulario Indiano: Reproducción facsímil de la edición única de 1596.* Con estudio e índices de Alfonso García Gallo. 4 vols. Madrid: Ediciones Cultura Hispánica, 1945–46.

Friede, Juan, and Benjamin Keen, eds. *Bartolomé de Las Casas in History: Toward an Understanding of the Man and His Work.* DeKalb: Northern Illinois University Press, 1971.

Fuentes y Guzmán, Francisco Antonio. *Recordación florida del reyno de Guatemala* [1882–83]. 3 vols. Biblioteca "Goathemala" de la Sociedad de Geografía e Historia. Guatemala: Tipografía Nacional, 1932–33.

Gage, Thomas. *Thomas Gage's Travels in the New World* [1648]. Edited and with an introduction by J. Eric S. Thompson. Norman: University of Oklahoma Press, 1969.

Gall, Francis. "Soconusco (Hasta la época de la Independencia)," *Anales de la Sociedad de Geografía e Historia* 35 (1962): 155–68.

———. *Título del Ajpop Huitzitzil Tzunún: Probanza de Méritos de León y Cardona.* Guatemala: Centro Editorial "José de Pineda Ibarra," 1963.

García, Genaro. *Carácter de la conquista española, en América y en México, según los textos de los historiadores primitivos.* Mexico: Oficina Tipográfica de la Secretaría de Fomento, 1901.

Gerhard, Peter. *A Guide to the Historical Geography of New Spain.* Cambridge: Cambridge University Press, 1972.

Gibson, Charles. "The Aztec Aristocracy in Colonial Mexico," *Comparative Studies in Society and History* (The Hague: Mouton & Co.) 2 (1960): 169–96.

———. *The Aztecs Under Spanish Rule: A History of the Indians of the Valley of Mexico, 1519–1810.* Stanford, Calif.: Stanford University Press, 1964.

———, ed. *The Spanish Tradition in America.* New York: Harper and Row, 1968.

———. *Tlaxcala in the Sixteenth Century.* New Haven, Conn.: Yale University Press, 1952.

Giménez Fernández, Manuel. "Fray Bartolomé de Las Casas: A Biographical Sketch." In *Bartolomé de Las Casas in History: Toward an Understanding of the Man and His Work,* edited by Juan Friede and Benjamin Keen, pp. 67–126. DeKalb: Northern Illinois University Press, 1971.

Greenleaf, Richard E. "Viceregal Power and the Obrajes of the Cortés Estate, 1595–1708," *Hispanic American Historical Review* 47 (1968): 365–79.

Guerra, Eduardo. "Quito y Pedro de Alvarado," *Anales de la Sociedad de Geografía e Historia de Guatemala* 25 (1951): 288–90.

Guillemin, Jorge. *Iximché, Capital del antiguo Reino Cakchiquel.* Publicaciones del Instituto de Antropología e Historia de Guatemala. Guatemala: Tipografía Nacional, 1965.

Hanke, Lewis U. *Aristotle and the American Indians.* Bloomington: Indiana University Press, 1970.

———. "A Modest Proposal for a Moratorium on Grand Generalizations: Some Thoughts on the Black Legend," *Hispanic American Historical Review* 51 (1971): 112–27.

———. "More Heat and Some Light on the Spanish Struggle for Justice in the Conquest of America," *Hispanic American Historical Review* 44 (1964): 293–340.

———. "The New Laws—Another Analayis." In *Indian Labor in the Spanish Indies,* edited by John Francis Bannon, pp. 55–64. Boston: D. C. Heath and Co., 1966.

———. "The 'Requerimiento' and its Interpreters," *Revista de Historia de América* 1 (1968): 25–34.

———. *The Spanish Struggle for Justice in the Conquest of America.* Boston: Little, Brown, 1965.

Haring, Clarence H. *The Spanish Empire in America.* New York: Oxford University Press, 1947.

Herrera y Tordesillas, Antonio de. *Historia general de los hechos de los castellanos en las islas i tierra firme del mar océano* [1601]. 4 vols. Madrid: La Imprenta Real de Nicolás Rodríguez Franco, 1726–30.

Hussey, Roland D. "Text of the Laws of Burgos," Hispanic American Historical Review 12: 301–27.

Juárez y Aragón, J. Fernando. 'En el homenaje de la Municipalidad de Antigua al Obispo Marroquín," Anales de la Sociedad de Geografía e Historia de Guatemala 36 (1963): 52–56.

Juarros, Domingo. Compendio de la historia de la ciudad de Guatemala. 3d ed. 2 vols. Guatemala: Tipografía Nacional, 1936.

Katz, Friedrich. Situación social y económica de los Aztecas durante los siglos XV y XVI. Mexico: Universidad Nacional Autónoma de Mexico, 1966.

Keen, Benjamin. The Aztec Image in Western Thought. New Brunswick, N.J.: Rutgers University Press, 1971.

—————. "The Black Legend Revisited: Assumptions and Realities," Hispanic American Historical Review 49 (1969): 703–19.

—————. "The White Legend Revisited: A Reply to Professor Hanke's 'Modest Proposal,'" Hispanic American Historical Review 51 (1971): 336–55.

Keniston, Hayward. Francisco de los Cobos, Secretary of the Emperor Charles V. Pittsburgh, Pa.: University of Pittsburgh Press, 1958.

Klein, Herbert S. "North American Competition and the Characteristics of the African Slave Trade to Cuba, 1790 to 1794," William and Mary Quarterly, Third Series, 1 (1971): 87–101.

Konetzke, Richard, ed. Colección de documentos para la historia de la formación social de Hispanoamérica, 1493–1810. 4 vols. Madrid: Consejo Superior de Investigaciones Científicas, 1958–62.

Kubler, George. Mexican Architecture in the Sixteenth Century. 2 vols. New Haven, Conn.: Yale University Press, 1948.

Lamadrid, Lázaro. "Bishop Marroquín, Zumárraga's Gift to Central America," The Americas 5 (1949): 331–341.

Las Casas, Bartolomé de. Historia de las Indias. Edited by Agustín Millares Carlo. 3 vols. 2d ed. Mexico: Fondo de Cultura Económica, 1965.

Landa, Diego de. Landa's Relación de las Cosas de Yucatán. Translation and notes by Alfred M. Tozzer. Papers of the Peabody Museum of American Archeology and Ethnology, Harvard University, vol. 18. Cambridge, Mass.: The Museum, 1941.

Lockhart, James. The Men of Cajamarca: A Social and Biographical Study of the First Conquerors of Peru. Austin: University of Texas Press, 1972.

—————. Spanish Peru, 1532–1560: A Colonial Society. Madison: University of Wisconsin Press, 1968.

López de Velasco, Juan. Geografía y descripción universal de las Indias, desde el año de 1571 al de 1574. Madrid: La Real Academia de la Historia, 1894.

Lozoya (Juan de Contreras), Marqués de. Vida del Segoviano Rodrigo de Contreras, Gobernador de Nicaragua (1534–1544). Biblioteca de Historia Hispano-Americana. Toledo: Imp. de la Editorial Católica Toledana, 1920.

Lutz, Christopher H. "Santiago de Guatemala, 1541–1773: The Socio-Demographic History of a Spanish American Colonial City." Ph.D. dissertation, University of Wisconsin, 1976.

MacLeod, Murdo J. "Algunos aspectos de la presencia Lascasiana en Centroamérica." In *Fray Bartolomé de Las Casas en Hispanoamérica*, edited by Manuel M. Velasco Suárez. San Cristóbal de Las Casas, Mexico: Editorial Fray Bartolomé de Las Casas, 1976.

————. *Las Casas, Guatemala, and the Sad but Inevitable Case of Antonio de Remesal.* Latin American Studies Occasional Paper, no. 5. Pittsburgh, Pa.: University of Pittsburgh, 1970.

————. "The Seventeenth Century Depression in the Audiencia of Guatemala." Paper read at the Rocky Mountain Social Sciences Association meeting, Colorado Springs, Colo., 1968.

————. *Spanish Central America: A Socioeconomic History, 1520–1720.* Berkeley and Los Angeles: University of California Press, 1973.

MacNutt, Francis A. *Bartholomew De Las Casas, His Life, His Apostolate, and His Writings.* New York: G. P. Putnam's Sons, 1909.

Markman, Sidney David. *Colonial Architecture of Antigua Guatemala.* American Philosophical Society Memoirs, vol. 64. Philadelphia, Pa., 1966.

————. *San Cristóbal de Las Casas.* Seville: Escuela de Estudios Hispano-Americanos, 1963.

Martin, Norman F. *Los Vagabundos en la Nueva España, Siglo XVI.* Mexico: Editorial Jus. 1957.

Martínez Peláez, Severo. *La patria del criollo.* Guatemala: Editorial Universitaria Centroamericana, 1973.

Miles, S.W. "Summary of Preconquest Ethnology of the Guatemala-Chiapas Highlands and Pacific Slopes," In *Handbook of Middle American Indians*, vol. 2, part 1. Austin: University of Texas Press, 1965.

Millares Carlo, Agustín, and J. I. Mantecón. *Indice y extractos de los Protocolos del Archivo de Notarias de México.* 2 vols. Mexico: El Colegio de México, 1946.

Millon, René. "When Money Grew on Trees: A Study of Cacao in Ancient Mesoamerica." Ph.D. dissertation, Columbia University, 1955.

Miranda, José. *El Tributo Indígena en la Nueva España Durante el Siglo XVI.* Mexico: Fondo de Cultura Económica, El Colegio de México, 1952.

Molina Argüello, Carlos. "Gobernaciones, Alcaldías Mayores y Corregimientos en el Reino de Guatemala," *Anuario de Estudios Americanos* 17 (1958): 105–32.

————. *El Gobernador de Nicaragua en el Siglo XVI: Contribución al Estudio de la Historia del Derecho Nicaragüense.* Seville: Escuela de Estudios Hispano-Americanos, 1949.

Montero de Miranda, Fray Francisco. "Descripción de la Provincia de la Verapaz" [1575], *Anales de la Sociedad de Geografía e Historia de Guatemala* 27 (1953–1954): 342–58.

Moreno, Fran Jay. "The Spanish Colonial System: A Functional Approach," *Western Political Quarterly* 20 (1967): 308–20.

Morley, Sylvanus G. *The Ancient Maya.* 3d. ed. rev. by George Brainerd. Stanford, Calif.: Stanford University Press, 1958.

Mörner, Magnus. *La Corona Española y los Foráneos en los Pueblos de Indios de América.* Stockholm: Almqvist & Wiksell, 1970.

———. "La Política e Segregación y del Mestizaje en la Audiencia de Guatemala," *Revista de Indias* 95–96 (1964): 137–51.

Motolinía, Fray Toribio. *Carta al Emperador: Refutación a Las Casas sobre la Colonización Española.* Mexico: Editorial Jus, 1949.

Muro Orejón, Antonio, ed. *Las Leyes Nuevas de 1542–1543: Ordenanzas para la gobernación de las Indias y buen tratamiento y conservación de los indios.* Seville: Escuela de Estudios Hispano-Americanos, 1961.

———, ed. *Las Ordenanzas de 1571 del Real y Supremo Consejo de las Indias.* Texto facsímil de la edición de 1585. Seville: Escuela de Estudios Hispano-Americanos, 1957.

Oviedo y Valdés, El Capitán Gonzalo Fernández. *Historia General y Natural de las Indias, islas y tierra-firme del mar océano.* 4 vols. Madrid: La Real Academia de la Historia, 1851–55.

Palacio, Diego García de. *Carta Dirigida al Rey de España, por el Licenciado Dr. Don Diego García de Palacio, Oydor de la Real Audiencia de Guatemala: Año 1576. Being a Description of the Ancient Provinces of Guazacapán, Izalco, Cuzcatlán, and Chiquimula, in the Audiencia of Guatemala: With an Account of the Languages, Customs and Religions of their Aboriginal Inhabitants, and a Description of the Ruins of Copán.* Translation by Ephraim G. Squier. Series of the "Collections of Rare and Original Documents and Relations Concerning the Discovery and Conquest of America, Chiefly from the Spanish Archives," no. 1. New York: Charles B. Norton, 1860.

———. "Relación hecha por el Licenciado Palacio al Rey D. Felipe II, en la que describe la Provincia de Guatemala, las costumbres de los indios y otras cosas notables [1576]," *Anales de la Sociedad de Geografía e Historia de Guatemala* 4 (1927): 71–92.

Pardo, José Joaquín. *Efemérides de la Antigua Guatemala, 1541–1779.* Guatemala: Union Tipográfica, 1944.

———. *Prontuario de Reales Cédulas, 1529–1599.* Guatemala: Union Tipográfica, 1941.

Parry, John H. *The Audiencia of New Galicia in the Sixteenth Century: A Study in Spanish Colonial Government.* Cambridge: Cambridge University Press, 1948.

Paso y Troncoso, Francisco del, ed. *Epistolario de Nueva España, 1505–1818.* 16 vols. Biblioteca Histórica Mexicana de Obras Inéditas, segunda serie. Mexico: Antigua Librería Robredo de José Porrúa e Hijos, 1939–42.

Peña y de la Cámara, José María de la. *A List of Spanish Residencias in the Archives of the Indies, 1516–1775.* Washington, D.C.: Library of Congress, 1955.

Pérez Valenzuela, Pedro. *Ciudad Vieja.* Guatemala: Imprenta Universitaria, 1960.

Pike, Ruth. "Sevillian Society in the Sixteenth Century: Slaves and Freedmen," *Hispanic American Historical Review* 47 (1967): 344–59.

Pineda, Juan de. "Descripción de la provincia de Guatemala, año de 1594," *Revista de los Archivos Nacionales* (San José, Costa Rica) 3 (1939): 557–79.

Poole, Richard Stafford. "The Franciscan Attack on the Repartimiento System (1585)." In *Indian Labor in the Spanish Indies*, edited by John Francis Bannon, Boston: D.C. Heath and Co., 1966.

Porras Barrenechea, Raúl, ed. *Cartas del Perú (1524–1543): Colección de Documentos Inéditos para la Historia del Perú*, vol. 3. Lima: Edición de la Sociedad de Bibliófilos Peruanos, 1959.

Puga, Vasco de, comp. *Prouisiones, cédulas, instrucciones de Magestad, ordenanças de difuntos y audiencia para la buena expedición de los negocios y administración de justicia y gouernación de esta Nueua España, y para el buen tratamiento y conseruación de los indios dende el año de 1525 hasta este presente de 63.* 2d ed. 2 vols. Mexico, 1878–79.

Quezada Toruño, Rodolfo. "Oración fúnebre del Ilustrísimo Reverendísimo Señor Obispo Licenciado Don Francisco Marroquín, en el IV Centenario de su fallecimiento, *Anales de la Sociedad de Geografía e Historia de Guatemala* 36 (1963): 385–91.

Radell, David R., and James J. Parson. "Realejo: A Forgotten Colonial Port and Shipbuilding Center in Nicaragua," *Hispanic American Historical Review* 51 (1971): 295–312.

Ramírez, José Fernando, ed. *Proceso de Residencia contra Pedro de Alvarado, 1529.* Mexico: Valdés y Redondas, 1847.

Recinos, Adrian. *Crónicas Indígenas de Guatemala.* Guatemala: Editorial Universitaria, 1957.

———. "La expansión hispánica en la América Central durante la primera mitad del siglo XVI," *Anales de la Sociedad de Geografía e Historia de Guatemala* 31 (1958): 73–79.

———. Delia Goetz, and Dionisio José Chonay, trans. *The Annals of the Cakchiquels, Title of the Lords of Totonicapán.* Norman: University of Oklahoma Press, 1953.

"Recopilación de las Reales Cédulas que gobiernan en el Supremo Tribunal de la Real Audiencia de Guatemala dispuesta y ordenada en virtud de comisión del mismo Tribunal, por don Miguel Ygnacio Talavera—Año de 1603," *Boletín del Archivo General de la Nación* (Guatemala), 1 (1967): 19–20.

Recopilación de leyes de los Reynos de las Indias [1681]. 4 vols. 2d. ed. Madrid: A. Balbas, 1756.

"Relación de la Verapaz hecha por los religiosos de Santo Domingo de Cobán, 7 de diciembre de 1574," *Anales de la Sociedad de Geografía e Historia de Guatemala* 28 (1955): 18–31.

"Relación de los caciques y principales del pueblo de Atitlán, 10. Febrero del Año 1571," *Anales de la Sociedad de Geografía e Historia de Guatemala* 26 (1952): 435–48.

"Relación hecha a su Majestad por el gobernador de Honduras, de todos los pueblos de dicha gobernación.—Año 1582," *Boletín del Archivo General del Gobierno* 11 (1946): 5–19.

Remesal, Antonio de. *Historia general de las Indias Occidentales, y particular de la gobernación de Chiapa y Guatemala* [1619]. 2 vols. Biblioteca "Goathemala" de la Sociedad de Geografía e Historia. Guatemala: Tipografía Nacional, 1932.

———. *Historia general de las Indias Occidentales, y particular de la gobernación de Chiapa y Guatemala.* Edited by Carmelo Sáenz de Santa María. Biblioteca de Autores Españoles. 3d ed. Madrid: Ediciones Atlas, 1964–66.

Riley, G. Micheal. *Fernando Cortés and the Marquesado in Morelos, 1532–1547.* Albuquerque: University of New Mexico Press, 1973.

———. "Labor in Cortesian Enterprise: The Cuernavaca Area, 1522–1549," *The Americas* 28 (1972): 271–87.

Rodríguez Becerra, Salvador. *Encomienda y conquista: Los inicios de la colonización en Guatemala.* Publicaciones del Seminario de Antropología Americana, vol. 14. Seville: Universidad de Sevilla, 1977.

Romoli, Kathleen. *Balboa of Darien: Discoveror of the Pacific.* Garden City, N.Y. Doubleday, 1953.

Rosenblat, Angel. *La Población Indígena y el Mestizaje en América, 1492–1950.* 2 vols. Buenos Aires: Editorial Nova, 1954.

Roys, Ralph L. *The Indian Background of Colonial Yucatán.* Washington, D.C.: Carnegie Institution of Washington, publication 548, 1943.

Rubio Mañé, Ignacio. "Alonso de Maldonado, Primer Presidente de la Audiencia de Guatemala," *Anales de la Sociedad de Geografía e Historia de Guatemala* 2 (1964): 163–65.

Rubio Sánchez, Manuel. "El añil o xiquilite," *Anales de la Sociedad de Geografía e Historia de Guatemala* 26 (1952): 313–49.

———. "El Cacao," *Anales de la Sociedad de Geografía e Historia de Guatemala* 31 (1958): 81–129.

———. *Comercio Terrestre de y entre las Provincias de Centroamérica.* Guatemala: Editorial del Ejército, 1973.

Saco, José Antonio. *Historia de la esclavitud de los indios en el Nuevo Mundo, seguida de la historia de los repartimientos y encomiendas.* 2 vols. Havana: Cultural, 1932.

Sáenz de Santamaría, Carmelo. *El Licenciado Don Francisco Marroquín, Primer Obispo de Guatemala (1499–1563).* Madrid: Ediciones Cultura Hispánica, 1964.

———. "Vida y escritos de don Francisco Marroquín, primer Obispo de Guatemala. (1499–1563)," *Anales de la Sociedad de Geografía e Historia de Guatemala* 36 (1963): 85–366.

Saint-Lu, André. *La Vera Paz: Esprit Évangélique et Colonisation.* Paris: Centre de Recherches Hispaniques, Institut D'Etudes Hispaniques, 1968.

Sanchíz Ochoa, Pilar. *Los hidalgos de Guatemala: Realidad y apariencia en un sistema de valores.* Publicaciones del Seminario de Antropología Americana, vol. 13. Seville: Universidad de Sevilla, 1976.

Santamaría, Francisco J. *Diccionario General de Americanismos.* 3 vols. Mexico: Editorial Pedro Robredo, 1942.

Schäfer, Ernesto. *El Consejo Real y Supremo de las Indias.* 2 vols. Seville: Escuela de Estudios Hispano-Americanos, 1936–1947.

————. *Indice de la Colección de Documentos Inéditos de Indias.* 2 vols. Madrid: Consejo Superior de Investigaciones Científicas, Instituto "Gonzalo Fernández de Oviedo," 1946–1947.

Scholes, France V. *The Spanish Conqueror as a Business Man.* University of New Mexico Fourth Annual Research Lecture, May 3, 1957. Albuquerque: University of New Mexico Press, 1957.

————, and Eleanor B. Adams. *Don Diego Quijada, Alcalde Mayor de Yucatán, 1561–1565.* Biblioteca Histórica Mexicana de obras inéditas, vols. 14, 15. Mexico: Antigua Librería Robredo de José Porrúa e Hijos, 1938.

————, and Ralph L. Roys. *The Maya Chontal Indians of Acalan-Tixchel: A Contribution to the History and Ethnography of the Yucatan Peninsula.* Washington, D.C.: Carnegie Institution of Washington, publication 560, 1948.

Scholes, Walter Vinton. *The Diego Ramírez Visita.* University of Missouri Studies, vol. 20, no. 4. Columbia: University of Missouri, 1946.

Schurz, William Lytle. *This New World: The Civilization of Latin America.* New York: E. P. Dutton, 1964.

Sherman, William L. "Abusos contra los Indios de Guatemala (1602–1605). Relaciones del Obispo," *Cahiers du monde Hispanique et Luso-Brésilien. Caravelle* 11 (1968): 4–28.

————. "A Conqueror's Wealth: Notes on the Estate of don Pedro de Alvarado," *The Americas* 26 (1969): 199–213.

————. "Indian Slavery and the Cerrato Reforms," *Hispanic American Historical Review* 51 (1971): 25–50.

————. "Porque Fray Bartolomé tuvo problemas con algunos funcionarios (Oficiales), en particular con el presidente Maldonado y el gobernador Contreras." In *Fray Bartolomé de Las Casas en Hispanoamérica,* edited by Manuel M. Velasco Suárez. San Cristóbal de Las Casas, Mexico: Editorial Fray Bartolomé de Las Casas, 1976.

————. "Tlaxcalans in Post-Conquest Guatemala" *Tlalocan* 6 (1970): 124–39.

————. "Viceregal Administration in the Spanish American Colonies: Some Neglected Sources," *Rocky Mountain Social Science Journal* 5 (1968): 143–51.

Simpson, Lesley Byrd. *The Encomienda in New Spain.* Berkeley and Los Angeles: University of California Press, 1950.

————. "A Seventeenth Century Encomienda: Chimaltenango, Guatemala," *The Americas* 15 (1959): 393–402.

————. *Studies in the Administration of the Indians in New Spain. I. The Laws of Burgos of 1512. II. The Civil Congregation.* Ibero-Americana, no. 7. Berkeley and Los Angeles: University of California Press, 1934.

————. *Studies in the Administration of the Indians in New Spain. III. The Repartimiento System of Native Labor in New Spain and Guatemala.* Ibero-Americana, no. 13. Berkeley and Los Angeles: University of California Press, 1938.

————. *Studies in the Administration of the Indians of New Spain. IV. The Emancipation of the Indian Slaves and the Resettlement of the Freedmen, 1548–1553.* Ibero-Americana, no. 16. Berkeley and Los Angeles: University of

California Press, 1940.

Solórzano y Pereyra, Juan. *Política Indiana* [1648]. 5 vols. Corregida, e ilustrada con notas por el licenciado don Francisco Ramiro de Valenzuela. Madrid: Compañía Ibero-Americana de publicaciones, n.d.

Squier, Ephraim George. *The States of Central America*. New York: Harper and Brothers, 1858.

Stone, Doris. "Some Spanish Entradas, 1524–1695," *Middle American Research Series* 4 (1932): 213–96.

Taplin, Glen W., comp. *Middle American Governors*. Metuchen, N.J.: The Scarecrow Press, 1972.

Torquemada, Fray Juan de. *Los veinte y vn libros rituales i Monarchia Indiana, con el origen y guerras, de los Indios Ocidentales, de sus Poblaciones, Descubrimiento, Conquista, Conuersion, y otras cosas marauillosas de la mesma tierra, distribuydos en tres tomos* [1615]. 3 vols. Madrid: Nicolás Rodríguez Franco, 1723.

Torre, R. P. Fray Tomás de la. *Desde Salamanca, España, hasta Ciudad Real de Chiapas: Diario del Viaje, 1544–1545*. Mexico: Editora Central, 1945.

Toussaint, Manuel. *Colonial Art in Mexico*. Translated and edited by Elizabeth W. Weisman. Austin: University of Texas Press, 1967.

Tovilla, El Capitán don Martín Alfonso. *Relación Histórica Descriptiva de las Provincias de la Verapaz y de la del Manché* [1635], *publicada por primera vez con la Relación que en el Consejo Real de las Indias hizo sobre la pacificación, y población de las provincias del Manché y Lacandón, el Licenciado Antonio de León Pinelo*. Guatemala: Editorial Universitaria, 1960.

Ulloa Ortiz, Berta. "Cortés escalvista," *Historia Mexicana* 2 (1966): 239–73.

Urbano, Victoria. *Juan Vázquez de Coronado y su ética en la conquista de Costa Rica*. Madrid: Ediciones Cultura Hispánica, 1968.

Vázquez, R. P. Fray Francisco. *Crónica de la Provincia del Santísimo Nombre de Jesús de Guatemala* [1714–1716]. 4 vols. Biblioteca "Goathemala" de la Sociedad de Geografía e Historia. Guatemala: Tipografía Nacional, 1937–44.

Vázquez de Espinosa, Antonio. *Description of the Indies (c. 1620)*. Translated by Charles Upson Clark. Smithsonian Miscellaneous Collections, vol. 102. Washington: Smithsonian Institution Press, 1968.

Vigil, Ralph H. "Alonso de Zorita, Crown Oidor in the Indies, 1548–1556." Ph.D. dissertation, University of New Mexico, 1969.

Vitoria, Francisco de. *Relectio de Indis o Libertad de los Indios*. Edición crítica bilingüe por L. Pereña y J. M. Pérez Prendes. Madrid: Consejo Superior de Investigaciones Científicas, 1967.

Wagner, Henry R., and Helen R. Parish. *The Life and Writings of Bartolomé de las Casas*. Albuquerque: University of New Mexico Press, 1967.

Warren, Dave. "The Nobility Element of the Matrícula de Huexotzinco," *Actas y Memorias*, XXXVII Congreso Internacional de Americanistas, 3. Buenos Aires: República Argentina, 1968.

———. "Some Demographic Considerations of the *Matrícula de Huexotzinco*," *The Americas* 27 (1971): 256–57.

Whetten, Nathan L. *Guatemala: The Land and the People*. New Haven, Conn.: Yale University Press, 1965.

Wolf, Eric. *Sons of the Shaking Earth*. Chicago: University of Chicago Press, 1959.

Ximénez, Fray Francisco. *Historia de la provincia de San Vicente de Chiapa y Guatemala de la Orden de Predicadores*. 3 vols. Biblioteca "Goathemala" de la Sociedad de Geografía e Historia. Guatemala: Tipografía Nacional, 1929–31.

Zamora Castellanos, Pedro. "Itinerarios de la conquista de Guatemala," *Anales de la Sociedad de Geografía e Historia de Guatemala* 20 (1945): 23–32.

Zavala, Silvio. *Contribución a la historia de las instituciones coloniales en Guatemala*. Jornadas, no. 36. Mexico: El Colegio de México, 1945.

———. *Estudios indianos*. Mexico: El Colegio Nacional, 1948.

———. "Los esclavos indios en Guatemala," *Historia Mexicana* 19 (1970): 459–65.

———. *Los esclavos indios en Nueva España*. Mexico: El Colegio Nacional, 1967.

———. *La filosofía política en la Conquista de América*. Mexico: Fondo de Cultura Económica, 1947.

———. *Los intereses particulares en la conquista de la Nueva España*. Instituto de Investigaciones Históricas, Serie Histórica, no. 10. Mexico: Universidad Nacional Autónoma de México, 1964.

———. *Servidumbre natural y libertad cristiana, según los tratadistas españoles de los siglos XVI y XVII*. Buenos Aires: Instituto de Investigaciones Históricas, 1944.

———. "Los Trabajadores Antillanos en el Siglo XVI," *Revista de Historia de América* 2 (1938): 31–68; 3 (1938): 60–88.

———, and María Castelo, eds. *Fuentes para la historia del trabajo en Nueva España* [1575–1805]. 8 vols. Mexico: Fondo de Cultura Económica, 1939–48.

Zorita, Alonso de. *Life and Labor in Ancient Mexico: The Brief and Summary Relation of the Lords of New Spain*. Translation by Benjamin Keen. New Brunswick, N.J.: Rutgers University Press, 1963.

Index

Acajutla, prehispanic town and Spanish port, 25, 227, 239, 242–43, 247
Acalán, 16, 19
Acatepeque, Indian town, 24
Achi Indians (Achies), 50
Adams, Eleanor B., x
Afán de Ribera, Diego, son of Per, 270
Afán de Ribera, Per (Pedro) (Perafán de R.), governor of Costa Rica and Nicaragua, 47, 230, 270
Agangasca, Indian town, 298
Aghauetic, 15
Agia, Fr. Miguel, Franciscan author of report, ca. 1600; defines "personal service," 87–88, 193–94; on Indian attitudes toward labor, 192; and negative opinion of caciques, 297; compares labor in central America with that in Peru, 339–42
Agricultural labor, 240–59
Agriculture, 91, 240–59
Aguacatepeque, Indian town, 203–4
Aguatega, Indian town, 46
Aguilar, Cristóbal de, 61
Alax, Indian town, 100
Alburquerque, duke of, 318, 344
Alcántara, Fernando de, lieutenant of governor, 57
Alcántara, Joan de, 62
Alcatoa, Indian town, 53

Almagro, Diego de, conquistador, 56
Alvarado, Diego, brother of Pedro, 60
Alvarado, Gonzalo, conquistador and brother (or cousin) of Pedro, 26, 144
Alvarado, Jorge, brother of Pedro and acting governor, 49, 71, 106, 288–89
Alvarado, Pedro de, conquistador and governor: career of, xiii; expeditions to Peru and Pacific, 8–9; conquest of Guatemala, 9, 21–27; maintains dominance of Central America, 9; character of, 9; called "Tonatiuh" by Indians, 9; as adelantado, governor, and captain general, 9; allows exploitation of natives, 9; death of, 11, 130; invades Soconusco, 21; dispute with Montejo, 31; slaves of, 38, 59–69, 67, 71; and black slaves, 42; and use of cannibalistic allies, 49–59; takes Indian slaves to Peru, 56, 59, 71; invades Puynmatlan, 73; and naborías, 107; and tamemes, 113, 118, 123; residencia of, 130; allows slave trading, 157; as a leader, 180; and shipbuilding, 237; and caciques, 226–67; and expedition to Quito, 281; and Indian women, 305, 308; and second wife, 318; political connections of, 344

479

Alvarez, Don Domingo, Indian principal, 201

Alvarez de Ortega, Juan, archdeacon, 218

Alvarez Osorio, Fr. Diego, bishop of Nicaragua, 275

Amapal, 239

Amanteca, 15

Amatique (Santo Tomás de Castilla), Spanish port, 365

Amatitlán, Indian town, 251

Angulo, Fray Pedro de, Dominican, 59, 130, 185, 273–74

Añil. *See* Indigo

Annals of the Cakchiquels, 137, 142

Antigua (Santiago de Guatemala), Spanish city, xv, 26, 237

Apinula, Indian town, 139

Apprentices, 178, 211–12

Architecture, 235–37

Archivo General de Indias, Seville, xiii

Argueta, Gaspar de, estanciero, 290

Arias de Avila, Pedro. *See* Pedrarias Dávila

Aristocracy, native, 263–303, 328

Arrieros, 208–10

Arteaga Mendiola, Lic., 244, 356

Atahualpa, 266–67

Atiquipaque, Indian town, 23, 139

Atitlán, Indian town, 22–23, 71, 106, 273, 275

Atlacatl, Cuzcatec ruler, 26

Audiencia de los Confines: jurisdiction of, 3; creation of, 11–12, 129; performance of, 1544–48, 12, 132; first meeting of, 129, and new laws, 131; Cerrato assumes presidency of, 135, Cerrato judges first audiencia, 135–52; site of moved to Santiago, 151–52

Audiencia judges (oidores): opinions of, xii; performance of, 1544–48, 12, 135–52; of Santo Domingo, 57; criticism of, 89, 149; first appointees,

129; business interests of, 152. *See also individual names*

Audiencia of Mexico: remiss in protecting Indians, 10; opposes branding of esclavos de rescate, 37; and tamemes, 116, 118, 122; and a case of murder, 270; Indian policies of, 343

Augustinians, 251

Avela, Fr., cattle dealer, 48

Avilés, Captain, encomendero and official, 169

Avyaque, province of, 270–71

Bancroft, Hubert H., xiv, 27, 162–63, 359, 363

Bañuelos, Francisco de, critic of Cerrato, 168–70

Barahona, Sancho de, conquistador and encomendero, 71, 99, 273

Bargas Lobo, Alonso, procurador síndico, 204

Barón Castro, Rodolfo, 360–61

Barreda, Hector de la, cattle importer, 240

Barrera, Diego de la, encomendero, 200

Barrionuevo, Francisco de, author of report, 56, 78

Belehe Qat, Cakchiquel ruler, 21

Beltrán, Dr. Diego, member of the Council of the Indies, 42, 344

Beneçiano, Lucas de, 61

Benzoni, Girolamo, Milanese chronicler, 185

Bibas, Alonso, encomendero, 319

Black death, 6

Blacks: importation of planned, 42, 109; as mining slaves, 56, 125, 235; sale price of slaves, 69, 79; bozales, 90; population of Honduras, 91; and road maintenance, 120; demand for, 109, 128, 177, 233, 248; belonging to judge Rogel, 143, belonging to